LIFE IN WORDS: ESSAYS ON CHAUCER, THE *GAWAIN*-POET, AND MALORY

This volume collects fifteen landmark essays published over the last three decades by the distinguished medievalist Jill Mann. Bringing together her essays on Chaucer, the *Gawain*-poet, and Malory, the collection foregrounds the common interest in the semantic implications of key vocabulary such as "authority," "adventure," and "price" that links them together.

Mann, one of the finest critics of Middle English literature in her generation, uses the concepts suggested by the language of medieval literature itself as a way into the masterpieces of Middle English, including *The Canterbury Tales*, *Troilus and Criseyde*, *Sir Gawain and the Green Knight*, and the *Morte d'Arthur.*

An extended introduction by Mark David Rasmussen brings out the nature of the themes that run through the collection, analyses the critical methods in play, and assesses their significance in the context of Middle English studies over the last thirty years.

JILL MANN is Emeritus Professor of English at the University of Notre Dame and a Life Fellow of Girton College, Cambridge.

MARK DAVID RASMUSSEN is Charles J. Luellen Professor of English at Centre College.

Life in Words: Essays on Chaucer, the *Gawain*-Poet, and Malory

JILL MANN

Edited and with an Introduction
by Mark David Rasmussen

UNIVERSITY OF TORONTO PRESS
Toronto Buffalo London

Toronto Buffalo London
utorontopress.com

Reprinted in paperback 2020

ISBN 978-1-4426-4865-4 (cloth)
ISBN 978-1-4875-2839-3 (paper)

Library and Archives Canada Cataloguing in Publication

Title: Life in words : essays on Chaucer, the Gawain-Poet, and Malory / Jill Mann ; edited and with an introduction by Mark David Rasmussen.

Names: Mann, Jill, author. | Rasmussen, Mark David, 1953– editor.

Description: Paperback reprint. Originally published: 2014. | Includes bibliographical references and index.

Identifiers: Canadiana 20200331388 | ISBN 9781487528393 (softcover)

Subjects: LCSH: English literature – Middle English, 1100–1500 – History and criticism. | LCSH: English literature – Middle English, 1100–1500 – Semantics. | LCSH: Literature, Medieval – Themes, motives. | LCSH: Chaucer, Geoffrey, –1400 – Criticism and interpretation. | LCSH: Chaucer, Geoffrey, –1400 – Language. | LCSH: Sir Gawain and the Green Knight. | LCSH: Gawain (Legendary character) – Romances – History and criticism. | LCSH: Arthurian romances – History and criticism. | LCSH: Malory, Thomas, Sir, active 15th century – Criticism and interpretation. | LCSH: Malory, Thomas, Sir, active 15th century – Language.

Classification: LCC PR255 .M35 2020 | DDC 820.9/001–dc23

University of Toronto Press acknowledges the financial assistance to its publishing program of the Canada Council for the Arts and the Ontario Arts Council, an agency of the Government of Ontario.

Contents

Author's Preface

Many years ago I knew a college bursar, by training an engineer, who had entered academe late in life, and perhaps in consequence had a rather narrow-minded dismissiveness towards the humanities. Quite often he would remark, "I think it's disgraceful that most people" (glancing meaningfully at any humanities scholar seated near him) "drive a car every day but have no idea of what goes on under the bonnet." One day I expressed my irritation by replying, "And I think it's disgraceful that most people use language every day and never think about what it is that they are using and how its vocabulary structures and determines their thoughts. That is what we literary scholars do." I was both surprised and delighted to see that he was quite taken aback by this simple impromptu answer. "*Well,*" he said, "I've never thought of that before. I'll have to think about it."

My comment reflected my own growing realization that the medieval narratives that I was studying and teaching used the rich implications of key words to focus their complex explorations of human experience. Furthermore, their medieval authors seem to have been fully conscious that this was the case: that is, the narratives themselves were constructed as if they were miniature laboratories for the investigation and testing of these key words: what, exactly, does "patience" mean? Why is it that both "anger" and "glosing" (i.e., glossing texts) are treated as its opposites? Why does "pitous" mean both "pitying" and "piteous"? What is it that holds together the whole range of meanings for the Middle English word "pris"? What do we mean by referring to both "aventure" ("chance") and "destiny" as agents of a sequence of events, and how do they relate to human agency? Why is it that Middle English "inogh" (like medieval Latin "satis") means not only "sufficiently, moderately," but also "abundantly, supremely, to the highest degree," and how does this shift in meaning help us to understand the concept of (self-)sufficiency? Whatever the richness of characterization and realistic representation of aspects of human life in these narratives, these elements seemed to me to be ordered and irradiated by thinking about the implications of everyday language and its possibilities.

The essays collected in this book represent some of my investigations of this topic. Without being committed to a rigorous methodology, they use words (and sometimes grammatical structures) as a way into understanding the aspects of human experience represented in medieval narratives. The title "Life in Words" thus has a double reference. It acknowledges that words have a life of their own, which can be explored for its significance, but it also acknowledges that human life is lived in words, and that experience is continually filling them with new depths of meaning.

The essays are substantially as they were originally published, but I have made occasional stylistic improvements and clarifications. Referencing styles have been harmonized throughout the volume, and editions used for citation and quotation have been extensively updated where relevant, as have major reference works. In order to avoid overburdening the text, I have not updated references to secondary criticism in a systematic way, but I have sometimes included references to recent criticism where it seemed they would be useful.

Finally, I would like to express my deep gratitude to Mark David Rasmussen for initiating this project, for selecting the essays to be included and writing the Introduction which perceptively traces the links between them and sets them in their scholarly context, and for negotiating publication of the book. Thanks are also due to Suzanne Rancourt and Barbara Porter at the University of Toronto Press for steering the book through production, and to Charles Stuart for exemplary copy-editing.

Jill Mann
Cambridge, June 2013

A Note on References

Quotations of Chaucer's *Canterbury Tales* are taken from the Penguin Classics edition by Jill Mann (London, 2005). Quotations of Chaucer's *Troilus and Criseyde* are taken from the Penguin Classics edition by Barry Windeatt (London, 2003). Other works of Chaucer are cited from *The Riverside Chaucer*, ed. Larry D. Benson, 3rd ed. (Boston, MA, 1987).

Quotations from *Sir Gawain and the Green Knight* are taken from the edition by J.R.R. Tolkien and E.V. Gordon, revised by Norman Davis (Oxford, 1968).

Quotations of Malory's *Morte d'Arthur* are taken from *The Works of Sir Thomas Malory*, ed. Eugène Vinaver, rev. P.J.C. Field, 3 vols, 3rd ed. (Oxford, 1990). Since pagination is continuous through all three volumes, the citation will be to page number only, followed (after a slash) by line number(s) when the text is quoted directly. Editorial brackets have been removed. Where reference is to the editorial matter in this edition rather than the text, for the sake of clear identification it is cited as "Malory, *Works*, 000."

Quotations from works by Boccaccio are taken from *Tutte le opere di Giovanni Boccaccio*, ed. Vittore Branca, 10 vols (Milan, 1964–98). Branca's edition is available online at http://digilander.libero.it/il_boccaccio. Translations of *Filostrato* are taken from *The Filostrato of Giovanni Boccaccio*, translated with a parallel text by Nathaniel Edward Griffin and Arthur Beckwith Myrick (Philadelphia, 1929; repr. New York, 1978).

Quotations and translations of Dante's *Divine Comedy* are taken from the edition by Charles S. Singleton, 3 vols in 6 (Princeton, NJ, 1970–5).

Translations of Aristotle's *Nicomachean Ethics* are from *The Complete Works of Aristotle: The Revised Oxford Translation*, ed. Jonathan Barnes, 2 vols (Princeton, NJ, 1984), II, pp. 1729–867 (trans. W.D. Ross, rev. J.O. Urmson).

Since book and chapter numbers of the Barnes translations do not always exactly match those in the *Aristoteles latinus*, they are cited by the Bekker references (references to Immanuel Bekker's standard edition [1831] of the Greek text of Aristotle, used by all Aristotle scholars), which are given in the margins of the *Revised Oxford Translation.*

Abbreviations

Cambridge Italian Dictionary	*The Cambridge Italian Dictionary*, edited by Barbara Reynolds. 2 vols. Cambridge, 1962–81.
Du Cange	Charles du Fresne du Cange, ed. *Glossarium mediae et infimae Latinitatis*. Rev. edn, 5 vols. Graz, 1883–7; repr. Graz, 1954.
EETS e.s., o.s.	Early English Texts Society, extra series, original series
Lewis and Short	Charlton T. Lewis and Charles Short, eds. *A Latin Dictionary*. Rev. ed. Oxford, 1907.
MED	*Middle English Dictionary*, edited by H. Kurath, S.M. Kuhn, and Robert E. Lewis. Ann Arbor, MI, 1954–2001.
Niermeyer	J.F. Niermeyer, ed. *Mediae Latinitatis Lexicon Minus*. Leiden, 1976.
OED	*The Oxford English Dictionary … edited by James A.H. Murray, Henry Bradley, W.A. Craigie, and C.T. Onions*, 16 vols. Oxford, 1933. 2nd ed. prepared by J.A. Simpson and E.S.C. Weiner. 20 vols. Oxford, 1989.
Oxford Latin Dictionary	*Oxford Latin Dictionary*. Oxford, 1968–82.
PL	*Patrologiae Cursus Completus, Series Latina*. Ed. J.P. Migne. Paris, 1844–64.
PMLA	*Publications of the Modern Language Association of America*
Tobler-Lommatzsch	Adolf Tobler, Erhard Lommatzsch, and Helmut Christmann, eds. *Altfranzösisches Wörterbuch*. Stuttgart, 1915– .

List of Essays, with Places of Original Publication

1 "Troilus' Swoon." *Chaucer Review* 14 (1980): 319–35.
Reprinted by permission of Penn State University Press.

2 "Shakespeare and Chaucer: 'What is Criseyde Worth?'" In *The European Tragedy of Troilus*, edited by Piero Boitani, 219–42. Oxford, 1989.
Reprinted by permission of Oxford University Press.

3 "Chance and Destiny in *Troilus and Criseyde* and the *Knight's Tale*." In *The Cambridge Chaucer Companion*, edited by Jill Mann and Piero Boitani, 75–92. Cambridge, 1986. Revised edition: *The Cambridge Companion to Chaucer*, 93–111. Cambridge, 2003.

4 "Chaucerian Themes and Style in the *Franklin's Tale*." In *The New Pelican Guide to English Literature*, edited by Boris Ford, vol. 1.1:133–53. Harmondsworth, 1982.
Reprinted by permission of David Higham Associates on behalf of the Estate of Boris Ford.

5 "Anger and 'Glosynge' in the *Canterbury Tales*" [Sir Israel Gollancz Memorial Lecture 1990]. *Proceedings of the British Academy* 76 (1990): 203–23.
Reprinted by permission of the British Academy.

6 "The Authority of the Audience in Chaucer." In *Poetics: Theory and Practice in Medieval English Literature: The J.A.W. Bennett Memorial Lectures, Seventh Series, Perugia, 1990*, edited by Piero Boitani and Anna Torti, 1–12. Cambridge, 1991.

7 "Parents and Children in the *Canterbury Tales*." In *Literature in Fourteenth-Century England: The J.A.W. Bennett Memorial Lectures, Perugia, 1981–1982*, edited by Piero Boitani and Anna Torti, 165–83. Tübingen and Cambridge, 1983.

8 "Satisfaction and Payment in Middle English Literature." *Studies in the Age of Chaucer* 5 (1983): 17–48.
Reprinted by permission of *Studies in the Age of Chaucer.*

9 "Price and Value in *Sir Gawain and the Green Knight.*" *Essays in Criticism* 36 (1986): 294–318.
Reprinted by permission of Oxford University Press.

10 "Courtly Aesthetics and Courtly Ethics in *Sir Gawain and the Green Knight.*" *Studies in the Age of Chaucer* 31 (2009): 231–65.
Reprinted by permission of *Studies in the Age of Chaucer.*

11 "Sir Gawain and the Romance Hero." In *Heroes and Heroines in Medieval English Literature: A Festschrift Presented to André Crépin on the Occasion of his Sixty-Fifth Birthday*, ed. Leo Carruthers, 105–17. Cambridge, 1994.

12 "Malory: Knightly Combat in *Le Morte D'Arthur.*" In *The New Pelican Guide to English Literature*, edited by Boris Ford, vol. 1.1:331–9. Harmondsworth, 1982.
Reprinted by permission of David Higham Associates on behalf of the Estate of Boris Ford.

13 "'Taking the Adventure': Malory and the *Suite du Merlin.*" In *Aspects of Malory*, edited by Toshiyuki Takamiya and Derek Brewer, 71–91, 196–207. Cambridge, 1981.

14 *The Narrative of Distance, The Distance of Narrative in Malory's* Morte Darthur. *The William Matthews Lectures 1991, Birkbeck College.* London, 1991.

15 "Malory and the Grail Legend." In *A Companion to Malory*, edited by Elizabeth Archibald and A.S.G. Edwards, 203–20. Cambridge, 1996.

Grateful acknowledgment is made to the institutions and publishers listed above for permission to republish the articles in question. Where no permission is specified, rights have either been waived or are held by the author.

Introduction

Jill Mann's Patience

BY MARK DAVID RASMUSSEN

This volume collects fifteen remarkable essays published between 1980 and 2009 by the distinguished scholar and critic of medieval literature Jill Mann. Individually, many of these essays have become landmark treatments of their topics, often cited in the critical literature, but they have never been brought together as a group. There are several advantages to doing so now. One is that of convenience. While some of these essays were first published in journals or edited collections that are relatively easy to find in academic libraries or online, others have been much harder to track down, published in Festschriften or volumes of conference proceedings that were not widely distributed and are now out of print. One piece that has been especially difficult even for scholars to come by is a revelatory essay on Malory, "The Narrative of Distance, The Distance of Narrative in Malory's *Morte Darthur*," originally delivered as a pair of lectures at Birkbeck College and privately printed by the college as a pamphlet. So one purpose served by this collection will simply be to make these path-breaking essays more broadly and readily available.

Much more important, though, bringing these essays together will allow readers to trace the shared themes and concerns that run among them, and that connect them to the body of Jill Mann's other published work. In the process they will be able to appreciate the full scope of her critical achievement for the first time. For as prominent a figure as Jill Mann has been within the field of medieval studies, I believe that the nature and significance of her accomplishment has not yet been generally understood. In truth, she has only herself to blame for this. Jill Mann is among the most erudite and self-possessed of scholar/critics – like Geffrey in the *House of Fame*, she knows at every moment where she stands – but she is constitutionally averse to making grandiose claims about the value of her own work or where it belongs on the critical map.[1] My own aim in assembling this collection has been not only to make these magnificent essays more widely available, but also (and primarily) to highlight the nature of Jill Mann's achievement over the course of her career, for I am certain that we have never been more in need of her critical example than we are right now.

To characterize Jill Mann's critical practice, I have adopted one of her own favourite words from the literature she studies. For Chaucer, in particular, as Jill Mann understands him, "patience" denotes a mode of responsiveness to the world, an openness to the fluctuating possibilities of change.[2] It involves putting aside the will to control events in favour of a surrender to their movement, but that very surrender possesses a kind of creative power, as one meets the vicissitudes of change with an answering flexibility of response. What do I mean, then, by Jill Mann's patience? I mean primarily her willingness to listen to what medieval authors have to say on their own terms, in the contexts of their history and culture – her willingness to let them speak for themselves. But I mean something more as well, for her patience also involves a second quality, a trust that the medieval author, once understood in his or her own context, will have something valuable to say to us in ours. It is not that she considers great literature to be a storehouse of unchanging human truths, in the manner of traditional humanist criticism; just the opposite, in fact. Her model for our engagement with the past is that of a dialogue between two different historical moments, and those differences must be carefully heeded.[3] But in the course of that patient listening we may find that the past, *precisely because of its difference from us*, has the power to "enlarge our perceptions of human life and its possibilities"[4] in ways that can surprise or trouble or inspire.

---

1 Of course, she is always aware of how her own work relates to what others have done, and when appropriate she makes that relationship clear. See, for instance, her preface to *Feminizing Chaucer* discussed below, as well as the opening paragraphs of "Excursus: Wife-Swapping in Medieval Literature" in the same volume, both of which deftly locate her own work within the contentious field of gender studies (Jill Mann, *Feminizing Chaucer* [Cambridge, 2002], vii–xix, 152–4). But making what is modishly called "a critical intervention" is never her initial aim in writing; rather, she wishes to engage the work itself and what it has to say.

2 The theme ramifies throughout Jill Mann's work and the essays in this collection, but see especially the fourth essay included here, "Chaucerian Themes and Style in the *Franklin's Tale*." The willingness of Malory's knights to accept what adventure may bring, a recurring topic in Jill Mann's essays on the *Morte d'Arthur*, represents a chivalric version of patience.

3 For the importance of dialogue as a model for her own critical work, with particular reference to Bakhtin, see Jill Mann, "Chaucer and Atheism," *Studies in the Age of Chaucer* 17 (1995): 5–19, especially 7–9.

4 *Feminizing Chaucer*, xviii.

The double movement of Jill Mann's thought, what I have called her patience, may be traced back to her earliest published work, the revision of her Cambridge dissertation that appeared in 1973 as *Chaucer and Medieval Estates Satire*.[5] That book permanently changed our understanding of its topic, the *General Prologue* to Chaucer's *Canterbury Tales*. At the time of its publication, a long-standing critical tradition had prized the *General Prologue* as a triumph of psychological realism, a splendidly realized gallery of idiosyncratic individuals.[6] (In the most extreme version of this critical approach, scholars combed the archives seeking real-life models for Chaucer's pilgrims.)[7] Basing her argument on a painstaking survey of the vast body of medieval poetry in the genre of estates satire, Jill Mann demonstrated conclusively that virtually all of the details that strike readers as especially vivid and lifelike – the Monk's hunting, the Prioress's lapdogs, the Wife of Bath's elaborate headgear – were lifted straight out of the estates satire tradition. Our sense of the pilgrims' lifelikeness, she argued, comes not from these details themselves, but from how they are presented to the reader: though the pilgrims are types, "Chaucer encourages us to *respond* to them as individuals."[8] By deliberately evoking in us contradictory responses to the pilgrims, by giving us a sense of them as characters who exist in time, and especially by showing how they are themselves aware of the typical attitudes toward their estates, "Chaucer forces us to feel that we are dealing with real people because we cannot respond to them with the absolute responses appropriate to the abstractions of moralistic satire."[9] In thus removing from estates satire the imperative to make moral judgments that is the genre's *raison d'être*, Chaucer reshapes its moral absolutism into a thoroughgoing relativism; he both draws upon the genre and uses it against itself.

So widely accepted has this argument been – so completely has it become part of what we think we know about the *Canterbury Tales* – that the headnote to the *General Prologue* in *The Norton Anthology of English Literature* amounts to a paraphrase of it.[10] Jill Mann's second critical study of Chaucer proved to be

5 *Chaucer and Medieval Estates Satire* (Cambridge, 1973).

6 Monuments of this critical tradition, which goes back at least to Dryden, include the accounts of the *General Prologue* offered in G.L. Kittredge, *Chaucer and His Poetry* (Cambridge, MA, 1915) and R.M. Lumiansky, *Of Sondry Folk: The Dramatic Principle in The Canterbury Tales* (Austin, TX, 1955).

7 See John M. Manly, *Some New Light on Chaucer* (New York, 1926).

8 *Chaucer and Medieval Estates Satire*, 189; italics in original.

9 *Chaucer and Medieval Estates Satire*, 189.

10 Stephen Greenblatt, gen. ed., *The Norton Anthology of English Literature*, 9th ed., vol. 1 (New York, 2012), 242–3. Through several previous editions the passage appears in substantially the same form.

more controversial. Originally published in 1991 in the Harvester–Wheatsheaf "Feminist Readings" series and assigned the unhelpful title *Geoffrey Chaucer*, this was one of four pioneering books on Chaucer and gender to appear in quick succession between 1989 and 1992.[11] Though the topic was different from that of her first book, there were some striking similarities of approach, for both studies suggest that what marks Chaucer off as an artist is his ability to make new meanings out of traditional norms.[12] In the first book, these are the normative values of estates satire, while in the second one they are the stereotypes about women current in Chaucer's day, and particularly the polarized image of women as falling into two categories, either like Eve, manipulative, shrewish, and lustful, or like the Virgin Mary, sexually pure and all-enduring – the so-called Eva/Ave split that came down to Chaucer from the antifeminist tradition. Even as he draws on these stereotypes, Mann suggested, Chaucer seeks to make us aware of their status as human constructions of meaning, fictions that help shape (and often distort) real lives. The Wife of Bath is an especially prominent case in point. As has long been recognized, for all of her evident vitality the Wife is essentially a literary composite, with many of her words and character traits drawn from the commonplaces of the antifeminist tradition. What Chaucer emphasizes, though, is the Wife's interaction with these stereotypes, not only when she self-consciously adopts them as a template for her own behaviour, fully exploiting their possibilities as she bullies her first three husbands into submission, but also (and most vividly) when she comes to experience their cost, as her beloved fifth husband, Jankin, both beats her and reads to her nightly from his "book of wikked wives," subjecting her to the images of women that earlier she had claimed as her own. In short, just as a typical character like the Monk in the *General Prologue* comments on the traditional attitudes toward

11 Carolyn Dinshaw, *Chaucer's Sexual Poetics* (Madison, WI, 1989); Priscilla Martin, *Chaucer's Women: Nuns, Wives, and Amazons* (Basingstoke, Hants, 1990); Jill Mann, *Geoffrey Chaucer* (Hemel Hempstead, UK, 1991); Elaine Tuttle Hansen, *Chaucer and the Fictions of Gender* (Berkeley, CA, 1992). For the most part, these four authors seem to have been unaware of one another's work at the time of writing. Mann lists the books of Dinshaw and Martin in her bibliography, but she does not cite them in her text or address their arguments, and Hansen's book, the last of the four to appear, contains no references to the other three. In 2002 Jill Mann's book was issued in a revised edition titled *Feminizing Chaucer*, and subsequent page references will be to this edition (see note 1).

12 This link between the two studies seems not to have been generally recognized, but see my review essay, "Feminist Chaucer? Some Implications for Teaching," *Studies in Medieval and Renaissance Teaching* 5, no. 2 (1997): 77–85, especially 83. My summary and evaluation of *Feminizing Chaucer* develops some points from this earlier essay.

his estate ("But thilke text heeld he nat worth an oystre") and thus becomes an individual, so the Wife becomes recognizably human when she interacts with the models that Chaucer has used to construct her. As we experience through her character "the imagined representation of an individual engagement with the stereotypes and their absorption into an individual life," we feel for ourselves how the stereotypes limit and confine.[13]

This view of the Wife as both reflecting and reflecting upon the antifeminist model had some precedents in earlier accounts, and it is probably the starting point for most readings of her character today.[14] Another of the book's claims was both more original and more controversial. According to Mann, not only does Chaucer critique the negative "Eva" pole of the stereotype, but he also refashions the stereotype's positive pole, with its conventionally feminine virtues of patience and pity, into an ethical ideal for all human beings, female and male. So, in addition to showing how this ideal is exemplified by such characters as Griselda (in the *Clerk's Tale*) and Constance (in the *Man of Law's Tale*), Mann also considered how it shapes the conduct of such male characters as Theseus in the *Knight's Tale* and Arveragus in the *Franklin's Tale*, so that each becomes a "feminized hero."[15] In the process, a model for imagining feminine identity becomes "the norm against which all human behaviour is to be measured," the basis for "a fully human ideal that erases male/female role divisions."[16] Susan Crane, among others, disagreed, objecting that since "the current does not run in reverse from masculine into feminine identity," with female characters adopting masculine virtues, Chaucer's gender ideal is "finally masculine."[17]

13 *Feminizing Chaucer*, 67. See also pages 65–6 on how Chaucer places the reader "in the Wife's position" as she hears the string of exempla from Jankin's book.

14 See Derek Pearsall, "Medieval Literature and Historical Enquiry," *Modern Language Review* 99, no. 4 (2004): xxxi–xlii, for the pervasiveness of this view: "I do not think that there are many readers of Chaucer now ... who cannot understand how the Wife of Bath, grotesque as she is, is portrayed as both a victim and a manipulator of the patriarchal system in which she lives" (xxxiii). Important anticipations of Mann's argument include Robert W. Hanning, "From *Eva* and *Ave* to Eglentyne and Alisoun: Chaucer's Insight into the Roles Women Play," *Signs* 2 (1972): 580–99; Hope Phyllis Weissman, "Antifeminism and Chaucer's Characterization of Women," in *Geoffrey Chaucer: A Collection of Original Articles*, ed. George D. Economou (New York, 1975), 93-110; Mary Carruthers, "The Wife of Bath and the Painting of Lions," *PMLA* 94 (1979): 209–22; and Lee Patterson, "'For the Wyves love of Bathe': Feminine Rhetoric and Poetic Resolution in the *Roman de la Rose* and the *Canterbury Tales*," *Speculum* 58 (1983): 656–95, revised and reprinted in *Chaucer and the Subject of History* (Madison, WI, 1991), 286–317.

15 This phrase provides the title for Mann's fifth chapter, *Feminizing Chaucer*, 129–44.

16 *Feminizing Chaucer*, 2, 144.

17 Susan Crane, *Gender and Romance in Chaucer's Canterbury Tales* (Princeton, NJ, 1994), 21.

In 2002, when Jill Mann published a revised edition of her book, now titled *Feminizing Chaucer*, she added a preface locating her book in relation to other work on Chaucer and gender, beginning with the monographs by Dinshaw, Martin, and Hansen that had appeared nearly simultaneously with her own and citing studies published through 2000. In that preface, she addressed Crane's criticism, countering that figures like Constance and Griselda do mirror certain masculine virtues in their conduct, so that the "current," to adopt Crane's metaphor, may be said to run in more than one direction. But she also made another distinction, one that is crucial for our purposes. For she observed that her readings of Chaucer's representations of gender had aimed especially to place them within "the larger network of ideas in which gender plays a part," particularly "his exploration of cosmic power, and his engagement with questions of chance, destiny, divine justice and free will" mediated to him by Boethius.[18] When Chaucer draws on positive stereotypes about women, his ultimate aim is not to make a statement about gender identity, but to use the stereotypes to address central aspects of human experience as he understands it. For Chaucer, change is the fundamental element of that experience, and the most urgent ethical question is how best to respond to change. In this context, "feminine" submissiveness, or patience, may be revalued as an acceptance of the inevitability of change and a relinquishing of control, while "feminine" pity becomes a movement of feeling that obeys the motions of change. Both positive stereotypes of patience and pity, ostensibly passive, often in Chaucer's works become modes of power, helping to generate an ethical ideal that not only merges elements of feminine and masculine identity, but also active and passive modes of conduct. For Mann, the signal advantage of a feminist or gender-based approach to Chaucer is that it helps us to recognize and sort out the various strands of this ideal and see how Chaucer interweaves them – helps us, in other words, to recover more "of the full human meaning of his work."[19]

It is this wish to understand Chaucer's engagement with gender, not as an end in itself, but as an important element of his thought as a whole, that has set Jill Mann's book apart from most others on the topic.[20] One effect of this larger perspective is that her readings of how gender operates in particular works and passages tend to be enormously persuasive *as* readings, because they harmonize with so many different aspects of the text. So, for instance, Mann's claim

18 *Feminizing Chaucer*, xviii.

19 *Feminizing Chaucer*, 3.

20 One relatively recent exception is Alcuin Blamires, *Chaucer, Ethics, and Gender* (Oxford, 2006), a book that frequently draws on Mann's work.

that both Criseyde's falling in love with Troilus and her subsequent betrayal of him emerge out of the same process of her ongoing accommodation to the demands of change seems deeply in touch with the workings of the poem, far more helpful for understanding it than a more narrowly gender-based anatomy of her character as a projection of masculine anxieties.[21] And Mann's pages on Constance in the *Man of Law's Tale* present her not as a clichéd image of feminine vulnerability and disempowerment, but as the vehicle for a searing engagement with the problem of suffering in a God-governed world. These are readings that take seriously all that the text is trying to say, and consider gender as one crucial element of that complex thought. Furthermore, Mann's interpretations are always advanced through a close scrutiny of particular passages, showing how Chaucer's meanings emerge from the texture of his words – how Criseyde's ongoing experience of change, for instance, is registered in the circlings and hesitations of her internal monologues, or how the narrator's awareness of the provisional nature of human happiness colours the last stanzas of the *Man of Law's Tale*, or how the ebb and flow of command and obedience are mirrored in the syntax of the Franklin's praise of the marriage agreement in his story.[22] Chaucer's language involves us in the experiences he depicts, calling on our identification. At times we may be surprised or have our assumptions tested by what we read, as when we see Chaucer pursuing a far more radical questioning of Christian theodicy than is normally thought possible for a medieval author, or when his ideal of powerful suffering challenges our unreflecting tendency to place absolute value on active modes of conduct.[23] Above all, perhaps, we may find ourselves identifying with Chaucer's own authorial practice, as he crafts his meanings out of inherited materials, sometimes critiquing those materials and sometimes recasting them in original ways, exploiting them to evoke new possibilities. It is part of Chaucer's wisdom to recognize that experience is not lived outside of pre-existing constructions of meaning; to make such ideational constructions, and to use them to organize our experience, is part of what it is to be a human being. We make the meanings for our lives largely by orienting ourselves within and against these constructions, and as we observe a creative artist doing so within his historical moment, "shifting and reworking traditional patterns into radically new forms," we may be fortified and encouraged as we make similar efforts within our own.[24] In the end, as Jill Mann puts

21 See, for instance, Elaine Tuttle Hansen, *Chaucer and the Fictions of Gender*, 156–74.

22 *Feminizing Chaucer*, 18–25, 111–12, 88–91.

23 *Feminizing Chaucer*, 103–5, 142–4.

24 *Feminizing Chaucer*, 151.

it, it is not any one configuration of meaning that Chaucer offers, "but simply the demonstration that reconstruction is possible, that is the most valuable contribution he has to make."[25]

Between these two books on Chaucer, then, a reasonably coherent picture of Jill Mann's scholarly and critical practice begins to emerge, one that is relevant both to those two studies and to the essays collected here. In her engagement with medieval literature, she is especially drawn to examining how great authors create new meanings within their own historical situation and existing systems of thought, reflecting on the nature of human experience as they understand it. In order to recover the process by which these meanings are shaped, the work must be attended to sympathetically, within its own structure of ideas. Often, as in the two books on Chaucer, this will involve studying the work in close connection with its sources or analogues, to highlight both the author's indebtedness and originality. Within this collection, the last three essays on Malory offer a particularly sustained example of this approach. Just as Jill Mann reads the *General Prologue* against the genre of medieval estates satire, or as she juxtaposes Chaucer's representation of women with what we find in Theophrastus and Jean de Meun, so these essays build their arguments on scrupulously detailed comparisons between Malory's tales and their French sources to show how Malory adapts those sources, and the assumptions they bear about the nature of human experience, to further his own very different ends. (A similar point might be made about Jill Mann's 2009 monograph on beast literature, *From Aesop to Reynard*, which analyses individual works against the existing norms established by beast fable and beast epic, and especially their divergent views of human behaviour and language.)[26] Other essays in the collection examine the uses that Chaucer makes of Boethius, or that the *Gawain*-poet makes of Aristotle's theory of value and the medieval commentary tradition.[27] One hallmark of all of these essays, and indeed of all Jill Mann's work, is masterful

---

25 *Feminizing Chaucer*, 151.

26 Jill Mann, *From Aesop to Reynard: Beast Literature in Medieval Britain* (Oxford, 2009). Medieval beast literature has been a particular focus of Jill Mann's scholarship throughout her career. In addition to this critical study, she has published numerous articles on the topic, as well as an authoritative edition of the twelfth-century beast epic *Ysengrimus*. (Jill Mann, ed., *Ysengrimus: Text with Translation, Commentary, and Introduction* [Leiden, 1987]; in 2013 a students' version of this edition appeared in The Dumbarton Oaks Medieval Library.)

27 See respectively "Chance and Destiny in *Troilus and Criseyde* and the *Knight's Tale*" and "Price and Value in *Sir Gawain and the Green Knight*."

learning worn lightly, conveyed in prose that is straightforward and clear, addressed equally to specialists in the field and to general readers who wish to learn more about, and from, the literature of the past.[28]

Jill Mann's patient engagement with the medieval text also involves a careful attention to the details of its language. To my mind, she is hands down the best close reader of medieval literature operating in the field today. I have already mentioned several enlightening passage analyses from *Feminizing Chaucer*, and I could have cited many more. Such readings may be found in virtually every essay in this collection, from the sensitive and entirely persuasive account of the consummation scene in *Troilus and Criseyde* offered in the first published of these essays, "Troilus's Swoon" (1981), to the intricate tracking of the *Gawain*-poet's images of physical and moral enclosure in the most recent contribution, "Courtly Aesthetics and Courtly Ethics in *Sir Gawain and the Green Knight*" (2009). These are close readings of familiar passages from canonical works, and like all great close readings, they leave us feeling that we have understood the passages and the works for the first time. Yet the remarkable attentiveness to language in Jill Mann's work is never in the service of a sheerly aesthetic formalism; it is integral to her historicist approach. Many of the preoccupations of twentieth-century formalisms, and especially of the New Criticism, are of little importance to her work. Persona and irony are not terms to conjure with in her critical vocabulary, and she tends not to interpret individual *Canterbury Tales*, for instance, as expressing the personalities of their tellers. Rarely does she seek to offer a comprehensive reading of a particular work – in this collection, her essay "Chaucerian Themes and Style in the *Franklin's Tale*" comes the closest to such a full-dress interpretation – and even the operation of character within

28 As I mention later, the general reader tends to be neglected in most criticism of medieval literature today, but Jill Mann's determination to address that reader's interests and needs has grown, if anything, more emphatic over time. When she and Piero Boitani compose the preface to their co-edited *Cambridge Chaucer Companion* in the mid-eighties, they address it to students, but seventeen years later, when the volume is reissued in a revised form as *The Cambridge Companion to Chaucer*, its preface is directed to an audience of readers. Compare "students approaching Chaucer for the first time," "students may test their responses," "the student is best served," and "the interested student," in *The Cambridge Chaucer Companion*, ed. Piero Boitani and Jill Mann (Cambridge, 1986), viii–ix, to "students, teachers, and all general readers who wish to approach Chaucer's work," "readers may test their own responses," "the reader is best served," and "the interested reader," in *The Cambridge Companion to Chaucer*, ed. Piero Boitani and Jill Mann (Cambridge, 2003), ix–x. This heightened emphasis on the needs of the general reader, at a time when the academic brigade is marching the other way, comes about as close as Jill Mann gets to critical polemics.

narrative is a relatively tangential concern.[29] Rather, what intrigues her is how medieval authors use language within their historical moment to reflect upon the conditions of general human experience as they understand it. In the introduction to her magisterial Penguin Classics edition of the *Canterbury Tales*, she uses the metaphor of the kaleidoscope to convey her sense of how Chaucer addresses the recurring conditions of general experience.[30] The different elements of that experience are like different shards of coloured glass, and each new work involves another shaking of the kaleidoscope, a fresh combination of the experiential themes. The metaphor might apply equally well to the essays in this volume, those on the *Gawain*-poet and on Malory as well as those on Chaucer.

The "key words" of which Jill Mann speaks in her "Author's Preface" are a crucial element of this historically specific engagement with general experience as refracted through language. Such words as "aventure" and "proces" and "hap" and "pris," to name only a few, hold within themselves multiple possible significances, some or all of which may be activated in any given use, and medieval authors often build their meanings out of these possibilities.[31] To take a relatively straightforward example, "suffraunce" in Middle English may mean "suffering" in the modern sense, but also "allowing, giving permission," an older meaning reflected in the now-archaic usage, "to suffer someone to do something." As Chaucer uses the word, these two strands of meanings coalesce in the figure of a Christian God who allows suffering to occur, but who also experiences it in the person of the son with whom he is consubstantial.[32] These embedded meanings make the word a valuable resource for Chaucer to draw on as

29 For an interest in character as a defining quality of E.T. Donaldson's criticism, as well as that of other Chaucerians influenced by the New Criticism, see Lee Patterson, *Negotiating the Past: The Historical Understanding of Medieval Literature* (Madison, WI, 1987), 20–6. For Jill Mann's contention that for Chaucer character is of relatively slight importance in determining an individual's fate, see the concluding section of "Chance and Destiny in *Troilus and Criseyde* and the *Knight's Tale*" included in this volume.

30 Geoffrey Chaucer, *The Canterbury Tales*, ed. Jill Mann (London, 2005), xxiii–xxvi.

31 An important (and acknowledged) precedent for Jill Mann's analyses of medieval key words is J.D. Burnley's too often neglected study, *Chaucer's Language and the Philosophers' Tradition* (Cambridge, 1979), cited in *Feminizing Chaucer*, 139. Mann's explication of the key words "pity" and "patience" owes a special debt to Burnley's work. More distantly in the background are C.S. Lewis, *Studies in Words* (Cambridge, 1960) and Raymond Williams, *Keywords: A Vocabulary of Culture and Society* (New York, 1976). More recently, Richard Firth Green, in *A Crisis of Truth: Literature and Law in Ricardian England* (Philadelphia, PA, 1999), offers a fascinating account of a single key word, "truth," whose evolving significances are vital to late fourteenth-century English culture and literature.

32 See chapter 7, "Parents and Children in the *Canterbury Tales*," 117–37 below.

he develops his own creative engagement with the problem of innocent suffering. For Chaucer, as for the *Gawain*-poet and Malory, the key words, freighted with inherited possibilities for meaning, are like traditional norms and systems of thought, conventional materials out of which new meanings may be crafted. As we observe these authors drawing upon the implications of these key words to articulate their own understandings of experience, we may learn from the past in at least two different ways. First, for all that we honour historical difference, within Western culture lived experience is not entirely discontinuous over time; reading historically, we still may find overlaps and intersections between what we discover from medieval works and what we experience in our own lives. And, second, the process of making meanings is itself a human universal. By reading historically, we put ourselves in touch with that human process, as transacted in the very different conditions of the past. When Jill Mann says of Chaucer that "the human is primary for him,"[33] she refers especially, I think, to the way that the author creates meanings within his given circumstances, and when she speaks of "Life in Words," this is the life that she has in mind. If we are careful to observe the medieval author orienting himself within these possibilities in his own historical moment, we may revive his work's capacity to speak to us in ours.

These, then, are the workings of Jill Mann's critical practice, both as realized in the two books under discussion and as displayed in the fifteen essays that you have before you now. In her criticism, it is the very difference of the past that allows it to speak to us today. And by incorporating in her critical practice her own version of the medieval ideal of patience, Jill Mann demonstrates how it is possible for someone in the present to have her life reshaped by the literature of the past. Why is her example so important to us now? Quite simply, because in recent years, apart from Jill Mann's work, reading historically in order to connect with the past has been the road not taken within medieval literary studies. To see how and why this is so, we might start with Lee Patterson's deservedly influential, indeed now canonical, 1987 essay of "Historical Criticism and the Development of Chaucer Studies."[34] Writing in the late eighties, Patterson saw Chaucer studies as divided between two main camps, an essentialist humanism heavily influenced by the New Criticism and most closely associated with the figures of E.T. Donaldson and Charles Muscatine, on the one hand, and on the other a fiercely anti-individualist, anti-humanist historicism, the exegetical

33 "Chaucer and Atheism," 16.

34 In *Negotiating the Past*, 3–39, revised and reprinted in *Acts of Recognition: Essays on Medieval Culture* (Notre Dame, IN, 2010), 1–30.

criticism practised by D.W. Robertson and his followers. One critical school, alert to verbal nuance and irony, looked to Chaucer for his insights into an unchanging human nature, and particularly into human psychology, while the other saw the medieval period as shaped by a set of values completely alien to those of most modern readers, values determined by an Augustinian aesthetic that needed to be recovered through a deliberate effort of historical retrieval that moved past the surface of the text to pursue allegorical meanings. For Patterson, this impasse between New Criticism and exegetics, between humanistic essentialism and anti-essentialist historicism, was the defining dilemma of Chaucer studies. Patterson's own plea was for a historicism that left room for individual agency, and in this he differentiated his own historicist work not just from the exegetical labours of Robertson and his followers, but also from the totalizing narratives of subversion and containment offered in the 1980s by such new historicist critics of Renaissance literature as Stephen Greenblatt and Louis Montrose.[35] In his subsequent book on Chaucer, Patterson showed the poet establishing an individual subjectivity by means of his own engagement with history, and claiming our interest today as a significant participant in the ongoing history of the human subject.[36]

During the more than twenty-five years since the publication of Patterson's essay, historicist work has increasingly come to dominate the field of medieval literary studies, and now its pre-eminence is virtually unchallenged.[37] But the historicisms currently practised by literary medievalists are very different from that advocated by Patterson in his essay. While Patterson's work is most indebted to Marxist social theory and aesthetics, and particularly to the work of

35 For Patterson's strictures on the new historicism, see *Negotiating the Past*, 60–70.

36 Patterson, *Chaucer and the Subject of History*.

37 For the current dominance of historicist approaches, see Pearsall, "Medieval Literature and Historical Enquiry." Even critics who approach medieval literature from perspectives sometimes stigmatized as "presentist," such as queer or postcolonial studies, are careful to articulate their arguments in historicized terms. See, for instance, the essays in *Queering the Middle Ages*, ed. Glenn Burger and Steven F. Kruger (Minneapolis, MN, 2001), and in *The Postcolonial Middle Ages*, ed. Jeffrey Jerome Cohen (New York, 2000), as well as Carolyn Dinshaw, "New Approaches to Chaucer," in Boitani and Mann, *The Cambridge Companion to Chaucer*, 270–89. Dinshaw's hermeneutic of queer "touching" is based on a recognition of historical difference; see Carolyn Dinshaw, *Getting Medieval: Sexualities and Conventions, Pre- and Postmodern* (Durham, NC, 1999), 1–54. The one significant strain of opposition to critical historicism has come from critics operating in a psychoanalytic mode; for a reflection on this controversy, see Elizabeth Scala, "Historicists and Their Discontents," *Texas Studies in Literature and Language* 44 (2002): 108–31, as well as Louise O. Aranye Fradenberg, *Sacrifice Your Love: Psychoanalysis, Historicism, Chaucer* (Minneapolis, MN, 2002).

Adorno, more recent work in the historicist mode is energized by the proliferating critical approaches made available by post-structuralism. Rather than History, these critics approach medieval works from the perspectives of multiple local histories, shifting contexts not necessarily reconcilable into a larger whole, indeed often resisting such totalization. The focus now is on discrete texts generated within peculiar circumstances, with meanings refracted through such processes as manuscript production and circulation, or dispersal among pluralist, multilingual communities. And the shift has been away from canonical authors like Chaucer and the *Gawain*-poet to more marginal figures and texts that fascinate largely because of their very marginality.[38] There is a great sense of excitement about this heterogeneous body of work, the excitement of challenging boundaries and marking new distinctions. But the move of medieval literary studies away from canonical authors and toward increasingly fragmented and localized histories has had at least two regrettable effects. One is the loss of any reasonable chance of engaging the interest of a non-specialist reader. For the most part, critics in this mode operate out of concerns that are too narrowly specialized, too parochial, to captivate anyone who is not already an expert in the field, engaged with its normative discourses. While a non-canonical author like Lydgate, or a non-canonical text like the *Ormulum*, can profitably be read in the light of the culture within which they were produced and the exigencies of their historical moments, they can never speak to readers who turn to literature for pleasure and look for meanings that they can apply to their lives.[39] And,

38 An important essay heralding the shift toward a postmodern plurality of histories is Stephen G. Nichols, "Writing the New Middle Ages," *PMLA* 120 (2005): 422–41. Patterson's second book on Chaucer, *Temporal Circumstances*, shifts into this postmodernist mode as well, replacing the concentration on a single career narrative in *Chaucer and the Subject of History* with attention to "a plurality of micronarratives" (Lee Patterson, *Temporal Circumstances: Form and History in The Canterbury Tales* [New York, 2006], 14). A similar progression may been seen in the work of another pioneering historicist in medieval literary studies, Paul Strohm, who goes from the uniform focus of *Social Chaucer* (Cambridge, MA, 1989) to the multiple histories traced in *Hochon's Arrow: The Social Imagination of Fourteenth-Century Texts* (Princeton, NJ, 1992) and *Theory and the Pre-Modern Text* (Minneapolis, MN, 2000). An excellent (and sympathetic) account of the diverse forms taken by the current "hunger to historicize" in medieval literary studies is offered by David Raybin, "Critical Approaches," in *A Companion to Medieval English Literature and Culture, c.1350–c.1500*, ed. Peter Brown (Oxford, 2007), 9–24; reference at 13.

39 For Lydgate as a previously marginal figure who becomes a critical cynosure, see James Simpson, *The Oxford English Literary History, Volume 2, 1350–1543: Reform and Cultural Revolution* (Oxford, 2002) and Derek Pearsall's riposte, "The Apotheosis of John Lydgate," *Journal of Medieval and Early Modern Studies* 35 (2005): 25–38. An extended reading of the *Ormulum* may be found in Christopher Cannon's study of early Middle English literature, *The Grounds of English Literature* (Oxford, 2004), 82–110. For both Simpson and Cannon, the emphasis on

second, one intended result of this pluralistic, deliberately fragmented historicism is to make medieval culture seem so elusive as to be virtually unknowable and thus inescapably remote from – or "other to" – our present concerns.[40]

It is this situation that gives Jill Mann's work the special pertinence that it must have for us today. I am not the first to express concern about the estranging effects of the current modes of historicizing, as well as their tendency to bypass the needs and interests of the non-specialist reader. Two distinguished medievalists of the generation before Jill Mann, Derek Pearsall and J.A. Burrow, have expressed similar reservations in essays that have circulated widely within the field.[41] But both essays end weakly, calling for a return to the literary (in the case of Pearsall) or for a renewed recognition of the claims of genius (in the case of Burrow). Such gestures seem formulaic and underdefined, an appeal to "mystified" categories, as a Marxist might put it. I think that the example of Jill Mann's work offers a far more rigorous and substantial alternative. If we return to Patterson's original contrast between Donaldson and Robertson, Jill Mann combines Donaldson's alertness to the effects created by language with a historicist determination to read the literary work within its own context. She looks for ways that we can connect works from the past with our own experience, but her respect for historical difference, her deep scholarship, and her unmatched

---

non-canonical texts is polemical, an effort to recover texts that they believe the ascendant category of "the literary" had forced into neglect. For Cannon, this dislodging of the non-literary occurred in the fourteenth century, while Simpson places it in the sixteenth, but in both instances the formidable efforts of these two critics are directed at retrieving the non-canonical texts that have been displaced. The first critical monument to this urge to reperiodize the literature of medieval England and to move away from canonical authors was the massive and enormously controversial volume edited by David Wallace, *The Cambridge History of Medieval English Literature* (Cambridge, 1999). For a conspectus of critical responses, see "Colloquium: *The Cambridge History of Medieval English Literature*," *Studies in the Age of Chaucer* 23 (2001): 473–519, with essays by Christine Chism, Theresa Coletti, Fiona Somerset, Sarah Stanbury, Anne Savage, and a response by David Wallace.

40 Compare David Wallace's preface to the *Cambridge History*: "The aim here is to defamiliarize the present, including present accounts of medieval and Renaissance culture, by achieving some sense of the strangeness, the unlikeliness, the historical peculiarity, of medieval compositional processes" (xiv).

41 Derek Pearsall, "Medieval Literature and Historical Enquiry," and J.A. Burrow, "Should We Leave Medieval Literature to the Medievalists?" *Essays in Criticism* 53 (2003): 278–83. In an earlier essay, "The Sinking Island and the Dying Author: R.W. Chambers Fifty Years On" (*Essays in Criticism* 30 [1990]: 1–23), Burrow had affirmed his own belief in the "distinction between writers or writings which live today in the minds of readers and those which do not" (19), a belief to which both Pearsall and Mann would surely subscribe.

capacity for sympathetic close reading act as checks against any tendency to lapse into unreflecting identification or solipsism. In the work that she has produced over the course of her career, including the essays contained in this volume, she has sustained an effort to remain responsive to the text within its own historical circumstances, and by this very means to allow it to speak to us in ours. In a 2010 essay, Steven Justice speaks of "literary criticism's recent allergy to its object of study."[42] That Justice himself was along with Patterson and Paul Strohm one of the trailblazing historicists in medieval literary studies of the 1990s, author of an influential study of the discourses of the English Rising, gives his remark additional point.[43] Jill Mann's work shows one way that this allergy can be avoided, perhaps even cured; one way that a humanist understanding of medieval literature (and of literature *tout court*) can continue to thrive, not by fleeing from history, but by engaging it more fully.[44]

In my remarks so far, I have touched briefly on a few of the essays included in this volume, and I have been especially concerned to show how the collection's emphasis on key words focuses the attention to historicized reading that animates Jill Mann's work. Let me shift my own focus now, to consider more fully the volume before you and the fifteen essays that it contains. I should begin by acknowledging that these represent less than a third of the over fifty essays published by Jill Mann to date, not counting book reviews, encyclopedia entries, and

42 Steven Justice, "Literary History," in *Chaucer: Contemporary Approaches*, ed. Susanna Fein and David Raybin (University Park, PA, 2010), 199–214; reference at 211.

43 Steven Justice, *Writing and Rebellion: England in 1381* (Berkeley, CA, 1994).

44 This last clause would characterize Lee Patterson's work as well as Jill Mann's, and in fact in their shared attention to the human significance of the medieval author's engagement with his own circumstances the two critics have much in common; in "Chaucer and Atheism" Jill Mann notes her own sympathy with Patterson's desire "to urge the claims of humanism" (18). Patterson and Mann differ in many other ways, of course, but especially, I think, in their abilities and inclinations as close readers. As extraordinary an achievement as *Chaucer and the Subject of History* is, its interpretations always take the form of inserting Chaucer's works within particular historical frameworks (placing the *Knight's Tale*, for instance, in relation to the paradoxes of chivalric identity). These juxtapositions are often exceptionally stimulating for one's understanding of the work as a whole and what it may be trying to do, but I honestly cannot recall a single instance where my understanding of a particular passage in Chaucer was transformed by reading Patterson's work, an experience that I regularly have while reading Mann. While both critics encourage us to learn from Chaucer by identifying with his activity as an author, only for Mann is this an identification achieved through the process of reading, rather than by reframing the substance of what has already been read.

the like.[45] In selecting the essays for this collection, I have chosen those I considered to be of exceptionally high quality, but I have also concentrated on the three canonical authors whose works Jill Mann has addressed most often: Chaucer, the *Gawain*-poet, and Malory. This has meant omitting many essays on more specialized topics that have powerfully engaged her critical intelligence, such as medieval Latin poetry, beast literature, textual scholarship, and Langland. However, of all those writing today about medieval literature Jill Mann speaks most directly to the needs and interests of the intelligent general reader, and for that reader these are the three authors who are most likely to matter. (Sadly, I have yet to meet a non-academic who truly cared for Langland.)[46] I am confident that all such readers, as well as specialists in the field, will come away from this volume with their understanding of these three writers tested, extended, and challenged, not just by what they find within individual essays, but also by the overlapping and connections among them. Some of these connections are among essays devoted to a single author, viewing his work from different angles. So, precisely half of the volume – seven and a half of its fifteen essays – is devoted to exploring the complex dynamic of the Chaucerian response to change in all of its implications, whether at the level of the human or of the divine.[47] Similarly, two of the essays on the *Gawain*-poet address different but

45 For a complete bibliography of Jill Mann's published work up to 2009, see the Festschrift for her edited by Christopher Cannon and Maura Nolan, *Medieval Latin and Middle English Literature: Essays in Honour of Jill Mann* (Cambridge, 2011), xi–xvi.

46 That said, the omission of three superb essays on that poet does cause a pang. They are "Eating and Drinking in 'Piers Plowman,'" *Essays and Studies* 32 (1979): 26–43; "Langland and Allegory," published by the Medieval Institute in pamphlet form as the second of the Morton W. Bloomfield Lectures in Medieval English Literature (Kalamazoo, MI, 1992); and "The Nature of Need Revisited," *The Yearbook of Langland Studies* 18 (2004): 3–29. All three essays, like so many in this volume, concentrate on how an author builds meanings out of the literal and even material implications of key words; in "Langland and Allegory" Jill Mann maintains that this process is fundamental to Langland's distinctive use of personification allegory, while the closing pages of "The Nature of Need Revisited" mirror the argument of several essays included here in proposing that Langland models his depiction of divine need upon human experience. Still, Langland's thematic concerns as addressed in these three essays overlap far less with those of the three authors considered in this volume than those three authors overlap with one another, so what the volume loses in breadth it may (I hope) gain in coherence. I take further consolation from the fact that "Langland and Allegory," which has long been the hardest of these three essays to obtain, has recently been republished in *The Morton W. Bloomfield Lectures, 1989–2005*, ed. Daniel Donoghue, James Simpson, and Nicholas Watson (Kalamazoo, MI, 2010), and thus become more widely available.

47 Many of these essays were originally envisioned as part of a larger study of central themes in the *Canterbury Tales*; although that study was never completed, its outline is sketched in Jill Mann's introduction to her Penguin Classics edition of *The Canterbury Tales*, xvii–xlix, especially xxiii–xlii.

complementary aspects of his singularly materialistic idealism, while the essays on Malory trace in careful detail the world view of the author and his knights, with their active embrace of the seemingly arbitrary nature of human experience, combined with a longing for both secular and spiritual wholeness. But the collection also highlights connections among its three authors, connections that are sometimes surprising. On the face of it, few authors could seem less similar than Malory and Chaucer, who shows little interest in scenes of battle and derring-do.[48] And yet the submission of Malory's knights to the unknowable processes of adventure, a submission that Malory emphasizes through his systematic deviations from his French sources, is an attitude similar in kind to the Chaucerian acceptance of chance and change. (Both authors also draw extensively on the implications of "aventure" or "adventure" as an important key word.) As Jill Mann demonstrates in her essay "Sir Gawain and the Romance Hero," the *Gawain*-poet shares elements of this attitude, too. But in other ways the *Gawain*-poet's values are distinct from, even opposed to, those of Chaucer and Malory, and these contrasts among the authors are at least as illuminating as their similarities. A recurrent theme of this volume is Jill Mann's provocative claim that medieval authors often deliberately present religious ideas as derived from, rather than transcending, worldly experience, with "the divine" expressing "an aspect of the human."[49] So, Chaucer bases his model of God's involvement with humanity on the relation between parents and their children, with its paradoxical combination of love and power, while Malory builds his own spiritual ideal, epitomized by the Grail, out of the worldly elements of chivalric fellowship, a desire for wholeness, and blood. As we discover in the essay "Satisfaction and Payment in Middle English Literature," though, the

48 As Jill Mann elsewhere remarks, the chivalric narrative that so preoccupies medieval authors, and pre-eminently Malory, where a single male protagonist sets off in search of adventure, is found only once in the entire body of Chaucer's poetry, when it is burlesqued in *Sir Thopas* (*Feminizing Chaucer*, 3).

49 See "Shakespeare and Chaucer: 'What is Criseyde Worth?'" 40–1 below. In "Chaucer and Atheism," Jill Mann speaks even more provocatively of "the divine [in Chaucer] ... as the superflux of the human" (16). And in a powerful recent essay, "In Defence of Francesca: Human and Divine Love in Dante and Chaucer," *Strumenti critici* 131 (2013): 3–26, she brilliantly extends this line of thought to Dante, arguing that Francesca's earthly love provides an indispensable and never fully abandoned model for the divine love associated with Beatrice, and that Chaucer so understands it, recognizing that "Beatrice *needs* Francesca if she is to mean anything" (25, italics in original). Mann's discussion in this essay of Troilus's use of Christian language to evoke his love for Criseyde, a language that she says he "spontaneously reinvents" (23), offers a fresh way in to this much-debated aspect of *Troilus and Criseyde*.

Gawain-poet's approach to spiritual truth is different. While Chaucer uses the complicated nuances of the key word "ynogh" to evoke the mirroring of the human in the divine, the *Gawain*-poet uses these same connotations to enforce an absolute break between mortal and heavenly realms. Along intriguingly parallel lines, when anatomizing human conduct the *Gawain*-poet draws on a mercantile vocabulary of price and value, based ultimately on Aristotle, that fails to stir Chaucer's interest.[50] One formative element of the *Gawain*-poet's practice, then, may be a desire to segregate realms that for Chaucer and Malory are mutually intelligible.

These are just a few of the thought-provoking connections that I have discovered among the essays and authors contained in this collection; other readers are sure to find more. Above all, though, the volume is unified by its exploration of the key words whose complex implications serve as vehicles of the thought of these three authors – words such as "aventure" and "patience" and "pitous," or "pris" and "suffraunce," or "proces" and "worship" and glose," and many more. Again, the consideration of these words overlaps and ramifies between essays and among authors, and so it may be helpful if I offer a brief overview of the volume and its contents to orient readers as they set off explore it on their own.

The volume opens with a cluster of seven seminal essays on Chaucer published between 1980 and 1991. Each of these pursues its own direction, but all are engaged in one way or another with the central Chaucerian topic of change. The first essay, "Troilus's Swoon," looks closely at the consummation scene in Book III of *Troilus and Criseyde*, proposing that Troilus's fainting in that scene is best understood, not as a sign of weakness, but as a crucial stage in the process whereby power continually shifts between one lover and the other, as Chaucer seeks to show the couple attaining a relationship built on the mutual submission to one another's will. The flexible nature of such a relationship may strike us as peculiarly modern, but in fact it is designed by Chaucer to meet the demands of the human condition as he understands it in his own historical moment, and especially to accommodate the perennial fluctuations of change. In this poem, and throughout Chaucer's work, the key word "proces" is used to evoke this central aspect of human experience. The collection's second essay, "Shakespeare and Chaucer: 'What is Criseyde Worth?'" begins by pondering the paradox that Chaucer seems to offer a more richly dramatic, "Shakespearean" presentation of Criseyde's behaviour in *Troilus and Criseyde* than Shakespeare himself does of the character of Cressida in *Troilus and Cressida*, but this

50 See "Price and Value in *Sir Gawain and the Green Knight*" and "Shakespeare and Chaucer: 'What is Criseyde Worth?'"

is because in this play Shakespeare is especially interested in the topic of value and exchange, and it serves this interest for Cressida to be presented undramatically as "a blank cheque on which men write their own estimates of value." Chaucer, on the other hand, wishes to show how Criseyde's behaviour negotiates the conflicting demands of private experience and public conduct, as we see in the first scene in the temple and in her early exchanges with Pandarus. Once again it is the need to accommodate change that drives human actions. When the question of value is introduced in Chaucer's poem, it is not in order to calculate Criseyde's worth, but to evoke the spiritual dimension of the "grete worthynesse" that she and Troilus experience in love, analogizing it to the bargain achieved by a redeemer who died "oure soules for to beye."

The next two essays, both landmarks of Chaucer criticism, offer more systematic accounts of the dynamics of change as Chaucer understands it, highlighting especially the importance of chance. The first of the two, "Chance and Destiny in *Troilus and Criseyde* and the *Knight's Tale*," begins with an extended reading of the scene in *Troilus and Criseyde* where Criseyde sees Troilus riding down the streets of Troy and recognizes that she is falling in love with him, an episode that demonstrates the importance of chance as a motivating force behind events in Chaucer's narrative poems. Chaucer derives much of his understanding of chance and destiny from Boethius's *Consolation of Philosophy*, focusing that understanding through his use of such key words as "hap," "aventure," and "cas." Chaucer, however, takes Boethius's thought one step further: while for Boethius Fortune and mutability are external to human experience, Chaucer views our inner lives as governed by the processes of change. Chaucer's unsurpassedly vivid representation of human speech and behaviour may encourage us to think that his characters determine their fates, but in fact "his deepest interest in investigating human psychology is to uncover the subtlest manifestations of time and change at work in human emotions, shaping the course of human lives." The collection's fourth essay, "Chaucerian Themes and Style in the *Franklin's Tale*," offers the first and most comprehensive account of the value of patience as a human surrender to the processes of change, a surrender that paradoxically creates power. Within the *Franklin's Tale*, a central work within Chaucer's oeuvre, this surrender is manifest in Arveragus's relinquishment of "maistrye" at the tale's beginning, in his bidding Dorigen to keep her promise at its crisis, and in Aurelius's releasing Dorigen from her bond at its close. Rather than adherence to a static moral ideal, what brings about the tale's happy ending is the flexibility of "the ideal of patience, which is founded on change, on the perpetual readiness to meet, to accept, and to transform the endless and fluctuating succession of 'aventures' that life offers." The true magic in the tale is that of Aurelius's "pitee," a responsive movement of the human heart.

The title of the volume's fifth essay, "Anger and 'Glosynge' in the *Canterbury Tales*," must come as something of a surprise. Just how are these two terms related, and what do they add to the preceding analyses of Chaucer's thought? In fact, within the *Canterbury Tales* Chaucer often presents the activity of glossing a text – of supplementing its literal meaning with interpretive commentary – as an excessive imposition of will, an act of anger. Both anger and glossing represent "a refusal of reality, a refusal to accommodate the self either to events in the world outside, or to the autonomous meaning of the text." Each stands, then, as the antithesis of patience, and this essay considers how the dynamic of anger, glossing, and patience plays out in no fewer than fourteen of the *Canterbury Tales*, making it the most widely ranging of the essays in the volume.

Just as the fifth essay supplements the earlier consideration of patience by attending to its opposites, so the sixth one, "The Authority of the Audience in Chaucer," considers how patience might manifest itself as a mode of authorial practice. The key words "auctor" and "auctoritee" are etymologically linked, but when Chaucer represents himself within his own poems it is most often as a reader of other people's works, rather than as a writer who crafts authoritative meanings. In so representing himself, Chaucer acknowledges the way that readers process texts by interpreting them in the light of their own preoccupations, a condition of authorship that he magnanimously (or patiently) accepts.[51]

These first six essays, then, examine the Chaucerian dynamic from a variety of viewpoints, considering the human response to change as manifested through patience and anger, and as an element of authorial practice. The last essay in the collection to be devoted exclusively to Chaucer, "Parents and Children in the *Canterbury Tales*," is an especially important essay within Jill Mann's oeuvre, one that offers a significant shift of perspective. Throughout the *Canterbury Tales*, Chaucer uses the motif of parents and children to explore the paradoxical relationship between love and power, a power that can verge on cruelty. Projected on to the level of the divine, that paradox allows Chaucer to ask such troubling questions as whether God's governance of our lives is "the loving control of a father, or the arbitrary tyranny of a despot," questions that might be thought unaskable by a medieval poet. Crucial to achieving at least a partial resolution of them is the key word "suffraunce," which (as we saw earlier) can mean both "suffering" and "allowing." Uniting the persons of parent and child, God both permits suffering to occur and endures it himself. This manifestation of divine patience mirrors the human activity of childbirth, when a woman gives herself over to pain to bring about new life.

51 In her introduction to the Penguin Classic *Canterbury Tales*, xliv–v, Jill Mann makes this link between patience and Chaucer's authorial practice explicit.

Among the essays in the collection, this one concentrates most closely on the crucial topic of the reciprocal modelling of the human and the divine, as it projects into the divine realm the human surrender to change. The eighth essay, "Satisfaction and Payment in Middle English Literature," also addresses the interplay between human and divine realms of value. This is a transitional essay within the collection, with its interest evenly divided between Chaucer's *Clerk's Tale* and the *Gawain*-poet's dream elegy *Pearl*. The essay considers the rich implications of a single key word, "ynogh," along with the Middle English words derived from its Latin equivalent, *satis* ("satisfaction," of course, but also "satiate," and even "sad"), for developing the thought of these two poems. To us today, "enough" seems a thoroughly ordinary word, but in late medieval literature it "vibrates with emotional and intellectual connotations." The word's power comes from its ability to modulate between two nearly opposite senses, "in moderation" and "to the utmost degree," and at pivotal moments in these two works these meanings converge, so that perfect moderation becomes utter fulfilment. In *Pearl* the narrator's mounting desire to receive "more and more" is answered by the maiden's vision of the heavenly Jerusalem, where all possess "ynogh": an appropriate share of unlimited bliss. Through the parable of the vineyard she directs the narrator from a fixation on payment to an acknowledgment of the supreme value of satisfaction. And the main narrative of the *Clerk's Tale* moves between two identical sentences spoken by Walter toward the beginning and end of the tale: "It is ynogh, Grisilde myn" (365, 1051). The sentence is first spoken when Walter accepts the sufficiency of Griselda's vow to obey him during their marriage, and then again when he acknowledges that her ability to suffer has outstripped his capacity to present her with further trials. In between these moments we behold the spectacle of Walter himself, driven by his insatiable need to test Griselda more and more, a need that is overridden only by Griselda's perfect self-sufficiency. Prompted by Chaucer's (or the Clerk's) allegorizing comments at the conclusion of the tale, critics have pondered the implications of imagining Walter as a God seeking to "prove" the virtues of humankind. But surely it is Griselda, "in the 'insatiability' of her willingness to suffer," who offers the truer image of Christian divinity.

No essay in the collection pursues the implications of its key words more searchingly, or more rewardingly, than this one. And we see again, as in earlier essays, the ways that spiritual values are derived from worldly ones, as the Christian paradox of fulfilment through self-denial is grounded in the paradoxes of earthly satisfaction, both as found in human experience and in the intricate significances of a cluster of key words. Yet the essay's juxtaposition of *Pearl* and the *Clerk's Tale* also establishes some key distinctions between the *Gawain*-poet and Chaucer, distinctions that are especially pertinent to the next pair of essays. While Griselda's self-sufficiency is at least as much a model for the divine as the divine is a model for it, in *Pearl* the maiden's heavenly wisdom remains beyond her father's reach: seeking to cross over the stream and enter the new Jerusalem, he wakes from his dream. The worldly and spiritual realms are not mutually intelligible for the *Gawain*-poet in quite the same way that they are for Chaucer. And as we see in the next pair of essays, when this poet chooses to concentrate on secular experience, his models of excellence are emphatically worldly.

The ninth and tenth essays, published twenty-three years apart, offer paired accounts of ways that the poet of *Sir Gawain and the Green Knight* builds his ethical values on worldly foundations. In the case of "Price and Value in *Sir Gawain and the Green Knight*," these foundations are the norms governing exchange in medieval economic theory, norms ultimately derived from Aristotle. Like the previous essay, this one begins by anatomizing a key word that encompasses two seemingly incommensurate meanings. In Middle English, "pris" may refer to monetary value, as "price" does today, but also to non-monetary worth, such as fame or moral excellence. (In Modern English these meanings are covered by the later derivatives, "praise" and "prize.") In *Sir Gawain and the Green Knight* the non-monetary meanings of the word are defined by the monetary ones; moral values are continually expressed in mercantile terms. Ultimately, Gawain must maintain the equilibrium between his own inner and outer "pris," but the terms of the market never entirely drop out of the equation.

The next essay, "Courtly Aesthetics and Courtly Ethics in *Sir Gawain and the Green Knight*," continues the exploration of the materialist idealism of that poem by examining how lavish courtly display is presented there as an emblem of inner virtue. Extravagant display – what Veblen called "conspicuous consumption" – was a notorious element of the court of Richard II, often attacked by contemporary satirists. Those who defended such extravagance claimed that it served a useful purpose by marking differences of social status. But the poet of *Sir Gawain and the Green Knight* celebrates and values such displays because they provide "a natural expression of the inner splendour of courtly virtues" and thus exemplify the "fusion of material splendour and ethics." Ornate descriptions of Gawain and the Green Knight enclosed within their bright array offer physical images of moral self-containment. And throughout the poem Gawain's inward virtue is presented as a matter for public scrutiny. Rather than critiquing or transcending its social milieu, as is sometimes claimed, the poem uses that milieu to celebrate the free-standing integrity of the chivalric ideal.

A final essay on the *Gawain*-poet, "Sir Gawain and the Romance Hero," prepares for the essays on Malory by showing how "the positive acceptance of submission" characterizes the romance ideal in the poem. While the epic hero is active, the hero of romance is typically passive: he submits himself to adventure. This very willingness to hand himself over to chance constitutes his heroism: the active embrace of passivity makes him a hero. The protagonist of *Sir Gawain and the Green Knight* exemplifies this heroism in his acceptance of the Green Knight's challenge, in his journey toward the Green Chapel, and in his splendid conduct throughout the bedroom scenes. The one moment when Gawain departs from this ideal is when he takes the green girdle in the hope that it will give him active control over events, for in doing so he "fatally qualifies the complete self-abandonment which passive heroism requires." Yet Gawain recovers the romance ideal with his final, uncompromising acceptance of his own failure, an acceptance that confirms his success.

While Jill Mann is best known for her work on Chaucer, she is also a major presence in Malory studies, thanks to the four influential essays with which this volume concludes. Together, these essays show how Malory's chivalric narratives convey a distinctive and powerful vision of human experience. As already remarked, there are elements here that remind us of what we find in Chaucer, especially Malory's fascination with the key word "adventure." As the first of these four essays, "Knightly Combat in Malory's *Morte d'Arthur*," demonstrates, "adventure" literally defines chivalric identity. Knights do not win their identities through heroic exploits – rather, the results of their adventures show them whom the mysterious operations of chance have proved them to be. To accept a quest or undertake an adventure is to submit to the arbitrary workings of chance, while knightly combat provides a formal structure within which "the revelatory movements of chance" may be realized. And the medium of combat is the human body, which in *Le Morte d'Arthur* possesses a unique range of significances. "In Malory, the body is not a clumsy encumbrance to the spirit, nor even its humble tool. It is the medium through which a knight's worship is revealed, and the testing-ground of its validity; it is what the knight opposes to his fellows and yet what unites him with them. It is a field of action, and a repository of truths."

This first essay on Malory introduces a number of key words – "adventure," "worship," "body," "departe," "hole," "felyship" – that are given much fuller development in the three subsequent essays, each of which is built on richly detailed comparisons between Malory and his French sources. In " 'Taking the Adventure': Malory and the *Suite du Merlin*," Jill Mann demonstrates how Malory's systematic changes to the French version of the Balin story reflect his wish to show how chance dictates the sequence of events, so that perceived connections among incidents will not be rational but aesthetic, a shape recognized after the fact and not determined by cause and effect. Recognizing Malory's emphasis on contingency allows us to discern his kinship with Chaucer, but also to feel the force of what he has to tell us about life. Ultimately, the knight's willingness to "take the adventure" involves not simple obedience to a cultural or narrative code, but "an attempt to stretch the self to embrace the utmost reach of possible events."

A new term introduced in this second essay on Malory, "distance," is developed much more fully in the next essay, "The Narrative of Distance, The Distance of Narrative in Malory's *Morte d'Arthur*." By comparing several episodes in Malory's *Book of Tristram* with their French sources, this essay demonstrates the centrality of distance as a theme in Malory's work, but also as its central narrative mode. Thematically, "the continual counterpointing of distance and wholeness" in the experience of the knights – their sense of their own distance from the events in which they participate, juxtaposed with a poignant desire for wholeness – constitutes the significance of Malory's narrative; it is its great subject. Paradoxically, the distance of characters' speeches from their emotions makes those speeches emotionally powerful; in this sense, the usual view that Malory is uninterested in portraying emotion (and particularly the emotion of love) is quite mistaken. Among the narrative devices that Malory adopts to enforce a sense of distance are the encounters of knights with the residue of past events, as if caught in an infinite narrative regress, as well as a tendency toward narrative divergence, with separate story lines presented in quickly alternating sequences and key narrative events related at second-hand. The final events of the *Morte* exemplify both the theme and the narrative mode of distance. Mordred's manner of death grotesquely parodies the knight's willingness to submit to adventure in the hope of achieving wholeness: by forcing himself upon Arthur's spear Mordred imposes his will on events, closing the gap between himself and Arthur, "but the result is a final negation of wholeness." And the death of Arthur himself is portrayed as an event perennially deferred: "The narrative finally passes away from us completely, receding into the past where we have always known it belongs."

The volume's final essay, "Malory and the Grail Legend," begins by asking a simple question: why should the quest for a Eucharistic vessel become "the goal and climax of knightly endeavour"? The usual answer, that the narrative of the grail quest was promoted by members of the clergy to elevate their interests over those of the knightly class, is unpersuasive. In fact, the opposite seems more nearly true, especially in Malory's elaboration of his French sources, where the religious associations of the Grail allow him to celebrate knightly endeavour by sacralizing it. In Malory the human body, like the Grail, is defined as a container for blood. And the movement from inner fragmentation toward wholeness that is the aim of the Grail Quest is modelled upon, rather than departing from, the narrative of knightly adventure, with its longing for identity and wholeness. In this sense the Grail symbolizes not the rejection of chivalric values, but their apotheosis. As this essay analyses the Grail Quest in the light of the narrative structures of knightly adventure delineated in the three preceding essays, the collection rounds to a close with one final return to the topic of the reciprocal modelling of the sacred and the secular that has been such an important unifying theme throughout.

In the first section of this introduction, I suggested some ways that the essays collected here demonstrate the value of Jill Mann's approach to medieval literature, both on its own terms and as an alternative to current tendencies within the field. In summarizing the essays themselves, I have concentrated on what they have to tell us about Chaucer, the *Gawain*-poet, and Malory, singly and in connection with one another. To bring matters to a close, I turn to a celebrated aphorism by Paul Ricoeur about the dialectical nature of interpretation at its best. "Hermeneutics," Ricoeur tells us, "seems to me to be animated by this double motivation: willingness to suspect, willingness to listen; vow of rigor, vow of obedience."[52] Ricoeur's double hermeneutic has always struck me as the standard toward which literary criticism must aspire, if it is to be worthy of the object it studies. In current work on medieval literature the hermeneutic of suspicion primarily holds sway, for reasons that are not hard to understand. No one wants to go back to a naive notion of literary value as defined by the work's fidelity to an unchanging human nature, outside of historical or cultural situation. But to let an anxiety about essentialism foreclose any possibility of identifying with the past is to risk losing what is most valuable in the reading of literature, the ability to learn from and be moved by its meanings as we apply them to our own lives. To this dilemma, I believe, Jill Mann's intellectually rigorous model of patient listening provides an answer, one that negotiates productively between Ricoeur's two poles of suspicion and trust. At this moment, she is an indispensable presence within the field of medieval literary studies, one whose example we especially need before us. In bringing together some of her best work from over a period of nearly thirty years, this volume clarifies the nature and scope of her critical achievement, as well as its implications for the future. For those who continue to believe that medieval literature has the power to challenge and to teach and to inspire, that its words can matter to us as we live our lives, the path leads forward from here.

52 Paul Ricoeur, *Freud and Philosophy: An Essay on Interpretation*, trans. Denis Savage (New Haven, CT, 1970), 27.

LIFE IN WORDS

Chapter One

Troilus's Swoon

Troilus swoons only once in the course of *Troilus and Criseyde.* It is important to remind ourselves of this fact, because this isolated instance is sometimes casually multiplied and generalized, as if it were a frequent testimony to the emotional intensity of Troilus's love. The swoon is also largely responsible for the popular impression of Troilus as a passive and ineffectual lover. The swoon is absent from the *Filostrato* at this point, since Chaucer's whole account of the consummation scene is radically different from Boccaccio's. Boccaccio's Troiolo does, however, swoon at a later point in the story – when he hears the request for the exchange of Criseida and Antenore in the Trojan parliament. This swoon Chaucer removes, while preserving Boccaccio's prefatory description of Troilus repressing his anguish with "mannes herte" (IV.154).[1] Why, then, does he introduce, at an earlier and apparently less disastrous point in the narrative, a swoon which provokes the questioning of Troilus's manhood ("Is this a mannes game?" III.1126)?

The functional role of the swoon can only be understood by seeing it within the context of Troilus's courtship as a whole – and, in particular, of that area of it which represents Chaucer's elaboration of Boccaccio's account, stretching from the arrangement of the meeting at Deiphebus's house to Pandarus's fictitious story of Horaste. (In Boccaccio, when the lovers meet in the consummation scene, it is the first time they have come face to face apart from an encounter at

---

This article originally appeared in a Festschrift for R.W. Frank, as a tribute to his wide-ranging and important contributions to medieval scholarship, and in particular to his work on medieval pathos.

1 Cf. *Filostrato*, IV.xiv.7–8: "ma con fatica pur dentro ritenne / l'amore e'l pianto, come si convenne" ("But with difficulty he restrained the love and grief within, as was fitting").

Criseida's window.) It is generally acknowledged that by protracting the preliminaries to the consummation in this way, Chaucer removes any impression that Criseyde is an easy conquest, and strengthens our sense of the natural growth of the relationship between the lovers, and hence of its solidity. What I want to draw attention to is that the developing relationship between Troilus and Criseyde is conceived and described in terms of power, and that the shifts and transformations in the way each of them either exerts or refuses to exert power over the other lead to the achievement of a mature and complex relationship on which the consummation can fittingly be based.

At the beginning of the poem, the power relationships between Troilus and Criseyde are simply the result of their social situations. Troilus is the king's son; Criseyde is not only his inferior in rank, but is also in an extremely precarious social position as the daughter of a traitor, in need of the protection of Hector in order to maintain any position in Trojan society at all. When Troilus first sees Criseyde in the temple, she is ready to assert herself ("With ful assured lokyng and manere," I.182) against any social opprobrium, but she prudently refrains from provoking it by standing humbly just inside the door, "ay undre shames drede" (I.180). Criseyde's position is also the weaker one just because she is a woman. When left alone to reflect on the news of Troilus's love for her, she is conscious of Troilus's power, as the king's son, to hurt or assist her (II.708–14), but even more prominent in her mind is the fear of masculine dominance and possessiveness, in their particular manifestations of jealousy and boastfulness. These fears are at first introduced in negative form: Criseyde reassures herself that not only is Troilus no boaster, but that she will never give him any opportunity to "bynde" her "in swich a clause" (II.728).[2] The idea that boasting is a linguistic "binding," an imprisonment of one partner within the linguistic freedom of the other, aligns it with jealousy, which is also conceived as a "binding." Criseyde congratulates herself on being without a jealous husband:

"I am myn owene womman, wel at ese –
I thank it God – as after myn estat,

2 The possibly relevant senses of the word "clause" given in the *Middle English Dictionary* are: 1. "a sentence or clause, a brief statement"; 2a. "an individual statement, allegation, admonition, etc. (in a series of such statements)"; 2b. [under which this line is cited] "a conclusion; ?an agreement; ?an inference." (*OED* clearly errs in interpreting this line as the first example of the use of the word in its legal sense.) The difficulty in glossing the word is, I think, due to the originality of the idea that Chaucer is developing: that one can bind by language. Cf. the notion in the *Manciple's Tale* (357) that by speech, by telling one's secrets to another, a person can become another's "thral."

> Right yong, and stonde *unteyd* in lusty leese,
> Withouten jalousie or swich debat:
> Shal noon housbonde seyn to me 'Chek mat!'
> For either they ben ful of jalousie,
> Or maisterfull, or loven novelrie." (II.750–6)[3]

Reflections on her present freedom, however, lead Criseyde inevitably to tremble at the idea of its surrender, and her confidence gives way to fear:

> "Allas! Syn I am free,
> Sholde I now love, and put in jupartie
> My sikernesse, and thrallen libertee?" (II.771–3)

Like Troilus before he falls in love, she finds the most striking aspect of the lover's life to be its servitude:

> "May I naught wel in other folk aspie
> Hire dredfull joye, hire constreinte, and hire peyne?" (II.775–6)

This fear of losing control of the self by submitting to love is countered, first, by Antigone's song – the joyous celebration of one "subgit" to love, which claims that love appears "thraldom" only to those who are outside its experience (II.828, 855–60)[4] – and, second, by Criseyde's dream of the eagle tearing her heart out without pain, which offers her (and us) a mysterious image of an aggression that is not felt as oppression.

Criseyde's fears of men are by no means unwarranted: ironically, she is eventually to give herself to a man whose behaviour certainly merits the term "maisterfull," whose desire to win her is spiced with the delight of wresting a treasured possession from another man (V.792–4), and who is also, it is suggested, a

---

3 My italics. The images of binding in Chaucer's poetry have been fully dealt with by Stephen A. Barney, "Troilus Bound," *Speculum* 47 (1972): 445–58, and John Leyerle, "The Heart and the Chain," in *The Learned and the Lewed: Studies in Chaucer and Medieval Literature*, ed. Larry D. Benson (Cambridge, MA, 1974), 113–45; repr. in *Chaucer's Troilus: Essays in Criticism*, ed. Stephen A. Barney (London, 1980), 181–209.

4 Ida L. Gordon has observed that Antigone's song provides an answer to Criseyde's fears, but she makes this observation part of an argument that Criseyde "has no understanding of love," with which I do not agree (*The Double Sorrow of Troilus* [Oxford, 1970], 98–102). See also Sister Mary Charlotte Borthwick, "Antigone's Song as 'Mirour' in Chaucer's *Troilus and Criseyde*," *Modern Language Quarterly* 22 (1961): 227–35, esp. 232–4.

boaster ("som men seyn he was of tonge large," V.804).[5] But Chaucer takes pains to show that in the case of Troilus, Criseyde's fears are unnecessary. So far from wishing to exert his control over Criseyde, Troilus has himself fallen "thral" to love (I.439), and has acknowledged that in the realm of love the power that he has in the everyday social world is his no longer.

> And to the God of Love thus seyde he
> With pitous vois, "O lord, now youres is
> My spirit, which that oughte youres be.
> Yow thanke I, lord, that han me brought to this.
> But wheither goddesse or womman, iwis,
> She be, I not, which that ye do me serve;
> But as hire man I wol ay lyve and sterve.
>
> "Ye stonden in hir eighen myghtily,
> As in a place unto youre vertu digne;
> Wherfore, lord, if my service or I
> May liken yow, so beth to me benigne;
> For myn estat roial I here resigne
> Into hire hond, and with ful humble chere
> Bicome hir man, as to my lady dere." (I.421–34)

In love, then, the ordinary power relationships are inverted; it is a sign of Love's supremacy that the weaker partner, the lady, wields power over the stronger. When Troilus and Criseyde first meet to talk in Deiphebus's house, we are made conscious of both sets of relationships and their conflicting distributions of power. Externally, the situation casts them in their social roles, with Criseyde as suppliant and Troilus as her powerful protector. So far is this from the emotional truth, and from Troilus's mind, however, that merely to hear Criseyde's formal request for his "lordshipe" throws his carefully rehearsed speech from his mind.

> This Troilus, that herde his lady preye
> Of lordshipe hym, wax neither quyk ne ded,
> Ne myghte o word for shame to it seye,
> Although men sholde smyten of his hed. (III.78–81)

5 John Leyerle shows perceptively how the images of binding denote a deep emotional commitment in Troilus, but with Diomede indicate merely the snares of the seducer ("The Heart and the Chain," 133).

The embarrassment of the word order in the relative clause demonstrates the unease with which Troilus entertains the idea that he might be Criseyde's "lord" rather than she his "lady." This humility works to his advantage: Criseyde, recognizing that his helplessness is a testimony to the genuineness of his feelings, loves him "nevere the lasse" for it (III.85–8). In accepting him as her servant, however, she emphasizes that this relationship suspends and supersedes the external social one:

"But natheles, this warne I yow," quod she,
"A kynges sone although ye be, ywys,
Ye shal namore han sovereignete
Of me in love, than right in that cas is;
N'y nyl forbere, if that ye don amys,
To wratthe yow; and whil that ye me serve,
Chericen yow right after ye disserve." (III.169–75)

It is on this basis that the courtship of Troilus and Criseyde continues up to the point of their meeting by night in Pandarus's house in Book III.[6] But while it is clear that this situation is in itself a good one, since it balances and contains the social power structure that would otherwise threaten to make of love a real "thraldom" for the woman, it also brings a problem: how is it possible for this situation to lead into a consummation of love? For either the lady must convict herself of previous hypocrisy and merely pretended innocence by initiating the process of sexual consummation from her commanding position, or the man must convict himself of hypocrisy and merely pretended submission by urging it upon her. What is important in solving this problem is Chaucer's perception that human emotions and relationships are never static; they are constantly subject to accidents from without and movements from within through which their nature is subtly and almost imperceptibly transformed. The word that Chaucer seems most frequently to associate with this imperceptible but ceaseless movement is "proces," which often serves to mark his reflections on the inevitable transmutations of human emotions and experiences in time. It is the key word, for instance, in the description of the gradual but inevitable slackening of Dorigen's first frenzy of grief at her husband's absence:

By proces, as ye knowen everychoon,
Men may so longe graven in a stoon

6 The inversion of external social relationships is emphasized again at the very beginning of this episode, in Pandarus's comment on Troilus's falling to his knees beside Criseyde's bed: "se how this lord kan knele!" (III.962).

Til some figure therinne emprented be.
So longe han they conforted hire til she
Received hath, by hope and by resoun,
Th'emprenting of hir consolacioun,
Thurgh which hir grete sorwe gan aswage;
She may nat alwey duren in swich rage.
(*Franklin's Tale*, 829–36)

It is significant, therefore, that at the very beginning of the awakening of Criseyde's feelings for Troilus, Chaucer turns aside from his narrative to assure us that the growth of her feelings was not a sudden occurrence, but a "proces."

For I sey nought that she so sodeynly
Yaf hym hire love, but that she gan enclyne
To like hym first, and I have told yow whi;
And after that, his manhod and his pyne
Made love withinne hire herte for to myne,
For which by proces and by good servyse,
He gat hire love, and in no sodeyn wyse. (II.673–9)

This passage has often been taken to be cynical or ambiguous; it seems to me to be neither,[7] but rather an acknowledgment and a warning of the difficulty of recreating the gradualness of an emotional "proces" within a narrative, where the selection of moments when the "proces" receives special stimulus or reaches recognizable stages may mislead us into thinking that these moments in themselves effect the whole movement from one point to another. The flowering of a plant may appear dramatic, but it depends on a long preceding period of slow and silent growth.

The aspect of the "proces" of love that is most important for the present discussion is that its minute and constant movement means that within the acknowledged structure of sovereignty and subjection there grows up another, alternative structure to the relationship, which will allow its consummation to take place, and allow it to mark a genuine transition, rather than an abandonment of hypocrisy which would also constitute a confession of hypocrisy. The part of the poem where we can see this happening is the summarizing description, near the beginning of Book III, of the tenor of the brief meetings between

7 For a different view, see E. Talbot Donaldson, "Criseide and her Narrator," in *Speaking of Chaucer* (New York, 1970), 65–83, at 66.

Troilus and Criseyde after the scene at Deiphebus's house, where Chaucer again refers to what is happening between them as a "proces" (470). In this passage, Chaucer emphasizes Criseyde's surprised delight at Troilus's ability to anticipate her every wish; so far from demonstrating any tendency to assert control over her, or to "bind her in the clause" of boasting, she finds in him that bending of the self to the contours of another's being which leads not to the issuing and execution of commands, the mimicking of one will by another, but the wordless and miraculous fusion of two wills into one, so that it is no longer possible to say whose will is dominant and whose is subjected. This view of the miraculous power of love to create "obeisaunce" to each other in lovers receives its fullest and, in some ways, most moving expression in the speech of the deserted falcon in the *Squire's Tale*, which I should like to quote in order to show how constant a part of Chaucer's view of love it is.

> "And I so loved him for his obeisaunce,
> And for the trouthe I demed in his herte,
> That if so were that anything him smerte,
> Al were it never so lite, and I it wiste,
> Me thoughte I felte deeth min herte twiste.
> And shortly, so ferforth this thing is went,
> That my wil was his willes instrument;
> This is to seyn, my wil obeyed his wil
> In alle thing, as fer as reson fil,
> Kepinge the boundes of my worship evere,
> Ne nevere hadde I thing so lief, ne levere,
> As him, God woot, ne nevere shal namo." (562–73)

(The last words of this speech echo Criseyde's protestation to Pandarus at III.869–70.) The obedience here is not a matter of subservience to rules of behaviour, but the spontaneous moulding of oneself to another – and it is this that enables Chaucer to use the word "obeye" in the description of the consummation itself: "ech of hem gan otheres lust obeye" (III.1690).[8] Troilus' subjection of himself ("So koude he hym governe in swich servyse," III.475) thus miraculously produces the subjection of Criseyde to his "governaunce."

8 The pathos of Chaucer's version of the Griselda story is increased if we see that Griselda is forced to reproduce by a deliberate and one-sided course of action that union of wills which in true love comes from a spontaneous and mutual "obeisaunce" (compare the *Clerk's Tale*, 501–11, 645–67, with the lines from the *Squire's Tale* quoted above).

For whi she fond hym so discret in al,
So secret, and of swich obëisaunce,
That wel she felte he was to hire a wal
Of stiel, and sheld from every displesaunce;
That to ben in his goode governaunce,
So wis he was, she was namore afered –
I mene, as fer as oughte ben requered. (III.477–83)

The repeated "so"s in this stanza seem to begin by being merely emphatic, but they then raise a sort of expectation of a result, a corresponding "that"; the onward movement of the syntax thus carries us on to the result, "she was namore afered," without this necessarily being envisaged at the beginning of the sentence. The movement of the syntax surely mimics the movement of Criseyde's mind: without any conscious decision to surrender the sovereignty she has reserved, Criseyde's emotions are led into enacting that surrender. The self-conscious correction of the stanza's last line – "I mene, as fer as oughte ben requered" – similarly imitates the mind's sudden consciousness of the point to which it has been led, and a return to the formally acknowledged version of the relationship. What these two lines reveal, in their forward movement and withdrawal, is the growth of an implicit trust, behind the formal structure of the relationship, which reverses that structure and prepares Criseyde to find herself in the power of another without feeling this as "thraldom." The importance of these lines is not only, however, in their demonstration of such a readiness for commitment: equally important is the fact that they show that this readiness is created by Troilus, not by Pandarus. It is not the response of weakness to insistent nagging or manufactured crisis, but a result of the trust that grows out of Troilus's "servyse."[9]

The commitment awaits, however, a formal summons, and the summons finally comes in the scene in Book III in Pandarus's house. But it comes in rather an unexpected form, and one that might well have worked to undo all the good effects of Troilus's "servyse." Pandarus enters Criseyde's chamber with an invented story about Troilus's supposed jealousy of one Horaste, and urges the need for her to see Troilus immediately to put his fears at rest. The

9 Cf. Charles Muscatine's comment on the consummation scene – that Criseyde's admission of surrender "is perhaps an ironic reflection on the labors of Pandarus. He ... has delivered the woman in the flesh, but she would not have been there if the woman in spirit had not yielded herself first. The spiritual woman yields to Troilus" (*Chaucer and the French Tradition* [Berkeley, CA, 1964], 161).

dangerousness of this fiction has not, I think, been fully appreciated in discussions of the poem. In the light of all that has gone before, it is clear that Pandarus's story about Troilus's jealousy represents a serious miscalculation. In Criseyde's eyes, it might well seem that this is the moment when the apparently "obeisaunt" lover throws off the mask of humility and asserts his "maistrye" over her.[10] We are alerted to this dangerous implication by Criseyde's long and passionate outburst against jealousy when she finally sees Troilus (III.1009–43), and her vehement denial that jealousy is a mark of love – an outburst which shows that the "proces" of courtship has in no way made this manifestation of masculine possessiveness less repugnant to her. Pandarus is clearly relying on the conventional view that "jalousie is love" (III.1024) in order to use this story as a stimulus towards the consummation. But he completely fails to understand, on the one hand, Criseyde's sensitivity to the threat of "thraldom," and, on the other, how remote from Troilus's nature is any tendency towards such possessiveness. So far from being necessary to bring about the consummation, Pandarus's story very nearly destroys the whole love affair.

What is it then that saves the situation? First, it is that the implicit trust which Troilus has created by his "obeisaunce" has power to carry Criseyde through this crisis. Secondly, the story of Horaste does, of course, contribute to the consummation in that the very anguish that it causes Criseyde reveals to her (and allows her to acknowledge to her uncle) the extent of her feeling for Troilus:

> "Hadde I hym nevere lief? By God, I weene
> Ye hadde nevere thyng so lief!" quod she. (III.869–70)

But were this to be the only basis on which the consummation were achieved, it would mean that Criseyde accepted, along with the depth of her feeling for Troilus, the "thraldom" of becoming his claimed possession. It is the swoon, the third and most important means by which the situation is saved, that is crucial in ensuring that when the consummation does take place it does not represent the manoeuvring of one partner into an admission of "thraldom" but the mutual surrender of each partner to the other.

In order to see this, we must also look at the swoon, and the situation immediately preceding it, from Troilus's point of view. When he is confronted with Criseyde in tears, protesting her innocence, he is not pleasantly surprised at the

10 For a medieval description of the lover's change from "serjant" to "mestre," see the speech of Amis, *Le Roman de la Rose*, ed. Felix Lecoy, Classiques Français du Moyen Âge, 3 vols (Paris, 1966–70), lines 9411–24).

extent of the obligation she acknowledges to him, but horrified at the pain she is suffering, and also at having provoked an anger which he assumes will destroy all her previous goodwill.

> This Troilus, whan he hire wordes herde,
> Have ye no care, hym liste nought to slepe;
> For it thoughte hym no strokes of a yerde
> To heere or seen Criseyde, his lady, wepe;
> But wel he felt aboute his herte crepe,
> For everi tere which that Criseyde asterte,
> The crampe of deth to streyne hym by the herte. (III.1065–71)

There is, moreover, at least a strong suggestion – in Pandarus's admonition to Criseyde to broach the question of his jealousy to Troilus since his delicacy will prevent him from raising it – that the horror of Troilus's situation is increased by his having had no prior knowledge of the story Pandarus was going to tell, so that he is presented with a fait accompli.[11] We can thus see the intensity of the pressures on Troilus immediately before the swoon. He is in his lady's bedroom for the first time, having had his hopes raised to the highest pitch. But instead of showing him the grace and kindness he has earned from her before, she is upbraiding him for his mistrust of her. He cannot excuse himself by revealing the truth – that the story is Pandarus's invention – since this would reveal the extent of Pandarus's guile and raise suspicions about the whole previous course of the affair. Equally, he cannot go through with the story and dredge up some support for his alleged suspicions,[12] because this would be to belie his own nature, to cause further grief to Criseyde, and to connive at the shifting

11 For the view that Pandarus's story is invented, see J. Milton French, "A Defense of Troilus," *PMLA* 44 (1929): 1246–51, at 1246–7. It is, of course, not unimportant that Chaucer refrains from telling us explicitly whether or not Troilus knew of Pandarus's scheme. The reason for this may be that he did not wish Troilus to be exonerated *simply* on the grounds of technical innocence of deception; on the contrary, he shows that Troilus cannot avoid some kind of deception, or what we may more accurately call "organized behaviour," from the moment he falls in love and has to disguise his feelings from those around him (I.320–50). He also cooperates in the fiction of his illness in the visit to Deiphebus's house (see especially III.206–7). But he makes the point, in that instance, that the fiction matches the truth (II.1527–30); the problem with the Horaste story is that it does *not* match the emotional truth of the situation or the relationship Troilus envisages with Criseyde, and it is perhaps this, rather than Troilus's technical innocence, that Chaucer wishes us to feel as dissociating him from Pandarus's fiction.

12 It may be objected that he later does this, but this is after the swoon has acted to withdraw the accusation, as it were, and to make the substantiation of merely historic interest.

of their relationship to one in which he could claim mastery over her. Unable to discover an issue in speech or action, Troilus's mind is turned in on itself, trapped in deadlock, and this condition of his mind is so acute that it transfers itself to his body.

> Therwith the sorwe so his herte shette
> That from his eyen fil there nought a tere,
> And every spirit his vigour in knette,
> So they astoned or oppressed were;
> The felying of his sorwe, or of his fere,
> Or of aught elles, fled was out of towne –
> And down he fel al sodeynly a-swowne. (III.1086–92)

The swoon is an expression of Troilus's acceptance of – and indeed absolute identification with – the contradictory and destructive implications of the situation, to which, unlike Pandarus, he is fully alive. Although "nought to blame" (1085), he seems unwittingly to have created his own destruction; he can neither identify with, nor dissociate himself from, the fictional Troilus in Pandarus's story. He is unable to find his real self in the external situation, and this loss of identity is mirrored in his loss of consciousness. The disorder in the outer world is transferred, by the completeness with which he perceives and accepts it, into his inner being, and the result is a dramatic and instantaneous loss of his own internal order. Troilus's swoon is comparable, in this respect, to the madness suffered by romance heroes – Yvain, Lancelot, Tristram; whatever the difference between the situations in which their madness occurs, those situations are all marked by an irresolvable disorder in the outside world to which the knight opens up his being, with a resulting dislocation of mental order.[13] It

13 Yvain's madness is provoked when he is accused of disloyalty in breaking his promise to return to his wife after a year (see Chrestien de Troyes, *Yvain*, ed. T.B.W. Reid [Manchester, 1942], lines 2704–809). The damsel who makes the accusation holds up to him and the court of Arthur an image of "Yvain / Le desleal, le traïtor, / Le mançongier, le jeinglor" ("Yvain the faithless, the treacherous, the liar, the light talker"), which he can neither reject nor (given the earnestness of his love for his wife) accept. Lancelot's madness, as described in the Prose *Lancelot*, is provoked by his realization that he has for the second time been tricked into making love to Helaine in the belief that she is Guinevere. When Guinevere hears him talking in his sleep, she realizes where he is and coughs to awake him; hearing her, Lancelot perceives that he has been deceived and is not with the real Guinevere. Like Yvain, he finds himself in a situation for which he must bear responsibility, but in which he cannot find an expression of his true self. Dismissed by the queen, Lancelot leaves without protest or explanation, and, taking to the woods, eventually becomes demented. See *Lancelot*, ed. Alexandre Micha, Textes

is, in all these cases, a mark of the hero's nobility of nature that he does not try to evade or diminish the horror of his external situation, even by such apparently acceptable means as an explanation or offered expiation of his own misdemeanours. He removes the horror from the external situation by the single expedient of taking it into himself.

Such a dislocation of rational consciousness is also a way of creating a fresh start in the narrative; it wipes out the first crisis by substituting a new one, and thus acts as a means of transition to the restoring of harmony and order in the external situation, even though that is not an end envisaged by the hero at the time. Troilus's swoon, similarly, although not designed to do so, offers Pandarus the opportunity to push the situation beyond the deadlock it has reached. But more important than this practical opportunity is the testimony it offers, of the most convincing and authentic kind, to the fact that Troilus has not in reality become the dominant possessive lover suggested by Pandarus's story. His swoon demonstrates, in the clearest possible way, his subjection to Criseyde and to his love of her, and his dissociation from the idea that she is not still her "owene womman." When he regains consciousness, under Criseyde's coaxing, he is still in this state of humble subjection (that is, their previous relationship has been restored), even though he finds himself in bed with his lady, and even his trumped-up substantiation of the Horaste story is due to the fact that "He most obeye" Criseyde's command to explain himself (III.1157). As a humble

---

Littéraires Français, vol. 6 (Paris, 1980), 173–7 (CV.33–8); Norris J. Lacy, *Lancelot-Grail: The Old French Arthurian Vulgate and Post-Vulgate in Translation*, vol. 3 (New York, 1995), 320–1. Tristan's madness has a rather different context, which offers some interesting analogies with Troilus's situation: initially, the imputed guilt is not his but Iseut's. He discovers a letter she has written to another knight and accuses her of infidelity, then takes to the forest in grief. To a friend called Fergus, he expresses his regret at having accused Iseut, and says that he has been guilty of "folie" and "vilenie" in speaking ill of her; if she has done anything wrong, he ought not to have accused her but pardoned her willingly. It is only after this confession – in which he dissociates himself from the self who accused Iseut and thus discovers that he has betrayed the true self who loves her without claiming rights over her – that Tristan's grief turns into madness. See *Le Roman de Tristan en prose*, ed. Renée L. Curtis, 3 vols (Cambridge, 1985) 3:140–5, 153–61, 166–76 (sections 836–42, 852–9, 866–75). A similar but slightly different case is that of Sir Orfeo, whose sojourn in the forest after the loss of his wife resembles those of the other romance heroes, but in whose case there is no question of guilt, either real or apparent; the dislocation originates entirely in the external order. On the other hand, this is the clearest example of a link between the hero's surrender to the disaster which overtakes him and the restoration of harmony and happiness (although the link does not imply a relationship of cause and effect on either a logical or a moral plane). See *Sir Orfeo*, ed. A.J. Bliss (Oxford, 1954), lines 227–329. For the probability that Chaucer knew *Sir Orfeo*, see Laura Hibbard Loomis, "Chaucer and the Breton Lays of the Auchinleck Manuscript," *Studies in Philology* 38 (1941): 14–33.

suppliant, he begs forgiveness and puts himself in Criseyde's "grace" (III.1176); she grants him forgiveness on condition he offends no more. Both are fulfilling their agreement that Criseyde should have the power to "wratthe" him for any misdemeanours.

At this point, therefore, the roles of the two lovers are still – or rather, have once more become, after the apparent threat of reversal – what they were at the beginning of the episode: Criseyde is lady and Troilus is servant. But now, at the end of a stanza, comes a sudden and entirely novel change:

> "And now," quod she, "that I have don yow smerte,
> Foryeve it me, myn owene swete herte." (III.1182–3)

With these words, Criseyde for the first time yields power over herself to Troilus; in asking him for forgiveness, she submits herself to him. Troilus sees immediately the implication of her words, and takes up the offer she has made him:

> This Troilus, with blisse of that supprised,
> Putte al in Goddes hand, as he that mente
> Nothing but wel; and sodeynly avysed,
> He hire in armes faste to hym hente. (III.1184–7)

Troilus at last takes on the role of the sexual aggressor: Criseyde in his arms is compared to the lark in the grip of the sparrowhawk, and trembles like an aspen leaf "Whan she hym felte hire in his armes folde" (1201). For the first time, the relationship between the two lovers conforms to the conventional pattern of sexual roles: the man aggressive and demanding, the woman submissive and yielding. But this is not a mere abandonment of the polite fictions of courtship in favour of the banal inevitability of a more "realistic" distribution of power. On the contrary, we can assent to and enjoy Troilus's insistence and Criseyde's submission precisely because this exercise of masculine power is based on, and still contains within itself, its opposite. Troilus exerts his dominance only *because* Criseyde has, of her own free will, made a submission, and her submission, read in context, does not imply a total surrender of power, once and for all, but a yielding on her part to match the yielding on his, and thus to make their relationship fully mutual. Moreover, even as Troilus takes up Criseyde's offer of power, of control, he is also making a submission: he "Putte al in Goddes hand, as he that mente / Nothing but wel" – trusting to God and the goodness of his own intention, he takes a chance, puts himself at the mercy of fate and the possibility of a truly final rebuff. Troilus's action is a leap in the dark, an impulse to make himself vulnerable to chance, rather than a calculated seducer's decision that he is safe in going further. And, with a similar paradox, for Criseyde the submission to Troilus does not bring about the "thraldom" she feared, but a liberation; there is no sense of her being manoeuvred or coerced, but rather of her finding the opportunity for the fullest expression of her being, and even finding for the first time a full understanding of her own being.

> And as the newe abaysed nyghtyngale,
> That stynteth first whan she bygynneth to synge,
> Whan that she hereth any herde tale,
> Or in the hegges any wyght stirynge,
> And after siker doth hire vois out rynge,
> Right so Criseyde, whan hire drede stente,
> Opned hire herte, and tolde hym hire entente. (III.1233–9)

It is in this light that we should read Criseyde's response to Troilus's claim of her surrender:

> "Now yeldeth yow, for other bote is non!"
> To that Criseyde answerde thus anon,
> "Ne hadde I er now, my swete herte deere,
> Ben yolde, ywis, I were now nought heere!" (III.1208–11)

Criseyde's words, like Troilus's, have been read as the dropping of a mask, a revelation of the truth behind an acted facade.[14] But if Criseyde uses the past tense here, it is surely because, like the earlier discovery that she was "namore

---

14 The comments of Donald W. Rowe (*O Love, O Charite! Contraries Harmonized in Chaucer's Troilus* [Carbondale, IL, 1976], 101) lend themselves to quotation here, not because they are unusual, but because they are conveniently compact and illustrate not only this point but also the general critical failure to understand the dynamics of the consummation scene. "[Criseyde] herself admits, in a moment of candor, that if she had not earlier yielded she would not be there, though it baffles the reader to determine the precise point at which she did. This is not to say, of course, that she went to Pandarus's house intending to seduce or be seduced. ... Troilus, for all his fainting and praying, is able to seize the prize, and he does so with vigor once Pandarus leaves the room, and immediately after the narrator asks, 'What myghte or may the sely larke seye, / Whan that the sperhauk hath it in his foot?' (III.1191–2). Implications of ravishing are not far away." See also Rowe's earlier comments that Troilus "suddenly demands that she yield" (ignoring the reason for this demand), and the "questionable intention in that demand" (ibid., 77). Cf. the account of the scene in Sanford B. Meech, *Design in Chaucer's Troilus* (Syracuse, NY, 1959), 70–1.

afered," this is a discovery that can only be made retrospectively. She cannot decide, prospectively, to yield; she can only discover that she has yielded. The liberty that is left to her is the liberty to acknowledge, frankly and generously, that the undefined pressures that have brought her to this moment of definition have been inner as well as outer, and that she takes responsibility, fully and delightedly, for the situation to which they have led her and the self they have discovered for her.[15] What she does by using the past tense is not to indicate a hypocrisy, a split in herself, but to discover a wholeness: she can integrate her present with her past.

It is, to me, significant of the difference between Diomede's wooing and Troilus's that the phrase which seals her surrender to the former is cast not in the past tense, but in the future: "To Diomede algate I wol be trewe" (V.1071). This assurance of future amendment clearly undermines itself: if Criseyde had learned anything from her experience, it ought to have been that firm statements about the future are luxuries that human beings cannot indulge in – or, at least, cannot allow themselves to believe to be actual descriptions of what will happen. But in addition to this general problem about the use of the future tense at this stage, there is a more particular one. With Diomede, as with Troilus, we do not see Criseyde making a clear decision beforehand; we only see her retrospective recognition of the situation into which she has moved. But in her reaction to Diomede's conquest, Criseyde's acknowledgment of the situation to which she has been led does *not* serve to integrate her past with her present, to enable her to look back at it and perceive a continuity between past actions, thoughts, wishes, fears, and the present situation in which they achieve full embodiment and meaning; in the case of Diomede, to look back at the past only emphasizes the gulf between the self that she used to be and the self she has become. She must abandon the past, and can thus only gesture towards the future in order to have some sense of the continuity of her self, and of the integrity of the self that is denoted by the word "trouthe." It is the later speech that is hypocritical, if either is, despite its apparently frank acknowledgment of guilt, since it tries to pretend that the future can be used to wipe out the past, and thus the split between the past and the present.[16]

---

15 Likewise, Troilus cannot decide beforehand to fall in love at first sight, but there is room for the exercise of his will in the generous acceptance of the loss of his old self: "For with good hope he gan fully assente / Criseyde for to love, and nought repente" (I.391–2).

16 In contrast, Henryson's *Testament of Cresseid*, despite its supposed cruelty to Cresseid, allows her to recuperate her past as she acknowledges her own falsity and dies of the resulting grief; see Jill Mann, "The Planetary Gods in Chaucer and Henryson," in *Chaucer Traditions: Studies in Honour of Derek Brewer*, ed. Ruth Morse and Barry Windeatt (Cambridge, 1990), 91–106, at 100.

The cruel irony is that it is Troilus's very sense of the necessity for Criseyde's love to be freely given if it is to be valuable that provides the opportunity for Diomede to urge it from her. Despite all counsels of wisdom, Troilus cannot in the last resort resist suggesting to Criseyde that they elope together before she is exchanged. If she cannot see the need for such drastic action, it is because she relies on the simple fact that she has no desire to do anything other than return to Troy and to Troilus as soon as she has left. Why, then, adopt a plan which seems to assume that, once in the Greek camp, she is bound to stay – and even worse, bound to want to stay? Troilus's further urging provokes a distraught response: if he insists on an elopement, it can only be because he mistrusts her. To this, Troilus can have no answer but to assent to her going.[17] An elopement might, to all practical purposes, have secured Criseyde's fidelity. But if she were only faithful because he had put it out of her power to be tempted, of what worth would be her fidelity? Troilus would then have taken on the role of the fabliau-husband, of such as the carpenter in the *Miller's Tale:* "Jalous he was, and heeld hire narwe in cage" (3224). Troilus is a different kind of lover; he takes only what Criseyde is willing to give, and her power to recall her gift must remain always with her, or it ceases to be a gift and becomes the tribute of a thrall.

Troilus's swoon is not, therefore, a piece of behaviour designed to show his ineffectuality, either as an individual or as a "courtly lover." It can only be properly interpreted within the whole context of Chaucer's examination of the complex evolution of the power relationships inevitably involved in the situation of any two people in love. In this context, we can see that it plays a crucial part in demonstrating that Troilus's "obeisaunce" to Criseyde is dictated by a deeply felt emotion, rather than by the empty conventions of courtship. Like the other major acts of surrender in medieval romance, its role is also creative: the disaster which is accepted, fully and completely, is miraculously dispelled by that acceptance.[18] In this case, the swoon, the demonstration of surrender, creates the opportunity for Troilus's exercise of dominance, his claim to Criseyde to yield; taken together with its causes and its consequences, it demonstrates the rich multiplicity of potential relationships in the love which here reaches its consummation, and the poise and responsiveness in both lovers which keep all the potentialities constantly in play.

---

17 See IV.1506–1652. Criseyde's plea – "Mistrust me nought thus causeles, for routhe" (1609) – recalls her pleading against baseless suspicion in Book III.

18 Other examples of the saving power of submission to threatened danger are Gawain's fulfilment of the beheading game promise in *Sir Gawain and the Green Knight*, which leads to the saving of his life, and Dorigen's resolve to fulfil her promise to Aurelius, which miraculously releases her from that promise. See "Sir Gawain and the Romance Hero," 221–34 below, and "Chaucerian Themes and Style in the *Franklin's Tale*," 62–79 below.

When we understand the consummation scene in this way, we also find that there is no need to attack or defend the love affair, and particularly Troilus's role in it, in historical terms. We not only can, but need to, respond directly to the emotions and instincts involved, examining Chaucer's representations of human relationships with no other preconceptions than our belief that a poet of profound humanity will have something complex and enriching to show us in them.[19] We may then see his fine sensitivity to what is true and what is false, what is liberating and what is enslaving, in the coming together of men and women in the special "binding" of love. We may also see that Chaucer's conception of their roles is based, not on literary conventions or religious doctrine or social orthodoxy, but on the "lawe of kinde," which he must have trusted would work as powerfully on his modern readers as on his fourteenth-century ones.

Love is a thing as any spirit free.
Wommen, *of kinde*, desiren libertee,
And nat to been constreined as a thral,
And so doon men, if I sooth seyen shal.
(*Franklin's Tale*, 767–70; my italics)

These words seem to me in no way outdated or untrue; nor are they "unmedieval." But our admiration for Chaucer should not be based merely on this affirmation of the desire for liberty, which is perhaps easy enough to make, so much as on the way he fulfils the far more difficult task of developing the image of a complex and binding relationship in which that liberty is nevertheless preserved.[20]

19 I have here excised half a sentence about "new directions" and "old directions" in Chaucer studies, which has been wrongly, if understandably, interpreted as a nervous reaction to "Robertsonianism" (see Lee Patterson, *Negotiating the Past* [Madison, WI, 1987], 5 n. 5. In fact, the title originally projected for the R.W. Frank Festschrift in which this article first appeared was *New Directions in Chaucer Studies*, and this sentence was a rather weak attempt to establish some connection with it. In the end, the Festschrift appeared as vol. 14 of the *Chaucer Review*, unobtrusively titled *Directions in Medieval Literary Criticism*, and the point of these remarks disappeared entirely.

20 Several recent articles have offered sympathetic discussions of swooning in *Troilus and Criseyde* and other medieval literary works; see Gretchen Mieszkowski, "Revisiting Troilus's Faint," in *Men and Masculinities in Chaucer's Troilus and Criseyde*, ed. Tison Pugh and Marcia Smith Marzec (Cambridge, 2008), 43–57; Judith Weiss, "Modern and Medieval Views on Swooning: the Literary and Medical Contexts of Fainting in Romance," in *Medieval Romance, Medieval Contexts*, ed. Rhiannon Purdie and Michael Cichon (Cambridge, 2011), 121–34; Barry Windeatt, "The Art of Swooning in Middle English," in *Medieval Latin and Middle English Literature: Essays in Honour of Jill Mann*, ed. Christopher Cannon and Maura Nolan (Cambridge, 2011), 211–30.

Chapter Two

Shakespeare and Chaucer: "What is Criseyde Worth?"

Chaucer's *Troilus and Criseyde* is a supremely *dramatic* poem. It is, indeed, a brilliant example of that ability to suggest a living, fluctuating personality behind the surface manifestations of speech, look, and gesture that we think of as characteristically "Shakespearean," and its influence on Shakespeare could therefore be traced far beyond the confines of a single play. Yet, if we do narrow the basis of comparison to the two versions of the Troilus story, a rather curious paradox emerges: in the presentation of Criseyde, Chaucer is more "Shakespearean" than Shakespeare – that is, his heroine has a depth of life denied to her stage counterpart. It is both the hows and the whys of this difference that I wish to examine.[1]

It is obvious at first glance that *Troilus and Criseyde* contains large stretches of dialogue, but it is not only the dialogue, vivid as it is, that constitutes the "dramatic" quality of the poem. Even more significant is the fact that Chaucer constantly writes in "stage directions" – minute indications of physical location, gesture, look, appearance.[2] A few – very few – of these indications he found

1 Quotations from *Troilus and Cressida* are taken from the third Arden edition by David M. Bevington (London, 1998). For more general comparisons of Chaucer's poem and Shakespeare's play, see Muriel C. Bradbrook, "What Shakespeare did to Chaucer's *Troilus and Criseyde*," in Bradbrook, *The Artist and Society in Shakespeare's England* (Brighton, Sussex, 1982), 133–43; Ann Thompson, *Shakespeare's Chaucer* (Liverpool, 1978), 111–65; E. Talbot Donaldson, *The Swan at the Well: Shakespeare Reading Chaucer* (New Haven, CT, 1985), 74–118, 148–57.

2 On Chaucer's use of gesture, see Barry Windeatt, "Gesture in Chaucer," *Medievalia et Humanistica* 9 (1979): 143–61; Robert D.G. Benson, *Medieval Body Language: A Study of the Use of Gesture in Chaucer's Poetry*, Anglistica, 21 (Copenhagen, 1980); John P. Hermann, "Gesture and Seduction in *Troilus and Criseyde*," *Studies in the Age of Chaucer* 7 (1985): 107–35.

already present in his own source, the *Filostrato* of Boccaccio, but he gave them a quite different role and meaning through his own additions and expansions. For example, in the opening scene in the temple, Boccaccio describes Criseida as standing near the temple door, "dignified, gracious, and amiable" ("negli atti altiera, piacente ed accorta").[3] In taking over these details, Chaucer makes them dramatically meaningful by relating them to Criseyde's present situation, turning them into a dialectical articulation of her consciousness of herself and her relation to other people. The dialectic begins to make itself felt in the "And yet" with which he follows his description of her beauty:

And yet she stood ful lowe and stille alone,
Byhynden other folk, in litel brede,
And neigh the dore, ay undre shames drede,
Simple of atir and debonaire of chere,
With ful assured lokyng and manere. (I.178–82)

Criseyde is sensitive to "shames drede" because she is the daughter of a traitor who has abandoned the city of Troy in the midst of a war; allowed by the generous patronage of Hector to live on unmolested in Troy, her humble attire and meek appearance signal an acknowledgment of the precariousness of her position and her wish to avoid offence by obtruding herself. This is also why she takes up a humble position near the door and "Byhynden other folk." But, at the same time, her assurance and dignity of manner indicate that her father's guilt is not her own, and she will therefore defend her right to the "litel brede" in which she stands, in the face of any public expression of hostility. The features of this description are not, that is, to be interpreted as a simple reflex of her character or her temperament; they are, rather, the result of what we may call "arranged behaviour." It is only by interpreting the semiotics of this "arranged behaviour" that we arrive at any understanding of Criseyde's inner self, of her sense of right and propriety and her ability to behave with poise and tact.

Troilus too "arranges" his behaviour with an eye to its effect on the beholder. After reporting Troilus's speech of contempt for the "blynde" lovers who cannot "war by other be," Chaucer adds an expressive facial gesture which has no counterpart in Boccaccio:

And with that word he gan caste up the browe,
Ascaunces, "Loo! is this naught wisely spoken?" (I.204–5)

3 *Filostrato*, I.xix.8.

The casting up of the brow, which Chaucer glosses for us, gives an "illocutionary force," in J.L. Austin's terms, to Troilus's statement, and provides us with the key to its tone (it is a young man's high spirits, rather than, for example, a gloomy philosophical profundity).

Troilus's gaze, ranging idly through the crowd, "smites" on Criseyde and is suddenly fixed there. When he recollects himself, he returns to "his firste pleyinge chere" (I.280), "arranged behaviour" becoming evident again as we contrast his outward manner with his inward confusion. Criseyde's glance too plays a part in this first contact between them, and Chaucer devotes two whole stanzas to describing it and its effect on Troilus:

> To Troilus right wonder wel with alle
> Gan for to like hire mevynge and hire chere,
> Which somdel deignous was, for she let falle
> Hire look a lite aside in swich manere,
> Ascaunces, "What, may I nat stonden here?"
> And after that hir lokynge gan she lighte,
> That nevere thoughte hym seen so good a syghte.
>
> And of hire look in him ther gan to quyken
> So gret desir and swich affeccioun,
> That in his hertes botme gan to stiken
> Of hir his fixe and depe impressioun.
> And though he erst hadde poured up and down,
> He was tho glad his hornes in to shrinke:
> Unnethes wiste he how to loke or wynke. (I.288–301)

The account of Criseyde "lightening" her expression is Chaucer's own addition to Boccaccio's description of her slightly disdainful ("sdegnosetto") glance and gesture.[4] The effect of the extra detail is not merely arithmetical – to suggest two character traits instead of one; it changes the whole meaning of Criseyde's glance. For in Chaucer's presentation it is clear that her first disdainful look is a reaction to her consciousness of Troilus's gaze; she interprets the fixity of his attention to her as a sign that he is critical of her presence, and responds first with self-defensiveness, and then with a placatory softening that indicates it is not to be taken as brazen aggressiveness. This first encounter between Troilus and Criseyde is thus conducted in the "language of looks," not of words; what is important is not only that we learn to decode the "language of looks" but that this decoding leads us into a vivid awareness of the constant trafficking

4 *Filostrato*, I.xxviii.2.

between a world of formed, coded, outer speech and behaviour, and an inner world of spontaneous thought and feeling. This interaction between the inner and the outer, between private reaction and social behaviour, interests Chaucer as much as or more than Criseyde's individual character.

It is this interest that leads to Chaucer's considerable expansion of Boccaccio's narrative in Book II of his poem, which recounts the wooing of Criseyde, and that gives it its dramatic quality. A few representative moments will serve as illustration. The first is the moment of Pandarus's arrival at Criseyde's house:

> Quod Pandarus, "Madame, God yow see,
> With al youre book and al the compaignie!"
> "Ey, uncle myn, welcome iwys," quod she;
> And up she roos, and by the hond in hye
> She took hym faste, and seyde, "This nyght thrie –
> To goode mot it turne – of yow I mette."
> And with that word she doun on bench hym sette.
>
> "Ye, nece, yee shal faren wel the bet,
> If God wol, al this yeer," quod Pandarus;
> "But I am sory that I have yow let
> To herken of youre book ye preysen thus.
> For Goddes love, what seith it? telle it us!
> Is it of love? O, som good ye me leere!"
> "Uncle," quod she, "youre maistresse is nat here."
>
> With that thei gonnen laughe ... (II.85–99)

We know, without prompting from Chaucer, that Pandarus is deliberately using any pretext to introduce the subject of love, and so to encourage thoughts of it in Criseyde's mind. We make this deduction instantaneously, "glossing" Pandarus's speech in the light of our knowledge of his concealed intention just as we should do if we were watching an actor in a play. But, over and above this, Pandarus's speech in another sense *proclaims* an insincerity of a less specific sort; the "high-flown," exaggerated earnestness in his request makes it obvious that "he doesn't really mean it." Criseyde deflates her uncle's mock solemnity, not by direct comment but by a joke. Skilled in the "language of looks," she is also adept in the art of civilized discourse, in the ability to use speech not as a transparent register of feeling but as an instrument which can be made to create relations of ease and frankness. The joking imputation of a concealed motive breaks through the surface of language only in order to flatter Pandarus with the implication that he too is adept in these arts, and will therefore relish this acknowledgment of the gap between its "arranged" surface and the private motives that are screened behind it.

Now it is *because* Pandarus really does have a concealed intention of a very specific sort, while Criseyde does not, that we can measure the difference between "hypocrisy" or "deception," and what I have called "arranged behaviour." Criseyde's behaviour is "arranged," not because she is playing a hidden game, but because any speech or action of hers represents a *selection* from a vast reservoir of thoughts and feelings that lie behind these surface manifestations – a selection in which a sense of propriety and a response to others will play as large a part as her own impulses. The more sophisticated her speech, that is, the more we have a sense of Criseyde *thinking behind* her speech, not expressing everything that is in her mind, nor thinking only what she expresses.

In what follows, we are continually aware of this reservoir of thought and feeling, because it is to it that Pandarus covertly addresses himself. His tantalizing hints of a splendid piece of news, which must nevertheless be withheld from his niece, aim to arouse her curiosity, and he keeps it aroused by commanding her not to question him further. Criseyde dutifully obeys, but when, after another hundred lines, Pandarus mentions her "faire aventure" again, her curiosity, welling up behind the barrier of her obedience like water behind a dam, at once breaks out through this offered chink:

> "A! wel bithought! For love of God," quod she,
> "Shal I nat witen what ye meene of this?" (II.225–6)

By leaving a gap between Pandarus's two references to Criseyde's "faire aventure" Chaucer does more than increase suspense (in Criseyde and the reader); the suppressed remembrance of the earlier exchange, which we share with Criseyde, instructs us in the *continuing* existence of a half-conscious mental life into which ideas and impressions are absorbed and from which they can surface into speech or action as occasion calls them forth. Pandarus's elaborate manoeuvring aims at making the fact of Troilus's love part of Criseyde's "mental furniture" in this way, so that it can be left to have its own effect. We can see it doing just that when, after the initial storms that greet Pandarus's revelation of the truth have subsided into Criseyde's agreement to offer Troilus "good chere" but nothing more, Criseyde introduces into their cheerful talk of other matters an apparently casual question:

> Tho fellen they in other tales glade,
> Tyl at the laste, "O good em," quod she tho,
> For his love, which that us bothe made,
> Tel me how first ye wisten of his wo?

Woot noon of it but ye?" He seyde, "No."
"Kan he wel speke of love?" quod she; "I preye
Tel me, for I the bet me shal purveye."

Tho Pandarus a litel gan to smyle ... (II.498–505)

Pandarus smiles because he can see that the idea he has introduced into Criseyde's mind is working in it with the silent but ceaseless action of yeast; his first task is done.

Among the facial expressions – such as the smile – which translate inner states into public signals (or, to put it the other way round, which offer a clue to the spontaneous responses within), the blush has a particularly important and interesting place, because it is involuntary.[5] It is given a key role in the scene that follows, when Criseyde, finally left alone by Pandarus, sits down to formulate the unformulated impressions she has received, but finds that there is yet another to add to them, for at that moment Troilus by chance rides past her window. The people admiringly hail the brave young defender of the city, and Troilus blushes in response. The blush in turn calls forth a spontaneous response in the watching Criseyde, and as she becomes conscious of this response she too blushes.[6]

For which he wex a litel reed for shame
When he the peple upon hym herde cryen,
That to byholde it was a noble game
How sobrelich he caste down his yën.
Criseyda gan al his chere aspien,
And leet it so softe in hire herte synke,
That to hireself she seyde, "Who yaf me drynke?"

For of hire owen thought she wex al reed,
Remembryng hire right thus, "Lo, this is he
Which that myn uncle swerith he moot be deed,
But I on hym have mercy and pitee."

5 Although Diomede seems able to blush at will, as he *mimics* the behaviour of the embarrassed lover (V.925–9).

6 This scene is invented by Chaucer; in the later window scene, which corresponds more closely to Boccaccio, the two lovers again blush (II.1256–8), whereas in the *Filostrato* they gaze at each other with unembarrassed complaisance (II.lxxxii–lxxxiii).

And with that thought, for pure ashamed, she
Gan in hire hed to pulle, and that as faste,
Whil he and alle the peple forby paste. (II.645–58)

The blush in each case represents an inward response to an image of the self that is offered from outside. Both Troilus and Criseyde suddenly perceive how they appear (or may appear) to others; Troilus sees himself reflected in the people's acclaim as the brave defender of Troy, Criseyde sees herself as the beloved of this young hero (and also sees that her own gaze might be attributed to her desire to assess his suitability as a lover). Because the blush is spontaneous and uncontrollable, it is the sincerest of testimonies to the inner being that it manifests.[7] Troilus's blush testifies to his modesty; it rebuts the possible accusation of vanity at his acclaim by very virtue of the fact that it acknowledges his consciousness of its possibility. Criseyde's blush rebuts the accusation of brazenness in the same way. The blush is a direct road of access to the heart and mind, a means of penetrating to the most instinctive movements of the inner self. It mediates between public and private; the public gaze is internalized within the mind, private impulses are laid bare to the outside world. Taking its origin in intimate and secret thoughts, the blush comes to birth as the thinker, suddenly taking the position of an outward observer, becomes conscious of those thoughts, and responds again to that consciousness with an instinctive emotion which instantaneously translates itself into an outward signal.

It is through this sense of the constant dialectic between an inner world of unformulated thought and emotion and an outer world of speech and behaviour that Chaucer convinces us of the existence of Criseyde's inner reservoir of thought and enlightens us as to its nature. When therefore she finally sits down to reflect once more and we are led deep into the private world of her thoughts and feelings, we are ready to see her reflections for what they are – not an insight into her "character," but a glimpse into that whole restless world of impulsive movement and response from which decisions and actions arise by a process as mysterious as the birth of Venus from the sea. We can understand, finally, how within this fluctuating process the idea that Pandarus has introduced into her mind begins to take hold and to grow in it, how it can be encouraged and nourished by following events, until it has become an acknowledged part of her willed behaviour. And we can see how, ultimately, the idea of betraying Troilus and giving herself to Diomede can gradually lodge itself in her mind by the same process.

7 See Windeatt, "Gesture," 151–3, and, on blushing generally, Christopher Ricks, *Keats and Embarrassment* (Oxford, 1974), esp. chs 2–3.

We take for granted the dramatic life of *Troilus and Criseyde*, performing instinctively and immediately the interpretative acts that I have had to trace so laboriously. But we take it for granted, I think, largely *because* we are early accustomed to it by our familiarity with Shakespeare.[8] The sense of a whole world of emotional response and unspoken thought which is only partially and tangentially reproduced in dialogue is one of the great strengths and pleasures of Shakespeare's plays; in the works of lesser dramatists we find all too often that what is said can be taken to be coextensive with what is thought. To take an example somewhat akin to the Chaucerian passages I have discussed, in the scene on the quay in *Othello* we can sense Desdemona's tension and anxiety – betrayed in her quick question "there's one gone to the harbour?" – lying behind her cheerful badinage with Iago, without needing her own gloss: "I am not merry, but I do beguile / The thing I am, by seeming otherwise" (2.1.122–3). But this only makes it the more surprising that when Shakespeare, in his turn, comes to represent Cressida, he carefully *suppresses* all that sense of a living human responsiveness lying behind speech by means of which we could make meaningful sense of dialogue and action. The few speeches she is given – and they are surprisingly few[9] – offer disconcertingly contradictory impressions of her.[10] Some critics interpret her early banter with Pandarus, which constitutes her most extended series of utterances, as evidence of shallowness or wantonness; others point out that it could as well come from one of Shakespeare's romantic heroines, from Beatrice or Rosalind.[11] But we are not, as we are with Beatrice or Rosalind, allowed a secure sense of a serious centre of being lying behind the verbal flippancy. For one thing, Cressida has no female friends or relatives, as they do, with whom she might reveal a more intimate self, and her witty exchanges with Pandarus keep both him and us at arm's length. We wait for this lone heroine to speak directly to the audience – as does Viola, say – but in the brief soliloquy in which she reveals that she values Troilus even higher than Pandarus's praise, and yet holds off, since "Things won are done" (1.2.277–86), we are still left in suspense to know how to resolve the apparent

8 "In the free flow of Shakespeare's world, motivation is never analysed or presented for inspection, but inferred by us instinctively, as we might infer that of real people around us"; John Bayley, *Shakespeare and Tragedy* (London, 1981), 106.

9 Donaldson, *The Swan at the Well*, 86, notes that "her speaking role in the play is small: she speaks only 152 times, and 128 of her speeches are of less than twenty words, 93 of less than ten."

10 For John Bayley Cressida is "discontinuous with any idea of personality" ("Time and the Trojans," *Essays in Criticism* 25 [1975]: 55–73, at 61).

11 Bayley, *Shakespeare and Tragedy*, 103; cf. Donaldson, *The Swan at the Well*, 87.

contradiction between her passionate admiration and her cool calculation. The passionate outburst in which she voices her agony at parting from Troilus and protests her eternal loyalty seems entirely sincere (4.2.97–110); we are therefore as surprised as Troilus to see her in the Greek camp accepting Diomedes's advances (5.2.1–118) – and even here the resurgence of tender memories of Troilus (5.2.83–7), at a time when a whore or a sexual politician would have nothing to gain from them, runs counter to the inference that might be drawn from her rapid transfer to the Greek's protection. Most important of all, the fact that we "eavesdrop" on this scene with Ulysses and Troilus, and hear only snatches of Cressida's conversation with Diomedes, means that we gain no inkling of what has brought about this devastatingly sudden change in her. We observe it from without, as uncomprehending as Troilus.[12] It is as if the new context automatically produces a new Cressida; she changes with her changing environment.

I want to suggest that the reasons why Shakespeare denies us access to Cressida's inner life lie in her crucial role in relation to a central theme of the play, the problem of value.[13] It is in making this theme the centre of his conception

12 On Cressida's "sudden move into opacity" when she goes to the Greek camp, see Janet Adelman, "'This Is and Is Not Cressid': The Characterization of Cressida," in *The (M)other Tongue: Essays in Feminist Psychoanalytic Interpretation*, ed. Shirley Nelson Garner, Claire Kahane, and Madelon Sprengnether (Ithaca, NY, 1985), 119–41, at 119–28.

13 On the theme of value, see: Winifred M.T. Nowottny, "'Opinion' and 'Value' in *Troilus and Cressida*," *Essays in Criticism* 4 (1954): 282–96; Frank Kermode, "Opinion, Truth, and Value," *Essays in Criticism* 5 (1955): 181–7; I.A. Richards, *Speculative Instruments* (London, 1955), 201–2; A.P. Rossiter, *Angel with Horns and other Shakespeare Lectures*, ed. Graham Storey (London, 1961), 141–5; Terry Eagleton, *Shakespeare and Society* (London, 1970), 14–38; R.A. Yoder, "'Sons and Daughters of the Game': An Essay on Shakespeare's 'Troilus and Cressida,'" *Shakespeare Survey* 25 (1972): 11–26, at 16–19; Douglas B. Wilson, "The Commerce of Desire: Freudian Narcissism in Chaucer's *Troilus and Criseyde* and Shakespeare's *Troilus and Cressida*," *English Language Notes* 21 (1983): 11–22; Frank Kermode, "'Opinion' in *Troilus and Cressida*," in *Teaching the Text*, ed. Susanne Kappeler and Norman Bryson (London, 1983), 164–79. None of these critics makes any attempt to relate the problem of value to philosophical/economic thinking on the subject; although the definition of "true worth" varies from critic to critic, its "objective" status is always assumed, not regarded as problematic. An exception is the article by Gayle Greene, "Shakespeare's Cressida: 'A kind of self,'" in *The Woman's Part: Feminist Criticism of Shakespeare*, ed. Carolyn Ruth Swift Lenz, Gayle Greene, and Carol Thomas Neely (Urbana, IL, 1980), 133–49, who follows Elton (see n. 15 below) in recognizing the subjective nature of value, and links this with the change in Cressida ("as opinion changes, so does she"), but follows him also in assuming that this subjectivity represents "the breakdown of an ordered, hierarchical notion of reality" reflecting "the transition in conceptions of value that was occurring in the Renaissance" (147n4), and so both sentimentalizing and misrepresenting the medieval thinking on price and value. David Bevington's introduction to his 1998 Arden edition perpetuates the erroneous assumption that the play depicts "an unsettling new

of the Troilus and Cressida story that Shakespeare departs most obviously from Chaucer, and an exploration of it will result in a sharper sense of the instructive differences between the two writers. But I shall suggest in conclusion the ways in which Chaucer's poem nevertheless contains the seeds from which Shakespeare's new interpretation could have germinated.

In response to Troilus's threatening insistence that the Greeks treat Cressida well, Diomedes gives the sober reply: "To her own worth / She shall be prized" (4.4.132–3). Coming as they do at the moment of Cressida's transition from Trojans to Greeks, from passionately committed lover to fickle mistress, Diomedes's words raise in acute form the question: What *is* Cressida's "own worth"? On which of her two selves are we to base our estimate of her? It is here that our lack of access to her inner thoughts and feelings becomes crucially important, for only through such access would we feel confident in identifying the "real Cressida" as (say) a calculating siren, a fickle whore, or a helpless victim of circumstance. By denying us this possibility Shakespeare frees us to notice that the question "what is Cressida worth?" has two problematic aspects, not one. Cressida is one element in the problem, the question of what constitutes worth is another.

This question runs through the whole play, and both Greeks and Trojans are confronted by it. On the Greek side, it is presented in male terms: it is the question of Achilles's worth. Achilles's estimate of his own worth becomes inflated; he overvalues himself, "grows dainty of his worth," as Ulysses tells the Greek council (1.3.145); "Imagined worth" disturbs his judgment (2.3.169–73). Overvaluing himself naturally leads Achilles to undervalue others – in particular, Agamemnon, who complains to Patroclus about the consequent derangement in the hierarchy that reflects and regulates relative worth: Achilles "overhold[s] his price," and forces those "worthier than himself" to dance attendance on him and humble themselves to his whims (2.3.131, 123–30). This blurring of relative value underlies the annihilation of degree vividly imagined in Ulysses's famous speech; degree is obscured when "th'unworthiest" are not distinguished from their betters (1.3.83–4).

Ulysses's plan to bring Achilles to his senses is of course to exalt the worth of Ajax in such a way as to devalue Achilles. Ulysses, that is, teaches Achilles a very valuable lesson in economics – that value is "subjective" rather than "objective." The value of an object is set by the level of desire for it in its potential buyers; it is not an inalienable property of the object itself. If gold ceased to be prized, it would cease to be valuable; if changes in human society create a new demand

ethic of subjective and commercial valuation" consequent upon "the shift from feudalism to early modern capitalism" (78; see also 67–73). It is *because* we cannot pin the blame for the play's theory of value on "the spirit of capitalism" characteristic of the modern world (Greene, "Shakespeare's Cressida," 137) that it is so challenging and disturbing. See also the following note.

for a commodity (oil, for example), its value will rise. Similarly, a man's worth is set by the value placed on him by others, as Ulysses explains:

> no man is the lord of anything,
> Though in and of him there be much consisting,
> Till he communicate his parts to others;
> Nor doth he of himself know them for aught,
> Till he behold them formed in th'applause
> Where they're extended. (3.3.116–21)

It must be grasped that what Ulysses is talking about is not simply the *recognition* of worth, but its very constitution. A man's qualities become valuable only in so far as others concur in so defining them; it is not that his worth is scorned, it is that it does not exist outside the applause of others. Thus, even he himself can gauge his own worth only by the measure of others' praise. Diomedes's suggestion that Cressida's "own worth" is intrinsic to her is therefore misleading; her value will depend not only on the qualities she possesses but on the qualities admired by her valuers. In economic terms, it is consumer demand that creates value in commodities.

Ulysses's notion that value is determined by the valuer rather than the object of valuation is neither original nor idiosyncratic, nor does it represent (as some critics assume) a cynical rejection of medieval idealism.[14] On the contrary, it is entirely in line with the orthodoxies of medieval economic thinking, as it developed in a series of commentaries on Aristotle.[15] The starting point for medieval

14 This is the line taken by Rossiter, who considers the "practical 'realist' argument" in this speech, which "denies the 'estimate and dignity' of intrinsic merit," to be in contradiction with the "universal, eternal values" asserted in Ulysses's speech on degree (*Angel with Horns*, 145); cf. his further remarks on "the questioning of values in [a] new and sceptical atmosphere," and the dismissal of "the old stable Medieval universals" (148). Ulysses's speech on degree is not however at odds with this theory of value. It is precisely because worth is established by general consensus that the undervaluing of Agamemnon instigated by Achilles is to be taken so seriously.

15 On this commentary tradition, which arose in the wake of Robert Grosseteste's translation of the *Ethics* into Latin in the mid-thirteenth century and continued into the Renaissance, see the excellent study by Odd Langholm, *Price and Value in the Aristotelian Tradition* (Bergen, 1979), especially 18–20; Grosseteste's translation was "gradually superseded by the Renaissance translations of Aretinus and Argyropulus; after 1530 there is a whole host of new ones" (Langholm, 16). See also Joel Kaye, *Economy and Nature in the Fourteenth Century* (Cambridge, 1998), chs 1–5, and especially 88–93 on the mistaken modern ideas about the idealizing nature of medieval theories of value. W.R. Elton, "Shakespeare's Ulysses and the Problem of Value," *Shakespeare Studies* 2 (1966): 95–111, interprets the value theory in the play on lines

discussions of the "just price" and the determination of value was Book V, chapter 5 of the *Nicomachean Ethics*, a text translated by Robert Grosseteste and thereafter interpreted by a series of medieval commentators. In this short passage Aristotle discusses justice in exchange as a subcategory of commutative justice. If a shoemaker and a builder are to make a just exchange of the goods they produce, the relative value of shoes to house must be established. Their monetary price is the conventional notation of this relative value, but money is only an index of worth, not its determiner. What in fact determines worth, for Aristotle, is need (the Greek word is *chreia*, which the medieval Latin translators and commentators render by *opus*, *necessitas*, or *indigentia* – all meaning "need"); it is the relative level of need for shoes as against a house in the parties making the exchange that will determine the relative value of the commodities. This "need" is not however to be identified with physical deprivation; the famous fourteenth-century philosopher John Buridan, recognizing that most objects of exchange are not needed in the sense of being essential to survival, interpreted *indigentia* as any consciousness of insufficiency, any sense of lack on the part of the consumer. Thus, we can say that rich men "need" luxuries because they demonstrate that need in their willingness to exchange other goods or money for them.[16] In Buridan's hands, "need" thus becomes virtually indistinguishable from the modern English "demand," and this emphasis on demand constitutes a recognition of the subjective desires of the consumer as the true determinant of value. "Objective" value is a chimera of the imagination in economic terms, since the objective utility of a commodity exists only in its usefulness to the consumer[17] – and "utility" must be defined not with reference to that which is necessary for survival, but as whatever men deem necessary for their existence.

---

broadly similar to my own, but uses as a basis of comparison Hobbes's views on value relativism, which are too late to have influenced the play and therefore less relevant to it than the mainstream Aristotelian tradition outlined here. Neither Elton nor any of the critics cited in n. 13 notices the connection between value theory and the exchange of Cressida.

16 Langholm, *Price and Value*, 123–7. Buridan's work was highly influential, and his *Quaestiones* on the *Ethics* were printed in 1489, 1513, and 1637; his ideas were also "kept alive in a number of summaries and paraphrases" from the fifteenth to the seventeenth centuries (ibid., 141–2). In following notes I give references to Langholm's survey to save space; I have however consulted Buridan's work at first hand.

17 Subjective value (*complacibilitas*) and objective value (*virtuositas*) are distinguished in the branch of value theory represented by San Bernardino of Siena (1380–1444); see Raymond de Roover, *San Bernardino of Siena and Sant'Antonino of Florence: The Two Great Economic Thinkers of the Middle Ages* (Boston, MA, 1967), 16–23; and for the misleading nature of the distinction, Langholm, *Price and Value*, 115.

"Res valet quantum vendi potest" ("a thing is worth what it can be sold for"), as the medieval canon lawyers put it, in a quite uncynical spirit.[18] Value is not determined by idealizing theories;[19] it is market value, determined by aggregate demand, and settled in the everyday operations of market exchange.

The influence of the *Nicomachean Ethics* on Shakespeare's *Troilus and Cressida* has been claimed by Kenneth Palmer,[20] but neither he nor (as far as I know) anyone else has recognized the fundamental importance of the *Ethics* to the play's exploration of the question of value. Ulysses, as we have seen, aims to teach Achilles the importance of demand in creating worth. Among the Trojans, Troilus too recognizes the crucial role of demand, the subjective desire of the consumer. "What's aught but as 'tis valued?" is how he answers Hector's argument that Helen "is not worth what she doth cost / The holding" – the cost being the "many thousand" Trojans who have died "To guard a thing not ours, nor worth to us / ... the value of one ten" (2.2.18–25, 51–2). For Troilus, the many thousand Trojan deaths *prove* Helen's value, since they measure the level of desire for her possession. Hector vainly appeals to a notion of intrinsic value which will justify the subjective estimate:

> But value dwells not in particular will;
> It holds its estimate and dignity
> As well wherein 'tis precious of itself
> As in the prizer. 'Tis mad idolatry
> To make the service greater than the god;
> And the will dotes that is inclinable
> To what infectiously itself affects,
> Without some image of th'affected merit. (2.2.53–60)

Hector, like the average layman reacting to the astronomical price fetched by a Picasso, indignantly tries to assert the idea of an inherent worth which is somehow to be defined by common sense. Many modern critics align themselves with this view, but economically speaking it is untenable by the standards of medieval and Renaissance thinking. Hector's insistence on objective worth

18 *Price and Value*, 130–1.

19 Thus Aquinas, following St Augustine, pointed out that in economic terms a pearl is more valuable than a mouse, although the mouse, as a living creature, has a higher status in the scale of being (Langholm, *Price and Value*, 87).

20 In particular he sees it as a source for Hector's speech, with its reference to Aristotle, in the Trojan council; see *Troilus and Cressida*, ed. Palmer (London, 1982), introduction, 48–9, and appendix III, 311–20.

would hold good only in cases of counterfeit – in cases, that is, where a gullible fool allows himself to believe a glittering metal is gold; in such a case, the commodity does not have the attributes that are agreed to constitute preciousness. But gold itself – real gold – is not "precious of itself"; it is precious *because* its human prizers agree in attributing value to it. (One could imagine a society in which it had no value at all.) Troilus answers Hector's charge of whimsical subjectivity by appealing to mercantile realities as proof that the subjective estimate of value becomes *binding;* there is no going back on the bargain once it is struck. Value may be determined by subjective desire, but it does not subsequently fluctuate with a change in the desiring subject, since the realities of the market fix it in the act of purchase.

> We turn not back the silks upon the merchant
> When we have soiled them; nor the remainder viands
> We do not throw in unrespective sieve
> Because we now are full. (2.2.69–72)

Helen is "a pearl / Whose price hath launched above a thousand ships"; if the Trojans judged her "Inestimable" when Paris brought her home, they cannot now "Beggar the estimation which [they] prized / Richer than sea and land" (2.2.81–92). The realities of commerce become one with the idealism of chivalry: since value is fixed by the commitment of the valuer to the prized object, to change one's estimate of value is to lose honour through the abandoning of that commitment. And the greater one's "bank" of honourable commitment, the higher the potential rise in value of the object on which it is expended. In response to Hector's first sober appraisal of the cost of keeping Helen Troilus protests not her worth but Priam's:

> Fie, fie, my brother!
> Weigh you the worth and honour of a king
> So great as our dread father in a scale
> Of common ounces? Will you with counters sum
> The past-proportion of his infinite
> And buckle in a waist most fathomless
> With spans and inches so diminutive
> As fears and reasons? Fie, for godly shame! (2.2.25–32)

Helen's "inestimable" value is guaranteed by Priam's "fathomless" worth; to count the cost of keeping her is to make of Priam a penny-pinching millionaire. Female worth and male worth thus enjoy a symbiotic relationship; the valuable object testifies to the wealth of the buyer, just as that very wealth raises the price of the object. The cautious buyer, on the other hand, depresses the price of the commodity. Just as Diomedes differs from Troilus as to how Cressida's worth is to be measured, so he "weighs up" the worth of Helen in exactly the calculating way that Troilus rejects:

> For every false drop in her bawdy veins
> A Grecian's life hath sunk; for every scruple
> Of her contaminated carrion weight
> A Trojan hath been slain. Since she could speak,
> She hath not given so many good words breath
> As for her Greeks and Trojans suffered death. (4.1.71–6)

Paris treats this as "sales talk" designed to disguise the real value attached to the object; the Greeks show what Helen is worth to them in their continued commitment to the cause of recovering her.

Cressida is as acutely aware as Troilus and Ulysses that value resides in the estimation of the valuer, as we see from her first soliloquy.

> Women are angels, wooing;
> Things won are done; joy's soul lies in the doing.
> That she beloved knows naught that knows not this:
> Men prize the thing ungained more than it is. (1.2.277–80)

The point of this soliloquy is not to expose feminine coquetry, but to make it clear that in the world of the Trojans as in the world of the Greeks the value of women is determined by men. Hector's challenge to the Greeks is a prime illustration of this unromantic truth, for all its apparent evocation of an outdated world of chivalric gallantry: the superior worth of Andromache over the women of Greece is to be proved, not by reference to the women themselves, but by male valour. If no Greek accepts the challenge, it will be proved that "The Grecian dames are sunburnt, and not worth / The splinter of a lance" (1.3.282–3).

Like the other women in this play, Cressida is a blank cheque on which men write their own estimates of value. For Troilus she is, like Helen, "a pearl," and he himself a merchant using Pandarus as "convoy" (1.1.96–100). For Diomedes, as we have seen, she is more coolly appraised. What is interesting here is that all the "language of looks" which in Chaucer's *Troilus and Criseyde* acts as a passport to the inner heart, revealing it in its interaction with the outer world, here becomes a series of external signs appraised by men in their determination of female value. Instead of seeing Cressida blushing on stage, we have Pandarus giving Troilus an account of her blushes and short breathing; the effect is to raise her erotic appeal for her lover – to raise the value of the commodity – rather than to give us direct access to her emotions (3.2.28–32, 96). In the Greek camp, when the Greek leaders kiss Cressida in turn, Ulysses perversely takes the kissing as indicative of *her* licentiousness, rather than that of the men, although it was in fact his own suggestion, and Cressida's only contribution to the scene is a witty refusal to kiss both him and Menelaus.[21] Apparently out of pique, Ulysses then instantly interprets her looks and gestures as unmistakable signals of wantonness. The "language of looks" is not so much decoded as constructed by the observer.[22]

> Fie, fie upon her!
> There's language in her eye, her cheek, her lip,
> Nay, her foot speaks; her wanton spirits look out
> At every joint and motive of her body. (4.5.55–8)

Ulysses's speech is immediately followed by the general cry "The Trojan's trumpet" (referring to the arrival of Hector); the punning alternative "The Trojan strumpet" has been noted since Rossiter,[23] but what critics fail to comment on is the irony in the fact that the trumpet announces Hector's arrival for the single combat which is, theoretically, to uphold the worth of Trojan womanhood

---

21 David Bevington inexplicably overlooks Ulysses's request for a kiss ("May I, sweet lady, beg a kiss of you?" 4.5.48), claiming that "alone among the Greek generals ... Ulysses refuses to beg a kiss" (*Troilus and Cressida*, ed. Bevington, introduction, 25). So far from being "appalled by the spectacle of grown men demeaning themselves before a woman" (ibid.), he is happy to join the queue, until Cressida wittily puts him off by replying, in effect, "Yes, you can *beg*."

22 Everything depends of course on how the scene is acted, but there is nothing elsewhere in the text to justify Ulysses's speech and a fair amount to suggest that the Greeks' coarse notions of "courtesy" are unpleasant to Cressida. In so far as we can check Ulysses's description against the text (e.g., on Cressida's readiness to "give accosting welcome ere it comes" 4.5.60) it is inaccurate. Donaldson, *The Swan at the Well*, 112–13, comments: "It seems clear that a pretty young woman should not defeat a middle-aged self-proclaimed thinker in a small battle of wits, or deny him a kiss that others have received. Sour are the grapes of his wrath." As elsewhere in Renaissance drama, female sharpness of tongue is taken as a sign of licentiousness (see Lisa Jardine, *Still Harping on Daughters: Women and Drama in the Age of Shakespeare* [Brighton, Sussex, 1983], ch. 4). Cressida's vulnerability to male interpretations of her words and actions has already given rise to some uneasy moments in an earlier scene with Troilus, when he imputes a *double entendre* to her invitation "come you again into my chamber" (4.2.37): see Donaldson, *The Swan at the Well*, 94.

23 *Angel with Horns*, 133.

(significantly, there is not a word of reference to this in the actual combat scene). Creating female worth with one hand, these battling men destroy it with the other.

Throughout the play, there is a strong sense of the separation between a man's world and a woman's world. We feel this instantly in the very first scene as Troilus is transformed from a languishing introspective lover into a brisk comrade-in-arms by the entry of Aeneas; dropping his flights of rhetoric, he takes on the brusque laconicism of the club or the locker room. The putting away of the woman's world appears in his answer to Aeneas's enquiry as to the reason for his absence from the battlefield: "Because not there. This woman's answer sorts, / For womanish it is to be from thence" (1.1.102–3). (In Chaucer's poem, where the war is kept very much out of sight, there is none of this sense of "men's talk" in the scenes between Troilus and Pandarus.) Male solidarity expresses itself also in willingness to "guarantee" the worth of other men and to interpret their outward behaviour as a sign of it. In the same scene in which he produces his hostile reading of Cressida's "body language," Ulysses represents Diomedes's gait as a sign of his "aspiration," and willingly passes on Aeneas's "translation" (as he calls it) of Troilus's nature to his fellow Greeks (4.5.15–17, 97–113). Aeneas interprets Hector's actions for the benefit of Achilles, the one figure who breaks this male solidarity by his willingness to sneer at enemies and friends alike (4.5.78–87). In contrast, Cressida, like the other women in the play, stands alone, bereft of interpreters of her own sex and open to the construction the men put on her.[24]

One could trace the separation of the male and female worlds throughout the whole play, but it is most clearly realized in Hector's parting from Andromache. Its ultimate source, in Book VI of the *Iliad* (VI.390–493), is a scene of great beauty and tenderness. Although Hector refuses Andromache's plea that he stay at home, he does so with a sense of tragic necessity, sorrowfully foreseeing her future capture and thraldom. He offers to kiss his baby son Astyanax, but the boy shrinks back into his nurse's arms, terrified by his father's helmet with its nodding crest; both father and mother laugh at the childish terror and Hector lays aside his helm to kiss the boy before turning back to his mother, smiling amid her tears. The hero seems all the more heroic for this touch of domestic tenderness. Shakespeare must have known this original version of the scene, if not from Chapman (whose first selection from the *Iliad* did not include

24 Donaldson, *The Swan at the Well*, 84–5, notes that "Cressida is one of Shakespeare's few unmarried women without a confidante."

Book VI), then from one of the earlier Renaissance translations of Homer,[25] but he preferred to follow the tradition established by Dares's Latin version of the *Iliad*, in which Andromache's pleas are fused with the much later appeals of Priam and Hecuba, addressed to Hector as he is about to fight Achilles (*Iliad* XXII.25–89). In this medieval tradition, Hector angrily scorns Andromache and the womanish fears created in her by a dream.[26] The medieval authors vary in the degree of harshness they attribute to Hector's rejection of Andromache, but the underlying point – the manly refusal to be cowed by womanish words (*muliebria verba*) – remains the same.[27] And so it does in Shakespeare; although not harsh in itself, Hector's rejection of his wife has a shocking effect precisely because it comes from the gentle Hector.

> Andromache, I am offended with you.
> Upon the love you bear me, get you in. (5.3.77–8)

This, be it remembered, is the wife whose worth Hector earlier fought for; her husband determines her value, but she is not to determine his fate.

It is thus the men who finally fix Cressida's worth; yet they do so not by verbal assessment, but by the same mechanism which determines market value. For Aristotle makes clear that it is by *exchange* that value is determined, since

25 See the list of translations of the *Iliad* available to Shakespeare in J.S.P. Tatlock, "The Siege of Troy in Elizabethan Literature: Especially in Shakespeare and Heywood," *PMLA* 30 (1915): 673–770, at 742.

26 *Daretis Phrygii De Excidio Troiae Historia*, ed. Ferdinand Meister (Leipzig, 1873), 28–9 (section XXIV). The *Ilias Latina* (ed. Emil Baehrens, *Poetae Latini Minores*, vol. 3 [Leipzig, 1881], lines 564–74) follows Homer, but later writers took their cue from Benoît and Joseph of Exeter, who follow Dares. See Benoît de Sainte-Maure, *Le Roman de Troie*, ed. Léopold Constans, Société des Anciens Textes Français, 6 vols (Paris, 1904–12), lines 15263–599; Joseph of Exeter, *Frigii Daretis Yliados Libri Sex*, in *Joseph Iscanus Werke und Briefe*, ed. Ludwig Gompf (Leiden, 1970), V.425–66; Guido delle Colonne, *Historia Destructionis Troiae*, ed. Nathaniel E. Griffin (Cambridge, MA, 1936), 172–3; John Lydgate, *Troy Book*, ed. Henry Bergen, Part II, EETS e.s. 103 (London, 1908), III.4896–5143; William Caxton, *The Recuyell of the Historyes of Troy*, ed. H. Oskar Sommer, 2 vols (London, 1894), 2.610–12.

27 "At ubi tempus pugnae supervenit, Andromacha uxor Hectoris in somnis vidit Hectorem non debere in pugnam procedere; et cum ad eum visum referret, Hector muliebria verba abicit. Andromacha maesta misit ad Priamum, ut ille prohiberet, ne ea die pugnaret. Priamus Alexandrum Helenum Troilum et Aenean in pugnam misit. Hector ut ista audivit, multa increpans Andromacham arma ut proferret poposcit nec retineri ullo modo potuit. maesta Andromacha summissis capillis Astyanactem filium protendens ante pedes Hectoris eum revocare non potuit. tunc planctu femineo oppidum concitat ..." (Dares, ed. Meister, 28–9 [section XXIV]). Shakespeare's picture of Hector chiding Andromache when out of temper because he has been worsted by Ajax (1.2.4–6) is probably also inspired by this scene.

there must be a "proportionate equivalence" between the goods exchanged.[28] The exchange of three apples for two pears establishes an equivalence of worth between the two sets of items, despite their disparity in nature and number. It is thus no accident that Shakespeare chose to articulate the question of value in a play that culminates in an exchange. The exchange of Cressida for Antenor functions in the imaginative fabric of the play as the point at which the Trojans fix her worth. Antenor appears on stage several times, but he never speaks. A.P. Rossiter romanticized this wordless bystander into an imaginative picture of Antenor as "Shakespeare's one strong silent man," the "one character [who] comes out of it without a scratch," the plain man of goodwill and limited comprehension caught up willy-nilly in the fortunes of war.[29] Rossiter's fanciful picture is either ignorant or wilful; for to anyone at all acquainted with the story of Troy in the Middle Ages and Renaissance, Antenor was notorious as the man by whom Troy was finally betrayed.[30] Chaucer, for example, exclaims at length upon the irony that the Trojans build their own destruction by exchanging Criseyde for the man who is to destroy them (*Troilus and Criseyde* IV.197–210). (When Shakespeare's Pandarus speaks approvingly of Antenor as "one o'th'soundest judgements in Troy whosoever, and a proper man of person" (1.2.185–7), the audience would have been conscious of a similar irony.) The exchange fixes Cressida's value as equivalent to the value of that for which she is exchanged – that is, as the value of a traitor. Troilus's assertions of her unquantifiable worth are irrelevant (4.4.122–4); she is valued by the market process that equates her worth with that of Antenor. His future treachery is balanced by hers.

We can see therefore why Shakespeare "externalizes" his presentation of Cressida; her value is brought to her from outside, without reference to her inner being. Chaucer conceives her shift from true lover to faithless mistress from within; although briefly presented, it is nevertheless shown to be the result of a slow erosion of her former self, her old allegiances and habits of mind fading gradually under the influence of new surroundings. We are emotionally distanced from the new Criseyde, but we are not debarred access to understanding her. In Shakespeare the change is accomplished instantly and from without, with the shift from Troilus's romantic rhetoric to Ulysses's misogynistic scorn. It

28 "Contrapassum secundum proportionalitatem, et non secundum aequalitatem"; Langholm, *Price and Value*, 167. Agamemnon's implied comparison between the testing of metal and the trial of human worth in adversity (1.3.21–5) invokes the idea of settling worth by "assay," but assay only fixes worth on a scale of values already determined by market forces.

29 *Angel with Horns*, 151.

30 See Guido's *Historia*, Books XXIX–XXX.

is tempting to moralize on Troilus's bitter disillusionment – tempting, that is, to say that here we do have a case of counterfeit: he took glittering metal for gold. But to do so involves constructing precisely that definition of the "real Cressida" that the play, as I have argued, withholds from us. If Shakespeare's Cressida is unlike Chaucer's Criseyde, Shakespeare nevertheless resembles Chaucer in refusing to take the easiest and most popular way of accounting for her defection by depicting her as a deceitful whore from the start.[31] What is fundamental for him as for Chaucer is the conception that her shift from Troilus to Diomedes is a *change*, rather than the dropping of a mask. Under the pressure of external events a new self comes into being. Chaucer shows how the noble and generous elements in Criseyde blossom in the association with Troilus; under the influence of Diomede another self, which is capable of cheapness and dishonesty, gradually takes shape. In Shakespeare the range of potentialities suggested is narrower, but it remains true that the transfer of allegiance to Diomedes is profoundly disturbing precisely because we cannot relate it to the old Cressida. "This is and is not Cressid" (5.2.153). What Criseyde/Cressida represents is not sensuality but change – the change that is indelibly rooted in human beings. "Men loven of propre kinde newfangelnesse" (*Squire's Tale* 610) is Chaucer's deep-held belief, and Shakespeare is clearly echoing Chaucer in Ulysses's similar identification of "newfangelnesse" as a fundamental trait of human nature:

> One touch of nature makes the whole world kin,
> That all with one consent praise new-born gauds. (3.3.176–7)

It is the propensity to change that makes the valuation of human beings even more hazardous than the valuation of commodities. What we ought to deduce from Troilus's appeal to the mercantile bargain as a model for knightly honour is the *riskiness* in the commitment to value – the risk that the merchant, piloting his convoy between "dangerous shores" (2.2.64), has to accept as wholeheartedly as any chivalric warrior facing "the chance of war" (Prol. 31). The risk increases when the commodities bargained for are human beings. The attributes of gold may cease to be valuable if the social consensus alters, but they do not cease to exist. In human affairs, a change in the valuer can effect a change in the

31 For evidence of the predominance of this view of Cressida in both medieval and Renaissance literature, see Gretchen Mieszkowski, "The Reputation of Criseyde 1155–1500," *Transactions of the Connecticut Academy of Arts and Sciences* 43 (1971): 71–153, and Hyder E. Rollins, "The Troilus-Cressida Story from Chaucer to Shakespeare," *PMLA* 32 (1917): 383–429. Rollins comments (427–8) that in comparison with his immediate predecessors and contemporaries Shakespeare treats Cressida gently.

object valued; demand creates supply. "This is Diomed's Cressida" (5.2.144); the self is transmuted into the forms the market requires. To set Cressida down as "a daughter of the game" (4.5.64) from the outset is to obliterate this significant process of change.[32] Shakespeare, like Chaucer, sees the importance of context in creating the wholeness of a person – the coalescence of inner and outer that makes up their "worth." "What is Criseyde worth, from Troilus?" (IV.766) is Criseyde's anguished question as she contemplates leaving Troy. Away from Troilus, she loses the esteem that constitutes her worth as a person.

This moment in Chaucer's poem is, however, an isolated one. We must look elsewhere in medieval literature – in the works of the *Gawain*-poet, for example – to find a literary exploration of the theme of value which has the same Aristotelian background as Shakespeare's, and is equally ingenious in giving it imaginative expression.[33] In Chaucer, the theme of value is confined to a few hints, and behind them we can sense a tradition quite different from the Aristotelian one. Chaucer's version of the consummation scene picks up Boccaccio's use of the word "valore" in his coy description of the physical union of the two lovers ("d'amor sentiron l'ultimo valore" – "they experienced love's utmost pleasure"; *Filostrato* III.xxxii.8;) and transforms its meaning:

> I kan namore, but thus thise ilke tweye
> That nyght, bitwixen drede and sikernesse,
> Felten in love the grete worthynesse.
>
> O blisful nyght, of hem so longe isought,
> How blithe unto hem bothe two thow weere!
> Why nad I swich oon with my soule ybought,
> Ye, or the leeste joie that was theere? (*Troilus and Criseyde*, III.1314–20)

Not only does Chaucer's "grete worthynesse" have an emotional resonance that goes far beyond Boccaccio's notion of physical rapture, but the meaning of the word is fully activated by the subsequent use of the metaphor of "buying" such

32 Cf. Donaldson, *The Swan at the Well*, 118: "for us to see from the beginning of the play no potentiality in Cressida for a future better than the one we know she will have ... is to reduce the play's vision to that of Thersites." For changing critical attitudes to Shakespeare's Cressida, see the excellent summary by Donaldson, 149–51 n. 13, which shows that the older view of her as shallow and vulgar has been replaced in recent criticism by more careful and discriminating appraisals.

33 See "Price and Value in *Sir Gawain and the Green Knight*," 167–86 below.

joys at the cost of one's soul. The extravagant language might well prompt a censorious reader to conclude that we are here to see Troilus as making a "bad bargain," as the epilogue to the poem invites us to lament the waste of "his grete worthynesse" in devotion to an unworthy object. Yet, in this same epilogue the metaphor of buying surfaces again, and this time it shows us a God who made what prudence might consider a "bad exchange," from a similarly uncalculating devotion to the unworthy:

> ... loveth hym the which that right for love
> Upon a crois, oure soules for to beye,
> First starf, and roos, and sit in hevene above. (V.1842–4)

Chaucer, in other words, links the question of value with the language of redemption ("buying back"), in keeping with his poem's exploration of the divine as an aspect of the human. Shakespeare – at least in this play – conceives the buying and selling of human lives in human, not divine, terms, and ties the problem much more closely to the complexities of late medieval and Renaissance economic thought. Nevertheless, if we look back to Chaucer's poem with Shakespeare's dramatization of the male valuation of women in mind, one striking line leaps into sudden prominence. It is the climax of Hector's response to the embassy that comes to request the exchange of Criseyde for Antenor – a response that acquires a depth of significance not only because of the manly dignity with which it affirms female dignity, but also because it seems to lie quite outside the mental world of the men of Shakespeare's play:

> "Syres, she nys no prisonere," he seyde;
> "I not on yow who that this charge leyde,
> But, on my part, ye may eftsone hem telle,
> We usen here no wommen for to selle." (IV.179–82)

I would like to thank my colleague Juliet Dusinberre for helpful comments on an earlier draft of this essay.

Chapter Three

Chance and Destiny in *Troilus and Criseyde* and the *Knight's Tale*[1]

At a crucial moment in Book II of *Troilus and Criseyde*, Criseyde is left alone to reflect on Pandarus's astonishing revelation that Troilus is dying with love of her. And as chance would have it, at this very moment Troilus rides past her window.

> But as she sat allone and thoughte thus,
> Ascry aros at scarmuch al withoute,
> And men cride in the strete, "Se, Troilus
> Hath right now put to flight the Grekes route!"
> With that gan al hire meyne for to shoute,
> "A, go we se! Cast up the yates wyde!
> For thorwgh this strete he moot to paleys ride;
>
> "For other wey is fro the yate noon
> Of Dardanus, there opyn is the cheyne."
> With that com he and al his folk anoon

1 The issues dealt with in this essay have been discussed by numerous other writers, and it is not possible to indicate in detail points where my own treatment corresponds to or diverges from theirs. The reader is referred to some particularly important contributions: Howard R. Patch, "Troilus on Determinism," *Speculum* 6 (1931): 225–43; Morton W. Bloomfield, "Distance and Predestination in *Troilus and Criseyde*," *PMLA 72* (1957): 14–26; Walter Clyde Curry, "Destiny in *Troilus and Criseyde*," in *Chaucer and the Mediaeval Sciences*, rev. ed. (New York, 1960), 241–98. All three articles are reprinted in *Chaucer Criticism*, ed. Richard J. Schoeck and Jerome Taylor, 2 vols (Notre Dame, IN, 1961), vol. 2; Bloomfield's article is also reprinted in *Chaucer's Troilus: Essays in Criticism*, ed. Stephen A. Barney (London, 1980). For a study of Chaucer's translation of Boethius in relation to the medieval afterlife of the *Consolatio*, see *Chaucer's Boece and the Medieval Tradition of Boethius*, ed. A.J. Minnis (Cambridge, 1993).

An esy pas rydyng, in routes tweyne,
Right as his happy day was, sooth to seyne,
For which, men seyn, may nought destourbed be
That shal bityden of necessitee. (II.610–23)

The vision that passes before Criseyde's eyes is a powerfully attractive one: a handsome warrior, young and strong, whose battered armour and wounded horse bear witness to his daring and bravery, and whose blushing response to the people's cheers bears witness to his humility. As she watches, Criseyde finds her emotions instinctively aroused by the sight.

Criseyda gan al his chere aspien,
And leet it so softe in hire herte synke,
That to hireself she seyde, "Who yaf me drynke ?"

For of hire owen thought she wex al reed,
Remembryng hire right thus, "Lo, this is he
Which that myn uncle swerith he moot be deed,
But I on hym have mercy and pitee." (II.649–55)

There is no such window scene at the corresponding point in Chaucer's narrative source, Boccaccio's *Filostrato*.[2] There, Pandaro's departure is immediately followed by a description of Criseida's solitary reflections, in which the handsome exterior of Troiolo exercises its due influence, but which are not interrupted by his actual appearance. Only after this do we hear how Pandaro goes to Troiolo to tell him that the wooing of Criseida has been begun, and Troiolo, full of gratitude and hope, allows Pandaro to lead him to Criseida's window, where he receives a favourable glance from his lady. His gentle and amiable looks remove her remaining fears, and henceforth she fixes all her desires on this new love (*Filostrato* II.lxxxii–lxxxiii).

On first comparing Chaucer's version with Boccaccio's, we might simply assume that Chaucer's change is made with an eye to dramatic immediacy. Instead of the imagined appearance of Troilus, Chaucer introduces the hero himself, and he places the window scene before rather than after Criseyde's internal deliberations so as to increase its influence on her thoughts. But Chaucer does not merely move the position of the window scene; he also doubles it. On returning

2 Comparison of the two texts is easiest in the edition of *Troilus and Criseyde* by B.A. Windeatt (London, 1984), which places the Italian text alongside corresponding passages in Chaucer; here no parallel is given, but the source of the scene in *Filostrato* II.lxxxii is noted.

to Troilus, Pandarus advises him to write Criseyde a letter, declaring his love; he suggests that Troilus should ride past Criseyde's window *as if* accidentally, while he is delivering the letter to his niece, so that he can draw her into the window to impress her with the sight of her admirer (II.1002–22). This plan is duly executed (II.1247–74), and Troilus's reward is an outward blush and inward admiration from Criseyde. This second window scene is clearly, like the first, born of the single window scene in Boccaccio, which indeed it resembles even more closely in being a calculated move on Pandarus's part, designed to establish contact and some kind of tacit understanding between the two young people.

Why did Chaucer go to such trouble to expand and duplicate the single brief window scene (described in only two stanzas) in Boccaccio? Why did he fashion his narrative in such a way that the interview carefully arranged by Pandarus is preceded by an earlier encounter, dictated by nothing more than chance? The first answer, I believe, is that he wanted the comparison of the two scenes to reveal human efforts as negligible when weighed against the role of chance. The second window scene confirms and strengthens Criseyde's attraction to Troilus (II.1271–4), but it is the first window scene that has created this attraction ("Who yaf me drynke?"), and it is of key significance in the process because of its crucial positioning, occurring as it does at the moment when Criseyde is momentarily thrown off balance by the novelty of the situation, and thus most vulnerable to impressions one way or the other. Having initiated Criseyde's internal deliberations by one chance occurrence, Chaucer follows them with two more, neither of which has any precedent in Boccaccio's narrative. Fluctuating between fear and desire, Criseyde goes to walk in her garden, and hears her niece Antigone sing a song, written by "the goodlieste mayde / Of gret estat in al the town of Troye" (II.880–1), which praises love in terms that answer all Criseyde's doubts and fears (II.899–903).[3] She then goes to bed, with the nightingale singing beneath her window, and dreams that a white eagle tears her heart from her body, without causing her any pain, and leaves his own in its place. These experiences too have a contributory role in the "proces" (II.678) by which Criseyde turns to love. We shall better understand the reasons for their introduction if we return to the initial account of Troilus riding past the window and scrutinize it more closely.

I have said that this first encounter is dictated by nothing more than chance; Chaucer makes this clear by using the adjective "happy" ("his happy day": II.621), whose root is the noun "hap," meaning "chance." As Chaucer presents it, Troilus's riding past the window at that particular moment is nothing more than "a piece

3 For a more detailed demonstration of this, see Jill Mann, "Troilus's Swoon," 3–19 above.

of good luck." In doubling the window scenes, Chaucer is emphasizing chance as the crucially important determinant in the course of the love affair. The scope of human agency is correspondingly restricted: Pandarus, fondly imagining himself the omniscient and omnipresent director of the drama, is in fact merely a contributor to, not the controller of, the dynamics of the narrative. The chance which he carefully simulates in the second window scene has already been independently at work, making his own efforts superfluous. His skilful manipulations begin to look less like vital contributions, and more like baroque flourishes on an independently worked design.[4] Looking back to the beginning of the story, we realize that chance appropriately guides the love affair, since it was chance that initiated it; it is "upon cas" (I.271) that Troilus's gaze falls on Criseyde in the temple, with such dramatic effects. Troilus himself thinks of his love as an "aventure" (another Middle English word for chance; see I.368), and it is consistently referred to as such by Pandarus (II.224, 288) and also Criseyde (II.742). Indeed, Pandarus's own intervention in the affair is dictated by the "cas" or "aventure" that causes him to break in on Troilus's solitary languishing (I.568).[5]

But no sooner has Chaucer established Troilus's ride-past as due to chance, than he goes on to refer this chance to an underlying "necessitee."

> Right as his happy day was, sooth to seyne,
> For which, men seyn, may nought destourbed be
> That shal bityden of necessitee. (II.621–3)

And it is of "necessitee" that Troilus complains at the other end of the narrative, in his much-discussed soliloquy on free will in Book IV. Here the sense of casualness associated with "luck" or "chance" has entirely disappeared; the relentless rhyming of "necessitee" and "destinee" that ushers in Troilus's lament (IV.958–9) expresses his sense of being imprisoned in a tyrannical world of fate which leaves no room for the exercise of the human will or the realization of human desires. What then is the nature of the "necessitee" that underlies the episode in Book II, and the "necessitee" confronting Troilus in Book IV? What is the nature of the connection between this destinal "necessitee" and chance? And what room is left for the exercise of free will in the face of these powerful forces?

---

4 This is even more true of his efforts in the bedroom scene of Book III; see Mann, "Troilus's Swoon," 10–11 above.

5 The role played by these and connected words in the development of this theme in *Troilus* may be traced in *A Concordance to the Complete Works of Geoffrey Chaucer*, ed. John S.P. Tatlock and Arthur G. Kennedy (Gloucester, MA, 1963), or *A Glossarial Concordance to the Riverside Chaucer*, ed. Larry D. Benson (New York, 1993).

Troilus and Criseyde itself testifies to the fact that Chaucer's thinking on these questions was stimulated and directed by his reading of Boethius's *Consolation of Philosophy*, which he himself translated.[6] Boethius, confronting disgrace, imprisonment, and possible death, is brought, like Troilus, to raise questions of cosmic order – "questiouns of the symplicite of the purveaunce of God, and of the ordre of destyne, and of sodeyn hap, and of the knowynge and predestinacioun devyne, and of the liberte of fre wil" (*Boece,* IV pr.6). As he ponders the arbitrary injustice manifested in his own loss of good fortune, he observes that such injustices would better sort with a theory that the world was governed by blind chance ("fortunows hap") than with a belief in the ordering control of divine providence (IV pr.5). Philosophy's answer to these doubts addresses itself first to the questions of providence and destiny (IV pr.6), and then to the question of chance (V pr.i–m.i); finally she reaffirms the freedom of the human will (V pr.2–pr.6).

Crucial to Philosophy's explanation of providence and destiny is the role of time. Providence, the "pure clennesse of the devyne intelligence," is outside of time – a separation expressed in the image of the tower, from the height of which the divine intelligence surveys all together the events which are for us arranged in temporal succession (IV pr.6). This atemporal providence disposes all things in an order; destiny is the manifestation of that order in time – it is a "temporel ordenaunce." To express this idea, Philosophy uses the analogy of a craftsman who first conceives the object he is to make, and then produces it according to his design; his conception of the object as a whole "governs" its final form, but exists separately from its execution at all stages of the process. Using a different analogy, we could say that the relation between providence and destiny is something like the relation between a bus timetable and the actual running of the buses. The analogy is not perfect in either instance, because it is difficult to rid ourselves of the notion that the workman's design, and the bus timetable, *precede* the temporal realization that they govern – in other words, that they too belong to a temporal process. The point at which the analogies hold good is the perception that the conception and its execution exist on different planes, and that the conception embraces as a whole and immediately what can only be executed as a reality gradually and over time.

The difference between providence and destiny can thus be expressed as a difference of *perspective* – as is suggested in the text by the image of the tower, and Philosophy's repeated use of the work "lokynge" for the divine thought (IV pr.6). Although Philosophy talks of destiny as "subgit" to providence, it is

6 The most comprehensive study of Chaucer's debt to Boethius is Bernard L. Jefferson, *Chaucer and the Consolation of Philosophy of Boethius* (Princeton, NJ, 1917).

misleading to think of them only as two separate links in a chain of command. On the contrary, destiny and providence are merely two different names given to the same thing, which is called providence when considered as a unity out of time, and destiny when it is manifested in the linear succession of events in time. It is precisely this difference of perspective that gives rise to human doubts about providence. Bound to a temporal existence, human beings are denied a vision of the unity in which the order of providence is visible; they can glimpse only a part of the whole pattern, which inevitably appears to them as fragmentary and confused. Philosophy speaks of "destinal ordenaunce" as "ywoven and acomplissid" (IV pr.6), and the image of weaving is a helpful one. In the weaving of tapestry, the design of the whole will be perceptible only when the weaving is completed; while it is in progress, the shifts in shape and colour may well seem random and confusing.

This conception of destiny helps solve the problem of necessity inasmuch as destiny is no longer perceived as the direct imposition of a divine will (whether the divinity be pagan or Christian) on helpless humanity. On Philosophy's definition, the free exercise of the human will is *part of* destiny; it is simply one of the " moevable thinges" (IV pr.6) whose constant interplay makes up the temporal unfolding of destiny. For us the term "destiny" implies a predetermining of the future, outside the human will, whereas for Boethius, events take their place in the "destinal cheyne" (V pr.2) as a result of their own natural developments. The existence or non-existence of "necessitee" is a matter of perspective; it exists only when the destinal chain is seen as a whole from the perspective of providence, since that which God sees must necessarily exist to be seen. As Philosophy puts it a little later (V pr.6): "thilke thing that is futur, whan it is referred to the devyne knowynge, than is it necessarie; but certis whan it is undirstonden in his owene kynde, men seen it outrely fre and absolut fro alle necessitee." It may help us to understand this differentiation between the freedom of events within the temporal process, and their necessity within the atemporal sphere of the divine intelligence, if we consider for a moment the status of the past, rather than the future, in relation to divine knowledge. Human beings are quite happy to think of the past as fixed and determined, merely by virtue of the fact that it has happened; it is only the future that they feel must be undetermined – that is, open to the influence of their own will. Now since divine providence "enbraceth alle thinges to-hepe" (IV pr.6), it makes no distinction between past, present, and future. If then it is to consider the future as undetermined, the past must be considered undetermined also; conversely, the future must be perceived as determined in exactly the same way that the past is. The future is "necessary" only in the sense that it exists (not pre-exists) in the atemporal vision of divine providence, which beholds past, present, and future in the timelessness of the eternal moment. "Thilke God seeth in o strok of thought alle thinges that ben, or weren, or schollen comen" (V m.2). From the human point of view, we could express the upshot of this argument by the paradoxical proposition that things are destined only when they have happened. ("The thingis thanne ... that, whan men doon hem, ne han no necessitee that men doon hem, eek tho same thingis, *first or thei ben don,* thei ben to comen withoute necessitee": V pr.4, my italics.) Only after they have happened are portions of the destinal pattern realized in time and made perceptible to human observers. "Necessitee," then, does not represent the intrusion of divine control into human affairs; it is the pattern achieved by the totality of temporal events, working according to their own causes and effects.

The role of chance in this scheme of things is easily explained. Like destiny and providence, chance is a matter of perspective. "Hap," explains Philosophy, is a name that men give to occurrences not embraced by their own intentions in initiating actions (V pr.1). If a man ploughs a field and discovers a buried cache of gold, the discovery was intended neither by himself nor by the burier of the treasure; we therefore call it chance. Yet the event is not without causes: in this case, the hiding of the treasure and the ploughing of the field, both of which play an instrumental role. It is simply that the result of these two actions was not envisaged by either of their human performers. "Hap" arises, therefore, from "causes encontrynge and flowynge togidere to hemself, and nat by the entencioun of the doere" (V pr.1). In the following metre, Philosophy illustrates this idea with the image of the two mighty rivers, Tigris and Euphrates, in whose waters a multitude of floating objects are swept together or pushed apart, as the whole mass rushes onward to the sea; in the same way, the shifts of Fortune are made one with the inexorable course of "destinal ordinaunce."

Turning back to our starting point, we can see how brilliantly Chaucer has fashioned the scene in which Troilus passes Criseyde's window so that it embodies Boethius's notion of "causes encontrynge and flowynge togidere to hemself," independent of human intention. The impression that Troilus makes on Criseyde is not only unintended by him, he is not even conscious of it; nor was it envisaged by Criseyde as she went into her closet for private thought. Even less was it foreseen or intended by Pandarus, despite his confidence that the whole world will proceed to execute his "purpos." Yet Pandarus is *one* cause within the larger confluence; it is his introduction of the idea of Troilus's love into Criseyde's mind that has created in her a susceptibility to a sight that would at other times have evoked no more than polite admiration. The "flowynge togidere" of causes is thus rightly called chance ("his happy day"), since it lies outside what was envisaged by the human actors. But it can also be accurately called "destiny," since the confluence of causes realizes a pattern. All the other occasions on which Troilus rode up this very street are not important; this one assumes significance because it connects with another contingent circumstance – Criseyde's first response to Pandarus's revelation – and thus forms part of the pattern which we are to call Troilus's destiny. The "opyn cheyne" of the gate of Dardanus is a surrogate for the chain of destiny: open as Troilus embarks on his ride home, it closes as his passing links with Criseyde's watching. Thus the term "necessitee" can be justified by reference of the event to its presence in the destinal pattern, out of time, in the divine thought.

The readers of Chaucer's poem are in a privileged position, since they can perceive this destinal necessity in a manner analogous to, although not identical with, that of the divine intelligence. For the pattern of destiny is, in literary terms, the pattern of the story. We feel it therefore as "inevitable" that Pandarus's revelation should be followed by Troilus's impressive appearance, and that this in turn should be followed by Antigone's song, the nightingale, and Criseyde's dream, all insensibly steering her towards love. But we feel it as inevitable only because we know already that this is a love story, and because we are observing these individual occurrences with their known end in mind; it is because the story has, in a sense, already happened for us – we see it in "o strok of thought" – that we can perceive its course as inevitable. The occurrences recounted are not necessary in themselves: Troilus could have ridden up some other street or returned an hour earlier; Antigone could have chosen to sing a melancholy song in which a lady lamented the loss of her lover or the torments of jealousy; it could have been a rainy night on which the nightingale uttered not a note and Criseyde fell into a dreamless sleep – the result of all this being that she woke next morning in a mood of bracing common sense determined to hear no more romantic tales. These are not undisciplined speculations; they are justifiable precisely because this is a narrative in whose dynamics chance plays a crucial role. In order to register with full appreciation the brilliance of Chaucer's depiction of "causes encontrynge and flowynge togidere to hemself," we must be alive to the possibility that the confluence of chance events could at every point have taken on a different form. The "openness" of the story, our present sensation of suspense as we live through each event as it happens,[7] gives us a sense of its fluidity, its vulnerability to chance, even as our knowledge of its eventual end gives us a sense of inevitability, of its final shape as destiny. Through narrative suspense, Chaucer makes us alert to the possibility of a different story – that is,

7 The most obvious example of suspense is the ending of Book II ("O myghty God, what shal he seye?": 1757), but the whole Horaste story, for example, increases narrative tension and our sense of precariousness up to the consummation scene.

a different destiny. For *this* destiny is realized only through the confluence of contingent events; it is not fixed in advance, but in retrospect, when the pattern of "temporel ordenaunce" (*Boece* IV pr.6) has been worked out.[8]

Love is an area of human experience in which the retrospective nature of the realization of destiny is particularly easy to grasp, precisely because it is an experience about which it is next to impossible to use the future tense. The future-tense formulation "I will/am about to fall in love with you" is patently absurd, while the present-tense "I am in love with you" implies not so much the consciousness of a present happening as of a past event – "I have fallen in love with you" – which is achieving belated recognition. That is why Criseyde's expression of surrender to Troilus in the consummation scene of Book III – "Ne hadde I er now, my swete herte deere, / Ben yolde, ywis, I were now nought heere!" (III.1210–11) – is not, as some critics have held, a coy revelation that her mind had been consciously made up at some earlier date; it is rather a realization that her present situation and feelings imply, and therefore reveal, an earlier unconscious surrender, now to be made explicit.[9] Thus it is, also, that after the consummation the lovers, like all lovers, rehearse the events that have led up to this climactic end:

> Thise ilke two of whom that I yow seye,
> Whan that hire hertes wel assured were,
> Tho gonne they to speken and to pleye,
> And ek rehercen how, and whan, and where
> Thei knewe hem first, and every wo and feere
> That passed was; but al swich hevynesse –
> I thank it God – was torned to gladnesse. (III.1394–1400)

They reinterpret previous events as part of the pattern of destiny, their significance – the direction in which they were tending – now being established by the end that has been reached.[10]

The lovers have here no complaints of a destiny being forced on them; when Troilus (echoing the lover's perennial cry, "we were meant for each other") tells

8 Mark Lambert ("Telling the Story in *Troilus and Criseyde*," in *The Cambridge Companion to Chaucer*, ed. Piero Boitani and Jill Mann, 2nd ed. [Cambridge, 2003], 78–92) shows how Chaucer deliberately fashioned the parting scene in Book IV as an "alternative ending" to the story; had Criseyde not revived from her swoon in the nick of time, we should have had a Romeo-and-Juliet-type ending, which would have made this a story of fidelity unto death, rather than a story of classic betrayal.

9 See further Mann, "Troilus's Swoon," 16–17 above.

10 I owe this point to Dr Philip Davis of the University of Liverpool.

Criseyde that "God hath wrought me for I shall yow serve" (III.1290), he is not expressing a consciousness of tyrannical control, but rather a sense of having discovered his true nature and function in life for the first time, of finding what it is that most fully expresses and engages his individual being. Their free assent, that is, is not only part of the "confluence of causes," it is also accorded to the confluence as a whole. Free will and destiny are thus inextricably united; destiny, as I said earlier, works through the will in the subtle coalescence of outward event and inward desire.

This subtle coalescence is portrayed with extreme delicacy by Chaucer in Book II, as he traces Criseyde's response to Troilus's love. So far I have concentrated on the external occurrences – Pandarus's revelation, Troilus's riding past, Antigone's song, the dream. But equally important in the confluence of causes are the inner workings of Criseyde's mind and emotions, which are as it were the eyes into which the hooks of external incident can fall. Between Troilus's riding past and Antigone's song, Chaucer places his long account of Criseyde's deliberations (II.703–812). *What* she thinks is less important than *how* she thinks: her mind appears as a seething mass of different possibilities, jostling and giving way to each other with the spontaneous movement of her emotions.[11] Within these possibilities, we can perceive the instincts towards love – and specifically, towards an ennobling love – which find an echo and a confirmation in Antigone's song. But we can also see the instincts *against* love – the fears of jealousy, emotional torment, and betrayal – which could equally have found a chance echo and confirmation in the outside world; the different nature of the coalescence would then have given a different turn to the story. The chances and changes that Boethius contemplates in the *Consolation* are chances and changes in the external world – loss of riches, family, or friends. Chaucer adds to his representation of these instances of "moevable destyne" (*Boece* IV pr.6) the *inner* mutations which are ceaselessly at work in every human being. It is on these inner mutations that the external occurrences work; from the coalescence of the two the shape of the action is born. A spherical object placed at the top of a slope will roll to the bottom because of its own sphericity as well as because of the declivity; its own nature is "expressed" in

11 For a subtle, sensitive, and full analysis of Criseyde's internal monologue and its relations to the surrounding narrative, which coincides very closely with the next section of my discussion, see Donald R. Howard, "Experience, Language and Consciousness: 'Troilus and Criseyde,' II, 596–931," in *Medieval Literature and Folklore Studies: Essays in Honor of Francis Lee Utley*, ed. Jerome Mandel and Bruce A. Rosenburg (New Brunswick, NJ, 1970), 173–92; repr. in *Chaucer's Troilus*, ed. Barney, 159–80.

the rolling just as much as the nature of the surrounding circumstances.[12] So Criseyde is "expressed" in her motions towards love, even though external circumstances are needed to bring her potentialities into being.

In describing this process, I am not merely saying that Criseyde chooses to fall in love, exercising her free will in a matter presented to her for decision. This description fits Boccaccio's Criseida fairly accurately, but not Chaucer's Criseyde. For Chaucer's brilliance lies precisely in the way he makes us alive to the involuntary elements involved in the exercise of the will. Criseyde certainly imagines that Pandarus has presented her with a case in which she is free to choose one way or the other; she comforts herself, when he has left her, that she need not fear because

> man may love, of possibilite,
> A womman so, his herte may tobreste,
> And she naught love ayein, but if hire leste. (II.607–9)

But it is at this very point that Troilus rides past, and Criseyde finds herself unable to view the sight with the detachment she has just described; she is inevitably affected by the new knowledge she possesses.

> For of hire owen thought she wex al reed,
> Remembryng hire right thus, "Lo, this is he
> Which that myn uncle swerith he moot be deed,
> But I on hym have mercy and pitee." (II.652–5)

Tolstoy's brother Nicholas used to tell him that his wishes would come true if he first fulfilled certain conditions; the first of these conditions was to stand in a corner and *not* think of a white bear. Tolstoy commented: "I remember how I used to get into a corner and try (but could not possibly manage) not to think of a white bear." Criseyde's case as she thinks about *not* falling in love with Troilus seems to me of the same sort; the more she considers not doing so, the larger the position occupied in her mind by the possibility. The revelation of Troilus's love inevitably creates a new entity in her mind, a new set of emotions, of circumstances ready to form a nexus with external incidents and thus to take on the configurations of destiny.

---

12 This analogy is based on those devised by the Stoics to express their theory of necessity and free will (see A.A. Long, *Problems in Stoicism* [London, 1971], 180); there is of course no question of Chaucer having direct knowledge of these theories, but he seems independently to have arrived at similar ideas.

The long and patient observation of this process in Books II and III teaches us to understand how it can be repeated, with contradictory results, in the movement towards betrayal in Book V. The changed external circumstances again exert their own pressure on Criseyde's mind, linking with her fears and her sense of emotional desolation to bring different possibilities to the fore. Again, there is no decision; the moment of betrayal is diffused through a long-drawn-out process that renders it invisible. The gloomy stanza describing the internal state of mind which is to coalesce with Diomede's external pressure in the shape of betrayal –

> Retornyng in hire soule ay up and down
> The wordes of this sodeyn Diomede,
> His grete estat, and perel of the town,
> And that she was allone and hadde nede
> Of frendes help; ...

– does not conclude "and thus she decided to stay." Rather, it emphasizes that this is the beginning of a process whose conclusion is dispersed through a series of minute readjustments:

> ... and thus bygan to brede
> *The cause whi*, the sothe for to telle,
> That she took fully *purpos for to dwelle*. (V.1023–9; my italics)

We are now in the position to appreciate not only Chaucer's debt to Boethius, but also his most original development of Boethian ideas. Boethius, as I have already suggested, sees Fortune as largely external; Chaucer on the other hand sees the processes of mutability as impregnating the inner life of humankind to the very depths of being. The adjective "slydynge," which Boethius applies to Fortune (I m.5), Chaucer applies to Criseyde's mind, telling us that she was "slydynge of corage" (V.825). Fortune, for Chaucer, is not merely apparent in the larger, more readily observable mutations in worldly affairs, it is a name we can also apply to the moment-by-moment mutations in Criseyde's mind, observable in her long soliloquy in Book II, to the opalescent shifts as one impulse or another spontaneously emerges. It is from these minute and ceaseless fluctuations that the larger movements of change are formed. In addressing Fortune with a capital F, human beings deceive themselves into thinking that Fortune is an independent entity, existing apart from themselves and from other agencies, whereas Fortune is simply the name for (what is to them) the random, the unplanned, the unforeseen, for mutability in all its manifestations, which include not only the accidents of the external world, but also the momentary oscillations within their own minds.

There is however a moment in *Troilus and Criseyde* where Fortune is associated with an external agency which apparently overrides human will – namely, the influence of the planets. At the moment when Criseyde is about to leave Pandarus's supper party, Chaucer suddenly breaks the cheerful mood with two stanzas of gloomy foreboding.

> And after soper gonnen they to rise,
> At ese wel, with herte fresshe and glade;
> And wel was hym that koude best devyse
> To liken hire, or that hire laughen made:
> He song; she pleyde; he tolde tale of Wade.
> But at the laste, as every thyng hath ende,
> She took hire leve, and nedes wolde wende.
>
> But O Fortune, executrice of wyerdes,
> O influences of thise hevenes hye!
> Soth is, that under God ye ben oure hierdes,
> Though to us bestes ben the causes wrie.
> This mene I now, for she gan homward hye,
> But execut was al bisyde hire leve
> The goddes wil, for which she moste bleve.
>
> The bente moone with hire hornes pale,
> Saturne and Jove, in Cancro joyned were,
> That swych a reyn from heven gan avale
> That every maner womman that was there
> Hadde of that smoky reyn a verray feere;
> At which Pandare tho lough, and seyde thenne,
> "Now were it tyme a lady to gon henne!" (III.610–30)

How does this view of planetary influence sort with the views on chance and destiny that I have already outlined? And does it contradict or undermine the supposition that human will is an element in the "causes flowynge togidere to hemself," in its assertion that "the goddes wil" is executed regardless of Criseyde's "leve"?

The first step in answering these questions is to identify the nature of the planetary conjunction described. Critics have, astonishingly, spent more time in trying to use this passage as a means of dating the composition of *Troilus and*

Criseyde (by relating it to the real occurrence of such a conjunction) than in attempting to analyse its poetic function.[13] Poetically, the most important feature of the conjunction is that it is a malevolent one. The benevolent influence of Jupiter is outweighed by the malign effects of Saturn (described at length by the planet himself in the *Knight's Tale*), in combination with the Moon, in the unpropitious house of Cancer.[14] The conjunction therefore bodes eventual ill for the love affair that is consummated under its auspices. But the description of the conjunction tells us more than this – it also tells us what it is that will bring about this ill. Saturn was traditionally interpreted in medieval mythic allegoresis as Time, since his Greek name, Cronos, was identified with the Greek word *chronos*.[15] The Moon is a traditional symbol of change, because of her constant waxing and waning.[16] Time and change hang threateningly over the love affair that is shortly to be consummated; time and change bring it into being, time and change will destroy it. When understood, the planets appear not as agents of an independently exercised "goddes wil," but as emblems (as well as representatives) of the natural forces through which the "goddes wil" – the pattern of destiny – realizes itself. As in the Boethian scheme of things, destiny is executed by Fortune ("executrice of wyerdes"), by the individual chances that weave together the "temporel ordenaunce" of destiny.

If this passage represents the planets as dominating human will, it is in order to show that the destinal ordinance that is being woven is one that *goes beyond* the wishes and predictions of the human contributors to it. Troilus and Criseyde

---

13 See the articles listed and discussed in the note to Troilus III.624–6, in the *Riverside Chaucer*, and J.D. North, *Chaucer's Universe* (Oxford, 1988), 369–78. John J. O'Connor ("The Astronomical Dating of Chaucer's *Troilus*," *Journal of English and Germanic Philology* 55 [1956]: 556–62) insists on the storial significance of the conjunction, but relates it to the fall of Troy and the heavy rain, rather than to the ultimate outcome of the love affair. Chauncey Wood (*Chaucer and the Country of the Stars* [Princeton, NJ, 1970], 47–8) also emphasizes the rain, which he sees as a bathetically deflatory result of so awe-inspiring a conjunction.

14 Cancer was the "domicile" of the Moon and would thus strengthen her influence; see North, *Chaucer's Universe*, 195, and 196, Fig. 30. Jupiter at first seems the odd man out in this predominantly malevolent grouping. I suggest that here, as in the *Knight's Tale*, he has a double role: first, as one of the seven planets (in which role he brings the short-term happiness experienced by the lovers), and second, as a mythic representative of the power of the Christian God, the providence which lies behind the whole conjunction and subjects it to its own ultimate plan.

15 Isidore of Seville, *Etymologiae* VIII.xi.31: "Vnde et eum Graeci Cronos nomen habere dicunt, id est tempus, quod filios suos fertur devorasse, hoc est annos, quos tempus produxerit, in se revolvit."

16 See *Romaunt of the Rose*, lines 5331–50; *House of Fame*, lines 2114–16; *Complaint of Mars*, line 235, for the Moon as an image of change.

are shortly to commit themselves to a consummated love as to their (beneficent) destiny, as we have seen; they assume that the pattern is now completed, it has achieved its final shape at that point. This passage reminds us that the destinal process will continue, and that the "cas or aventure" (IV.388) of Criseyde's exchange for Antenor will be the first in a different confluence of causes that will seal the final destiny of Troilus. The planetary conjunction images to perfection this "double destiny"; its immediate effect is to bring the rain, cause of Criseyde's decision to stay the night, and thus, eventually, of the blissful consummation, while its ultimate effect is to subject the love affair to the forces of time and change by which it is destroyed. Pandarus sees only the immediate effect; he rejoices in the rain that enables the execution of his will. Forgetful of the astrological calculations that he had taken care to complete before making his first approach to Criseyde (II.74–5), he sees only that portion of the cosmological whole which is useful to his immediate purposes. The description of Pandarus's preparations for the supper party shows his powers of control at their apparent zenith: directing Troilus, coaxing Criseyde, picking a moonless night when rain is threatening, so that the cosmos itself seems merely a tool of his grand design. The words used of him at this point represent him as a kind of mini-providence: his planning is referred to as "purveiaunce," and it is "Forncast and put in execucioun" just as divine providence is executed by destiny (III.533, 521). The stanzas on the planetary conjunction reveal that this appearance of all-embracing control is a pathetic sham. The solemn apostrophe of Fortune introduces not only a note of foreboding but also a sobering shift in perspective, as our vision widens with dramatic speed from the cosy domestic interior of the dinner party to the dizzying heights of the cosmos, whence we glimpse humans crawling like "bestes" on the surface below. This dramatic effect makes clear with unforgettable impact the limitations of human control. Pandarus's grand design is merely a feeble fragment of a far vaster pattern, woven by mightier forces than he.

Chaucer's attempt to render the operations of chance and destiny in human affairs was not confined to *Troilus and Criseyde*. They assume importance in several of the *Canterbury Tales* – notably the *Man of Law's Tale*, the *Wife of Bath's Tale*, the *Franklin's Tale*, and the *Nun's Priest's Tale*, but most of all in the *Knight's Tale*, to which I shall devote the brief remaining space of this essay.

As in *Troilus*, Chaucer takes pains in the *Knight's Tale* to alter his Boccaccian source in order to emphasize the role of chance in the events of the narrative.[17]

17 A detailed summary of Boccaccio's *Teseida*, with excerpts of those passages that are closely paralleled in the *Knight's Tale* (and accompanying translations), can be found in *Sources and Analogues of the Canterbury Tales*, ed. Robert M. Correale and Mary Hamel, 2 vols (Cambridge, 2002–5), 2:87–214.

The most striking example can be found in his altered account of Palamon's escape from prison. In the *Teseida,* Palemone is driven to make the attempt by discovering that Arcita has returned to Teseo's court in disguise and is serving Emilia as her page (V.1–8). The mechanics of the escape are carefully and plausibly recounted, and once he is free, Palemone goes straight to the grove outside Athens because he knows that it is a favourite haunt of Arcita (V.22, 33). Chaucer patiently unravels this logically knit narrative sequence, in order to produce a narrative dominated by chance. Knowing nothing of Arcite's presence in Athens, Palamon simply happens (after seven years!) to escape:

> Were it by aventure or destinee –
> As whan a thing is shapen, it shal be ... (1465–6)

The occurrence is, like Troilus's riding past the window, referred equally to chance and destiny. Chaucer's apparent casualness in proposing the two as alternatives is a mere narrative disguise, for here as in *Troilus* we shall see that the one is a component of the other. Palamon goes to the grove to hide himself, and "by aventure" (1506) Arcite makes for the same place. Not only that, but "by aventure" (1516) he wanders into the very path by whose side Palamon lies hidden, and then reveals his true identity in soliloquy. Chaucer's motive in creating this inherently improbable narrative can only have been to illustrate "causes flowynge togidere to hemself" and creating destiny out of "fortuit hap." The final chance necessary to complete the pattern – in that it turns the knights' private squabble over Emily into a public contest capable of practical resolution – is the arrival of Theseus, which is duly heralded by an emphasis on destiny.

> The destinee, ministre general,
> That executeth in the world overal
> The purveiaunce that God hath sein biforn,
> So strong it is, that thogh the world had sworn
> The contrarye of a thing by ye or nay,
> Yet somtime it shal fallen on a day
> That falleth nat eft withinne a thousand yeer. (1663–9)

The thousand-to-one chance fixes the shape of the destinal pattern for good or ill.

The rest of the narrative is equally full of chance events, most often signalled as such by the use of the key words "aventure," "cas," or "hap." It is "by aventure or cas" (1074) that Palamon first sees and falls in love with Emily, his fate, like that of Troilus, being sealed by chance – and Chaucer here alters the *Teseida,* in which the first glimpse belongs to Arcita (III.11–12), as if to stress that it *is* simply the chance of being first-comer that will often determine a man's success in love. It is chance ("it happed," 1189; cf. "aventure" at 1235) that brings Perotheus to Athens and thus effects Arcite's release. We are made conscious also of the alternative stories that chance could dictate, as Palamon and Arcite each speculate on various ways in which Fortune might produce events to favour the other's suit (1240–3, 1285–90). Finally, the tournament that Theseus decrees shall determine who is to marry Emily is a vast amphitheatre for chance ("falling nis nat but an aventure"; 2722). Acknowledging, with true wisdom, the limitations of human control, Theseus eschews making the choice himself; not denying or combatting the role of chance, he merely provides a civilized context within which it can operate. The final chance of Arcite's death after victory is thus a blow, but not a crushing one, since Theseus's role throughout the narrative constitutes an acknowledgment of the powers of chance and an illustration of readiness to adapt to it.[18]

However, in the *Knight's Tale* as in *Troilus,* at an important moment in the poem we might be tempted to think that the course of events is *not* dictated merely by chance, but by the will of higher powers. For the *Knight's Tale,* like *Troilus,* represents human affairs as subject to planetary influence.[19] Just before the tournament, Palamon and Arcite pray to Venus and Mars respectively to grant their wishes, and Chaucer temporarily abandons the human plane of his narrative to show us the heated debate that then breaks out between the conflicting celestial powers. For Palamon and Arcite, Venus, Mars, Saturn, and the rest are "gods"; when we look closer, however, we can see that it is not as deities but as planets that they exert power. Saturn's speech makes this plain:

> "My cours, that hath so wide for to turne,
> Hath moore power than woot any man.
> ...
> I do vengeance and plein correccioun
> Whil I dwelle in the signe of the Leoun." (2454–5, 2461–2)

It is because Saturn's sphere is the outermost in the planetary order (his course thus being widest of all) that his influence dominates the planets beneath him.[20]

---

18 See Jill Mann, *Feminizing Chaucer* (Cambridge, 2002), 133–40.

19 For an astrologically based interpretation of the whole poem, see Douglas Brooks and Alastair Fowler, "The Meaning of Chaucer's *Knight's Tale,*" *Medium Aevum* 39 (1970): 123–46.

20 In the medieval cosmological scheme, the planets were thought to move in concentric spheres, arranged in the order: Moon, Mercury, Venus, Sun, Mars, Jupiter, Saturn. Then came the sphere of the fixed stars, and finally the Primum Mobile or First Moving Sphere, which moves

His overruling influence means that the lesser influences exerted by Mars and Venus will resolve themselves into a malevolent pattern; his sending of a "furye infernal" (2684) to startle Arcite's horse is an anthropomorphic representation of a cosmological phenomenon. It is *because* Mars and Venus are planets, and not independent pagan deities, that Palamon and Arcite win their favour: both knights take care to make their pleas at the astrologically correct hour, when the planet's power is at its height,[21] and response to human prayers follows according to a quasi-physical law of cause and effect. The importance of this is that we perceive that the planets act according to their nature, not according to their whims. Their representation in human shape means we can "read" their behaviour in two ways: first, as the result of their own independent wishes, and second, as the result of inevitable natural processes. As we shift between these two views, from free agents to naturally impelled forces, we are instructed in the illusions of control; we see that the apparently independent movers are themselves moved by other powers.[22]

The shift from the human to the cosmological plane has a similarly instructive effect. Like the dramatic widening of vision in the passage concerning the planets in Book III of *Troilus,* it expands way beyond the possible reach of any sort of human control the kinds of causes that we conceive as flowing together to make up the pattern of human destiny. We are allowed, by poetic licence as it were, a fleeting glimpse of the hidden causes behind what appears to the human onlookers as the chance ("aventure"; 2703) of Arcite's fall (as if, in Boethius's example, we were privileged to see the man burying the gold and thus to know the "cause" of its being found). But in being vouchsafed this glimpse, we are only being shown one more cause, not the final cause that lies behind all of them. We have a shift in perspective, not the complete vision that belongs only to providence, seeing "alle thinges to-hepe." We have left the human plane, but we have not left the cosmos, or the realm of time. It is in Theseus's final speech that we perceive this most fully. His opening reference to the "Firste Moevere" reminds us that there is a power beyond the planets, by which they are moved. They do not operate of their own volition; their power is only a secondary one. A fortiori, the same holds good for human beings. Only from the perspective of

---

all those beneath it. God is the First Mover of the whole cosmos. For a brief account, see Edward Grant, *Physical Science in the Middle Ages* (Cambridge, 1971), ch. 5, "Earth, Heavens and Beyond."

21 See John Livingston Lowes, *Geoffrey Chaucer* (London, 1934), 10–13.

22 See also Jill Mann, "The Planetary Gods in Chaucer and Henryson," in *Chaucer Traditions: Studies in Honour of Derek Brewer*, ed. Ruth Morse and Barry Windeatt (Cambridge, 1990), 91–106, at 91–5.

the First Mover, which is forever inaccessible to mortals, could the final causes of events be understood, and the shape which would give them final meaning be perceived. Theseus emphasizes our perception of "temporel ordenaunce" as a series of individual destinies, whose end is determined by the natural processes of change and decay – the tree falls, the river runs dry, men and women die. The larger shape, the whole of which these individual experiences are part, remains hidden; human beings can perceive only what Boethius calls the "entrechaungeable mutacioun" (IV pr.6) by which the processes of decay and renewal work themselves out. The planets too are part of this "entrechaungeable mutacioun"; they are not the agents by which it is set in motion.

Since human beings are bound to time and change, they must embrace these conditions of their existence, for good or ill. But time and change do not always bring disaster. Theseus's humble acknowledgment of the inevitability of change and death concludes with an attempt to realize the beneficent possibilities created by the shifting kaleidoscope of chance. Arcite's death is irreversible, but it provides the chance to create a new configuration with the marriage of Palamon and Emily. Whereas at the end of *Troilus* chance works to close off possibilities, here there survives the opportunity, gladly perceived and acted upon by Theseus, to move forwards, to allow the process of mutability to carry one on to happiness. Caught in the realization of his tragic destiny, Troilus perceives "necessitee" as a cruel trap; in the more optimistic configurations of the *Knight's Tale,* we can see that it is possible to "maken vertu of necessitee" (3042) – not merely to "grin and bear it," but to transform necessity *into* "vertu," to respond to the pattern as it forms with a recognition of its passing chances for good, as well as the faith that its final shape will be revealed as concordant with the "cheyne of love."

Chaucer's thinking on the question of whether the world is governed by "fortunows hap" or by a benign ordering power is fundamental to his most serious poetry. In reading that poetry, we must in consequence give due attention to his presentation of *event,* rather than focusing on the "characters" of Criseyde and Troilus, or Palamon and Arcite, as sole determinants of the narrative development. We must be alive to his use of words like "cas," "aventure," or "destinee" (and to others, such as "entencioun," "purveiaunce," "ordinaunce," "governaunce," which also belong to his exploration of Boethian problems)[23] as signalling his reflections on the nature of the forces which work on human

23 For a discussion of Chaucer's use of the last three words to develop Boethian themes, see Jill Mann, "Parents and Children in the *Canterbury Tales,*" 120–8, 132–7 below.

beings, and the extent of their own possibilities for action. Chaucer is outdone by none in his ability to reproduce the idiosyncratic details of human speech and action, but his deepest interest in investigating human psychology is to uncover the subtlest manifestations of time and change at work in human emotions, shaping the course of human lives.

Chapter Four

Chaucerian Themes and Style in the *Franklin's Tale*

The *Franklin's Tale* is not only one of the most popular of Chaucer's tales, it is also one whose emotional and moral concerns lie at the centre of Chaucer's thinking and imaginative activity. It is usually thought of as a tale about "trouthe" – or perhaps about "gentillesse" – but it is equally concerned with the ideal of patience and the problems of time and change, which are subjects of fundamental importance not in this tale alone but in the *Canterbury Tales* as a whole. What follows is intended to be not only a close discussion of the *Franklin's Tale*, but also an attempt to indicate how a proper reading of it can help with a proper reading of the rest of the *Tales* – and indeed, of Chaucer's work in general.

The *Franklin's Tale* begins by introducing a knight who has, in best storybook fashion, proved his excellence through "many a labour, many a gret emprise" (732) and thus finally won his lady who, likewise in best storybook fashion, is "oon the faireste under sonne" (734). "And they lived happily ever after" is what we might expect to follow. And so far from trying to dispel the reader's sense of the familiar in this situation, Chaucer takes pains to increase it. He refers to the actors only in general terms ("a knight," "a lady"), and attributes to them the qualities and experiences normally associated with tales of romantic courtship (beauty, noble family, "worthinesse," "his wo, his peine and his distresse"; 737–8). Only after eighty lines are the knight and the lady given the names of Arveragus and Dorigen. This generality cannot be accidental, for Chaucer's apparently casual comments are designed precisely to emphasize that this individual situation takes its place in a plural context:

But atte laste she, for his worthinesse,
And namely for his meke obeisaunce,
Hath swich a pitee caught of his penaunce
That privELY she fel of his acord

To take him for hir housbonde and hir lord,
Of swich lordshipe *as men han over hir wives.* (738–43; my italics)

What is more, they stress this plural context even in describing the feature of the situation that seems to make it an unusual one: the knight's promise to his lady that he

Ne sholde upon him take no maistrye
Again hir wil, ne kithe hire jalousye,
But hire obeye, and folwe hir wil in al,
As any lovere to his lady shal. (747–50; my italics)

And after the lady's delighted promise of her own faithfulness and humility, we have a warm outburst of praise which again consistently sets this mutual understanding in the context of a whole multiplicity of such relationships.

For o thing, sires, saufly dar I seye,
That freendes everich oother moot obeye,
If they wol longe holden compaignye.
Love wol nat be constreined by maistrye;
Whan maistrye comth, the God of Love anon
Beteth his winges, and farwel, he is gon!
Love is a thing as any spirit free.
Wommen, of kinde, desiren libertee,
And nat to been constreined as a thral,
And so doon men, if I sooth seyen shal. (761–70)

"Love ... maistrye ... freendes ... wommen ... men" – the terms are abstract, plural, general. They relate general human experience to this situation, and this situation to general human experience, with no sense of conflict or discontinuity between the two.

I stress the importance of the general here for two reasons. The first is that this interest in the common features of human experience is characteristic of Chaucer. The parenthetical comments that transform the singular of the story into the plural of everyday experience are not confined to this passage or this tale alone; on the contrary, they are so ubiquitous in Chaucer that the reader may take them for granted and fail to question their significance. The second reason is that the unusualness of the relationship between Arveragus and Dorigen has often been taken as a sign that it is aberrant – that it represents an attempt to break away from the normal pattern of marital relationships which inevitably invites problems to follow.[1] Against this view we should note that however unusual the *degree* of generosity and humility in this relationship, Chaucer very firmly roots it in the normal desires and instincts of men and women.

Nor is there any reason given for supposing that these desires and instincts are merely human weaknesses. Chaucer's own comments, some of which have been quoted, constitute an unhesitating endorsement of the wisdom of this situation and of the participants in it. The relationship between the knight and his lady is called "an humble, wis acord" (791), and the knight himself "this wise, worthy knight" (787). It would not affect this point were anyone to argue that the comments are the Franklin's, not Chaucer's. For in either case any reader who wishes to dissociate him- or herself from the warm approval in these lines will face the same difficulty – and that is the difficulty of finding a location in the tale for true wisdom and worthiness, if both characters and narrator offer only false images of these qualities. The only way out of this difficulty would be to claim that the reader already knows what true wisdom and worthiness are, and brings this knowledge to bear on the tale, in criticism of its values. But this idea assumes that it is possible for his or her knowledge to remain detached from the tale in a way that the passage we are considering simply refuses to allow. For if the reader is a woman, to refuse to acknowledge the truth of what is said about her sex is, *ipso facto*, to accept the legitimacy of her own "thraldom":

> Wommen, of kinde, desiren libertee,
> And nat to been constreined as a thral. (768–9)

If, on the other hand, the reader is a man, and feels inclined to respond to these lines with a knowing smile at the ungovernable nature of women, then the following line – "And so doon men, if I sooth seyen shal" (770) – immediately challenges him in turn to measure the reasonableness of the female desire for liberty by matching it against his own. The result is that both men and women readers are made aware of the need for the liberty of the opposite sex through the recognition that it is a need of their own. The use of the plural, the appeal to the general, is indeed an invitation to readers to bring their own experience and feelings to bear, but it invites them to an identification with the narrative, not to a critical dissociation from it.

Chaucer's use of the plural is thus intimately connected with his use of the second person, an equally pervasive and significant feature of his style. His appeals to the reader as judge have often been discussed – "Who hath the worse,

---

1 See, for example, D.W. Robertson, *A Preface to Chaucer* (Princeton, NJ, 1962), 470–2.

Arcite or Palamoun?" (*Knight's Tale*, 1348); "Which was the mooste free, as thinketh yow?" (*Franklin's Tale*, 1622). But to emphasize these formal appeals alone is to imply, again, that the reader, in the role of judge, remains detached from and superior to the narrative. If, on the other hand, we look at the whole series of addresses to the audience in Chaucer, we shall see that the situation is more complicated. Certainly it is true that the narrative is subordinate to the reader, in the sense that it acknowledges that it relies on a particular experience of the reader for its life and depth; the appeal for judgment on the situations of Arcite and Palamon, for example, is specifically addressed to "Yow loveris" (1347). The opening of *Troilus and Criseyde* (I.22) similarly invites "ye loveres" to read the narrative in the light of their own experience. This call for supplementation of the narrative from one's own experience is often implicitly, as well as explicitly, made. Such an appeal can, for example, be felt in the rhetorical question that concludes the praise of the marriage in the *Franklin's Tale:*

> Who koude telle, but he hadde wedded be,
> The joye, the ese, and the prosperitee
> That is bitwix an housbonde and his wif? (803–5)

The rhetorical question here makes a space for the reader's own experience to give full meaning to the description, just as it makes space for a very different kind of experience to give a very different kind of meaning to the apparently similar question in the *Merchant's Tale* (1337–41). But if the story needs the reader, it can also make claims on the reader. Precisely because the narrative is based on common knowledge, on experiences and feelings shared by the narrator, the readers, and the characters in the story, it is possible for its third-person generalizations to issue into second-person imperatives. Thus, when Troilus falls in love, the generalizations about Love's all-conquering power ("This was, and is, and yet men shall it see"; I.245) issue naturally into a command:

> Refuseth nat to Love for to ben bonde,
> Syn, as hymselven liste, he may yow bynde. (I.255–6)

So we can see that in the narrator's comments on the marriage of Arveragus and Dorigen, the apparently casual insertion of "sires" in the first line is a deliberate preparation for the intensification of the narrative's claims on the reader – claims which make themselves known not only as commands but also as threats.

> Looke who that is moost pacient in love,
> He is at his avantage al above.

> Pacience is an heigh vertu, certein,
> For it venquisseth, as thise clerkes seyn,
> Thinges that rigour sholde never atteine.
> For every word men may nat chide or pleine.
> Lerneth to suffre, or elles, so moot I gon,
> Ye shul it lerne, wherso ye wole or non.
> For in this world, certein, ther no wight is,
> That he ne dooth or seyth somtime amis. (771–80)

The command "Lerneth to suffre" does not stand alone; if we disobey it, we face a threat, an "or elles." If we search for the authority on which we can be thus threatened, we find it, I think, in the appeal to *common* human experience that I have been describing, in the generalizations from which the imperative issues and into which it returns. And because the experience is common, the speaker himself is not exempt from it; it is perhaps possible to detect in the parenthetical "so moot I gon" a rueful admission that he has learned the truth of his statement the hard way. At any rate, the phrase stands as an indication that the speaker offers his own individual experience as a guarantee of the truth of the generalizations.

It is because Chaucer wishes to appeal to the general that he so often uses proverbs as the crystallizations of episodes or whole narratives. The proverb which underlies the description of the marriage in the *Franklin's Tale* is perhaps the most important one of all to him; the attempt to understand the paradoxical truth "Patience conquers" is at the heart of the *Canterbury Tales* and much of Chaucer's other work besides. It animates the stories of Constance and Griselda; it is celebrated in Chaucer's own tale of *Melibee*. It undergoes, as we shall see, a comic-realistic metamorphosis in the *Wife of Bath's Prologue*, and it also stimulates Chaucer's exploration of the qualities that represent a rejection of patience: "ire," "grucching," "wilfulnesse." It is tinged with a melancholy irony in *Troilus and Criseyde*, where Criseyde quotes another version of the proverb – "the suffrant overcomith" (IV.1584) – in the course of persuading Troilus of the wisdom of letting her go to the Greeks. This latter instance shows us that an understanding of the truth to be found in such proverbs does not give us clues to the instrumental manipulation of life – quite the reverse, in fact. The parallel truism that Criseyde also quotes – "Whoso wol han lief, he lief moot lete" (IV.1585) – does not become the less true because in this case Troilus fails to keep possession of his happiness even though he follows her advice. It is precisely the knowledge that proverbs carry with them the memory of human miseries as well as human triumphs and joys that gives depth and emotional power to the apparently worn phrases.

But of course it is also the story, the new setting which will give fresh meaning, that gives new depth and emotional power to the old words, and we should therefore look to the rest of the *Franklin's Tale* to see how much it can help us to understand the nature of patience and "suffrance." The first thing that the story shows us is the link between patience and change. In the first place, it is because human beings are inevitably and constantly subject to change, not just from day to day but from moment to moment, that the quality of patience is needed. In his list of the influences that disturb human stability, Chaucer makes clear that they come both from within and without the person.

> Ire, siknesse, or constellacioun,
> Win, wo, or chaunging of complexioun
> Causeth ful oft to doon amis or speken.
> On every wrong a man may nat be wreken;
> After the time moste be temperaunce
> To every wight that kan on governaunce. (781–6)

All these things disturb the stability of a relationship by altering the mood or feelings or behaviour of an individual. Thus, the only way that the stability and harmony of a relationship can be preserved is through constant adaptation, a responsiveness by one partner to changes in the other. The natural consequence of this is that patience is not merely a response to change; it *embodies* change in itself. And this is at first rather surprising to us, since we tend to think of patience as an essentially static quality, a matter of gritting one's teeth and holding on, a matter of eliminating responses rather than cultivating them. But it is the responsive changeability of patience that is emphasized in Chaucer's final lines of praise for the marriage of Arveragus and Dorigen.

> Heere may men seen a humble, wis acord!
> Thus hath she take hir servant and hir lord –
> Servant in love, and lord in mariage;
> Thanne was he bothe in lordshipe and servage.
> Servage? – nay, but in lordshipe above,
> Sith he hath bothe his lady and his love;
> His lady, certes, and his wif also,
> The which that lawe of love acordeth to. (791–8)

It is often said that this passage illustrates Chaucer's belief in an ideal of equality in marriage. But the patterning of the language does not give us a picture of equality; it gives us a picture of alternation. The constant shifts in the vocabulary suggest constant shifts in the role played by each partner: "servant ... lord ... servant ... lord ... lordshipe ... servage ... servage ... lordshipe ... lady ... love ... lady ... wif." The marriage is not founded on equality, but on alternation in the exercise of power and the surrender of power. The image it suggests is not that of a couple standing immutably on the same level and side by side, or marching in step, but rather of something like the man and woman in a weather house, one going in as the other comes out. Except of course that this image gives a falsely mechanical idea of what is, as Chaucer describes it, a matter of a living organic responsiveness, and that it is also incapable of expressing an important aspect of the relationship – that the ceaseless workings of change lead to an unchanging harmony, and to the creation of a larger situation in which each partner simultaneously enjoys "lordshipe" and "servage," as the passage itself stresses. The result of these constant shifts could be called equality (though I should prefer to call it harmony), but the term "equality" is too suggestive of stasis to be an accurate description of the workings of the ideal involved here. The ideal of patience better befits the way human beings are, because the simplest and most fundamental truth about people, for Chaucer, is that they change. "Newefangelnesse," the love of novelty, is part of their very nature ("propre kinde"; *Squire's Tale*, 619).

Human beings are not only subject to change in themselves; they also live in a changing world. The opening of the *Franklin's Tale* might seem at first to belie this, since it reads more like an ending than a beginning, so that the story seems, with the long pause for the eulogy of the marriage, to have reached a full stop before it has begun. What prevents a sense of total stagnation is that the unusualness of the situation – of Arveragus's surrender of absolute control – creates a powerful expectation that *something is going to happen*. This is not just a stratagem for holding our interest; on the contrary, Chaucer uses narrative expectation as a way of indicating the persistence of change even when events have apparently reached a standstill, a way of making us feel the potentiality for change within the most apparently calm and closed of situations. Thus, as Chaucer allows himself his leisured commentary on the "humble, wis acord," we find ourselves asking not "Is this a good thing?" but "How will this turn out?" We await the completion that the development of events will bring to our understanding and evaluation, and we are thus taught to expect development, the breaking of stasis, as natural.

The stasis is first broken in a very simple way: Arveragus departs for England, and Dorigen's contentment changes into a passionate grief. This grief is described in a long passage (815–46) which takes us from her first agonies, through her friends' attempts at comfort, to her final subsidence into a kind of resignation which creates a new, if provisional, stasis. Two features of this passage are important: the first is that Dorigen's experience is, once again, placed in a general context.

> For his absence wepeth she and siketh,
> *As doon thise noble wives whan hem liketh.* (817–18; my italics)

Secondly, her experience is not only generalized, it is also abbreviated: "She moorneth, waketh, waileth, fasteth, pleineth" (819). Dorigen experiences her grief intensely and at length, but it is described summarily and – *ipso facto* – with a sort of detachment. This does not mean, however, that we need to qualify what was said earlier about the identification established between character, writer, and reader; the detachment here is not due to lack of sympathy or to criticism, but to a difference of position in time. Dorigen moves slowly through a "proces" (829) which is for her personally felt and unique; the image of the slow process of engraving on a stone emphasizes its gradualness, its almost imperceptible development. The teller of the story (and the reader of it), on the other hand, can from the outset see Dorigen's experience in a general context of human suffering, and from a knowledge of the general human experience which is embodied in the formulae of traditional wisdom – "Time heals," "It will pass" – can appreciate not only what is pitiable about Dorigen's misery but also the inevitability of its alleviation, and thus what is slightly comic about it. The amusement denotes no lack of sympathy, no sense that Dorigen's grief is melodramatic or insincere; it is the kind of amusement that Dorigen herself might well feel, looking back on her former agonies six months after her husband's safe return. As time goes on, and Dorigen succumbs to the natural "proces" of adjustment, she herself comes nearer to this view, so that the passage ends with a rapprochement between her position and that of the storyteller and the reader, and the calmer wisdom of "wel she saw that it was for the beste" (846) is shared by all three.

The celebrated Chaucerian "ambiguity of tone," of which this passage might well be taken as an example, is often regarded as an equivocation between praise and blame, a confusion in our impulse to approve or disapprove. Complex the tone may be, but it does not lead to confusion if we read it aright. The complexity is often due, as it is in this case, to Chaucer's habit of fusing with the narrative account of an event or situation the differing emotional responses it would provoke – and with complete propriety – at different points in time. Different contexts of place and time allow and even demand quite different emotional and intellectual responses. In common experience we take this for granted: we find it entirely proper and natural that a widow should be consumed with grief at her husband's death and equally proper and natural that several years later she should have found equanimity. Time thus affects not only decorum, but also morality: were the widow to show at the time of her husband's death the reactions of a widow several years later, we should find her behaviour unfeeling and wrong. Chaucer's complexity arises from the fact that he encourages us to bring to bear our knowledge of both points in the process at the same time. He is helped in this by the fact that a story always abbreviates experience; the protracted timescale of real-life experience is condensed in the timescale of the narrative, so that we can more easily and more swiftly achieve those shifts of perspective that are in life so laboriously accomplished. This is, of course, even more true in short narrative, because in such a narrative the disparity between the timespan of the occurrences and the timespan of the relation of them is most striking. Chaucer's interest in short narrative, the beginnings of which can be seen in the *Legend of Good Women*, and which finally achieved success in the *Canterbury Tales*, seems to me, therefore, to be a natural consequence of what he sees as interesting in human experience. The short narrative is a powerful way of provoking reflection on the process of change and of vitalizing our sense of the moral and emotional complications created by change, by our existence in the "proces" of time. And a multiplicity of short narratives can suggest the multiple individual forms in which a common experience manifests itself, and the constitution of common experience out of a multiplicity of variant instances.

The processes of time and change are not all, however, a matter of the development of inner feeling; change, as we have already observed, can equally originate in the outer world – in its most dramatic form, in the kind of sudden chance or accident for which Chaucer uses the Middle English word "aventure." This is a word that can be used with deceptive casualness to refer to the most mundane and minimal sort of occurrence, but also, more emphatically, to refer to the strange and marvellous. The other words that Chaucer uses to mark the operations of chance are "hap," "cas," and "grace," the last of these being usually reserved for good luck unless accompanied by an adjective like "evil" or "sory." Chaucer's concern with the problems of chance, with human helplessness before it, and with the difficulties it opposes to any belief in the workings of a co-ordinating providence, is something that can be observed throughout his literary work. The operations of "aventure" are often examined (as they are in the *Franklin's Tale*) in the sphere of love, and for good reason. The disruptive, involuntary, unforeseeable, and unavoidable force of love is perhaps the most powerful reminder of the power of chance over human lives. What is more, it increases human vulnerability to other chances, as Dorigen, in her persistent fears for her husband's possible shipwreck on the "grisly rokkes blakke" (859), is only too well aware. What she at first fails to perceive is her possible vulnerability to an "aventure" which is closer at hand: the "aventure" of Aurelius's love for her.

> This lusty squier, servant to Venus,
> Which that ycleped was Aurelius,
> Hadde loved hire best of any creature
> Two yeer and moore, as was his aventure. (937–40)

Chaucer's description of the wearing away of Dorigen's grief means that we can dimly see several possible patterns into which the coalescence of inner "proces" and outer "aventure" might fall. Were Arveragus's ship in fact to be wrecked, we could visualize not only Dorigen's passionate grief but also its susceptibility to slow assuagement, so that when the healing processes of time have done their work, Aurelius *might* hope at last to win his lady (as Palamon wins Emily). Or Arveragus might simply be forced to stay away so long that by the same process of imperceptible adaptation, Dorigen finds Aurelius a more vivid and powerful presence to her thoughts and feelings than her husband, and changes her initial rejection into acceptance – in which case the story would come closer to the pattern of *Troilus and Criseyde*. The openness of Chaucer's stories to other possible developments makes us aware that they are not fixed into inevitable patterns; like life itself, they are full of unrealized possibilities. In this case, the menace symbolized in the black rocks is not realized, and the other possibilities thus evaporate. "Aventure" does not take the form of shipwreck and Arveragus returns. But that there is no other kind of disaster is due also to the power of patience, of the ability to "suffer" the shocks of "aventure."

In order to understand this conception of "suffering" more fully, I should like to make some comparisons with another example of the genre to which the *Franklin's Tale* belongs, the Breton lay. This comparison will have the incidental advantage of suggesting why Chaucer assigns the tale to this genre, even though his source was probably a tale of Boccaccio.[2] The *Franklin's Prologue* suggests that the Breton lays are centrally concerned with "aventures":

> Thise olde gentil Britouns in hir dayes
> Of diverse aventures maden layes ... (709–10)

2 Boccaccio tells the story in the *Filocolo* (IV.4) and the *Decameron* (X.5). See the section on the *Franklin's Tale* in *Sources and Analogues of the Canterbury Tales*, ed. Robert M. Correale and Mary Hamel, vol. 1 (Cambridge, 2002), 211–65.

The notion that this is the proper subject of the lays can be traced back to one of their earliest composers, the late twelfth-century writer Marie de France, who says that each lay was written to commemorate some "aventure."[3] There is no direct evidence that Chaucer knew Marie's work,[4] but a brief comparison with some aspects of the lay of *Guigemar* will help to illustrate the literary tradition which lies behind Chaucer's thinking on "aventure," and also to understand the imaginative core of the *Franklin's Tale*, the underlying pattern of experience that it shares with a lay like *Guigemar*. Like the *Franklin's Tale*, *Guigemar* deals with "aventure" in relation to love: it is interested both in the way that love is challenged by "aventure," by the shocks of chance, and equally in the way that love itself *is* an "aventure," a force which is sudden and overwhelming in its demands, and to which the only fitting response is surrender or commitment of the self. What we also find in Marie's lays is the idea that such a surrender acts as a release of power. It is this pattern – surrender to "aventure" followed by release of power – that can be linked with the "Patience conquers" of the *Franklin's Tale*.

The hero of the lay, Guigemar, is a young man endowed with every good quality, but strangely resistant to love. One day while out hunting he shoots a white deer; the arrow rebounds and wounds him in the thigh, and the dying deer speaks to him, telling him that he will be cured of this wound only by a woman who will suffer for love of him greater pain and grief than any woman ever suffered, and that he will suffer equally for love of her. Guigemar's actions indicate an immediate and unquestioning acceptance of the doom laid on him by the deer. He invents an excuse for dismissing his squire, and rides off alone through the wood, not following any predetermined direction, but led by the path. That is, he follows not the dictates of his own wishes, but the dictates of chance. Eventually he comes to a river estuary, and finds a very rich and beautiful ship, with no one on board. Having boarded the ship, Guigemar finds in the middle of it a bed, sumptuously and luxuriously arrayed. The bed is an emblem of an invitation to rest, to relax, to surrender control – or rather to surrender it still further, since he in fact lost control at the moment when he shot the white deer. He climbs into the bed and falls asleep; the boat then moves off of its own

3 I cite the edition of Marie's *Lais* by A. Ewert (Oxford, 1944). For an English translation of Ewert's text, see Glynn S. Burgess and Keith Busby, *The Lais of Marie de France*, 2nd ed. (London, 1999). For Marie's statement about the *lais* and *aventures*, see her Prologue, 35–6.

4 Although her *lais* achieved a high degree of popularity; see Ewert's introduction, xviii. For a full discussion of the fortunes of the lay in England, see John B. Beeston, "How Much was Known of the Breton Lai in Fourteenth-Century England?" in *The Learned and the Lewed: Studies in Chaucer and Medieval Literature*, ed. Larry D. Benson (Cambridge, MA, 1974), 319–36.

accord, taking him to the lady who is to be his love, and who is kept imprisoned by her jealous husband in a castle surrounded by a high-walled garden, open only to the sea. The castle and the sea, and their relation to each other, are images that the tale endows with symbolic meaning. The sea (as often in medieval literature) is an image of flux or chance, of something vast and unpredictable that can carry one with the force of a tide or a current to strange harbours. The image of the imprisoning castle which is nonetheless open to the sea suggests the openness of even the most restrictive marriage relationship to the threat of "aventure." The jealous husband cannot shut out the power of chance; his marriage – and equally the generous marriage of the *Franklin's Tale* – must remain vulnerable to the assaults of chance.

Guigemar, in contrast, surrenders to the dictates of chance. When he wakes from his sleep on the boat, he finds himself in mid-ocean. Marie's comment on this situation brings a new extension to our notion of "suffering"; she says "Suffrir li estut l'aventure" (199). Both the infinitive "suffrir" and the noun "aventure" seem to call for a double translation here. "Aventure" simply means, in the first place, "what was happening"; but the word also emphasizes the chance nature of the event, its lack of background in a chain of causes. "Suffrir" seems to ask to be translated not only as "suffer, endure," but also as "allow," a usage now familiar to us only in archaic biblical quotations such as "Suffer the little children to come unto me." So that the line cannot be confined to a single interpretation: "He had to endure / allow what was happening / chance." Guigemar prays to God for protection, and goes back to sleep, another acknowledgment that control is not in his hands. So it is in the surrender or abandon of sleep that he arrives at the lady's castle, is found by her, and becomes the object of her love.

Guigemar's "suffering" can help with the understanding of the "suffering" urged on the readers of the *Franklin's Tale:*

> Lerneth to suffre, or elles, so moot I gon,
> Ye shul it lerne, wherso ye wole or non. (777–8)

This sort of "suffering" is not simply a matter of enduring pain or vexation; it is a matter of "allowing," of standing back to make room for, the operations of "aventure," and thus of contributing to the creation of something new by allowing the natural process of change to take effect. It is the generous in spirit who do this, in both Marie's work and Chaucer's, and it is the mean-spirited, such as the lady's jealous husband, who vainly try to close off possibilities for change, to wall up what they have and to preserve it in a state of fixity.

It is a later moment in the lay, however, that provides the most powerful image of a surrender of the self that miraculously releases power. After Guigemar and the lady have enjoyed each other's love for some time, his presence is discovered by the lady's husband, and he is put back on to the magic ship (which has miraculously reappeared) and sent back to his own country. After his departure, the lady suffers intensely, and finally she cries out with passion that if only she can get out of the tower in which she is imprisoned, she will drown herself at the spot where Guigemar was put out to sea. As if in a trance, she rises, and goes to the door, where, amazingly, she finds neither key nor bolt, so that she can exit freely. The phrase that Marie uses is another that seems to call for a double translation: "Fors s'en eissi par aventure" (676). "Par aventure" is a casual, everyday phrase, meaning simply "by chance, as it happened"; thus on one level, all this line means is "By chance she got out." But the miraculous nature of the event together with the way that the phrase recalls the other miraculous "aventure" of the ship suggest something like "By the power of 'aventure,' she got out." The intensity of the lady's surrender to her grief, which is imaged in her wish to drown herself, to "immerse" herself in her love and sorrow, magically transforms external reality. "Aventure," which had earlier been a force that impinged on people and acted on them, here becomes something which is itself acted on by emotion, which miraculously responds to its pressure. When the lady goes down to the harbour she finds that the magic ship is once again there, so that instead of drowning herself, she boards it, and is carried away to an eventual reunion with Guigemar. Her readiness to "suffer," the depth of her surrender, magically transforms her external situation and releases the power for a new departure. A surrender paradoxically creates power.

The surrender that leads to the release of power is also at the heart of the narrative in the *Franklin's Tale.* It can be seen, first of all, in Arveragus's surrender of "maistrye," which wins in return Dorigen's promise of truth and humility. Neither of them knows what their promises are committing them to, and it is precisely such ignorance that makes the commitments generous ones. But the underlying principle can operate in far less noble and generous situations, as Chaucer shows us by repeating such a pattern of reciprocal surrender in varying forms, through the rest of the *Canterbury Tales.* The most comic and "realistic" version is to be found at the end of the *Wife of Bath's Prologue*, in the quarrel provoked by the Wife's fifth husband, who insists on reading to her his "book of wikked wives" (685). The Wife, in fury, tears three leaves from his book, and he knocks her down. With instinctive shrewdness, the Wife exploits the moral advantage that this gives her, and adopts a tone of suffering meekness.

> "O, hastow slain me, false theef?" I saide,
> "And for my land thus hastow mordred me?
> Er I be deed, yet wol I kisse thee!" (800–2)

Such a display of submissiveness elicits a matching submissiveness from the aghast Jankin, and he asks for forgiveness. The quarrel ends with the establishment of a relationship that follows, in its own more robust way, the pattern of that between Arveragus and Dorigen: the husband's surrender of "governance" is met by unfailing truth and kindness on the part of his wife. The description of this reconciliation stays within the sphere of comic realism, however, not least because every gesture of surrender carries with it an accompanying gesture – albeit softened and muted – of self-assertiveness: the "false theef" of the Wife's first speech; Jankin's excusing of himself for striking the blow by insisting that she provoked him; the Wife's final tap on his cheek to settle the score and establish their kind of equality. The generosity here is a matter of letting these last little pieces of self-assertiveness pass, of "allowing" them to be submerged in the larger movements of self-abasement which are being enacted. Such a comic-realistic version of the notion that surrendering power gives one back power enables us to see that although its operations may be "magical" in the sense that they are not easy to rationalize, the roots of this principle lie in the everyday world of instinctive interaction between human beings. The fairyland world where wishes come true is not an alternative to this everyday experience, but a powerful image of its more mysterious aspects.

Such an image is offered us, of course, by the end of the Wife's tale, in the account of the working out of the relationship between the knight and the ugly old lady he has been forced to marry. After lecturing the knight on the value of age, ugliness, and poverty, the old lady offers him a surprising choice: whether he will have her "foul and old," but a "trewe, humble wif," or whether he will have her "yong and fair," and take the chance ("take the aventure") that others will compete to win her favours away from him (1219–26). The knight's response is to make the choice over to her, to put himself in her "wise governaunce," and the miraculous result of this is that the ugly old lady is transformed into a beautiful young one, who promises to be faithful in addition. As in the lay of *Guigemar*, a mental surrender has magical effects on physical reality. But the magical transformation in physical reality is the manifestation of an equally magical inward transformation that accompanies and causes it: the knight who began the tale with a particularly brutal assertion of masculine "maistrye," the rape of a young girl, is transformed into a husband who humbly relinquishes control to his wife. What is more, he must accept that possession can never be complete in the sphere of human relations; to accept happiness is to accept the possibility of its loss, and to take a beautiful wife is to incur the risk of unhappiness at losing her ("Whoso wol han lief, he lief moot lete," as Criseyde puts it).

In the *Franklin's Tale*, the magic has rather a different role to play. It does not bring about the denouement of the tale: on the contrary, it creates the problem.

The clerk from Orléans uses it to remove all the rocks from the coast of Brittany so that Aurelius may fulfil the apparently impossible condition for winning Dorigen's love. As Dorigen herself says of their removal: "It is agains the proces of nature" (1345). The magic is used to create an "aventure" – a sudden, disruptive happening that interrupts the gradual rhythms of natural change. It is as an "aventure" that the situation created by the removal of the rocks presents itself to Arveragus: he says to Dorigen, "To no wight tel thow of this aventure" (1483). But he has also told her, "It may be wel, paraunter, yet today" (1473). There is the same kind of hidden pun in the qualifying "paraunter" here as there is in Marie de France's use of the phrase "par aventure." On the face of it, it simply means "perhaps." But it also suggests a deeper appeal to the power of chance – the power of "aventure," which has created the problem and which has, therefore, also the power to resolve it *if* it is allowed to operate. Arveragus allows it; he stands back, as it were, to make room for it, subduing his own claims and wishes. The test of his relinquishment of "maistrye" is that he must submit himself to his wife's independently made promise so far that he is forced to order her to keep it; the test of Dorigen's promise to be a "humble trewe wif" is that she must obey her husband's command that she fulfil her independent promise to be unfaithful. The structure of their relationship at this point, therefore, is a poignant illustration of the simultaneity of "lordshipe" and "servage" described earlier: each of the marriage partners is following the will of the other and yet at the same time acting out an assertion of self. And just as this moment in the tale provides an illustration of the fusion of "lordshipe" and "servage," so it provides an illustration of what is meant by the command "Lerneth to suffre." Arveragus "suffers" in the double sense of enduring pain and "allowing"; in bidding his wife to keep her promise, he provides a compelling example of patience in Chaucer's sense of the word, of adaptation to "aventure," of allowing events to take their course. And he shows us very clearly that such an adaptation is not, as we might idly suppose, a matter of lethargy or inertia, of simply letting things drift. The easy course here would be to forbid Dorigen to go; Chaucer makes clear the agonizing effort that is required to achieve this adaptation.

> "Trouthe is the hyeste thing that man may kepe."
> – But with that word he brast anon to wepe. (1479–80)

In this tale, as in *Guigemar*, a surrender to "aventure" is met by a response of "aventure." In this case, it takes the form of the meeting between Dorigen and Aurelius, as she sets out to keep her promise. Chaucer emphasizes the chance nature of this meeting: Aurelius "Of aventure happed hir to meete," he says, and a few lines later, "thus they mette, of aventure or grace" (1501, 1508). Yet nothing is more natural, since we are told that Aurelius was watching and waiting for Dorigen's departure. These comments point, therefore, not so much to the fact that this meeting is an amazing coincidence, as to the operation of "aventure" within it. The intensity of Dorigen's surrender to the situation in which she has been trapped is perceptible in her anguished cry "half as she were mad,"

> "Unto the gardin, as min housbond bad,
> My trouthe for to holde, allas! allas!" (1512–13)

And this surrender has a dramatic effect on Aurelius; it mediates to him Arveragus's surrender to "aventure" and stimulates him to match that surrender with his own. He releases Dorigen from her promise and sends her back to her husband. He accepts the chance by which he has come too late, by which his love for Dorigen post-dates her marriage – one of the arbitrary cruelties of time – and having perceived the inner reality of the marriage, the firmness with which each is linked in obedience to the other in the very act of consenting to Dorigen's "infidelity," Aurelius "allows" that relationship its own being, undisturbed; he too exercises patience and "suffers" it.

But what if he had not? What if he had insisted on the fulfilment of the promise? For if Chaucer is pointing to the power of chance in human lives, he is bound to acknowledge that chance might well have had it so. One critic who correctly observes the perilous ease with which either development could realize itself at this point has written a conclusion to the episode in which Aurelius does just that.[5] The freedom and openness of events in the Chaucerian world means that romance is always open to turn into fabliau – or into tragedy. But I think that in this tale the nature of such a tragedy would be qualified by our sense that Aurelius would have "enjoyed" Dorigen in only a very limited sense; his possession of her would have been as much a matter of "illusioun" and "apparence" (1264–5) as the removal of the rocks that made it possible. The magic, in this tale, suggests the illusory, forced quality of Aurelius's power over Dorigen (in contrast to the natural power won by Arveragus, spontaneously springing into life at the end of the long process of his courtship). That is why the magic removal of the rocks is presented as a laborious, technologically complex operation, rather than the wave of a sorcerer's wand.[6] The *real* magic in this tale is Aurelius's change of heart, which is as miraculous as that of the knight in the

5 Ian Robinson, *Chaucer and the English Tradition* (Cambridge, 1972), 195–6.

6 The magic in the *Filocolo* story is of a much more traditional kind, involving the concoction of a magic potion from exotic herbs, roots, stones, etc.

Wife of Bath's Tale. The magic removal of the rocks is merely a means by which we can measure the immensity of this "human magic"; we can gauge, as it were, the size of the problem it is able to solve. And this "human magic" is nothing other than the human power to change. What the development of the tale brings to our notion of the human tendency to change is that it is not just an everyday, humdrum matter of our moods fluctuating with the passage of time, but that it is a source of power; its role can be creative.

As I have already suggested, Chaucer is well aware of the tragic aspects of the human propensity to change, as his constant preoccupation with the theme of betrayal shows. He is also aware of the saving power of human resilience, a sort of comic version of patience, which can nullify the tragic aspects of "aventure"; thus beside the serious transformation of the rapist knight in the *Wife of Bath's Tale* we can set the figure of Pluto in the *Merchant's Tale*, the ravisher who has clearly been worn down by feminine rhetoric so that he presents the ludicrous picture of a henpecked rapist. Romances such as the tales of the Knight and Franklin, however, offer us a serious celebration of patience, of the creative power of change. "Pitee" may be the quality that leads Criseyde's emotions away from Troilus to Diomede (V.824), or it may be ironically appealed to as the cause of May's amazing readiness to respond to Damian's advances (*Merchant's Tale*, 1986), but it is also the quality that enables Theseus to adapt himself to each new claim that chance events impose on him (*Knight's Tale*, 953, 1761), or that leads Dorigen to accept Arveragus's suit (740), and it is "routhe" (another word for pity) that leads Aurelius to release Dorigen (1520). Moreover, as the passage on patience makes clear, the responsiveness implied in the ideals of patience and "pitee" must be exercised continually; the balance and poise achieved at the end of the *Franklin's Tale* is reached by a "proces," a chain of ceaseless adjustment in which the magician-clerk, as well as the other three figures, must play his part.[7] Ceaseless adjustment is, as we saw, something that characterizes the marriage, with its endless alternation of "lordshipe" and "servage," and it is for that reason that it can survive "aventure"; it is founded on it. Only through ceaseless change can there be stability. Only through a perpetual readiness to adapt, to change, in each of the actors in the tale, can the status quo be preserved. Or, in Chaucerian language, "trouthe" is the product of patience.

Chaucer's strength is that he gives us a *creative* sense of order. He makes us aware that static formulae, of whatever nature – the husband's sovereignty,

7 Even this has its comic version, in the *Shipman's Tale*, where a chain of unshaken selfishness creates the same sort of final balance and poise.

equality in marriage – are inappropriate to human beings, since they are subject to change from within and chance from without. What is needed instead is an ideal such as the ideal of patience, which is founded on change, on the perpetual readiness to meet, to accept, and to transform the endless and fluctuating succession of "aventures" that life offers.

Chapter Five

Anger and "Glosynge" in the *Canterbury Tales*

Prudentius's *Psychomachia*, as is well known, describes a battle between seven Vices and seven Virtues. The third of the seven encounters is between Patience and Wrath ("Ira"), whose character is manifest in her frenzied and violent appearance.

> hanc procul Ira tumens, spumanti fervida rictu,
> sanguinea intorquens subfuso lumina felle,
> ut belli exsortem teloque et voce lacessit,
> inpatiensque morae conto petit, increpat ore,
> hirsutas quatiens galeato in vertice cristas.[1] (113–17)

[From a distance swelling Wrath, raging with bared teeth and frothing mouth, darts her eyes, all shot with blood and gall, at her [Patience], and challenges her with weapon and with speech for taking no part in the fight; fretting under the delay, she hurls a pike at her, meanwhile assailing her with abuse and tossing the shaggy crests on her helmeted head.]

Patience remains unmoved under Wrath's onslaughts, protected by a hidden coat of mail; frustrated at the failure of all her weapons to pierce this defence, Wrath eventually turns her violence on herself, committing suicide with her own sword.

If we were called upon to represent Wrath and Patience, this is probably how we would do it; the witty touch of having Wrath commit suicide, instead of

1 Quotations from the *Psychomachia* are taken from the Loeb Classical Library edition and translation of Prudentius's works by H.J. Thomson, 2 vols (London, 1953–62), 1:274–343. I have altered the translation slightly.

being killed by the opposing virtue, is probably the only unexpected element in this little episode. But when Langland pictures the Seven Deadly Sins making their confessions to Repentance in Passus V of *Piers Plowman*, his treatment of Wrath takes a quite different form. All the other sins are represented in the most obvious way: that is, their portraits are composed of samples of human behaviour illustrating the sin in question. Sloth is slothful in various ways, Avarice is avaricious, Envy is envious, and so on. But Wrath is *not* represented as wrathful. There is none of the rage and frenzy that characterizes Prudentius's Ira; instead, Wrath introduces himself as one who practises two of the most peaceful occupations imaginable: a gardener and a cook.

> "I am Wrathe," quod he, "I was som tyme a frere,
> And the coventes gardyner for to graffen impes ..." (V.135–6)[2]

Of course, he turns out to be a *metaphorical* gardener: he "grafts" lies on to friars, so that they eventually bear leaves of "lowe speche" to please lords, and then "blossom" in private chambers where the lords confess to the friars rather than to their parish priests. The "fruit" of this metaphorical tree is a large-scale quarrel between the friars and the parish priests, who resent their loss of power and income. Wrath is also a metaphorical cook, this time in the kitchen of a nunnery, where he cooks up "joutes of janglyng" (stews of gossip); he spreads rumours that one sister is a bastard, another the offspring of her mother's adultery, or that another "hadde child in chirie-tyme," until a full-scale quarrel breaks loose.

> "Of wikked wordes I Wrathe hire wortes made,
> Til "Thow lixt!" and "Thow lixt" lopen out at ones
> And either hitte oother under the cheke.
> Hadde thei had knyves, by Crist! hir either hadde kild oother." (V.160–3)

What is interesting in this portrait is that Langland represents Wrath as working, not through direct physical action, but through the corruption of words – words which are not in themselves angry in the first instance but which include the "low speech" and smooth lies traditionally associated with the friars.[3]

This collocation of anger, the corruption of words, and the friars, recurs in Chaucer's *Summoner's Tale*. It tells of a friar visiting the house of a sick man, to

2 Quotations from *Piers Plowman* are from A.V.C. Schmidt, *The Vision of Piers Plowman: A Critical Edition of the B-Text*, 2nd ed. (London, 1995).

3 For this traditional association, see Jill Mann, *Chaucer and Medieval Estates Satire* (Cambridge, 1973), 37–9.

whom he is less welcome than to his wife. The friar boasts of his skill in "glosing," which turns out to mean interpreting the words of the Bible in such a way as to encourage people to give charitable donations to friars.

> "I have today been at youre chirche at messe,
> And seid a sermon after my simple wit –
> Nat al after the text of holy writ,
> For it is hard to yow, as I suppose,
> And therfore wol I teche yow al the glose.
> Glosing is a glorious thing, certein,
> For lettre sleeth, so as we clerkes seyn.
> Ther have I taught hem to be charitable,
> And spende hir good ther it is resonable." (1788–96)

The *Middle English Dictionary* gives three main branches of meaning for the verb "glose": first, "to gloss, comment on, interpret, explain, paraphrase." Even this first meaning has a pejorative subcategory: "to interpret falsely," and this pejorative meaning is to the fore in senses 2 and 3: "to obscure the truth ... falsify ... gloze over," and "to use fair words, speak with blandishment, flattery or deceit ... cajole, flatter." In its "pure" sense, "glosing" means getting out of a text the meaning it contains; it is an act of disciplined enquiry in which (in theory at least) the interpreter is subordinate to the text. But, as the semantic development of the word shows, it is all too easy for this act of interpretation to become a matter of reading something *into* the text, especially when the text in question – the Bible – is one that is believed to have the power to generate a limitless number of spiritual truths. The text then becomes no more than a tool to serve the interests of the interpreter, meaning whatever he or she wishes it to.

The friar of the *Summoner's Tale* thus reads the biblical words "Blessed are the poor in spirit" as a prophetic reference to the mendicant order.

> "But herkne now, Thomas, what I shal seyn:
> – I ne have no text of it, as I suppose,
> But I shal finde it in a manner glose –
> That specially oure swete Lord Jesus
> Spak this by freres, whan he seide thus:
> 'Blessed be they that povre in spirit been.' " (1918–23)

The friar uses this piece of "glosing" to support the mendicants' side in their quarrel with the beneficed clergy, who (he claims) give themselves over to gluttony and good living. (The friar's specifications to Thomas's wife of what he would like to eat show that his own gluttony takes the subtler form of "nouvelle cuisine" – fastidious delicacy rather than gross quantity.)

The friar's ability in "glosing" is soon demonstrated. The sick man's wife has complained about her husband's anger ("He is as angry as a pissemire"; 1825); when she tries to cuddle him in bed at night, he makes no other response than to groan like a pig (1827–31). Reading between the lines, one can see Thomas's point of view: his sickness is a good enough reason to make the wife's physical advances unwelcome. One can also guess that her aim in bringing the matter up is to advertise her lack of sexual satisfaction to the friar, in the hope that he may live up to the traditional reputation of his kind and do something about it. For the moment, however, the friar directs his attention to the husband, promising a short sermon on the theme of anger – at which point the wife hurriedly excuses herself to go and make dinner. Her husband is left to endure the friar's solemn rebukes for his anger against his wife, "the sely innocent / ... that is so meke and pacient" (1983–4). However the main reason for him to exhibit patience towards this gentle innocent turns out to be the danger that the slightest provocation will turn her into a raging fury.

> "And, Thomas, yet eftsoones I charge thee:
> Be war from hire that in thy bosom slepeth!
> War fro the serpent that so sleighly crepeth
> Under the gras, and stingeth subtilly.
> Be war, my sone, and herkne paciently,
> That twenty thousand men han lost hir lives
> For striving with hir lemmans and hir wives.
> Now sith ye han so holy meke a wif,
> What nedeth yow, Thomas, to maken strif?
> Ther nis, iwys, no serpent so cruel
> Whan man tret on his tail, ne half so fel,
> As womman is whan she hath caught an ire.
> Vengeance is thanne al that they desire." (1992–2004)

This association of women and wrath is traditional in medieval satirical and antifeminist literature;[4] it is probably the reason why Langland chooses a nunnery for his second example of quarrelsomeness.

The friar's long sermon on wrath is not very successful, since its major result is to make the sick man violently angry: "This sike man wex wel neigh wood for

4 See Mann, *Chaucer and Medieval Estates Satire*, 123 and n. 82.

ire" (2121). He takes his vengeance by pretending that he has one last gift to give the friar, a treasure which he has concealed down his back at the level of his buttocks, and which he will bestow on him on condition that he shares it equally with the other twelve friars in his convent. As the excited friar gropes for this treasure, Thomas lets fly an enormous fart. The fart is not a simple obscenity; in the context of the narrative it makes a precise point. The standard grammars of the Middle Ages commenced with a definition of the basic unit of language ("vox") as the breaking of air ("aer ictus").[5] As the Eagle explains to Chaucer in the *House of Fame*, "Soun ys noght but eyr ybroken; / And every speche that ys spoken, / ... In his substaunce ys but air" (765–8). The fart reproduces this purely physical aspect of speech, separated from its signifying capacity. Thomas's fart makes a point about the friar's sermon: that its semantic content is, as far as he is concerned, nil. It is merely so much "hot air," worthy to be countered only by another blast of hot air, the fart.

The friar's words not only fail to connect with reality by their lack of effect on the hearer, they also have no effect on their own author. For on receiving the fart, the friar in his turn becomes violently angry; he leaves Thomas's house in a furious rage.

> And forth he gooth with a ful angry cheere,
> And fette his felawe theras lay his stoor.
> He looked as it were a wilde boor;
> He grinte with his teeth, so was he wrooth ... (2158–61)

His anger is still apparent when he reaches the house of the lord of the village, where he is a regular guest:

> This frere cam as he were in a rage
> Whereas this lord sat eting at his bord.
> Unnethes mighte the frere speke a word,
> Til atte laste he seide, "God yow see!" (2166–9)

The sermon on anger thus has no effect whatever, on either its hearer or its deliverer; it is free-floating, a verbal balloon punctured by Thomas's gross physical

5 See *Grammatici Latini*, ed. H. Keil, 7 vols (Leipzig, 1857–80), 2:5 (Priscian: "Philosophi definiunt, vocem esse aerem tenuissimum ictum"), and 4:367 (Donatus: "Vox est aer ictus sensibilis auditu"). For a discussion of the elaboration of these simple definitions in medieval linguistic philosophy, see Jean Jolivet, *Arts du langage et théologie chez Abélard* (Paris, 1969), 22–36.

response. The tale ends with the solution of the problem posed by the condition Thomas attaches to his gift: the twelve friars are to be assembled round the spokes of a cartwheel with the chief friar at its centre, and Thomas is to administer the fart at the hub of the wheel, so that each friar receives an equal amount of its "soun" and "savour" (2226). The suggested resolution parodies visual representations of the bestowal of the "gift of tongues" on Christ's disciples at Pentecost;[6] the pretentious verbalism of the friars is brought back to its most basic physicality.

Yet despite its ineffectuality, the sermon on ire does have something to tell us about anger. The anecdotes selected to illustrate the theme derive ultimately from Seneca's *De Ira* (perhaps by way of John of Wales).[7] What is interesting about them is that (as with Langland's Wrath) they do not conceive anger as frenzied rage. One is the story of Cambises, who was not only "irous" but also a drunkard; when one of his lords exhorted him to temper his drinking, because wine deprives a man of control over his mind and limbs, Cambises flatly denied this assumption. Having drunk even more than before, he had the lord's son brought before him, and taking up bow and arrow, shot him in the heart, to prove the steadiness of his hand. Another is the story of an "irous potestat" (2017) called upon to judge a knight who had gone out with a companion and returned alone, giving rise to suspicions that he had murdered his fellow. The potentate finds him guilty and orders another knight to put him to death, but on the way to the execution, they meet the man supposed dead, and therefore return to the judge to report that no murder has taken place. So far from acquitting the prisoner, however, the judge condemns all three to death: the first because he has already been sentenced and therefore must die; the second because he is thus the cause of his fellow's death and should therefore be punished for it; and the third, the knight charged with the execution, because he has been given an order and failed to carry it out. The third story tells how Cyrus the Great, emperor of Persia, furious that one of his horses had drowned in the river Gindes, had his men cut a multitude of channels into which the river was dispersed and dried up.

What these stories show us about the "irous" man is that he insists on enforcing his own version of reality; or, to put it another way, he imposes himself on the world even in the teeth of the world's resistance. Cambises obliterates the

6 See Alan Levitan, "The Parody of Pentecost in Chaucer's *Summoner's Tale*," *University of Toronto Quarterly* 40 (1970–1): 236–46 (with accompanying illustrations), and Penn R. Szittya, *The Antifraternal Tradition in Medieval Literature* (Princeton, NJ, 1986), 231–8.

7 Seneca, *De Ira* I.18 (the "irous potestat") , III.14 (Cambises), and III.21 (Cyrus the Great), in Seneca, *Moral Essays*, ed. J.W. Basore, Loeb Classical Library, 3 vols (Cambridge, MA, 1958), vol. 1. On John of Wales, see R.A. Pratt, "Chaucer and the Hand that Fed Him," *Speculum* 41 (1966): 619–42, at 627–31.

lord's picture of the consequences of drunkenness along with the lord's son. The moral the friar draws from this story recommends accepting the fictions of the powerful as reality, never disturbing them with the brutal truth.

"Beth war, therfore, with lordes how ye pleye.
Singeth '*Placebo*,' and 'I shal if I kan,'
But if it be unto a povre man.
To a povre man men sholde his vices telle,
But nat to a lord, thogh he sholde go to helle." (2074–8)

As for the "irous potestat," so far from accommodating himself to reality, he reshapes reality to fit his own arbitrary mental construction of it, insisting that reality conform with his words rather than vice versa. The chain of causality is reversed: the potestate's death sentence makes the knight a murderer, and if there is a murderer, there must be a victim. Cyrus reacts to the accident of his horse's drowning as if the river were a conscious agent, punishing it in revenge for its natural function. We can thus see what anger and "glosing" have in common: both are a refusal of reality, a refusal to accommodate the self either to events in the world outside, or to the autonomous meaning of the text. They share a blinkered insistence on reducing the world or the text to a mirror-image of one's own narrow desires, instead of opening the self to the impact of an external reality.

The themes of the *Summoner's Tale* are widened and intensified in the rest of the Canterbury collection. We can see this already in the linking passages which introduce it, for this is not only a tale *about* anger, it is also *produced* by anger. It forms part of the quarrel between the Friar and the Summoner which breaks out at the end of the *Wife of Bath's Prologue* when the Summoner takes exception to the Friar's mockery of the length of the Wife's prologue.[8] The Host puts a temporary stop to their squabble, telling them that they "fare as folk that dronken ben of ale" (852) – a link between anger and drunkenness that we shall find elsewhere. But at the first opportunity – that is, when the Wife has finished her tale – the Friar tells an insulting story about a summoner which reduces the pilgrim Summoner to apoplectic fury:

This Somnour in his stiropes hye stood;
Upon this Frere his herte was so wood
That lik an aspen leef he quook for ire. (1665–7)

8 The animosity between Friar and Summoner is an example of the general hostility between the friars and the secular clergy, as Frederick Tupper noted; see "The Quarrels of the Canterbury Pilgrims," *Journal of English and Germanic Philology* 14 (1915): 256–70, at 258.

His tale about the "glosing" friar is the fruit of his anger; it is both fuelled and shaped by hostility to the pilgrim Friar. This is not the only example where anger is the stimulus that produces a tale; odd as it may seem, anger is one of the most important creative impulses in the *Canterbury Tales* (drunkenness is another). The *Miller's Tale* leaves "a litel ire" in the heart of the Reeve (3862), who, as a carpenter himself, feels offended by the duping of the Oxford carpenter in the tale, and who lists "anger" as one of the four live passions still smouldering in the ashes of old age (3884). He gives vent to his anger, and takes his revenge, by telling his own tale about the duping of a miller. The *Reeve's Tale* is followed by a skirmish between the Cook and the Host in the *Cook's Prologue*, in which anger lurks beneath an apparently playful banter; the Host tries to laugh off his blunt remarks about the standard of hygiene in the Cook's shop with the entreaty "be nat wrooth for game" (4354), and the Cook maliciously replies that by the same token he hopes that the Host will not be "wrooth" if he tells a story about a "hostileer" (4359–60). The later altercation between the Cook and the Manciple I shall deal with presently.

Of course these quarrels between the pilgrims have always attracted critical attention, but they have usually been regarded as one of the anarchic, unplanned elements that give the *Canterbury Tales* its verisimilitude, dissolving the neat and ordered framework of the tale collection into the unpredictable collisions and developments of real life. This is undoubtedly true on the level of the fiction, but I wish to suggest that at the level of theme these manifestations of anger are nevertheless part of a structure of contrasts which underlies the whole work. The Friar-Summoner sequence of tales is a key example. In 1911, G.L. Kittredge outlined his theory that the tales in Groups D-F of the *Canterbury Tales,* running from the *Wife of Bath's Tale* to the *Franklin's Tale*, constituted a "Marriage Group" which advanced different views of the relationships between the sexes in marriage, and this theory has become so widely accepted that it is received wisdom even today.[9] Yet the Friar-Summoner sequence has always been something of an embarrassment to this theory, for although it occurs immediately after the Wife of Bath's contribution, which is supposed to open the marriage debate, it quite clearly has nothing to do with marriage at all. Kittredge could only explain it by saying that Chaucer was "too good an artist" to tie himself to a "frigidly schematic" development of the Marriage theme, and so allowed "the talkative members of the company" to thrust themselves forward.[10] I want to suggest an alternative way of looking not only at the D-F

9 "Chaucer's Discussion of Marriage," *Modern Philology* 9 (1911–12): 435–67; repr. in *Chaucer: Modern Essays in Criticism*, ed. Edward Wagenknecht (New York, 1959), 188–215.

10 Wagenknecht, *Chaucer*, 194.

sequence, but at the *Tales* as a whole, which will make perfect sense of the placing of the Friar's and Summoner's tales where they are. I want to suggest that the central theme of this group of tales, and others besides, is not Marriage but Patience.

In Seneca's *De Ira*, the agent that controls anger is reason;[11] but for Prudentius, and for most of the Christian Middle Ages, anger is counteracted by patience.[12] The *Parson's Tale* tells us that

> The remedye agains ire is a vertu that men clepen mansuetude, that is debonairetee, and eek another vertu that men callen pacience or suffraunce ...
>
> Pacience, that is another remedye agains ire, is a vertu that suffreth swetely every mannes goodnesse, and is nat wrooth for noon harm that is doon to him. The philosophre seyth that pacience is thilke vertu that suffreth debonairely alle the outrages of adversitee and every wikked word. This vertu maketh a man lik to God, and maketh him Goddes owene deere child, as seyth Crist. This vertu disconfiteth thin enemy; and therfore seyth the wise man, "If thow wolt venquisse thin enemy, lerne to suffre." (654, 659–61)

The Parson's words find an echo in the long lyrical passage celebrating patience at the opening of the *Franklin's Tale*:

> Pacience is an heigh vertu, certein,
> For it venquisseth, as thise clerkes seyn,
> Thinges that rigour sholde never atteine.
> For every word men may nat chide or pleine;
> Lerneth to suffre, or elles, so moot I gon,
> Ye shul it lerne, wherso ye wole or non.
> For in this world, certein, ther no wight is,
> That he ne dooth or seyth somtime amis.
> Ire, siknesse, or constellacioun,
> Win, wo, or chaunging of complexioun
> Causeth ful ofte to doon amis or speken. (773–83)

---

11 *De Ira* I.17.2–18.2. (This passage immediately precedes the anecdote told of the "irous potestat" in the *Summoner's Tale*.) The opposition between reason and anger is also implicit in the tripartite division of the soul into rational, concupiscible and irascible elements, which was commonplace in medieval thought; see, for example, Thomas Aquinas, *Summa Theologiae* Pars Ia.Q.81. Art. 2–3.

12 See J.D. Burnley, *Chaucer's Language and the Philosophers' Tradition* (Cambridge, 1979), 23: "Seneca despised pity as irrational. Whilst he was willing to recommend *clementia* as preferable to *crudelitas* wherever possible, Seneca's conception of equity was thoroughly dependent

"Ire" stands at the head of the list of things that may cause human beings to speak or act amiss; patience counteracts these disturbances and restores harmony and equilibrium. The *Franklin's Tale* shows patience in action in Arveragus's response to the claims of his wife's ill-fated promise. And other tales of the D-F group likewise make patience a central theme. The *Clerk's Tale* is a narrative study of patience, exemplified in Griselda's "suffraunce" of her husband's cruelty. The *Wife of Bath's Tale*, which begins the group, shows a masculine example of patient acceptance of "aventure" in the knight who is transformed from a rapist into a husband who meekly surrenders "governaunce" to his wife (1230–8).

All of these three tales are also tales about promises – promises which commit the person who makes them to unpleasant consequences which could not be foreseen at the time they were made. The knight in the *Wife of Bath's Tale* promises the Loathly Lady who saves his life by telling him what women most desire that he will grant the first request she makes him thereafter, and finds to his horror that she asks him to marry her. Griselda promises to obey her husband in thought and deed without protest or "grucching" (351–7), and finds that she is required to surrender her two children to be murdered (as she thinks) and finally to acquiesce in her own repudiation. Dorigen promises Aurelius her love if he removes all the rocks from the coast of Brittany, and finds to her consternation that she is held to her word when he fulfils this apparently impossible condition. The tales that celebrate patience thus also celebrate a literalism of the most austere sort. Dorigen's answer to Aurelius clearly *means* "no," but she accepts that she is bound by the letter of her promise rather than its spirit. No such problems for the friar of the *Summoner's Tale*, who as we have seen rests confidently on the principle that "lettre sleeth, so as we clerkes seyn" (1794). It is no accident that the friar's declaration that "Glosing is a glorious thing, certein" (1793) echoes and travesties the "Pacience is an heigh vertu, certein" of the *Franklin's Tale*. The submission involved in patience is a submission to words as well as to external "aventure"; it represents the polar opposite of "glosing." "Glosing" of the kind practised by the friars represents the imposition of the interpreter's bias on the words of the text, whereas with these promises the very person who utters the words must accept that he or she is not in control of their meaning. It is events that "glose" these words by filling them with a meaning that imposes itself on those who have spoken them.

---

on reason. The Christian middle ages, however, placed a different value upon emotion, and particularly upon pity and compassion." In Chaucer, reason occasionally appears in alliance with patience (see n. 18 below on the *Knight's Tale*, and cf. *Merchant's Tale* 2369), but its role is a minor one.

It is often said that the fabliaux "call a spade a spade" – that whereas the romance relies on elevated language to invest human behaviour with a noble idealism, fabliau employs a verbal directness which fearlessly acknowledges the basic realities of life. In fact, in the *Canterbury Tales* at least, almost exactly the reverse is the case. In Chaucer's romances, the word is taken *au pied de la lettre*, however uncomfortable that might be. Besides the literalism in the rigorous interpretation of promises which I have already cited, there is the literalism exploited by Saturn in order to resolve the planetary debate in the *Knight's Tale*; although both knights clearly *mean* the same thing when they make their prayers in the temples of Mars and Venus, the fact that Arcite asks for victory and Palamon asks for Emily makes it possible to "satisfy" each of them in a strictly literal sense. In contrast, in Chaucer's fabliaux, words are mere counters in a cynical game; wise players can manipulate them precisely because they always keep them separate from reality. Whether it is Nicholas embellishing his full frontal grab at his landlord's wife with the elegant phrases of love poetry, or the students of the *Reeve's Tale* faking a passionate intellectual interest in the workings of a mill in order to make sure that the miller does not cheat them of their corn while it is being ground, or the monk and merchant's wife of the *Shipman's Tale* negotiating a one-night stand and the price to be paid for it without ever mentioning the sex or explicitly linking it with the money, the inhabitants of the world of fabliau use language merely as a stalking horse under whose cover they can advance on their real desires. "Glosing," in the sense of interpreting, is a perennial necessity in such a world; both the actors in the story and its readers have to be continually reading between the lines. What is said has to be decoded in the light of its context and the covert intentions of the speaker. The *Friar's Tale* is appropriately paired with the *Summoner's Tale* because it is a textbook illustration of this kind of "glosing." The summoner who rides in company with the devil takes a literalist line on language when it is in his interests to do so (although he is unable to take in the literal force of the devil's remarks about his future knowledge of hell). When the carter whose horses are failing to pull his cart out of the mire curses them and wishes the devil may fetch them, the summoner (presumably mindful of the devil's agreement to share with him his winnings) urges the devil to claim his prey (1551–4). The comedy of this is surely that whereas we would expect the devil to tempt the summoner, in fact it is the summoner who tempts the devil – a piece of ingenious malice on the part of the pilgrim Friar to demonstrate the moral baseness that characterizes summoners. But the devil resists the temptations of literalism; he patiently explains that the carter's words are not a literal reflection of his "entente" (1556), as is proved when the horses finally succeed in pulling the cart out of the mud and the carter rewards them with blessings instead of curses. "The carl spak o thing, but he thoghte another" (1568) is the devil's wise comment. When, however, the old woman who is being harassed by the summoner wishes that the devil may fetch him, *then* the devil perceives that this is no mere figure of speech but a heartfelt desire; her words are spoken in deadly earnest (1626–38).

Dorigen would have been quite safe with the devil of the *Friar's Tale*; he would have glossed her words according to the "entente" behind them rather than holding her to their literal form. The summoner is treated more leniently than she is; for she must exercise patience in freely submitting to the mere form of her words rather than their inner meaning, whereas it is only when form and meaning are proved to be united that the summoner must exercise a similar submissiveness to his fate (he is urged by the devil to "be noght wrooth"; 1634). Yet Dorigen's ultimate fate is more benign than the summoner's: submission to literalism proves to be her salvation, while the summoner who attempts to make literalism serve his own ends is damned for all eternity.

The tales told by the Friar and Summoner are thus tales of anger and "glosing," and as such they fit perfectly into the group of tales initiated by the Wife of Bath, as a contrast to the tales of patience. But Kittredge was of course right to the extent that it is in the context of relations between the sexes that these themes are often worked out. Women, in particular, are given a special relationship to patience.[13] Chaucer's own tale of *Melibee*, for example, embodies patience in Melibee's wife Prudence, who by a lengthy process of reasoned argument persuades him to renounce the "ire" that he feels for his enemies (1009, 1121–7, 1246) and instead to "suffre and be pacient" (1480). The *Clerk's Tale* sees Griselda's patience as characteristic of her sex: however much clerks may boast of Job's great patience, we are told, no man can ever be half as patient as a woman can (932–8). But elsewhere in the *Tales* it is made clear that women also have a special relationship to anger, as we have already seen; the friar of the *Summoner's Tale* does no more than repeat a commonplace when he warns Thomas not to cross his wife because a woman's anger is more terrifying than a serpent's (2001–3). The friar's view of the irascibility of women is one shared by medieval writers, from one of whom Chaucer culled the vignette of female anger that he inserts into the Wife of Bath's portrait in the *General Prologue*:[14]

> In al the parisshe wif ne was ther noon
> That to the offringe bifore hire sholde goon –

13 See Jill Mann, *Feminizing Chaucer* (Cambridge, 2002), 125–8, 141–2.

14 *Les Lamentations de Matheolus et le Livre de Leesce de Jehan le Fevre, de Ressons*, ed. A.G. van Hamel, 2 vols, Bibliothèque des Hautes Études 95–6 (Paris, 1893–1905), 1:82, lines 1431–40.

And if ther dide, certein, so wrooth was she
That she was out of alle charitee. (449–52)

In one sense therefore it can be said that the Wife represents anger; her *Prologue* supports this picture of her by showing her in action as scold and shrew, berating her three old husbands and making sure that the exercise of patience is all on their side.

Thanne wolde I seye, "Goode lief, taak keep
How mekely looketh Wilkin, oure sheep!
Com neer, my spouse, lat me ba thy cheke.
Ye sholden be al pacient and meke,
And han a swete spiced conscience,
Sith ye so preche of Jobes pacience.
Suffreth alwey, sin ye so wel kan preche ...
Oon of us two moste bowen, doutelees,
And sith a man is moore resonable
Than woman is, ye mosten been suffrable." (431–7, 440–2)

Her fourth husband is tormented by her "angre" and "verray jalousye" (488); he becomes the traditional henpecked husband who alone "knows where his shoe pinches" (486–94). Her account of life with her fifth husband climaxes with the violent quarrel precipitated by his persistent reading aloud from his antifeminist book; the Wife rips three leaves from the offending volume and knocks her husband backwards into the fire, whereupon he in turn floors her with a blow to the head that leaves her permanently deaf.

Yet this picture of the Wife as the classic example of the wrathful woman is complicated in various ways. In the first place, her wrath does not come out of the blue, as a merely natural characteristic: one way or another, it is the result of masculine hostility. Her tirades against her three old husbands are actually composed of antifeminist insults which she presents as what her husbands said to her when they were drunk.[15] Masculine aggression is turned back on the sex that produced it. Her fourth husband is made to "fry in his own grease" as a punishment for his infidelities. And the violent outburst against Jankin is caused by his relentless antifeminist abuse; the antifeminist material *creates* the wrathful woman that it pretends merely to describe. Female anger here is a result of masculine "glosing," of Jankin's subordination of the text to his own

15 See Mann, *Feminizing Chaucer*, 62–4.

malicious purposes. Whatever the antifeminist material assembled in Jerome's treatise *Against Jovinian* in its defence of virginity, we may assume that Jerome did not have it in mind that it should be used as an instrument of marital torture.

At the opening of her *Prologue*, the Wife declares herself a vigorous opponent of the masculine/clerical "glosing" which attempts to define the meaning of a text in accordance with its own interests. Thus she disputes the gloss that reads Christ's words to the Samaritan woman at the well as a prohibition against multiple marriages.

> "Thow hast yhad five housbondes," quod he,
> "And that ilke man which now hath thee
> Is nat thin housbonde" – thus seide he, certein.
> What that he mente therby, I kan nat seyn ...
> Men may divine and glosen, up and doun,
> But wel I woot, expres, withouten lie,
> God bad us for to wexe and multiplye.
> That gentil text kan I wel understonde! (17–20, 26–9)

The Wife returns to the literal text as a way of rejecting masculine "glosing." She likewise rejects the "glosing" that interprets the genital organs as created for the "purgacioun / Of urine," or to enable us to distinguish a male from a female (120–2); "Glose whoso wole," she proclaims, experience teaches that "it is noght so" (119, 124). Yet this appeal to experience is itself a kind of alternative "glosing," an attempt to read data from her own point of view, and the Wife shows herself every bit as accomplished a manipulator of texts as the clerics she despises because of their monopoly over books and their interpretation.[16] As her anger counters masculine aggression, her own brand of "glosing" counters clerical interpretations which restrict and humiliate women. Ptolemy's recommendation on indifference to Fortune, for example ("Of alle men his wisdom

16 David Aers comments on the resemblance between the Wife's procedures and those of orthodox exegetes: "the standard practices of medieval exegesis included the sustained pulverization and fragmentation of Biblical texts, the utter dissolution of their existential and historical meanings, and the imposition of pre-determined dogmatic propositions." *Chaucer, Langland and the Creative Imagination* (London, 1980), 86. Similar comments are made by E.T. Donaldson, "Designing a Camel; Or, Generalizing the Middle Ages," *Tennessee Studies in Literature* 22 (1977): 1–16, at 5–7. For discussion of the Wife of Bath as a practitioner of "alternative" exegesis, see also R.W. Hanning, "Roasting a Friar, Mis-taking a Wife, and Other Acts of Textual Harassment in Chaucer's *Canterbury Tales*," *Studies in the Age of Chaucer* 7 (1985): 3–21, and Alcuin Blamires, "The Wife of Bath and Lollardy," *Medium Ævum* 58 (1989): 224–42.

is hieste / That rekketh nat who hath the world in honde"; 326–7), is brazenly "glossed" so that it becomes an exhortation to her old husbands not to worry about who else is enjoying her sexual favours, so long as they are getting all they want. Like the characters in the fabliaux, the Wife avoids calling a spade a spade. She has a string of euphemisms for male and female genitals: "oure bothe thinges smale" (121), "sely instrument" (132), "harneis" (136), "instrument" (149), "*bele chose*" (447, 510), "*quoniam*" (608), "chambre of Venus" (618). Her repeated invitations to her listeners to divine "what I mene" behind coy formulations (90, 200), likewise align her firmly with the "glosing" that is characteristic of the fabliau and against the literalism of the romance tales.

Yet (and this is the second qualification to the picture of the Wife as representative of anger) neither anger nor "glosing" brings her final relief; instead it is her own version of patience that does so. She wins more by pathos, that is, than by anger. Finding herself flat on the floor as a result of Jankin's blow, she acts the role of pathetic victim to the hilt, exploiting his remorse and horror at his own violence until finally he hands over the "governaunce" of their affairs to her and burns his book (813–16). Destruction of the text is safer than "glosing." Henceforth the only kind of "glosing" between them is presumably that which Jankin practises so well in bed:

> ... so wel koude he me glose,
> Whan that he wolde han my *bele chose*,
> That thogh he hadde me bet on every bon,
> He koude winne again my love anon. (509–12)

In the quarrel between the Wife and Jankin we see something exemplified elsewhere in the *Canterbury Tales*: that anger creates a deadlock, an impasse, from which patience or "suffraunce" offers an escape – patience, and its associate pity, which is likewise an antidote to anger.[17] I want briefly to illustrate this from the *Knight's Tale*, in order to reinforce the point that these are themes by no means limited to the D-F sequence of tales, but found from the beginning of the collection to its end. Theseus, who is in a sense the hero of the *Knight's Tale*, is portrayed at its opening as a representative of pity, in opposition to the "ire" and "tyrannye" of Creon (940–1). The appeal of the widow ladies that he should show them "Som drope of pitee thurgh thy gentillesse" is met by an instant

17 See Burnley, *Chaucer's Language and the Philosophers' Tradition*, for a full exploration of the opposition between patience and pity on the one hand, and anger on the other, in medieval structures of language and thought.

response: he dismounts from his horse "With herte pitous" and promises to do vengeance on Creon (920, 953). Yet the "ire" that Theseus here combats in Creon he later has to combat in himself, and Chaucer deliberately alters his source (Bocaccio's *Teseida*) in order to bring this about. When Theseus and his party come across Palamon and Arcite fighting in the grove, Theseus first reacts with violent anger to the discovery that the one has escaped from his prison, and the other returned to Athens against his express prohibition. It is only when the Queen and her ladies beg for mercy, weeping and falling to their knees, that he changes his mind, "For pitee renneth soone in gentil herte" (1761). "And thogh he first for ire quook and sterte," says Chaucer, his reason and his compassion unite to dispel his anger (1762–82).[18] All this is in striking contrast to Boccaccio's Teseo, who feels no more than a passing twinge of irritation, and accepts the situation without intervention from any women.[19] Chaucer not only wishes to show his hero as "pitous," he wishes to show pity counteracting and vanquishing anger. And he also wishes, I think, to show how anger closes off narrative possibilities. Putting Palamon and Arcite to death would bring the story to a halt; it is Theseus's pity that allows the story to move on, giving it space for further developments.

Anger can, as we have seen, paradoxically perform the function of a creative impulse in the *Canterbury Tales*. But it also threatens, on two occasions, to bring the action to a halt, to close off possibilities, by breaking the contract of "game and play" that holds the pilgrim company together. And in each of these cases anger in one pilgrim follows on from a rejection of "glosing" in the other. The first occasion is at the end of the *Pardoner's Tale*, when the Host refuses the Pardoner's offer to let him kiss his relics, using a violent bluntness of speech that resembles Thomas's response to the "glosing" friar in that it confronts the Pardoner's professional rhetoric with the most basic physical realities:

> "Lat be!" quod he, "It shal nat be, so thee'ch!
> Thow woldest make me kisse thin olde breech,
> And swere it were a relik of a seint,
> Though it were with thy fundement depeint.
> But, by the crois which that Seint Eleine fond,
> I wolde I hadde thy coilons in my hond
> In stede of relikes or of seintuarye!
> Lat kutte hem of; I wol thee helpe hem carye.
> They shul be shrined in an hogges toord!" (947–55)

18 The inclusion of reason shows the influence of the Senecan tradition (see n. 12 above).

19 *Teseida* V.88.

This bursting of his linguistic bubble makes the Pardoner speechless with anger (as it does the friar of the *Summoner's Tale*):

> This Pardoner answerde nat a word;
> So wrooth he was, no word ne wolde he seye.
> "Now," quod oure Hoost, "I wol no lenger pleye
> With thee, ne with noon oother angry man." (956–9)

This quarrel is patched up by the Knight, and the tale-telling goes on.

The second near-breakdown is in the *Manciple's Prologue*, and again it is caused by plain speaking: the Host calls on the Cook for a tale, but he is so drunk he can hardly stay on his horse. The Manciple then jeeringly suggests he be excused, ridiculing his gaping mouth and stinking breath; "Of me, certein, thow shalt nat been yglosed" (34), he assures him. Again the abandonment of "glosing" produces speechless anger:

> And with this speche the Cook wax wrooth and wraw
> And on the Manciple he gan nodde faste
> For lakke of speche, and doun the hors him caste ... (46–8)

Drink and anger, which had earlier acted as a stimulus to tale-telling, here totally incapacitate the Cook and reduce him to silence. Once again the quarrel is patched up, this time by the Host; the Manciple appeases the angry Cook ("I wol nat wrathe him": 80), and the atmosphere of "game" is restored by giving the Cook yet more to drink. Yet the tale the Manciple goes on to tell answers to the menacing resonances of this introductory episode rather than its playful ones; it constitutes the bleakest picture of anger and "glosing" in the whole of the Canterbury collection.

The tale tells of the crow who was punished for tale-telling. Chaucer must have known it in the first place from Ovid's *Metamorphoses* (II.531–632), but it is also very likely that he knew Gower's version of it in Book III of the *Confessio Amantis* (783–817) – which is, significantly, the section devoted to the sin of Wrath.[20] Chaucer alters the slant and the significance of the story about the crow, but he retains the connection with anger. This book of the *Confessio* also includes the story of Alexander and the pirate (III.2363–417) that likewise reappears in the *Manciple's Tale*, where it is made into a story about "glosing," as we shall see. The *Manciple's Tale* opens in an apparently paradisal world, when

20 *The English Works of John Gower*, ed. G.C. Macaulay, 2 vols, EETS e.s. 81–2 (London, 1900–1).

the god Phebus lived on earth. The "mooste lusty bachiler" and the best archer in the world, he was also master of music, both as singer and as a player of instruments (105–15). His pet crow, who in those days was as white as a swan, likewise sang like a nightingale and imitated human speech (130–8). Phebus also had a wife, of whom he was exceedingly fond and also exceedingly jealous. Chaucer – or the Manciple – then comments on the futility of jealousy: a good wife does not need invigilation, and a bad wife will always manage to elude it (148–54). Phebus's wife is thus unfaithful to him despite his watchfulness, and what is more, she chooses as her lover a man "of litel reputacioun" who cannot stand comparison with her husband (199–200). The crow who is witness to her adultery reveals it to Phebus, who "in his ire" seizes his bow and arrows and slays his wife, and then breaks to pieces both his musical instruments and his bow (264–9). *Then* he repents and blames everything on the crow, who is punished by being turned black, deprived of his song, and tossed out of doors to become a figure of ill omen (270–308).

This simple story is elaborated in Chaucer's telling by the addition of several extended passages of narratorial comment. First, Phebus's attempts to police his wife's behaviour provoke a lengthy digression on the ineradicability of Nature, beginning with the maxim

> ... ther may no man embrace
> As to destreine a thing which that nature
> Hath naturelly set in a creature. (160–2)

This is followed by the illustrative example of the bird in the cage which is used by Boethius to make the same point: however well you feed it on dainties and decorate its cage, if the cage door is left open it will be off to the wood to eat "wormes and swich wrecchednesse" (163–74). Similarly a cat is never so pampered that it will not abandon all its titbits to run after a mouse (175–80). It is significant in this connection that the opening two narratives in Gower's section on Wrath present anger as a refusal of *nature*: in the first, nature takes the form of the incestuous love between Canacee and her brother Macharius, which their father's wrath refuses to accept as natural (III.143–360). In the second (III.361–80), Tiresias sees two snakes coupling sexually "so as nature hem tawhte" (III.367), and angrily strikes them with his stick; he is then "unkindeliche" ("unnaturally") transformed into a woman as punishment for having disturbed nature ("for he hath destourbed kinde": III.373–5). Like Gower, Chaucer sees anger as a refusal of nature, a fundamental refusal to accept the way things are. Phebus refuses to accept the adultery of his wife, which although as illicit as the incestuous love of Canacee and Macharius, resembles it in being a reflex of the inexorable power of nature.

No sooner is the Manciple's narrative resumed after this digression than it is abandoned again, as the narrator backtracks on the word "lemman" which he has just used of Phebus's wife's lover:

Hir lemman? Certes, this is a knavissh speche!
Foryeveth it me, and that I yow biseche. (205–6)

Yet he defends this "knavissh speche" on the principle that the word should be cousin to the deed. "I am a boistous man," he explains (211); as far as he is concerned, the only difference between a high-born lady who commits adultery and a poor wench who does the same lies in the language used to describe them: the "gentile" woman will be called her lover's "lady," while the poor woman will be called his "wenche" or "lemman."

And, God it woot, min owene deere brother,
Men leyn that oon as lowe as lith that oother. (221–2)

The story of Alexander and the pirate told by Gower is then cited to underline the point: a tyrant such as Alexander is just as much a thief as the leader of a band of outlaws; the only difference is that his ravages are on a larger scale (223–34).

In the *Confessio Amantis* this story illustrates the destructiveness of war. In the *Manciple's Tale* it is used to make a point about "glosing" – about the use of language to camouflage the squalid indignities of human behaviour. The thief is "glosed" into a conqueror; the wench is "glosed" into a lady love. Chaucer has already shown us this kind of "glosing" in action in the *Merchant's Tale*, where the romantic language used to describe the incipient love affair between "fresshe May" and the young squire Damian seems increasingly at odds with the very unromantic events it is called upon to describe. "Pitee" here is not the meaningful term it was in the *Knight's Tale*, but merely a euphemism for violent sexual desire; the maxim that "pitee renneth soone in gentil herte" is invoked to account for May's instantaneous yielding to Damian's advances (1986). Yet the climax of the tale, the brisk coupling in the pear tree, is something that virtually defies "glosing," and the Merchant is temporarily deflected into describing it in plain terms:

And caughte hire bv a twiste, and up she goth –
Ladies, I pray yow that ye be nat wroth;
I kan nat glose, I am a rude man –
And sodeinly anon this Damian
Gan pullen up the smok and in he throng. (2349–53)

But given a little time the Merchant recovers himself magnificently, as he describes January, his sight newly restored by Pluto, taking in what is going on over his head:

> Up to the tree he caste his eyen two,
> And saugh that Damian his wif had dressed
> *In swich manere, it may nat been expressed,*
> *But if I wolde speke uncurteisly.* (2360–3; my italics)

It looks at first as if the Merchant will be obliged to repeat his earlier crudeness, but with a superb verbal body swerve he triumphantly defies our expectations. His linguistic avoidance of blunt statement parallels January's refusal of reality: even though a miracle restores to him the power to see his wife's adultery with his own eyes, he nevertheless allows himself to be persuaded that his eyes deceived him. Stylistic "glosing" answers to this wilful blindness on the narrative level;[21] it shows us how the operations of physical appetite can, with a different kind of linguistic embodiment, be disguised as the manifestations of romantic passion.

In the *Manciple's Tale*, Phebus's romantic illusions are shattered by the brutal simplicity of the one word with which the crow reveals his wife's adultery:

> And whan that hoom was come Phebus the lord,
> This crowe sang "Cokkow! Cokkow! Cokkow!" (242–3)

The message hovers at the very limits of human language, already passing over the boundary to become a mere bird call; human dignity is confronted by animal reality. Even when the crow is called upon to expand on the meaning of his jeering call, his phrasing is unsoftened by euphemism ("on thy bed thy wif I sey him swive"; 256). And just as the narrator of the *Merchant's Tale* fears that his inability to find a suitable "glose" will provoke anger in his hearers, so

---

21 Cf. the comments of Priscilla Martin, *Chaucer's Women: Nuns, Wives and Amazons* (Basingstoke, Hants, 1990), 118: "The fabliau mocks the romance, the squalid defiles the sacred, low style ruptures high. The narrator's 'rude' (2351) speech at the crucial moment, 'in he throng' (2353), January's 'Ye, algate in it wente!' (2376) compromise the elevated and allusive style of the rest of the Tale, as if the noble diction were merely a gloss on the vile reality. Understood properly, suggests the narrator, the wonderful cadences, sensuous imagery and holy symbolism of the *Song of Songs* are nothing but 'olde lewed wordes' (2149). In this re-vision of the *Song of Songs* words are the only covering for the creatures' nakedness and words are showily deceptive."

the unmitigated directness of the crow's revelation plays a part in creating the violence of Phebus's anger; he cannot withstand the assault of bald and unmitigated truth.[22] His "ire" is the attempt to obliterate this intolerable reality, to destroy it by destroying his wife. But once he has killed her, he attempts to obliterate reality a second time, not by anger, but by "glosing." In an astonishing flow of sentimental rhetoric, he recreates his wife as an innocent victim. His remorse at his own anger does not indicate an acceptance of his wife's infidelity, but on the contrary refuses it a second time in the pretence that she was innocent after all.

"Allas, that I was wroght! Why nere I ded?
O deere wif, o gemme of lustihed,
That were to me so sad and eek so trewe,
Now listow deed, with face pale of hewe,
Ful giltelees – that dorste I swere, iwys!
O rakel hand, to doon so foule amis!
O trouble wit! O ire recchelees,
That unavised smitest giltelees!
O wantrust, ful of fals suspecioun!
Where was thy wit and thy discrecioun?
O, every man be war of rakelnesse!
Ne trowe nothing withouten strong witnesse.
Smit nat to soone, er that ye witen why,
And beth avised wel and sobrely,
Er ye doon any execucioun
Upon youre ire for suspecioun.
Allas, a thousand folk hath rakel ire
Fully fordoon, and broght hem in the mire!
Allas, for sorwe I wol myselven sle!" (273–91)

Anger is rejected only because its role has been taken over by "glosing"; both are a means of shutting out reality, retreating into a world of private illusion. Those who try to break through the boundaries of this cosy world, such as the crow, are viciously punished, turned into the villain of the piece, and summarily ejected.

The ending of the tale does nothing to lighten this gloomy picture of the human commitment to illusion. Like the friar of the *Summoner's Tale*, the Manciple concludes one should never tell unpleasant truths to powerful people:

22 For a similar example of anger provoked by a refusal to "glose," see the story of Ahab and Micaiah in Gower's *Confessio Amantis*, ed. Macaulay, V.2527–685, esp. 2531, 2631, 2664–9.

Lordinges, by this ensample I yow preye,
Beth war, and taketh kepe what that ye seye:
Ne telleth nevere no man in youre lif
How that another man hath dight his wif. (309–12)

And he reiterates the advice to keep one's mouth shut for a further fifty lines, quoting his mother's exhortations in his childhood to "keep wel [his] tonge." The alternative to "glosing," it seems, is silence. It is not a very comforting moral for the poet who, like the crow, is committed to telling tales; it is not surprising that this dour onslaught against tale-telling is followed by the prose *Parson's Tale*, which renounces both poetic form and fiction.[23] This time the refusal of "glosing" ("I wol nat glose"; 45) is not a sign of aggressive confrontation, but of an austere rejection of "fable" in favour of plain prosaic "Moralitee and vertuous matere" (31, 38). For those who cannot follow the Parson in rejecting poetic fiction along with the less attractive kinds of "glosing," comfort is to be had only by retreating to the heart of the *Tales* – for example to the *Nun's Priest's Tale,* the other animal tale in the collection, where a barnyard incident is "glosed" into a drama of cosmic significance in a way that makes the disparity between rhetoric and action into a source of comic celebration rather than tragic gloom. Comfort can also be had by retreating to tales such as those of the Knight or the Franklin, with their counterposing images of patience and pity. But the power of these ideals rests precisely with the sharpness and clarity of vision with which Chaucer focuses the human impulses towards their contraries, anger and "glosing," and records with unblinking honesty both the comedy and the bleakness of their manifestations in human life.

23 Cf. B.J. Harwood, "Language and the Real: Chaucer's Manciple," *Chaucer Review* 6 (1971–2): 268–79.

Chapter Six

The Authority of the Audience in Chaucer

The authority of the literary text seems, by the laws of etymology, to belong to the author. "Auctour" glides insensibly into "auctoritee"; indeed, the word "auctour" itself can mean "a source of authoritative information or opinion, an authority" (*MED* 2a). And as a natural result the problematic aspects of literary authority, much discussed in recent years,[1] have been generally considered in relation to the author. Indeed, they have been considered first and foremost as a problem *for* the author. Jacqueline Miller's study of "Authority and Authorship" in medieval and Renaissance literature, for example, identifies the central concern of Chaucer's *House of Fame* as the pressing need felt by "Chaucer and many of his contemporaries ... to define the (often uneasy) relationship between the status of their individual authorial positions and the authorizing principles of their art – to find the proper balance between their claims for poetic independence and their reliance upon the sanction of traditional *auctoritee*."[2] This author-centred approach to the *House of Fame* goes back to J.A.W. Bennett's book on the poem, which sees it as "the one work of the poet that dwells on the nature and rewards of poetic achievement ... the work in which [Chaucer] presents himself as a seeker after fresh poetic inspiration, new poetic 'tidings.' "[3] John Norton-Smith describes the *House of Fame* as delineating "the hidden

1 See especially Alastair Minnis, *Medieval Theory of Authorship: Scholastic Literary Attitudes in the Later Middle Ages* (London, 1984).

2 *Poetic License: Authority and Authorship in Medieval and Renaissance Contexts* (New York, 1986), 35. Chapter II incorporates Miller's earlier article, "The Writing on the Wall: Authority and Authorship in Chaucer's House of Fame," *Chaucer Review* 17 (1982–3): 95–115. The same author-centred approach characterizes the essays in the collection edited by Kevin Brownlee and Walter Stephens, *Discourses of Authority in Medieval and Renaissance Literature* (Hanover, NH, 1989).

3 *Chaucer's Book of Fame: An Exposition of "The House of Fame"* (Oxford, 1968), 3.

sources which urge him, as a poet, to both write and think about certain problems."[4] Piero Boitani's magisterial study of the poem likewise climaxes with the questions: "What gives a poet his inspiration? What makes him a poet?"[5]

With none of this have I any quarrel. Yet as Piero Boitani also observes elsewhere, when Chaucer gives us a self-portrait, he represents himself as a "fanatic bibliophile"[6] – that is, not as a writer but as a *reader*. The vivid and intimate picture of Chaucer's everyday life which is given us by the eagle in the *House of Fame* describes him coming home from his daily work only to bury himself in his books.

> "For when thy labour doon al ys,
> And hast mad alle thy rekenynges,
> In stede of reste and newe thynges
> Thou goost hom to thy hous anoon,
> And, also domb as any stoon,
> Thou sittest at another book
> Tyl fully daswed ys thy look;
> And lyvest thus as an heremyte,
> Although thyn abstynence is lyte." (652–60)

Nor is this an isolated case. In the *Parliament of Fowls*, Chaucer represents himself as busy all day in reading, not in writing. In the *Book of the Duchess*, his relation to books is not that of the creative writer, but that of the casual bedtime reader. True, in the *Legend of Good Women*, his role as a writer is brought into play by the God of Love's accusations against him, but even so it is as an assiduous reader, perpetually poring over his books, that he first introduces himself. The idea of linking the dream vision to the reading of a book was, indeed, as A.C. Spearing has observed, Chaucer's special contribution to the genre.[7] The much-discussed Narrator of *Troilus and Criseyde* ought perhaps to be called not the Narrator but the Reader, since he reminds us at every stage that he is getting all this out of a book and is unable to alter the story he is telling or fill in its lacunae. These persistent intrusions of a reading presence within the text dramatize Chaucer's relationship to a literary past – to the authors whose

---

4 *Geoffrey Chaucer* (London, 1974), 39.

5 *Chaucer and the Imaginary World of Fame* (Cambridge, 1984), 216.

6 "Old Books Brought to Life in Dreams: the Book of the Duchess, the House of Fame, the Parliament of Fowls," in *The Cambridge Companion to Chaucer*, ed. Piero Boitani and Jill Mann, 2nd ed. (Cambridge, 2003), 58–77, at 59.

7 *Medieval Dream-Poetry* (Cambridge, 1976), 58.

influence must be reconciled with his own creative independence; they also dramatize his relationship to a literary future – to the readers on whom the continuing life and meaning of his work depends. That is, Chaucer's role as reader of others' works is a covert surrogate for our own role as readers of his own. His representations of the reading process constitute – I shall argue – an acknowledgment of the essential role played by the reader in the creation (or destruction) of literary authority, and show his interest in some of its more important implications for the writer.[8]

The reinstatement of the reader as the neglected third in the "triangle of author, work and public" was an important project in twentieth-century criticism – in, for example, the work of Stanley Fish, of Wolfgang Iser, and in the "reception theory" outlined by Hans Robert Jauss.[9] In this triad, writes Jauss, the reading public "is no passive part, no chain of mere reactions, but rather itself an energy formative of history."[10] Jauss, like Mikhail Bakhtin before him, stresses the "dialogical character of the literary work,"[11] which enables it to acquire new significances as new historical contexts – in practice, new readers – bring to light new structures of meaning. "A literary work," says Jauss, "is not an object that stands by itself and that offers the same view to each reader in each period. It is not a monument that monologically reveals its timeless essence. It is much more like an orchestration that strikes ever new resonances among its readers and that frees the text from the material of the words and brings it to a contemporary existence."[12] In approaching Chaucer's work with these words in mind, it is no part of my intention to congratulate him for having cleverly anticipated modern reception-theory; his own analysis of the reading process, though equally sophisticated, is animated by different interests and aims. Nor am I proposing to apply reception theory to Chaucer's work. There is the world of difference between analysing the representations of the reading process in Chaucer's text, and analysing the reading processes that his text itself implies or

8 The subject is broached by Susan Schibanoff, "The New Reader and Female Textuality in Two Early Commentaries on Chaucer," *Studies in the Age of Chaucer* 10 (1988): 71–108, at 96–103.

9 See Stanley Fish, *Is There a Text in This Class? The Authority of Interpretive Communities* (Cambridge, MA, 1980); Wolfgang Iser, *The Implied Reader: Patterns of Communication in Prose Fiction from Bunyan to Beckett* (Baltimore, MD, 1974); id., *The Act of Reading: A Theory of Aesthetic Response* (Baltimore, MD, 1978); Hans Robert Jauss, *Toward an Aesthetic of Reception*, trans. Timothy Bahti (Brighton, Sussex, 1982).

10 *Aesthetic of Reception*, 19.

11 Ibid., 21. On Bakhtin, see Tzvetan Todorov, *Mikhail Bakhtin: The Dialogical Principle*, trans. Wlad Godzich (Manchester, 1984).

12 *Aesthetic of Reception*, 21.

provokes – an excellent subject but one for another paper. I wish only to draw attention to Chaucer's various imagined representations of the reader's role; and if reception theory has a part to play, it is perhaps that it has prepared us to appreciate Chaucer's interest in this subject, and to recognize the originality, the honesty, and above all magnanimity, which mark his reflections on it.

Let us go back to the conversation between Chaucer and the eagle in the *House of Fame*, and in particular to the point where the bird offers to identify all the different constellations for the airborne poet, so that when he next reads about them in books he will be able to relate his reading to what he has seen. Chaucer nonchalantly rejects this kind offer, because, he says, he believes everything the books say without having to verify it, and what is more, it might hurt his eyes to look at the stars directly.

> "No fors," quod y, "hyt is no nede.
> I leve as wel, so God me spede,
> Hem that write of this matere,
> As though I knew her places here;
> And eke they shynen here so bryghte,
> Hyt shulde shenden al my syghte
> To loke on hem." (1011–17)

Every author must at times have wished for a reader like this – docile, credulous, ready to take on trust everything the books tell him. This is, if you like, the passive reader whose existence is rejected by Jauss. And likewise, of course, by Chaucer, for his appearance here is nothing other than a joke, his acknowledgment that the passive reader has no existence outside of this comic fantasy.

How a typical reader is actually likely to behave we can see in the immediately preceding passage, where Chaucer, in direct contrast to his stated attitude, immediately begins checking off what he sees around him against the information he has gathered from his reading. Looking back through the heavens at the world he has left behind, he thinks first of Boethius's account of Philosophy's imaginary flight through the spheres on the wings of thought (972–8; cf. *De Cons. Phil.* IV m.l). Then he thinks of Martianus Capella's *Marriage of Philology and Mercury* and Alan of Lille's *Anticlaudianus*, and observes that they too have accurately described the celestial regions.

> And than thoughte y on Marcian,
> And eke on Anteclaudian,
> That sooth was her descripsion
> Of alle the hevenes region,

As fer as that y sey the preve;
Therfore y kan hem now beleve. (985–90)

The implications of this passage for the truth claims of literature have been thoroughly discussed in Chaucer criticism. What is important about it as an illustration of the reading process is not only that it shows us the constant interaction between literature and life in which the reader is engaged, but also that it shows us books *meshing with other books* in the mind of the reader. As Gillian Beer puts it in her introduction to *Arguing with the Past*: "Books once read do not stay inside their covers. Once in the head they mingle, forming networks of allusion with other reading and other experiences of the time."[13] Chaucer's heavenly flight draws Boethius, Martianus, and Alan into a collage whose significance is created and sealed by the experience of the moment.

This observation is not negated but given an extra dimension of complexity by the circumstance that in this particular case the "experience" which serves as the nodal point of literary meaning is of course one that no human being has ever had outside the pages of a book. The "network of allusion" in this case makes no contact with reality; it remains a purely literary phenomenon. And yet in a strange way, to find something repeated in *another* book carries something of the same evidential power as finding it confirmed in experience. Reading about an ascent through the cosmos in Boethius, Martianus, and Alan – and one might add, in other authors such as Dante, whose influence on this scene is palpable even though he is not named – leaves the same kind of residue in the memory as experience itself.[14] "A thousand tymes have I herd men telle / That ther ys joy in hevene and peyne in helle" says Chaucer at the opening of the *Legend of Good Women* (F 1–2), and he proclaims his willingness to believe it; but nevertheless he also knows that there is no living soul who has ever been to either place. So when at the end of Book I of the *House of Fame* he refers us, if we want a detailed description of Hell, to Virgil or Claudian or Dante, it is as if the correspondences between these three separate reports must inevitably arise from and bear witness to the independent reality of what they describe – whereas what they in fact testify to is nothing other than a chain of literary influence (that is, both Claudian and Dante model their descriptions on Virgil). Chaucer focuses the question of literary truth on these "non-existent" experiences not only, I think, because of his concern with the kind of belief

13 *Arguing with the Past: Essays in Narrative from Woolf to Sidney* (London, 1989), 9.

14 Iser quotes Henry James's observation that reading gives us the illusion "that we have lived another life" (*The Act of Reading*, 127).

that literature can command, but also because of his awareness of the *priority* of books over experience – his interest in the way that they prepare us to recognize experiences when we have them, to give them a predetermined shape and name. We shall certainly recognize Hell if we ever see it. To see literature performing this preparatory role with experiences that people have never had makes it easier to see it performing the same role with the ones that they do have. Love, for example. At the opening of the *Parliament of Fowls*, Chaucer tells us that he knows not Love "in dede," but the poem nevertheless constitutes a packed storehouse of impressions on the subject, garnered from innumerable books and awaiting the confirmatory experience that will activate them.

It is in the *Parliament of Fowls* that we find the best and fullest example of books mingling with each other and forming networks of allusion in the reader's head. What we enter in this poem is not so much a garden of Love as a reader's mind, in which Macrobius and Cicero, Boccaccio, Dante, Alan of Lille, and the *Romance of the Rose* mesh and entangle themselves into a bizarre configuration. It is rather like those films that begin with a hand turning the pages of a book, whose pictures suddenly begin to move and fill the screen with their own autonomous reality. Jauss speaks of the reader approaching each new work he reads with a "horizon of expectations" created by a knowledge of pre-existing literary works – a horizon whose boundaries may be confirmed or dramatically thrown open by the act of reading.[15] The *Parliament of Fowls* could be seen as a sort of animated version of one reader's "horizon of expectations." But the mental world that lies within this horizon is not such a tidy and well-ordered affair as one might suppose from Jauss's account of it; it is more like a literary Disneyland. Books collapse into each other in an unpredictable and undisciplined sort of way, forming unexpected alliances and idiosyncratic patterns; they are linked by haphazard association rather than by the laws of genre or subject. Cicero's Africanus seems to have assimilated himself to Dante's Virgil; the gate to Dante's Hell does not open on to a world regulated by divine justice but on to the amoral frivolities of Guillaume de Lorris's garden. The texts take on a life of their own: the birds depicted on Nature's robe in Alan of Lille's *Complaint of Nature* come to life and start squabbling at her feet.[16] What is more, this variegated literary kaleidoscope could at any moment be shaken into a new pattern by the arrival of a new book on the horizon, creating a new network of allusions with those already in place and changing expectations yet again.

---

15 *Aesthetic of Reception*, 25.

16 The point is made by Peter Dronke, "Chaucer and the Medieval Latin Poets: Part A," in *Writers and their Background: Geoffrey Chaucer*, ed. Derek Brewer (London, 1974), 154–72 at 164–5.

This is all great fun for readers. But it creates certain problems for writers. Iser discusses the "asymmetry" in the dialogic relation between text and reader arising from the fact that the text cannot answer back, and is therefore in some sense at the mercy of the reader's ability to make sense of it. For Iser, this potential imbalance is regulated by controlling mechanisms in the text: "the reader's activity must be controlled in some way by the text."[17] The multitextual jumble of the *Parliament of Fowls* shows that the reader's activity is not so easily regimented. We have here no disciplined concentration on the individual literary work as a thing-in-itself, carefully analysed in terms of the rules it establishes for itself, its relations with other literary material and with life scrupulously curtailed and regulated by notions of literary decorum and methodological consistency. This is not professional reading, this is *real* reading, producing a mishmash of half-remembered words and images whose arrangement is orchestrated by the reader rather than the writer. That Chaucer was conscious of the potential problems in the dialogic relation between writer and reader can be seen, I think, from the various cases where he imagines different sorts of dislocation in this relation, cases where one voice in the dialogue could be said to drown out the other. Let us start with an example where the problem is on the reader's side: *Troilus and Criseyde.* Here it is the writer – the fictional Lollius – who assumes dominance over the reader – the dramatized projection of Chaucer himself. Knowing the outcome of the story from the beginning, Chaucer nevertheless represents himself as being drawn in by the moment-by-moment excitement of the reading process to an emotional identification with the happiness of the two lovers which gives way — like theirs – to a progressive dismay at the way the story is going in the last two Books. In Book III, the reader's passionate involvement in the story instantly realizes the words on the page as a scene of dramatic immediacy:

> Criseyde, which that felte hire thus itake,
> As writen clerkes in hire bokes olde,
> Right as an aspes leef she gan to quake ... (III.1198–200)

So far from being felt as an intrusion that breaks the illusion of present experience, the reference to "bokes olde" makes us aware of how live an experience reading can be, the words filling themselves out with our imagined participation (as Chaucer appeals to his readers to fill out his report of the scene with their own experience of love). Yet by Book V, the story has become distasteful to

17 *The Art of Reading*, 167.

the reader, and Chaucer's disaffection from what he reads registers itself in the terse reportage with which he rehearses its bare essentials.

And after this the storie telleth us
That she hym yaf the faire baye stede
The which he ones wan of Troilus ...
I fynde ek in the stories elleswhere ...
But trewely, the storie telleth us,
Ther made never womman moore wo
Than she, whan that she falsed Troilus. (V.1037–9,1044,1051–3)

"The storie telleth us," but we don't really want to hear it, because the information is at odds with the matrix of meaning we have been encouraged to prepare by the ecstasies of Book III, and are reluctant to discard for another, gloomier version. Trapped by the story he reads, the reader finds it too late to retract his commitment to the characters and experiences it has offered, and can only respond by throwing the book away altogether. The ending of the poem rejects not only human love but also reading.

Lo here, the forme of olde clerkis speche
In poetrie, if ye hire bokes seche. (V.1854–5)

Chaucer's role here is not that of the writer revealing to us the hidden meaning of the story he has told; it is rather that of the reader, registering his disgust and disappointment with the story he has read, and regretting that he ever started on it.

In *Troilus* it is the reader who is alarmed by a lack of control, his role curtailed and restricted by the unpalatable nature of the text. Elsewhere in Chaucer it is the writer's inability to control what the reader does with his text that is a potential cause of alarm. Chaucer is possibly the only English poet to have been more troubled by the anxiety of *exerting* influence than by the anxiety of undergoing it; the burden of the future can be more worrying than the burden of the past.[18] Consider, for example, the relationship between Virgil and Dante from Virgil's rather than (as is more usual) Dante's point of view, and it becomes apparent that for all Dante's reverence and love for the poet who is his "maestro" and "autore" (*Inferno* I.85), he is nevertheless making Virgil *mean* something

18 For these terms see W. Jackson Bate, *The Burden of the Past and the English Poet* (London, 1971), and Harold Bloom, *The Anxiety of Influence: A Theory of Poetry* (London, 1973).

that the Roman writer not only never conceived of but would have actively disliked. Virgil would doubtless have been as uncomfortable with his role as a forerunner and guide to Christianity as St Bernard would be were he to return from the grave and find he had been made a precursor of Islamic fundamentalism.

Chaucer's own anxieties, as least as he dramatizes them, centre particularly on the effect of his writings on women. In the God of Love's accusations against him in the Prologue to the *Legend of Good Women*, he projects a concern that reading *Troilus and Criseyde* might reinforce men in a low opinion of women:

> And of Creseyde thou hast seyd as the lyste,
> That maketh men to wommen lasse triste,
> That ben as trewe as ever was any steel ... (F 332–4)

Already in *Troilus and Criseyde* itself, Chaucer shows Criseyde ruefully prophesying that when her story becomes known, women will hate her most because her actions will be used to discredit the sex as a whole (V.1063–6). It is of no use for Chaucer to protest, as he does at the end of *Troilus*, that it is not his intention to blacken women's reputation; an author's intentions, as every modern critic knows, cannot control the meaning of his work. And if this axiom allows for the free play of critical subtlety, it also allows for a crude reductivism that can turn the story of Criseyde into an antifeminist anecdote. We can see the problem in the famous *querelle* over the *Romance of the Rose*: the male humanists vainly appealing to literary subtleties – to Jean de Meun's urbane irony, or his use of dramatic monologue in order to distance himself from antifeminist points of view, while for Christine de Pisan all this means nothing beside the simple fact that the text is *read* as antifeminist; one husband, she says, used to read the poem aloud to his wife and shower her with blows as he did so.[19] Chaucer gives us a similar situation in his picture of the Wife of Bath forced to endure her fifth husband reading aloud day and night from his "book of wikked wives" (685).[20] Loath as I am to say a good word for St Jerome, it must I suppose be admitted that his *intention* in writing the treatise *Against Jovinian* was to persuade his readers to celibacy, not to encourage them to torment their wives. But to the Wife of Bath this is a distinction she is not in a position to appreciate; she might be forgiven for thinking, like Hilaire Belloc's illiterate Sarah Byng, that the sole function of literature is to breed distress. Her response to Jankyn's onslaughts

19 Christine de Pisan, Jean Gerson, Jean de Montreuil, Gontier et Pierre Col, *Le Débat sur Le Roman de la Rose*, ed. Eric Hicks (Paris, 1977), 139–40.

20 It is tempting to think that it was the *Wife of Bath's Prologue* that Christine had in mind.

is not to suggest he take a course in literary criticism, but simply to attempt to destroy the book.

We can reject Jankyn's use of literary texts as immoral, but it is less easy to prove that it is illegitimate. If meaning is determined by interpretive communities, as Stanley Fish tells us it is, then men must surely make up one of the largest and most cohesive communities of this sort, whose interpretive values were accepted without protest and indeed without notice for centuries. But Chaucer, with his sharp eye for the way literature interacts with life, noticed them. In the figure of Pluto in the *Merchant's Tale*, he gives us a brilliant vignette of the male reader observing life through the spectacles of literature – spectacles which have special blinkers on the side. Seeing May and Damian about to commit adultery in the tree, Pluto comments sententiously not on Damian's ungrateful betrayal of his kind master, but on the general and deplorable treacherousness of womankind. He supports these strictures with reference to "Ten hundred thousand tales" of women's "untrouthe and brotelnesse" (2240–1), and also to the antifeminist proverbs in the Solomonic books of the Bible. Pluto assumes that experience provides the evidence and literature plays a merely confirmatory role ("Th'experience so preveth every day / The treson which that womman dooth to man"; 2238–9). But it is of course the other way round: it is the antifeminist material he has read, converging with his personal bias towards his own sex, that shapes his expectations and conditions him to respond to experience in a particular way. As in the *House of Fame* and the *Parliament of Fowls*, reading is *prior* to experience and disposes us to approach it selectively, preparing us to recognize familiar forms while unfamiliar ones fall outside the range of vision. Pluto is blind not only to Damian's role in the adultery but also to his own past: the wife whom he so pompously lectures on the treasons that women inflict on men was won by a rape, as Chaucer reminds us by referring to Claudian's *De Raptu Proserpinae*, and its account of how he "ravisshed" her on the slopes of Mount Etna, when he introduces the pair (2229–33). The reading of Pluto's own story might suggest that a few remarks on the brutalities men inflict on women might not come amiss. Proserpina does not point this out directly, but she mounts a parallel attack on Solomon, whose "auctoritee" (2276) as a critic of women is similarly undermined by the facts of his personal life, since he was a "lechour and an idolastre" (2298). Like the Wife of Bath commenting on St Jerome, she unearths the personal "auctour" buried in the impersonal "auctoritee," as an interpretive strategy that will reveal masculine bias. Moreover, she claims that when Solomon said he had never found a good woman, what he *meant* was that nobody is truly good but God alone (2286–90). We might be tempted to dub this last simply a *mis*interpretation, but Proserpina has lifted it from the entirely sober context of the *Melibee* (1076–80), where it is less easy to ascribe to female unscrupulousness in argument. As with the Wife of Bath's cavalier handling of biblical and patristic authorities in defence of multiple marriages, it is not possible to distinguish intrinsically between the creative exegesis practised by men (and therefore taken seriously) and the creative exegesis practised by women (and therefore regarded as unlicensed); St Jerome, Pluto, the Wife of Bath, and Proserpina all use identical interpretive methods.[21]

If these last examples of the reading process have shown its potential reductivism, we can turn back to the *House of Fame* for an example of its more creative aspects, and see them, what is more, exercised in women's favour rather than to their detriment. Chaucer's picture of Dido in Book I is, as has often been pointed out, a blend of Virgil and Ovid; emerging from a narrative summary of the *Aeneid*, her lament over Aeneas's departure swells to proportions that remind us of Ovid's *Heroides*, and insensibly persuades us to see it from the female point of view – that is, as an act of treacherous desertion rather than a self-sacrificing submission to a heroic destiny. The immediate cause of this emotional involvement in Dido's position is not, however, Ovid (who makes surprisingly little contribution to the *material* of Dido's lament), but the fact that her story makes contact with certain proverbial commonplaces in the mind of the narrator. Or rather, here again we should say in the mind of the reader, for in narrating the train of images he "sees" on the wall of the temple Chaucer is also "reading" a written text, as his opening quotation of Virgil's words makes clear; as in any reading process, the words transform themselves insensibly into a series of vivid pictures to which the reader imagines he is responding directly. Dido's trust in Aeneas's seeming goodness thus activates in him a whole stream of generalizations that relate her story to his own store of ideas on life.

> Allas! what harm doth apparence,
> Whan hit is fals in existence!
> For he to hir a traytour was;
> Wherfore she slow hirself, allas!
> Loo, how a woman doth amys
> To love hym that unknowen ys!
> For, be Cryste, lo, thus yt fareth:
> "Hyt is not al gold that glareth."
> For also browke I wel myn hed,

21 See E. Talbot Donaldson, "Designing a Camel; Or, Generalizing the Middle Ages," *Tennessee Studies in Literature* 22 (1977): 1–16, at 5–7, and David Aers, *Chaucer, Langland and the Creative Imagination* (London, 1980), 86.

Ther may be under godlyhed
Kevered many a shrewed vice.
Therfore be no wyght so nyce
To take a love oonly for chere,
Or speche, or for frendly manere,
For this shal every woman fynde,
That som man, of his pure kynde,
Wol shewen outward the fayreste,
Tyl he have caught that what him leste;
And thanne wol he causes fynde
And swere how that she ys unkynde,
Or fals, or privy, or double was.
Al this seye I be Eneas
And Dido, and hir nyce lest,
That loved al to sone a gest;
Therfore I wol seye a proverbe,
That "he that fully knoweth th'erbe
May saufly leye hyt to his yë" –
Withoute drede, this ys no lye. (265–92)

This interpretation of Dido as simply one in a long line of female victims of male heartlessness, and an example of the need to look before you leap, liberates Chaucer from the Virgilian original; when he returns to Dido and reports her long lament, he emphasizes its independence from any "auctour," locating its origin in the imaginative autonomy of the dream.

In suche wordes gan to pleyne
Dydo of hir grete peyne,
As me mette redely –
Non other auctour alegge I. (311–14)

The Dido passage has been discussed – most notably by Sheila Delany – in terms of "Chaucer's experience as a poet," illustrating his sense of "the validity of conflicting truths" and the unreliable basis of literary authority.[22] This it doubtless is, but what particularly interests me is what it has to tell us of the reading process. For the importance of Ovid to Chaucer is not simply that he offers us another version of Dido – as if he and Virgil were presenting alternative accounts

22 *Chaucer's House of Fame: The Poetics of Skeptical Fideism* (Chicago, 1972), 57.

of the same historical events; it is that his version of Dido is recuperated from a *reading* of Virgil's text. As the text frees itself into images in the reader's mind, so it assumes a quasi-reality, permitting it to be restructured into a new meaning. So Virgil's Dido is reconstructed as Ovid's Dido, and both are read in the light of Chaucer's own knowledge of the everyday experience stored in proverb and commonplace, until Dido takes on a different form again, rooted in the authority of the reader, and "non other auctour." The dialogical character of the literary work is here seen in action; literary authority passes from the author to the reader.

Dido miserably foresees her imprisonment within a literary text – "alle myn actes red and songe / Over al thys lond" (347–8), the meaning of her story fixed as simply the tale of a loose woman liable to give herself to anybody. In imagining Dido and Criseyde foreseeing their own afterlife in story, Chaucer implicitly confronts the writer's responsibilities towards the human subjects whose living complexities he reduces to the outline of a meaning. But what frees him from the full weight of these responsibilities as writer is the autonomy of the reader, who can always read *through* the story to recuperate a structure of meaning unperceived by the author. If Chaucer's reading is not faithful to Virgil, it is at least faithful to Dido.

Chaucer's reading of Dido perhaps qualifies as an instance of creative misprision, in Harold Bloom's terms; I want to end by looking at some examples of less dignified kinds of misreading. The first is in the *Book of the Duchess*, in Chaucer's reading of the story of Ceyx and Alcyone. This is, in Ovid, a pathetic and moving tale, but in Chaucer's retelling, as has often been noted, the pathos is oddly muted by passages of brisk summary or bluff comedy, especially in the account of Juno's messenger visiting the cave of Morpheus and having to bellow in the god's ear to wake him up (178–83).[23] Although Chaucer tells us that Alcyone's grief at the loss of her husband affected him so much that he felt bad about it all the next morning (95–100), this is not represented as being his immediate reaction to the story. What primarily interests him about it is that there is such a thing as a god of sleep, a fact in which his present insomnia gives him an overriding interest. He promptly vows to the god a sumptuous feather bed, and gold-leaf decoration for his cave, if only he will send him to sleep – and of course his prayer is instantly granted. Modern critical theories are rarely, in my experience, so honest about the reading process as Chaucer is here, but we are all familiar, I think, with the kind of tangential reaction he is describing. In modern times it is perhaps easier to illustrate in relation to films: we all know the men who never seem to see anything in a film but the cars or the guns ("Did you *see* that 1959 Cadillac?"). We weep buckets as we watch Anna Karenina prepare to

23 A.C. Spearing notes the imbalances of tone created by these comic elements; *Medieval Dream-Poetry*, 71

throw herself under the train, reflecting all the while that a little fur muff like hers is just what we need for next winter. The undisciplined and arbitrary nature of the reader's response must be the despair of the writer; his best efforts will be negated or unbalanced by the reader's immediate needs and obsessions, or even simply indelibly coloured by them, as Gillian Beer reports that her reading of *Anna Karenina* is permanently intertwined with "the plains of Yugoslavia and the bleak clangour of Tottenham Court Road" in the "repertoire of memory."[24] Yet although Chaucer's first response to the story of Ceyx and Alcyone is thus both contingent and tangential, the story nevertheless seems to work its way into his mind, metamorphosing itself into his dream of the Black Knight's grief for his lost mistress, and hanging over his thoughts and feelings all next day. Again the story expands within the reader's mind, taking on its own life and fashioning itself into new shapes, realizing its effects obliquely and over time.

Finally, what of the *Canterbury Tales*? In the oral tale-telling of the pilgrims, the reading process seems to disappear entirely; and yet it could be said that this is also a means of bringing the writer into direct confrontation with his audience, providing direct access to their response. When we examine these responses, it becomes clear that the Canterbury pilgrims react to literary fiction in a manner fairly typical of the Great British Public: they want above all to be entertained, and are restive with the unrelieved solemnity of the *Monk's Tale* (they like their pathos simple, as in the *Prioress's Tale*). Their interest in a story is focused by their individual circumstances: the main point of the *Miller's Tale* in the eyes of the Reeve is that it is about a carpenter (because he is one); the Clerk's final ironic advice to wives to let their husbands "weep and wail" strikes a chord with the unhappily married Merchant; the Franklin is struck by the Squire's eloquence because it contrasts with the graceless behaviour of his own son. The spokesman for the pilgrims' reactions to the tales is most often Harry Bailly, whose literary responses are well described by Alan Gaylord: "When Harry reacts to a story, he never treats it as a thing-in-itself; it serves rather to mirror his own likes and dislikes, or to point to something which is already known."[25] Adapting Marianne Moore's observation that the poet gives us "imaginary gardens with real toads in them,"[26] Gaylord says of Harry that "He expects to hear about real toads in real gardens; he is most pleased if it turns out the toads and the gardens belong to someone he knows, and if what is said about them confirms what he had always thought about gardening. To the

24 *Arguing with the Past*, 2.

25 Alan T. Gaylord, "Sentence and Solaas in Fragment VII of the Canterbury Tales: Harry Bailly as Horseback Editor," *PMLA* 82 (1967): 226–35, at 232.

26 "Poetry," in *Collected Poems* (London, 1951), 41.

extent that the stories remind him of familiar things he is willing to respond with familiar emotions."[27]

This, then, is how Chaucer imagines his readers to be, how he imagines them responding to what he writes. One might suppose this to be no more than humorous condescension on his part, were it not that in the *Book of the Duchess* he has represented himself as just such a reader. And these are the readers whose authority over the text he is willing to acknowledge, with the magnanimity I mentioned earlier. When the time comes for Chaucer to tell his own tale, he modestly obliges with the rhyme of *Sir Thopas*, which he says is the only one he knows (708–9). After two hundred lines of bathetic tail-rhyme, he is stopped in his tracks by the Host's inability to endure any more, and is told in words of one syllable and four letters exactly what his "drasty ryming" is worth (929–30). He is then grudgingly allowed to tell a tale in *prose*, whose importance, as he stresses, lies in its "sentence" rather than in its verbal felicities. The authority of the audience here becomes absolute; the author is not simply misinterpreted or underappreciated but actually hooted off the stage. The best commentator on this passage is still G.K. Chesterton, who emphasizes that the joke here is of far larger scope than a satire on bad romances; it is a joke encompassing Chaucer's entire relation to his literary creation and his audience. "Chaucer is mocking not merely bad poets but good poets; the best poet he knows; 'the best in this kind are but shadows.' "[28] This last comment is of course a quotation of Theseus's remarks on the play produced for his wedding in *A Midsummer Night's Dream*, and Bottom and his mechanicals getting to work on the story of Piramus and Thisbe are probably the authentic heirs of Chaucer's pilgrims in their roles as literary critics. But the conclusion of Theseus's comment is relevant too: "The best in this kind are but shadows; and the worst are no worse, if imagination mend them." And Hippolyta answers: "It must be your imagination then, and not theirs" (5.1.211–14). It is in the reader's imagination that the literary work finds the fullness of its meaning. For Chaucer, the literary process is not completed with the production of a literary work. It is not complete without the reader – that is, until it has been absorbed by a living consciousness into a pattern formed by experience and other books that will give it meaning – not a fixed meaning, but one that will shift and grow with new readings. The authority of the writer is realized in the effect of his work on the reader, but however great that authority is, it is incapable of controlling precisely what that effect will be. The creative autonomy – or plain cussedness – of the reader must be the despair of the writer, but it must also be, on the other hand, his abiding consolation.

27 "Sentence and Solaas," 232.

28 *Chaucer* (1932; repr. London, 1962), 21.

Chapter Seven

Parents and Children in the *Canterbury Tales*

The aim of this essay is to show that the parent-child relationship is one of the central motifs of the *Canterbury Tales*.[1] It is a motif whose repetition and variation through the individual tales that I shall discuss – those of the Monk, Man of Law, Physician, Prioress, and Clerk – allows Chaucer to explore not only the relations of human beings to each other, but also their relation to the universe in which they find themselves and to the forces governing it. Although the discussion that follows first brings out the cruelty apparently inherent in the parent's right to exercise power over the child, and then tries to show how the cruelty is transmuted as it is subsumed into a larger vision, it is not intended to suggest that Chaucer propels his reader by ineluctable logic from "problems" to "answers." Taken together, these tales do not suggest a debate with a formal resolution, but an extended and extendable meditation on different manifestations of a mystery – the mystery of the relation between power and love. This mystery is explored within the context of another – the mystery of kinship. Kinship not only binds human beings to each other, it also links them with the God who became kin to them in the Incarnation. To use the parent-child image to express man's relation to God is therefore to invoke more than the idea of dependence alone. Some comments made by Peter Dronke in a different context are also relevant here: "Children not only depend on their parents for existence, they resemble their parents, and are a continuation of their parents in time." The children of a divine father, therefore, are "god-like"; "they are theophanies."[2] Chaucer's stories are founded on the assumption that such a revelation

1 For a more general treatment, see Derek S. Brewer, "Children in Chaucer," in Brewer, *Tradition and Innovation in Chaucer* (London, 1982), 46–53.

2 Dronke, *Fabula: Explorations in the Uses of Myth in Medieval Platonism* (Leiden, 1974), 113.

works in both directions: if these stories make manifest a god-like dimension within ordinary human existence, it is also true that in the story embodying the central Christian mystery – the Crucifixion – certain human potentialities find their fullest expression and most meaningful place. In stressing the divine resonances of these tales of Chaucer, therefore, I am not in any way claiming that their "real" subject is the divine, that they are mere vehicles for the rehearsal of Christian truths. Rather, they seek to penetrate a fundamental experience that generates both secular legend and Christian gospel, and which is common to both man and God.

Chaucer's most moving presentation of the father-child relationship is the story told in the *Monk's Tale* of Ugolino di Pisa ("Erl Hugelin of Pize"), who was shut up with his children in a tower by his enemy, archbishop Ruggieri, and starved to death. As Chaucer himself indicates (2459–62), his authority for this story was Dante, who has Ugolino describe his cruel end in canto 33 of the *Inferno.*[3] Dante's Ugolino tells how his children begged him for bread – echoing, as Piero Boitani has suggested, the prayer daily addressed by men to their heavenly father: "give us this day our daily bread."[4] Chaucer gives this prayer to one son in particular, a three-year-old child, and expands it to a whole stanza's length, increasing the pathos of the story through our sense of the father's helplessness in the face of this childish importunity. When the young child eventually dies, Ugolino gnaws his arms in the misery of his grief, and his children, misinterpreting this action as due to his hunger, beg him to eat their flesh rather than his own:

> "Fader, do nat so, allas,
> But rather ete the flessh upon us two.
> Oure flessh thow yaf us, taak oure flessh us fro,
> And ete inow." – Right thus they to him seide.
> And after that, withinne a day or two,
> They leide hem in his lappe adoun and deide. (2449–54)

The words of the children are based on those in Dante:

> "Padre, assai ci fia men doglia
> se tu mangi di noi: tu ne vestisti
> queste misere carni, e tu le spoglia." (*Inferno* XXXIII.61–3)

---

3 Chaucer's version of the story is compared with Dante's by Piero Boitani, "Two Versions of Tragedy: Ugolino and Hugelyn," in Boitani, *The Tragic and the Sublime in Medieval Literature* (Cambridge, 1989), 20–55.

4 Ibid., 36, 49–50.

["Father, it will be far less painful to us if you eat of us; you did clothe us with this wretched flesh, and do you strip us of it!"]

Behind these words (as Piero Boitani has likewise shown)[5] there lie the words of Job:

> Nudus egressus sum de utero matris meae, et nudus revertar illuc. Dominus dedit, Dominus abstulit; sicut Domino placuit, ita factum est. Sit nomen Domini benedictum. (Job 1:21)
>
> [Naked came I out of my mother's womb, and naked I shall return thither. The Lord gave, and the Lord has taken away; as it pleased the Lord, so was it done. Blessed be the name of the Lord.]

It is significant that these words are Job's response to the death of his children; expressing his simple resignation to the will of God, he recognizes that not even his children can be claimed as possessions to which he has a right. Chaucer was evidently alive to the reminiscence of Job at this point, because he made it even clearer in his own text; the clothing image, which Dante does not use quite as in Job, is left out, and instead the focus is entirely on Job's contrast between giving and taking away. But the expression of Job's resignation undergoes a strange inversion when thus set in the Ugolino story: instead of the father's acceptance of the loss of his children, we have the children accepting their own reabsorption into their father. It seems to be suggested that they are so much a mere continuation of him that he may consume them. The religious resonances of the story, which prompt us to see the human father in this tale as analogous with the divine father who gives and takes away fleshly life, thus raise a silent disquiet. Beneath the tender poignancy of this scene in Chaucer, as in Dante, there lurks a potential horror: the suggestion that the power of a father over his children may extend to a right to devour them, and furthermore, that such power may belong to the God who is daily addressed as "Our Father." The Christian God threatens to transform himself into the pagan god Saturn, the god who devoured his own children.

Chaucer completely omits any suggestion that Ugolino did in fact eat the bodies of his children before he died, and even in Dante this suggestion is merely implicit.[6] The image of the cruel father lurks like a shadow behind the *Monk's*

5 Ibid., 33–4, 52–3.

6 For the pointers to this implication in Dante's version, see Piero Boitani's *lectura* of Inferno XXXIII, in *Cambridge Readings in Dante's Comedy*, ed. Kenelm Foster and Patrick Boyde (Cambridge, 1981), 83–4. Rachel Jacoff outlines the history of objections to this interpretation, and convincingly accounts for the critical resistance to it; see "The Hermeneutics of Hunger," in *Speaking Images: Essays in Honor of V. A. Kolve*, ed. Robert F. Yeager and Charlotte Morse (Asheville, NC, 2001), 95–110.

Tale story, but it is only a shadow. In the *Man of Law's Tale*, however, there is a quite unambiguous sense of the suffering that can attend the subordination of child to parent. Constance, the central figure of the tale, expresses with pitiable clarity her grief at having to leave her home and marry a stranger in obedience to her father's will. Weeping, she commends to her father's and mother's "grace" their "wrecched child Custaunce," who will, she believes, never see them again.

> "Allas, unto the Barbre nacioun
> I moste anon, sin that it is youre wille!
> But Crist, that starf for oure redempcioun,
> So yeve me grace his hestes to fulfille.
> I, wrecche womman, no fors thogh I spille.
> Wommen are born to thraldom and penaunce,
> And to been under mannes governaunce." (281–7)

Constance's words on the destiny of women are based on God's decree that as a punishment for eating the apple, Eve and her daughters should suffer the enmity of the serpent, the pains of childbirth, and subjection to the domination of men (Genesis 3:15–16). It is the prospect of being "bounde" under the "subjeccioun" of her new husband that stimulates Constance's sorrow (267–71). The key words she chooses to articulate her experience of this "subjeccioun" are "thraldom" and "governaunce." To understand the implications of these terms, it is necessary to realize that it is not women alone who are under "governaunce," or who experience bewilderment and misery at the forms it takes. In his translation of the *Consolation of Philosophy*, Chaucer consistently uses the verb "govern," and its associates "government," "governor," and "governaunce," to indicate the subordination of mankind to God. Boethius's initial outbursts against God are a passionate accusation of *mis*governaunce, as can be seen from the following example:

> "O thou governour, governynge alle thynges by certein ende, whi refusestow oonly to governe the werkes of men by duwe manere? Why suffrestow that slydynge Fortune turneth so grete enterchaungynges of thynges? So that anoyous peyne, that scholde duweliche punysche felons, punysscheth innocentz; ... Thow governour, withdraugh and restreyne the ravysschynge flodes, and fastne and ferme thise erthes stable with thilke boonde by which thou governest the hevene that is so large." (I m.5, 31–7, 54–8)

In answer to Boethius's complaint, Philosophy works to demonstrate that God "governeth alle thinges by the keye of his goodnesse," and that "we foolis that reprehenden wikkidly the thinges that touchin Godis governaunce, we aughten ben asschamid of ourself (III pr.12, 87–8, 126–9). To show how Philosophy establishes the benign character of this "governaunce" would mean summarizing the whole of the *Consolation*, but it is important in this context to note that in celebrating God's role as creator and regulator of the cosmos, she conceives this role as that of a father.

> "O thow Fadir, soowere and creatour of hevene and of erthes, that governest this world by perdurable resoun, that comaundest the tymes to gon from syn that age hadde bygynnynge; thow that duellest thiselve ay stedefast and stable, and yevest alle othere thynges to ben meved, ne foreyne causes necesseden the nevere to compoune werk of floterynge matere, but oonly the forme of sovereyn good iset within the withoute envye, that moevede the frely." (III m.9, 1–11)

The word "governaunce" thus constantly carries a Boethian colouring in Chaucer; even when it denotes human domination or power, it connotes the greater power of God over his creation. This connotation may be used seriously: it may lead us to see human authority as the copy, and the agent, of God's. So women attract attention because their subjection to male "governaunce" is a model of the human subjection to God.

The word may, however, be used ironically, in such a way that it leads us to reflect on the vain pretensions of men to be in control of their world. The same double possibility of seriousness or irony applies to two other self-consciously Boethian words which Chaucer frequently rhymes with "governaunce": "purveiaunce" and "ordinaunce." It is the ironic possibility that is realized, for example, in the lines describing the preparations made by Constance's father for her wedding:

> Now wolde som men waiten, as I gesse,
> That I sholde tellen all the purveiaunce
> That th'Emperour, of his grete noblesse,
> Hath shapen for his doghter, dame Custaunce.
> Wel may men knowe that so greet ordinaunce
> May no man tellen in a litel clause,
> As was arrayed for so heigh a cause. (246–52)

The "purveiaunce" and "ordinaunce" with which God disposes the cosmos are here shrunk so as to refer only to the provision of material comforts and a retinue, and the shrinking is a measure of the circumscribed area within which human, as opposed to divine, power can operate.

The word "governaunce" in Constance's speech cannot, however, be interpreted in quite this way. Constance's utterance is an expression of resignation, so that her view of "governaunce" cannot be explained away as stemming from the kind of impatience initially expressed by Boethius. But neither can it be aligned with the benign view of "governaunce" in Philosophy's hymn. Constance's experience leads her to equate "governaunce" with "thraldom and penaunce." The "mannes governaunce" to whose "subjeccioun" she is bound is not only that of her future husband, but also that of her father, as her words make clear ("Allas, unto the Barbre nacioun / I moste anon, *sin that it is youre wille!*"). The use of the Boethian "purveiaunce" and "ordinaunce" presents the Emperor as a kind of mock-God, wielding power within his small domain; Constance's helplessness before her father's will follows the pattern of human helplessness before the will of the divine father. She is sent forth into "hethenesse" as the soul is exiled on earth, separated from its true heavenly home – a conception that Chaucer would also have found in Boethius (I pr.5; IV m.l). Through Constance's experience, the *Man of Law's Tale* invests the concept of "subjeccioun" to a higher "governaunce" with a sense of poignancy and bewilderment.

As a natural corollary of this, Philosophy's vision of the harmonious motions of the universe, expressed in her hymn to God as father and governor, gives way to an astonishing vision of the cosmos which presents an unnatural cruelty as fundamental to its structure and operation. It is a vision that arises from Chaucer's description of the malignant stellar influence blighting Constance's wedding.

O Firste Moeving, cruel firmament!
With thy diurnal sweigh that crowdest ay
And hurlest al from est til occident
That naturelly wolde holde another way,
Thy crowding set the hevene in swich array
At the biginning of this fiers viage,
That cruel Mars hath slain this mariage.

Infortunat ascendent tortuous,
Of which the lord is helplees falle, allas,
Out of his angle into the derkest hous!
O Mars, o atazir, as in this cas!
O fieble moone, unhappy been thy pas!
Thou knittest thee ther thow art nat received;
Ther thow were wel, fro thennes artow weived.

Imprudent Emperour of Rome, allas!
Was ther no philosophre in al thy toun? (295–310)

These stanzas refer to the contradictory motions within the cosmos, as its operations were conceived in the Middle Ages. Whereas the natural movement of the planets was from West to East, they were daily dragged from East to West by the superior force of the Primum Mobile, the "Firste Moeving" sphere which lay beyond the planetary spheres. Consequently, the planets managed to win back in the course of a year only a small degree of advancement in the direction of their natural movement, which acted as resistance to this "crowding." Although this cosmological model was developed to provide a quite neutral scientific explanation of physical phenomena, numerous medieval writers – including some known to Chaucer, such as Alan of Lille and Dante – gave it a moral or emotional colouring. But in doing so, they usually interpreted the subjection of the planets to the Primum Mobile as a *good* thing; Alan, for example, saw it as an analogue to the subjection of the senses to reason. So far as I know, Chaucer is the *only* medieval writer to use this cosmological model as an image of violence and unnaturalness at the core of the universe's movement, or to call the Primum Mobile "cruel."[7] A hint of the idea is there, perhaps, in Chaucer's translation of Boethius' complaint, which emphasizes the irresistible force to which the heavens are subject ("O thow makere of the wheel that bereth the sterres ... and turnest the hevene with a *ravysschynge* sweighe, and *constreynest* the sterres to *suffren* thi lawe ..."; I m.5, 1–5), but the complaint as a whole contrasts the order of the heavens with the disorder of human life, and does not link the anarchy of human existence with a cosmic derangement.

In both human and cosmological terms, then, the *Man of Law's Tale* raises in painful clarity the question of the nature of the "subjeccioun" in which mankind finds itself bound. The question it poses is: are we God's children, or his thralls? Is his "governaunce" the loving control of a father, or the arbitrary tyranny of a despot?

In answering this question, Chaucer has recourse to two principal motifs. The first is one that I would call the motif of the "enthralled lord" – a motif which is apparent in the frequent use of images that suggest a *chain* of

7 See Alan of Lille, *De Planctu Naturae*, prose 3, ed. Nikolaus M. Häring, *Studi medievali*, 3rd ser. 19.2 (1978), 797–879, at 826–7; Alan of Lille, *Distinctiones dictionum theologicalium*, s.v. *Mundus*, *PL* 210, col. 866. Dante's clearest exposition of the function of the Primum Mobile is given in *Convivio* II.xiv, where it is compared, in its ordering function, to the science of moral philosophy. For further references to the development of the tradition, see John Freccero, "Pilgrim in a Gyre," in Freccero, *Dante: The Poetics of Conversion* (Cambridge, MA, 1986), 70–92; and A.B. Chambers, "Goodfriday, 1613. Riding Westward: The Poem and the Tradition," *ELH* 28 (1961): 31–53. The starting point for the development of the idea of the dual motion in the medieval West was the passage in Plato's *Timaeus* on the Demiurge's creation of the world through the contrasting motions of the Same and the Different (see the Latin translation by Calcidius, ed. J.H. Waszink [London, 1962], 28–9 [36B–7C]) – and it is this Platonic idea that is reflected in Lady Philosophy's account of the "moevynge into two rowndes" by which the world-soul "gooth to torne ayen to hymself" in her hymn to God the Creator (III m.9, 28–30).

command. Two such images have already passed before us. The first is Constance's father, whose power, as it turns out, is subordinate to the influence of the planets, which make a mockery of his "purveiaunce." But what is strange about the stanzas describing this planetary influence is that they emphasize the impotence of the planets at the same time as they complain about their power. The lord of the ascendant – the dominant planet in any conjunction, as the very name suggests – "is helplees falle"; the moon is "fieble." The planetary influence which blights Constance's wedding operates, as we have seen, under the greater influence of the Primum Mobile. Both the Emperor and the planets, then, at first look like figures of authority but turn out to be figures of subordination; they are what we might call "enthralled lords."

There are numerous other examples of such "enthralled lords" in the tale; for example, Alla's constable, who exerts the authority of his office over Constance, sending her back out to sea, but who laments the fact that he is compelled to do so by a higher authority – and in doing so, significantly, echoes Boethius's central question about the just "governaunce" of the universe.

> "O mighty God, if that it be thy wille,
> Sith thow art rightful juge, how may it be
> That thow wolt suffren innocentz to spille,
> And wikked folk regne in prosperitee?
> O goode Custaunce, allas, so wo is me,
> That I moot be thy tormentour, or deye
> On shames deeth; ther is noon oother weye." (813–19)

It might be objected that the tale offers examples of the untrammelled exercise of power, in the two mothers-in-law who usurp male "governaunce" and insist on bending events to their own will. The mother of Constance's first husband, the Sultan, vigorously asserts her own will, rejecting "thraldom and penaunce" in words that are a deliberate echo of and contrast with Constance's resignation (337–40). Yet her independence is a delusion; she too is subject to a greater power, which uses her as a mere instrument, as Chaucer's comment makes clear.

> O Sathan, envious sin thilke day
> That thow were chaced from oure heritage,
> Wel knowestow to wommen the olde way!
> Thow madest Eva bringe us in servage.
> Thou wolt fordoon this Cristen mariage.
> Thin instrument – so weilawey the while! –
> Makestow of wommen, whan thou wolt bigile. (365–71)

By the same token, Donegild's "tyrannye" (779) leads to her own death, not Constance's; the extent of her "ordinaunce" (805) is as circumscribed as the Emperor's.

If the figures of evil are instruments of Satan, Constance is the instrument of Christ. We can see this instrumentality in, for example, Chaucer's account of Hermengild's conversion to Christianity:

> This constable, and dame Hermengild his wif,
> Were payens, and that contree everywhere.
> But Hermengild loved hire right as hir lif,
> And Custaunce hath so longe sojourned there,
> In orisons, with many a bitter teere,
> Til Jesu hath converted thurgh his grace
> Dame Hermengild, constablesse of that place. (533–9)

Almost imperceptibly, the subject of the sentence shifts from Constance to Jesus, so that her role, while essential, is felt as mediatory; Jesus works through her. The same pattern is repeated in the account of Hermengild's healing of the blind man:

> "In name of Crist," cride this blinde Britoun,
> "Dame Hermengild, yif me my sighte again!"
> This lady weex affrayed of the soun,
> Lest that hir housbonde, shortly for to sayn,
> Wolde hire for Jesu Cristes love han slain;
> Til Custaunce made hire boold, and bad hire wirche
> The wil of Crist, as doghter of his chirche.
>
> The constable weex abasshed of that sight,
> And seide, "What amounteth al this fare?"
> Custaunce answerde, "Sire, it is Cristes might,
> That helpeth folk out of the feendes snare." (561–71)

The actual cure seems to take place between the stanzas, so that Chaucer need not commit himself to a sentence which presents Hermengild as the sole performer of the action. Her healing power is exerted in obedience to Constance's command, and as a manifestation of Christ's will. But Christ's power is transmitted through a filial relation; it is as "doghter of his chirche" that she can do His will. Equally significantly, it is as "doghter of holy chirche" that Constance is defended from false accusation by the divine voice (675).

This brings us to the second motif by which Chaucer explores the question of "governaunce" – the motif of parenthood and childhood. It is a motif which can intertwine with the first, as we can see in Constance's prayer to Mary to save her from false condemnation:

"... thow, merciful maide,
Marye I mene, doghter to Seint Anne,
Biforn whos child aungeles singe Osanne,
If I be giltlees of this felonye,
My socour be, for ellis shal I die!" (640–4)

The dual presentation of Mary as mother and daughter is a reminder that every parent is also a child; we can thus perceive one possible fusion of authority and subservience. But in order to understand the full intertwining of the two motifs, we need to explore further the nature of parental "governaunce." The cruel effect of the Emperor's "governaunce" we have already noted, but there are far crueller images in the malevolent mothers of Constance's two husbands, the first of whom goes so far as to murder her own son. Satan, himself banished from the "heritage" (366) which has been transferred to mankind, the "sons of adoption," works through women, his instrument and traditional object of malice, to destroy the hereditary links of family love.[8] The cruel parent can create a cruel child: when Alla discovers his mother's treachery, he has her put to death. But Alla himself offers a more complicated and interesting image of parenthood, since he *appears* to be a cruel parent; the letter forged by his mother makes it appear that he has ordered his newborn son to be cast on to the mercy of the waves with Constance. Constance's lament to her little child, as she walks to the boat that is to take her out to sea, focusses on this paternal cruelty:

"O litel child, allas, what is thy gilt,
That nevere wroghtest sinne as yet, pardee?
Why wil thin harde fader han thee spilt?
O mercy, deere constable," quod she,
"As lat my litel child dwelle here with thee!
And if thou darst noght saven him, for blame,
So kis him ones in his fadres name!"

Therwith she looked bakward to the londe,
And seide, "Farewel, housbonde routhelees!" (855–63)

8 See Galatians 4:5 for the link between sonship and inheritance, and the idea of man's "adoption."

Against this image of the cruel father, Constance's opening appeal to the Virgin, which aligns her suffering with Mary's, sets an image of maternal tenderness.

"Moder," quod she, "and maide bright, Marye,
Sooth is that thurgh wommans eggement
Mankinde was lorn, and dampned ay to die,
For which thy child was on a crois yrent.
Thy blisful eyen sawe al his torment;
Thanne is ther no comparison bitwene
Thy wo, and any wo man may sustene.

"Thow saw thy child yslain bifore thine eyen,
And yet now liveth my litel child, parfay.
Now lady bright, to whom alle woful cryen,
Thow glorye of wommanhod, thow faire may,
Thow haven of refut, brighte sterre of day,
Rewe on my child, that of thy gentillesse
Rewest on every reweful in distresse." (841–54)

Constance's words assume the identity of mother and child in suffering; they also provide the basis for generalizing this experience, by assuming a similar identity of pain between sufferer and beholder, founded on pity – the bond between "every reweful" and those who "rewe" being indicated by the verbal echo itself.[9] Behind Constance's words stirs memory of the words spoken to Mary by Simeon at the Presentation in the Temple: "Yea, a sword shall pierce through thy own soul also" (Luke 2:35).

The parallel of Constance's experience with Mary's even greater suffering makes us aware of the disturbing fact that Constance's plaintive question to her child – "Why wil thin harde father han thee spilt?" – is one that could have been addressed to Jesus by Mary at the Crucifixion. Alla's cruelty is, as we know, only apparent; he has not, in fact, ordered his child's death. But what about God? Is he not a father who *did* slay his own son? This idea was by no means "unthinkable" in fourteenth-century England: Langland speaks of laymen who presume to discuss theology, and "tellen ... of þe Trinite hou two slowe þe thridde."[10] But merely to pose this

9 For further discussion of the role of "pitee" in these tales, see Jill Mann, *Feminizing Chaucer* (Cambridge, 2002), 108–10, 112, 114–15, 119. The medieval Latin word "pietas" captures the link between the notions of "compassion" and "family feeling."

10 This phrase is in both the A version (XI.40) and the C version (XI.37) of *Piers Plowman*, but it has been smoothed away in the manuscripts of B, doubtless because it was found too shocking. See A.V.C. Schmidt, *William Langland. Piers Plowman: A Parallel-Text Edition of the A, B, C and Z Versions*, vol. I (London, 1995).

question is to realize its inevitable answer, and to realize the point to which the tale's exploration of "governaunce" and "subjeccioun" has led – a point at which the two motifs we have been tracing make their most significant fusion. For God the Father *is* God the Son; he both ordains the suffering and suffers. The identity of parent and child in suffering takes on in him an utterly complete and utterly literal realization. As we move up through the "chain of command" in the cosmos, and find that every exercise of power is subject to higher control, we increasingly come to feel that the final responsibility for the "governaunce" of the world and its cruel consequences must rest with God – but when we reach the top of the chain of command we find that we are immediately returned to the bottom again. God is the last in the line of "enthralled lords." The God to whose "governaunce" creation is subject enters his own creation and becomes subject to the "governaunce" of his creatures.[11] To translate this perception into the terms of the *Monk's Tale*, it is not God who eats the bodies of his children, but his children who in the Eucharist eat the body of their father and receive life from it.

The *Man of Law's Tale* ends, fittingly enough, with the moving reunion between Constance and her father – a reunion which is, significantly, prepared for by the revivification of the image of the lost daughter in her father, through sight of her son. But this family reunion does not mark the end of Chaucer's exploration of the theme of parents and children; this tale is only one of the possible narrative structures through which we can try to understand the mysterious relationship between suffering and a benevolent providence, the apparently cruel operations of omnipotent love. Another image of paternal cruelty is offered in the *Physician's Tale.* Again, however, the cruelty is apparent. Virginius kills his daughter because it is the only way to save her from the plots of Apius, who desires to enjoy her sexually. The tale is briefly told, and its focal point is undoubtedly the poignant exchange between Virginius and Virginia in which he tells her she must die, and in which the tragic conflict between action and feeling is stressed by the insistent repetition of "father" and "doghter." Virginius is another "enthralled lord"; he expresses the agony of being compelled to be his daughter's executioner:

> "Doghter," quod he, "Virginia, by thy name,
> Ther been two weyes, outher deeth or shame,
> That thou most suffre – allas, that I was bore!

11 Cf. G.K. Chesterton's comments on Chaucer's entry into his own creation, the *Canterbury Tales* (*Chaucer* [London, 1932; repr. 1962], 21–2); Jill Mann, "The Authority of the Audience in Chaucer," 116 above, and *Feminizing Chaucer*, 98–9.

For nevere thow deservedest wherfore
To dien with a swerd or with a knif.
O deere doghter, endere of my lif,
Which I have fostred up with swich plesaunce
That thou were nevere out of my remembraunce,
O doghter, which that art my laste wo,
And in my lif my laste joye also,
O gemme of chastitee, in pacience
Tak thow thy deeth, for this is my sentence." (213–24)

The tale shows us that the Marian experience expressed in the words "a sword shall pierce through thy own soul also" is not an exclusively feminine one, by echoing those words in the description of Virginius "With fadres pitee stikinge thurgh his herte" (211). The mother is absent from the scene, and cruelty and pity are lodged in the same parent. And this time, the cruelty is seen as an *expression* of the "pitee":

"For love, and nat for hate, thow most be deed;
My pitous hand moot smiten of thin heed." (225–6)

The tale also offers another variation on the theme of "thraldom." Apius bribes Claudius into claiming in his court that Virginia is not Virginius's "doghter" (187), but a "thral" of Claudius who has been stolen away from him (183, 189), hoping thus to win her away from her father's custody. Virginius thus kills his daughter to save her from "thraldom"; the struggle over Virginia is precisely a struggle over whether she shall be daughter or thrall. Virginia herself chooses to die as a daughter rather than to live as the thrall of Apius:

She riseth up, and to hir fader saide,
"Blessed be God that I shal die a maide!
Yif me my deeth, er that I have a shame.
Dooth with youre child youre wil, a Goddes name!" (247–50)

Her submission to her father's will matches the resignation of Ugolino's sons.

Whereas the *Physician's Tale* simplifies the family to father and daughter, the *Prioress's Tale* simplifies it to mother and son, since the mother of the little boy who is its central figure is a widow. The emphasis all the way through the tale is on motherhood. The *Prologue* is addressed to Mary as mother of Christ. The little boy learns to sing the antiphon *O alma redemptoris* because it celebrates "Cristes moder," and he sings it as he goes to and from school each day because

"On Cristes moder set was his entente" (538, 550). After he has been murdered by the Jews, the anguish of his mother as she searches for him prompts her to appeal to Mary for help:

> With modres pitee in hir brest enclosed,
> She gooth, as she were half out of hir minde,
> To every place wher she hath supposed
> By liklihede hir litel child to finde;
> And evere on Cristes moder meke and kinde
> She cride, and at the laste thus she wroghte:
> Among the cursed Jewes she him soghte. (593–9)

The mother's agony as she searches for her child is subtly reminiscent of the anxiety of Mary and Joseph, seeking for their lost son while he argues with the doctors in the Temple (Luke 2:48); and this raises, again like a shadow, the possibility of another variation in the parent-child theme – that the parent may be abandoned by the child (as God is by his children).[12] But the last line of the stanza brings the widow nearer to Mary's experience at the Crucifixion; it is the Jews who are responsible for the murder of her son as of Mary's. The image of the bereaved mother is multiplied in the tale; its constant echoes of the Mass for the Holy Innocents recall the grief of the mothers of the children slain for the sake of Mary's child.[13] Those mothers are themselves the fulfilment of Jeremiah's prophecy of the voice that is to be heard in Rama, "Rachel weeping for her children" (Jer. 31: 15; Matt. 2:18), and Chaucer refers to the widow as "this newe Rachel" (627). The chorus of lamenting mothers stretches from the Old Testament through the New to the world of present experience, embracing human and divine in a single experience of pain.

The boy's body is eventually found because, miraculously, he continues to sing *O alma redemptoris* after death, and he explains to the abbot who questions him that Jesus allows this miracle "for the worship of his moder deere" (654). Mary, he says, had come to him and laid a seed on his tongue, bidding him sing until it was removed.

---

12 I am grateful to Loretta Minghella, a former student at Clare College, Cambridge, for this suggestion.

13 See Marie Padgett Hamilton, "Echoes of Childermas in the Tale of the Prioress," in *Chaucer: Modern Essays in Criticism*, ed. Edward Wagenknecht (New York, 1959), 88–97.

"And after that thus seide she to me:
'My litel child, now wol I fecche thee
Whan that the grein is fro thy tonge ytake.
Be nat agast, I wol thee nat forsake.'" (667–9)

The death of the child is thus represented as the entry into relationship with a new mother – a mother, who, unlike the father to whom is addressed the cry "My God, my God, why hast thou forsaken me?" will not forsake her child.[14] The absence of the father in this tale is in fact an important element in its structure. The world of the tale is a world of women and children. The absence of any father, human or divine, allows concentration on the tenderness that binds mother and son; the mother's tender protectiveness for the weakness of childhood is matched by the grown-up son's tender reverence for the relative weakness of womanhood – a reciprocity which is expressed in visual art by the balancing of Madonna and Child with the Coronation of the Virgin. But this isolation of mother and child raises also, I think, something like a yearning for the presence of a strong, protective father who might act as a powerful opponent of Satan and his human instruments, in this case not women but the Jews. Transferred on to the divine level, we can see that this yearning could easily become a sense of indignation that the father had forsaken mother and child, had withdrawn his protective power; there exists here the possibility of the same questioning of God's cruelty as in the *Man of Law's Tale*. But here, as in the *Man of Law's Tale*, the counter to this indignation is the tale's demonstration of the *power* of helpless innocence. The comment on the miracle focuses on this:

O grete God, that parfournest thy laude
By mouth of innocentz, lo here thy might! (607–8)

And in the *Prioress's Prologue*, where the father is briefly introduced, it is as one subject to the compelling power of innocence, who is "ravished" by Mary's humility (469).

The miraculous power of weakness and suffering is even more profoundly demonstrated in the *Clerk's Tale*. In the *Man of Law's Tale*, the cruelty of the father, Alla, turned out to be merely apparent. In the *Clerk's Tale*, Walter's

14 Matt. 27:46; Mark 15:34. Cf. Piero Boitani's comments on Dante's evocation of this cry in the Ugolino episode (*Cambridge Readings*, 82–3).

behaviour to his children is also, in one sense, only apparently cruel, since he does not kill them, as Griselda believes, but sends them away to be brought up by his sister, and later returns them to her. Walter is not, however, innocent of cruelty in the same sense that Alla is; he really is cruel to his wife and children. He *claims* to be an "enthralled lord," acting under compulsion, but his words are a hollow parody of the speeches of Alla's constable or Virginius, where both the compulsion and the grief are genuine. His claim that "in gret lordshipe ... / Ther is gret servitute," and that he "may nat do as every plowman may" (797–9) fits into the pattern established by other examples of the fusion of "governaunce" and "subjeccioun" only as a perverted mimicry of them, since it is not true that his people object to Griselda as their mistress, and it is the dictates of his own will to test her that he is following. Similarly, the servant who protests that he is acting under orders, when removing Griselda's children, is a debased parallel to Alla's constable. But in a different way, Walter really is an "enthralled lord," as well as pretending to be one. He is a victim of his own obsessive desire, as Chaucer makes clear in describing it:

> But ther been folk of swich condicioun,
> That whan they have a certein purpos take,
> They kan nat stinte of hire entencioun,
> But right as they were bounden to a stake,
> They wol nat of that firste purpos slake.
> Right so, this markis fulliche hath purposed
> To tempte his wif, as he was first disposed. (701–7)

There is nothing in Chaucer's source, the Latin tale of Petrarch, corresponding to the words "as they were bounden to a stake." Walter is "bounden" to his cruel obsession; appearing to enjoy complete independence, he is in fact helplessly enslaved to his own will. Griselda, in contrast, turns "subjeccioun" into "governaunce" by the complete absorption of her vow to be obedient to Walter into her own will:

> "This wil is in min herte and ay shal be;
> No lengthe of time or deth may this deface,
> Ne chaunge my corage to another place." (509–11)

And if Walter is bound by his own will, he is liberated from it by Griselda's patience. The miracle of the tale is that Walter's apparently endless desire to test Griselda does in fact come to an end, that her apparently helpless suffering inexorably breaks down his will to inflict torment.

In examining this suffering more closely, we should begin by noting that for the first time in the tales we have been examining, we have an apparently cruel mother. The critics who complain of Griselda's "unfeeling" relinquishment of her children are in fact focusing, albeit uncomprehendingly, on one of the problems that the tale exists to contemplate. Chaucer's awareness of this possible interpretation of Griselda's behaviour is made clear in the way he carefully points out that Walter would have thought this himself if he had not known of her love for her children (688–93). It is faith – the trust in the constants of characteristics, rather than external behaviour – that counteracts the outward image of cruelty. Walter's faith in Griselda's continuing love for her children convinces him that her obedience is not merely inertia, and enables him finally to abandon the test and restore her children. It is her own "benignity" that, unconsciously, she meets and reaps in the joy of her reunion with her children:

> "O tendre, o deere, o yonge children mine,
> Youre woful moder wende stedfastly
> That cruel houndes, or som foul vermine,
> Hadde eten yow; but God, of his mercy,
> And youre benigne fader tendrely
> Hath doon yow kept!" – and in that same stounde
> Al sodeinly she swapte adoun to grounde. (1093–9)

But Griselda's faith in Walter as "benigne fader" is more difficult to maintain than his belief in her as benign mother. And the difficulty is again a measure of the difficulty in maintaining belief in the benign nature of God's "governaunce." The final stanzas of the tale parallel Griselda's position in relation to Walter with the human position in relation to God.

> For, sith a womman was so pacient
> Unto a mortal man, wel moore us oghte
> Receiven al in gree that God us sent.
> For greet skile is, he preve that he wroghte;
> But he ne tempteth no man that he boghte,
> As seyth Seint Jame, if ye his pistel rede;
> He preveth folk al day, it is no drede,
>
> And suffreth us, as for oure excercise,
> With sharpe scourges of adversitee
> Ful ofte to be bete in sondry wise;
> Nat for to knowe oure wil, for certes he,
> Er we were born, knew al oure freletee.
> And for oure beste is al his governance;
> Lat us thanne live in vertuous suffrance. (1149–62)

It would seem, once again, that the only role allowed to mankind is the patient "suffrance" of God's "governance," whether its results are cruel or beneficent.

Yet, as I have already suggested, it is the power of "suffrance" that the tale exists to represent. It is a power that the Crucifixion evidences. And the words in which Griselda refers to the Crucifixion show how the problem of the apparent cruelty of the father is answered on a divine level, as in the *Man of Law's Tale*, by the identification of father and son; when bidding her daughter farewell "in hire benigne vois," she says

"Farewel, my child! I shal thee nevere see.
But sith I thee have marked with the crois
Of thilke fader – blessed mote he be –
That for us deide upon a crois of tree,
Thy soule, litel child, I him bitake,
For this night shaltow dien for my sake." (555–60)

She does not refer – as she most naturally might – to the Son who died for us, but to the Father who died for us.[15] The oddity of phrasing draws attention, once again, to the fact that God's role embraces that of both father and child; his cruelty is visited on himself. Like Chaucer's Ugolino, who gnaws his own arm, he eats himself rather than his children. The human follows the pattern of the divine; Griselda's "this night shaltow dien for my sake" places her own child's suffering in line with Christ's, as well as aligning her own parental sorrow with that of God the Father.

But Griselda's suffering is also Christ-like. The profundity of its resonances is established, first, by the linking of Griselda's resignation with Job's. The same speech of Job that lies behind the words of the children in the Ugolino story is echoed in her words to Walter:[16]

"Naked out of my fadres hous," quod she,
"I cam, and naked moot I turne again.
Al youre plesance wol I folwen fain." (871–2)

And she is explicitly linked with Job by the stanza claiming that even his "humblesse" is outstripped by that of women (932–8). It is relevant here that the suffering of Job was interpreted in the Middle Ages as a type of the suffering

15 I am grateful to Lars Engle for first drawing my attention to this.

16 It was Petrarch who introduced the echo of Job into Griselda's words at this point; see *Sources and Analogues of the Canterbury Tales*, ed. Robert M. Correale and Mary Hamel, 2 vols (Cambridge, 2002–5) 1:125/320.

of Christ. In late medieval art the type-figure known as "Christus im Elend" represents Christ in the attitude of Job on his dunghill.[17] And Griselda too can be seen as a type of Christ. Pondering the apparent invitation at the end of the tale to equate God's role with Walter's, we can see that this is, in fact, appropriate only so far as the apparent cruelty of the divine father is concerned; if we plumb appearances, as the tale prompts us to do, we see that it is Griselda who offers a far truer and profounder image of divine suffering. It is her experience that gives depth of meaning of the Clerk's statement that God

> suffreth us, as for oure excercise,
> With sharpe scourges of adversitee
> Ful ofte to be bete in sondry wise. (1156–9)

The evocation of Christ's physical suffering which is made by Griselda's experience causes us to link the noun "suffrance" at the end of the last stanza back to the verb "suffreth" at the beginning, and to give the latter a new meaning. God not only "suffers" in the sense of "allowing," he also suffers in the simplest sense, the experience of pain. And it is precisely the identity of father and child that leads to the fusion of the two kinds of "suffering." Chaucer must, we realize, have pondered the deeper implications of the word he chose to translate Boethius's questions in the passage I quoted earlier: "Why *suffrestow* that slydynge Fortune turneth so grete enterchaungynges of thynges ... ?" For God to "allow" the world to be as it is, is for God to suffer, to endure its cruelties as their victim.

Julian of Norwich identifies the nature of the second Person of the Trinity with "moderhed." The identification is made, first, on the basis of mercy, the quality that characterizes both Christ and mothers. But it is also made on the basis of suffering, and in particular, the suffering undergone in childbirth, as Julian shows in a passage that exploits as Chaucer does the ambiguity in the Middle English word "suffer." Its sharply physical sense is uppermost in the fusion of the Passion with the pains of childbirth:

> Thus he sustaineth us within him in love, and traveyled into the full time that he wolde suffer the sharpest throwes and the grevousest paines that ever were or ever shalle be, and died at the last. And whan he had done, and so borne us to blisse, yet might not all this make aseeth to his mervelous love.[18]

17 See G. von der Osten, "Job and Christ: The Development of a Devotional Image," *Journal of the Warburg and Courtauld Institutes* 16 (1953): 153–8.

18 *The Writings of Julian of Norwich*, ed. Nicholas Watson and Jacqueline Jenkins (University Park, PA, 2006), *A Revelation of Love* (= Long Text), chapter 60, 17–21.

And it is the testimony of love in this suffering which provides the assurance that the second kind of "suffering" carries with it the first:

> The kinde, loving moder that woot and knoweth the neede of her childe, she kepith it full tenderly, as the kinde and condition of moderhed will. And ever as it waxeth in age and in stature, she changeth her werking, but not her loue. And when it is wexid of more age, she suffereth it that it be chastised in breking downe of vicis, to make the childe to receive vertues and grace. [19]

To speak of human beings as God's children is a cliché, but it is less usual to think of them as brought to birth in pain. For Chaucer, as for Julian, however, this idea is crucial. It is childbirth that determines the nature of the mother's role, and founds it in a different experience from that of the father – that is, the experience of pain. And Chaucer is like Julian too in seeing in childbirth a powerful image of "suffraunce" in both its senses, "suffering" and "allowing." One of his most hauntingly enigmatic alterations of Petrarch's Latin story is Griselda's response to the command that she relinquish her second child. In Petrarch, she adds to her acquiescence the comment: "nor do I have any part in these children beyond the bearing of them" ("neque ... in hiis filiis quicquam habeo preter laborem").[20] In the *Clerk's Tale*, Griselda's words, though close, are subtly different:

> I have nat had no part of children tweine
> But first, siknesse, and after, wo and peine. (650–1)

Chaucer's addition – the reference to "siknesse," "wo and peine" – is a deliberate reminder of the pain of childbirth. Brief though it is, the reminder gives a reality to the experience which enables us to link it with Griselda's "suffraunce," and thus, through her, with God's.

There is a similarly brief but suggestive hint in the line describing Constance's pregnancy in the *Man of Law's Tale*: "She halt hir chambre, abiding Cristes wille" (721) – Christ's will, not her own or her husband's. The woman in childbirth is necessarily passive; she allows herself to become the instrument of a process, the vehicle of a power she cannot initiate and can control only by

19 Ibid., chapter 60, 45–9. On the medieval tradition of "Christ as mother," see *A Book of Showings to the Anchoress Julian of Norwich*, ed. Edmund Colledge and James Walsh (2 vols, Toronto, 1978), introduction, 1:150–5, and Caroline Walker Bynum, *Jesus as Mother* (London, 1982), 110–69.

20 Correale and Hamel, eds, *Sources and Analogues*, 1:121/249.

full acceptance of and identification with it. In Chaucer's tales, childbirth can thus become an image of the necessary surrender of the self to an external will, to a larger "governaunce," and in doing so it shows how the experience of child and parent can meet and become one, as they do in the God who is both Father and Son.

The childbirth which had seemed in Genesis merely punitive, a punishment for the sin in Paradise, thus finds a creative role – and by the same token, suggests one for human "suffrance." And just as there can be no control over the process of birth, so there can be no control over its result. The child is not the property of the parent. Beside the Job-like resignation of the children in the *Monk's Tale*, therefore, we may set the Job-like resignation of the parent in the *Clerk's Tale*:

> I have nat had no part of children tweine
> But first, siknesse, and after, wo and peine.

For Chaucer, the pains and resignation of childbirth are a model in which we can see and understand that an acknowledgment of powerlessness is a necessary accompaniment of the exercise of "governaunce," and in which we can see also the necessity for God to allow to his children their independent existence, whatever the pain he – and they – must then suffer.

Chapter Eight

Satisfaction and Payment in Middle English Literature

In the debate between the Four Daughters of God in Passus XVIII of *Piers Plowman*, Peace, in the course of justifying the redemption of man, describes the need for opposites to define each other. Without woe, we should not know the meaning of "weal"; without night, we should not be able to understand the meaning of "day." Just so, she concludes,

> "... til *modicum* mete with us, I may it wel avowe,
> Woot no wight, as I wene, what is ynogh to mene." (XVIII.215–16)[1]

It is the meaning of "enough" – more specifically, the meaning attached to the word in Middle English poetry – that I should like to explore in this paper. "Enough" is a simple, everyday word that is easily passed over, a prosaic word for a rather prosaic concept, we probably feel, thinking of the cautious, common-sense attitude expressed in such proverbial phrases as "Enough is enough," or "Moderation in all things." But in late medieval literature it becomes a poetic word, a word that vibrates with emotional and intellectual connotations, as a close examination of two texts in particular, *Pearl* and Chaucer's *Clerk's Tale*, will show.

An earlier version of this paper was delivered as the Tucker-Cruse Lecture at Bristol University in spring, 1982, and I gratefully acknowledge comments received on that occasion. The section devoted to the *Clerk's Tale* was delivered as the Annual Chaucer Lecture to the conference of the New Chaucer Society held in San Francisco in April, 1982. I am glad to have this opportunity of expressing my gratitude to Paul Ruggiers and the Society's Board of Trustees for inviting me to deliver this lecture and would also like to thank the participants in the conference for their comments.

1 William Langland, *The Vision of Piers Plowman: A Critical Edition of the B-Text*, 2nd ed., ed. A.V.C. Schmidt (London, 1995).

The term "enough," as the words of Peace make plain, makes sense only in relation to other terms, and setting out some of them will provide an appropriate framework for the analysis of these texts and a guide to their significant key words. In the first place, "enough" is, by definition, the midpoint between "too much" and "too little," or between "more" and "less." To locate and to adhere to this midpoint is, according to the *Nicomachean Ethics* of Aristotle, to achieve virtue; "vertu is the mene, / As Etik seith," as Chaucer puts it in the *Legend of Good Women* (F 165–6).[2] Obvious enough in itself, this observation is worth making because it alerts us to the less obvious need to bring other words into relation to the word "enough" by virtue of their grammatical forms, as well as by virtue of their meanings. The comparative forms of adjectives and adverbs assume importance because they represent a movement along the scale from "too little" to "too much"; they can serve as markers of an increase that may be an approach to satisfaction or an urge toward excess, and they likewise serve as markers of a decrease that may be a retreat to moderation or a lapse into deficiency. Superlatives too take on a special interest and have a particular ambivalence of their own. On the one hand, they seem to imply excess, in that they represent a movement beyond the midpoint represented by "enough." On the

2 John Livingston Lowes, "Chaucer's "Etik,"" *Modern Language Notes* 25 (1910): 87–8, claimed that Chaucer's reference is not to the Aristotelian *Nicomachean Ethics*; he drew attention to John of Salisbury's use of the term "ethicus" for writers of sententious tendency in general, and among them, Horace, one of whose recommendations to moderation is cited by John with the preface "ut enim ait ethicus" (*Policraticus* VIII.13, ed. C.J. Webb, 2 vols [Oxford, 1909] 2:317). Interesting as this suggestion is, it is a perhaps unnecessarily complicated way of accounting for the line in the *Legend*, particularly since Lowes does not discuss the evidence for Chaucer's knowledge of the *Policraticus*, and other studies of this question have not been able to demonstrate more than a very limited indebtedness to this work; see W.W. Woollcombe, in *Essays on Chaucer* (London, 1896), 295–8; Eleanor Prescott Hammond, *Chaucer: A Bibliographical Manual* (New York, 1908), 93; and Thomas R. Lounsbury, *Studies in Chaucer*, 3 vols (London, 1892), 2:362–4. A further parallel with the *Policraticus* suggested by John Fleming, in "Chaucer's Clerk and John of Salisbury," *English Language Notes* 2 (1964): 5–6, is likewise not conclusive. As for the *Ethics*, on the other hand, Burgundio of Pisa's Latin versions of Books 2 and 3 (known as Ethica vetus) and of Book 1 (known as Ethica nova) were in circulation in the twelfth/early thirteenth century, and Grosseteste's complete translation was produced in (?)1246–7 (see Bernard G. Dod, "Aristoteles latinus," in *The Cambridge History of Later Medieval Philosophy*, ed. Norman Kretzmann, Anthony Kenny, and Jan Pinborg [Cambridge, 1982], 45–79, especially 61). I have, therefore, thought it worthwhile to quote some passages of the *Ethics* at relevant points in the following discussion. I quote from René Antoine Gauthier's edition of the Ethica vetus and Ethica nova, *Ethica Nicomachea*, *Aristoteles Latinus* XXVI.1–3, fasc. 2 (Leiden, 1972). I have also used the four manuscripts of the *Latin Ethics* preserved in the library of Gonville and Caius College, Cambridge, to whose Librarian I am grateful for permission to consult them.

other hand, they share the stability of the mean, in that they represent a limit, a termination of the increase signified by the comparative "more."[3]

If we look for the Middle English nouns corresponding to these points on the scale, we find that corresponding to the idea of "too little," for example, are the nouns "defaute" and "nede." It is need that stimulates the drive toward satisfaction, and it is the fulfilling of primary need that marks the boundary line of "mesure" or "temperaunce" – the nouns corresponding to "enough"; to carry on taking more, beyond the point where need is satisfied, is to turn satisfaction into excess (the function of need in determining what constitutes temperance is clearly explained in Passus XX of *Piers Plowman* by the personified figure of Need himself). To put it the other way round, need is eradicated by enough; to quote Henryson's fable of the town mouse and the country mouse, "Quha hes aneuch, of na mair hes he neid."[4] The Middle English nouns corresponding to the idea of "too much," on the other hand, are "excesse" and "superfluitee." Less obvious but more interesting is the embodiment of the concept of "too much" in the word "outrely" (meaning "utterly, completely, quite": *MED* 2), which I shall, for convenience in discussion, represent by the word "outrance," even though the *MED* records this noun as appearing in English texts only after the fourteenth century; it would, of course, have been familiar from medieval French. As we have already noted of superlatives, the idea of doing something "à outrance" involves an ambivalence; it seems to imply "going to excess, going too far," but

3 Cf. *Nicomachean Ethics*, Ethica vetus II.6 (*Aristoteles Latinus* XXVI.1–3, fasc. 2 (14): "Est igitur virtus, habitus voluntarius in medietate existens que ad nos determinata racione; et ut sapiens determinabit. Medietas autem, duarum maliciarum, huius quidem secundum superfluitatem, huius vero secundum indigenciam. Et adhuc, quoniam hee quidem deficiunt, hee autem superhabundant, eius quod oportet, et in passionibus et in operacionibus, virtus autem medium et invenit et vult. Ideo secundum substanciam et racionem que quid est esse significat, medietas est virtus. Secundum autem perfectum et bonum, extremitas" ("Excellence, then, is a state concerned with choice, lying in a mean relative to us, this being determined by reason and in the way in which the man of practical wisdom would determine it. Now it is a mean between two vices, that which depends on excess and that which depends on defect; and again it is a mean because the vices respectively fall short of or exceed what is right in both passions and actions, while excellence both finds and chooses that which is intermediate. Hence in respect of its substance and the account which states its essence [it] is a mean, with regard to what is best and right it is an extreme"; 1106b–1107a). Grosseteste's translation is very similar; see *Aristoteles latinus* XXVI.1–3, fasc. 4 (Leiden, 1973), II.5 (404).

4 *Fables* II.375, in *The Poems of Robert Henryson*, ed. Denton Fox (Oxford, 1981). The examples from Langland and Henryson testify to the consistency through medieval literature generally of the vocabulary sets that I describe, though the prominence given to the set, and to particular elements within it, varies, of course, between one literary text and another. Langland's own emphasis is on the concept of need; see Jill Mann, "The Nature of Need Revisited," *Yearbook of Langland Studies* 18 (2004): 3–29.

it can also mean simply "going to the absolute limit, to the fullest extent"[5] – the point at which a potential is most fully realized, so that all fears of deficiency, and all pressures toward future increase, fall away in the stability of perfection.

Pearl

It is the dreamer's desire for "more" that governs the development of the dream in *Pearl.* At the beginning of the poem he is represented in a state of deprivation, bereft of the pearl that was his highest treasure; he is at the "too little" end of the scale. Paradoxically, however, this first section of the poem simultaneously represents the state of deprivation as a *good* thing; to be "wythouten spot" (48), as the pearl is, is to enjoy complete perfection.[6] That the pearl is without defect means that the potential beauty of its form is most fully realized. Absolute deprivation is in this instance a condition of absolute perfection. The contrast between these two kinds of deprivation at the beginning of the poem is an intimation of the two extremes – human need, heavenly fulfilment – that the poem will try to bring into relation; it is also an intimation that the one may be mysteriously transformed into the other.

The dreamer's vision instantly and lavishly repairs his loss, in one sense, by offering to him not a single pearl alone but an entire landscape of jewels. He is given much *more*, that is, than he is represented as having lost. And the idea of "more" is further emphasized by the fact that the "blys" to which the light and beauty of his surroundings restore him (123) is a bliss that is continually increasing:

> Doun after a strem þat dryȝly halez
> I bowed in blys, bredful my braynez;
> þe fyrre I folȝed þose floty valez,
> þe more strenghþe of joye myn herte straynez. (125–8)

The persistent increase of riches is emphasized by the doubling of "more":

> As Fortune fares þeras ho fraynez,
> Wheþer solace ho sende oþer ellez sore,

5 The phrase "à outrance" is glossed by Godefroy (*Dictionnaire de l'ancienne langue française*) as "excessivement, violemment," and by Tobler-Lommatzsch as "zum Äussersten."

6 All quotations from *Pearl* are taken from *The Poems of the Pearl Manuscript: Pearl, Cleanness, Patience, Sir Gawain and the Green Knight*, ed. Malcolm Andrew and Ronald Waldron, 5th ed. (Exeter, 2007).

Þe wyȝ to wham her wylle ho waynez
Hyttez to haue ay more and more.[7] (129–32)

In accordance with the complicated verse scheme of the poem, since the word "more" is here used in the last line of the stanza, it then becomes the link word in the whole stanza section, and in almost every instance it is similarly intensified by being doubled (144, 156, 168, 180). The link phrases emphasize, however, not only the increase of riches but also an accompanying increase of desire: "And euer me longed ay more and more" (144). Mounting desire is expressed in the tripling of "more":

More and more, and ȝet wel mare,
Me lyste to se þe broke byȝonde,
For if hit watz fayr þer I con fare,
Wel loueloker watz þe fyrre londe. (145–8)

As the dreamer's pleasure grows, so does his expectation, and his longing for the opposite bank, which is even *more* lovely than the side on which he finds himself. It is this focus on the opposite bank, created by the desire for "more," that leads to the dreamer's perception of the child sitting at the foot of the crystal cliff. And, once perceived, the child attracts to herself the link phrase "more and more":

On lenghe I loked to hyr þere;
þe lenger, I knew hyr more and more.

The more I frayste hyr fayre face,
Her fygure fyn quen I had fonte,
Such gladande glory con to me glace
As lyttel byfore þerto watz wonte. (167–72)

We might expect the mounting joy to reach a simple climax and complete fulfilment in the rediscovery of the lost pearl. But this is not the case. The dreamer is, in fact, torn between "glory" and "baysment" (171, 174), so that the last use of "more" in this part of the poem ironically works against the dreamer's pleasure, not for it: "More þen me lyste my drede aros" (181).

---

7 The interpretation of the phrase "hytte to haue" given by *MED* (s.v. hitten, 3b) – "to happen to get (sth.), obtain by chance" – is preferable to the *OED*'s interpretation of "hytte" in this line as meaning "aim, seek, strive" (s.v. hit, v., 18).

"More" cannot, then, be always and simply linked with pleasure. The comparative can signal an increase of discomfort as well as an increase of joy. And it can also signal the possibility of a direct link between the two emotional states. The dreamer's joy at seeing the girl again is in proportion to the comparative closeness of their relationship: "Ho watz me nerre þen aunte or nece; / My joy forþy watz much þe more" (233–4). But his grief is likewise in proportion to his former joy: "My blysse, my bale, ȝe han ben boþe, / Bot much þe bygger ȝet watz my mon" (373–4). With this recognition that increase of happiness brings with it an increase of vulnerability, the problem of "more" is left suspended, and a new phase in the poem's movement is opened.

The new phase is initiated by the idea of "too much." The dead girl informs the dreamer that she leads the life of a queen in heaven. Rather than being pleased by this news, the dreamer is rendered puzzled and uncertain, even when she assures him that the sovereign place of the Virgin Mary is in no way diminished by her own high position. Despite his love for her, the dreamer feels that she has been given too much:

> "That Cortayse is to fre of dede,
> ȝyf hyt be soth þat þou conez saye.
> Þou lyfed not two ȝer in oure þede;
> Þou cowþez neuer God nauþer plese ne pray,
> Ne neuer nawþer Pater ne Crede –
> And quen mad on þe fyrst day!
> I may not traw, so God me spede,
> Þat God wolde wryþe so wrange away.
> Of countes, damysel, par ma fay,
> Wer fayr in heuen to halde asstate,
> Oþer ellez a lady of lasse aray;
> Bot a quene! – hit is to dere a date." (481–92)

The preceding stanza has made clear that the dreamer's objection is based on his assumption that others will have deserved more and will therefore be treated unjustly – given too little – if allotted only the same reward that she enjoys:

> "Þyself in heuen ouer hyȝ þou heue,
> To make þe quen þat watz so ȝonge.
> What more honour moȝte he acheue
> Þat hade endured in worlde stronge,
> And lyued in penaunce hys lyuez longe
> Wyth bodyly bale hym blysse to byye?

What more worschyp moȝt he fonge
Þen corounde be kyng by cortaysé?" (473–80)

The maiden does not attempt to solve the dreamer's difficulties directly; instead, she relates the biblical parable of the workers in the vineyard – which may seem to be no answer at all, since the parable has usually produced in its readers the same kind of baffled protest that prompts the dreamer's questions. Even though the workers that he has hired in the course of the day have worked for different lengths of time, when the day is over, the lord orders his reeve to set the workers in line and give each of them "inlyche a peny" (546). The reaction of the workers who have toiled all day on seeing the latecomers receive the same payment is predictable:

"Þese bot on oure hem con streny;
Vus þynk vus oȝe to take more." (551–2)

These lines conclude the first stanza of a new section of the poem, and the word "more" thus again becomes the link word for an entire section. It is the cornerstone of the workers' complaint:

"More haf we serued, vus þynk so,
Þat suffred han þe dayez hete,
Þen þyse þat wroȝt not hourez two,
And þou dotz hem vus to counterfete." (553–6)

The complaint is answered by the lord's mild reminder that they had originally contracted for a penny. Their comparatives are negated by an appeal to the limiting stability of the bargain: "Fyrre þen couenaunde is noȝt to plete; / Wy schalte þou þenne ask more?" (563–4)

When it is used at the beginning of the next stanza, "more" means "moreover," and thereafter in the section the word is used in ways that move it out of the context of the workers' demand, yet still its insistent repetition seems to reiterate their claims with increasing urgency. And at the end of the section, when the dreamer restates the original problem, the word "more" is supported by a whole battery of other comparatives. We are told that God rewards everyone according to their deserts; if, then, the maiden comes "to payment" (598) before someone who has laboured in God's service longer than she has, the dreamer says, "Þenne þe lasse in werke to take more able, / And euer þe lenger þe lasse þe more" (599–600).

The maiden's reply begins a new section of the poem, and with it a new link word makes its appearance. The word "more" is discarded, and its place is taken by "enough":

> "Of more and lasse in Godez ryche,"
> Þat gentyl sayde, "lys no joparde,
> For þer is vch mon payed inlyche,
> Wheþer lyttel oþer much be hys rewarde.
> For þe gentyl Cheuentayn is no chyche,
> Queþersoeuer He dele – nesch oþer harde:
> He lauez Hys gyftez as water of dyche,
> Oþer gotez of golf þat neuer charde.
> Hys fraunchyse is large: þat euer dard
> To Hym þat matz in synne rescoghe –
> No blysse betz fro hem reparde,
> For þe grace of God is gret inoghe." (601–12)

Four more times, with only two slight variations in form, the maiden repeats the same refrain: "For þe grace of God is gret innoghe" (624, 636, 648, 660). The apparently relentless tide of reiterations of "more" is stemmed by the firm steadiness of "enough."

Yet the shift in rhythm and mood effected by this change in link word is not in itself the answer to the dreamer's question; it is merely a key to an understanding of that answer. Full understanding comes with perception of the meaning carried by the Pearl maiden's statement that all those in God's kingdom are "payed inlyche," whether they receive little or much (603). The crucial word in what she says is "payed." It is a word that naturally assumes importance in the parable of the vineyard, which is all about payment. But "pay" also assumes importance at the beginning and end of the whole poem: it appears in the very first line – "Perle plesaunte, to prynces paye" – and it is the link word of the stanzas in the last section of the poem – which means that it also links the last line of the poem to the first, forming (as has often been noted) a circular structure. If we place these uses of "pay" beside the uses of the word and its associates in the parable, what is thrown into prominence is the simple fact that the word has two main branches of meaning: in the fourteenth century, as now, it meant "payment" in the monetary sense, but it also carried its older meaning of "satisfaction." When the poet calls the pearl "plesaunte, to prynces paye" (1), or when at the end of the poem he says "Now al be to þat Pryncez paye" (1176), it is this older meaning that is uppermost.

The use of the word "paye" in the sense of "satisfaction" at the beginning and end of the poem inevitably colours the use of the word "payed" in the maiden's statement that everyone is "payed inlyche" in the kingdom of heaven and makes it into a kind of pun: all are equally "paid," because all are equally "satisfied" – that is, everyone has *enough*. The earthly notion of "payment" is transformed into the heavenly notion of "satisfaction," with the emphasis on the element "*satis*," that is, on the idea of "enough." The idea of "more" then becomes an absurdity; once one is satisfied, there is no need for more – indeed, there is no room for its absorption. It is no accident, I think, that in the stanzas linked by "innoghe" the maiden uses the image of water pouring out in abundance to express the copiousness of God's grace, for as we think of human beings as the receptacles of this outflowing grace, we realize that when such a receptacle is full it cannot be any fuller. It takes different amounts of water to fill a large bowl and a small bowl, but once it is poured in, they are both equally full. Accordingly, as we shall see, the idea of satisfaction becomes linked with the idea of fullness.

The substitution of the idea of satisfaction for the idea of payment and the activation of the double meaning of the word "payed" are not, of course, the only means by which the poet seeks to transform the normal mundane categories of measurement into terms more suitable to the "unquantifiable" bliss of heaven. The substitution of the pearl, the central image of the poem, for the penny that is paid to the workers in the vineyard is equally important.[8] The pearl and the

8 I must here acknowledge a debt to Marie Borroff, who has commented perceptively on the contrast between the circularity of the penny, figuring eternity, and the line of workers set "vpon a rawe" to receive it, figuring linear time ("Pearl's 'Maynful Mone': Crux, Simile, and Structure," in *Acts of Interpretation: The Text in its Contexts 700–1600. Essays on Medieval and Renaissance Literature in Honor of E. Talbot Donaldson*, ed. Mary J. Carruthers and Elizabeth D. Kirk [Norman, OK, 1982], 159–72, at 162–4). Some further comments of Borroff admirably express the transcendence of earthly scales of comparison within eternity: "Having the form of a circle, the pearl ... stands for eternity, the existence of God in a timeless present from the perspective of which human history is a completed, static pattern. Human beings are trapped in progressive time, looking back from the present to the past and forward to an unknown future. Eternity is not perpetual duration, 'longer than' time; it is the absence of time. So too with the worth of the heavenly pearl. It is not 'greater than' the worth of anything on earth; it is absolute, literally 'beyond measure.' Nearer and farther, earlier and later, lower and higher, less and more, all are interdependent manifestations of a dimensional mode of being in which men, under the governance of a changing fortune, move toward certain death ... The inner dissatisfaction and perpetual striving inevitable in such a world have their otherworldly counterparts in the peace of heaven. To dwell there is to possess a happiness which, again, is not 'greater than' human happiness, but perfect, without qualification." Marie Borroff, *Pearl: A New Verse Translation* (New York, 1977), xiii.

penny are alike in the roundness that symbolizes the eternity of the heavenly kingdom,[9] and alike also in their role as valuable objects, as indices and repositories of worth. But the difference between them can be measured by the transformation of the two-dimensional flatness of the penny into the three-dimensional roundness of the pearl. Even more important is that the pearl's value is dependent on its completeness. In the Middle Ages a penny cut in two became two half pennies, so that it retained its original value; to cut a pearl in two, on the other hand, would be to destroy its original value.[10] The image of the penny, therefore, corresponds to the earthly notion that to share something of value involves splitting it and sharing it out in quantifiable portions. Its replacement by the image of the pearl enables the reader to understand that the kingdom of heaven is not a divisible good of this sort – that heavenly bliss can be given only in its entirety or not at all.

The image of the pearl can also help us understand the place finally found within heaven for the concept of "more." For when the Pearl maiden describes the life of the blessed in the heavenly Jerusalem, we find, contrary to our expectations, that the idea of "more" is not scorned or discarded. Quite the opposite: each of the 144,000 virgins who are brides of the Lamb wishes the company to increase:

> "And þaȝ vch day a store He feche,
> Among vus commez nouþer strot ne stryf,
> Bot vchon enlé we wolde were fyf –
> Þe mo þe myryer, so God me blesse!
> In compayny gret our luf con þryf,
> In honour more and neuer þe lesse." (847–52)

Following on from this usage, the word "lesse" becomes the link word of this section – but in negative form: "*neuer* þe lesse." The introduction of the key

9 The Pearl maiden later explains that the pearl is like the kingdom of heaven because it is "endelez rounde" (738). See also the excellent analysis in Cary Nelson, *The Incarnate Word: Literature as Visual Space* (Urbana, IL, 1973), "Pearl: The Circle as Figural Space"; and on the background to this idea in medieval thought, see Georges Poulet, *The Metamorphoses of the Circle*, trans. Carey Dawson and Elliott Coleman (Baltimore, MD, 1966), introduction.

10 For the (illegal) medieval habit of halving pennies, see the twelfth-century Latin beast poem *Ysengrimus*, ed. Jill Mann (Leiden, 1987), VII.679–84, and George C. Brooke, *English Coins from the Seventh Century to the Present Day*, 3rd ed. (London, 1950), 81, 103–4. Jewellers do use "half pearls," but these are stones which were not perfect in the first place and are, therefore, set with only part of their surface visible; see George Frederick Kunz and Charles Hugh Stevenson, *The Book of the Pearl* (London, 1908), 354.

word "innoghe" has negated the idea of "less," but it has not completely negated the idea of "more"; on the contrary, "the more the merrier" is the principle on which the happiness of the blessed company is founded.[11] How can this be?

It will, I think, be easier to see the answer to this question if we briefly consider the answer that Dante represents as being given to him when he asks a similar question in canto XV of *Purgatorio.* Virgil tells him that in the highest sphere "the more they are who say 'ours,' the more of good does each possess, and the more of charity burns in that cloister." Dante, understandably, then asks: "How can it be that a good distributed can make more possessors richer with itself than if it is possessed by a few?"[12] Virgil's reply (in C.S. Lewis's words) restates the "distinction between goods that are, and goods that are not, objects of competition: he uses the image of light which gives of itself in proportion as the body it falls on is more highly polished, with the consequence that the greater the number of such bodies, the more light there is for all."[13]

The *Pearl*-poet, unlike Dante, does not make this idea explicit, but its relevance to his description of the heavenly Jerusalem, which is even more

11 On this point I differ from Marie Borroff, who sees the link word "nevertheless" as an indication of the same "habit of insatiable desire" in the dreamer that is evidenced in the use of "more" as link word in sections 3 and 10; Borroff, *Pearl*, xiii.

12 *Purgatorio* XV.55–63.

13 C.S. Lewis, *Studies in Medieval and Renaissance Literature* (Cambridge, 1966), 71. For the Aristotelian distinction, see *Nicomachean Ethics* IX.8 (1168b, 1169b), and *Eudemian Ethics* VII.15 (1248b). Even closer to the idea in *Pearl* is Augustine (*De civitate dei*, ed. B. Dombart and A. Kalb, 2 vols [Turnhout, 1955], XV.5): "Nullo enim modo fit minor accedente seu permanente consorte possessio bonitatis, immo possessio bonitas, quam tanto latius, quanto concordius indiuidua sociorum possidet caritas. Non habebit denique istam possessionem, qui eam noluerit habere communem, et tanto eam reperiet ampliorem, quanto amplius ibi potuerit amare consortem" ("The possession of goodness is not diminished when it is shared, either temporarily or permanently, with another; on the contrary, goodness is a possession that grows the more, the more harmonious the love between the comrades who possess it. For no one will have this possession unless he is willing to share it, and he will find it the greater to the extent that he is able to love to share it"). The following comments of Georges Poulet (*Metamorphoses*, xxiv) are also of interest in this connection: "All medieval philosophy of light is a long commentary on the spherical diffusion of every luminous point. (Omne agens multiplicat suam virtutem sphaerice ["Every force diffuses its strength spherically"]). This phrase of Grosseteste is applicable to all activity, but first of all, to God. God is a light propagating Itself, a force that multiplies and diffuses itself." The image of light is thus naturally linked with the image of the circle. It may also be noted that Dante's response to Virgil's explanation is "Tu m'appaghe" (*Purgatorio* XV.82), which is of interest here since the Italian word *appagare*, like the Middle English "paye," means "to satisfy" as well as "to content, please."

dominated by the image of light than that in Revelation, is clear. The light of the Lamb (1046–7) is reflected by "þe borȝ al bryȝt" (1048), including the pearls. It is thus a light that increases continually as they increase, so that their own share of it is never diminished. As the maiden explains to the dreamer, in the City of God "glory and blysse schal euer encres" (959). In this continual increase the first thing to fall away is earthly need: "Hem nedde nawþer sunne ne mone. / Of sunne ne mone had þay no nede ..." (1044–5). But this transcendence of earthly need can be expressed only by the use of comparatives; the heavenly city is "schyrrer þen sunne" (982), the river flowing from God's throne is "bryȝter þen boþe þe sunne and mone" (1056). The increasing excitement of the description culminates in the superlatives lavished on the description of the Lamb: "Best watz he, blyþest, and moste to pryse" (1131); the heavenly increase is terminated and fully realized in him. Yet, again, the superlatives are not used to imply a ranking order, a hierarchy in which more and less can be measured along a scale; perfection belongs to all. "Tor to knaw þe gladdest chere" (1109). In this context "too much" no longer indicates the dreamer's indignant sense of unmerited reward but conveys his humble sense of inadequacy in describing the joys of the heavenly kingdom: "Delyt þat Hys come encroched / To much hit were of for to melle" (1117–18). The superlatives indicate not the last point on a linear scale but a perfect fullness corresponding to the perfection of the circle: "Þis noble cité of ryche enpresse / Watz sodanly ful, wythouten sommoun ..." (1097–8). The crowd of virgins, "Hundreth þowsandez" strong (1107), makes up the superabundant fullness of the heavenly city, a fullness that is itself a source of joy.[14]

The image of "innoghe" in this poem, then, involves no renunciation, no settling for second-best, but rather an endlessly sufficient abundance. As the dreamer says of the pearl on the young girl's breast: "A mannez dom moȝt dryȝly demme / Er mynde moȝt malte in hit mesure" (223–4). In this abundance of bliss human capacity will founder before it even approaches the midterm of "enough"; even "mesure" is beyond a man's wildest imaginings. "Vrþely herte" cannot "suffyse" for the extent of heavenly happiness (135–6). The dreamer's human insufficiency means that the "melting" of his mind at

14 Thus in the first three (interconnected) definitions of God in the pseudohermetic Book of the Twenty-Four Philosophers discussed by Poulet (*Metamorphoses*, p. xi), the first conceives God in terms of light, the second conceives him in terms of a sphere, and the third conceives him in terms of fullness ("Deus est totus in quolibet sui" ["God is entirely complete in every part of himself"]). Cf. Col. 2.9–10: "quia in ipso [sc. Christo] inhabitat omnis plenitudo divinitatis corporaliter, et estis in illo repleti" ("for in him dwelleth all the fullness of the Godhead bodily, and ye are complete in him").

the sight of heavenly bliss (1153–4) leads him to overstep the boundaries of “mesure,” imposed by his still-human existence. Impatient for his own satisfaction, and careless of that of his “Prince,” he wants to see more than is allowed him and tries to cross the stream that separates him from the heavenly company. The result is the loss of his dream – as if in illustration of the principle earlier enunciated by the maiden that “Ofte mony mon forgos þe mo” through the inability to suffer “lurez lesse” (339–40). In confirmation of this we are told at the end of the poem that had the dreamer not grasped after more he would have received it; “more” is not a right to be claimed but an unsolicited, gratuitous experience of increase.

> To þat Pryncez paye hade I ay bente,
> And ʒerned no more þen watz me geuen,
> And halden me þer in trwe entent,
> As þe perle me prayed þat watz so þryuen,
> As helde, drawen to Goddez present,
> To mo of His mysterys I hade ben dryuen. (1189–94)

In the heavenly kingdom renunciation is paradoxically rewarded with satisfaction. In its fullness the desire for “more” falls away, not because one prudently settles for “less” but because that endless desire is endlessly satisfied, and it is the completeness of that satisfaction that constitutes “enough.”

This identification of “enough” with both moderation and superlative completeness is, however, no idiosyncratic vision of the *Pearl*-poet; it is founded in the everyday English usages of the word, as I shall try to show in the following section on the *Clerk's Tale.* We shall then see that the refrain “þe grace of God is gret innoghe” draws on the double significance of “innoghe” just as the parable in which it is set draws on the double significance of “paye.”

The Clerk's Tale

The vocabulary associated with “enough” appears from an early date in Chaucer's works. We can see it, for example, in his translation of Boethius. Philosophy explains to Boethius that riches do not provide “suffisance”; although rich men have “inoghe” to make them safe against hunger, thirst, and cold, the “nede” that they experience in common with all other men “ne mai nat al outrely be doon awey; for thoughe this nede that is alwey gapynge and gredy, be fulfild with richesses, and axe any thyng, yit duelleth thanne a nede that myghte be fulfild. I holde me stille and telle nat how that litel thyng suffiseth to nature; but certes to avarice inowghe suffiseth nothyng” (*Boece* III, pr.3.90–6).

It is just such a "gapynge and gredy" desire for more and still more that we can recognize in Walter in the *Clerk's Tale*, which I shall make the focus for study of the idea of "enough" in Chaucer's work. For although the complex of ideas surrounding the notion of "enough" recurs throughout the Canterbury collection, it is in the *Clerk's Tale* that it is given fullest and profoundest expression. The word "enough" appears in this tale more often than in any other; even more important than its frequency is its key placement in the structure of the narrative. It is, in the first place, used to seal the marriage compact between Walter and Griselda: Griselda's acceptance of the condition that she must be obedient to Walter's every desire and command is greeted by the immediate reply, "This is inogh, Grisilde min" (365). But, of course, the whole point of the story is that it is *not* enough – that Walter insists on testing Griselda to see whether he can make her give still more.[15] He is, in other words, insatiable. Chaucer's comments on the beginning of Walter's obsession emphasize this inability to rest content with "enough"[16] – the desire for "more" that is inexcusable because it is unprompted by need:

> Ther fil, as it bifalleth times mo,
> Whan that this child had souked but a throwe,
> This markis in his herte longeth so
> To tempte his wif, hir sadnesse for to knowe,
> That he ne mighte out of his herte throwe
> This merveillous desir, his wyf t'assaye;
> Nedelees, God woot, he thoghte hire for t'affraye!
>
> He hadde assayed hire inow bifore,
> And fond hire evere good; what neded it
> Hir for to tempte, and alwey moore and moore,
> Thogh som men preise it for a subtil wit?
> But as for me, I seye that ivele it sit
> T'assaye a wif whan that it is no nede,
> And putten hire in angwissh and in drede. (449–62)

15 The desire for more initiates not only the testing of Griselda but also Walter's marriage (and thus the whole story); in this instance, it is his tenants' desire for the "o thing" that could give them "moore felicitee" that leads them to request his marriage (lines 109–10).

16 I call these comments "Chaucer's" rather than "the Clerk's" partly to avoid cumbersomeness but also because I think that the function of the pilgrim-narrator is not present to our imagination at this point – and precisely because it has no essential role to play in our response. Continuity of style throughout the *Tales* is enough to show that Chaucer fuses himself with each of his narrators in turn.

Chaucer likewise emphasizes the needlessness of the next stage of Griselda's trial – the loss of her second child – and adds a comment on Walter's contempt for "mesure":

O nedelees was she tempted in assay!
But wedded men ne knowe no mesure
Whan that they finde a pacient creature. (621–3)

And after the loss of this child Chaucer yet again intrudes into the narrative with similar comments on it:

But now of wommen wolde I asken fain
If thise assayes mighte nat suffise?
What koude a sturdy housbond moore devise
To preve hir wifhod and hir stedfastnesse,
And he continuinge evere in sturdinesse? (696–700)

And yet at the close of the story Walter's obsessive urge to test Griselda *does* miraculously come to an end – and what is striking is that he brings her trials to a close with exactly the same words that he had used to initiate them:

"This is inogh, Grisilde min," quod he;
"Be now namoore agast ne ivele apaied.
I have thy feith and thy benignitee,
As wel as evere womman was, assayed,
In greet estaat, and povreliche arrayed.
Now knowe I, deere wif, thy stedfastnesse!"
And hire in armes took and gan hir kesse. (1051–7)

The question is, how is it that Walter's insatiability is finally satisfied? How is it that enough finally *is* enough for him – that his obsessive desire for more does not lead him on to devise yet further torments and humiliations?

In repeating the word "inogh" at the beginning and end of the tale in such a way as to raise this question, Chaucer is following the lead given in Petrarch's Latin prose version of the Griselda story, which he identifies in the *Clerk's Prologue* as his main source for the tale.[17] That Chaucer probably also knew *Le livre*

17 Petrarch, *Epistolae seniles*, XVII.3. The Latin text, with accompanying translation, is given in *Sources and Analogues of the Canterbury Tales*, ed. Robert M. Correale and Mary Hamel, 2 vols (Cambridge, 2002–5), 1:108–29. Since the Latin text is lineated consecutively, citations will be given in the form of line numbers, inserted in parentheses in my text. Translations are my own.

Griseldis, one of the French prose translations of Petrarch, is of less concern to us,[18] since it was the artistic shaping of Petrarch's version to which Chaucer responded, as becomes evident from the sensitive recreation of it in his own tale.[19] In Petrarch, as in Chaucer, Walter proclaims that he has "enough," both when Griselda makes her promise to him before marriage and when he finally brings her trials to an end. The word in the Latin text is *satis*: "satis est," he says, in the first instance (161), and, in the second, "satis ... mea Griseldis, cognita et spectata michi fides est tua" ("I have, my Griselda, well known and observed your fidelity"; 376–7). We can see at once that in making these speeches identical, rather than merely similar, Chaucer sharpens our sense of the question they pose. Petrarch repeats the word *satis* elsewhere in his narrative in ways that make it carry a deliberate weight of significance. It is, for example, used ironically by Walter in a bland pretence of satisfaction, even as he is pursuing his desire for more; he prefaces the announcement that he is going to have Griselda's daughter taken away by saying "Michi quidem cara satis ac dilecta es" ("To me you are dear and beloved enough"; 197–8). He likewise introduces the news that he plans to divorce her by saying "Satis ... tuo coniugio delectabar" ("I was happy enough in my marriage with you"; 299–300). Again these uses underline the fact that enough is precisely *not* enough for Walter.

But to translate *satis* merely as "enough" in these latter instances is of course to be guilty of inaccuracy or translationese; in such expressions the Latin *satis* does not qualify but intensifies. *Satis cara* means not "moderately dear" but "very dear" – even "wholly, completely dear."[20] The Italian *assai* and the medieval French *assez* share the same characteristics; both can mean "rather, moderately" – indicating a kind of halfway house – but can also mean "fully, completely, abundantly" – indicating the end of the line, the fullest realization of some possibility.[21] And the same is true of the Middle English "inogh"; in adverbial use it means not only "sufficiently ... moderately ... adequately," but also "extremely ...

18 See the detailed study of J. Burke Severs, *The Literary Relationships of Chaucer's Clerke's Tale* (New Haven, CT, 1942), updated in the section on the *Clerk's Tale*, by Thomas Farrell and Amy Goodwin, in Correale and Hamel, *Sources and Analogues*, 1:101–67, which includes the French text and an accompanying English translation.

19 The French translator does reproduce many elements in the complex vocabulary pattern that Petrarch builds around the word "*satis*," but in a haphazard fashion that suggests that he was not consciously aware of its significance. The vocabulary pattern is completely absent from Petrarch's own model, the tenth tale of the tenth day of Boccaccio's *Decameron*.

20 This meaning is not acknowledged in Lewis and Short or the *Oxford Latin Dictionary*, but see the entries for "*satis*" in Du Cange ("Valde, omnino"), and Niermeyer ("very").

21 For medieval French, see Tobler-Lommatzsch, s.v. assez ("viel, reichlich," as well as "genug"); for Italian, see the *Cambridge Italian Dictionary*, s.v. assai ("very, ... very much; a great deal; ... plenty," as well as "quite").

fully, completely, entirely" (*MED*) – "as much as well could be," as the *OED* puts it.[22] Thus the refrain in *Pearl* – "þe grace of God is gret innoghe" – means not only that God's grace is "sufficiently" great, reaching to the limit of the demand made on it, but also that it is "abundantly" great, limitless, acknowledging no boundaries but those of the radiating sphere of perfection.

Following Petrarch's practice with *satis*, Chaucer exploits this possible sense of the word "inogh" many times in his tale. We are told at the opening that Walter is "Discret inogh his contree for to gye" (75). Griselda is described as "fair inogh to sighte" (209), and Walter, in his married life, enjoys "outward grace inow" (424). And, as in Petrarch, it is with a blandly cruel pretence of satisfaction that he introduces his plans for divorce:

> "Certes, Grisilde, I hadde inogh plesance
> To han yow to my wif for youre goodnesse ..." (792–3)

The semantic ambivalence in the word alerts us to an ambivalence in the concept of "inogh." In one sense it represents a point of balance between extremes. But in another sense "inogh" is itself a superlative; it indicates "outrance" – fullness, abundance, satisfaction to the utmost limits. Walter's desire to test Griselda "To the outreste preve of hir corage" (787) is matched by her willingness to pursue obedience to its limits; "inogh," for Griselda, is not "a moderate amount" but everything that it takes to satisfy him.

Following through the use of the word *satis* and its associates shows us that Walter's obsessive insatiability has, however, one oddly positive corollary – that is, he does *not* become "sated" with Griselda in the manner characteristic of men of rank who amuse themselves by taking up with low-born girls. This is pointed up by the use of the word *sacietas* ("satiety") in the Latin text at the point where Walter sends Griselda back to her home; her father gloomily reflects that he had always expected such a consequence to the marriage, "that a man so exalted, and proud after the fashion of nobles, would at some time send her back home, satiety with so low-born a wife having arisen" ("sacietate sponse tam humilis exorta"; 333).[23] But the father's reading of the situation is, of

22 Sense 2a. For the other glosses, see *MED*, s.v. "inough," adv., senses (b) and (e) for the meaning "moderately," and senses (a) and (d) for the meaning "fully."

23 Chaucer's use of conventional phrases of the "bothe lasse and moore" type for the meaning "everybody" (67, 940) reminds us that the scale from "more" to "less" is realized in social as well as emotional terms. The union of Walter and Griselda reconciles and mediates between the social polarities designated by the superlatives "gentileste" (72) and "povrest" (205), achieving the point of balance that represents "enough."

course, mistaken: paradoxically, Walter's very insatiability preserves him from this more usual kind of satiation. We learn to make a crucial distinction here, in recognizing that, while we want Walter to have "had enough," it is not in this cruder, more vulgar sense. We want him to be satisfied, not sated.

The chain of significant words through which Petrarch explores the concepts of insatiability and satisfaction extends further. Prominent in it are the noun *cupiditas* (indicating a greedy, selfish desire), and its associates, the adjective *cupidus* and the verb *cupio*. *Cupiditas* is the term Petrarch applies to Walter's desire to test over and over again his wife's already proven loyalty: "Cepit, ut fit, interim Walterum ... mirabilis ... quedam ... cupiditas, sat expertam care fidem coniugis experiendi altius et iterum atque iterum retemptandi" ("An amazing desire to prove further, and to test over and over again the loyalty of his wife, which had already been proved enough, seized hold of Walter"; 192–4). Surprisingly, however, the words that denote Walter's insatiability are also used of Griselda. When Walter orders her to make ready his house for the reception of his new bride, she answers that she will, now and always, obey him "Non libenter modo ... sed cupide" ("not only willingly ... but avidly"; 349). Similarly, when the new wife and her brother arrive, we are told that Griselda "could never be sated with praising them" ("ipsa in primis puelle pariter atque infantis laudibus saciari nullo modo posset"; 364–5). But Griselda's "insatiability" is unlike Walter's in that it is founded on satisfaction. Walter asks her whether she finds his new wife "beautiful and noble enough" ("Satis pulcra atque honesta"), to which she replies emphatically "Certainly" ("Plane"; 368), signalling her rejection of any suggestion of possible increase by the negation of comparatives: "nor can any more beautiful or noble be found" ("nec pulcrior ulla nec honestior inveniri potest"; 369). With her, if with anyone, she goes on, Walter will be happy, "and I desire ("cupio") and hope that it may be so"; 370–1). It is Griselda's "satisfaction," her full and wholehearted acceptance of the woman who is, she believes, to take her place, that carries its own kind of "insatiability"; her desire to do Walter's will can never reach a termination, never be sated. And so it is Walter, not Griselda, who finally reaches the limit of endurance; "ferre diucius non valens" ("able to bear it no longer"; 376), he is brought to his final acknowledgment that he has enough. As is signalled by the negation of another comparative ("diucius"), his insatiability is terminated. Or, rather, it is transformed; for, with a final deliberate use of the adjective *cupidus*, Petrarch tells us that Walter embraced Griselda "cupidis ulnis" ("with greedy arms"; 379). The *cupiditas* that drove him to send Griselda away is henceforth transformed into an insatiable desire for union.

Chaucer was fully alive to these subtleties in Petrarch. He used his own network of vocabulary to recreate them and even, I think, to go beyond Petrarch in subtlety. We have seen already that the central position in this network of words is occupied by the word "inogh." The adverb "outrely" also belongs to it; it is used several times in connection with Walter, emphasizing his "extremism," his urge to go to the limits (639, 768, 953).[24] The words "ful," "fulliche," and "fulfild" fit into the pattern too; for example, at the point when Walter sends Griselda back home, Chaucer uses the word "fulfild" to do the work of Petrarch's *sacietas*, saying that Griselda's father believed she would be sent back home "whan the lord fulfild hadde his corage" (907). The deliberate debasement of the richer, more satisfying possibilities in the word "fulfild" here is paralleled in the use of the adverb "fulliche" in the lines telling us that Walter "fulliche hath purposed / To tempte his wif, as he was first disposed" (706–7) or of his desire "his wif to tempte moore / ... Fully to han experience and loore / If that she were as stedefast as bifore" (786–9). Petrarch's structuring of the final scene of the tale is likewise imitated by Chaucer: when Walter asks whether his new wife pleases her, Griselda negates a comparative – "A fairer saw I nevere noon than she" – to indicate the fullness of her appreciation, and wishes that God may send to her and to Walter "Plesance *inogh*, unto youre lives ende" (1033, 1036; my italics). The only place for "more" in Griselda's mind here is the consideration that the new bride has been brought up "Moore tendrely" than she has and therefore could not bear the same harsh treatment (1040–2); when Griselda asks for more, it is not for herself but for her supplanter.

This scene also includes, however, another, crucially important word that needs to be linked into the pattern, and that is the adjective "sad," the word that Chaucer constantly associates with Griselda. Derek Brewer has drawn attention to the importance of the word in this tale and to its dissociations from any of the modern connotations linking it to the visible expression of emotion; here, on the contrary, it implies the suppression of emotion, meaning "firm, steadfast, constant" (*MED* 2c).[25] When Petrarch talks about Griselda's steadfastness, he uses words like *constancia*, *robur*, *paciencia*, *equanimitas*. Chaucer too uses words like "constance" and "pacience," but he much prefers "sad" and "sadnesse." Walter's urge to tempt Griselda "moore and moore" arises from the desire "hir sadnesse for to knowe" (451–9). And it is her "sadnesse" that finally conquers him:

24 *OED* glosses the word (sense 1) as meaning "In an utter or extreme degree; entirely, absolutely; in an unqualified manner."

25 Brewer, "Some Metonymic Relationships in Chaucer's Poetry," *Poetica* 1 (1974): 1–20.

And whan this Walter saw hir pacience,
Hir glade cheere, and no malice at al,
And he so ofte had doon to hire offence,
And she ay sad and constant as a wal,
Continuinge evere hir innocence overal,
This sturdy markis gan his herte dresse
To rewen upon hir wifly stedfastnesse. (1044–50)

Chaucer's use of the word "sad" offers a minor puzzle. For the word goes back etymologically, as the *OED* testifies, to a root that means "sated, satisfied"; it is, in fact, a distant cousin of the Latin *satis* and likewise of *satur*, "satiated." Are we to imagine that Chaucer had – among his other bookish dreams – a prophetic vision of the *OED* entry for "sad"? Or should we see it as no more than a bizarre coincidence that he builds his poem on the word "sad" as Petrarch builds his prose version on the word *satis*? In fact, neither of these desperate hypotheses is necessary. For the earliest meaning of "sad" in English was, of course, "sated; surfeited; satisfied," and it had not completely lost that meaning in late Middle English (*MED* 1a). Chaucer himself uses the word in this sense on one occasion, saying in the *Canon's Yeoman's Tale* of the practitioners of alchemy that "of that art they kan nat wexen sadde" (877). Chaucer could also have found reinforcement for the idea of a connection between steadfastness and satisfaction, had he needed it, in the word "suffisaunce" – a word common to medieval French and Middle English – and this too is a word that assumes importance in the vocabulary patterns of the *Clerk's Tale*. In Chaucer's usage the word "suffisaunce" has a wide range of applications. There is, first, the concrete sense of "enough to eat and drink," exemplified in the "homly suffisaunce" of the friar of the *Summoner's Tale* (1843). The word can also denote the quality that monitors the amount necessary for bodily sufficiency – "moderation" or "temperance"; the Parson, who himself "koude in litel thing have suffisaunce" (*General Prologue* 490), tells us that "suffisance ... seketh no riche metes ne drinkes, ne dooth no fors of to outrageous apparaillinge of mete" (*Parson's Tale* 833). But the word also stands, as has been well demonstrated by J.D. Burnley, for the grander, more comprehensive ideal of Stoic self-sufficiency.[26] As Chaucer's *Balade of Fortune* tells us:

26 J.D. Burnley, *Chaucer's Language and the Philosophers' Tradition* (Cambridge, 1979), 72–3, 78–9. Burnley emphasizes that the Stoic notion naturally took on a Christian colouring in medieval writings. The definition of "felicitas" as "sufficientia" in the *Nicomachean Ethics* is also

No man is wrecched, but himself it wene,
And he that hath himself hath suffisaunce. (25–6)

Griselda's "sadnesse" is clearly a version of this kind of "suffisaunce"; at the lexical level it acts as an English equivalent of the French term. Last, we may note that "suffisaunce" is also a word that Chaucer uses in describing relationships between men and women as an indicator of what we would probably term in modern English "fulfilment." In the consummation scene of *Troilus and Criseyde*, Criseyde says to Troilus, "Welcome, my knyght, my pees, my suffisaunce!" (III.1309). Burnley finds this use by Criseyde a perverted one; the "philosophical significance" of the word is lost, he says, since it no longer denotes self-sufficiency but means "a kind of dependence."[27] My own feeling is that Burnley is too harsh here, and not quite alive to the complexity of the love experience that Chaucer delicately suggests – that is, that in love there *is* a kind of self-sufficiency, a steadiness of self, a sense of the fulfilment of one's own identity for the first time, achieved through the mirroring of that identity in the other person's love. At any rate, it is significant that Burnley does not disapprove when Chaucer uses the word in a similar way to describe Griselda's love for Walter:

But she, ilike sad for everemo,
Disposed was, this humble creature,
Th'adversitee of Fortune al t'endure,

---

relevant here: "Videtur autem et ex autarchia [gloss: .i. per se sufficiencia] idem contingere; perfectum enim bonum per se sufficiens esse videtur. Per se sufficiens enim dicimus non se solo vivente vitam solitarem, set et parentibus et filiis et uxor<i> et universis amicis et civibus, quoniam natura civilis homo ... Set per se sufficiens ponimus quod solum effectum eligibilem facit <vitam>, et nullo indigentem. Tale autem felicitatem existimamus esse ... Perfectum utique quid et per se sufficiens videtur felicitas, operatorum existens finis" (Burgundio of Pisa, Ethica nova, I.5, *Aristoteles Latinus* XXVI.1.2) ("From the point of view of self-sufficiency the same result seems to follow; for the complete good is thought to be self-sufficient. Now by self-sufficient we do not mean that which is sufficient for a man by himself, for one who lives a solitary life, but also for parents, children, wife, and in general for his friends and fellow citizens, since man is sociable by nature ... the self-sufficient we now define as that which when isolated makes life desirable and lacking in nothing; and such we think happiness to be ... Happiness, then, is something complete and self-sufficient, and is the end of action"; 1097b). Following the alternative manuscript readings given by Gauthier, and also those of the Caius College manuscripts, I read *uxori* for *uxore*, and alter the punctuation of the last sentence.) The insistence that "self-sufficiency" includes friends and family as well as oneself is of special interest in connection with Griselda; that is, Griselda's "suffisaunce" extends to Walter's happiness.

27 Burnley, *Chaucer's Language and the Philosopher's Tradition*, 95–6.

Abidinge evere his lust and his plesance
To whom that she was yeven, herte and al,
As to hire verray worldly suffisance.[28] (754–9)

These lines link "suffisaunce" with "sadnesse," and more, they show us Griselda's apparently unemotional "sadnesse" as linked with her emotional "suffisaunce," the fulfilment that she finds in her love. "Sadnesse" arises from emotional "suffisaunce," and it also concludes in it; Griselda's steadfastness, arising from her love, leads to the satisfaction of that love in Walter's final change of heart. To return to the question of how it is that Walter finally "has enough," I think that Chaucer saw the answer in the concept of "sadnesse"; denoting "steadfastness," in this tale "sadnesse" takes on connotations of "satisfaction." The lines I quoted earlier on Walter's final surrender to pity for Griselda's "stedfastnesse," with his full realization that she is "ay sad and constant as a wal," are followed immediately by his second and last "This is inogh, Grisilde min."[29] It is Griselda's "sadnesse" that is finally "inogh" for Walter. This may seem paradoxical – even impossible – since "sadnesse," strictly interpreted, would have passive, rather than active, force – would signify "being satisfied," rather than "power to satisfy." But what Chaucer's delicate linking of words and concepts perhaps suggests is that "sadnesse" in this story comes to participate in the strange kind of "transferability" characterizing "suffisaunce" in love relationships; matching the paradoxical ability of a lover to derive "self-sufficiency" from the "satisfaction-fulfilment" offered by a mutual love is the paradoxical ability, demonstrated in this tale, for one partner's stoical self-sufficiency to issue in the other's emotional satisfaction and hence in mutual fulfilment.

At any rate, by perceiving that Chaucer grasped the connections between "sad" and "inogh," we can see that it is entirely appropriate that it is the "unsad" people of the city (995) who welcome Walter's new wife in a greedy desire for "more" – marked by a battery of comparatives:

For she *is fairer*, as they demen alle,
Than is Grisilde, and *moore* tendre of age,

28 Ibid., 88. We may note at this point that the word "sad" is also associated with Walter's love for Griselda; he contemplates the humble peasant girl "noght with wantowne looking of folye" but in "sad wise" (235–8).

29 It may be noted at this point that *MED*, s.v. "inough," n., sense (f), classifies this phrase with the use of "inough" to mean "no more of this matter, that will do." In my view this is incorrect. First, the citations given in the *MED* show that in this sense the more usual expression is the simple word "enough." Second, the narrative context of the *Clerk's Tale* gives Walter's words full lexical weight in both instances.

And *fairer* fruit bitwene hem sholde falle,
And *moore* plesant, for hire heigh linage. (988–91; my italics)

The true function of "more" is to be found not in such greedy yearnings, or in Walter's desire continually to "tempte moore" (786), but in its quasi-magical growth out of the acceptance of "inogh." This growth can be seen in the description of Griselda's at first apparently static constancy.

He waiteth if by word or contenance
That she to him was chaunged of corage.
But nevere koude he finde variance;
She was ay oon in herte and in visage.
And ay the ferther that she was in age,
The *moore* trewe, if that it were possible,
She was to him in love and *moore* penible. (708–14; my italics)

It is this spontaneous generation of increase that finally finds its counterpart and its reward in the increased splendour of the feast that celebrates the reunion of Walter and his wife:

... *moore* solempne in every mannes sight
This feste was, and *gretter* of costage,
Than was the revel of hir mariage. (1125–7; my italics)

Chaucer's last use of the idea of "sadnesse" shows a subtlety that marks one of the points at which he goes beyond even Petrarch. Readers over the centuries have found it tempting to take Griselda's "sadnesse," the calmness with which she relinquishes her children, as due to the absence, rather than the control, of emotion. But Chaucer shows the mistakenness of this interpretation by the way he uses the word "sad" in the reconciliation scene. When she is reunited with her children, Griselda's feelings at last find expression:

"O tendre, o deere, o yonge children mine,
Youre woful moder wende stedfastly
That cruel houndes, or som foul vermine,
Hadde eten yow; but God, of his mercy,
And youre benigne fader tendrely
Hath doon yow kept!" – and in that same stounde
Al sodeinly she swapte adoun to grounde.

And in hire swough so sadly holdeth she

Hir children two, whan she gan hem t'embrace,
That with greet sleighte and greet difficultee
The children from hir arm they gonne arace. (1093–1103)

We may note, first, the poignancy given to the idea of "stedfastnesse" by the application of the adverb "stedfastly" to Griselda's belief that her children are dead; the deep conviction of loss has a numbing steadfastness of its own. But even more striking is the use of the adverb "sadly." In the swoon that marks the overwhelming deliverance from her steadfast belief in the death of her children, Griselda holds them "sadly" – firmly, tightly, closely, so closely that they can barely be torn from her grasp.[30] Griselda's love for her children has the same steadiness and depth as her acceptance of their loss. Chaucer, I think, took the hint from Petrarch's paradoxical idea of Walter embracing his wife "cupidis ulnis" and transformed it into something that is even more profound and subtle, precisely because it brings us closest to the mysterious ability of "suffisaunce" to encompass both steadfast self-sufficiency and the ecstatic fulfilment of reciprocated love.

No account of the *Clerk's Tale* could be complete if it did not at some point follow its final move on to the plane of divine-human relationships, and I want to end, therefore, with some comments on what happens in this context to the complex of words and ideas that I have been discussing. Chaucer repeats Petrarch's comment that the tale is told not as an inducement to wifely obedience but to encourage human "suffrance" of whatever God sends us – and Chaucer offers us this encouragement, we may note, in terms of a movement from positive to comparative:

For, sith a womman was so pacient
Unto a mortal man, wel *moore* us oghte
Receiven al in gree that God us sent. (1149–51; my italics)

Readers have often wanted, naturally but mistakenly, to make these comments a basis for equating God's role with Walter's. The emphasis is, however, all on Griselda; it is the nature of the suffering, not the nature of the testing, that forms the basis of the transition into allegorical meaning. And for that reason, and others besides, I have argued elsewhere that it is in fact Griselda, not Walter, who gives us the truer image of the God who suffers not only the cruelty

30 The swoon is not in Petrarch; in the French version Griselda faints, but she is not holding her children when she does so.

that men inflict on him but also the cruelty that they inflict on each other.[31] And it is precisely in the "insatiability" of her willingness to suffer that Griselda offers an image of this aspect of the divine.

I would like to bring this out more clearly by quoting Julian of Norwich. In Julian's work we are first shown the insatiability of the human longing to be satisfied by the divine – a satisfaction that will meet every need:

> This saw I bodely, swemly and darkely, and I desyred mor bodely light to have seen more clerly. And I was answerede in my reason: "If God will shew thee more, he shal be thy light. Thee nedeth none but him." For I saw him and sought him. For we be now so blinde and so unwise that we can never seke God till what time that he of his goodnes sheweth him to us. And whan we see ought of him graciously, then are we stered by the same grace to seke with great desire to see him more blissefully. And thus I saw him and sought him, and I had him and wanted him. And this is and should be our comen working in this life, as to my sight.[32]

The insatiable desire that in the *Clerk's Tale* is Walter's "gapinge and gredy" wish for "moore and moore" is here transformed into the soul's endless desire for God. And just as Walter's desire is met by Griselda's endless offer of more, until it culminates in his acknowledgment of satisfaction, so the soul's desire is met

---

31 See "Parents and Children in the *Canterbury Tales*," 134–7 above. As this article demonstrates a close relationship between the *Clerk's Tale* and the Ugolino episode in the *Monk's Tale*, the pathos of parental resignation in the first being matched by the pathos of filial resignation in the second, it is worth noting here that the word "inogh" is also of importance in the brief Ugolino story. Ugolino's children beg him to save himself from starvation by eating them: "Oure flessh thow yaf us, taak oure flessh us fro, / And ete inow" (2451–2). The poignancy comes partly from the double meaning of "inogh" – the clash between the surface suggestion of moderation and the measurelessness of the filial sacrifice. Chaucer's use of the word here may have been prompted by Dante's use of the word *assai* at the corresponding point in *Inferno* XXXIII.61, though Dante uses it in a different way.

32 *The Writings of Julian of Norwich*, ed. Nicholas Watson and Jacqueline Jenkins (University Park, PA, 2006), A Revelation of Love (= Long Text), 159 (ch. 10/8–15. Further references are given in the text. On the soul's "insatiable" appetite for God, cf. Augustine, *Confessions*, ed. L. Verheijen, 2nd ed. (Turnhout, 1981), X.6.8: "... ubi fulget animae meae, quod non capit locus, et ubi sonat, quod non rapit tempus, et ubi olet, quod non sparget flatus, et ubi sapit, quod non minuit edacitas, et ubi haeret, quod non diuellit satietas. Hoc est quod amo, cum deum meum amo" ("... where my soul is floodlit by light which space cannot contain, where there is sound that time cannot seize, where there is a perfume which no breeze disperses, where there is a taste for food no amount of eating can lessen, and where there is a bond of union that no satiety can part. That is what I love when I love my God"; trans. Henry Chadwick, *Saint Augustine. Confessions* [Oxford, 1992], 183).

by Christ's willingness to suffer more, and it too is limited only by an acknowledgment of satisfaction:

> Then saide oure good lorde, asking: "Arte thou well apaid that I suffered for thee?" I saide: "Ye, good lorde, gramercy. Ye, good lorde, blessed mot thow be." Then saide Jhesu, our good lord: "If thou arte apaide, I am apaide. It is a joy, a blisse, an endlesse liking to me that ever I sufferd passion for the. And if I might suffer more, I wolde suffer more." (ch. 22/1–5)
>
> ... And in these wordes – "if I might suffer more I wolde suffer more" – I saw sothly that as often as he might die, as often he wolde, and love shulde never let him have rest tille he had done it. And I behelde with grete diligence for to wet how often he wolde die if he might. And sothly the nomber passed my understanding and my wittes so ferre that my reson might not, nor cold not, comprehende it ne take it. (ch. 22/21–6)

Like Griselda, Christ not only is willing to suffer more and more, to unimaginable limits, but is also willing to suffer "nedelees":

> He saide not, "if it were nedfulle to suffer more" but, "if I might suffer more." For though it were not nedfulle, and he might suffer more he wolde. This dede and this werke about oure salvation was ordained as wele as God might ordaine it ... And heerin, I saw a fulle blisse in Crist, for his blisse shuld not have ben fulle if it myght ony better have ben done than it was done. (ch. 22/42–7)

It is the willingness to suffer "outrely" that creates satisfaction, the "fulnesse" of bliss, in the divine vision of Julian as in the human tale of Griselda. And the emotions aroused by the tale of Griselda, the fullness of satisfaction that is created in us by Walter's final "This is inogh, Grisilde min," can help us understand why Julian can imagine God as having no more eloquent appeal than the words "Let me alone, my derwurdy childe, intende to me, I am *inogh* to the. And enjoy in thy saviour and in thy salvation" (ch. 36/39–40; my italics). In her sufficiency, as in the miraculous power of her suffering, Griselda is God-like.

Coda

In the complex panorama of the *Canterbury Tales*, all serious concepts undergo comic transformations, and the concept of "inogh" is no exception. A brief glance at the *Shipman's Tale*, which provides the richest example of such a transformation, will indicate the range of possible variations on this theme.

Like *Pearl*, the *Shipman's Tale* links the idea of "inogh" with the idea of "payment" – but it does so, needless to say, in a quite unspiritual context. The opening of the tale puts the emphasis on payment:

> But wo is him that payen moot for al!
> The sely housbonde, algate he moot paye;
> He moot us clothe, and he moot us arraye,
> Al for his owene worshipe, richely,
> In which array we dauncen jolily.
> And if that he noght may, paraventure,
> Or ellis list no swich dispence endure,
> But thinketh it is wasted and ylost,
> Thanne moot another payen for oure cost ... (10–18)

The other elements in the now familiar lexical set duly make their appearance in this new context. Prominent among them is "nede," which now signifies business transactions:

> The thridde day this marchant up ariseth,
> And on his nedes sadly him aviseth ... (75–6)
> Now gooth this marchant faste and bisily
> Aboute his nede, and byeth and creaunceth. (302–3)

"Incres" is similarly conceived in financial terms (81). And "sadnesse," as the picture of the merchant "sadly" calculating what he needs, has here a quite different meaning from that which it bears in the *Clerk's Tale*. It stands here not for the self-sufficiency of the stoic but for the sobriety of the businessman.[33] The merchant's "sadnesse" has, however, this in common with Griselda's: it entails the suppression of private emotion, to create a serene facade for the outer world. But what was, in the *Clerk's Tale*, a supremely heroic endeavour to meet misfortune with serenity becomes in the *Shipman's Tale* an attempt to make the keeping up of appearances into a bulwark against mishap. When the merchant's wife protests impatiently at the length of time he spends on his "rekeninges," because he already has "inogh ... of Goddes sonde" (216–19), he reprovingly insists on the "curious bisinesse" of "us chapmen," on the fear of "hap and Fortune" that must be concealed beneath "cheere and good visage," so that the

33 On "sadnesse" as a characteristic quality of merchants, see Gardiner Stillwell, "Chaucer's 'Sad' Merchant," *Review of English Studies* 20 (1944): 1–18.

financial realities may be kept "in privetee" (224–37). His response makes the concept of "inogh" elusive of definition in this world. It is not (as the wife assumes) what it takes to satisfy present needs, whether physical or emotional; rather, it stands for the resources that will enable one to meet the vicissitudes of "this queinte world" (236) with resilience (and is thus something like a commercial version of Stoic "suffisaunce"). And because they have a crucial role to play in maintaining one's credit, appearances constitute just such resources. Hence the merchant's parting charge to his wife:

"... for to kepe oure good be curious,
And honestly governe wel oure hous.
Thou hast inow, in every manere wise,
That to a thrifty houshold may suffise.
Thee lakketh noon array ne no vitaille;
Of silver in thy purs shaltow nat faille." (243–8)

The role played here by "inough" is played by "payment" in the opening passage already quoted; the husband's "owene worship" is established by the "aray" for which he pays, because it testifies to the solidity of his credit (12–13). It is perhaps fortunate for the merchant that his wife and her lover are every bit as committed to the world of appearances, and as skilled in manipulating it, as he is. If the merchant's success depends on the concealment of his "privetee" behind a facade of "sadnesse," so does his wife's. Thus, for the wife and the monk, the ideas of "inogh" and of "nede" are mainly important for the role they can play in the superficial emotional drama behind which the real hard-headed agreement between them can be reached (100, 109); the pressure of real need or "defaute" never makes itself felt:

"A Sonday next I moste nedes paye
An hundred frankes, or ellis am I lorn ...
Pardee, I wol nat faille yow my thankes,
If that yow list to doon that I yow praye.
For at a certein day I wol yow paye ..." (180–1, 188–90)

Yet, as in the serious world of *Pearl*, so here too in the fabliau universe the apparently barren cancelling-out of obligation which is represented by "payment" is transformed into the notion of a miraculous increase which is represented by "inough." The Wife of Bath, in a comic version of the Pearl maiden's lesson to the dreamer (including its light imagery), spells out the power of sex to provide a never-failing satisfaction:

"Have thow inogh, what thar thee rekke or care
How mirily that othere folkes fare?
For, certes, olde dotard, by youre leve,
Ye shal han queinte right inogh at eve.
He is to greet a nigard that wil werne
A man to lighte a candel at his lanterne;
He shal han never the lasse light, pardee!
Have thow inogh, thee thar nat pleine thee."
(*Wife of Bath's Prologue*, 329–36)

The geniality of the *Shipman's Tale*, its adroit evasion of a cynical or harshly moralizing conclusion, depends not only on the smooth maintenance of the facade that keeps the adulterous affair, like the merchant's business, "in privetee," but also on the inexhaustible "credit" constituted by sex, its power to provide "inogh" to fill the needs created by misfortune. Just as the merchant's "chevissaunce" magically causes barren metal to multiply itself, so that "nede," paradoxically, comes to stand for the inevitability of profit (371), so sexuality constitutes a source of wealth that magically replenishes itself and cancels the "dette" between husband and wife. The wife at first again protests that her husband has "inough" (380), but this apparent limitation on sexual satisfaction soon gives way, as she recognizes the newly created debt, to the offer to "paye ... abedde" (424), producing the endless supply that constitutes enough. Sex has the same careless abundance, the same inexhaustible outpouring, as God's grace. With a final triumphant appeal to the double meaning of "inogh," the Shipman cheerfully wishes for himself and his audience access to these never-failing resources (433–4):

Thus endeth my tale, and God us sende
Taillinge inough unto oure lives ende! Amen.

Chapter Nine

Price and Value in *Sir Gawain and the Green Knight*

At the end of *Sir Gawain and the Green Knight*, the Green Knight reveals his complicity in the attempted seduction of Gawain by the lady of the castle (his wife), and voices his whole-hearted admiration for Gawain's resistance to it:

> "I sende hir to asay þe, and sothly me þynkkez
> On þe fautlest freke þat euer on fote ȝede;
> As perle bi þe quite pese is of prys more,
> So is Gawayn, in god fayth, bi oþer gay knyȝtez." (2362–5)

The pearl is a fitting image for the spotless purity of "the most faultless of men." But this idea remains latent; the quality of the pearl on which the Green Knight explicitly bases his comparison is not its purity but its value. "As a pearl is of greater value than a white pea, so is Gawain by comparison with other fair knights." The subject of value in general, and Gawain's value in particular, is central to the poem. I wish to show first, that the poet posed himself the questions "what does value consist in? how is value to be determined?" and second, that it is against the background of medieval economic thought, as it developed within the tradition of Aristotelian commentary, that we can best appreciate the intensity, precision, and witty ingenuity with which the poet conducts his own exploration into the difficulties involved in answering them.

The word "pris" is itself an ideal base from which to launch such an exploration. Its radical meaning is "price" (from Latin *pretium* via Old French *pris*) – the only meaning it retains in modern English. In the medieval period it meant "value" or "worth" in a more general, non-monetary sense as well, and it also had a range of functions now taken over by the later formations "praise" and "prize." That is, it denoted the applause or esteem which is accorded to excellence, "fame, renown or good reputation" (*OED* 9, 10; *MED* 9), and also "preeminence, superiority," the "prize" of coming first in an imaginary contest of excellence (*OED* 11–13; *MED* 7–8). In the chivalric context of *Sir Gawain and the Green Knight*, where moral excellence and knightly renown are of obvious importance, we are not surprised to find the word used in all these transferred senses; what is surprising is to find how alive the poem is to the basic, commercial sense of the word, and how this awareness of its economic centre animates the interrelations between its other meanings.

It is obvious from the first that the *Gawain*-poet uses "pris" to denote both monetary and non-monetary value, and that in doing so he makes the one the mirror of the other. Material splendour and moral worth share a common vocabulary, as a glance at the entries for "dear" and "rich" in Kottler and Markman's *Concordance* immediately makes clear.[1] The description of Gawain's arming provides a formal illustration of this paralleling of the material and the moral. Gawain's armour and accoutrements glitter with gold (569, 577, 587, 591, 598, 600, 603); the pentangle on his shield is "of pure golde hwez" (620), and his helmet is crowned with diamonds "o prys" (615). The jewels and precious metals externalize and communicate his intangible inner worth, the links between the two being suggested by metaphor and simile:

> For ay faythful in fyue and sere fyue syþez
> Gawan watz for gode knawen, and *as golde pured*,
> Voyded of vche vylany, wyth vertuez *ennourned* ... (632–4; my italics)

When the poet later says of Gawain that "alle prys and prowes and pured þewes / Apendes to hys persoun" (912–13), this earlier description of jewels and precious metals hovers behind the word "pured" like a concealed metaphor. The "pured þewes" match the "pured gold"; inward "prys" and outward value are in perfect harmony. And it is not only in being "highly prized" that gold and knightly worth are analogous. The evolution of the "pure" of line 620 into the "pured" of line 633 combines with the surrounding emphasis on the demonstration of Gawain's qualities in action ("watz for gode *knawen*," "watz *funden* fautlez"; 633, 640; my italics), to suggest that knightly worth, like precious metals, can be subjected to a process of "refining," accomplished by the trials of knightly adventure. This suggested analogy gives a punning quality to the Green Knight's use of the word "assay" – the process by which the value of precious

1 *A Concordance to Five Middle English Poems*, ed. Barnet Kottler and Alan M. Markman (Pittsburgh, 1966).

metals is ascertained – in referring both to his own challenge to Arthur's court and to his wife's temptation of Gawain:

> " ... to *assay* þe surquidré, ȝif hit soth were
> Þat rennes of þe grete renoun of þe Rounde Table." (2457–8; my italics)
> "I sende hir to *asay* þe ..." (2362; my italics)

The trial both tests and enhances value. It functions as refining to gold or polishing to a jewel; the past participles used by the Green Knight of Gawain's confession are again pregnant with metaphor:

> "I halde þe *polysed* of þat plyȝt, and *pured* as clene
> As þou hadez neuer forfeted syþen þou watz fyrst borne." (2393–4; my italics)

If this were all, however, it would still leave us with a very romantic conception of "prys" – would leave it, that is, in the glamorous world of jewels and precious metals, forming a flattering parallel to and appropriate focus of interest for an aristocratic class secluded and sheltered from the less dignified aspects of economic life. Yet the very first use of the word "prys" in the poem reminds us of these aspects in a quite unembarrassed way. The tapestries adorning the dais on which Guinevere sits are said to be set with "þe best gemmes / Þat myȝt be preued of prys wyth penyes to by'" (78–9). "Preued," like "assay," suggests a process of testing, the expert establishment of value by a method resembling an ordeal. But the added phrase "wyth penyes to bye" takes us away from the solitary, respectful confrontation of expert and valuable material, and into the world of the market. What "proves" the value of these jewels is purely and simply the amount of cash that has to be paid for them.

This early mention of market realities prepares the way for the much more prominent role to be assumed by the language and practices of the market later on, in Fitt Three of the poem. The presence of a consistent strain of mercantile or commercial vocabulary, running throughout the poem but especially prominent in this Fitt, has been noted several times before, and has even had a whole monograph devoted to it.[2] By their bantering use of words like "bargayn,"

2 R.A. Shoaf, *The Poem as Green Girdle: Commercium in Sir Gawain and the Green Knight* (Gainesville, FL, 1984); for earlier discussions of the commercial imagery in the poem, see note 2 to Shoaf s introduction, 81.

"chaffare," "chepe," and "chevisaunce,"[3] Gawain and the lord of the castle turn their daily exchange of winnings into a mock-barter, in which profit and loss are reckoned up on each side. This mercantile language can be most succinctly illustrated by the conversation following Gawain's proffer of the three kisses in the third and final exchange:

> "Bi Kryst," quoþ þat oþer knyȝt, "ȝe cach much sele
> In *cheuisaunce* of þis *chaffer*, ȝif ȝe hade goud *chepez*."
> "ȝe, of þe *chepe* no charg," quoþ chefly þat oþer,
> "As is pertly *payed* þe *chepez* þat I *aȝte*." (1938–41; my italics)

Most critics have linked this mercantile language in one way or another with Gawain's failings in his test – as representing his "spiritual penury,"[4] for example, or as a sign that he is sinking into "consumerism and merchandising" to such an extent that "he comes to resemble the archetypal shady dealer."[5] In my view, the mercantile language is not a mere stratagem, a means of tarring Gawain with the brush of anti-commercial snobbery, but a subject in its own right; it takes the exchange of winnings out of the world of party games and into the real world of barter and bargaining. Within the playful banter, serious questions about the establishment of market value can be raised and reflected on.

The events of Fitt Three are utterly appropriate to the exploration of these questions. For it is exchange, and not "assay," that is the crucial process in determining value. "Assay" can locate a precious metal on a scale of values, but cannot determine that precious metals will be per se valuable. Medieval thought on the questions of price and value was in no doubt that the process in which value is determined, both relatively and absolutely, is exchange. The fact that *both* Gawain's tests take the form of an exchange (exchange of winnings, exchange of blows) thus assumes a startling significance.[6] The reader's interest is directed not just towards the moral quality of Gawain's performance in these exchanges, but also towards what they can tell us about "prys" and its determination.

3 A full list of words belonging to the linguistic register of trade and commerce is provided in Shoaf's appendix, 77–80. I agree with Shoaf (55–6) that the word "cost" is drawn into this linguistic field although technically it is a different word from "cost" meaning "expense" (see *MED*, s.v. cost, n., senses 1 and 2); it suggests its homonym by a quasi-pun. Cf. also P.B. Taylor, "Commerce and Comedy in *Sir Gawain*," *Philological Quarterly* 50 (1971): 1–15, at 10–12.

4 Taylor, "Commerce and Comedy," 3.

5 Shoaf, *The Poem as Green Girdle*, 59.

6 As does the fact that the *Gawain*-poet seems to have been the first to bring these two motifs together; see the introduction to Tolkien and Gordon's edition, xix–xx.

Medieval thinkers learned that value is essentially exchange value from their study of Book V, Chapter 5 of Aristotle's *Nicomachaean Ethics*. The *Ethics* was translated into Latin by Robert Grosseteste in the mid-thirteenth century, [7]and commentaries on the work began to appear almost immediately, continuing unabated until the end of the Middle Ages. The analyses of *Ethics* V.5 in these commentaries constitute the most important line of development in medieval economic thought.[8] Aristotle's main interest in this section of the *Ethics* is not in economic questions per se, but in commutative justice, of which justice in exchange is a subcategory; his discussion is in consequence brief. It is also occasionally obscure, but from our point of view the meaning of the original text is less important than the way the medieval commentators interpreted it. Aristotle's concern is to show that justice in exchange is not a matter of tit-for-tat equivalence (simple "contrapassum"), but rather of "proportionate requital" ("contrafacere proportionale"). Since men need to exchange objects of different kinds for their mutual benefit, the kind of exchange which cements the bonds of human society is not a matter of identical return (a blow for a blow, for example), but of maintaining a *proportionate* equivalence between non-identical things. Aristotle cites shoes and a house. In order to effect a just exchange, the builder and the shoemaker must be able by some means to establish the "proportionate equivalence" between the shoes and the house – i.e., their relative worth – and this means that despite their disparity as objects, they must be capable of being referred to a common measure of value: "all things that are exchanged must be somehow commensurable." In practical terms, this end is achieved by the use of money: "it is for this end," Aristotle says, "that money has been introduced, and it becomes in a sense an intermediate; for it measures all things, and therefore the excess and the defect – how many shoes are equal to a house or to a given amount of food." But money is an index of value, not its

7 Grosseteste's translation exists in a "pure" and a "revised" version, both of which are edited by René Antoine Gauthier, *Ethica Nicomachea. Translatio Roberti Grosseteste Lincolniensis sive "Liber Ethicorum," A. Recensio Pura; B. Recensio Recognita, Aristoteles Latinus* XXVI.1–3, fasc. 3–4 (Leiden, 1972–3).

8 An excellent and scholarly account of this commentary tradition is given in Odd Langholm, *Price and Value in the Aristotelian Tradition* (Bergen, 1979); see Langholm also for further bibliography. Langholm provides in an appendix the Latin translation of the crucial passage of *Ethics* V.5 in Grosseteste's "pure" version, with interlinear variants of revision. My exposition is based on this composite text; translations are my own.

For a fuller account of medieval economic thought, see Odd Langholm, *Economics in the Medieval Schools* (New York, 1992), and Joel Kaye, *Economy and Nature in the Fourteenth Century* (Cambridge, 1998), chs 1–5, and especially 88–93 on the mistaken modern ideas about the idealizing nature of medieval theories of value.

source: the real creator of value is not money, but need. "All goods must therefore be measured by some one thing ... Now this unit is in truth demand [*chreia*], which holds all things together ... but money has become by convention a sort of representative of demand." What exactly Aristotle meant by "chreia" is a matter of debate, but its medieval meaning was fixed by the translators and commentators of the *Ethics*, who rendered it variously as "opus," "necessitas," or "indigentia," all meaning "need."[9] Need makes things "commensurable" for purposes of exchange – that is, it establishes their relative value.

The medieval commentary tradition developed different aspects of this theory in turn. Albertus Magnus, whose first commentary on the *Ethics* followed hard on the heels of Grosseteste's translation, introduced a new element into the explanation of the relative value of shoes and a house by referring it to the difference in "labour and costs" ("in labore et expensis") expended by the shoemaker and the builder in producing them.[10] Later commentators saw the role of the consumer as more important than the role of the producer in fixing value, and turned their attention to elucidating the nature of *indigentia*.[11] The most important advance on this front found expression in the influential commentary of the fourteenth-century philosopher John Buridan, who answered the potential objection that many (indeed most) objects exchanged are not "needed" in the sense of being necessary for basic survival, by glossing *indigentia* in Stoic terms as *any* felt lack or consciousness of insufficiency.[12] In this sense, rich men show their "need" of luxuries simply by their willingness to exchange other goods for them. As interpreted by Buridan, the term comes very close to the modern English "demand"; the emphasis is on the subjective desires of the consumer, rather than the objective utility of the commodity. Medieval canon lawyers expressed a similarly hard-headed perception of the role of the consumer in creating value in the maxim "Res valet quantum vendi

9 See Langholm, *Price and Value*, 37–50.

10 Ibid., 61–84.

11 The emphasis on *indigentia* characterizes the *Ethics* commentary of Thomas Aquinas (see Langholm, *Price and Value*, 85–95); it was Thomas who clarified another of Aristotle's obscurities by developing the theory of the "double measure" of value, in which the true measure, need, is reflected in terms of money, the practical measure.

12 Langholm, *Price and Value*, 123–7. Buridan's contribution to economic theory is contained in Quaestiones xiv–xvii of his commentary on *Ethics* Book V (*Quaestiones super Decem Libros Ethicorum Aristotelis ad Nicomachum*); I have consulted the Paris editions of 1513 and 1518 and the Oxford edition of 1637. For the earlier sources of these four Quaestiones, see Langholm, 107, 118, 125. The Stoic influence appears in Buridan's quotation of Seneca's second letter to Lucilius (*Epistulae Morales* II): "Non qui parum habet, sed qui plus cupit, pauper est" (*Quaestiones* V.xv) – one among several Senecan quotations in the *Quaestiones*.

potest" ("a thing is worth what it can be sold for").[13] Scarcity, whose role was acknowledged in maxims such as "omne rarum est carum,"[14] is not enough to create value in itself; it must be combined with demand – as is well understood by Chaucer's Wife of Bath:

> Great prees at market maketh deere ware,
> And to greet cheep is holde at litel pris. (*Wife of Bath's Prologue*, 522–3)

Buridan also introduced into general circulation another important refinement of the Aristotelian theory – namely, the explanation that the need in question is not a merely individual need (otherwise starving men would have to pay more for bread than well-fed ones), but the generalized demand for a particular commodity felt by a whole community, considered in the aggregate;[15] the importance of this definition for *Gawain* will become clear later.

The Aristotelian commentary tradition was quite clear about the fact that the scale of market values established by *indigentia* is completely independent of other, more idealistic, types of value hierarchy. Aquinas, borrowing from St Augustine, pointed out that in economic terms a pearl is more valuable than a mouse, but in the scale of being the mouse must be rated higher, as living creatures are superior to insensate minerals.[16] In a chivalric romance such as *Gawain*, we might expect that value would be established by an appeal to idealistic hierarchies of just this sort – that the analogous "prys" of the knight and gold depends on their analogous positions at the top of their respective ontological categories. But the exchange of winnings sequence pushes beyond such abstract schematizations, and brings us uncompromisingly up against the recognition that it is in the operations of the market – in exchange – and not in the tidy classifications of moralists or theologians, that value is determined.

A closer look at this section of the narrative will illustrate the point. On the first day of the exchange, Gawain offers a kiss as his "winnings" for the day. In return the lord produces the mounds of venison he has brought home from the hunting field. The lord's excited demand for an assessment of the relative worth of the two contributions insists on their commensurability: "How payez yow þis play? Haf I prys wonnen? / Haue I þryuandely þonk þurȝ my craft serued?" (1379–80). But how is the lord's question to be answered? The market

13 Langholm, *Price and Value*, 130–1.

14 Ibid., 155; cf. 113–17.

15 Ibid., 109, 125; Buridan, *Quaestiones* V.xvi.

16 Langholm, *Price and Value*, 87; cf. Augustine, *De Civitate Dei*, ed. B. Dombart and A. Kalb, 2 vols (Turnhout, 1955), XI.16.

imagery with which the whole exchange of winnings is permeated rules out any recourse to idealistic value hierarchies in pondering the question; we are not encouraged to answer, for example, that the kiss is superior to the venison since it is food for the spirit rather than the body, or that the venison is better than the kiss because it represents a communal rather than an individual good. We have to turn to other possible means of defining value, more appropriate to the rules of everyday bargaining.

The wit and ingenuity with which the poet has constructed the exchange of winnings in such a way as to dramatize this central problem now becomes clear. In the first place, he has made the disparity between the objects exchanged far more extreme in nature than Aristotle's comparison of shoes and a house. The substantial is matched with the insubstantial, the corporeal with the incorporeal. Only Buridan's hypothetical example of the exchange of verbal thanks for a gift of £10 comes close to it.[17] The poet has also created an extreme contrast between the methods by which the respective winnings are acquired: the lord's hunting spoils are won by dint of long and energetic physical effort, while Gawain's kisses are accumulated as he lies comfortably in bed. Yet this difference is not allowed to determine their worth. When the question of cost is raised by the lord on the third day (Gawain's three kisses represent an impressive profit "ȝif ȝe hade goud chepez": 1939) – Gawain evades the question ("of þe chepe no charg": 1940). The "labour and costs" theory of comparative value is invoked only to be serenely (and wisely, according to the lights of modern economists) dismissed. The question of value is kept within the confines of the exchange itself.

Turning our attention to the objects themselves, it seems at first that the venison is obviously the more valuable, since it has what can be called an "objective" utility, accessible and beneficial to the majority of potential consumers, while the kiss has only a "subjective" value in the sense that it is dependent on the attitude of the individual receiver.[18] The value of the venison appears to be

---

17 *Quaestiones* V.xiv; Buridan explains that a rich man would need "honour," and would therefore regard £10 as a fair exchange for it.

18 A distinction between "objective" and "subjective" value (termed respectively *virtuositas* and *complacibilitas*) is a feature of the value theory of the Franciscan San Bernardino of Siena (1380–1444); see Raymond de Roover, *San Bernardino of Siena and Sant'Antonino of Florence: The Two Great Economic Thinkers of the Middle Ages* (Boston, MA, 1967), 16–23; the terms originated with the thirteenth-century Franciscan Petrus Olivi, of Serignan in Languedoc (Langholm, *Price and Value*, 115, 153–4), but his association with heresy impeded the circulation of his ideas until they were taken over by Bernardino. It is unlikely that either could be considered a source for the *Gawain*-poet, but they show that this line of thinking was a perfectly possible development within medieval economic thought.

more stable in that it appears to inhere in the object itself, rather than in the unpredictable responses of the consumer. Moreover, a kiss does not remain constant through a series of exchanges; when given by Gawain to the lord it is a very different thing from a kiss offered by a lady to Gawain. This point is comically and paradoxically emphasized by Gawain's scrupulous efforts to reproduce as exactly as possible the kiss he has received:

> He hasppez his fayre hals his armez wythinne,
> And kysses hym as comlyly as he couþe awyse. (1388–9)

The harder Gawain tries, the more it becomes apparent that the value of the kiss he bestows cannot be intrinsically the same as that of the one he received. One could say that it has a purely "notional" value, such as is possessed by paper money; its value is referential, guaranteed by the original it represents as paper money is guaranteed by gold.[19] However, even the value of the original kiss would have depended on the identity of its bestower, as the lord points out:

> "Hit is god," quoþ þe godmon, "grant mercy þerfore.
> Hit may be such hit is þe better, and ȝe me breue wolde
> Where ȝe wan þis ilk wele bi wytte of yorseluen." (1392–4)

A kiss from a serving wench is not as valuable as a kiss from a lady; a kiss from an ugly woman not as valuable as a kiss from a pretty one; a kiss from a stranger not as valuable as a kiss from a woman one loves ... [20] But, as modern economists point out, a distinction between "objective" and "subjective" value is both naive and misleading – and their opinion was shared by the *Gawain*-poet. The desiderated commodity and the desiderating consumer are inseparable elements in the attribution of value; one cannot say whether it is the desire in the consumer that creates desirability in the object, or the desirability in the object that arouses desire in the consumer. The *Gawain*-poet uses the freedom offered by the world of romance to construct an artificial situation which wittily opposes the two kinds of value – but which collapses the opposition as soon as it is perceived. For if the kiss has no "objective" value for the lord (as it might have

19 Cf. the notion of "ascribed value" discussed in William J. Courtenay, "The King and the Leaden Coin: The Economic Background of 'Sine Qua Non' Causality," *Traditio* 28 (1972): 185–209.

20 "What is a kiss worth? It depends who has given it" (J.A. Burrow, *A Reading of Sir Gawain and the Green Knight* [London, 1965], 88). Burrow contrasts the kiss with the "solid winnings" represented by the venison, and adds "The kisses are like merchandise ("cheuicaunce"), their value conditional upon the state of the market" (ibid., 88–9).

if passed on by a woman), the venison has no "subjective" value for Gawain; he cannot eat it, store it, take it away. Despite its solid substantiality, his "profit" remains purely notional.[21] And despite the apparent disadvantages of "subjective" value, illustrated in the uncertain and elusive worth of the kiss, the exchange of winnings demonstrates how indispensable is the role of the subjective element. For even the "objective" utility of the hunting spoils needs to be realized in Gawain's subjective "appreciation" of them. It is here that the connection between "prys" and "prayse" assumes significance, emerging in the alliterating cluster of words expressing Gawain's admiration for the boar killed by the lord on the second day:

> Þat oþer kny3t ful comly comended his dedez,
> And praysed hit as gret prys þat he proued hade ...
> Þenne hondeled þay þe hoge hed, þe hende mon hit praysed,
> And let lodly þerat þe lorde for to here. (1629–30,1633–4)

The lord's "prys" is "proued" first in the boar itself, and then in Gawain's praise of it; they are the external manifestations of, and testimonies to, the lord's worth. Gawain's praise establishes the value of the lord's offering, despite the fact that it is of no objective utility to him. And similarly, the lord's admiration for the kisses is sufficient to establish their value as equal and in his view superior to that of his own offerings. On the third and last day he proclaims himself vanquished; his "foule fox felle" is "ful pore for to pay for suche prys þinges / ... suche þre cosses / so gode" (1944–7). This time it is his own gift which is redeemed by the function of the exchange that makes it equal in worth to such treasures.

It is the exchange alone that makes the different types of "winnings" commensurable in value, creating a "proportionate equivalence" between the two – as Gawain implies when on the second day he gives the lord his two kisses with the comment "Now ar we euen" (1641). It is the exchange that guarantees the equivalence of the worth *attributed to*, not inherent in, the respective winnings, since it implies a judgment of such equivalence in the minds of the consenting parties. So far, the exchange conforms impeccably to the classic model, on the basis of which the poet must have worked out his own bizarre demonstration of the magic power of the exchange to realize a commensurable value in commodities of the most heterogeneous sort.

21 Cf. the comments of Thomas D. Hill, "Gawain's Jesting Lie: Towards an Interpretation of the Confessional Scene in *Gawain and the Green Knight*," *Studia Neophilologica* 52 (1980): 279–86, at 283.

Yet the more we see the exchange as the only means by which the relative value of kisses and venison can be established, the more we become aware that it diverges from the classical model in one crucial aspect – that is, in the absence of *indigentia* as its motivating force. The agreement to exchange is not instigated by the need of either party (even if we take the term in Buridan's extended sense). It *could* not be, for at the time the bargain is made, neither of the parties to it knows what the next day's winnings will be, and is thus not in a position to calculate the level of his own desire for the objects to be exchanged. We cannot therefore explain or justify the "proportionate equivalence" of the exchange by reference to the role of *indigentia*. There are important strategic reasons behind the creation of this non-realistic, "pure" exchange: to remove the unifying force of *indigentia* revives our sense of the heterogeneity of the goods which that unifying force can hold on the same scale, and brings the central problem of defining the nature of value into focus. The "exchange of winnings" sequence thus equips us with some ideas, albeit doubtful and conflicting ones, about the different ways of defining value, and in particular about the double nature of "prys" – subjective and objective, internal and external. It is these ideas that we are to carry with us into the rest of the poem.

The question of "prys" looms large in the bedroom conversations between Gawain and the lady of the castle, where the word itself becomes a weapon in a duel of wits. It is first used by Gawain in a conventional formula of politeness: he calls the lady "your prys" ("your excellence"; 1247). The lady immediately seizes on the word, and insists that the "prys" is not hers but his:

> "In god fayth, Sir Gawayn," quoþ þe gay lady,
> "Þe prys and þe prowes þat plesez al oþer,
> If I hit lakked oþer set at lyȝt, hit were littel daynté;
> Bot hit ar ladyes innoȝe þat leuer wer nowþe
> Haf þe, hende, in hor holde, as I þe habbe here,
> To daly with derely your daynté wordez,
> Keuer hem comfort and colen her carez,
> Þen much of þe garysoun oþer golde þat þay hauen.
> Bot I louue þat ilk lorde þat þe lyfte haldez,
> I haf hit holly in my honde þat al desyres,
> þurȝe grace." (1248–58)

The lady's speech brings to the forefront of the poem the question it is designed to raise and to answer: what is Gawain's "prys," and how is it established? The lady is aware that exchange measures value, and invents a hypothetical exchange by which to evaluate the worth of Gawain's company (as in the exchange of winnings, the insubstantial – "daynté wordez" – is held to outweigh in value objects of a more solidly material sort – "garysoun oþer golde"). The lady also shows herself a good medieval economist in her consciousness that "prys" is established by *indigentia* in the sense of "demand": the value of Gawain's company is determined by the simple fact that all women desire it. As in the exchange of winnings, "prys" is guaranteed by praise, the connection between the two having already been established by the description of the enthusiastic response to Gawain's first arrival at the castle:

> ... alle *prys* and prowes and pured þewes
> Apendes to hys persoun, and *praysed* is euer;
> Byfore alle men vpon molde his mensk is þe most. (912–14; my italics)

The praise follows on the "prys" (in the sense of "worth"), but it also *is* the "prys" (in the sense of "renown"). The lady's first remarks to Gawain put a similar emphasis on universal praise as the basis of his reputation:

> "For I wene wel, iwysse, Sir Wowen ȝe are,
> Þat alle þe worlde worchipez quere-so ȝe ride;
> Your honour, your hendelayk is hendely praysed
> With lordez, wyth ladyes, with alle þat lyf bere." (1226–9)

Gawain's response to the lady's flattery is to protest that the honour bestowed on him by the world in general and the lady in particular reflects not so much his own intrinsic value, as the honourable worth of the lady (in the terms used earlier, he protests that it is purely "subjective"). His own merits are "no match for" their praise, and the exchange is therefore "uneuen":

> "... þe daynté þat þay delen, for my disert nys euen,
> Hit is þe worchyp of yourself, þat noȝt bot wel connez." (1266–7)[22]

The lady rejects this emphatically, asserting that her own experience has shown that the valued qualities are inherent in the admired object, and not just in the imagination of the admirer:

> "Bi Mary," quoþ þe menskful, "me þynk hit an oþer;
> For were I worth al þe wone of wymmen alyue,

22 The first of these lines should probably be emended to read "Bot for þe daynte þat þay delen, my disert nys euen" ("But my worth is not equal to the lavish treatment they give me"). This would make the b-verse regular (with only one strong dip).

> And al þe wele of þe worlde were in my honde,
> And I schulde chepen and chose to cheue me a lorde,
> For þe costes þat I haf knowen vpon þe, kny3t, here,
> Of bewté and debonerté and blyþe semblaunt,
> And þat I haf er herkkened and halde hit here trwee,
> Þer schulde no freke vpon folde bifore yow be chosen." (1268–75)

She inverts another hypothetical market exchange to establish Gawain's value: were she in herself worth all the women alive, and the possessor of all the world's wealth besides, she could not "barter" herself for a better husband than him. Gawain repeats his insistence that this high valuation is a mere subjective whim on her part – while delicately reminding her that so far as she is concerned, the marital bartering process is over:

> "Iwysse, worþy," quoþ þe wy3e, "3e haf waled wel better,
> Bot I am proude of þe prys þat 3e put on me ..." (1276–7)

I do not think that this reply reveals Gawain falling prey to the temptation to value himself at the flatteringly high rate the lady attributes to him, or that "he finally believes that value is subjective only and takes thus the making of his life into his own hands."[23] On the contrary, his remark constitutes a humble acknowledgment that his "prys" is not his to determine; it is for others to furnish the "proof" of his value by their praise. But his clear-sighted insistence on the importance of the subjective response in establishing value opens up a gap between "prys" as inner worth and "prys" as outer reputation; he refuses to identify himself with the Gawain who figures in the gossip picked up by the lady. He needs to do this because the lady is herself opening up such a gap for her own ends. In the conversations that follow, she projects his "prys" as a reputation for philandering and ubiquitous gallantries, rather than renown for "clannes" and "trawþe" (1512–29). And so far from resulting from Gawain's behaviour, this reputation is used to determine it: at the end of the first interview, she doubts whether he is, in fact, Gawain ("Bot þat 3e be Gawan, hit gotz in mynde"; 1293), since "So god as Gawayn gaynly is halden" could not have failed to beg a kiss from her (1297–1301). Gawain's insistence that his "prys" has its source in others, not himself, is to a large extent motivated by his desire to dissociate himself from this false definition of what constitutes his "worth."

23 Shoaf, *The Poem as Green Girdle*, 40–1, 42; cf. 63.

The problem posed by this scene is thus more complex than the question of whether Gawain will be able to resist the lady's demands. It is the problem of the relative roles played by Gawain's inward quality and his outward reputation in defining his "prys." Modern high-mindedness might incline to disregard reputation altogether, but the market imagery of the poem forestalls this hasty conclusion. Desire is as necessary an element in the creation of value as desirability; what people think of Gawain, and what they consider desirable in him, are not irrelevant to his "prys." If Gawain were universally scorned and belittled, could he be said to have "prys" at all? "What's aught but as 'tis valued?" as Shakespeare's Troilus puts it (in a play which also shows the influence of the *Nicomachean Ethics*).[24] If gold were universally scorned, it would be of no value. On the other hand, if there is a generalized "demand" for skill in "luf-talkyng" and flirtatious gallantries, do not these qualities become *ipso facto* valuable? If we argue that Gawain's "prys" is *simply* his inward worth, as he himself defines it, we appear to be insisting on a naive theory of "objective" value which ignores the realities of the market in favour of an idealistic belief in inherent worth.

Gawain, however, resists the lady's suggestions that he adapt his sense of his own worth in terms of a prevailing demand. He clings desperately to his own sense of his "prys," both in the bedroom scenes and also when he is faced with the guide's suggestion that he run away from the encounter with the Green Knight. "If I ran away," he says, "I *would be* a coward" ("I were a knyȝt kowarde"; 2131) – even if no one ever knew about it. It seems that the irrelevance of reputation to fundamental worth could hardly be more uncompromisingly expressed. And the definition of this worth also seems to be developed in isolation from the rest of the community; the comments of the other knights at Gawain's departure from Arthur's court suggests that they see the exploit as folly rather than heroism (674–83). If this were all, we could conclude that the poet was endorsing Gawain's faith in his own private, individual definition of "prys," in eccentric defiance of market demand – that outward reputation was being discarded as irrelevant and unimportant. But matters are not so simple. For what is being defended in this solitary quest *is* reputation – the "renoun" or "los" of the Round Table (258, 313; cf. 2457–8), which the Green Knight wished to have substantiated. Gawain's acceptance of the Green Knight's challenge makes it clear that renown is not merely derivative of prowess; it is an external standard against which the knight may measure his worth, an outer mould within which knightly endeavour may shape itself. A knight's "prys" is

24 See "Shakespeare and Chaucer: 'What is Criseyde Worth?'" 20–41 above.

the result of a collaboration between inward worth and outward renown;[25] his "trawþe" – the integrity or "wholeness" imaged in the pentangle – commits him to the attempt to keep the two in matching harmony. The values expressed in the device of the pentangle are externalized *in order that* Gawain may match himself to their high standards, even more than to show that in the past he has done so. Gawain is thus not only concerned that his reputation should accurately match his inward state (as with his final confessions), he is also concerned that he should match his reputation. He is sensitive to any suggestion that he is falling short of it – such as the lady's reproach "Bot þat ȝe be Gawan, hit gotz in mynde" (1293), or the Green Knight's taunt "Þou art not Gawayn ... þat is so goud halden" (2270).

This concern for "prys" in both senses explains the complicated shifts in the redefinitions of the value of the girdle as the poem moves to its close. At its first appearance, Gawain prizes it very highly as a "juel" (1856). He is persuaded to think his motives for taking it honourable by his previous rejection of the "objectively" valuable ring. Taking the girdle, in contrast, seems a trivial matter: "symple in hitself ... and lasse ... worthy" (1847–8), the girdle appears to have only "subjective" value. It is only "þe jopardé þat hym iugged were" (1856) that gives the girdle the value of a "juel" *for Gawain*; others have no need of its protection so no one will suffer loss if he takes it. "Need" raises its head for the first and last time – and paradoxically, it motivates the only unfair exchange in the poem; Gawain takes the girdle knowing that he will not render it to the lord at the end of the day. Gawain is not to know, of course, that what makes the girdle the poem's most glaring example of "subjective value" is that its life-saving powers apparently exist entirely in Gawain's mind; they are attributed to and not inherent in it. Since the value of the girdle is subjective, it can shift dramatically when the Green Knight makes his revelation, and Gawain's private decision to default on the exchange of winnings is brought into the public domain. Gawain is first made conscious of his fault through its externalization. While his inner conscience acts as its own imaginary "audience" in respect of the exchange of blows, it is less vigilant in the apparently more frivolous context of the exchange of winnings. But as soon as he sees himself reflected in the Green Knight's gaze, Gawain acknowledges the stain on his inward worth. The girdle thus becomes the visible sign of his invisible loss of "prys"; he declares he will wear it as a corrective of "renoun" (2434). For the Green Knight, however, Gawain's flaw

25 Cf. Derek Brewer's comments in "Honour in Chaucer," in *Tradition and Innovation in Chaucer* (London, 1982), 89–109, 167–8, at 90.

disappears, paradoxically, as soon as it is externalized – first, in the nick on his neck, and second, in his frank "confession":

> "I halde it hardily hole, þe harme þat I hade.
> Þou art confessed so clene, beknowen of þy mysses,
> And hatz þe penaunce apert of þe poynt of myn egge,
> I halde þe polysed of þat ply3t, and pured as clene
> As þou hadez neuer forfeted syþen þou watz fyrst borne." (2390–4)

These outward manifestations mend the rupture between inner state and external appearance, make them once again "match" each other. The integrity of Gawain's "prys" is recreated – as is confirmed by the symbolic healing of the nick on his neck during his journey home ("Þe hurt watz hole þat he hade hent in his nek"; 2484). But Gawain's inner state must then be externalized once again for the benefit of his fellow knights, and he uses both the scar and the girdle as means to this externalization.

> "Þis is þe token of vntrawþe þat I am tan inne,
> And I mot nedez hit were wyle I may last;
> For mon may hyden his harme, bot vnhap ne may hit,
> For þer hit onez is tachched twynne wil hit neuer." (2509–12)

The second confession, like the first, recreates a continuum between inner state and outward reputation; Gawain's "prys" is redefined for the court. And so the value attached to the girdle can be altered yet again. The court's brilliantly imaginative and tactful reaction empties it of its significance as a badge of shame: they wear such a girdle as an *honour*, "For þat watz acorded þe renoun of þe Rounde Table" (2519). What Gawain considers "blame" the other knights consider "renoun"; the discrepancy is not cynical but reflects an awareness of the role of the valuer in creating value. Gawain's "prys" is not to be established by himself alone; it is by the community as a whole that it is to be fixed. And for them, to have only so small a fault is a state to be desired. As the nick on Gawain's neck heals, so the "wounding" significance of the girdle disappears as it is absorbed into the wholeness of the Round Table. There is no attempt to conceal or to dismiss Gawain's one failure, but its significance shifts as it is evaluated by the outside world. And it is only in this communal context – in the fixing of "prys" as "renoun" – that Gawain's value is externalized and stabilized. The end of the poem reaffirms the importance of renown as the external definition of "prys" – as the beginning and end of a long and subtle commerce between the internal and the external through which value is not merely recognized but is realized.

Gawain's "prys" is identified with his "trawþe," its worth imaged in the "pure golde hwez" of the pentangle. When he takes the girdle, he "exchanges" for it his "trawþe." In the privacy of his own thoughts, he counts the cost a small one; it is only when the watching gaze of a concealed audience is revealed to him – when his inner state is mirrored in outward fame – that he takes the true measure of his "losse" (2507). I should now like to make some more speculative suggestions about the role of "trawþe" in the exchanges of the poem.

Truth cannot be the object of exchange, since it is one of the "goods of the soul" which, Buridan argues, are by nature insusceptible of valuation in terms of external goods, because they are "ends in themselves" ("fines ipsorum")[26] – a definition nicely matched in the self-enclosed impenetrability of the pentangle. How, then, is its value to be established? Only, I think, by the negative route taken in its exchange for the girdle – that is, by estimating the cost of its *loss*. The method has some similarities with that by which medieval commentators argued for the "value" of items such as air and water, which were not scarce, were not sold for a high price, and yet were of the greatest value for human existence. The value of such goods, it was said, can be measured by the value that men would place on them if they lacked them; it depends on imagining a "demand which might have been."[27] The *Gawain*-poet, we may say, imagines something like a "demand which might have been" for "trawþe." The exchange of blows makes it quite clear that had Gawain abandoned "trawþe" entirely, he would have lost his head. Its "worth" is thus realized in the preservation of his life.

The explanation usually given for Gawain's acceptance of the girdle and surrendering his "trawþe" for so poor a return is that he succumbs to a desire for life; this interpretation is supported by the Green Knight's comments at 2367–8. But as a knight, Gawain risks his life daily, against human and non-human foes. Why should he give way to cowardice in this particular instance? (The fact that he flinches at the first swing of the axe suggests that his faith in the girdle has evaporated by the time he confronts the Green Knight, so that he is proved both to possess and to exercise the courage necessary for the ordeal.) I would suggest that in this particular instance Gawain is under pressure not merely from his physical fear – which he can and does master – but also from an intellectual rebelliousness. That is, he is driven to take the girdle by his consciousness that the initial agreement is unfair, and is tempted to *equalize the exchange* by matching

26 *Quaestiones* V.xv.

27 Langholm, *Price and Value*, 138–9; the commentators in question belong to the late fourteenth and early fifteenth century, so that the *Gawain*-poet could not have known them, but he seems to have followed an analogous line of thought.

the magic powers of the Green Knight with his own. For the exchange of blows is unlike the exchange of winnings in that it involves an exact (rather than a "proportionately equivalent") return – the return of one blow for another being the classic example of simple *contrapassum* in both the *Ethics* and the medieval commentaries on it.[28] In *Gawain*, however, the ostensible fairness of the exact exchange conceals an underlying imbalance: the Green Knight can replace his head if it is cut off, but Gawain cannot. That Gawain himself is only too conscious of this monstrous inequality in the exchange becomes clear when the Green Knight tauntingly contrasts his own steady endurance of the axe blow with Gawain's flinching, and receives the tight-lipped rejoinder:

> " ... þaȝ my hede falle on þe stonez,
> I con not hit restore." (2282–3)

So that when Gawain takes the girdle, it seems to even up the exchange, to create the tit-for-tat correspondence which the Green Knight infuriatingly pretends that it represents.

The exchange of blows is thus not only an excellent illustration of simple *contrapassum*, but also of Aristotle's argument that simple *contrapassum* is not *ipso facto* just. Aristotle himself gives as an example the difference between a ruler striking one of his subjects (in his official capacity) and a subject striking his ruler (in an unofficial capacity) – an example which seems to have been translated into extreme and melodramatic terms by the *Gawain*-poet, so that the point is made in the absolute way that only the romance allows.[29] Gawain is held to the exchange of blows not because its terms are (as the Green Knight pretends) just, but because he has agreed to it; as with the exchange of winnings, the agreement to exchange of itself creates an equivalence between the two sides. "Trawþe" takes over the role of need as the regulator of exchange; it is the matching honesty on both sides that makes the exchange "euen" (1641). This balancing role of truth creates a *contrapassum* which *is* just, expressed in the Green Knight's words to Gawain:

> "Trwe mon trwe restore
> Þenne þar mon drede no waþe." (2354–5)

28 See, for example, Buridan, *Quaestiones* V.xiv.

29 An interesting hint for such an "impossible exchange" is given in Buridan's passing reference to the theory that death is not commensurable with external goods, "for no one of sane mind would agree for all the money in the world that his head should be cut off" (*Quaestiones* V.xv).

Truth cannot be exchanged for external goods, but it *can* be exchanged for itself. Like the kiss, it "returns itself, pays its own debt, and keeps its own balance."[30] The exchange of winnings lies behind the exchange of blows, controlling and determining its outcome by an invisible power. To perceive the shadowy presence of the one behind the other teaches us to perceive yet another shadow beyond both – the exchange of "trawþe" which fills the apparently futile or frivolous bargaining with serious meaning. The "need" in the exchange is not a need for the goods exchanged; it is a need for "trawþe," and "trawþe" alone.

It is therefore in the form, not the content, of the bargain that its equilibrium is to be found. In the exchange of blows as in the exchange of winnings, punctiliousness in keeping to the terms of the bargain must be accompanied by insouciance as to the inequality in their realization. When Gawain reproaches himself, at the end of the poem, with having abandoned "larges and lewté þat longez to kny3tez" (2381), he puts his finger on the twin qualities that the exchange calls for: "lewté" in the scrupulous fulfilment of exchange, "larges" in the uncalculating nature of the initial agreement. Profit and loss are to be determined by chance; acceptance of the riskiness of the enterprise is a condition of the bargain.

Thus if the poet removes the role of need in stimulating exchange, it is to get nearer to the fundamental realities of mercantile life, not to negate them. For the merchant sending his argosies to the sea commits himself, like the knight, to the vagaries of chance, allowing it to determine his final balance of profit and loss, to make him "even now worth this, / And now worth nothing."[31] The line describing the second agreement to exchange winnings – "Wat chaunce so bytydez hor cheuysaunce to chaunge" (1406) – is a beautiful embodiment of this overlap between the mercantile and the knightly; the knightly bravado of the first half of the line informs the mercantile phraseology of the second, so that we feel both "larges" and "lewté" in it, and feel them to be characteristic of both classes. The merchant values "trawþe" as highly as the knight – for him too, his word is his bond. He too treasures his reputation, as the source of his credit, his "worth." He understands as well as the knight does the intangible and elusive nature of "prys," and shares a reverence for the gold and jewels which are mysteriously agreed to possess it, though they minister to no bodily comforts. If the merchant of the parable is so well able to understand the value of the "pearl of great price" that he surrenders all he has in order to possess it, then the real-life merchant will well understand Gawain's willingness to sacrifice everything for the sake of the "trawþe" that gives him the value of a pearl.

30 Taylor, "Commerce and Comedy," 5.

31 *Merchant of Venice*, 1.1.35–6.

This overlay of knightly and mercantile values suggests that the audience for which the poem was intended was not an exclusively courtly one – that the poet was speaking to both classes, and attempting to create an ideal to which both could aspire. The obvious location for such an audience of sophisticated and wealthy merchants and knights in the late fourteenth century is London – and the last twenty years of that century saw indeed the creation of merchant-knights who in themselves embodied the fusion adumbrated in the poem. My analysis of the poem may therefore lend literary support (though not of course proof) to the theory, originally advanced on historical grounds, that London is the likeliest location for its audience.[32] If the *Gawain*-poet was acquainted with Aristotle's theory of value and the medieval commentaries on it – as I believe we must conclude he was – then it is most probable that he himself was a cleric and a scholar. But if so, he put his clerkly learning to good use in the imaginative creation of a romance world which could act as a model for both knights and merchants and harmonize the potential conflict between them. So far from seeing the commercial world as contaminating knightly values, he accords it an equal dignity, and takes its realities as the firm basis on which to build his ideal of knightly "prys."

32 Michael J. Bennett, "*Sir Gawain and the Green Knight* and the Literary Achievement of the North-West Midlands: The Historical Background," *Journal of Medieval History* 5 (1979): 63–88; *Community, Class and Careerism: Cheshire and Lancashire Society in the Age of Sir Gawain and the Green Knight* (Cambridge, 1983), 231–5. It is important to distinguish here between the *author* (who certainly, as the dialect of the poem shows, came from the north-west Midlands) and the *audience*; Bennett's case rests on the absence of any local courts important enough to have exercised literary patronage on the one hand, and on the substantial numbers of men from Cheshire and Lancashire gathered in London in the king's service on the other. For more recent opinions on the likely location of the poem's audience in London, see my article "Courtly Aesthetics and Courtly Ethics in *Sir Gawain and the Green Knight*," 187–220 below.

Chapter Ten

Courtly Aesthetics and Courtly Ethics in *Sir Gawain and the Green Knight*

Late medieval chivalric and courtly culture was characterized by display – or, to use Thorstein Veblen's term, "conspicuous consumption."[1] Splendid clothing, armour, jewels, lavish food and table settings, ritual and spectacle of all kinds (tournaments, theatrical entertainments, pageants, processions, royal entries) – all these things were means by which the courtly class defined itself and presented itself to the world. Malcolm Vale has spoken of "the increasing sacralization of the secular" in the courts of the period: "A more formal, ritualized element gradually invaded the domestic life of princely courts, receiving its most marked – and often extravagant – expression at court feasts in which vows were taken, elaborate interludes and *entremets* introduced, and a more dramatic and theatrical dimension brought to the holding of 'full' or 'solemn' courts."[2] The court of Richard II was notorious for this kind of extravagant

---

Early versions of this essay were delivered as papers to the aesthetics seminar at Trinity College, Cambridge; to Mary Clemente Davlin's students at Dominican University, River Forest; and to the medieval graduate seminar at the University of Oxford. I would like to thank the audiences on all these occasions for their enthusiastic interest and comments. I would also like to thank Maura Nolan and Chris Cannon, who read later drafts with special care and comments.

1 Thorstein Veblen, *Theory of the Leisure Class: An Economic Study in the Evolution of Institutions* (New York, 1899; repr. London, 1970). In the first sentence of his introductory chapter, Veblen states that "The institution of a leisure class is found in its best development at the highest stages of the barbarian culture; as, for instance, in feudal Europe or feudal Japan." He discusses conspicuous consumption as a mark of the leisure class in Chapter 4.

2 Vale, *The Princely Court. Medieval Courts and Culture in North-West Europe 1270–1380* (Oxford, 2001), 300.

display.[3] Nigel Saul calls him "an extravagant, luxury-loving prince. His tastes were expensive and he took a delight in beautiful objects. He owned a large and valuable collection of goldsmiths' work and plate. He was lavish in his spending on clothing, jewellery, tapestry and *objets d'art* generally: according to the Evesham chronicler, on one occasion he spent no less than £20,000 on a robe [decorated] with precious stones."[4] Already in the early years of his reign, there were complaints about the costs of Richard's household, although at this period, according to Chris Given-Wilson, they were not, comparatively speaking, excessive. There were cutbacks in the 1380s, but from 1393 onwards, domestic expenditure climbed dramatically, reaching more than £35,000 in each of the last three years of his reign.[5]

Royal extravagance attracted criticism and controversy from some quarters. The alliterative poem known as *Richard the Redeles* (written around the time of

3 The romanticized and enthusiastic account of courtly culture presented by Gervase Mathew (*The Court of Richard II* [London, 1968]) was followed by a more sceptical and cautious attitude in the essays included in *English Court Culture in the Later Middle Ages*, ed. V.J. Scattergood and J.W. Sherborne (London, 1983); see especially the essays by Sherborne ("Aspects of English Court Culture in the Later Fourteenth Century," 1–27), Scattergood ("Literary Culture at the Court of Richard II," 29–43), and J.J.G. Alexander ("Painting and Manuscript Illumination for Royal Patrons in the Later Middle Ages," 141–62). Latterly, the pendulum has swung back again; see Michael J. Bennett, "The Court of Richard II and the Promotion of Literature," in *Chaucer's England: Literature in Historical Context*, ed. Barbara Hanawalt (Minneapolis, 1992), 3–20, especially 7–10; Nigel Saul, *Richard II* (New Haven, CT, 1997), ch. 14, "The King and His Court"; and John M. Bowers, *The Politics of Pearl: Court Poetry in the Age of Richard II* (Cambridge, 2001).

4 Saul, *Richard II*, 354–5; I have substituted "decorated" for "lined" in Saul's text, as it seems more probable that the stones would appear on the outer side of the garment. For the Evesham chronicler's comment, see *Historia Vitae et Regni Ricardi Secundi*, ed. George B. Stow (Philadelphia, 1977), 156: "inter alias huius mundi diuicias, fecit sibi fieri unam tunicam, de perillis, et aliis lapidibus preciosis, et auro ex propria ordinacione factam, ad 30,000 marcarum in ualorem appreciatam." Despite the obviously exaggerated estimate of the monetary value of the garment, this comment gives a good idea of how Richard's magnificent clothing was perceived by contemporaries. See also Kay Staniland, "Extravagance or Regal Necessity? The Clothing of Richard II," in *The Regal Image of Richard II and the Wilton Diptych*, ed. Dillian Gordon, Lisa Monnas, and Caroline Elam (London, 1997), 85–93, and Marian Campbell, "'White Harts and Coronets': The Jewellery and Plate of Richard II," ibid., 95–114.

5 Chris Given-Wilson, *The Royal Household and the King's Affinity: Service, Politics and Finance in England 1360–1413* (New Haven, CT, 1986), 80–4 and 139–40; see 113 on parliamentary complaints about royal expenditure; for tables showing the relative costs of the royal household for the period 1360–1413, see 94 and 268–72. Truce with France in 1389 meant that more funds became available for luxury items: "Royal expenditure now shifted from armourers and bowyers to painters and goldsmiths". Caroline M. Barron, "Richard II and London," in *Richard II: The Art of Kingship*, ed. Anthony Goodman and James Gillespie (Oxford, 1999), 129–54, at 139–40.

Richard's deposition)[6] contains an indignant account of the extravagant attire favoured by courtiers. Citing the text from Matthew's gospel (11:8), "They that are clothed in soft garments, are in the houses of kings," the author complains that the courtiers care for nothing other than "quentise of clothinge" (elegance of clothing) (III.176; cf. 120, 122). Their cloaks are wide and their sleeves are so long that they "slide on the erthe" (III.131, 152). They wear gold chains and ornament their belts and drinking horns with silver (III.140). They run themselves into debt in order to buy expensive furs (III.148–51). Their garments are ornamented with "dagging," the edges cut into elaborate shapes, which costs ten times more for the stitching than for the cloth itself (III.162–9). These complaints are, as Patricia Eberle has put it, an indication that "the tradition of dress as a form of investment had become at the court of Richard II what we would now call investment dressing."[7] Towards the end of *Richard the Redeles*, the personified figure of Wisdom appears at court, clad in "the olde schappe," "in an holsum gyse" (III.212–13); predictably, he is rudely ejected by the well-dressed courtiers.

So much for the prosecution, but there was also a contemporary case for the defence. In the same article, Patricia Eberle also drew attention to the justification of courtly luxury found in a Latin treatise written by Roger Dymmok, a Dominican friar, in response to the twelve Lollard propositions contained in a document (purportedly) fixed to the door of Westminster Hall during the session of Parliament in 1395.[8] His treatise is dedicated to Richard II, and the

---

6 For an edition of the poem, see *The Piers Plowman Tradition*, ed. Helen Barr (London, 1993), 99–133. Citations included in my text refer to Passus and line numbers. Barr dates the poem shortly after Richard's deposition (Introduction, 14); David Carlson inclines to place it in late summer 1399, just before the deposition; "English Poetry, July–October 1399, and Lancastrian Crime," *Studies in the Age of Chaucer* 29 (2007): 375–418, at 379–80. The poem survives in a single manuscript, Cambridge, University Library Ll.4.14, of the second quarter of the fifteenth century.

7 Patricia Eberle, "The Politics of Courtly Style at the Court of Richard II," in *The Spirit of the Court. Selected Proceedings of the Fourth Congress of the International Courtly Literature Society (Toronto 1983)*, ed. Glyn S. Burgess and Robert A. Taylor (Cambridge, 1985), 168–78, at 171.

8 *Rogeri Dymmok Liber Contra XII Errores et Hereses Lollardorum*, ed. H.S. Cronin (London, n.d.). The twelve Lollard propositions survive only in the writings of their opponents, viz.: *Fasciculi Zizaniorum*, ed. Walter Waddington Shirley, Rolls Series 5 (London, 1858), 360–9 (Latin), and Dymmok's refutation (Latin and English); for a separate edition of the English version of the propositions, see Anne Hudson, ed., *Selections from English Wycliffite Writings* (Cambridge, 1978), 24–9, 150–5. For a discussion of Dymmok's treatise and its intended audience, see Fiona Somerset, *Clerical Discourse and Lay Audience in Late Medieval England* (Cambridge, 1998), 103–34.

manuscript, now at Trinity Hall, Cambridge (MS 17), was evidently a presentation copy. Most of the Lollard propositions criticized the failings of the established Church, but the twelfth concerned secular life: it claimed that "þe multitude of craftis nout nedful" (such as goldsmiths and armourers) should be abolished, because they encourage "wast, curiosite and disgysing" (that is, elaborate display and fancy clothing).[9] In answer to this, Dymmok distinguished between two types of "necessity": first, there are those things needed simply to sustain life, but second, there are those things necessary to live decently ("conuenienter"). Drawing on Aristotle's discussion of "magnificence," or "the art of spending money lavishly," in the *Nicomachaean Ethics* (IV.ii; 1122a–1123a), he argues that differences in social status need to be manifested in differences in food, clothing, and housing, and for this many crafts are necessary. As far as clothing is concerned, he explains that "princes and nobles" ("principes ac nobiles") should be distinguishable by their more elaborate dress, since it flies in the face of reason that the servant should be dressed like the master, a simple knight like a prince, or a monk like a layman. Furthermore, it is a way of striking fear into the lower orders and so it prevents them from rebelling against their betters ("ad incuciendum metum populis, ne nimis faciliter insurgant contra suos superiores").[10] Dymmok cites the advice given by Aristotle to Alexander in the *Secretum Secretorum* that he should never appear in public except in "fine and splendid dress," so that he should be held in greater reverence. Dymmok also cites the visit of the queen of Sheba to the court of King Solomon; having attempted to impress him with her own wealth, she was forced to recognize in the superior splendour of Solomon's court the superiority of his wisdom. [11]

As Dymmok's defence suggests, the lavish display of Richard's court was not simply the result of a taste for soft living. It had a serious political purpose: it was designed to enhance the prestige of the monarch and to induce an almost religious sense of awe in those who beheld him.[12] The most famous

9 *Dymmok*, ed. Cronin, XII, 292.

10 On the role of clothing laws in reinforcing the social order in the fourteenth and fifteenth centuries, see Claire Sponsler, "Narrating the Social Order: Medieval Clothing Laws," *Clio* 21:3 (1992): 265–83.

11 *Dymmok*, ed. Cronin, XII.1, 293–5.

12 Nigel Saul (*Richard II*, 355–6) speaks of the "element of political calculation" in Richard's lavish expenditure; his aim "was to present a particular set of messages about himself." Display conveyed "the reality and effectiveness of his power," and also "bore visible witness to wisdom" (Saul quotes Dymmok's comparison with Solomon as evidence for the latter point). Richard Firth Green also points out "the propaganda value of a large and sumptuous household" (see *Poets and Princepleasers. Literature and the English Court in the Late Middle Ages* [Toronto,

visual artefact of Richard's reign, the Wilton Diptych, illustrates Richard's sense of the religious dimensions of his kingship: on the left-hand panel, Richard is presented to the Christ Child not only by John the Baptist, to whom he was specially devoted, but also by his two sainted predecessors, King Edward the Confessor and King Edmund of Anglia, while on the right-hand side of the panel the heavenly angels accompanying the Virgin and Child all wear Richard's livery badge, the white hart.[13] The full-size (2.13 × 1.10 m.) portrait of Richard, robed, crowned, and holding the sceptre and orb, which was placed in Westminster Abbey, with its awe-inspiring "hieratic frontal pose," gave solemn authority to his kingship in a more public way.[14]

In this essay I propose to examine *Sir Gawain and the Green Knight* against the background of this conscious cultivation of royal and courtly display, and to argue that the poet is aiming to identify the raison d'être of courtly luxury in a far more sophisticated and interesting way than Dymmok. Instead of justifying courtly magnificence in terms of realpolitik, as a means of intimidating the lower classes and maintaining social order by a visible display of wealth and power, the poet sees it as a natural expression of the inner splendour of courtly virtues (especially "trawþe" and "clannes") and a reflection of their special qualities. Outward display and inward virtues are mirror images of each

1980], 17–18). Staniland ("The Clothing of Richard II," 92), noting that Richard's "ostentatiously rich dressing" was "by no means a new departure and parallels can be found among his English and Continental peers," suggests that it could have provided "reassurance and [a] sense of authority ... in the hostile environment of the English court." Lynn Staley emphasizes that Richard's attempts to create this awe-inspiring image of kingship belong to the last decade of his reign, and result from his desire to claw back the power wrested from him by the Appellants in 1388 (*Languages of Power in the Age of Richard II* [University Park, PA, 2005], 22, 75–6, 111–39).

13 For detailed discussions of the techniques, functions, and iconography of the Diptych, see the essays in Gordon, Monnas, and Elam, *The Regal Image of Richard II*. The Diptych was probably intended for private use, but it testifies to the image of kingship that Richard wished to associate with himself. Its date is uncertain, but internal indications have suggested a date in the late 1390s (1395–9); see Nigel Morgan, "The Signification of the Banner," in Gordon, Monnas, and Elam, *The Regal Image of Richard II*, 179–88, especially 187–8, and Maurice Keen, "The Wilton Diptych: The Case for a Crusading Context," ibid., 189–96, especially 189.

14 See Jonathan J.G. Alexander, "The Portrait of Richard II in Westminster Abbey," in Gordon, Monnas, and Elam, *The Regal Image of Richard II*, 197–206, quotation at 205. Cf. Paul Binski, *Westminster Abbey and the Plantagenets. Kingship and the Representation of Power, 1200–1400* (New Haven, CT, 1995), 206. As with the Diptych, the date of the portrait is uncertain, but it has been generally thought to belong to the 1390s (Alexander, 201, 204; Binski, 205).

other.[15] This fusion of material splendour and ethics is effected by significant strands in the vocabulary of the poem, and discussion of these strands will form the core of my argument. I shall, however, preface this discussion with a synthesis of recent work that points toward the Ricardian court, rather than the north-west of England, as the most probable context for this poem, and show how some features of the Cotton Nero poems become more readily comprehensible in this context. As a coda to the main discussion, I shall return to the political functions of the poem's fusion of courtly splendour and courtly virtues and make some suggestions as to why the particular ethical qualities celebrated in the poem are appropriate to the Ricardian context.

First, then, a brief consideration of the likely home of the poem. Not so long ago, it would have been thought self-evidently pointless to connect it with the royal court, since this poem and the three others that accompany it in the sole surviving manuscript (London, British Library Cotton Nero A.X) were confidently located, on the grounds of their dialect, in the north-west of England – even more precisely, in "a very small area either in SE Cheshire or just over the border in NE Staffordshire."[16] The poet's description of Gawain's journey

---

15 Cf. Elizabeth Keiser, *Courtly Desire and Medieval Homophobia* (New Haven, CT, 1997), 24: "The *Cleanness*-poet does not attempt to spiritualize and desecularize the class-specific behavior of his listeners. Rather, he incarnates the conception of the ethical and the divine in forms of life appealing to an aristocratic mentality."

My argument does not depend on a claim that the *Gawain*-poet necessarily knew Dymmok's treatise (which would mean that *Gawain* was written after 1395), but on the other hand the possibility cannot be excluded. Cotton Nero A.X (which lies at least one remove from the author's holograph) is dated on paleographical grounds to the last quarter of the fourteenth century; its illustrations were added some time later (c. 1400–1410). See Kathleen L. Scott, *Later Gothic Manuscripts, 1390–1490*, 2 vols (London, 1996), 2:66–8, and A.S.G. Edwards, "The Manuscript: British Library MS Cotton Nero A.x," in *A Companion to the Gawain-Poet*, ed. Derek Brewer and Jonathan Gibson (Cambridge, 1997) 197–219. Although it is not the main concern of this article to argue for a date of composition in the 1390s, it is worth noting that other indications (such as Richard's assembly of his Cheshire bodyguard) offer cumulative support for such a date; see further nn. 5, 12, 19, 31, 36.

16 Angus McIntosh, "A New Approach to Middle English Dialectology," *English Studies* 44 (1963): 1–11, at 5; see also *A Linguistic Atlas of Late Mediaeval English*, ed. Angus McIntosh, M.L. Samuels, and Michael Benskin, 4 vols (Aberdeen, 1986), 3:37–8. On the basis of an analysis of the "disjunction between the poet's dialect and the scribe's," H.N. Duggan suggested that "if the *LALME* localization of the manuscript is correct and if the poems are not substantially earlier than the manuscript," then the poet's dialect is more likely to derive from Staffordshire than from Cheshire, Lancashire, or Derbyshire ("Meter, Stanza, Vocabulary, Dialect," in *Companion to the Gawain-Poet*, 221–42, at 242). Duggan's proviso turns out to be important, since Ad Putter and Myra Stokes have since conducted a very thorough re-examination and critique of *LALME*'s evidence for localizing the dialect of Cotton Nero A.X and have concluded that

through the Wirral, which demonstrates a knowledge of this part of the country, pleasingly harmonized with this indication of the poet's place of origin and served to confirm it.[17] The provincial court to which, it was supposed, the poet belonged, and for whose entertainment he wrote, was imagined as the counterpart of Bertilak's court in the poem, a baronial castle in the countryside.[18] This picture was first seriously troubled by the historian Michael Bennett, who, after a thorough study of Cheshire and Lancashire society in the later Middle Ages, concluded that it is "difficult to document any major centres of cultural life in the region" that would provide a plausible source of patronage and audience for the author of such a poem as this.[19] The major landholders in the region – such as John of Gaunt or the earls of Arundel and Salisbury – had their main residences elsewhere. On the other hand, Bennett pointed out, Richard II, who was earl of Chester, had strong connections with the region. In the late 1380s and 1390s, he came to rely on the earldom of Chester as a power base from which he

---

(at least until such time as further evidence is produced) Cheshire is more likely than Staffordshire ("The *Linguistic Atlas* and the Dialect of the *Gawain* Poems," *Journal of English and Germanic Philology* 106 [2007]: 468–91).

17 For a recent attempt to read *Gawain* as a "border text," see Rhonda Knight, "All Dressed Up with Someplace To Go: Regional Identity in *Sir Gawain and the Green Knight*," *Studies in the Age of Chaucer* 25 (2003): 259–84.

18 See James R. Hulbert, "A Hypothesis Concerning the Alliterative Revival," *Modern Philology* 28 (1931): 405–22, especially 414 (though Hulbert on 406, n. 1, acknowledged that he had found no castle in the north-west Midlands that could be identified with the Green Knight's abode).

19 Michael J. Bennett, "Courtly Literature and Northwest England in the Later Middle Ages," in *Court and Poet. Selected Proceedings of the Third Congress of the International Courtly Literature Society (Liverpool 1980)*, ed. Glyn S. Burgess (Liverpool, 1981), 69–78, at 70. See also Bennett, "*Sir Gawain and the Green Knight* and the Literary Achievement of the North-West Midlands: The Historical Background," *Journal of Medieval History* 5 (1979): 63–88; *Community, Class and Careerism: Cheshire and Lancashire Society in the Age of Sir Gawain and the Green Knight* (Cambridge, 1983), 231–5; "The Court of Richard II and the Promotion of Literature" (cited in n. 3); "The Historical Background," in Brewer and Gibson, *Companion to the Gawain-Poet*, 71–90.

Edward Wilson suggested that *Gawain* might have been composed for the Stanley family ("*Sir Gawain and the Green Knight* and the Stanley family of Stanley, Storeton, and Hooton," *Review of English Studies* n.s. 30 [1979]: 308–16), but Ad Putter has pointed out that the most likely candidate for patron of the *Gawain*-poet is Sir John Stanley (d.1414), who belonged to the Lathom branch of the family, and who "left his native area to pursue a career in the service of Richard II"; "he was appointed Deputy to the Lieutenant of Ireland, Robert de Vere, and soon afterwards Lieutenant in his own right; in the 1390s [he] presided over Richard II's recruitment of his Cheshire bodyguard, becoming Controller of the Wardrobe in 1397" (*An Introduction to the Gawain-Poet* [London, 1996], 35). For further information on the Stanley family, see Michael J. Bennett, *Community, Class and Careerism*, 215–19; " 'Good Lords' and

could draw loyal support.[20] In 1397, he raised Chester from a county palatinate to a principality (thus making himself prince of Chester). What is particularly relevant here is that at the same time he recruited a large retinue of men from Cheshire (estimated at around 750), from whose numbers was chosen the personal bodyguard of 311 archers who accompanied him everywhere.[21] The king's partiality for his Cheshire men was widely resented and criticized (it was one of the articles offered in justification for his deposition).[22] Lately, scholars have been more and more willing to entertain the possibility that the *Gawain*-poet might have formed part of this major translocation of Cheshire men to London, and that his poems might have been addressed to a London audience – more precisely, the royal court.[23]

King-Makers: The Stanleys of Lathom in English Politics, 1385–1485," *History Today* 31, no. 7 (July 1981): 12–17, especially 13; Barry Coward, *The Stanleys, Lords Stanley and Earls of Derby, 1385–1672* (Manchester, 1983), 2–3. Ralph Hanna's rejection of a Cheshire connection, on the grounds that the information in *LALME* showed that the author's dialect was not that of Cheshire ("Defining Middle English Alliterative Poetry," in *The Endless Knot: Essays on Old and Middle English in Honor of Marie Borroff*, ed. M. Teresa Tavormina and R.F. Yeager [Cambridge, 1995], 43–64, at 56 n. 39), is countered by Putter and Stokes (see n. 16 above), especially 471–2.

20 Richard spent some time in Cheshire and the north-west Midlands in July 1387; see Saul, *Richard II*, 172, 471. He and his household also spent Christmas and New Year 1398–9 at Lichfield, with his Cheshire retainers in attendance, and Michael Bennett has suggested that *Gawain* would have made an excellent entertainment on this occasion ("The Court of Richard II," 13–14).

21 These figures are taken from R.R. Davies, "Richard II and the Principality of Chester 1397–9," in *The Reign of Richard II. Essays in Honour of May McKisack*, ed. F.R.H. Du Boulay and Caroline M. Barron (London, 1971), 256–79, at 268–9; for a more detailed discussion of the composition and numbers of the Cheshire retinue, see James L. Gillespie, "Richard II's Cheshire Archers," *Transactions of the Historic Society of Lancashire and Cheshire* 125 (1975): 1–39, especially 11.

22 See Gillespie, "Cheshire Archers," 23 and 31–3; Saul, *Richard II*, 393–4.

23 The poem *St Erkenwald*, which is written in a dialect similar to that of the poems in Cotton Nero A.X, is "emphatically a London poem, written in praise of the capital's patron saint" (Malcolm Andrew, "Theories of Authorship," in Brewer and Gibson, *Companion to the Gawain-Poet*, 23–33, at 26). For evidence that other alliterative works were copied in the capital, see Putter, *Introduction to the Gawain-Poet*, 29–31, and A.I. Doyle, "The Manuscripts," in *Middle English Alliterative Poetry and its Literary Background*, ed. David A. Lawton (Cambridge, 1982), 88–100. Putter concludes: "Perhaps the group of royal household servants from the north west would offer the sort of milieu most consistent with the characteristics of the *Gawain*-poet's work and his imagined audience: cosmopolitan, but not oblivious to regional identity; sophisticated and courtly, but no more socially exclusive than the circle of Cheshire courtiers at Richard II's court. To this tight network belonged not only knights like Sir John Stanley or Sir Richard Craddock, to whom Richard II entrusted his presentation copy of Jean

In the context of the Ricardian court, a number of puzzling features of the *Gawain*-poet's works become more comprehensible. The poem *Cleanness*, for example, contains a passage of enthusiastic praise (voiced by God himself) for sex between a man and a woman, which is said to be a bliss exceeding that of Paradise itself. This unqualified praise of the sexual act, with no mention of the procreation of children (the usual *sine qua non* for an account of sinless sex) is without parallel or precedent in medieval literature. But Elizabeth Keiser has argued that it needs to be understood as the obverse of the poem's attack on male homosexuality.[24] Its context is the story of God's destruction of Sodom, as a punishment for the sexual perversions of the Sodomites. The two angels whom God sends to Sodom, and whom the Sodomites want to rape, are described as beardless youths of surpassing beauty (789–94), with skin like the briar-rose and radiant complexions. In contrast, the Sodomites are stout men, uncouth and rowdy. Keiser argues – persuasively, to my mind – that this scene makes sense if it is related to the style of elegant luxury adopted by the courtiers of Richard II, and exemplified in the angels of the Wilton Diptych, who are depicted (like Richard himself) as beardless youths, with long flowing hair and rosy complexions.[25] The message that *Cleanness* speaks on behalf of these elegant courtiers is: "we are feminized, but we are *not* effeminate." In other words, the poem deliberately differentiates the elegant courtier from the homosexual. Carolyn Dinshaw has argued that *Sir Gawain and the Green Knight* similarly – and probably for the same reason – raises the spectre of homosexuality only to

---

Froissart's poems, but also clerics of the chancery and the privy seal like John Clitheroe and John Macclesfield, and the goldsmith Christopher Tildesley, clerk of the royal works" (36). Cf. Bennett, *Community, Class and Careerism*, 233–4, and Bowers, *Politics of Pearl*, 82 n. 26.

Thorlac Turville-Petre has expressed resistance to "the attempt to make a Londoner out of the *Pearl*-poet," but this is not because he wishes to deny a connection with the Ricardian court; rather he argues that *Gawain* "embraces a national audience and claims a status within the culture as central as the work of Chaucer, Gower, and Langland ... the implied audience for *Gawain* ... is neither northern nor southern, but national" ("The *Pearl*-Poet in his 'Fayre Regioun,'" in *Essays on Ricardian Literature in Honour of J.A. Burrow*, ed. A.J. Minnis, Charlotte C. Morse and Thorlac Turville-Petre [Oxford, 1997], 276–94; quotations from 286 and 287–8).

Lynn Staley (*Languages of Power*, 196–263) has recently proposed that the *Gawain*-poet's works were produced under the patronage of John of Gaunt and his brother Thomas of Woodstock (see n. 34 below), but her case is avowedly no more than speculative and to my mind the evidence for Richard's court is stronger.

24 Keiser, *Courtly Desire*, 65–70, 149–59.

25 Cf. the Green Knight's contemptuous reference to Arthur's courtiers as "berdlez chylder" (line 280).

reject it.[26] The kisses exchanged between Gawain and the lord of the castle – kisses that Gawain passes on as "comlyly," as "hendely," as "sauerly and sadly" as he can manage (1389, 1639, 1937) – so far from suggesting the possibility of a homosexual relationship between them, are designed to make it unthinkable – as unthinkable as the possibility of Gawain's actually having sex with his host's wife and finding himself in the position of having to pass on this favour to her husband.[27] The poem establishes heterosexuality as normative, as "the only legitimacy, the only intelligibility";[28] only the courtly game, not personal predilections, can impel Gawain into simulated erotic behaviour with another man.

The careful distancing of homosexual imputations assumes importance for the poem's context when we recall that Thomas Walsingham insinuated that Richard II had homosexual relations with his close friend Robert de Vere.[29] In

26 "A Kiss Is Just a Kiss: Heterosexuality and its Consolations in *Sir Gawain and the Green Knight*," *Diacritics* 24 (1994): 205–26. Dinshaw cites Walsingham's accusation of homosexual relations between Richard II and Robert de Vere (222–3); as she says, even if the accusation was unfounded, there would be a point in Richard's supporters trying to deflect it. However, Dinshaw still sees the poem's "probable audience" as the regional society of Cheshire and Lancashire, and she does not make clear how she reconciles this with the link to the household of Richard II that she calls "very likely" (222).

For an interesting parallel to the idea that the illicit is flaunted only in order to be dismissed as irrelevant, see C. Stephen Jaeger, "L'amour des rois: structure sociale d'une forme de sensibilité aristocratique," in Jaeger, *Scholars and Courtiers: Intellectuals and Society in the Medieval West* (Aldershot, Hants, 2002), VIII.547–71, which takes as its starting-point the loving intimacy between Richard the Lionheart and Philip Augustus, king of France, who slept in the same bed and ate from the same plate, and ends with the (legendary) story of the founding of the Order of the Garter, and the role of the girdle in *Sir Gawain and the Green Knight*. Like Dinshaw, Jaeger sees the suggestion of illicit behavior as introduced simply in order to be rejected. Such a reaction belongs to the vulgar; true aristocrats inhabit a world of exalted feeling and emotional self-control that elevates them far above such ignoble thoughts (562).

27 Social kissing was of course conventional between men in this period; see *Piers Plowman* B XVI.148–49 (I am grateful to Carl Schmidt for drawing my attention to this passage), and cf. *Gawain* 2472 (at 596 and 1118 kisses of farewell seem to be exchanged with both lords and ladies). But Dinshaw's point is that the fact that the kisses were originally given by the lady, in a heavily charged erotic context, gives them a *potentially* erotic character when they are handed on to her husband. Edward Wilson has also drawn my attention to *The Vision of Edmund Leversedge* (ed. W.F. Nijenhuis [Nijmegen, 1991], 122–3), written c.1465–70, which testifies to the popularity of social kissing between men and women, and its potentially erotic character (see Wilson's review of Nijenhuis's edition in *Review of English Studies* n.s. 46 [1995]: 255–7, at 257, for further evidence of the prevalence of social kissing in England.) See also J.A. Burrow, *Gestures and Looks in Medieval Narrative* (Cambridge, 2002), 32–3, 50–7.

28 "A Kiss Is Just a Kiss," 222.

29 *The St Albans Chronicle. The Chronica maiora of Thomas Walsingham, I: 1376–1394*, ed. and trans. John Taylor, Wendy R. Childs, and Leslie Watkiss (Oxford, 2003), (anno 1386) 798: "[rex] tantum afficiebatur eidem, tantum coluit et amauit eundem, non sine nota, prout

this connection it becomes startlingly significant that the distinguishing feature of Robert de Vere's heraldic arms was a five-pointed star ("mullet"), blazoned on the upper left-hand quarter of his shield (quarterly or and gules in the first quarter a mullet argent).[30] Although it lacks the criss-crossing internal lines of the pentangle, the "mullet" is otherwise identical with Gawain's own heraldic blazon, and it is hard to imagine that fourteenth-century readers would have failed to note the resemblance. I am not proposing that *Gawain* should be read as a *roman à clef*, with Gawain himself as a covert stand-in for de Vere, but simply that assigning him the pentangle as his heraldic blazon might have been a

---

fertur, familiaritatis obscene" ("The king was very devoted to him, and greatly respected and loved him, but not without the ignominy, it is said, of an impure relationship"). These words belong to the revisions that Walsingham seems to have made to his chronicle to make it more acceptable to the Lancastrians after their rise to power; see George B. Stow, "Richard II in Thomas Walsingham's Chronicles," *Speculum* 59 (1984): 68–102, at 86, and John Taylor, *English Historical Literature in the Fourteenth Century* (Oxford, 1987; repr. 2000), 68, 74–6. But there is no reason to suppose that he was not belatedly putting on record gossip that had circulated much earlier and which (as Walsingham demonstrates) was remembered to the end of Richard's reign.

Robert de Vere also had Cheshire connections: in the summer of 1387, he "ensconced himself in Chester Castle," where he "lived in some style, giving the region for a while the feeling of a real court. His fine furniture and tapestries at Chester were inventoried in 1388" (Bennett, "The Historical Background," in Brewer and Gibson, *Companion to the Gawain-Poet*, 83). In September of the same year, Richard appointed him to the office of justice of Chester, and in December 1387 de Vere raised a force of Cheshire men who fought on the king's behalf at the battle of Radcot Bridge (Saul, *Richard II*, 172).

30 These arms are recorded in several medieval armorial rolls, which are most conveniently accessed via the link "European Rolls of Arms of the Thirteenth Century" at http://www.medievalgenealogy.org.uk/links/herrefs.shtml#rolls. See The Falkirk Roll, H99; Glover's Roll, B11; The Camden Roll, D30; St George's Roll, E15; The Heralds' Roll, HE 58; Charles's Roll, F17; Vermandois, VE 973. Derek Brewer mentions that the "mullet" is the shield device of the de Vere family, but he does not draw any further conclusions from this ("Armour II: The Arming Topos as Literature," in Brewer and Gibson, *Companion to the Gawain-Poet*, 175–9, at 178). Brewer points out that the most usual blazon for the French Gauvain in Arthurian romance was the two-headed eagle (ibid., p 177), which makes the choice of the pentangle for the English Gawain all the more striking.

For the history of the pentangle figure, and discussion of its possible significance, see Richard Hamilton Green, "Gawain's Shield and the Quest for Perfection," *ELH* 29 (1962): 121–39, repr. in *Middle English Survey: Critical Essays*, ed. Edward Vasta (Notre Dame, IN, 1965), 71–92, at 83–8), and Theodore Silverstein's edition of *Sir Gawain and the Green Knight* (Chicago, 1974), note to line 619 ff. Silverstein's comment that no attempt so far has "succeeded in associating [the pentangle], or its supposed heraldic equivalent the mullet, with any contemporary circumstance or patron of the poet" obviously reflects scholarly concentration on the north-west as the poem's main context; had the scope of scholarly enquiry been expanded to include the Ricardian court, the potential significance of de Vere's blazon might have been noticed earlier.

graceful way of associating Richard's beloved friend (or, perhaps, his memory) with the romance hero's virtues.[31]

The celebration of courtly magnificence that plays so large a role in three of the four Cotton Nero poems (*Sir Gawain and the Green Knight*, *Pearl*, *Cleanness*) fits easily into the context of the Ricardian court. For example, there seems to have been a fashion for pearls, perhaps stimulated by a spectacular crown brought to England by Anne of Bohemia;[32] at the end of Gower's *Confessio Amantis*, some of those in the assembly summoned by Cupid wear "grete Perles," according to "the newe guise of Beawme" (VIII.2469–70). The pearl is of course the central image in the poem that bears its name, and it also appears as a significant metaphor in *Gawain* (2364–5) and *Cleanness* (1117–32). More generally, John Bowers's book *The Politics of Pearl* has linked the Cotton Nero poems with the courtly display cultivated by Richard II. These poems not only describe such courtly display, but can themselves be seen as courtly artefacts – highly wrought, intricate verbal constructions, decorated with vivid and colourful descriptions.[33] Bowers is, however, mainly concerned with *Pearl*,[34] and he pays almost no attention to *Sir Gawain and the Green Knight*, probably because he is hampered by an assumption that this poem is "a sophisticated satire on the

31 De Vere was sent into exile in 1388 and died in 1392, but these dates do not necessarily provide a *terminus ante quem* for the poem; Richard's affection for him survived undiminished, and the pentangle might have been a tribute to his memory (perhaps at the time of his reburial at Earl's Colne in 1395).

32 The crown is currently in Munich; for photographs, see Saul, *Richard II*, Plate 16, and Gordon, Monnas, and Elam, *The Regal Image of Richard II*, Colour Plate 19.

33 Bowers, *Politics of Pearl*, 152 (he is speaking of *Pearl*, but the description applies equally well to the other poems). Cf. Felicity Riddy, "Jewels," in Brewer and Gibson, *Companion to the Gawain-Poet*, 143–55, at 147–8: "As a jewel, the poem [*Pearl*] locates itself among other highly-wrought, prestigious art-objects, religious and secular, of the late fourteenth century: the elaborate reliquaries, caskets, crowns, brooches, and cups that were the products of the jeweller's craft ... The poem about jewels which is itself a jewel thus associates poetry in the English language for the first time with prestige art; *Pearl* associates itself with the international aristocratic luxury system – including fine food and wines, expensive horses, costly fabrics, tapestries and art works of various kinds – that is the matrix for one kind of high culture in the late Middle Ages."

34 Bowers makes some interesting suggestions (for example, he connects the procession of 144,000 virgins in the heavenly Jerusalem with the fraternity processions of late fourteenth-century London, and he sees the pearl emblems worn by these virgins as heavenly counterparts of the livery badges that were so popular at the time, the most notorious being of course Richard's badge of the white hart). But I am unable to accept his suggestion that the Pearl maiden is a figure designed to fuse reminiscences of Richard's two queens, the dead Anne of Bohemia and the child-bride Isabelle of France. Staley's suggestion (*Languages of Power*,

Ricardian court."[35] In his eyes, it reflects and responds to a "crisis of chivalry" in Richard's court. The "unusual immaturity of King Arthur and his courtiers" reflects (he claims) "the adolescent profile as well as the headstrong adolescent attitudes that prevailed at Richard's own court during most of the 1380s."[36]

> The dazzling array of rich details in *Gawain* matches the opulence of the royal court ... Even Fitt III's extended description of the hunting, killing, and dressing of game corresponds closely with Richard II's own well-attested enjoyment of the hunt. Indeed, the whole of Fitt III can be read as a wicked satire of Ricardian excesses, on the one hand devoting long passages to minute accounts of hunting as an aristocratic leisure-pastime, on the other hand focussing upon the unmanliness of Gawain's bedroom adventures – as if replying to Thomas Walsingham's famous contempt of Richard II's courtiers as "knights of Love rather than War, more capable in the bedchamber than on the battlefield." [37]

213–51) that *Pearl* was written for Thomas of Woodstock, and the Pearl maiden is to be identified with his daughter Isabel, who did not die but was donated to a convent of Minoresses in infancy, seems equally implausible. In neither case would the discussion of the rights of "innocents" to salvation, which occupies the central space of the poem, have any point (since none of the three women was an infant, and the two Isabel(le)s were not dead).

35 *Politics of Pearl*, 172.

36 *Politics of Pearl*, 17. It may well be the case that Arthur's youthfulness is meant to recall Richard's, but if so, it might plausibly be linked with Richard's impetuous bravery (recorded by Thomas Walsingham, Froissart and others) in dealing with Wat Tyler and the rebels of 1381, when he was only fourteen years old (Saul, *Richard II*, 72). In that case, it would be a matter for admiration rather than criticism.

An allusion to Richard's youthful bravery would not necessarily imply that *Gawain* was composed in the 1380s; the Wilton Diptych, which has been assigned to the late 1390s (see n. 13 above), still portrays him as a beardless youth, suggesting that youthfulness was a part of the image he cultivated.

37 *Politics of Pearl*, 17–18. Cf. Bowers's comments on *Pearl* on 22: "With even greater delicacy than was invested in the critique of chivalric ethics in *Gawain*, the poet adroitly manages to satirize Ricardian practices, whose public glitter scarcely concealed devious and self-serving motives, while he seems steadily to invoke heavenly models to validate and imbue with majesty these same social practices."

For Walsingham's comment, see *Chronica maiora* (anno 1387) 814: "Et hii nimirum milites plures erant Veneris quam Bellone, plus ualentes in thalamo quam in campo, plus lingua quam lancea premuniti, ad dicendum uigiles, ad faciendum acta marcia somnolenti." For a more sympathetic assessment of Richard's martial abilities, see James L. Gillespie, "Richard II: King of Battles?" in *The Age of Richard II*, ed. James L. Gillespie (Stroud, 1997), 139–64. For an argument that "bedroom adventures," so far from being unmanly, are designed as emblematic representations of the "passive heroism" characteristic of the medieval romance hero (as opposed to the battlefield adventures of the traditional warrior ethic), see Jill Mann, "Sir Gawain and the Romance Hero," 221–34 below.

While I am entirely at one with Bowers in seeing Richard's court as an illuminating context for the Cotton Nero poems and as providing important clues for their understanding, I take a diametrically opposed view of the poet's attitude to courtly culture. My own analysis of *Gawain* starts from the conviction that the courtly splendour represented by Arthur and his knights is not being satirized but celebrated.

Courtly splendour takes many forms in *Sir Gawain and the Green Knight*, from feasting to architecture to the rituals of hunting, and as already noted, the descriptions of these things adds to the sense of the poem itself as a carefully crafted *objet de luxe*. I shall however focus on the descriptions of the courtly dress and armour worn by Gawain and the Green Knight, because it is here that the poet's concept of the relation between outward appearance and inner qualities manifests itself most fully. I take my cue from a comment by Michel Stanesco on the late medieval chivalric class: "The aim of the gothic show is to indicate without mediation a qualitative and generalized truth. The splendid fashions of dress in the late Middle Ages, for example, are designed to reveal to the gaze the reality of the one who wears them."[38]

Splendid dress, that is, does not *cover up* or overlay an underlying reality; rather, it *manifests* an underlying reality and because of this it is not superfluous but essential. In "Price and Value in *Sir Gawain and the Green Knight*"[39] I discussed the outer/inner connotations of the Middle English word "prys": it is applied both to the material value of gold, jewels, and rich cloth ("prys" as "price" or monetary value), and also to Gawain's inner worth ("prys" as moral worth), which is both matched and challenged by his outward reputation ("prys" as "praise").[40] In this essay I propose to extend that discussion into a consideration of other vocabulary sets in the poem that identify outer with inner, material splendour with moral worth.

38 "Le but de la *monstration* [gothique] est d'indiquer sans médiation la qualité normative et vraie. La splendeur des modes vestimentaires, par exemple, à l'époque du Moyen Âge flamboyant doit révéler au regard la réalité de celui qui les porte"; *Jeux d'errance du chevalier médiéval: Aspects ludiques de la fonction guerrière dans la littérature du moyen âge flamboyant* (Leiden, 1988), 222. Stanesco contrasts the splendid clothing of the French court in the baroque period, which aimed simply at effect at any cost, thus turning the royal court into "an immense opera" (ibid.). The English translations of quotations from Stanesco are my own.

39 See "Price and Value in *Sir Gawain and the Green Knight*," 167–86 above. At the conclusion of this article I commented that the fusion of the knightly and the mercantile in the vocabulary of the poem suggested London as the most likely location for its audience (186).

40 See *MED* senses 1 ("monetary value, price"), 4 ("non-monetary value, worth"), and 9 ("fame, renown; good reputation").

These vocabulary sets are most concentrated in the poet's description of the arming of Gawain at the beginning of Fitt 2.[41] This long passage establishes relations between exterior and interior by applying the same vocabulary to both (as with the word "prys").

He dowellez þer al þat day, and dressez on þe morn,		
Askez erly hys armez, and alle were þay broȝt.		
Fyrst a tulé tapit tyȝt ouer þe flet,		
And miche watz þe *gyld* gere þat *glent* þeralofte;	gilt	glinted
Þe stif mon steppez þeron, and þe stel hondelez,		
Dubbed in a dublet of a dere tars,		
And syþen a crafty capados, closed aloft,		fastened
Þat wyth a *bryȝt* blaunner was bounden withinne.	shining	adorned
Þenne set þay þe sabatounz vpon þe segge fotez,		
His legez lapped in stel with luflych greuez,		wrapped
With polaynez piched þerto, *policed ful clene*,	attached	very brightly polished
Aboute his knez knaged wyth knotez of *golde*;	fastened	knots
Queme quyssewes þen, þat coyntlych closed		enclosed
His thik þrawen þyȝez, with þwonges to tachched;		attached
And syþen þe brawden bryné of *bryȝt* stel ryngez		
Vmbeweued þat wyȝ vpon wlonk stuffe,		enveloped
And wel *bornyst* brace vpon his boþe armes,		polished
With gode cowters and gay, and glouez of plate,		
And alle þe godlych gere þat hym gayn schulde		
þat tyde;		
Wyth ryche cote-armure,		
His *gold* sporez spend with pryde,		fastened
Gurde wyth a bront ful sure		girt
With silk sayn vmbe his syde.		
When he watz hasped in armes, his harnays watz ryche:		clasped
Þe lest lachet oþer loupe *lemed* of *golde*.	thong loop	shone
So harnayst as he watz he herknez his masse,		
Offred and honoured at þe heȝe auter.		
Syþen he comez to þe kyng and to his cort-ferez,		
Lachez lufly his leue at lordez and ladyez;		

41 The description of a hero arming is a *topos* in classical and medieval literature; see Derek Brewer, "The Arming of the Warrior in European Literature and Chaucer," in Brewer, *Tradition and Innovation in Chaucer* (London, 1982), 142–60, 170–3.

And þay hym kyst and conueyed, bikende hym to Kryst.
Bi þat watz Gryngolet grayth, and gurde with a sadel
Þat *glemed* ful gayly with mony *golde* frenges,
Ayquere naylet ful nwe, for þat note ryched;
Þe brydel barred aboute, with *bryȝt golde* bounden; studded
Þe apparayl of þe payttrure and of þe proude skyrtez,
Þe cropore and þe couertor, acorded wyth þe arsounez;
And al watz rayled on red ryche *golde* naylez,
Þat al *glytered* and *glent* as *glem* of þe sunne. glinted ray
Þenne hentes he þe helme, and hastily hit kysses,
Þat watz *stapled* stifly, and stoffed wythinne. fastened
Hit watz hyȝe on his hede, hasped bihynde, fastened
Wyth a *lyȝtly* vrysoun ouer þe auentayle, gleaming
Enbrawden and bounden wyth þe best gemmez studded
On brode sylkyn borde, and bryddez on semez,
As papiayez paynted peruyng bitwene,
Tortors and trulofez entayled so þyk
As mony burde þeraboute had ben seuen wynter
in toune.
Þe cercle watz more o prys
Þat vmbeclypped hys croun, encircled
Of diamauntez a deuys
Þat boþe were *bryȝt* and *broun.* [42] shining

This description emphasizes two important aspects of the knight's appearance: brightness and enclosure. I have indicated brightness by italicizing words, and enclosure by underlining them.[43] Brightness is emphasized in the words used for the shining metal of Gawain's armour: steel, gilded, polished, tied with golden thongs. His spurs are gold and his helmet is encircled with diamonds. Enclosure is evident in the frequent emphasis on the encasing of the body in armour, and the fastening of one piece of armour to another, clasped, knotted, tied. The image that this long passage presents is an image of the knight *enclosed* in his armour, protected by its impenetrable and glittering surface. The

42 I have added marginal glosses for the less familiar words.

43 I have included the word "bounden" in the "enclosure" group; its primary meanings are those of modern English "bind," but in *Sir Gawain and the Green Knight* it is also used to mean to "trim" or "embellish," and to "stud" with jewels or precious metal. It thus has links with both brightness and enclosure, but it seems to me that the primary meanings colour the transferred sense and reinforce the vocabulary of enclosure.

description of his horse forms part of the impression of brightness, its draperies glimmering and gleaming, its saddle studded with golden nails.

But this is by no means the end of the long description of Gawain's arming. It continues with a detailed account of the device on his shield, the pentangle that symbolizes his "trawþe." In this latter part of the description, enclosure and brightness take on an ethical character as they become linked with the pentangle virtues.

THEN þay schewed hym þe schelde, þat was of *schyr* goulez   bright
Wyth þe pentangel depaynt of *pure golde* hwez.
He braydez hit by þe bauderyk, aboute þe hals kestes,
Þat bisemed þe segge semlyly fayre.
And quy þe pentangel apendez to þat prynce noble
I am in tent yow to telle, þof tary hyt me schulde:
Hit is a syngne þat Salamon set sumquyle
In bytoknyng of trawþe, bi tytle þat hit habbez,
For hit is a figure þat haldez fyue poyntez,
And vche lyne ymbelappez and loukez in oþer,   overlaps   locks
And ayquere hit is endelez; and Englych hit callen
Oueral, as I here, þe endeles knot.
Forþy hit acordez to þis kny3t and to his *cler* armez,   bright
For ay faythful in fyue and sere fyue syþez
Gawan watz for gode knawen, and as *golde pured*,   refined
Voyded of vche vylany, wyth vertuez ennourned
in mote;
Forþy þe pentangel nwe
He ber in schelde and cote,
As tulk of tale most trwe
And gentylest kny3t of lote.

....

...Þe fyft fyue þat I finde þat þe frek vsed
Watz fraunchyse and fela3schyp forbe al þyng,
His *clannes* and his cortaysye croked were neuer,
And pité, þat passez alle poyntez, þyse *pure* fyue
Were harder happed on þat haþel þen on any oþer.   fastened
Now alle þese fyue syþez, for soþe, were fetled on þis kny3t,   fixed
And vchone halched in oþer, þat non ende hade,   linked
And fyched vpon fyue poyntez, þat fayld neuer,   fixed
Ne samned neuer in no syde, ne sundred nouþer,

Withouten ende at any noke I oquere fynde,
Whereeuer þe gomen bygan, or glod to an ende.
Þerfore on his *schene* schelde schapen watz þe knot bright
Ryally wyth *red golde* vpon rede gowlez,
Þat is þe *pure* pentaungel wyth þe peple called
with lore.

The pentangle first appears as a material image of brightness, with its "pure golde hwez" (620). It also embodies enclosure; it is a "knot" (630 and 662). Each of its lines "vmbelappes" (overlaps) and "loukez" (locks) into the others (628). The five virtues that are represented by the five lines of the pentangle are also described in the vocabulary of enclosure (see lines 655–62): the words "halched" (linked) and "fyched" (fixed) express the interlocking quality of these virtues (657–8), and the words "happed" (fastened) and "fetled" (fixed) indicate the tightness with which they are attached to Gawain's person (655–6) – knotted to him, as it were. The interlocking quality of the five virtues makes up Gawain's truth (loyalty, fidelity, integrity); the virtues are, as it were, loyal to each other, linked in mutual bonds of relation. The loss of one is the loss of all, as critics have often noted.[44] The effect of this enclosure, I would suggest, is to create a clean central space, emptied of debasing elements: "Voyded of vche vylany" (634). The adverb "clene," used in line 576 of Gawain's brightly polished leg armour, is here transformed into the noun "clannes," the moral purity that this cleared space represents. "Clene" is thus a word that represents both the cleansed centre of enclosure and its glittering surface.[45] And since the adjective "clene" also means "complete, whole,"[46] it has the potential to evoke enclosure itself, as represented in the impenetrable intactness of the pentangle; this potential will be realized (in the adverbial form meaning "completely") later in the poem. The "pure golde hwez" of the pentangle are also transposed into moral terms: Gawain's virtue makes him "as golde pured" (633) (purified like gold). And finally, Gawain's moral character is "wyth vertues ennourned" (634) (adorned); his inner qualities share the splendour of his outer appearance.

The medieval French *Livre de l'ordre de chevalerie* contains a section on the significance of the knight's equipment and armour which provides an

44 See, for example, J.A. Burrow, *A Reading of the Gawain-Poet* (London, 1965), 49–50, and A.C. Spearing, *The Gawain-Poet. A Critical Study* (Cambridge, 1970), 198.

45 For a discussion of the resonances of the word "clene" in the *Gawain*-poet's works, and the other words with which he commonly links it, see Keiser, *Courtly Desire*, 23 and 265 n. 25.

46 *MED* sense 6.

instructive contrast with this passage.[47] Like *Gawain*, it gives moral significance to the closure represented by the knight's armour: the hauberk is "clos & fermé" on all sides to signify that treachery, pride, and disloyalty cannot gain entrance to the knight's "noble couraige." But its general procedure is to establish a set of metaphorical equivalents between the material and the moral, in a manner that reads like an inversion of St Paul's "armour of God" passage (Ephesians 6:11–18): for example, the knight's sword signifies the cross, and its two edges mean that a knight should maintain chivalry and justice. His lance signifies truth, because truth is straight and upright. The helmet signifies his shamefulness and fear of reproof, for it obliges a knight to cast his eyes downward just as a shamefast person does. The spurs signify diligence and swiftness, the gorger signifies obedience.[48] The description of Gawain's arming does not work from exterior equipment to interior meaning through a set of one-to-one correspondences in this way. Instead, the ethical and the material merge into a single dazzling image of knightly excellence, embracing "clannes" in all its senses, and the connection between them appears to be not metaphorical, but intrinsic. Moreover, the movement is not only from outward adornment (the gold-embroidered pentangle) to inward virtue ("trawþe"), but also back again, as virtue is reconceived as adornment (Gawain is purified like gold and adorned with virtues).

The interlocking quality of Gawain's five virtues is not the only reason why the pentangle is a fitting symbol of his knightly worth. Another reason is that the language of enclosure is an indication of the self-sufficient nature of chivalric virtue. Gawain's task is not motivated or supported by any external considerations – there are no maidens to be rescued, no countries to be delivered from the oppressions of a giant or a dragon, no wrongs to be righted.[49] The only reason he has for keeping his promise is the promise itself. Although his immediate motivation in taking on the Green Knight's challenge is the need to rescue Arthur from the threat of decapitation,[50] Arthur himself has risen to the challenge in order to defend the "renoun" of the Round Table, which is

47 See *Livre de l'ordre de chevalerie*, ed. Vincenzo Minervini, Biblioteca di filologia romanza 21 (Bari, 1972), ch. VI. This work is a late fourteenth-century French translation of Ramón Lull's *Libre del orde de cavalleria*. Caxton's translation of the French version was edited by A.T.P. Byles, *The Book of the Ordre of Chyualry*, EETS o.s. 168 (London, 1926).

48 *L'ordre de chevalerie*, ed. Minervini, 144–6.

49 For further discussion of this point, see Mann, "Sir Gawain and the Romance Hero," 225–6 below.

50 This immediate motive defers the question of why the challenge should be accepted, but the question recurs as Gawain leaves to search for the Green Knight, and the other courtiers criticize Arthur for letting their best knight go off on a frivolous and pointless mission (674–83).

itself a self-reflexive act. To uphold one's renown is to prove oneself to be what one asserts one is. Chivalric virtue is its own *raison d'être*; it is not supported by practical utility or even by divine command. Like the pentangle, it thus stands clear of external support, locked in itself; its driving aim is the maintenance of its own purity and integrity within an incomprehensible and threatening world, to which it offers a dazzling surface, brilliant in its perfection.

One last comment on Gawain's arming: the poet calls the pentangle a game ("gomen"; 661), which is also what the Green Knight calls the challenge he offers to Arthur's court (273, 283). This word too can be linked to the language of closure, as Stanesco's account of the chivalric game makes clear: "Game is an activity which is localized, and above all closed. The preliminary to every game is the delimitation of a precise space or trajectory, which must be different from the rest of the world. It matters little whether the limits of this space are material or imaginary, the essential thing is that the player of the game finds himself in a protected space."[51] Yet this "protected space" is not designed to exclude danger or instability, but, on the contrary, to provide a place within which they can operate.

> In so far as it contains an unforeseen element, the tournament permits the player the liberty to envisage himself at the end of the game as different from what he was at its beginning. What determines the at times extremely complicated structure of a combat in a closed arena is precisely the sense of game: the possibility of becoming other, not by virtue of being masked, but in relation to what one was beforehand. The "principle of incertitude" creates the distance between what one is and what one can be; it is in this problematic interspace that the knight of the late Middle Ages installs himself.[52]

Stanesco's comments on the tournament help us to understand the relation between enclosure and incertitude in the "gomen" to which Gawain has

---

51 *Jeux d'errance*, 134: "le jeu est une activité localisée et, surtout, fermée. Le geste préalable à tout jeu est la délimitation d'un endroit ou d'un trajet précis, qui doit être différent du reste du monde. Peu importe que les limites de cet espace soient matérielles ou imaginaires, l'essentiel est que le joueur se trouve dans un lieu protégé."

52 *Jeux d'errance*, 122: "tant qu'il comprend une part d'imprévu, le tournoi permet au joueur la liberté de s'envisager à la fin du jeu comme différent de ce qu'il était au début. Ce qui détermine la structure parfois extrêmement compliquée d'un combat en champ clos, c'est justement le sens du jeu: la possibilité de devenir autre, non pas tant derrière un masque, mais par rapport à ce qu'on a été auparavant. Le 'principe d'incertitude' crée la distance entre ce qu'on est et ce qu'on peut être; c'est dans cet entre-deux problématique que s'installe le chevalier du Moyen Âge flamboyant."

committed himself; although it takes a unique form and leads him at first on unconfined wanderings, its rules nevertheless hold him within their imaginary bounds, creating by their very nature the principle of uncertainty that constitutes knightly adventure.[53]

However, the account of Gawain's arming is not the only, nor even the first description of courtly dress that we have encountered in the poem. That honour belongs to the description of the Green Knight at his entrance into Arthur's court. And in that description the same vocabulary sets betokening brightness and enclosure appear, presenting the reader with a puzzle similar to the one he presents to Arthur's courtiers. Again I have italicized the words for brightness and underlined those indicating enclosure.

Ande al grayþed in grene þis gome and his wedes:
A strayte cote ful stre3t, þat stek on his sides, clung to
A meré mantile abof, mensked withinne
With pelure pured apert, þe pane *ful clene* very splendid
With blyþe blaunner ful *bry3t*, and his hod boþe,
Þat watz la3t fro his lokkez and layde on his schulderes;
Heme wel-haled hose of þat same,
Þat spenet on his sparlyr, and *clene* spures vnder clung shining
Of *bry3t golde*, vpon silk bordes barred ful ryche,
And scholes vnder schankes þere þe schalk rides;
And alle his vesture uerayly watz *clene* verdure, pure
Boþe þe barres of his belt and oþer blyþe stones,
Þat were richely rayled in his aray *clene* splendid/shining
Aboutte hymself and his sadel, vpon silk werkez.
Þat were to tor for to telle of tryfles þe halue
Þat were enbrauded abof, wyth bryddes and fly3es,
With gay gaudi of grene, þe *golde* ay inmyddes.
Þe pendauntes of his payttrure, þe proude cropure,
His molaynes, and alle þe metail anamayld was þenne,
Þe steropes þat he stod on stayned of þe same,
And his arsounz al after and his aþel skyrtes,
Þat euer *glemered* and *glent* al of grene stones; gleamed glinted
Þe fole þat he ferkkes on fyn of þat ilke,
sertayn,

53 Cf. the poet's description of the knightly joust as a place where Fortune determines the outcome of events, at lines 96–9.

A grene hors gret and þikke,
A stede ful stif to strayne,
In brawden brydel quik –
To þe gome he watz ful gayn.

Wel gay watz þis gome gered in grene,
And þe here of his hed of his hors swete.
Fayre fannand fax vmbefoldes his schulderes; enfolds
A much berd as a busk ouer his brest henges,
Þat wyth his hiȝlich here þat of his hed reches
Watz euesed al vmbetorne abof his elbowes,
Þat half his armes þer-vnder were halched in þe wyse enclosed
Of a kyngez capados þat closes his swyre; encloses
Þe mane of þat mayn hors much to hit lyke,
Wel cresped and cemmed, wyth knottes ful mony
Folden in wyth *fildore* aboute þe fayre grene, gold thread
Ay a herle of þe here, an oþer of *golde*;
Þe tayl and his toppyng twynnen of a sute, twined/plaited
And bounden boþe wyth a bande of a *bryȝt* grene,
Dubbed wyth ful dere stonez, as þe dok lasted,
Syþen þrawen wyth a þwong a þwarle knot alofte, bound tight
Þer mony bellez ful *bryȝt* of *brende golde* rungen.
Such a fole vpon folde, ne freke þat hym rydes,
Watz neuer sene in þat sale wyth syȝt er þat tyme,
with yȝe.
He loked *as layt so lyȝt*, as bright as lightning
So sayd al þat hym syȝe;
Hit semed as no mon myȝt
Vnder his dynttez dryȝe.

Wheþer hade he no helme ne hawbergh nauþer,
Ne no pysan ne no plate þat pented to armes,
Ne no schafte ne no schelde to schwue ne to smyte,
Bot in his on honde he hade a holyn bobbe,
Þat is grattest in grene when greuez ar bare,
And an ax in his oþer, a hoge and vnmete,
A spetos sparþe to expoun in spelle, quoso myȝt.
Þe lenkþe of an elnȝerde þe large hede hade,
Þe grayn al of grene stele and of *golde* hewen,
Þe bit *burnyst bryȝt*, with a brod egge brightly polished

As wel schapen to schere as scharp rasores,
Þe stele of a stif staf þe sturne hit bi grypte,
Þat watz wounden wyth yrn to þe wandez ende, — wound round
And al bigrauen with grene in gracios werkes;
A lace lapped aboute, þat louked at þe hede, — wrapped; fastened
And so after þe halme halched ful ofte, — looped
Wyth tryed tasselez þerto tacched innoghe — fastened
On botounz of þe *bryȝt* grene brayden ful ryche.

Although he is not wearing armour, the description of the Green Knight's clothing emphasizes knotting, plaiting, encasing, enveloping, on the one hand, and on the other, the surface brilliance of his array, glittering with gold, jewels, and gold embroidery, The axe that he carries is of brightly polished gold and steel, and the lace that is wound round it is described in the vocabulary of enclosure: "lapped, louked, halched, tacched." The word that is insistently repeated in this passage is the adjective "clene," used in several senses that relate to surface brilliance. The edging of the Green Knight's mantle is "ful clene" (*MED* sense 5b: "splendid, elegant; shapely, comely, excellent"); he wears "clene spures" (*MED* sense 4b: "bright, shining, gleaming, sparkling"); his clothing is all "clene verdure" (*MED* sense 1a "pure, unmixed, unalloyed, unadulterated, unpolluted"); his "aray" is "clene" (a mixture of "splendid" and "shining"?). The Green Knight's appearance has all the surface brilliance of courtly display. Nothing, it seems, is hidden; there is no shabby "underneath." The lining of his cloak is "apert," plainly visible (154), and it is no less splendid than the outside of his garment: it is "mensked," adorned, with "pelure pured" (153), trimmed fur.[54]

As with the words used to describe Gawain's arming, the words used to describe the Green Knight are given moral senses elsewhere in the poem. "Pured" and "mensk" appear in close proximity again in Fitt 2, when the poet is describing the joy expressed in Bertilak's castle at Gawain's arrival; "mensk" is returned to its original meaning, "honour," while "pured" is used in a transferred sense of Gawain's "purified" virtues.

And alle þe men in þat mote maden much joye
To apere in his presense prestly þat tyme,
Þat alle prys and prowes and *pured þewes*

54 Cf. the manuscript illumination of the wedding of Richard II and Anne of Bohemia in Oxford, Bodleian Library MS Lat. liturg. f. 3, fol. 65v, which shows Richard wearing an ermine-lined mantle, with its lining proudly visible (Staley, *Languages of Power*, Figure 4).

Apendes to hys persoun, and praysed is euer;
Byfore alle men vpon molde his *mensk* is þe most. (910–14; my italics)

The adjective "clene" is used in a moral sense ("morally clean, pure, innocent, guileless") to describe the courtly conversation between Gawain and the lady of the castle at dinner on the night of his arrival, and significantly, it alliterates with "closed."

Bot ȝet I wot þat Wawen and þe wale burde
Such comfort of her compaynye caȝten togeder
Þurȝ her dere dalyaunce of her derne wordez,
Wyth *clene* cortays carp *closed* fro fylþe,
Þat hor play watz passande vche prynce gomen,
in vayres. (1010–15; my italics)

Like the pentangle, their talk is described as a "gomen," a game, and here too "vylany" ("fylþe") is kept outside its bounds. The journey through the wilderness of north-west England was only the apparent scene of Gawain's testing; the real test takes place, fittingly, within the enclosed space of the bedroom,[55] bounded by the rules of courtly game (the exchange of winnings as well as "cortays carp"). Enclosure excludes filth, maintaining the "voided" central space of cleanness. Excluding filth, enclosure also sets protective bounds around virtue, as we see when the lady refers to courtesy as "closed" within Gawain, again alliterating on "clene," here in its adverbial sense of "completely."

"So god as Gawayn gaynly is halden,
And cortaysye is *closed* so *clene* in hymseluen, so completely enclosed
Couth not lyȝtly haf lenged so long wyth a lady,
Bot he had craued a cosse, bi his courtaysye,
Bi sum towch of summe tryfle at sum talez ende." (1297–1301; my italics)

The alliterating words suggest that enclosure creates wholeness, completeness, perfection. Unfortunately for the lady's attempt to seduce Gawain, however,

55 Stanesco, *Jeux d'errance*, 134: "L'espace dans lequel se meut le chevalier à la fin du Moyen Âge est essentiellement un espace clos: lice, château, chambre, lit, cour, jardin, prison. Il ignore ou méprise la nature, les étendues illimitées, les chevauchées sauvages, les routes qui s'allongent à perte de vue." *Gawain* does of course include nature, a long and wild journey, and "limitless spaces," but these are designed precisely as distractions, disguising the real knightly test, which takes place indoors.

the completeness with which courtesy is enclosed in Gawain also makes him "clean" in the sense of "chaste," "morally clean."

It would be easy, at this point, to draw a contrast between the use of words such as "clene," "mensk," and "pured" in their material senses in the Green Knight's portrait and in their moral senses as used of Gawain. Easy, but mistaken, as the description of Gawain's arming has already shown; there the language of moral worth emerges from, and is continuous with, the language of courtly splendour. What we might say is that the Green Knight represents a dazzling surface which it is Gawain's task to round out with moral content. The Green Knight presents Arthur's court with an unsettling mirror image of themselves, rendered unfamiliar and alien by his green colour, implicitly challenging the courtiers with the question of whether their brilliant surface *does* make visible an inner truth, whether their dazzling reputation ("los") is matched by reality.[56] The combination of his greenness with the most sophisticated luxury of courtly dress turns him into an enigmatic *spectacle*, one whose appearance is scrutinized in exhaustive detail over three long stanzas, as the courtiers (and the reader) try to decipher its meaning. He is at once totally open to inspection and totally opaque.[57]

The Green Knight's description associates courtly splendour with the idea of the public gaze.[58] Courtly display, that is to say, depends on an audience; it presents itself for visual consumption by beholders, in whom it finds its point and the realization of its meaning. Vance Smith has some perceptive remarks (made in discussion of *Sir Launfal*) about the social anxiety surrounding the notion of value (the outward manifestation of wealth), resulting from "the

56 It will be clear that I disagree with the critical view represented by Larry D. Benson (among others), that the Green Knight "clearly champions a set of values completely opposite to those of the polished courtier, and that "he comes from another world altogether, from the world of nature" (*Art and Tradition in "Sir Gawain and the Green Knight"* [New Brunswick, NJ, 1965], 81, 93). For a shrewd dismantling of the attempts to interpret the Green Knight as a version of the natural figure of the Green Man, see Bella Millett, "How Green is the Green Knight?" *Nottingham Medieval Studies* 38 (1994): 138–51.

57 As J.A. Burrow argues (*A Reading*, 13–17), the Green Knight's appearance is disturbing, not because it represents the polar opposite of the Arthurian courtly world, but because its combination of the civilized human (his fashionable dress and adornments) with hints of the supernatural (his greenness and his size) makes him *uncategorizable*; it is thus hard to see how he should be treated. In the event, Arthur's decision to treat him as a knight ("Sir cortays knyȝt"; line 276) turns out be the right one.

58 There is a brief anticipation of this in the early description of Guinevere (74–84), surrounded by canopies and hangings, offered up to the public gaze, so that she becomes part of the splendid spectacle of the feast.

knowledge that one is being watched, and always being watched, interpellated as not only an economic subject but especially as a sumptuary subject."[59] So important is this public audience that in its absence the subject will mentally supply it: to quote again from Vance Smith, "value brings with it an audience, the consciousness that its form is not just made visible in public, but that it *is* a kind of public, bearing with it its own logic of surveillance."[60]

These remarks will, I think, help us to understand how the theme of courtly display is extended into the account of Gawain's testing in Bertilak's castle, where it might seem to have disappeared entirely. For of course this testing is carried out when he is completely divested not only of his armour but also of his courtly clothing, as he lies naked in bed.[61] Yet the sense of *being watched*, of being subject to the "logic of surveillance" that is implied in courtly display, persists. This sense is very cleverly established on the first morning when Gawain is awakened by a little noise at his bedroom door, and, peeping through the bed curtains, sees the lady entering his room. When she nears the bed, he hastily lies down and pretends to be asleep; she sits on his bed and waits for him to wake up. Gawain's initial role as watcher is thus neatly inverted; he is now conscious of *being watched*, and I think that this sense of scrutiny persists throughout the encounters with the lady. Gawain watches himself constantly, sensitive to any suggestion that he may have failed to live up to his outward reputation. It is now his inner worth that is "on display," with enclosure and cleanness both manifested in his bodily intactness, his chastity, and in the integrity or wholeness of his moral persona, manifest in the simultaneous maintenance of both his "trawþe" and his courtesy. The word "vnlouked," which is used of Gawain at last opening his eyes (1201), vividly conveys the idea of the unarmed body as itself an enclosure, making itself vulnerable but protected by its inner virtues. And this idea is also evident when Gawain meets the Green Knight's challenge, wearing his armour but renouncing its protection by removing his helmet and offering his naked neck to the axe blade. At this point, his only armour is the "trawþe" that the pentangle symbolizes, enclosing him within its locked boundaries.

---

59 D. Vance Smith, *Arts of Possession. The Middle English Household Imaginary* (Minneapolis, 2003), 169.

60 Ibid., 175. See also my remarks about value being established only in terms of the valuation accorded by others, "Price and Value in *Sir Gawain and the Green Knight*," 167–86 above.

61 The poet does not make this explicit, but the illumination in Cotton Nero A.X (fol. 129) which shows the lady at Gawain's bedside while he pretends to sleep depicts him as naked (Brewer and Gibson, *Companion to the Gawain-Poet*, 215, illustration 10). It is true that the illuminations do not always represent the events of the poem with entire accuracy, but it seems that the illuminator thought it natural for people to sleep naked.

The moment at which Gawain stops watching himself is of course the moment when he accepts the green girdle. He assumes that this action can be *hidden*, unaware that it is as available to the lord's gaze as his rejection of the lady's advances. In that sense he betrays the obligation to be always on display, to make himself fully manifest. Yet of course he does unwittingly make his fault manifest by wearing the green girdle in open view of the Green Knight. He wraps it twice round his body, attempting to enclose himself in its protection rather than that of the "trawþe" which has the truly magic power that the girdle only fakes.[62] The Green Knight makes his fault manifest in a different way, in the tiny nick that he makes in Gawain's neck by way of punishment for this minor lapse (had he truly failed, he would of course have lost his head). For Gawain, of course, any breach of his knightly integrity destroys the perfect enclosure represented by the pentangle. His inner self no longer matches the brilliant perfection of his outer display. The ending of the poem is taken up with a series of moves designed to restore the intimate connection between interior and exterior. First, Gawain's immediate and uncompromising acceptance of his guilt both internalizes and displays for public inspection his new image of himself. Second, the Green Knight treats this confession as recreating the continuity between his inner and outer selves. And the word used to describe this newly constituted self is the word "clene," used in its full richness of meaning:

Thenn loȝe þat oþer leude and luflyly sayde:
"I halde hit hardily hole, þe harme þat I hade.
Þou art confessed so *clene*, beknowen of þy mysses,
And hatz þe penaunce apert of þe poynt of myn egge,
I halde þe *polysed* of þat plyȝt, and *pured as clene*
As þou hadez neuer forfeted syþen þou watz fyrst borne. (2389–94; my italics)

Gawain's hidden fault becomes susceptible to healing precisely as it comes to the surface in the form of the nick that makes it visibly manifest – "apert," the word last used of the lining of the Green Knight's cloak. The word "clene" in line 2393 is most naturally taken to be an adverb meaning "completely," but it also suggests the sense "to a state of cleanness" (*MED* 1a). That is, the completeness of Gawain's confession has made him once more "clean," and not only in the sense of being freed from pollution but also in the sense of becoming "splendid, radiant." As in the scene of his arming, his virtues are conceived as courtly adornments: he is "pured" like gold and "polysed" like the shining steel

62 See Jill Mann, "Sir Gawain and the Romance Hero," 233–4 below.

of his armour. Gawain's confession has also restored his moral wholeness, his integrity (whose etymological sense is "wholeness"), making him "clene" in the sense of "complete." The Green Knight compares Gawain to a pearl, in comparison to other knights who are like white peas. The pearl, like the pentangle, offers an image of enclosure – an unbroken circle, an intact, inviolate sphere, which cannot be cut into without destroying its value, and which displays a smooth, shining surface to the world.[63]

By the time Gawain returns to Arthur's court, the nick in his neck is healed; it is "hole" as the Green Knight says his "harme" is. But Gawain insists on wearing the girdle as a permanent sign of his shame. Significantly, its vocabulary incorporates the twin elements of brightness (italicized) and enclosure (underlined):

Þe hurt watz hole þat he hade hent in his nek,
And þe *blykkande* belt he bere þeraboute — shining
Abelef as a bauderyk bounden bi his syde,
Loken vnder his lyfte arme, þe lace, with a knot, — fastened
In tokenyng he watz tane in tech of a faute. (2484–8)

Recounting his adventures, Gawain once again confesses his fault, expressing his sense of enduring shame in the vocabulary of enclosure:

"Þis is þe token of vntrawþe þat I am tan inne,
And I mot nedez hit were wyle I may last;
For mon may hyden his harme, bot vnhap ne may hit, — unfasten
For þer hit onez is tachched twynne wil hit neuer." (2509–12) — attached

Instead of the five virtues, disgrace is (in Gawain's eyes) "fastened" to him, like a shameful travesty of the fringes and tassels of courtly dress. But Arthur's court agree with the Green Knight in emphasizing Gawain's major success rather than his minor failure. For them, to have done as well as Gawain did would be no failure but an unimaginably high level of success.[64] They therefore

---

63 See further Jill Mann, "Satisfaction and Payment in Middle English Literature," 146–7 above.

64 At the risk of crudely simplifying the poet's subtle combination of perspectives, one might compare their reaction to Gawain's account of his failure with the likely reaction of an average student to a friend's lament that she had scored "only" 98 out of 100 in a recent test. Bertilak and the court focus on the 98% success, while Gawain focusses on the 2% failure, but this very fact recasts his performance as a perfect success. On acceptance of failure as a challenge that the romance hero must meet, and by so doing, demonstrate his heroism (a situation that occurs in four of Chrétien's five romances), see Mann, "Sir Gawain and the Romance Hero," 231–3 below.

determine that if Gawain wears the green girdle as a surface manifestation of the disgrace that is inwardly "attached" to him, they will wear it likewise, but as a token of honour.[65] They thus recreate the significance of the girdle by making it a courtly adornment, comparable to the knots and fringes and plaits that ornament courtly attire. This gesture gives the girdle an honorific status as part of the splendour of courtly display, one of the ways of making visible the inner qualities of Arthurian knighthood.[66] Enclosure is here realized not only in the form of the knotted girdle but also in the form of the unbroken circle of community that unites the members of the Round Table.

It should by now be clear how great a difference there is between the *Gawain*-poet's conceptualization of courtly display and Dymmok's notion of its role as political stratagem, a way of awing the lower classes into submission or surrounding the king with a mystique that will enhance his prestige and power. Instead, what we have in this poem is a truly imaginative spiritualization of courtly splendour, an attempt to read it as a material manifestation of the ethical qualities embodied in the courtly life and as itself constituting a challenge to be lived up to. The poem offers, in other words, a perfect example of Stanesco's definition of gothic display. Though its initial motivation was probably a celebration of the courtly magnificence cultivated by Richard II, it goes far beyond that aim, forging an ideal of knightly virtue as dazzling as the luxury of any court. This does not mean, however, that this particular ideal of knightly virtue transcends political function altogether. It remains to ask, therefore, in what way the particular ethical qualities that the poet links with courtly display might serve the interests of the court of Richard II, and also of the poet himself. "Trawþe" is a traditional knightly (and kingly) virtue, but "clannes" may seem a rather more surprising choice as a courtly quality. There are several ways of accounting for it, some more speculative than others.[67] One might look for a

65 Nicholas Perkins points out to me that the crown of thorns, referred to in the penultimate line of the poem (2529), is similarly a badge of shame which has been turned into a badge of honour (as it is in the Wilton Diptych, where the Christ Child's golden halo has the crown of thorns punched within it).

66 Susan Crane discusses the pentangle and the girdle as outward signs of Gawain's inner identity (*The Performance of Self. Ritual, Clothing, and Identity during the Hundred Years War* [Philadelphia, PA, 2002], 134–9), but she argues that "the difference between the meaning Gawain attributes to the girdle and the meanings urged by Bertilak and Arthur's courtiers marks the point where Gawain is, finally, estranged from his community" (136).

67 It may have appealed on an immediate and personal level to Richard himself, whose personal devotion to Edward the Confessor, and the fact that his marriage with Anne of Bohemia was affectionate but childless, have prompted modern speculations that he might have imitated the chaste marriage practised by his royal predecessor. See C.M. Barron, "Richard II: Image and Reality," in *Making and Meaning. The Wilton Diptych*, ed. Dillian Gordon (London, 1993), 13–19, at 15, and John M. Bowers, "Chaste Marriage: Fashion and Texts at the Court

reason in terms of the poet's own social status and ideology. If, as seems likely, he was a cleric,[68] the poem may be seen as part of a general reshaping of the knightly ideal in accordance with clerical values.[69] In the poem that goes by the name of *Cleanness*, a striking role is played by the prophet Daniel, who admonishes and counsels the erring king Belshazzar, interpreting the writing on the wall as the Chaldean clerks could not. The commanding figure of Daniel, whose "derne coninges" (1611) give him a moral ascendancy over his royal master, and who is rewarded with purple garments and gold adornment fit for a royal courtier, may be taken as a projection of the role the *Gawain*-poet aspired to play in Richard's court. The implication in this poem is that the holder of earthly power needs the cleric to guide his life. In inflecting courtly culture with clerical values, the poet is enhancing his own prestige and importance.

On the other hand, he can also be seen as enhancing the prestige of knighthood by associating it with the mystique of religious sanctity The rejection of insistent amorous advances, the heroic virtue that provokes such admiration from the Green Knight, is in origin a hagiographic motif. Stories are told of women forcing themselves on several saints, of whom Bernard of Clairvaux is the most notable. The *Vita prima*, written in Bernard's lifetime by his friend William of St Thierry, tells of two occasions in his youth when his striking good looks made him the object of aggressive female seduction. In the first case, a girl climbed naked into Bernard's bed as he lay sleeping; becoming aware of her presence, he turned away from her and went back to sleep. Even when she began to caress him, he made no response, so that eventually, confused and awed, she got up and left him. The second occasion more closely resembles Gawain's temptation by the lady of the castle: a married woman, in whose house Bernard was spending the night, three times in the course of the night crept into his bedroom. Each time, Bernard roused the household by shouting "Thieves! thieves!" and after the third failed attempt she gave up. (Bernard explained to

of Richard II," *Pacific Coast Philology* 30 (1995): 15–26. Nigel Saul thinks that "the suggestion certainly makes sense in the context of the king's piety," but "what counts against it is Richard's need for a male heir" (*Richard II*, 457). The association of courtly culture with sexual restraint would also have served as a refutation of the contemporary gossip about homosexuality that I mentioned earlier.

68 This is suggested by his probable range of reading (in Latin as well as French); see Putter, *Introduction to the Gawain-Poet*, 4–11, 14–17. Putter concludes that a cleric in minor orders, employed in an administrative capacity in a lay household, would best fit the evidence.

69 Ad Putter has given a very thorough and convincing account of *Sir Gawain and the Green Knight* in these terms; see *Sir Gawain and the Green Knight and French Arthurian Romance* (Oxford, 1995), ch. 5.

his companions next day that his cry was apt because she had been trying to steal the priceless treasure of his chastity.)[70] It seems to have been Chrétien de Troyes who first transposed this motif into a chivalric context, in the scene from *Le chevalier de la charete* in which Lancelot is obliged to go to bed with an amorous hostess, but lies stiffly far apart from her, making clear his unwillingness to touch her.[71] As in *Gawain*, the scene demonstrates that the courtly hero can control his desires as well as any saint.[72] And it also invests the courtly hero with the prestige that accrues to the saint, showing him as set apart from the common run of men. Gawain's chastity, however, is even more impressive than Lancelot's, since Lancelot is restrained by his single-minded devotion to Guinevere,[73] whereas Gawain's devotion is to his own inner "clannes" and his "trawþe" to his host. His allegiance is not to an earthly lady but to the Virgin Mary. And whereas St Bernard rejected his amorous hostess by setting the

---

70 *Vita prima*, *PL* 185, col. 230 D–231 B. For a translation, see *St Bernard of Clairvaux. The Story of his Life as recorded in the Vita Prima Bernardi by certain of his contemporaries, William of St. Thierry, Arnold of Bonnevaux, Geoffrey and Philip of Clairvaux, and Odo of Deuil*, trans. Geoffrey Webb and Adrian Walker (Westminster, MD, 1960), 20–2. For a critique of the *Patrologia* edition, and a list of surviving manuscripts (over 120) of the *Vita*, see Adriaan Hendrik Bredero, "Études sur la 'Vita prima' de Saint Bernard," *Analecta sacri ordinis cisterciensis* 17 (1961): 3–72. Similar stories are related of Bishop William of St Brieuc (d. 1234), *Acta Sanctorum* Iul. VII, 122D–E, and the Spanish Dominican saint Peter Gonzales (d. 1246), *Acta Sanctorum* Apr. II, 393E–394E. For further examples, see Donald Weinstein and Rudolph M. Bell, *Saints and Society. Christendom, 1000–1700* (Chicago, 1982), 81–3, 86–7. The motif is much older than the twelfth century; it occurs, for example, in Jerome's *Life of Paul of Thebes*, *PL* 23, cols 19–20; trans. Carolinne White, *Early Christian Lives* (Harmondsworth, 1998), 76.

71 *Le chevalier de la charrete*, ed. Mario Roques (Paris, 1968), lines 1192–280. Ad Putter discusses this scene in relation to *Sir Gawain and the Green Knight*, as well as two other instances in which it is Gawain who is fending off sexual advances from ladies; see Putter, *Sir Gawain and the Green Knight and French Arthurian Romance* (Oxford, 1995), 123–6 (Lancelot) and 101–2, 112–13 (Gawain). Other examples of romances in which "men turn down the advances of demanding women" are listed by Susan Crane, *Gender and Romance in Chaucer's Canterbury Tales* (Princeton, NJ, 1994), 40 n. 17. In contrast, some Anglo-Norman romances show women as active wooers whose advances are (sooner or later) welcome to the men concerned; see Judith Weiss, "The Wooing Woman in Anglo-Norman Romance," in *Romance in Medieval England*, ed. Maldwyn Mills, Jennifer Fellows, and Carol M. Meale (Cambridge, 1991), 149–61.

72 Chaucer parodies knightly chastity in "Sir Thopas": "Ful many a maide bright in bour, / They moorne for him *par amour*, / Whan hem were bet to slepe. / But he was chaast and no lechour" (742–5).

73 As Andreas Capellanus says, "love makes a man to be as it were adorned with the virtue of chastity" ("amor reddit hominem castitatis quasi virtute decoratum"; *On Love*, ed. P.G. Walsh [London, 1982] I.iv, 38).

household in an uproar, Gawain's task is much harder: he has to reject Bertilak's wife so courteously that he is not noticeably doing so. Saintly chastity is inflected with courtly manners.

The fusion of clerical and chivalric values thus works to the benefit of both sides. If, on the one hand, clerical values find a lodging-place in courtly life, on the other hand, religion itself is reconceived in aristocratic terms. The poet exploits the full semantic range of the word "clene," which provided a perfect opportunity to link the clerical and the courtly. "Clannes" embraces not only chastity but also the cleanliness, elegance, and dazzling beauty of courtly adornment. In a discussion of the *Gawain*-poet as "vernacular theologian," Nicholas Watson commented on the "specifically aristocratic articulation of the Christian life" that is contained in the four Cotton Nero poems, and identified the poet's project as "the displacement of the traditional categories of Christian heroism (embodied in virgins, martyrs, and preachers) to make way for a new set, embodied in a figure closer to the aspirations and capacities of the poet's audience, Gawain himself."[74] In *Cleanness* and *Pearl*, heaven is conceived as a court, adorned by material luxury, organized along hierarchical lines, and presided over by a God whose autocratic power would be the envy of Richard II. In *Cleanness* as in *Gawain*, the word "clene" effects the linking of the material and the moral, the combination of courtly luxury and moral restraint.[75] In *Sir Gawain and the Green Knight*, "clannes" likewise unites material and moral. Linked by alliteration with "cortaysye," it expresses the knight's freedom from "vylany," and is the quality that presides over courtly relations with women, which take the form of "clene cortays carp" rather than grossly physical relations. Here too it has important associations with the restraint that is symbolized in the knots and plaits of courtly attire, and with the maintenance of order and social decorum. So far from being an indication of extravagance and excess, the poet seems to be saying, courtly splendour incorporates self-discipline and self-control.

Finally, "clannes" in the form of chastity is important not only because it is a Christian virtue but because it can itself function as a metaphor, an image of bodily and spiritual intactness/integrity, of the knightly self-sufficiency represented by the hero encased in his armour, proof against the world. It represents

74 "The *Gawain*-Poet as a Vernacular Theologian," in Brewer and Gibson, *Companion to the Gawain-Poet*, 293–313, at 297, 311.

75 A.C. Spearing has shown the importance of boundaries and order to the notion of cleanness in this poem; see "Purity and Danger," in Spearing, *Readings in Medieval Poetry* (Cambridge, 1987), 173–94.

the *mode* of virtue as much as its content, signalling an absoluteness of commitment to one's own "prys." It is in this respect that it resembles the virtue of "trawþe," which exhibits the same sort of self-sufficiency in the form of the pentangle, locked within itself. Although "trawþe" undoubtedly involves a sense of what is owed to others, and fidelity in one's relations with them, the source of this externally directed behaviour is an inner integrity, a truth to oneself that is to be maintained as a primary duty. Gawain's disgust when he learns of his failure does not express itself as a consciousness of the way his behaviour affects others (as indeed it hardly does), but as a consciousness that he has fallen short of his conception of himself.

> "For care of þy knokke, cowardyse me taȝt
> To acorde me with couetyse, *my kynde to forsake*,
> Þat is larges and lewté þat longez to knyȝtez.
> Now am I fawty and falce, and ferde haf ben euer
> Of trecherye and vntrawþe ..." (2379–83; my italics)

Knightly virtue in this poem is non-utilitarian; it involves being true to one's conception of what one is. It may be compared with the solemn self-display evident in the hieratic image of Richard's kingship in the Westminster portrait, which displays kingship not as function but as being: a king, it seems to say, is simply what Richard *is*.

With all this, it should be added that the reshaped courtly ideal is probably as important for what it is *not* as much as for what it is. *Cleanness* offers a clue to this significance, in the contemptuous reference to the giants of the book of Genesis, fathered on the daughters of men by the "sons of God," who were characterized by a love of battle:

> Þose wern men meþelez and maȝty on vrþe,
> Þat for her lodlych laykez alosed þay were;
> He watz famed for fre that feȝt loued best,
> And ay the bigest in bale þe best watz halden. (273–6)[76]

What *Gawain* conspicuously rejects is the warrior ethic that defines heroism as fighting. In its place it sets the gentler and more sophisticated virtues that

76 I quote *Cleanness* from *The Poems of the Pearl Manuscript*, ed. Malcolm Andrew and Ronald Waldron, 5th ed. (Exeter, 2007).

rule the civilized and courtly life, celebrated and articulated in courtly display. In the context of Richard's court, this would align the poet with the rejection of the war party represented (among others) by the Appellants, and with support for Richard's more conciliatory attitude to his "cousin" the king of France.[77] This conciliatory attitude persisted into the 1390s: the three-year truce with the French agreed at Leulingham in 1389 was renewed several times, and finally in 1396 a twenty-eight-year truce was agreed as a prelude to Richard's marriage with Isabelle, daughter of the French king.[78] *Sir Gawain and the Green Knight* harmonizes with this desire for peace by showing that heroism can take other forms than physical prowess or martial aggression, manifesting itself in situations that demand even more physical courage than battle, but which also demand tact, diplomacy, humility, and self-restraint. With Richard's deposition and death, this attempt at promoting a different sort of heroism vanished like the wind, and hopes for peace with France were replaced by Lancastrian belligerence.[79]

---

77 According to Henry Knighton, when under threat from parliament in October 1386, Richard horrified Thomas Woodstock, duke of Gloucester (later one of the five Lords Appellant), and Thomas Arundel, bishop of Ely, by saying that he could look for assistance from "cognatum nostrum regem Francie." *Knighton's Chronicle 1337–1396*, ed. and trans. G.H. Martin (Oxford, 1995), 352–61. On opposing attitudes to war with the French in Richard's reign, see Saul, *Richard II*, 140–2, 196–8, 204, 219, 312, 439. Richard of course engaged in military campaigns against the Scots and the Irish, but he seems to have regarded these as internal struggles which were different from continental warfare. Gillespie says he "used military force as a tool, not an end" ("Richard II: King of Battles?" 160).

78 Saul, *Richard II*, 205–34 (the chapter is called "The Quest for Peace, 1389–98"). Saul comments that the truce of 1389 "inaugurated the longest break in hostilities since the resumption of the war in 1369" (205). Philippe de Mézières's *Letter to King Richard II* (ed. G.W. Coopland [Liverpool, 1975]) is a passionate plea to Richard to put an end to the Anglo-French war and accept Isabelle as his bride.

79 Thanking the people of London for their splendid reception of him in 1400, Henry IV reportedly swore that "neither my grandfather King Edward, nor my uncle the Prince of Wales, ever advanced so far in France as I shall do, if it please God and St George, or I shall die there in torment" ("vous jure et promech que monseigneur mon grant-pere le roy Edouard ne mon oncle le prince de Galles nallerent oncques sy avant en France comme je feray, sil plaist a Dieu et a monseigneur Saint George, ou je y morray en la paine"). See *Recueil des croniques et anchiennes istories de la Grant Bretaigne, a present nomme Engleterre, par Jehan de Waurin, seigneur de Forestel ... 1399–1422*, ed. William Hardy, Rolls series 39, vol. 2 (London, 1868), 45. Although Henry was distracted by other concerns from mounting a full-scale campaign against the French, his son Henry V more than made up for the lack.

Chapter Eleven

Sir Gawain and the Romance Hero

The poet of *Beowulf*, having begun his narrative by describing the nightly ravages inflicted by the monster Grendel on the household of the Danish king Hrothgar, introduces the hero of his poem as follows:

> At home, a great man among the Geats, a thane of Hygelac, heard of Grendel's deeds. In strength he was the mightiest among mankind in that day and age, noble and powerful. He ordered a good seagoing vessel to be made ready for him; he said that he wished to seek out over the swan's road the war-king, the famous prince, since he had need of men. Wise men in no way reproached him for that venture, though he was dear to them; they encouraged the man renowned for his spirit, examined the omens. From the people of the Geats the great man had picked champions, the bravest he could find; he went down to the water-borne timbers as one of fifteen. A skilled seaman pointed out the line of the coast. The time came; the boat lay on the waves, afloat beneath the cliff. Eager heroes stepped aboard at the prow; the tide turned, sea against the sand; soldiers carried bright trappings, splendid battle-gear, into the bosom of the vessel; men shoved out the well-braced timbers, warriors on a willing journey. Then driven by the wind, the ship travelled over the sea-waves, floating foamy-necked, just like a bird, until in due course on the following day its curved prow had come to where the voyagers could sight land, shining sea-cliffs, steep promontories and broad headlands. The sea then was crossed, the voyage at an end. The men of the Weders quickly set foot on level ground, moored the sea-borne timbers; their mail-shirts, the garments of war, rang out. They thanked God that the sea voyage had been easy for them.[1]

1 *Klaeber's Beowulf*, 4th ed., ed. R.D. Fulk, Robert E. Bjork, and John D. Niles (Toronto, 2008), lines 194–228; translation from *Beowulf*, ed. and trans. Michael Swanton (Manchester, 1978), 43–5.

The concept of heroism illustrated in this passage is one that is readily understood. The hero learns of a wrong that needs to be righted, distress that needs to be alleviated. His strength and bravery are just the qualities the enterprise demands, and he makes a rational decision to undertake it, choosing similarly qualified companions to support him. His heroism is not a vainglorious display of courage, but a mature plan of action, approved by his fellow countrymen. He sets off for a known destination, with a known end in view. He may succeed or fail, but the nature of his task, and the means by which he is to perform it, are not in doubt.

This "active" model of heroism, straightforward and obvious as it may seem, is not the one that is most characteristic of romance. The example used by Erich Auerbach in *Mimesis* to illustrate the romance ethos is Calogrenant's story of his search for adventures at the opening of Chrétien de Troyes's *Yvain*[2] – a narrative that shows us no purposeful journeying, but a random wandering through the forest in search of unspecified adventures, whose direction is dictated not by his own will but by the path he is following. When he at last finds an adventure with which he can engage, its nature is entirely enigmatic and its purpose seems to be only to test his own courage. A Giant Herdsman describes a mysterious "adventure" at a nearby fountain, which can be initiated by throwing water from the spring on to an emerald slab. The mysterious consequence of this action is a tremendous storm which devastates the entire forest; it is then succeeded, equally mysteriously, by the arrival of a flock of birds singing with exquisite beauty. Calogrenant throws the water on the slab and endures the storm; the singing birds arrive as predicted by the Herdsman. But what was *not* predicted was the arrival of a strange knight who indignantly accuses Calogrenant of laying waste his woodland and insists on avenging the injury in combat; so far from righting a wrong, the romance hero seems if anything to have created it. This impression is strengthened when Yvain repeats Calogrenant's actions, and kills the Knight of the Fountain, turning his beautiful young wife into a widow. Yet it is impossible to assess the rights and wrongs of the situation, because of the completely enigmatic nature of everything to do with the fountain. If it needs to be "defended" to avoid the destruction to the forest created by the storm, why not discourage the water-casting by removing the basin hanging above the slab? Or why not have the fountain constantly guarded? Or put up a large notice outlining the socio-economic consequences of the storm provoked by casting water on the stone, so as to appeal to the knight's better

2 Auerbach, *Mimesis: The Representation of Reality in Western Literature*, trans. Willard Trask (Princeton, NJ, 1953), ch. 6. *Yvain*, ed. T.B.W. Reid (Manchester, 1942), lines 175–580.

nature? The adventure of the fountain seems to invite the knight to set in motion the mysterious sequence of storm–singing birds–challenge to combat, and yet to hold him guilty for having done so. Its relation to any comprehensible sequence of cause and effect, or to any realistic context, is as mysterious to the reader as to Calogrenant.

The enigmatic nature of the romance world gives a new character to romance heroism. John Stevens recognizes this in contrasting the epic hero and the romance hero. "The hero of an epic, it seems, can never be at a loss to understand what is happening to him. He lives and fights in a known land against declared enemies." The romance hero, in contrast, is "like a man fighting ghosts in a mist ... [he] is involved in a mystery; he is on a quest but does not know what he has to look for; he is engaged in a struggle but does not know who his adversary is."[3] The mysteriousness of the romance world means that even when the romance hero has a specific aim in view, he is denied understanding both of the mechanics of his adventure and of its meaning. He is summoned to act without being able to make a rational calculation of the likely consequences of his action, or of what is the most effective way to proceed.

The differences between the romance hero and the "active" model of heroism that I outlined at the outset could be expressed by describing romance heroism as a fundamentally *passive* heroism. The romance hero does not seek to execute a consciously developed plan; rather, he seeks "adventures" in general, and allows chance (which is of course the fundamental meaning of "aventure" in both Old French and Middle English) to dictate the shape they will take. His role is to respond rather than to initiate, to suffer rather than to struggle. Even where he is most active, he must at the same time passively submit to the larger forces which determine whether he is the hero destined to "achieve" this adventure, and which will likewise determine its consequences. The measure of his heroism is his willingness to hazard himself without claiming control over these larger forces – indeed, without even being able to identify them.

The role of the sea in romance is a useful index of the contrast with the "active" model of heroism. In the passage from *Beowulf*, the sea is something to be navigated, the road that brings one to the end envisaged by one's desire. In romance, when the hero or heroine puts out to sea, he or she is characteristically

3 John Stevens, *Medieval Romance* (London, 1973), 78–80. See also Morton W. Bloomfield's contrast between the "rational" motivation of narrative episodes in epic, and the "irrational" character of romance narrative: "Episodic Motivation and Marvels in Epic and Romance," in Bloomfield, *Essays and Explorations: Studies in Ideas, Language and Literature* (Cambridge, MA, 1970), 97–128; cf. also Jill Mann, "'Taking the Adventure': Malory and the *Suite du Merlin*," 243–74 below.

at its mercy, set adrift in a rudderless boat, allowing its winds and currents to set a course, challenged and thwarted by its storms. King Horn set adrift in a boat without rudder or sail by the Saracens who have killed his father,[4] the wounded Guigemar asleep in the deserted boat which of its own accord takes him to the woman who will be his love,[5] the wounded Tristan allowing his ship to go where "God and chance" may take it, in the hope that he may be brought to a place where his wounds will be cured,[6] are all powerful images of passive heroism. And it is necessary to grasp this essential passivity as a mark of heroism if we are not to misunderstand the romance hero by judging him against the "active" heroic model,[7] and seeing his passivity as something that the romance writer aims to ridicule or criticize.

The opening of *Sir Gawain and the Green Knight* is a potential locus for such misunderstanding. It shows Arthur's knights engaged in feasting rather than fighting, their celebrations rudely interrupted by the entry of the Green Knight whose challenge – that one of their number should strike off his head now, and accept similar treatment himself in a year's time – leaves them in silent bewilderment. This has led some critics to see Arthur's court as sunk in lethargy and decadence, content to rest on their laurels, and readier to pass the time in party games than in earning their reputation as fighting men. Such a reading ignores the swirling energy that characterizes the poet's description of the feast, and even more important, it ignores the significance of Arthur's decision – a custom of his on such occasions – not to participate in it until some "adventure" has been recounted or has occurred. He therefore does not take his place at table, but leaves his seat empty, and stands in front of the table talking to his guests.[8] This picture of Arthur consciously *waiting* for an adventure, inviting it without dictating what form it will take, emblematizes heroic passivity. In *Beowulf*, the warriors' hall is a bulwark against the dangers outside; Grendel

4 *King Horn: An Edition Based on Cambridge University Library MS Gg.4.27 (2)*, ed. Rosamund Allen (New York, 1984), lines 103–58, 189–96.

5 *Guigemar*, lines 151–208, in Marie de France, *Lais*, ed. A. Ewert (Oxford, 1944).

6 *Le Roman de Tristan en prose*, ed. Renée L. Curtis (Cambridge, 1985), 1:155–7 (sections 308–11). "Diex et aventure" at section 311/3.

7 Thus, Morton W. Bloomfield finds an almost complete absence of heroes in the later Middle Ages (that is, the period between *Beowulf* and Spenser), because he is looking for the type of heroism I have called "active": "The Problem of the Hero in the Later Medieval Period," in *Concepts of the Hero in the Middle Ages and the Renaissance*, ed. Norman T. Burns and Christopher J. Reagan (London, 1975), 27–48.

8 This essential detail is overlooked by those who assume that the Green Knight is being deliberately insulting when he asks where the king is (224–7). Since the king's seat is conspicuously vacant, the question is a perfectly reasonable one.

creates such fear and terror precisely because he penetrates the hall itself and carries off the sleeping thegns. In *Gawain*, the court is deliberately and ostentatiously open to the outside world; its dangers are not excluded, but on the contrary are incorporated into the very texture of courtly life. Arthur's empty seat is an emblem of the centrality of adventure in the life of his court; adventure is, as it were, enthroned in his place, and he can assume his seat only when its superior claims have been acknowledged. So, when the Green Knight carries his challenge into the very heart of the court, he does not disrupt the courtly ceremonial so much as complete it, by providing the adventure that the king is waiting for. The unexpected, in this society, is precisely what is always expected, and what romance heroism holds itself in readiness to meet.

The Green Knight's challenge has two parts, one of which (striking off the Green Knight's head) is active, and the other of which (undergoing the same treatment) is passive. It is obvious from the outset that it is the passive part of the test that is the harder. The image of the knight baring his neck to the axe, without protection and without protest, is again a powerful emblem of passive heroism. It was surely for this reason that the French romance writers borrowed this motif from Irish sources and incorporated it into their narratives.[9] It appears in the *Gawain*-poet's probable source, the Caradoc episode in the First Continuation of Chrétien's *Perceval*; it also appears in *La Mule sans Frein* (where the hero is Gawain) and the *Perlesvaus* (where the hero is Lancelot).[10] In all these cases, the knight's passivity is increased by the fact that there are no reasons other than his own promise to motivate his submission. He cannot find a motive for it in the reflection that his own self-sacrifice will lead to the saving of other lives, or to any other visible benefit to the world at large. Nor can his submission be made meaningful by being conceived as a just "punishment" for wrongdoing; although the ordeal is represented as a fair requital for the original decapitation of the challenger, that act is itself so little an expression of the knight's independent volition that it hardly justifies his consequent death. The submission that Gawain makes to the Green Knight is thus an intellectual as well as a physical submission; it involves not only baring his neck to the axe, but also renouncing any understanding of the whole situation in which he finds himself, anything that could provide support by answering the "why"

9 For a discussion of the motif in Irish, French, German, and English literature, see Larry D. Benson, *Art and Tradition in Sir Gawain and the Green Knight* (New Brunswick, NJ, 1965), 11–25.

10 See Elisabeth Brewer, *Sir Gawain and the Green Knight: Sources and Analogues* (Cambridge, 1992), 25–32, 36–57.

that so urgently presents itself. The only motivation that he has comes not from without but from within – his own "trawþe," which is to be preserved, paradoxically, only by his commitment to his own destruction. The knight's field of action, one could say, is not the outside world, over which he claims to exercise no control, but himself; the outside world is the means of testing and revealing his selfhood.

It may seem that Gawain is "active" at least to the extent that he chooses to take up the Green Knight's challenge, judging himself fit to meet it. But a close attention to the poem will show that this is not really the case. The Green Knight's challenge is directed at Arthur, and when the king quite reasonably hesitates to rush into it, the Green Knight taunts him and his knights with cowardice to the point where his own reputation – that is, his commitment to the acceptance of adventure – demands that he take it up. It is now apparent that Arthur cannot be allowed to go through with the Beheading Game – that is, the court cannot allow its king to commit himself to what looks like certain death. One of them must relieve him of the commitment. And it is quite clear which one it must be. What makes it clear is the seating plan for dinner, which the poet has carefully outlined in the course of describing the feast. The seating is arranged, as the poet makes plain, according to rank: "þe best burne ay abof" (73). Arthur's seat is in the centre of the "high table" which is placed at one end of the hall, at right angles to the "sidbordez" at which the rank and file sit. On Arthur's right, in the place of honour, sits Bishop Baldwin, with Ywain on his other side. On Arthur's left is Guinevere, next to whom sits Gawain and then his brother Agravain (both of them the king's nephews). That is, Gawain has the highest place of honour after Bishop Baldwin. The bishop, being a cleric, cannot accept a knightly challenge, which means that it falls to Gawain to give the lead in extricating the king and the court from the difficult situation which has arisen. Just as the court was constrained by "cortaysye" (247) to allow Arthur to determine how to respond to the Green Knight's challenge, so, once he has accepted it, the court is similarly obliged to wait until its highest-ranking member speaks on its behalf. And Gawain is obliged to protect his lord, and to save the court from incurring the reproach that they allowed their king to die to save their reputation.

The displacement of the challenge from Arthur to Gawain is therefore not the result of an unconstrained decision on Gawain's part; rather, it is quasi-inevitable (that is, it could be avoided only if Gawain failed to display the necessary heroism). However little it was envisaged by the Green Knight (whose original target, we later discover, was Arthur, and through him, Guinevere), the finger of destiny ends up pointing very clearly at Gawain. And in the tradition of passive heroism, he responds, accepting the claims that the situation makes on him, with a heroic disregard for anything outside its immediate boundaries. The speech in which he requests that the challenge be transferred to him is a perfect illustration of passive heroism. It is carefully constructed so as to allay any suspicion of personal aggrandizement, or any slight to the king and the other courtiers.[11] The ostensible basis of Gawain's claim is not that he is the bravest and strongest of the knights, but on the contrary, that since he is "þe wakkest ... and of wyt feblest" (354), this "foolish" challenge (using Arthur's own description of it) is most appropriate to him (323, 358). But at the same time the real basis of his claim is made clear:

"Bot for as much as ȝe ar myn em I am only to prayse,
No bounté bot your blod I in my bodé knowe." (356–7)

["Only inasmuch as you are my uncle am I to be esteemed; I know no good qualities in myself other than your blood."]

In the most tactful manner possible, he makes clear that as the king's nephew, he is highest in rank and thus the inevitable heir to the challenge once Arthur has been persuaded to relinquish it.

The challenge having been transferred to Gawain, he proceeds to chop off the Green Knight's head, only to find that the Knight picks it up, remounts, delivers a final speech to the court through its mouth, and rides off. "Active" heroism has been made part of the challenge, one might say, only so that it may fail of any effect. The remaining part of the test is entirely passive, not only in the requirement that Gawain submit to the axe, but also in the requirement that he find the Green Knight's home, the green chapel, without being given the least inkling of its location. He cannot, that is, *direct* himself to a known goal; he can only travel at random, hoping that the green chapel will, as it were, find *him* in the course of his wanderings.

This is not all: the passivity required by the challenge is underlined yet again, in that the real test (as we discover at the end of the poem) does not take place when Gawain faces the Green Knight's axe, but when he is undergoing sexual harassment from the lady of the castle, in what had appeared to be a mere digressive episode. That is, the image of knightly heroism that we are to carry away from this poem does not show us the hero on his feet, armed, bravely battling against monsters or dangerous male adversaries; instead it shows us the hero naked, flat on his back in a comfortable bed, fending off the seductive

11 See the fine analysis of this speech by A.C. Spearing, *Criticism and Medieval Poetry*, 2nd ed. (London, 1972), 45–6.

assaults of a woman, and using no more dangerous weapons than words. Yet once again, physical action begins to look like the easy option when it is compared with the effort involved in dealing with the lady, and the discomfort that is increased by the need to pretend that one is having an enjoyable time. Passivity, that is, requires just as much energy as activity. Just as we can measure the effort required in Gawain's passivity before the Green Knight's axe by the lightning speed with which he springs around the minute the third stroke has been given, grabbing his weapons in readiness for active combat, so we can recognize the effort required to maintain his easy affability with the lady by the speed with which he gets out of bed and clothes himself the minute she has gone (1308–10) – his appetite for lying in, presumably, much diminished. The world of physical action outside, where the lord is hunting, seems a refreshingly uncomplicated place in comparison with the supposedly restful world of the bedroom.

The poet is of course well aware – and makes his readers aware – of the comedy inherent in Gawain's undignified posture in the bedroom scenes. But that does not mean that he is not serious about the kind of heroism Gawain displays there.[12] Nor is this conception of heroism something new in courtly romance. If we look at the twelfth-century romances of Chrétien de Troyes, which were the model for the genre, we find that the bed is a conventional site for knightly adventure. In Chrétien's *Knight of the Cart*, for example, Lancelot spends the night in a sumptuous bed which he has been explicitly warned off.[13] In the middle of the night, a lance shoots down from the rafters like a thunderbolt, passing straight through the bedding, and narrowly missing Lancelot himself. The lance has a blazing pennon which sets fire to the bed. Lancelot sits up, puts out the fire, and throws the lance into the middle of the hall – all without leaving the bed (507–38). He then goes back to sleep. Gawain has a similar adventure in Chrétien's *Perceval*, when he expresses a wish to sit for a while on an extremely luxurious bed.

> In the centre of the hall was a bed with nothing of wood about it, for it was made entirely of gold except for the cords, which were all of silver ... At each intersection of the cords a bell was hanging. Over the bed was spread a great coverlet of heavy

12 *Pace* Larry Benson, who has said that "comedy is not the stuff of which romance heroes are made" (*Art and Tradition*, 209).

13 *Le chevalier de la charrette*, ed. Mario Roques (Paris, 1968), lines 459–534. Similar encounters with a "Lit Aventureux" occur in the Prose *Lancelot*, ed. Alexandre Micha, 9 vols (Paris, 1978–83), 2:379–80 (LXVI.17–18) (Gawain), and 5:259–60 (XCVIII.29–30) (Bors); trans. in *Lancelot-Grail. The Old French Arthurian Vulgate and Post-Vulgate in Translation*, ed. Norris J. Lacy, vol. 3 (New York, 1995), 100, 269.

> silk material; and in each of its posts was set a carbuncle that shone more brilliantly than four brightly burning candles. The bed stood on little carved dogs that were pulling grotesque faces, and the dogs on four castors that moved so freely and swiftly that if anyone gave the bed a slight push with just one finger it would run all over the hall from one end to the other.[14]

This bed, described with the enthusiastic detail of a furniture catalogue, turns out to constitute a knightly challenge: Gawain is told that to sit on it means certain death. He nevertheless persists in his intention and sits on the bed, whereupon the bed cords screech, all the windows fly open, and in pours a hail of arrows, striking Gawain's shield and also inflicting numerous wounds on his body. Next, a lion bounds through a door and attacks Gawain, who promptly swipes off its head. He then resumes his seat on the bed, and is congratulated on having passed the test. As a result, he is told, he has freed the castle from enchantment and thus (though the causal connection is not apparent) resolved the problems inflicting its inhabitants: a troop of damsels waiting to be married, widowed ladies deprived of their lands, and squires waiting to be made knights. However socially useful the result of Gawain's action has turned out to be, this was not his aim when he sat on the bed, but an unforeseen consequence.

In both these scenes, the bed, like the rudderless boat, is a visual image of the essentially passive nature of romance heroism. (In *Guigemar*, the two images are combined into one: the bed is in the centre of the boat, and it is when the hero lies on the bed that the boat moves off of its own accord.)[15] The knight's courage shows itself not in combat, but in his willingness to hazard himself, to shed the protection of his armour, to surrender physical control. The outcome of the adventure is determined not by purposefully directed action, but by the adventure itself. The lance does not miss Lancelot because he takes any evasive action, but simply (it would appear) because he is Lancelot. In *Perceval*, Gawain is told that the knight who is to release the castle from its enchantments must be "ideally handsome and wise, quite free of greed, valiant and bold, with a

---

14 *Le Roman de Perceval ou le conte du graal*, ed. Keith Busby (Tübingen, 1993), lines 7692–712. English translations of the romances of Chrétien are taken from *Arthurian Romances: Chretien de Troyes*, trans. D.D.R. Owen (London, 1987; reissued 1991).

15 Cf. the similar pattern of events in *Partenopeu de Blois*, ed. Joseph Gildea, 2 vols. (Villanova, PA, 1967–8), lines 701–2. A variation on the same theme occurs in *Le Roman de Jaufre* (lines 3017–61), where the hero falls asleep on horseback and is carried by his horse to the castle of a lady with whom he falls in love (*Les Troubadours*, ed. and trans. René Lavaud and René Nelli, vol. 1 (Paris, 1960). See also Michel Stanesco's illuminating discussion of these and other examples of the motif of "dorveille" (sleep/reverie) in chivalric narratives; *Jeux d'errance du chevalier médiéval* (Leiden, 1988), 148–72.

noble and loyal heart, without baseness or wickedness."[16] So long as the knight *is* all these things, success will follow as a matter of course; it is not the result of organized effort. Moreover, Gawain does not decide to sit on the bed because he thinks he matches the description of the ideal knight, since he does not know that it is sitting on the bed that will dispel the enchantment. He simply pursues his own inclination, leaving the adventure to take its own course. The active element in both tests (putting out the fire, killing the lion) is introduced only to emphasize its subordinate role; both scenes emphasize the fundamentally passive nature of the heroism involved by ending with the knight lying or sitting on the bed as at the beginning. Activity is merely superficial; it does not imply abandonment of the hero's fundamental passivity in the face of adventure.

The Knight of the Cart contains another episode in which Lancelot undergoes an ordeal in a bed in circumstances more similar to Gawain's in the Middle English poem.[17] Lancelot accepts hospitality from a damsel who imposes the condition that he sleep with her. At bedtime, the damsel stage-manages a scene in which she is apparently being raped by a knight, the door to her room guarded by a line of armed men. When Lancelot rushes in to rescue her – oddly, his motive is said to be not his desire to save her, but his desire to keep his promise to her – the damsel sits up and dismisses all the men (who are members of her own household) without further ado. Lancelot then has to fulfil his original promise to sleep with the girl. Sweating with apprehension, he takes off his clothes, but retains his shirt, as she retains her chemise. He lies down beside her, but takes care not to touch her, keeping his back turned, and saying not a word. Seeing his discomfort, the damsel gives in, and gracefully withdraws. Chrétien refers to Lancelot's unwilling performance of his promise as "force," which in a sexual context was one of the Old French terms for rape.[18] That is, having initially been called upon to save the damsel from rape, Lancelot then has to submit to a quasi-rape himself. The full significance of this episode within *The Knight of the Cart* is too large a subject to discuss here; what is important for present purposes is that once again active heroism is gently marginalized, and replaced by a novel picture of heroism exercised in bed rather than in combat, in a refusal to act rather than in action. And again, it is a picture that shows passivity as *effort*.

The Perilous Bed whose sumptuousness invites relaxation and surrender, but which then unleashes a spectacular display of physical violence, is a deliberately

16 *Perceval*, ed. Busby, lines 7593–6.

17 *Le chevalier de l charrette*, ed. Roques, lines 931–1280.

18 Ibid., lines 1209–11. See Tobler-Lommatzsch, s.v. *force*, "Gewalt, Gewalttat."

paradoxical image, designed to express the new kind of heroism characteristic of romance. The challenge does not take the form of combat, but of the ordeal: knightly courage consists in a hazarding of the self whose condition is a surrender of control. The subjection to female demands which is evidenced in Lancelot's "rape" (not only in the fulfilment of his promise to his hostess, but also in the devotion to Guinevere which keeps him chaste) likewise emblematizes passivity as the core of the new heroism. The physically stronger is subordinated to the physically weaker. The *Gawain*-poet "naturalizes" this image; eschewing both the marvellous (the enchanted bed) and the improbable (the arbitrarily imposed obligation to sleep with the hostess), he invents a situation which in the most natural of ways makes the bed the locus of knightly endeavour. But the result is the same: "active" heroism is marginalized, and the maintenance of personal integrity within a framework that keeps the knight's role essentially passive is set in its place.

The one failure of which Gawain is guilty is to succumb to the temptation to assume some kind of control – that is, to accept the girdle which will (he believes) affect the outcome of the Beheading Game. Acceptance of the girdle, however sensible it might seem, fatally qualifies the complete self-abandonment which passive heroism requires. It represents Gawain's desire to have some *input* into the situation he confronts – and by the same token, testifies to the effort involved in renouncing that desire – allowing oneself to drown, as it were, without even clutching at a straw.

The relation between Gawain's (small) failure and romance heroism can however be viewed in another perspective – a perspective in which failure itself becomes an important test of knightly heroism. Of Chrétien de Troyes' five romances, no fewer than four show their heroes as incurring the charge of failure in one way or another, and in three of these cases the failure becomes an important pivot in the narrative. In *Erec and Enide*, the whole second part of the romance constitutes Erec's response to the criticisms of him for abandoning knightly exploits and devoting himself to his wife. Conversely, the whole second part of *Yvain* is set in motion by the dramatic denunciation of Yvain, before Arthur and his court, as a liar and a traitor, because he failed to fulfil his promise to return home to his new wife Laudine at the end of a year spent in tourneying. And finally, Perceval, while trying his hardest to obey all the instructions in polite behaviour he has been given, fails to ask any question about the Grail procession, and finds himself denounced next day as "Perceval le chetis" for having failed to bring about the cure of the Maimed King, which would, he is told, have been the consequence of his enquiry.

The inexplicable forms an important element in all these knightly "failures." It is not made clear whether the other knights are right to criticize Erec for his uxoriousness (they may be as blinkered as the courtiers who criticize Arthur for letting Gawain ride off to keep his promise to the Green Knight), or whether Erec's response, which consists of setting out on adventures with Enide as his companion, but prohibiting her from speaking to him, constitutes an acceptance or a rejection of their criticism. We are not told why or how Yvain manages to forget his promise to the wife he loves so much; the action cannot be plausibly explained by what we know of his character. And in Perceval's case, it seems unfair that his strenuous attempts to do the right thing should lay him open to blame, particularly when it is impossible to see any connection between the posing of the question and the healing of the king. The inexplicable in all these instances is an indication that the response to these failures is not to take the form of an investigation of their causes, an analysis of the nature and degree of the hero's responsibility, the role of intention, mitigating circumstances, consideration of what could have been foreseen at the time, and so on. Rather, the failure is something like a fait accompli, something as arbitrary but inevitable as the dangers produced by the Perilous Beds, and yet even more challenging to the knight, since what he is called upon to endure is not an external threat but a degrading image of himself. In response to this challenge, passive heroism means accepting this image without protest or self-defence, abandoning self-justification and explanation. Erec's practical acceptance is shown in his instant abandonment of domestic life for the quest; Perceval's acceptance is manifested in his confession to the hermit who turns out to be his uncle. Yvain's acceptance of the image of himself as the very antithesis of knightly honour is so complete that he loses his mind, running naked in the woods as a madman. The "folie" which forms an episode in the lives of Lancelot and Tristan as well as of Yvain is a measure of the grandeur of the romance hero's surrender to adventure.[19] Failure in all these instances is not the result of a desire for "realism" – that is, the wish to show that the knightly hero is not a plaster saint. Rather, it is an occasion for the demonstration of passive heroism in the acceptance of failure. So the final test of Gawain's heroism comes when the Green Knight confronts him with his own failure. And his acceptance is total: in his own eyes, he has betrayed everything that makes him a knight.

> "For care of þy knokke cowardyse me taȝt
> To acorde me with couetyse, my kynde to forsake,
> Þat is larges and lewté þat longez to knyȝtez.
> Now am I fawty and falce, and ferde haf ben euer

19 Cf. Mann, "Troilus's Swoon," 13n.13 above.

Of trechery and vntrawþe: boþe bityde sorȝe
and care!" (2379–84)

["Out of fear of your blow, cowardice taught me to reconcile myself with covetousness, betraying my nature, the generosity and faithfulness that belong to knights. Now I am faulty and false, and have always been afraid of treachery and disloyalty; curse them both!"]

For the Green Knight, Gawain's acceptance of his failure is so complete that it reconstitutes him as a hero.

"Þou art confessed so clene, beknowen of þy mysses,
And hatz þe penaunce apert of þe poynt of myn egge,
I halde þe polysed of þat plyȝt, and pured as clene
As þou hadez neuer forfeted syþen þou watz fyrst borne." (2390–4)

["You are confessed so completely, acknowledging your faults, and have the visible penance of my axe-blade, that I hold you absolved of that sin, and cleansed as completely as if you had never sinned since you were first born."]

But Gawain's acceptance persists beyond the scene of his confession; it extends into his further confession to Arthur's court, and his insistence on wearing the girdle ever after as a permanent sign of his fault. So far from trying to forget his failure, or to wipe it out by future improvement, he makes it into a central element of his identity. The knights of Arthur's court recognize this uncompromising acceptance as the final proof of Gawain's passive heroism, and perceive that it makes the girdle a badge of honour as well as of shame, which they themselves will wear to show their sense of the honour Gawain has brought on their number. Acceptance of failure becomes the badge of success.

One final point about passive heroism remains to be emphasized. I have throughout been trying to distinguish passive heroism from a laissez-faire inertia by stressing the effort that is necessary to relinquish attempts at control; action is always the easier option. Passive heroism, that is, is not a merely negative failure to act, but a positive acceptance of submission. Yet this might make it sound as if passive heroism is simply stoicism under another name. To some extent, of course, stoicism is an appropriate term to describe the knight's uncomplaining acceptance of suffering and death. But the passive heroism of romance differs from stoicism in that it is conceived as exerting its own kind of active power. Although it does not aim at results in the same way as the "active" model of heroism, it can nevertheless produce them, even though it is by unforeseeable and often incomprehensible processes. So, if Gawain bares his neck to the axe in expectation of certain death, he finds, miraculously, that the threat of death dissipates itself. If we ask what creates this result, the Green Knight's explanation of the test hardly provides a satisfactory answer. For if Morgan le Fay and he were motivated by so much malice against Arthur and his court that they aimed to terrify them all, and frighten Guinevere to death, with the ghoulish resuscitation of the Green Knight, there seems no reason why this malice should not find expression in decapitating Gawain, particularly when neither he nor the court would raise a protest. Sparing Gawain is "just," in moral terms, but there is no evidence that the Green Knight/Bertilak is in general animated by a strict sense of morality. The only explanation he gives for Gawain's release shows his own "trawþe" as a response to Gawain's:

> "Trwe mon trwe restore,
> Þenne þar mon drede no waþe." (2354–5)

["Truth must meet truth; then no peril need be dreaded."]

The continuing enigma of the nature and motivation of Bertilak and Morgan leaves us to find "trawþe" itself as the active power that works to save Gawain's life. It is his own "trawþe," exemplified in his passive surrender to the claims of his nonsensical promise, that is reflected back to him in the justice that spares him. Passive heroism here exerts a power no less magical than when it confounds the enchanted beds on which Chrétien's knights hazard themselves. As the rudderless boat comes safely to land of its own accord, so the hero who casts himself adrift on the sea of adventure finds that it brings him to a safe harbour.

Chapter Twelve

Knightly Combat in Malory's *Morte d'Arthur*

Malory's popularity is undoubted, but in some ways surprising, for the simple reading of his work presents considerable difficulties. The events of the narrative are repetitive and hard to connect with each other; since it is difficult to see them as a meaningful sequence, it is difficult to remember them, even over the span of a few pages. The vast numbers of people to whom we are introduced are barely differentiated from each other in terms of individual personality, and what distinguishing traits they have are liable to shift in a disconcerting fashion. Gawain is now a traitor and murderer, now a noble knight, and we cannot see what governs the change from one role to the other. Although Malory is a master in conveying human emotion, and at catching the rhythms of human speech, terse or plangent, dignified or touching, he seems to have little interest in "character," in the web of emotions and motives that lie behind human speech and action. Furthermore, this means that it is difficult for us to assess these actions in moral terms – and yet moral terms are by no means banished from the narrative. The knightly world is a world dedicated to abstract moral values – to "worthynes," "jantylnes," and "trouthe" – and yet the knight's most characteristic activity is within the physical sphere, in physical combat, often undertaken for its own sake, or as the result of a randomly imposed "custome." At the end of the work, the relation between the physical and the moral becomes an acute problem when Lancelot offers to prove Guinevere's "truth" to Arthur by means of bodily combat.

Clearly we cannot read Malory with the equipment of expectations and responses that we bring to other kinds of narrative. What modern Malory criticism needs to do – and has to some extent begun to do[1] – is to work out a

1 I have in mind in particular Mark Lambert, *Malory: Style and Vision in Le Morte Darthur* (New Haven CT, 1975).

critical vocabulary and a way of reading that is appropriate for the structure and nature of his particular kind of narrative. We could begin, in my view, by banishing from this critical vocabulary the word "character," as inappropriate to his representation of human figures, and also by ceasing to impose on his work the opposition between feudal loyalty and romantic love that critics have for so long tried to read into it, but for which the text itself provides little or no evidence. Instead, the terms on which we should build our reading of Malory are those suggested by the work itself: the (deliberate, as I believe) narrowness and simplicity, of his vocabulary directs our attention, by insistent repetition, to the key words and concepts of his narrative. I cannot discuss or even list them all here, but some of the most important are: *aventure, worship, body, departe, hole, togidir, felyship.* These words are not, for Malory, a decorative clothing for his subject; rather, they form the skeletal structure of his work. For example, Malory invests with import the double significance of the word "departe" in Middle English: it means both "to leave" and "to separate."[2] The reiteration of this word (and its variants) lays cumulative stress on this double significance, and this means that we feel the poignancy of separation as an emotional pressure behind even the most routine of knightly departures. It also creates in us a corresponding yearning for that which negates separation, for "wholeness" – both the wholeness of the individual person, and the wholeness of the Round Table fellowship.[3] Each individual departure adumbrates that final division of fellowship, and departure from life itself, which is realized at the end of the work. Correspondingly, at the end we are also reminded of the wholeness once achieved, and now passed away, in the solemn recording of the number of the Round Table knights "whan they were holé togyders" (1260/18). The deepest division at this point, however, is not that which separates them from each other, but that which separates us from them, locked in the past. Yet even as we register this, we are made conscious that only by means of this intervening distance can a different kind of wholeness be achieved – that of the "hoole book," which is only now made complete (1260/16).

Study of the use of "departe" leads logically, if to us somewhat surprisingly, to a realization of the importance of what might be called the "choreography" of Malory's narrative. What I mean is that in this work, emotional and moral aspirations, frustrations, and satisfactions are expressed simply by movement, by

2 Malory's use of the word in both senses is noted by P.J.C. Field, *Romance and Chronicle* (London, 1971), 82.

3 Mark Lambert has sensitively analysed the way that the two kinds of "wholeness" are brought into relation in "The Healing of Sir Urry," which is based on a "kind of pun" on the word "whole" (*Style and Vision*, 63–5).

motion away and toward, by departure and return. The Grail Quest, for example, is initiated because of Gawain's desire for greater closeness to the Grail, the sight of it without the distancing veil; it is a "movement towards." Yet Galahad, the knight who does achieve full contact with the presence of the Grail, is separated from his fellows not only geographically, by the sea journey to the city of Sarras, but also by the "departure" of his soul "to Jesu Cryste" (1035/14–16), and his integration into the new fellowship of the son of Joseph of Arimathaea (1034/14; 1035/1). Our longing for wholeness must instead be satisfied by the return of Bors to the Round Table fellowship, and by Lancelot's assurance to him: "ye and I shall never departe in sundir whylis oure lyvys may laste" (1037/5–6).

A discussion of these key words and concepts in Malory which was in any way adequate to the richness and subtlety of his use of them would, however, be a full-length study, and it would have to go far beyond vocabulary alone. As a preliminary, what I should like to sketch here is the role of the knightly combat in Malory, to show how it acts as a focus for two of his key concepts: "aventure" and the body.

Knights are, of course, dedicated to adventures. But it is important in Malory, as in Chaucer, to remind ourselves that the primary meaning of the Middle English word "aventure" is "chance." The knight's dedication is therefore a dedicated submission to chance. The knight puts himself at the disposal of chance; he does not decide his exploits in advance, but rides out so as to expose himself to the claims that chance may lay on him in his travels – or, alternatively, he responds to chance intrusions into the sphere of the court. The adventure is beyond the knight's control; it is something that comes to him. The knights who are least successful in the Grail Quest are not those who fail in adventures, they are those who simply do not have any. Nor can the knight ensure his success by effort; it is determined by "aventure." The most concisely formulated example with which this aspect of Malory's work can be illustrated is to be found in one of his French sources; King Pellinore explains to Arthur that he hunts the Questing Beast because it is destined to be killed by the best knight of his lineage,

> and because I wanted to know for a truth whether I was the best of our lineage, I have pursued it for so long. And I haven't said this to exalt myself, but to know the truth about myself.[4]

4 This is my translation of the French *Suite du Merlin*, ed. Gilles Roussineau, 2nd ed., 2 vols in one (Geneva, 2006), 5 (section 8): "Et pour chou que je voloie connoistre se j'estoie li mieudres de nostre lignage, pour chou l'ai jou si longement sivie et alés aprés lui, si ne l'ai mie dit pour vantance de moi, mais pour savoir la verité de moi meesmes."

Normally, we assume that titles follow on actions, and are merely their consequence, that it would be the action of killing the Questing Beast that gave rise to and justified the title of "best knight." But here the situation is reversed: the action is reduced to a mere sign that the title is to be claimed, and any knight to whom it is not destined to be awarded will not be able to kill the Beast. The title and the ability to perform the action are granted simultaneously by some mysterious third agency. It is the discovery of self, not the creation of self, that is the function of knightly "aventure."

The importance of knightly combat is that it offers a structure within which "aventure" can operate, within which the revelatory movements of chance can realize themselves. With this notion of combat we can compare the ideas underlying the historical tradition of the judicial combat – that is, the use of battle in deciding cases of law. The judicial combat was introduced to England by the Normans, and it was never a major element of English law; in Malory's time, it had long fallen into disuse. But the ideas on which it was founded seem to have had a more vigorous life in imaginative literature than in historical actuality. To us, the recourse to a judicial combat might look like a cynical decision to let physical force settle a quarrel, but this was far from being the governing principle. As the authors of the standard history of early English law put it, "the judicial combat is an ordeal, a bilateral ordeal," and like the ordeal, it constitutes an "appeal to the supernatural." "It was a sacral process. What triumphed was not brute force but truth."[5] As in the ordeal, the exposure of the body to hazard is the medium through which non-physical realities are revealed.

So it is with the knightly combat in Malory: the knight realizes himself and his destiny, the nature and the events that chance has willed to him, in the long succession of physical engagements with his fellows. But to see the relation of Malory's combats to the judicial combat of history is also to see the need to distinguish between them. The ideas that lie behind the judicial combat remain within the realm of historical interest. The notions behind the knightly combat in Malory, by contrast, take on a serious and perennially relevant significance. The significance of the battle in Malory is metaphysical; it becomes a means of asking "why?" If we regard the question "why did that knight win that battle?" as answered when we say "because he was the stronger," or "because he was the better fighter," we are obscuring the fact that the "why" is only put back a stage.

5 Sir Frederick Pollock and Frederic William Maitland, *The History of English Law Before the Time of Edward I*, 2nd ed., 2 vols (Cambridge, 1968) 2:598–600. For a full account, see George Neilson, *Trial by Combat* (Glasgow, 1890). For a perceptive account of the historical ordeal, see Robert Bartlett, *Trial by Fire and Water: the Medieval Judicial Ordeal* (Oxford, 1986).

If we pursue it and ask "*why* was he the stronger?" we shall see that ultimately there is no possibility of answering except that so it is, for reasons we do not understand. The world that Malory constructs is a world that manages to perform the nigh-impossible task of bringing us face to face with the unanswerable nature of these questions, of making us feel and accept the arbitrariness that lies at the very roots of experience and existence. Because the physical is made the medium for the revelation of the non-physical, the very absoluteness of the gulf between them teaches us to recognize how mysterious are the sources of the immaterial qualities which reside in the bodily person or the material world, and how unidentifiable are the agencies that assign them to one resting place or another.

It is not only in combat, of course, that the bringing together of the physical and the non-physical is used to make us conscious of this mysterious arbitrariness; it is also in the multifarious tests and ordeals which likewise rank as "aventures." The physical act of pulling a sword from a sheath, for example, mysteriously signals that Balin is the knight "moste of worship withoute treson, trechory, or felony" (64/2–3). His possession of these qualities cannot be explained, nor can the statement that he possesses them be seen as a derivative of his actions, since his success in the test of the sword is its only basis. The sword test makes clear that it is as a result of the uncomprehended mechanisms of existence that these qualities reside in him.

The combat, then, is a way of engaging with "aventure," and this engagement is accomplished through the body. The knight "puts his body in aventure," or he "jeopardies" it, or he offers to prove his truth against an accuser "my body to his body." Over and over again Malory introduces the word, in phrases like these, in his alterations of his French sources. When Tristram takes his leave of the Irish court, for example, he challenges any knight who has a grievance to declare it "now or ellys never, and here is my body to make hit good, body ayenste body!" (392/27–8). It is true that the Middle English word "body" has a wider meaning than its modern English counterpart; it can refer to the person as a whole, rather than his or her physical aspect alone. But Malory's insistent use of the word in physical contexts places an emphasis on the corporeal as that within which the non-corporeal person mysteriously resides. The connections between the two are not fully explicable, but (as in the ordeal) they are strong; the condition of the body signals the condition of the person.

It is not only the knight's own body that is important in this process, it is also the body of his opponent. Tristram declares to Sir Marhalt that he proposes "to be worshypfully proved uppon thy body" (381/30–1). Through engagement with the body of his opponent the knight "proves" or "assays" his own quality; but equally he "proves" that of his fellow. It is this, and not a sort of military

Blutbruderschaft, that leads to the paradoxical situation in which conflict becomes the means to achieve fellowship. We naturally think of combat either as strategic (designed to fend off aggression or oppression), or as expressive (venting anger or malice). In Malory, the role of knightly combat is often purely neutral; it is unrelated to the affective state of its participants. On two occasions in the *Book of Tristram*, a knight about to engage in combat is asked whether he requests it "of love othir of hate" (604/33), or "in love other in wrathe" (696/5). In both cases, the answer is "for/in love." Understandably puzzled by this response, critics have sought to explain it as a sign of decadence infecting the chivalric world. But this explanation fails to understand the nature of combat in Malory – the way in which acceptance of battle, just as much as renunciation of it, demonstrates an acceptance of the arbitrary in the qualities and destiny assigned to one.

There is a particularly good illustration of this in the account of the opposition between Tristram and Lamorak and its reconciliation. The form taken by the arbitrary here is the creation of Lamorak's ill will towards Tristram; it is formed not by any voluntary action of Tristram's, but by Mark's command that he belatedly enter a tournament to engage with Lamorak, who has had the upper hand in it all day. Tristram's protests that this is "ayenste knyghthode" (428/17) are overruled, but having technically complied with Mark's order by jousting with Lamorak and unhorsing him, he refuses to fight further. Lamorak, who is eager to win back the honour he has lost, is enraged by this refusal (and rightly, since from his point of view it looks like an unknightly refusal to follow through "aventure" to the end, an attempt to use it opportunistically by shaping it to the pattern of one's own advantage). Later, therefore, he takes his revenge on Tristram by sending to Mark's court a magic horn, drinking from which will reveal adulterers (429/28–430/29). (We may note in passing that this is another example of the revelation of moral states by physical means.) When Tristram and Lamorak next meet, in the "Ile of Servage," however, Tristram refuses to protract this hostile relationship; he accepts, as it were, the arbitrary in Lamorak's enmity; or we could say that he accepts it as the "aventure" that comes with his own obedience to Mark's commands. Tristram's renunciation of hostility wins from Lamorak an instant admiration for his "knighthode": "Hit may nat be false that all men sey, for of youre bounté, nobles, and worshyp of all knyghtes ye are pereles" (444/9–11).

Renunciation of battle here leads to reconciliation, and this we find unsurprising (though we might ponder on the paradox that renunciation of battle had of course created the hostility in the first place). What is surprising is that later in the narrative we find that the reconciliation is to be achieved all over again, and this time not through renunciation of battle, but through insistence on it. This time, on meeting, instead of expressing a spirit of mild forgiveness, Tristram in fury admonishes Lamorak "bethynke the now of the despite thou dedist me of the sendynge of the horne unto kynge Markis courte," and asserts "the tone of us two shall dy or we departe" (483/5–9). Here, Tristram's refusal to allow separation without battle to the death is a grim travesty of the "togetherness" achieved earlier, signalled by the recurrence of two key terms, "departe" and "togidirs." It is not that Malory has simply forgotten the earlier episode, because Lamorak's response is the mild reminder: "that tyme that we were togydirs in the Ile of Servage ye promysed me bettir frendeship" (483/10–11). Lamorak's reminder is perhaps designed to point to the fact that this time it is he who accepts the arbitrary – which is the belated expression of Tristram's violent fury. And he demonstrates this acceptance by entering the proffered battle. This time it is Tristram who comes to feel Lamorak's knighthood, through his bodily qualities.

> So sir Trystramys wolde make no lenger delayes, but laysshed at sir Lamerok, and thus they faught longe tylle aythir were wery of other. Than sir Trystrams seyde unto sir Lamorak,
>
> "In all my lyff mette I never with such a knyght that was so bygge and so wellbrethed. Therefore," sayde sir Trystramys, "hit were pité that ony of us bothe sholde here be myscheved." (483/12–18)

Lamorak's response is to offer his sword in surrender, but Tristram insists that the surrender is to be his. The image of fighting men on their knees offering their swords to each other is, when we think about it, an odd one, but it is a frequent one in romance, and expresses the spirit of the romance world. It does not imply a rejection of battle; on the contrary, it symbolizes the acceptance of engagement with the unknown that is at the heart of battle. Thus opposition becomes a means of achieving union. It is fitting, then, that the climax of the relationship between Tristram and Lancelot should be their (unwitting) battle against each other; it is likewise fitting that at the end of the Tristram book it should be battle that brings about Palomides' final reconciliation with Tristram, his acceptance of the arbitrariness that makes Tristram his superior and the beloved of Isolde, and leads to his final integration into Christian fellowship.

From this vantage point, we can see that it is significant that the phrases used of combat are phrases implying union. Often, as in the passage just quoted, the knight talks of "meeting" his opponent; in another favourite phrase, they "come together" like thunder; battle is "joined." The destruction of their bodily wholeness paradoxically reveals – and in that sense brings into being – the wholeness of their selves (their "integrity," to use the etymologically appropriate word), the wholeness of fellowship between them, and the integration with the external world that comes from acceptance of the independence and inexplicability of its operations. Malory's image of the body has its roots in romance, but his development of it, and the uses to which he puts it, are, I think, unique. In Malory, the body is not a clumsy encumbrance to the spirit, nor even its humble tool. It is the medium through which a knight's worship is revealed, and the testing ground of its validity; it is what the knight opposes to his fellows and yet what unites him with them. It is a field of action, and a repository of truths.

Malory's image of the body is a deliberately stylized one; there is none of the Rabelaisian sense of the body's functions, of eating, excreting, giving birth, of bodily fecundity or decay. Its most important element in Malory is blood, which is the creator of wholeness in two ways: first, as the creator of kinship, the fellowship between those of the same blood, and second, as the creator of personal wholeness through its powers of healing. The images of the body and of blood find their apotheosis in the Grail book, which gives a central position to the mystery of the Eucharist, the recreation of the Body and Blood of Christ, and the commemoration of his suffering. If, then, we are tempted to think of the body as a crude irrelevance to the spiritual, we are powerfully reminded in this book that it is through *bodily* suffering that human kind is redeemed. Through the shedding of God's blood human beings are healed, made whole in their own nature, and united with the divine.

The Grail book, then, does not represent an indictment or even a qualification of the values of chivalry; on the contrary, it is their sublimation. It is the profoundest example of the mysteries accomplished in the body. Like a true knight, God (in Langland's phrase) "auntrede hymself."[6] , and by exposing his body to suffering, by "accepting" human sin, miraculously reconstituted the wholeness between himself and his creation.

6 *Piers Plowman* B XVIII.221.

Chapter Thirteen

"Taking the Adventure": Malory and the *Suite du Merlin*

The growth and increasing elaboration of Arthurian material in the Middle Ages, from individual stories such as those told by Chrétien de Troyes to complex narrative groupings such as the Vulgate Cycle, is often explained as due to a desire for elucidation of what was in the early stories left baffling or unexplained.[1] Early Arthurian romances contained gaps to be filled, inconsistencies to be ironed out, mysteries to be unravelled, and allusions to be explained. They could also provoke repeatedly the question "what happened next?" and thus give rise to sequels and continuations as well as (by a kind of back-formation) proto-histories.

The impulse to elucidate (rather than to make mere factual additions) is one that Eugène Vinaver found especially characteristic of the *Suite du Merlin*[2] – not

1 See, for example, Fanni Bogdanow's comments on Robert de Boron (fl. 1191–1212), the first writer to conceive "the idea of a coherent scheme of romances," in *The Romance of the Grail* (New York, 1966), 2–3.

On the composition and development of the Vulgate Cycle, see *The Arthur of the French: The Arthurian Legend in Medieval French and Occitan Literature*, ed. Glyn S. Burgess and Karen Pratt (Cardiff, 2006), section VII, "Lancelot With and Without the Grail: *Lanceolot do Lac* and the Vulgate Cycle," by Elspeth Kennedy et al., 274–324.

2 Malory, *Works*, 1270–75. The most recent edition of the *Suite* is by Gilles Roussineau, *La Suite du Roman de Merlin*, 2nd ed., 2 vols in one (Geneva, 2006); this supersedes the older edition by Gaston Paris and Jacob Ulrich, under the title *Merlin: Roman en Prose du XIIIe Siècle, publié avec la mise en prose du Merlin de Robert de Boron d'après le manuscrit appartenant à M. Alfred H. Huth* (Société des Anciens Textes Français, 2 vols [Paris, 1886]), which includes the prose *Merlin* to which the *Suite* is a sequel. An English translation of the Paris-Ulrich edition of the *Suite* is included in *Lancelot-Grail: The Old French Arthurian Vulgate and Post-Vulgate in Translation*, ed. Norris J. Lacy, vol. 4 (New York, 1995), 161–277. Roussineau's edition is based on London, BL, MS Add. 38117 (the so-called Huth manuscript) for sections

the continuation of the *Merlin* found in the Vulgate Cycle, but the more "romantic" version sometimes known as the *Huth Merlin* – which is the French original on which Malory based his *Tale of King Arthur*, and the work I should like to use for detailed illustration of his relationship with his French sources. As an example of the impulse to elucidate, Vinaver cites the way the *Suite du Merlin* handles the Vulgate Cycle's account of Arthur's sword.[3] In the Cycle, Arthur acquires the sword by pulling it out of an anvil (and thus proving himself king); at his death, however, he has it thrown into a lake, whence a hand rises to catch it, and after brandishing it thrice, disappears with it beneath the water. This discrepancy between the origin of the sword and its final destiny is removed in the *Suite du Merlin* by the simple expedient of introducing a second sword. A complicated series of events leads up to a battle in which the first sword – the one from the anvil – breaks. Merlin then undertakes to provide Arthur with a sword adequate to his prowess, and leads him to a lake in which they see a hand holding a sword; a damsel appears and walks across the water to fetch it.[4] If we ask, "why must the sword be thrown into a lake?" the *Suite du Merlin*'s version of the story thus provides for the answer "because that is where it came from." It is the narrative elaboration provoked by this impulse to elucidate and clarify that accounts, in Vinaver's view, for "the prodigious growth of cyclic romances in the late medieval period."[5]

1–443, and on Paris, BNF, fr. 112 for sections 444–581. The version of the *Suite du Merlin* in Cambridge UL MS Add. 7071 (fols 230ra–342vb) is in certain respects closer to Malory (see Malory, *Works*, 1280–2), and my quotations from the *Suite* will be taken from this manuscript, but I shall also give references to the corresponding passages in Roussineau's edition, cited by page number and section number. The two texts differ constantly in verbal detail, but never substantially, in the cases I shall discuss.

For a discussion of the *Suite du Merlin*, and a reconstruction of the Post-Vulgate *Roman du Graal* (formerly known as the "pseudo-Robert de Boron Cycle") of which it formed part, see Fanni Bogdanow, *The Romance of the Grail*, especially 23–39 (for a brief description of the Cambridge manuscript, see 271–2), and also Bogdanow's contribution on "The Post-Vulgate *Roman du Graal*," in Burgess and Pratt, *The Arthur of the French*, 342–52.

For identification of Malory's other French sources, see the introductions to the relevant sections of Vinaver's Commentary (vol. 3), and Ralph Norris, *Malory's Library* (Woodbridge, Suffolk, 2008).

3 Discussed by Vinaver several times: see his introduction to *Le Roman de Balain*, ed. M.D. Legge (Manchester, 1942), xv–xvi; "La Genèse de la 'Suite du Merlin,'" *Mélanges de philologie romane et de litterature médiévale offerts à Ernest Hoepffner* (Paris, 1949), 295–300, at 287–8; "King Arthur's Sword or the Making of a Medieval Romance," *Bulletin of the John Rylands Library* 40 (1957–8): 513–26, at 522–5; *The Rise of Romance* (Oxford, 1971), 106, and Malory, *Works*, 1270–1.

4 Cambridge, UL, MS Add. 7071 fols 242vb–243va; Roussineau, 48–51 [sections 61–4].

5 Malory, *Works*, 1275.

Against this background Malory presents a case worthy of study, because, although his work spans the whole history of Arthur's reign, and thus aims at the kind of comprehensiveness characteristic of the cyclic romances, his work differs strikingly from them, for the simple reason that he threw out many of the explanations and clarifications that earlier writers had taken pains to provide. Or rather, so as not to prejudge the point at issue, I should perhaps say that they disappear in the course of Malory's drastic condensation of his sources. It has been noted before (again by Vinaver) that Malory "reversed, or attempted to reverse, the whole process" of narrative elaboration in Arthurian romance, by substituting for the interwoven "polyphonic" narrative of his French sources a series of short, independent narrative units, disentangled from interruptions and subplots, and obscurely related to each other, even in terms of chronology.[6] Vinaver thus aligns Malory with the late-medieval fondness for short narrative exemplified by the Italian *novella* – or, for that matter, by the *Canterbury Tales*.[7] Vinaver sees this desire to create compact, independent narratives as Malory's main motive in altering his sources, and presumably interprets the loss of explanation as an unfortunate by-product of it. I should like to argue the opposite case: that it was because Malory wished to remove explanations that he condensed his sources. And, with respect to Vinaver's view that Malory's narrative units are so far separated from each other as to constitute a series of independent literary works,[8] I shall try to show that, once the reason why Malory takes such pains to separate his narratives into discrete units is understood, we shall also see that they must nevertheless be taken together to achieve their full meaning.

We can see the way that explanation is lost as a result of condensation in Malory's account of the first arrival at court of the woman who is to entomb Merlin alive, which I shall analyse in order to establish some terms in which to discuss "Balin." This is how Malory describes the "adventure" of her arrival:

> Than was thys feste made redy, and the kynge was wedded at Camelot unto dame Gwenyvere in the chirche of Seynte Stephyns with grete solempnité. Than as every man was sette as hys degré asked, Merlion wente to all the knyghtes of the Rounde Table and bade hem sitte stylle, "that none of you remeve, for ye shall se a straunge and a mervailous adventure."

6 Malory, *Works*, 1275–8.

7 Vinaver, *Rise of Romance*, 95, 127–8.

8 See Malory, *Works*, xli–li, "The Problem of 'Unity.'" For a full discussion and bibliography of the scholarly argument as to whether Malory wrote one book or many, see Stephen Knight, *The Structure of Sir Thomas Malory's Arthuriad* (Sydney, 1969), chs 1–2.

Ryght so as they sate there com rennynge inne a whyght herte into the hall, and a whyght brachet nexte hym, and thirty couple of blacke rennynge houndis com afftir with a grete cry. And the herte wente aboute the Rounde Table, and as he wente by the syde-bourdis the brachet ever boote hym by the buttocke and pulde outte a pece, wherethorow the herte lope a grete lepe and overthrew a knyght that sate at the syde-bourde. And therewith the knyght arose and toke up the brachet, and so wente forthe oute of the halle and toke hys horse and rode hys way with the brachett.

Ryght so com in the lady on a whyght palferey and cryed alowde unto kynge Arthure and seyd, "Sir, suffir me nat to have thys despite, for the brachet ys myne that the knyght hath ladde away."

"I may nat do therewith," seyde the kynge.

So with thys there com a knyght rydyng all armed on a grete horse, and toke the lady away with forse wyth hym, and ever she cryed and made grete dole. So whan she was gone the kynge was gladde, for she made such a noyse.

"Nay," seyde Merlion, "ye may nat leve hit so, thys adventure, so lyghtly, for thes adventures muste be brought to an ende, other ellis hit woll be disworshyp to you and to youre feste."

"I woll," seyde the kynge, "that all be done by your advice."

Than he lette calle sir Gawayne, for he muste brynge agayne the whyght herte.

"Also, sir, ye muste lette call sir Torre, for he muste brynge agayne the brachette and the knyght, othir ellis sle hym. Also lette calle kynge Pellynor, for he must brynge agayne the lady and the knyght, othir ellis sle hym, and thes three knyghtes shall do mervayles adventures or they com agayne." (102/22–103/24)

At the corresponding point in the *Suite du Merlin*, the lady is wearing hunting dress, which is described at some length, and this, together with a prefatory account of the forest-like gardens in which Arthur's palace is set, serves to suggest a fairly natural explanation for her unruly intrusion.[9] Malory omits this description of the lady, and likewise the *Suite du Merlin*'s assurance as to her outstanding beauty, which is presumably mentioned to account for Merlin's later infatuation.[10] Perhaps the most important omission, however, is of the *Suite du Merlin*'s "explanation" for the court's lack of immediate reaction to the strange sequence of events. The damsel there complains to Arthur at the

9 The full version of this episode in the *Suite* is given in an appendix to this article.

10 In the French, the lady's passion for hunting also plays a part in the later development of her story, and the way in which she conceives the idea of burying Merlin alive (see Cambridge, UL, MS Add. 7071 fols 302ra–303vb, and fols 314ra–315vb; Roussineau 282–8 [sections 322–9]; 329–36 [sections 379–86]), but this too is all omitted in Malory (125–6). Malory,

loss of her stag and brachet, and urges that some of the knights should recover them for her. Merlin refuses to allow this, however, because, he says: "henceforth there will be in this house the custom that whatever adventure occurs, however dangerous or deadly it may be, no knight who seats himself at table shall move before he has eaten. But when the tables are taken away, then the knights to whom the adventures are allotted can pursue them." This "custom" seems to be invented to explain away the strangely quiescent attitude of the Arthurian court towards the adventures played out before it. As a would-be rational explanation, it is decidedly clumsy; still, it takes its place with the other features of the episode in the *Suite du Merlin* as material for the reader to work on in coming to understand what we might call the mechanics of the episode. (Similarly, the French text's earlier comment that all the knights were "stunned at the stag having passed through them" seems designed to explain why no one stops the knight carrying off the brachet.) Malory deliberately omits the attempt to provide a pseudo-realistic reason for the court's inaction, and keeps only Merlin's initial command to "sitte stylle ... for ye shall se a straunge and a mervailous adventure" – a command which makes the knights' role as spectators a condition, though not a rationally based one, of the whole episode.

All the differences between Malory's version of the episode and that of the *Suite du Merlin* seem to me to lead one way: towards an emphasis on the *distance* between the court and the events it beholds – and likewise, on the distance between those events and the reader. In the *Suite du Merlin*, the episode is more than once punctuated with the beginnings of a reaction from the court, and the material for a preliminary interpretation by the reader is scattered all the way through it. The three knights have their tasks assigned to them before the adventure even begins, so that we can recognize that their involvement in it exists, even though its expression is delayed. In Malory, the whole scene is played out like a tableau, with the reactions and judgments of both knights and reader suspended until it is finally completed. The only response that is voiced (which is Malory's addition) is a *lack* of response: " 'I may nat do therewith,' seyde the kynge." And Malory's other addition – the strangely comic comment that Arthur was glad at the lady's removal "for she made such a noyse" – also emphasizes an emotional distance between the adventure and its spectators.

---

moreover, breaks the connection between the hunting episode and the episode of Merlin's entombment by referring to the damsel as "the damesell that kynge Pellynore brought to courte," identifying her in terms of the end of the adventure of the white hart, rather than of her first appearance (contrast the *Suite du Merlin*'s title for her, "la damoisele chaceresce"; Cambridge, UL, MS Add. 7071 fol. 299vb; Roussineau 273 [section 313]).

It is not because of any direct emotional involvement in the human situation of the lady that the adventure is followed up.

An intellectual understanding of the rationale behind the unfolding of these events; an ability to identify motives or consequences in such a way as to feel confident in categorizing actions or people as right or wrong; a corresponding ability to establish intuitive sympathy with a victim – any of these things would give us the opportunity to take up a position in relation to these events, would put their spectators (that is, both us and the court) "in touch" with them. But the distance between the court and the adventure is not to be bridged by any of these means: it is to be bridged by "worship." If the adventure is not brought to an end, "hit woll be disworshyp to you and to youre feste." Merlin locates the reason for action not in the events of the adventure, but in the knights themselves. Despite the fact that its remoteness, the distance between them and it, suggests that it has nothing to do with them, paradoxically this very distance acts as a challenge; they cannot continue to be as they were without coming to terms with the adventure. Their "worship" becomes identified with their essence – with the continuity and integrity of their being, and with the continuity between their essential being and the exterior world.[11]

The adventure of the damsel can perhaps best be compared with the briefly fashionable and now long outmoded concept of a theatrical "happening" (a word which is a literal translation of the Middle English *aventure* in one of its meanings):[12] that is, a bizarre event which, *because* it does not fit into familiar patterns of occurrences, *because* it strikes the spectators as something remote and alien, challenges them to find some way of coming to terms with it. The tasks given to Sir Gawain, Sir Torre, and King Pellinore offer them a way of engaging with the adventure, but it involves accepting its inconsequentiality and mysteriousness, and demonstrating that acceptance empirically in the pursuit of the adventure's consequences. The knights are not told to find out who the lady is, or why the knight has carried her off (we never, in fact, learn more about the adventure than we are told here); they are told to bring back to the court the various actors in the drama – that is, to remove the physical distance between

11 This interpretation of "worship" can, I believe, solve some of the difficulties created by the distinction between honour and goodness as referents for the term in Malory's usage; see R.T. Davies, "The Worshipful Way in Malory," in *Patterns of Love and Courtesy*, ed. John Lawlor (London, 1966), 157–77, at 174, and the introduction to Derek S. Brewer's edition of *The Morte Darthur: Parts Seven and Eight* (London, 1968), 23–31, especially 26.

12 Cf. Derek Brewer's remark that "the passing modern fad of the 'happening' " may "give encouragement to those who value medieval romance" ("The Present Study of Malory," *Forum for Modern Language Studies* 6 [1970]: 83–97, at 96).

them and the court. It is a demonstration of the fact that participation in the adventure is not to be based on understanding that in the assigning of the three tasks, the return of the stag and of the dog are given parity of importance with the return of the lady. The lack of explanation means that one cannot be sure which is more important. Thus the final observation we can make on this scene is that the "lack of explanation" in Malory's narrative creates a difficulty in arranging the features of both narrative and the events it describes in a hierarchical order of importance.[13]

I should now like to test these observations – of the lack of explanation in Malory's narrative, the consequent difficulty of assigning relative importance to its various episodes or details, and the usefulness of "distance" as a key word in describing both its structure and its emotional quality – within the confines of a single narrative unit, "Balin or the Knight with Two Swords."[14] I choose this tale in particular because, although it comes early in Malory's work and must therefore represent the ideas with which he was working from the beginning,[15] it offers a miniature version of the tragedy which is to engulf the whole

---

13 The paratactic, co-ordinating nature of Malory's style also works to the same end; cf. the comments of Stephen Knight, "Style and the Effects of Style in Malory's Arthuriad," *Parergon* 9 (Aug. 1974): 3–27, at 9: "the co-ordinating conjunctions often have a very limited connecting function ... [so that] the units of information often have only a tenuous relation with each other, and we get reasons for very little that happens ... The arbitrary qualities of the action in a large way derive from, or are created by, the nature of the syntax, and the fact that actions rarely appear to be more important than other actions is largely a result of the even balance of the prose's progress." This is again different from the diffuse periods of the *Suite du Merlin*. Vinaver has commented that just as the interweaving narrative of Malory's French sources is replaced by a series of brief, disconnected episodes, so "the smooth symmetry of the French *période*" gives way to "a succession of abruptly divided clauses" ("Sir Thomas Malory," *Arthurian Literature in the Middle Ages: A Collaborative History*, ed. Roger Sherman Loomis (Oxford, 1959), 541–52, at 550). On Malory's paratactic style and its effects see also P.J.C. Field, *Romance and Chronicle: a Study of Malory's Prose Style* (London, 1971), 38–46.

14 This tale has already been compared with the corresponding version in the *Suite du Merlin* by Laura A. Hibbard [Loomis] ("Malory's Book of Balin," in *Memorial Studies in Memory of Gertrude Schoepperle Loomis* [Paris, 1927], 175–95]. I choose this same section for study because it offers a limited area of the text within which the relationship between Malory's normal episodic style and the rarer linear narrative movement can be examined. Mrs Loomis's comparison also concentrates mainly on the very end of "Balin" and does not deal with, for example, the sword-drawing or the Dolorous Stroke. She does, however, comment on many aspects of "Balin" which I have not room to mention, but which demonstrate convincingly the "superior power, purpose and artistry" of Malory's version.

15 Even if one were to accept Vinaver's view that the *Tale of King Arthur* was written after the *Tale of Arthur and Lucius* (Malory, *Works*, li–lvi), this would still put it early in Malory's production.

Arthurian world, and shows that Malory had already conceived the terms in which he was to describe that tragedy.

"Balin" begins with the news of king Royns's attack on Arthur's subjects and Arthur's summons of his knights to take counsel for his realm's defence. A damsel then arrives at court, girt with a noble sword which, she says, can be drawn from its sheath only by a knight who "muste be a passynge good man of hys hondys and of hys dedis, and withoute velony other trechory and withoute treson" (61/34–62/2). King Royns's knights have tried and failed. Arthur offers to try himself, to set an example for his barons, but he and they likewise fail. There is present, however, a poor knight named Balin. He offers to try the test, but is at first rejected by the damsel, who "for hys poure araymente ... thought he sholde nat be of no worship withoute vylony or trechory" (63/17–18). Balin's reply is a reproof:

> "A, fayre damesell," seyde Balyn, "worthynes and good tacchis and also good dedis is nat only in araymente, but manhode and worship ys hyd within a mannes person; and many a worshipfull knyght is nat knowyn unto all peple. And therefore worship and hardynesse ys nat in araymente." (63/23–7)

The damsel is convinced by this reply, and Balin's attempt to withdraw the sword is successful.

> Than Balyn toke the swerde by the gurdyll and shethe and drew hit oute easyly, and whan he loked on the swerde hit pleased hym muche. (63/30–2)

The damsel's response is immediate and emphatic:

> "Sertes," seyde the damesell, "thys ys a passynge good knyght and the beste that ever y founde, and moste of worship withoute treson, trechory or felony. And many mervayles shall he do." (64/1–4)

There are many baffling aspects of this episode, but I suppose one of the first questions to arise, if we took an honest view of it, might be: "why Balin?" The adventure can be achieved only by him; what is the reason for this? The answer, in one sense, is obvious: because he is "a passynge good knyght and the beste that ever y founde, and moste of worship withoute treson, trechory or felony." What is strange, however, is that this estimate of Balin is made only after he has succeeded in the test, and his success in the test is the only basis for making it. The damsel's prefatory objection to Balin's attempt, contrasting strongly with her judgment after he has succeeded, powerfully underlines this. In the *Suite du Merlin*, on the other hand, we are told when Baalin is first mentioned that "although he was poor in wealth, he was so rich in spirit and boldness that in all the realm of Logres there was no better knight at that time."[16] This assurance acts as an explanation for Baalin's success in the adventure, and in doing so it gives the adventure a different function. The fact that we can already be assured, before the test, that Baalin is all these things, means that this judgment can be based on other, more natural, sources of knowledge (close acquaintance with Baalin and his behaviour). The adventure then becomes merely a device for drawing public attention to the merit which is there to behold, but masked by the poverty of its possessor.[17] In Malory, the test is the *only* assurance of Balin's pre-eminence. It is not even possible to claim that this judgment is proved valid by Balin's later behaviour, since none of his actions in the rest of the tale is conspicuously a proof of the absence of treachery, and many of them might well suggest the reverse. In Malory, therefore, the adventure does not confirm Balin's nature, it reveals it.

In making the role of the adventure revelatory rather than confirmatory, Malory is seizing on one significant aspect of it in its original form: the relationship between the action (pulling out the sword) and its significance (being without treachery) is a symbolic rather than a natural relationship. Jumping into a river to save a drowning child "signifies" bravery or unselfishness – but the significance is intrinsic to the action. Pulling a sword out of a sheath, on the other hand, has no natural or intrinsic connection with a lack of treachery.[18]

16 "Mais s'il estoit povres d'argent il estoit si riches de cuer e de hardement e de pruesce que en tut le reaume de Logres n'avoit pas a ce tens nul meillor chevalier" (Cambridge, UL, MS Add. 7071 fol. 247va; Roussineau 68 [section 94]). Malory reduces this assurance to the incidental remark that Balin was "a good man named of his body," sandwiched between the account of his delivery from prison by the good offices of the barons, and the information that he was born in Northumberland (62/33–63/2). P.J.C. Field has commented on the way the syntactical disconnectedness here deludes us temporarily into assuming that Balin's regional origins have something to do with his prowess or with the barons' goodwill to him – which they do not (*Romance and Chronicle*, 152). Malory creates a narrator who simply hands on the scraps of information he has, without vouching for their connection with each other or with the narrative.

17 This is explicitly emphasized by the author's comment: "Mais pur ceo que povres resembloit ne faisoit home entre les autres nul mencion de lui, car home ne tient pas de povre gent grant conte entre riches" (Cambridge, UL, MS Add. 7071 fol. 247va; Roussineau 68 [section 94]).

18 This is clearly true of all the multiple variations of this test: healing wounds, pulling swords out of anvils, and so on. In Arthur's case, we tend to read the test as confirmatory rather than revelatory, since we already know that he is Uther's son and heir and has in fact been announced as such (12). But the very gratuitousness of the test in this case, and the use of a symbolic method rather than, say, the consulting of midwives or examining of birthmarks, is a

Again we discover a distance – this time between the nature of the act and the nature of its significance. The connection between them is not clear, and neither is the nature of the agent that creates this connection. Mark Lambert has pointed out that the use of magic devices gives the sanction of objectivity to the titles they bestow (king of all England, best knight in the world, and so on), since swords fixed in stones or sheaths, enchanted wounds, perilous sieges and the like, can hardly be accused of subjective or idiosyncratic judgment.[19] These devices impress us, however, not only with the objectivity of the titles they confer, but also with the arbitrariness and mystery of their bestowal. The exchange between Balin and the damsel seems to me designed to empasize this mystery. Balin's assertion that "manhode and worship ys hyd within a mannes person" (which is original with Malory) conveys more than a high-minded rejection of the decadence of late medieval chivalry.[20] Taken together with the test, it serves rather as an affirmation of the hidden mysteriousness of a man's nature – or "essence," as I should prefer to call it – and the arbitrariness of its assignation, worship being found where we might least expect it and so far "hyd within a mannes person" that it may bear no relation to the actions he performs.

For Balin's lack of treachery is not the only thing revealed by his drawing of the sword; it also reveals that he is destined to kill the man he most loves in the world. To the damsel's request that he hand back the sword, he replies:

> "Nay ... for thys swerde woll I kepe but hit be takyn fro me with force."
>
> "Well," seyde the damesell, "ye are nat wyse to kepe the swerde fro me, for ye shall sle with that swerde the beste frende that ye have and the man that ye moste love in the worlde, and that swerde shall be youre destruccion."
>
> "I shall take the aventure," seyde Balyn, "that God woll ordayne for me. But the swerde ye shall nat have at this tyme, by the feythe of my body!" (64/6–14)

Is this revelation in a different category from the revelation that Balin is without treachery? That is, can his destiny be connected with his insistence on keeping

way of revealing what we might otherwise miss: the determining force of birth, which allots us a destiny (as male or female, king or peasant) on principles which, if they exist at all, remain mysterious. It is for this reason that in Malory the inscription on the sword says that whoever withdraws it will be "rightwys kynge borne of all Englond" (12/36), making birth the sole determining factor, whereas in the prose *Merlin* it says that whoever withdraws it will be king "par l'aleccion Jhesu Crist" (*Merlin*, ed. Paris and Ulrich, I, 135).

19 *Malory: Style and Vision in Le Morte Darthur* (New Haven, CT, 1975), 28.

20 This is how Vinaver interprets it (Malory, *Works*, 1305).

the sword, and "explained" by his greed or obstinacy?[21] There are several reasons for thinking that it cannot.[22] First, Malory removes from the text any real clue to Balin's motive in retaining the sword, so that it is not possible to relate this action or Balin's later destiny to any specific "tragic flaw" in his character.[23] Second, when this scene is over, Merlin makes a belated arrival, and delivers a commentary on the damsel and the adventure, which, although too confused to function as an "explanation," makes it plain that whoever drew the sword out of the sheath was thereby *bound* to kill his brother (67/22–68/15). And third, the connection between keeping the sword and killing with it the man one most loves is also symbolic rather than natural; the warning is of a different nature from the type "If you smoke in bed you will burn yourself to death." In the second type of warning, the connection between the action which provokes the warning and the threatened disaster, the linear sequence of events which would lead from the one to the other, can be clearly envisaged; in the first type it is obscure and dependent on contingency.

We may see the test of the sword, therefore, as bringing about two revelations which are not logically or naturally related with it or with each other. Balin is distinguished above all men as being without treachery, but simultaneously as being the man who will kill the friend he loves most in the world. The adventure reveals a distance between Balin's essence and his destiny. We are given no "map" of Balin's personality, nor any understanding of the dynamic of events, which might show the relationship between these two facts. It is as if the adventure of the sword throws two spotlights on to these two facts, and leaves all that is between in darkness. The only connection that can be made between them is irony – the irony that it *should* be the man most without treachery who will

21 For example, Marilyn Corrie argues that the characters in both Malory and his French sources bring their misfortunes on their own heads ("Self-determination in the Post-Vulgate *Suite du Merlin* and Malory's *Le Morte Darthur*," *Medium Ævum* 73 [2004]: 273–89).

22 In the *Suite du Merlin*, the damsel says that the knight with the necessary qualities "porra desnoier les rengnes del espée e emporter l'espée ovec soie e deliverer moi de ceste dont jeo sui encombré malement" – which might seem to suggest that he could expect to keep the sword (Cambridge, UL, MS Add. 7071 fol. 247rb; Roussineau 66 [section 93]).

23 A further impediment to this interpretation is Malory's general lack of interest in characterization (by which I do not mean that he is incapable of rendering human reactions or emotions). Cf. Vinaver's comment that the authors of romances did not think of their works as "examples of 'psychological characterization through action,'" but as "narratives consisting of themes and patterns of themes" ("King Arthur's Sword," 526). Despite this warning, criticism of Malory still tends to look primarily for "character ... displayed in action" in his work (the phrase is taken from Stephen Knight, *The Structure of Sir Thomas Malory's Arthuriad*, 93).

kill his best friend. That is, the only connection between them is not rational, but aesthetic. It consists not in a logical sequence of cause and effect in the facts themselves, but in the perception of a kind of pattern in them on the part of the beholder.

What I have called an "aesthetic" connection between events is also characteristic of some episodes in the *Suite du Merlin*; the return of Arthur's sword to the lake from which it came, which I mentioned earlier, is aesthetically satisfying, but it does not "explain" the sword or identify the agent of its appearance and disappearance. In the *Suite du Merlin*, however, this kind of relationship between events is accompanied by connections of a more natural and rational kind, whereas in Malory, the "loss of explanation" I have been referring to removes so many of the other connections between events that it leaves the aesthetic relationship – structuring by similitude or contrast – as the predominant one.[24] Because it is so prominent in Malory's narrative, it raises a disquieting question for the reader: is the relationship between events any more than aesthetic? Does the pattern we perceive have any meaning? – is it a clue to some ultimate "explanation"? – or is it merely created by the ordering mind of the beholder working over the myriad operations of chance?[25]

For Malory makes it quite clear that it is chance that dictates the sequence of events, both in this episode and elsewhere. Since "chance" is one of the meanings – in fact in Middle English the primary meaning – of the word "adventure,"[26] the role of chance is emphasized in the very naming of an episode as (for example) "the adventure how Balyne gate the swerde." "Grace" – which when used without a qualifying adjective is the Middle English word for

24 Cf. Vinaver's chapter on "Analogy as the Dominant Form," in *Rise of Romance*, 99–122, especially 101–10. It will be seen however that I take a rather different view of the *Suite du Merlin*, and also do not agree with Vinaver's (perhaps unintentional) suggestion that the development of analogical structures reveals an underlying confidence in the ordered structure of the universe (100).

25 Robert O. Payne has commented on "the uncertain human struggle to read out of time a significant illusion which may somehow acquaint us with the timeless" and which "reflects a constant fear that epistemology may turn out to be only aesthetics" (*The Key of Remembrance:A Study of Chaucer's Poetics* [New Haven, CT, 1963], 217). The manifestations of this preoccupation in *Troilus and Criseyde*, which is the major subject of Payne's concern (ch. 7), have a different form from those that it assumes in Malory's work, but he could have found it explored in terms of *aventure* and *destine* in Chaucer's *Knight's Tale*.

26 *OED* s.v. *Adventure* n. 1, "That which comes to us, or happens without design; chance, hap, fortune, luck," better fits Malory's usage than *MED*'s rather muddled definition "Fate, fortune, chance; one's lot or destiny" (s.v. aventure 1a).

a good or benign chance[27] – is what determines Balin's success ("in hys herte he was fully assured to do as well, *if hys grace happed hym*, as ony knyght that there was"; 63/6–8; my italics), and it is lack of grace that determines the failure of the other knights. To the damsel's distressed complaint, "I wente in this courte had bene the beste knyghtes of the worlde withoute trechory other treson," Arthur replies: "here ar good knyghtes as I deme as ony be in the worlde, but their grace ys nat to helpe you" (62/28–32). We must not be betrayed, therefore, by phrases such as "to do an aventure" ("Than had the kynge and all the barownes grete mervayle that Balyne had done that aventure"; 63/32–3) into thinking that the knight who undertakes an adventure has it in his control; since it is chance, it cannot be controlled, or predicted, any more than we can control or predict whether a coin will come down heads or tails. The knight who undertakes an adventure submits to chance, in order to discover what chance has allotted him.[28]

This is by way of a long prelude to the final observations I want to make on Balin's drawing of the sword, before moving on to the rest of the tale. The test of the sword provides an image of the strange combination of activity and passivity which characterizes the knight's willed acceptance of the control of chance. The sword does not respond to any force exerted by the knight, but comes of itself to the man to whom it is allotted; it thus images his passivity. Yet once drawn, it is active, at the knight's disposal and ready for use; it confers on him a certain power.[29] (In order to achieve this double-edged image Malory alters the form of the test from the *Suite du Merlin*, where it involves untying the "hangings" of the sword.) The test likewise offers an image of the fusion of chance with destiny; the selection of Balin as the one who will succeed has the arbitrariness of chance, but the unerring specificity of its aim gives it the character

27 *MED* 3b; *OED* 10. Because this sense has become obsolete, we tend to misinterpret some medieval examples of it as meaning "God's favour" (*MED* 1; *OED* 11).

28 This is neatly made clear in the *Suite du Merlin*, when king Pellinore explains to Arthur that he hunts the questing beast because it is destined to be killed by the best knight of his lineage, "e pur ceo que jeo voloie de voir savoir e conoistre si jeo estoie le meillor de nostre lignage ai jeo si longement alé apres lui. Si ne l'ai mie dit pur vantance de moi, mais pur savoir la verité de moi meismes" (Cambridge, UL, MS Add. 7071 fol. 231ra–b; Roussineau 8, 5). There is obviously no question of Pellinore *making himself into* the best knight by undertaking the quest. This speech of Pellinore's is not included in Malory's version of the episode (42–3), but the idea it enshrines is one that he clearly understood and took over from his source.

29 There is the same ambivalence in Malory's references to "naked" swords; the word "naked" suggests vulnerability, but a naked sword is a dangerous one.

of destiny.[30] Balin's acceptance of the one with the other is indicated not only by his willingness to undergo the adventure of the sword, but also by his reply to the damsel's warning. In the *Suite du Merlin*, he simply reaffirms his intention to carry off the sword, even were his death to be the result, so fine and beautiful does it seem to him.[31] In Malory, he replies: "I shall take the aventure ... that God woll ordayne for me" (64/12–13); he simultaneously accepts a destiny laid on him, not created by him, and affirms its contingency, that it is not necessary until it has happened.[32]

In the multitude of events following the sword-drawing it is contingency that is very much to the fore. Like most of Malory's narratives, the tale moves by fits and starts from episode to episode, without giving us a sense of any necessary connection between them. There is a "distance" between the events of the narrative, as well as between those events and the people caught up in them. The episodic nature of Malory's narrative has been noted often enough, but the reasons for it are not often clearly perceived.[33] It is because the narrative is dominated by chance that the separation between one episode and another is emphasized, and that it does not follow the smooth linear order of a plot.[34]

---

30 In an article surveying the different manifestations of the motif of sword-drawing ("L'épreuve de l'épée," *Romania* 70 [1948–9]: 37–50), Alexandre Micha suggested that its original source may have been Aeneas's plucking of the golden bough, which will come easily to his hand "si te fata vocant" (*Aeneid* VI, 145–8). In romance also, the motif acts as a sign of destiny.

31 "E sil dist que si sa mort i devoit estre si l'enporteroit il, car trop li semble l'espée e bone e bele" (Cambridge, UL, MS Add. 7071 fol. 248ra, Roussineau 70 [section 96]). This is the third in a series of refusals; in the first, he refuses to return the sword even were he to be held "vilains" by all the court, and in the second (after being warned), he refuses to return it even were his death to result (Roussineau 69 [section 96]). The coarseness of feeling in the *Suite du Merlin*'s assumption that a noble knight would regard his own death as a worse calamity than slaying the man he loved most is entirely avoided by Malory.

32 On destiny and free will in the Vulgate Cycle, see Madeleine Blaess, "Predestination in Some Thirteenth-Century Prose Romances," *Currents of Thought in French Literature: Essays in Memory of G.T. Clapton* (Oxford, 1965), 3–19. She argues that the author(s) of the *Estoire* and the *Queste del Saint Graal* treat the fates of their characters as divinely predetermined, whereas the *Lancelot* and the *Mort Artu* show "the compulsion of character, environment, upbringing and heredity" in determining action. She does not consider the relations between chance and destiny in the "everyday" adventures of these romances, or indeed the significance of the knight's engagement in "aventures."

33 Thus, for example, Stephen Knight discusses at length the episodic structure of Malory's work up to the "Launcelot and Elaine" section of the Tristram story (*The Structure of Sir Thomas Malory's Arthuriad*, ch. 3), but finds it limiting and inferior as a narrative style.

34 This has been recognized, to my knowledge, only in the important article by Morton W. Bloomfield, "Episodic Motivation and Marvels in Epic and Romance," printed in his *Essays and Explorations: Studies in Ideas, Language and Literature* (Cambridge, MA, 1970), 97–128.

Occasionally a pattern of sorts – or rather some tentative links that may begin to suggest a pattern – appears to be emerging, but it dissolves again into randomness almost at once. A second damsel appears at court and demands a reward from Arthur for procuring his sword Excalibur for him. She claims that Balin slew her brother and the first damsel caused the death of her father, and asks for the death of either in revenge. Balin kills her (claiming that she caused the death of his mother), and having thus offended Arthur, decides to win back his favour by attacking king Royns. Some recurring figures and features here – king Royns, damsels, swords, parents, brothers – seem to begin linking themselves into an untidy pattern, but its very untidiness indicates its unfinished, unrealized nature; the linking never proceeds far enough to become meaningful. The consequences of an action in this tale, as in the rest of Malory, do not follow from it in sequence, as a chain of events: they radiate and proliferate in a manner that defies any attempt to arrange them in a hierarchical order of importance. As an example of this, I should like to take the events following Balin's killing of one of Arthur's knights, called Launceor (68–73). Launceor is attempting to avenge the insult offered to Arthur when Balin killed the lady in his court. Balin is reluctant to fight, and we again register in this reluctance (as in his unintentional offending of Arthur) a distance, between what he intends or wants to do, and what he does. This sense of distance becomes even sharper when the fight takes place and Balin kills Launceor without intending to, and, indeed, without even being aware that he has done so.

> And Balyne smote hym agayne thorow the shylde, and the hawbirk perysshed, and so bore hym thorow the body and over the horse crowpen; and anone turned his horse fersely and drew oute hys swerde, and wyst nat that he had slayne hym. (69/12–16)

The disappearance of the grammatical subject after the words "the hawbirk perysshed" reflects syntactically the "absence" of Balin from his action, from precisely this point in the sentence on; the action seems to take place of its own accord, without "expressing" Balin.

Without any pause in the narrative, Launceor's mistress Columbe arrives, gives vent to her grief, and commits suicide. The speed of this incident contrasts

---

Bloomfield stresses both the lack of "horizontal motivation" (i.e., the generation of one event from another) and the importance of chance in the structuring of medieval romance. He also remarks that the "genuine power" produced by the sense of mystery thus created is particularly evident in Malory's work (110), although it does not fall within the scope of his article to examine Malory's text closely in this light.

with the leisure with which it is mulled over for several pages. First Balin's brother Balan arrives, and on hearing of the lady's death and Balin's regret at it, replies "ye must take the adventure that God woll ordayne you" (70/19–20) – a suggestive echo of Balin's earlier words, which, like them, is not to be found in the French source. Both brothers then agree to attack king Royns in an attempt to win back Arthur's still further alienated favour. Second, a dwarf arrives and predicts that Launceor's kin will exact vengeance for his death. Third, king Mark arrives and builds a tomb for the two dead lovers. Fourth, Merlin arrives and predicts that on this spot there will take place the "grettist bateyle betwyxte two knyghtes that ever was or ever shall be, and the trewyst lovers" – that is, Lancelot and Tristram – and writes their names on the tomb (72/5–11). Finally, Merlin predicts that Balin will strike the Dolorous Stroke as a result of Columbe's death.[35]

It is difficult to decide either at this point or later the relative importance of the items in this miscellaneous series of consequences. The decision to fight King Royns does lead to a successful attack on him, and the regaining of Arthur's favour, but this is in no way connected with the tragic climax of the tale; it leads nowhere. Nothing ever comes of the dwarf's prediction of vengeance (which would be the most natural consequence to expect from the point of view of any development of a plot). King Mark appears to have wandered in from another story altogether.[36] The most memorable and impressive consequence of Launceor's death are in fact not those which are linked to it by any development of events, but the ones linked to it by the aesthetic connections of echo and reminiscence. It is in the repetition of the pairs of lovers – Launceor and

35 Vinaver (1277) attributes the responsibility for the Dolorous Stroke to Balin's slaying in Arthur's court of the Lady of the Lake (and mistakenly identifies her with the lady sent as a messenger from the Lady of the Isle of Avalon – i.e., the one girt with the sword), but Merlin's reference to "the dethe of that lady" clearly relates to the death of Columbe, following as it does immediately on Balin's protest "I myght nat save hir, for she slewe hirselff suddenly" (72/23–4). Vinaver is followed in this misinterpretation by Thomas L. Wright, "'The Tale of King Arthur': Beginnings and Foreshadowings," in *Malory's Originality*, ed. R.M. Lumiansky (Baltimore, MD, 1964), 9–66, at 45–6. The mistakes are pointed out by Robert L. Kelly in "Malory's 'Tale of Balin' Reconsidered," *Speculum* 54 (1979): 85–99, at 91–2.

36 The *Suite du Merlin*, in contrast, emphasizes that king Mark is part of the *same* story: "li rois Marcs de Cornewaille qui puis out a femme Ysout la blounte, si com cist contes meismes le devisera apertement pur ceo que conter en covient pur une aventure dont li graax parole" (Cambridge, UL, MS Add. 7071 fol. 251vb; Roussineau 84 [section 114]). It also mentions that Mark has recently been crowned, thus clarifying the temporal relationship of one part of the story to another. For Mark's later appearance in the Post-Vulgate *Queste*, see Fanni Bogdanow, *The Romance of the Grail*, 123–4.

Columbe, Lancelot and Guinevere, Tristram and Isode – or of battles between those who love each other – Lancelot and Tristram, Balin and his brother – or of the affirmed necessity to "take the adventure," that we are most strongly tantalized with the suggestion of meaning.

The most emphatic assertion of a link between events – Merlin's prediction that Balin will strike the Dolorous Stroke because of the death of Columbe – merely serves to draw attention to the absence of any justification for this link in terms of cause and effect. In the *Suite du Merlin*, Merlin does not give Columbe's death as a reason why Baalin will strike the blow; he simply contrasts Baalin's slowness in preventing the suicide with his precipitateness in striking the blow.[37] The reader is thus tempted to see in them (even if this was not the author's intention) signs of Balin's insensitivity to circumstances, which would "explain" and link them. In making the connection between the Dolorous Stroke and Columbe's suicide more emphatic, Malory also makes it more of an enigma. Our sense of Balin's responsibility is not diminished, but the nature of this responsibility is more mysterious.

The account of the striking of the Dolorous Stroke in no way clarifies the nature of this responsibility. Balin, together with a damsel whose knight has been slain by an invisible assailant, arrives at King Pellam' s court, and finds the invisible knight present in temporarily visible form. He kills him, not as the result of a premeditated decision, but as an immediate response to an unprovoked insult. He is then attacked by King Pellam, who is the invisible knight's brother; in the fight with Pellam, Balin's sword breaks and he runs from room to room seeking another weapon. (It here seems to be ignored – in both versions – that Balin should be well provided for such an emergency, since he is the Knight with Two Swords.)[38] This is how the *Suite du Merlin* describes his predicament:

> When the Knight with the Two Swords sees this happening [i.e. the breaking of his sword], he is not a little dismayed, and he leaps swiftly into another room, thinking to discover some weapon. But when he comes there, he finds neither that nor

37 "Tu ne serras mie si lenz" fait Merlin "quant tu ferras le doluruse coup par qui .iii. reaume en serront en poverte e exille .xxii. anz tut plains e sachez que si doluruse colps ne si lais ne ferist onques nul home com cist ert e toutes dolurs e totes misers en avendront ... [Merlin compares the evil consequences of Baalin's misdeed with those of Eve's] ... Si n'avendra mie cest dolur pur ceo que tu ne soies le meillor chevalier que orendroit soit par tut le reaume de Logres, mais pur ceo qe tu trespasseres le comandement que nuls ne doit trespasser. Car tu en mahaigneras le plus prudome que orendroit soit en vie ..." (Cambridge, UL, MS Add. 7071 fol. 252rb; Roussineau 85–6 [section 116]). Notice that Baalin's fault is here envisaged as belonging to the future, and not as one to which he is already committed by the death of the lady.

38 Cf. Laura A. Hibbard [Loomis], "Malory's Book of Balin," 192 and n. l, and see below, 271.

anything else, and then he is even more dismayed than before, for he sees that the king is still following him, his cudgel raised. And he leaps into yet another room, which was even further on, but he doesn't find there anything more than in the other, except that he sees that they are the most beautiful chambers in the world, and the richest he had ever seen. And he looks, and sees open the door of the third chamber, which was even further on, and goes in that direction to enter it, for he thinks all the time that he will find some weapon with which he can defend himself against the man who is pursuing him closely. And when he tries to enter, he hears a voice which cries to him: "Cursed is your coming in, for you are by no means worthy to enter so high a place!" He hears the voice well, but he doesn't alter his direction because of that; he presses into the chamber and finds that it is so beautiful and so rich that he would never have thought it had its equal in beauty in the world. The room was square and marvellously large, and sweet smelling as if all the spices in the world had been brought there. And [in the middle of] the room was a table of silver, very large and high in proportion, and resting on three pillars of silver; and on the table, right in the middle, there was a vessel of silver and gold, and in this vessel a lance was set with the point downwards and the hilt upwards. And whoever beheld that lance carefully, he would wonder greatly how it kept upright, for it was not supported on any side. The Knight with the Two Swords looks at the lance, but he does not fully recognize it, so he goes in that direction and hears another voice which calls to him very loudly: "Touch it not, sinner!"[39]

39 Quant cis as .ii. espéez voit cest aventour, il n'est pas petite esbahis, si saute erraument en un chambre, car il i quid trover armeure acun. Mais quant il est venus, il n'i troeve ne ce ne quoi, et lors est il plus esbaïs que devant, car il voit que lui rois le sueut touz voiez le fust levé. E il saut encor en un autre chambre qui estoit encore plus long, mais il n'i troeve nient plus qu'en l'autre, fors tant qu'il voit bien que lez chambrez sont [les] plus belez du monde et lez plus richez que onques mais vaist. Et il regarde, si voit l'uis overte de la tierce chambre qui estoit encore plus loing, si s'adresche cele part por entrer dedenz, car il i quid totez voiez trover aucune armoure, dont il se peust defender vers celui qui de prez l'en chace. E quant il veut entre dedenz, il out .i. vois qui li crie: "Mar i entrez, car tu n'es mie dignez d'entrer en si haut lieu." Il entent bien la voice, mais pur ceo ne laisse il pas sa voie, ainz se fiert en la chamber et troeve que ele est si bele et si riche qu'il ne quidast mie qu'en toute le monde eust sa paraille de biauté. La chamber estoit quarré et grans a mervaille et soef flerant ainsi cum se toutez lez espicez du monde i fussent aporteez. En mi [MS vn] lieu de la chamber avoit un tabel d'argent mult grante [et] haute par raison, et seoit sor .iii. pilerez d'argent. E desus la tabel, droit en mi lieu, avoit .i. orçuel d'argent et d'or, et dedenz cele orçuel estoit .i. lance drescié, la point desoz et le haut desuz. E qui regardast a mult la lanche, il merveillaist coment ele tenist droite, car ele n'estoit apoié ne d'un part ne d'autre. Lui chevalier as .ii. espeez regarde [MS legarde] le lanche, mais il ne [la] conoist pas trez bien, si s'adresse cele parte et ot un auter voiz qui li escrie mult haute: "Ne la touchie, pechierez!"

It is immediately clear from this description that anyone who touches that lance is not just courting disaster, but positively soliciting it. The progressive narrowing of focus, both architecturally and stylistically, emphasizes the lance as the centrepiece of the symmetrical arrangement and its most important element. The supernatural voice removes the last possibility of doubt as to the sacred importance of the place. All this is altered in Malory's account:

> Than kynge Pellam caught in his hand a grymme wepyn and smote egirly at Balyn, but he put hys swerde betwyxte hys hede and the stroke, and therewith hys swerde braste in sundir. And whan Balyne was wepynles he ran into a chambir for to seke a wepyn and so fro chambir to chambir, and no wepyn coude he fynde. And allwayes kyng Pellam folowed afftir hym. And at the last he enterde into a chambir which was mervaylously dyght and ryche, and a bedde arayed with cloth of golde, the rychiste that myght be, and one lyyng therein. And thereby stoode a table of clene golde with foure pelours of sylver that bare up the table, and uppon the table stoode a mervaylous spere strangely wrought.
>
> So whan Balyn saw the spere he gate hit in hys honde and turned to kynge Pellam and felde hym and smote hym passyngly sore with that spere, that kynge Pellam felle downe in a sowghe. And therewith the castell brake rooffe and wallis and felle downe to the erthe. And Balyn felle downe and myght nat styrre hande nor foote, and for the moste party of that castell was dede thorow the dolorouse stroke.

(Cambridge, UL, MS Add. 7071 fol. 270va-b; Roussineau 160–1 [sections 202–3]). BL Add. 38117 is lacunose at this point, and most of the Dolorous Stroke section is missing (Roussineau's text is based on the Cambridge manuscript for this passage). The folios containing it in the Cambridge manuscript are not part of the original manuscript either: fols 269–73 (fol. 273v is blank), 276 and 335–42 (the latter group being the last in the manuscript, which seems to end incomplete) are fifteenth-century replacement leaves. However the extent of the text covered by these replacement leaves is not identical with the lacuna in Add. 38117, so that the lacunae in these two manuscripts do not seem to indicate a lacuna in their common original. Moreover the evidence of the collation of the Cambridge MS does not oppose the view that the fifteenth-century leaves are indeed replacements and not additions; presumably the originals were worn or damaged and their contents were transferred to new folios. I am grateful to David Dumville for confirming this analysis. The Dolorous Stroke episode is printed by Fanni Bogdanow in an appendix to *The Romance of the Grail*, 241–9, and the emendations in the above version are hers, except for the correction of the manuscript reading "En vn lieu" (followed by Roussineau), which I have made on the assumption that the phrase parallels the "en mi lieu" of the following sentence. I can find no use of the word "lieu" in Tobler-Lommatzsch that would fit the former reading, and nothing would be easier than to misread four minims in the original script of the manuscript as "un" instead of "mi."

Ryght so lay kynge Pellam and Balyne three dayes.

Than Merlion com thydir, and toke up Balyn and gate hym a good horse, for hys was dede, and bade hym voyde oute of that contrey.

"Sir, I wolde have my damesell," seyde Balyne.

"Loo," seyde Merlion, "where she lyeth dede." (84/27–85/20)

The series of chambers, building up to a climax, has disappeared; Balin "at the last" finds himself in *a* chamber, whose features are presented in a jumble, not in the logical sequence of the *Suite du Merlin.* An absence of hierarchical order is again apparent, in Malory's telling, this time at the level of narrative detail. From this jumble, the spear "leaps out" and catches Balin's eye, but its prominence is accidental – it is created by the circumstance that Balin needs a weapon. It is chance that makes the spear the most important item in the room for Balin. This is emphasized even further by the presence in Malory's version of the man in the bed. Normally on entering a room we give primary attention to any people in it; the fact that this man is of no importance to Balin emphasizes the overturning of a normal hierarchical ordering of perception.[40]

The apparent explanation of the room, the lance, and the stroke that follows in Malory's text is characterized by a similar lack of hierarchical order, so that again it explains nothing. None of its pieces of information – that in the room was part of Christ's blood, that the man in the bed was Joseph of Arimathaea, that the lance was Longinus's spear, that King Pellam was kin to Joseph, and so on – will help us to identify the dynamic of the episode, the link between the action and its effect. The "explanation" merely emphasizes that chance has precipitated Balin into a different realm, a different set of "adventures" of which he knows nothing, but in which his simple action has tragic effects.

The sequel to this episode, and preface to Balin's destiny, is another in the whole series of actions in which Balin does what he did not want or intend to do; intending to cure the hopeless passion of a knight called Garnysshe of the Mownte by showing him his lady in the arms of another man, he instead stimulates Garnysshe into murdering both of them and then committing suicide. The sense of hopelessness generated by this episode brings to the point of anguished climax our sense of the distance between Balin's untreacherous essence and the apparently treacherous actions for which he is forced to accept responsibility: the outrage of Arthur's or Pellam's hospitality, the death of Launceor, the suicide of Columbe, the destruction of an entire country through the Dolorous Stroke.

40 Vinaver finds it "difficult to believe" that it was Malory who added the bed and its occupant to the description of the chamber (Malory, *Works*, 1316); I find it difficult to believe that it was not.

None of these actions, we may say, expresses Balin; they do not manifest his self, they merely manifest his destiny.

It is thus with a sort of grim desperation that the narrative rebounds from this last example of the split between self and destiny, and plunges straight into the account of the final action that Balin would not will, the slaying of his brother.

> When Balen sawe that, he dressid hym thensward, lest folke wold say he had slayne them, and so he rode forth. And within thre dayes he cam by a crosse; and theron were letters of gold wryten that said: "it is not for no knyght alone to ryde toward this castel." Thenne sawe he an old hore gentylman comying toward hym that sayd,
>
> "Balyn le Saveage, thow passyst thy bandes to come this waye, therfor torne ageyne and it will availle the," and he vanysshed awey anone.
>
> And soo he herd an horne blowe as it had ben the dethe of a best. "That blast," said Balyn, "is blowen for me, for I am the pryse, and yet am I not dede." Anone withal he sawe an honderd ladyes and many knyghtes that welcommed hym with fayr semblaunt and made hym passyng good chere unto his syght, and ledde hym into the castel, and ther was daunsynge and mynstralsye and alle maner of joye. Thenne the chyef lady of the castel said,
>
> "Knyghte with the Two Suerdys, ye must have adoo and juste with a knyght hereby that kepeth an iland, for ther may no man passe this way but he muste juste or he passe."
>
> "That is an unhappy customme," said Balyn, "that a knyght may not passe this wey but yf he juste."
>
> "Ye shalle not have adoo but with one knyghte," sayd the lady.
>
> "Wel," sayd Balyn, "syn I shalle, therto I am redy; but traveillynge men are ofte wery and their horses to, but though my hors be wery my hert is not wery. I wold be fayne ther my deth shold be."
>
> "Syr," said a knyght to Balyn, "methynketh your sheld is not good; I wille lene yow a byggar, therof I pray yow."
>
> And so he tooke the sheld that was unknowen and lefte his owne, and so rode unto the iland and put hym and his hors in a grete boote. And whan he came on the other syde he met with a damoysel, and she said,
>
> "O, knyght Balyn, why have ye lefte your owne sheld? Allas! ye have put yourself in grete daunger, for by your sheld ye shold have ben knowen. It is gret pyté of yow as ever was of knyght, for of thy prowesse and hardynes thou hast no felawe lyvynge."
>
> "Me repenteth," said Balyn, "that ever I cam within this countrey; but I maye not torne now ageyne for shame, and what aventure shalle falle to me, be it lyf or dethe, I wille take the adventure that shalle come to me."
>
> And thenne he loked on his armour and understood he was wel armed, and therwith blessid hym and mounted upon his hors. (88/1–89/7)

We seem suddenly to have left the world of contingency, of inconsequential episodes, and to be firmly carried along in the grip of destiny. Yet the pattern of destiny is formed (as Boethius tells us it is) by chance. The custom which Balin is forced to comply with is "unhappy" (unlucky), and his brother has, he later says, been forced into maintaining it because "I had never grace to departe fro hem syn that I cam hyther, for here it happed me to slee a knyght that kept this iland" (90/19–21). The knight who suggests that Balin leave behind the shield by which he might be recognized is called an "unhappy knyght" (90/15), and when Balin smites his brother it is, we are told, with "that unhappy swerd" (89/22–3).[41] And this chance formation of events is one that the knight must accept as he accepts the others, for, being a knight, he is committed to "take the adventure." For the third and last time in the tale, the phrase is used, making the final element in a pattern of repetition that links Balin's taking of the sword, the death of Columbe, and Balin's slaying of his brother.

But here we have for the first time a full realization of the implications in the phrase. We can sense as Balin uses it a closing of the gap between self and action, an obliteration of the distance between Balin and the adventures which have come to him. We have instead a sense of Balin coming together with his destiny: "I wold be fayne ther my deth shold be." The sentence is syntactically ambiguous. It would conform more easily to expected patterns of utterance if "fayne" were interpreted as an adjective – "I would be content [if] my death were destined to occur in that place" – and we perhaps unconsciously assimilate it to this meaning; but the syntax suggests rather that "fayne" is an adverb and "ther" a relative – "I would gladly be in the place where my death were destined to be."[42] It is this latter meaning especially that gives a powerful sense of Balin's death as something separate from him, waiting for him, and a kind of aesthetic satisfaction in the coming together of the two. What drives Balin into this union with the adventure awaiting him is his worship ("I may not torne now ageyne

41 In the *Suite du Merlin*, the tragedy is referred to as a "mesaventure" and "mesqueance," but it is said to be sent by God as punishment for the striking of the Dolorous Stroke (Cambridge,UL, MS Add. 7071 fols 272va and 276vb; Roussineau 168 [section 209]; 183 [section 226]).

42 The first interpretation takes "ther" as an adverb, and "shold be" as a periphrastic subjunctive in a noun clause following an expression of sorrow or pleasure, etc. See Tauno Mustanoja, *Middle English Syntax*, Part I (Helsinki, 1960), 458–9. The second interpretation takes "ther" as a relative adverb (ibid., 337–8) and "shold be" as a periphrastic subjunctive depending on the preterite subjunctive "wold" (*OED* s.v. *Shall*, 36). For the use of *shall* to express "to be destined to," see *OED* s.v., 20a. There is a fairly close parallel to this second interpretation at 26/29–30: "they lette brenne and destroy all the contrey before them there they sholde ryde" – although the *sholde* here has less modal colouring.

for shame"), which bridges the distance between self and adventure as it did in the episode of the lady and the white hart.

The pattern formed by chance has not, even now, assumed a meaning (as it would, for example, were Balin's slaying of his brother to be attributed to his obstinacy or rashness). The lament of the two dying brothers – "We came bothe out of one wombe, that is to say one moders bely, and so shalle we lye bothe in one pytte" (90/26–8) – is an aesthetic linking, a recognition of a shape in events, but not of cause and effect. And even here, the pattern is not completely fulfilled; the *wombe*/*tombe* echo which clearly determines the form of the lament is nevertheless avoided by the use of the word *pytte*, so that the pattern is felt as present but veiled.[43] There is still an obliquity, a swerving aside from complete union, which preserves the poignancy of distance. The pattern of events which finally emerges from the random adventures of the tale and the tantalizing repetitiveness of their features – tombs, suicides, pairs of sorrowing lovers, swords fixed in stones or sheaths, brothers, battles between friends – this pattern has the force of destiny, but no meaning in itself; the random adventures organize themselves into destiny of their own accord. It is, in fact, their very multiplicity and disconnectedness through most of the tale which acts as our guarantee that the shape they finally assume does not result from the effort of an organizing author – or even of an organizing God – but is the chance completion of a single pattern among the countless others which remain unfulfilled.

It is for this reason that I think mistaken the general critical preference for the linear, connected narrative of the last two sections of Malory's work (the *Book of Launcelot and Guinevere* and the *Tale of the Death of Arthur*) over the episodic, fragmented narrative of its earlier parts, and likewise disagree with the generally held view that they represent some mysterious crystallization of Malory's artistic insight or skill in the course of his writing.[44] On the contrary, it is essential to his conception of the forces shaping the destinal forward movement of the last two books (as of the end of "Balin") that this movement, this connectedness, emerges only rarely from the random fluctuations of chance, and then *by* chance. Even in the last two books, the half-formed

43 The French version at this point juxtaposes two senses of the word "vessel," rather than relying on an echo: "Car tut ausi com nos cors issirent d'un vessel ausi reserront il en un vessel mis" (Cambridge, UL, MS Add. 7071 fol. 278va, echoed on fol. 279ra; Roussineau 190 [section 234]; 192 [section 236]).

44 See R.T. Davies, "Worshipful Way in Malory," 159; Derek S. Brewer, "The Present Study of Malory," 89; Stephen Knight, *The Structure of Sir Thomas Malory's Arthuriad*, ch. 4; Mark Lambert, *Malory: Style and Vision*, 124.

pattern of destiny is often broken up; if Guinevere is threatened three times with death and three times rescued by Lancelot, it is not, I think, so that we shall be prompted into moral discriminations between his defence of her in a rightful or a wrongful quarrel, hut so that we may see that the first two rescues are end-stopped, do not necessarily lead on to disaster, while the third initiates the formation of a destinal pattern through the chance slaying of Gareth and Gaherys. In this case Malory inherited the arrangement of events from the *Mort Artu*, and it is the events themselves which refuse to come to a climax. But we can see the same dissipation of a destinal climax as the result of narrative method, and of Malory's own deliberate decision, in, for example, his breaking off the Tristram section two-thirds of the way through, its traditional content. Another example of avoidance of a destinal climax, on a different scale, is evident in the way that the deaths of Lamorak and Tristram happen "off-stage," and are only reported to us incidentally, in the course of quite other episodes (715–16; 1149–50) They are, that is, distanced from the reader, by virtue of being distant from the narrative in the course of which they are related. Paradoxically, in creating these distances Malory creates contact; it is because the deaths of Lamorak and Tristram are distanced from their own stories that they touch other stories. Conversely, if they were linked closely into the events of their own stories they would be artificially distanced from the myriad contingencies with which life surrounds them. There is a similar paradox, it may be noted here, in the knight's attempt to obliterate the distance between himself and an *aventure*; in pursuing a quest, he separates himself from the court and the fellowship of the Round Table, so that while the distance is closed in one direction, it opens in another. That Malory was quite conscious of this paradox can be seen on the one hand, in his ubiquitous and punning use of the word "depart" (and its derivatives), meaning both "to leave" and "to separate,"[45] and on the other, in his stress on the joyful return of the knight to the court, reuniting himself to it when the adventure is over. The Grail book is the most elaborate development of these paradoxical patterns of separation and union, both physical and spiritual, and it culminates fittingly in Lancelot's moving assurance to Bors (which is Malory's own addition): "wete ye well, gentyl cousyn sir Bors, ye and I shall never departe in sundir whylis oure lyvys may laste," and Bors's answering affirmation of unity "Sir ... as ye woll, so woll I" (1037/4–7).

To read Malory's work in this way, in terms of the dominance of chance and the distances and unions which it creates in experience, is to see more clearly

45 The pun, and the cumulative effects of Malory's use of the word, are noted by Field, *Romance and Chronicle*, 82.

his relationship to his historical context, to the late medieval obsession with chance and destiny, nourished by the study of Boethius and given powerful stimulus by the writings of Chaucer.[46] But it is also to see more clearly that what Malory has to say is of greater and more continuing importance than the expression of ideas about knighthood, past or contemporary, which might command merely polite or antiquarian interest. Malory uses the world of chivalry because its conventions embody – and were in fact designed to express – certain features of actuality, an actuality which exists for us as for him.[47] In his French sources, he found an interest in *aventure* and the notion that a knight stood in a special relation to it. He found also that the operations of *aventure* for weal and for woe were powerfully illustrated in the story of Arthur, the *roi aventureux*. The passage that gives Arthur this title is a speech of Merlin's in the *Suite du Merlin*, which is quoted by Fanni Bogdanow as an illustration of "the theme of 'aventure' and 'mescheance' which links the *Suite du Merlin* and Post-Vulgate *Queste-Mort Artu*":[48]

> "Rois Artus, qui es rois par aventure e fus conceus par aventure, e fus norris par aventure tele que cil qui te norissoient ne savoient qe tu estoies, et quant tu venis jovens enfés entre les homes le quele que ne te conoissoient e Nostre Sires [te] reconoie bien e t'aleva par sa grace desor toz et te fist seignur si com tu le devoies estre, e si fus engendrés par aventure e par aventure receus tu la corune, car ensi plaisoit il a Nostre Seignor. Et sachez que tanz aventures ne si merveilluses ne t'est pas avenues pur nient, ainz estoient signefiances e comencemenz de ceo qu'il devoit avenir en ton ostel e en ta subjection e en mainte autre lieu, et pur ceo te di jeo que tu dois estre apellés rois aventurus e li teons realmes [li realmes] as aventures. E sachiez que tut einsi com aventure te dona le realme, si le te toudra aventure."[49]

46 Cf. Bloomfield's comments on the role of the revived interest in Boethius in the twelfth century shift from epic to romance ("Episodic Motivation," 123). The need to consider more closely Malory's relationships with *English* literature is emphasized by Derek S. Brewer, "The Present Study of Malory," 84 and 90, and Larry D. Benson, "Sir Thomas Malory's *Le Morte Darthur*," in *Critical Approaches to Six Major English Works*, ed. R.M. Lumiansky and Herschel Baker (Philadelphia, PA, 1968), 81–131, at 107–11. They are probably thinking in the first instance of the English Arthurian romances, but the influence of Chaucer should also be considered, not only because of the importance of *aventure* in his works, but also because it is hard to conceive of a literary Englishman in the fifteenth century *not* having read Chaucer.

47 Cf. Bloomfield, "Episodic Motivation," 108: "Life is both rational and irrational. The typical epic stresses the first, the typical romance the second."

48 *The Romance of the Grail*, 153–5.

49 Cambridge, UL, MS Add. 7071 fol. 289va–b; Roussineau 234 [section 278]. The emendations are those made by Fanni Bogdanow, *The Romance of the Grail*, 153.

["King Arthur, who are king by hap, and were conceived by hap, and by hap were fostered so that those who fostered you knew not what you were, and when you came as a boy among the men who did not recognize you Our Lord knew you well, and raised you above all others by His grace, and made you lord as you were destined to be, and so you were born through hap and through hap received the crown, for so it pleased Our Lord. And know that so many and such marvellous happenings did not befall you for nothing, but they were tokens and beginnings of what was to occur in your house and in your realm and in many another place; and therefore I tell you that you ought to be called king of hap and your realm the realm of happening. And know that just as hap gave you the kingdom, so hap will take it away."]

But we can already see from this passage the difference between the *Suite du Merlin*'s conception of *aventure* and Malory's. For the author of the *Suite du Merlin*, the adjective which most often and most appropriately accompanies the word *aventure* is *merveilleuse*; he does not share Malory's conception of the mystery and power in the ordinary operations of chance. The emphasis all the way through the *Suite du Merlin* is on a special period of time, with a distinct beginning and ending, within which unusual adventures occur as a sign of God's special favour to Arthur.[50] The sense that the adventures are sent – and thus rigorously subordinated to the intentions of the sender – is pervasive in the *Suite du Merlin*, and it gives them a quite different significance from the one they carry in the autonomous and uncertainly organized world of Malory.[51] Nor is the conception of *aventure* in the Vulgate *Mort Artu* like that of Malory, despite Frappier's claim that this is the first medieval work in which

50 This attitude characterizes the other French prose romances also; in the *Mort Artu*, for example, the period of adventures is conceived as over, and the arrival of the mysterious ship of the lady of Escalot raises false hopes that they might be recommencing (*La Mort Le Roi Artu*, ed. Jean Frappier [Geneva, 1964], 88, 70, 21–4). Malory omits all such references to a special time of adventures, and likewise all the *Suite du Merlin*'s many references to the first institutions of chivalric customs (see, for example, Roussineau 29 [section 38]; 44 [section 56]; 209 [section 255]; 216 [section 260]; 222 [section 266]; 235 [section 278]; 375 [section 426]).

51 It is this equivocation that blurs the otherwise forceful presentation of *mescheance* in the *Suite du Merlin*'s version of the Balin story. When dying, the two brothers lament "Ha! Deus, pur quoi avez vus suuffert que si grant mesaventure nus avenist?" (Cambridge, UL, MS Add. 7071 fol. 278vb; Roussineau 190 [section 234]). Vinaver's comment on the French version of the Balin story – "No rational explanation relieves the gloom of Balin's fate, no comfort exists for his *mescheance*, and no reason for his death beyond the remarkable recurrence of the tragic pattern" – is thus an apter description of Malory's version than of the *Suite du Merlin* (*The Rise of Romance*, 110).

Fortune becomes "l'âme invisible et présente d'un ensemble."[52] For it is clear from Frappier's discussion of the author of the *Mort Artu* as "psychologue adroit" that in his view Fortune here represents the enmeshing of human decisions and passions, and that these are much more directly expressed in events than in Malory's version: "le conflit qui s'engage est purement moral. Seule l'erreur humaine permet au Destin d'exercer son impitoyable rigueur."[53] In working out his own narrative style and structure, Malory found (and found from the beginning of his work) a medium fit to express a far more powerful and profound idea of *aventure* than any in his sources.[54] And he also showed his originality in his new emphasis on *taking* the adventure.[55] The triple repetition of the phrase in "Balin" becomes the tale's dominant motif, but its importance is by no means restricted to that tale alone. It can, for example, be argued (although I have not the space to do it here) that it underlies Malory's treatment of the Tristram story: Tristram is *par excellence* the knight who "takes the adventure," and who thus turns his enemies (Segwarydes, Lamorak, Palomides) into his friends, transforming the distance created by hatred into the closeness of reconciliation. It also determines Malory's interpretation of the *Morte Arthure*; its reverberations can, for example, be deeply felt in the assertion of Arthur's determination to attack Mordred, although he is warned (as Balin is warned) of the danger:

> "Now tyde me dethe, tyde me lyff," seyde the kyng, "now I se hym yondir alone, he shall never ascape myne hondes! For at a bettir avayle shall I never have hym." (1237/5–7)

---

52 Jean Frappier, *Étude sur la Mort le Roi Artu* (Paris, 1936), 264.

53 Frappier, *Étude sur la Mort le Roi Artu*, 276. He also comments (262) on the way that the concept of Fortune is limited in the French *Queste del Saint Graal* by its role as an expression of God's will.

Robert L. Kelly points to "Malory's emphasis, not on the ethics of knighthood, but on the more philosophical problem of destiny," but sees his particular interest as being in "the role that choice plays in shaping one's destiny," and interprets Balin's words about taking the adventure as an expression of *hubris*, an "Oedipus-like challenge to providence" which is justly punished in what follows ("Malory's 'Tale of Balin' Reconsidered," 90).

54 Laura Hibbard [Loomis] rightly points out that the specific references to Fate or misfortune in the *Suite du Merlin* are "simply windy asseverations, such as might occur in any story of knightly mischance," whereas in Malory, "the sense of Fate ... depends not upon an outward word, but upon an inner mood and atmosphere, an emphasis, that is wholly and uniquely his own" ("Malory's Book of Balin," 179).

55 See *MED* aventure n. 1b: taken ~, to take (one's) chances; to endure (one's) fate; the first example listed under this heading is, significantly, *Knight's Tale* (I) 1186. See also *Complaint of Mars* 21; *House of Fame* 1052.

Of the other developments of the concept of "taking the adventure" in the *Morte Arthure*, I shall mention only the perverted mimicry of it by the two "unhappy" knights, Mordred and Aggravain. Aggravain's rejection of Gawain's counsel not to tell Arthur of his wife's infidelity parallels Arthur's phrase in form:

> "Falle whatsumever falle may," seyde sir Aggravayne, "I woll disclose hit to the kynge!" (1162/1–2)

But the similarity in form merely shows up the difference in meaning; Aggravain's words betray a reckless obstinacy in the assertion of his own will, rather than a submissive acceptance of contingency. As for Mordred, it has often enough been noted that the macabre manner of his death is unique to Malory, but it has escaped notice that it is invented as a grotesque parody of "taking the adventure." Mordred "accepts" his death, to the extent of pushing himself all the way up the "burre" of Arthur's spear; he closes the distance between himself and his father, but only in order to destroy – to impose, for the last time and even in defeat, his own destructive will on the world, rather than to take the adventure of defeat (1237/12–22).

The only hint for the concept of "taking the adventure" in Malory's French sources is a rather prosy lecture given by a hermit to Baalin in the *Suite du Merlin* (at a not particularly crucial point in the narrative):

> "I tell you," said the good man, "that there is no knight errant who does not consider adventures as they happen, be they good or bad. But certainly, these two which have so suddenly befallen you, I am greatly amazed by. Nevertheless, you do not seem to be a man who would grieve at anything that may befall him, but console himself and take heart. For truly, anyone who is upset by any adventure that he sees happen does not seem to me a man of great spirit."[56]

56 "Jeo vus di" fait li prudomes, "qu'il n'i a chevalier errant fors qu'il regarde les aventures ensi com eles avendront, soient beles, soient laides. Mes de ces .ii. sanz faille qui si soudainement sont avenues me merveille jeo mult durement. E neporquant vus ne semblez pas home qui si deust doluser de ceo que li aveigne, mais reconforter ceo e prendre cuer en lui meismes, car certes il ne semble pas home de grant cuer qui pur aventure qu'il voie avenir se desconforte" (Cambridge, UL, MS Add. 7071 fol. 266rb; Roussineau 143 [section 181]). Baalin says much the same thing to his damsel companion a little later "ensi covient prendre les aventures com eles avienent el siecle" (Cambridge, UL, MS Add. 7071 fol. 267ra; Roussineau 146 [section 184]). Much more frequent in the French sources is the phrase (*se*) *metre en aventure*, which Malory also takes over.

Malory's conception of "taking the adventure" is not to be identified with this rather prosaic idea of keeping a stiff upper lip. It is not a matter of stoic suffering or iron resistance; it is an attempt to stretch the self to embrace the utmost reach of possible events. The knight does not try to close the distance between himself and events by fitting them to himself, mastering them so that they become a mere expression of himself; instead he achieves union with them by matching himself to them, by taking into himself, accepting without understanding, their mysterious inevitability and his enigmatic responsibility for them. It is this submission of self which paradoxically means that his essence, his "worship," remains whole despite the fragmentation in his experience. Balin "takes the adventure" by which he is the knight most without treason and the slayer of his brother – an irreconcileable bifurcation of the path of adventure in which the name given to him, the Knight with Two Swords (as it were, the knight with two destinies), seems to find the significant role that it lacks in terms of plot. The pattern of Balin's adventures is closed and completed at his death, but the larger pattern of chance goes on without him: Merlin puts his sword into a stone, and it is left to float down the river until, as Merlin prophesies, "by adventure" it will come to Camelot, be "achieved" by Galahad, and used by Lancelot to slay Sir Gawain, the man he loves most (91/24–5). The episodes which lie between this point and that are as disconnected, as much dominated by chance, as those in "Balin"; the route that connects them is dark and winding. But "Balin" teaches us to recognize that this final cataclysmic adventure, in which the whole of the Round Table is destroyed, is one which is equally impossible to link with any will or intention, human or divine, but which the knight must equally accept.

Appendix

Mult fu grant la joie que li baron du realme de Logres firent le jour en la cité de Camaalot. Li granz palais ou li rois tenoit ses noces estoit en tele manere assis qu'il seoit el chief de la cité par devers le grant foreste près del bois as .ii. archiés, e tut entour a la reonde estoit enclos de gardins granz e merveilleuses e haus e ausi espes com si/ [fol. 284v] ceo fust une foreste. E en ceo que li rois seoit au disner e il avoient par laeinz près mangié, Merlin dist "Seignurs barons qui caeinz estes, ore ne vus movez pur chose que vus voiez, e jeo vus die que vus verrez ja caeinz venir .iii. des greignurs merveilles qe vus onques veissiés. E pur ceo qu'il n'en avera nule caeinz achevée, doins jeo le don a .iii. chevaliers des chevaliers de cainz qui les acheverorent. Si avera Gavain la primere aventure a mener a chef, e Tor le filz Arez avera la seconde. E li rois Pellinors avera la tierce. E sachiez que chescun endroit soi vendra bien a chief de la sue." De ceste parole s'en merveillerent mult cil del palais. E en ceo qu'il parloient entr'ex il voient venir par laienz un cerf qui venoit devers le gardin qui mult estoit grant e merveilluse, e un brachet apres, e une damoisele venoit après que amenoit .xxx. muetes des chiens, si les avoit tuz descouplés e les aloit huant e esmovant après le cerf qui tut estoit blanc, e li brachet autresi tut blanc, mais tuit li autre chien estoient tout noire. Mais de la damoisele vus di jeo bien que c'estoit une des plus beles damoiseles du monde ne que onques fust entree en la court le roi Arthur. Ele estoit vestu d'une robe vert assez court e avoit pendu a son col un corn d'ivoire e tenoit un arc en sa main e un seat e estoit trop ben apparaillé com veneresce; e ele venoit si grant aire com ele porroit traire del chaval e si grant noise faisant que ceo n'estoit si merveille non.

Quant li cerf aprocha la court il se fiert dedenz le palais ne nel lessa onques pur nule chose, e li braches apres. E li cerf s'en remet outre en la sale la ou li chevaliers estoient assis as tables. E lors li saut li braches e l'aert par deriere a la quise e le tire si fort qu'il en porte la pece. E quant li cerf s'en veet navrés il se launce outre par desus une table. E lors saut avant un chevalier qui laeinz mangoit, si prent le brachet e vient a son cheval e monte qui estoit en mie la court e s'en vait a tout si grant pas outre com si tut li mondes le chaçoit, e vait disant a soi mesmes que mult a bien fait sa bosaigne pur qui il vient a court. E la damoisele qui deriere venoit, quant ele en voit [MS soit] son brachet enporter, ele dist a celui qui l'emporte, "Sire chevaliers, meuz le vus venroit lessier que porter l'ent. Car vus le rendrez maugré le vostre." E cil ne respondi onques riens, ainz s'en voit totes voies. E la damoisele s'en entre el palais entre les chevaliers, qui tuit estoient esbahi du cerf qui s'en estoit par mie eus entrez, e tut li levrier s'en aloient apres lui e s'en estoient sailli par desus les tables e par desus les chevaliers, si qu'il s'estoient ja mis es gardins par d'autre part le palais e ravoient commencé lor chace. E quant ele ne trove le cerf ne les levriers ele s'areste ausi com tut esbahi e gette jus son arc e ses seates, e demande li queus est lui rois, e home li mustre tantost. E ele descent maintenant e vient devant le roi e li dist: "Ha! roi Artus, jeo me plaing trop malement de vus e de vostre ostel. Car j'ai primerement perdu mon brachet que jeo n'amoi pas petit, e sui desturné de sivre e le cerf e les braches que jeo chasoie, e qe jeo eusse prise en poi de tens, e ore en sui esloignié que jeo ne sai quele part il sont torné. Tut cest damage, rois Artus,/ [fol. 285r] m'est avenu par vostre hostel, pur qui jeo m'en plaing a vus meisme. Ore i parra coment vus le me restores." Lors saut avant Merlin e dist "Damoisele, ore vus suffrez autant, car assez en avez dit. E jeo vus die que vus n'en perderes ja caeinz chose que bien ne vus soit rendu." "Ore move donque" fait ele "auquns des chevaliers de caeinz qui aille apres le brachet, e autre apres le cerf, car il n'ont que demorer s'il les voelent attendre." "Ha! dame," fait Merlin, "ore hastez les chevaliers si durement, car nule haste n'i vaudroit riens. Car desoremes averra en ceste hostel tel custume: ore ja pur aventure qu'il aveigne ne si perilluse ne si mortele devoit avenir ne se remuera plus chevaliers qui a la table siece devant qu'il ait mangié. Mes quant les tables serront levées, lors purra les chevaliers lor aventures quere, cil a qui eles serront jugié. E jeo prie le roi qui ci est qu'il tiegne ceste coustume tant com il vivera." E lui rois li creaunte, voiant tuz les barons, qu'il le tendra. Lors dist Merlin a Gavain, "Gavain, l'aventure du cerf est vostre. Si tost com vus averez mangié, pren vos armes e montes en vostre cheval, e sives tant le cerf que vus l'aiez pris, si en aportes caeinz la teste e gardes que nuls des leverers ne vus faille quant vus revendrez en ceste court si'il ne morent en la chace, car autrement ne serroit pas l'aventure menée a fin." E il respont que il ne serra jamais a aise devant qu'il se soit a la voie mis. E Merlin redist a Tor: "Prennes vos armes si tost com les tables seront levées, e alez apres le chevalier qui le brachet enporte. E gardes que vus ne revenes james devant que vus aiez le brachet e le chevalier ou mort ou vif." E cist dist que de cest commandement faire est il tut prest. E lors dient li autre prodome, "Ha! Merlin, ceo est pechié quant vus ces .ii. enfanz mettes si tost en aventure de mort." "Seignurs," fet il, "onques ne vus esmaiez. Jeo les conoisse mult meuz que vus ne faites. Sachiez que chescuns vendra bien a chief de s'aventure a l'aide de deu." En ceo qu'il parolent par laeinz de ceste chose, es vus un chevalier armé de totes armes e fu montés sur un cheval blanc mult grant, e entra en tele manere el palais. E la ou il voit la damoisele, il se turne cele part tout ausi montés com il estoit, e la prent par les .ii. braz e la [MS le] mette desor le col de son cheval. Si se deffendoit ele au meux qu'ele porroit, e quant il out montée en tiele manere il s'en returne vers l'uis de la sale e s'en ist fors, e puis s'en vait si grant aleure com il poet traire del destrer; e cele qui s'en vait porter en tele guise crie toutes voies "Ha! rois Artus! jeo sui mort e honie par l'aseurance que j'en avoie en toi, e en ton ostel, si tu ne fas tant que jeo soie osté des mains a cest chevalier." Ensi s'en vait li chevaliers qui la damoisele enporte, e cele voit totes voies criant au roi Artu qu'il la [MS se] socore. E lors dist Merlin as barons de la cort, "Ore beau seignors, ne vus est bien avenu ceo que jeo vus promis des .iii. aventures que caeinz averoient hui en cest jour?" E il dient, "Merlin, que en dirroms nous? Vus en estes ausi voirdisant com vus estes de vos autres paroles." E Merlin dist tantost au roi Pellinor, "Rois, qu'en dirraiez vus, ceste daarraine aventure est vostre a achevier. Montes quant il vus plarra e alez apres le chevalier pur ramener la damoisele, e faites le si que vus en aiez honur." E il l'en mercie mult de cest doun e dist qu'il se mettra a la voie au plus tost que il purra. En tele manere com vus avez ci oi e en autre lieu commencierent/ [fol. 285v] les aventures a avenir en la court le roi Arthur.

(Cambridge, UL, MS Add. 7071 fols 284rb–285va; cf. Roussineau, 214–18 [sections 259–63]). I have silently expanded abbreviations, added punctuation, made a few necessary emendations, and modernized the spelling of u and v, i and j, in this and other quotations from the *Suite du Merlin.* I am grateful to the late Ruth Morgan, my former colleague at Girton College, for suggesting corrections and improvements in both text and translation of the quotations from the *Suite du Merlin* in this article.)

It will be seen how much lengthier the French narrative is than Malory's version. For the "prehistory" of this episode, and its development, see Malory, *Works*, 1269–70.

Chapter Fourteen

The Narrative of Distance, The Distance of Narrative in Malory's *Morte d'Arthur*

I. The Narrative of Distance

In the previous essay I tried to characterize the nature of adventure, and the knight's relation to it, in Malory's *Morte d'Arthur.*[1] I took as an example the strange incident that interrupts Arthur's wedding feast. Merlin instructs all the assembled knights to sit still, because they are about to see "a straunge and a mervailous adventure" (102/27). A white hart then rushes into the room, followed by a white brachet (a kind of hound), biting at the hart so that it gives a great leap and knocks over a knight at the side table. The knight takes up the brachet, leaves the hall, and rides away with it. A lady on a white horse then rides in and appeals to Arthur to retrieve her brachet, but he responds that he "may nat do therewith" (103/8). Finally an armed knight rides in on a great horse, seizes the lady, and carries her off, crying and wailing as she goes. "So whan she was gone," Malory concludes, "the kynge was gladde, for she made such a noyse" (103/11–12).

I suggested that what was striking about this scene was the sense of distance between the knights and the events played out before them. They watch like spectators at a play, obedient to Merlin's command, without intervening in the action. Arthur's response to the lady emphasizes this lack of connection between event and spectators, and his oddly inappropriate reaction to her howls as she is forcibly carried off manifests an emotional distance from the incident which matches the lack of physical intervention. The completely enigmatic nature of the whole sequence of events also increases our own sense of distance from what is happening; as I showed, Malory removes all the narrative details

1 See "'Taking the Adventure': Malory and the *Suite du Merlin*," 243–74 above.

in his French source which might help us to understand how and why this strange intrusion has come about, and where one's sympathies, as between the lady and either of the two knights, should lie. Once the sequence is over, Merlin at last encourages the knights to involve themselves in the adventure, but this involvement does not imply any attempt to solve its enigmas; they are simply to eliminate the physical distance between the adventure and the court by pursuing the hart, the knight with the brachet, and the lady, and bringing them back to Camelot. The ensuing narrative which relates the accomplishment of these tasks does nothing to bring us into closer touch with the original adventure by virtue of yielding any enlightenment as to the hows and the wherefores of its action, or the rights and wrongs of the situation. The Arthurian knight's acceptance of the adventure that confronts him "closes the gap" between himself and events in one sense, but it also involves his acceptance of their distance from him. His action is predicated on the assumption that the world in which he moves is not accessible to his understanding or his control; such revelation as he is vouchsafed follows his action rather than preceding and determining it, and what is revealed to him has the character of an arbitrary destiny. Arthur's drawing of the sword from the stone reveals that he is righteous king born of all England; Balin's drawing of the sword from the sheath reveals that he is "moste of worship withoute treson, trechory or felony" (64/2–3) and that he is destined to kill the man he loves most in the world.[2] In this latter case, the distance is not only between the knight and the external world, it is internal to the knight himself. The "adventure" he must accept is the tragic split between his two identities, the gap between the self and the action he will perform.

In this two-part essay I want to develop this account in an attempt to show that distance is a key concept in Malory's writing.[3] This is, first of all, a "narrative of distance" – that is, it represents distance as a pervasive and permanent element in human experience of all kinds. In the first part I shall concern myself with distance as narrative subject. In the second part I shall turn my attention to distance as narrative mode, to show how the romance style itself

---

2 That the second part of this dual destiny is intrinsic to the sword-drawing, and not a punishment for Balin's refusal to hand back the sword, is made clear by Merlin's explanation a little later: "And so thys lady Lyle of Avylion toke hir this swerde that she brought with hir, and tolde there sholde no man pulle hit oute of the sheethe but yf he be one of the beste knyghtes of thys realme, and he sholde be hardy and full of prouesse; and with that swerd he sholde sle hys brothir. Thys was the cause, damesell, that ye com into thys courte. I know hit as well as ye" (67/33–68/6). See further " 'Taking the Adventure,' " 250–6 above.

3 I shall also be developing some of the ideas briefly discussed in my article "Knightly Combat in Malory's *Morte d'Arthur*"; see 235–42 above.

replicates the character of the experience it describes. And I want to suggest that the emotional power of Malory's writing, the power that has made it the most influential and enduring of the many medieval versions of the Arthurian story, has its roots in the poignancy that comes from this sense of distance, and from its inevitable corollary – a longing for wholeness, for the obliteration of fissures, gaps, fragmentation, both within the self, and between the self and the outside world.

Distance can be apprehended as a narrative subject in the most routine incidents of the knightly world. The incessant physical movement which is the essence of knightly activity keeps the sense of motion *towards* and motion *away from* continually at the threshold of reading consciousness. Such phrases as "So they departed," "And so sir Lancelot departed," "Then he departed," punctuate the narrative with the regularity of bar markings in music. The dual sense of the word "depart," which in Malory's usage means "to separate" as well as "to leave," endows every knightly departure with a sense of severance.[4] Given the indeterminate geography of the romance world, the unfixed location of the goal of the knightly quest, and the random nature of knight-errantry, the sense of movement *away from* is always stronger than the sense of movement *towards*; we know what the knight is leaving but are not sure what he is going to. Distance is constantly opened up on one side without any certainty that it is being reduced on the other. Movement *towards* is experienced almost exclusively in the knightly combat, registered in the formulaic repetitions of the phrase "come together": "Wyth this every knyght departed in sundir and cam togydir all that they myght dryve" (309/21–2). The knights "depart" from each other *in order* that they might "come together"; an artificial and arbitrary distance is created so that it can be obliterated in the knightly encounter. Each knightly encounter thus functions as a symbol of a fundamental quest for "wholeness"; yet it also testifies to its elusiveness, for the combat destroys bodily wholeness even as it satisfies the knightly desire for engagement by bringing it together with a mirror image of itself. It is only when the knight is finally healed of his wounds that the wholeness of his bodily self matches the wholeness of coming together in the combat.

As in the adventure, so in the combat, distance is obliterated by physical rather than intellectual or emotional means. More often than not, the knight engages in combat without any clear sense of his opponent's motives or – when

4 P.J.C. Field comments on the "special overtones" given to the word "depart" by Malory's "constant use of it in tragic contexts": *Romance and Chronicle: A Study of Malory's Prose Style* (London, 1971), 82.

he is fighting on behalf of someone else – any detailed knowledge of the situation in which he is embroiling himself. More often than not, the identity of his opponent is also unknown to him. The visored knight is the very embodiment of distance; his armour is the condition of his engagement with his fellows, yet it maintains his distance from them by concealing his identity. The distance is of course frequently increased even further by the adoption of disguise, as when Lancelot rides in the armour of Sir Kay or the like. The narrative's obsession with identification is another expression of the quest for wholeness – to identify is to identify *with* one's experience, to grasp its nature and its meaning. But it too testifies to its elusiveness: recognition is not a climactic anagnorisis, accomplished once and for all; no sooner have knights been identified than they slip back into anonymity, so that the whole process must be gone through again.

I want to illustrate these staple features of Malory's narrative, and the way they articulate the experience of distance, from a relatively brief narrative sequence that occurs at the end of the section devoted to Sir Lamorak de Galys in the *Book of Sir Tristram*. I choose this sequence because most of it is made up of the apparently random and inconclusive incident that constitutes so much of Malory's narrative, and which his detractors take to be evidence of his pedestrian quality. The sequence begins with the characteristic mark of separation: "So on the morne Sir Lameroke departed" (447/16). As he rides, he sees four knights engaged in battle with a single opponent, whom they finally overcome. Lamorak rides between the knights and their victim, protesting that four to one is not a fair fight. They defend their action by saying that their opponent is false, which he denies, offering to prove his innocence in combat with the best of them, "my body to his body" (447/30). The four knights refuse the challenge, whereupon Lamorak proclaims he will rescue the knight from them. He slays two of the four, and the others flee. Lamorak then asks the knight he has rescued for his name, and is told it is Sir Froll of the Oute Ilys. Sir Froll then rides along with Lamorak and bears him company.

So far, the movement of this episode is towards the elimination of distance. Lamorak moves from being a spectator of the battle to being an active participant in it. Anonymity is replaced by identification; solitude gives way to fellowship as the two knights ride on together. But the fellowship does not last long. They meet another anonymous knight, all in white, with whom, Sir Froll says, he jousted a short while ago and was struck down. He proposes therefore to joust with him again. Lamorak counsels Froll not to do so, especially since the former joust had been at his own request, but Sir Froll rejects this advice, challenges the white knight, and is overthrown a second time. Sir Lamorak, having watched all this from the sidelines, rides after the white knight and asks his name, "for mesemyth ye sholde be of the felyshyp of the Rounde Table."

"Sir, uppon a covenaunte, that ye woll nat telle my name, and also that ye woll tell me youres."

"Sir, my name is sir Lamerok de Galis."

"And my name is sir Launcelot du Lake."

Than they putt up their swerdys and kyssed hertely togydirs, and aythir made grete joy of other.

"Sir," seyde sir Lameroke, "and hit please you I woll do you servyse."

"God deffende, sir, that ony of so noble a blood as ye be sholde do me servyse." Than seyde sir Launcelot, "I am in a queste that I muste do myselff alone."

"Now God spede you!" seyde sir Lameroke.

And so they departed. (448/31–449/11)

On Sir Lamorak's return to Sir Froll, the latter asks the name of the strange knight, which Lamorak refuses to give; at this Sir Froll takes offence and leaves him.

"Ye ar the more uncurteyse," seyde sir Froll, "and therefore I woll departe felyship." (449/16–17)

Lamorak acquiesces; and "So they departed" is the inevitable conclusion. Froll's initial separation from Lamorak's company to joust with Sir Lancelot is proleptic of the complete severance of their fellowship. Distance, briefly eliminated, opens up again. But these motions towards severance frame and contrast strikingly with the scene of mutual identification and affirmation of fellowship between Lamorak and Lancelot, where random adventure suddenly knots itself into a climax of recognition and emotional unity. Yet if this is the climax of the sequence of events so far, it cannot be said that the narrative line leads directly to it; its relation to the incidents concerning Sir Froll is curiously marginal. Lamorak enters the narrative line of Froll's adventures obliquely, in a physical as well as a metaphorical sense; the tangential trajectory on which he arrives at the scene expresses his tangential relationship to what is going on. His relationship to Froll's joust with Lancelot is even more tangential; he watches from the sidelines, disapproving of Froll's insistence on encounter. The narrative issues in an emotional climax that seems not fully to belong to it, to stand somehow apart from the surrounding events. A sudden movement of epiphany emerges obliquely from a series of random encounters with the unknown.

The narrative sequence is not yet concluded, despite the apparent disjunction created by the departure of Sir Froll. Two or three days later (the events of these days remaining a narrative blank), Lamorak comes across a knight sleeping by a well, with his lady sitting beside him. Sir Gawain arrives on the scene, takes up the lady, and places her on horseback behind his squire. Lamorak challenges him, but Gawain reminds him that he is King Arthur's nephew, and for the king's sake Lamorak holds back. Gawain then attacks the lady's knight with his spear; he is struck down, and the knight reclaims his lady (449). In the light of his previous objection, one would expect Lamorak to feel satisfied with this turn of events, but instead, he feels obliged to revenge his "felow," Sir Gawain, lest Gawain say dishonour of him in Arthur's court. He challenges the knight, and kills him on their first encounter (450/1–8). Once again a tangential relationship to events has been metamorphosed into a central involvement; but the sense of distance persists, in the shape of the gulf between Lamorak's initial response to Gawain's abduction of the lady and his final actions in defence of Gawain. He is distanced from himself, one might say, in his role in the combat.

The dead knight's lady rides in haste to his brother, Sir Bellyaunce le Orgulus, and tells him what has occurred. Swearing revenge for his brother's death, he rides after Lamorak, overtakes and challenges him. And the challenge reveals that the dead knight was none other than Sir Froll; "thow haste slayne my brother sir Froll that was a bettir knyght than ever was thou," says Sir Bellyaunce (450/16–17). The separate episodes of the narrative sequence are suddenly rendered continuous by the simple act of naming, the two or three days' interval that divides them proving a merely illusory separation. Yet if Bellyaunce's revelation discloses their linkage as a chronological sequence, it also disrupts their coherence at the level of meaning: the knight whom Lamorak had so recently been at pains to rescue from death is the very same one that he himself turns out to have killed – for no very compelling reason, as it seems to us – a few days later. Lamorak's second tangential entry into a sequence of events negates the effect of his first; the pattern created by his adventures, when revealed, proves to be one with which he cannot identify himself either in terms of motive or in terms of consistency with his own past actions.

This feeling of alienation from events is increased even further when Lamorak's identity is revealed to Sir Bellyaunce. They fight "myghtyly as noble knyghtes preved the space of two owres" (450/21–2), and finally Sir Bellyaunce asks Lamorak's name. Its revelation brings on another, which takes the narrative into its final phase.

> "A," seyde sir Bellyaunce, "thou arte the man in the worlde that I moste hate, for I slew my sunnys for thy sake where I saved thy lyff, and now thou haste slayne my brothir sir Froll. Alas, how sholde I be accorded with the? Therefore defende the! Thou shalt dye! There is none other way nor remedy."

"Alas!" seyde sir Lameroke, "full well me ought to know you, for ye ar the man that moste have done for me." And therewithall sir Lamerok kneled adowne and besought hym of grace.

"Aryse up!" seyde sir Bellyaunce, "othir ellys thereas thou knelyste I shall sle the!"

"That shall nat nede," seyde sir Lameroke, "for I woll yelde me to you, nat for no feare of you nor of youre strength, but youre goodnesse makyth me to lothe to have ado with you. Wherefore I requyre you, for Goddis sake and for the honour of knyghthode, forgyff me all that I have offended unto you."

"Alas!" seyde sir Bellyaunce, "leve thy knelynge, other ellys I shall sle the withoute mercy."

Than they yode agayne to batayle and aythir wounded othir, that all the grounde was blody thereas they fought. And at the laste sir Bellyaunce withdrew hym abacke and sette hym downe a lytyll uppon an hylle, for he was faynte for bledynge, that he myght nat stonde.

Than sir Lameroke threw his shylde uppon his backe and cam unto hym and asked hym what chere.

"Well," seyde sir Bellyaunce.

"A, sir, yett shall I shew you favoure in youre male ease."

"A, knyght," seyde sir Bellyaunce unto sir Lamerok, "thou art a foole, for and I had the at suche avauntage as thou haste me, I sholde sle the. But thy jantylnesse is so good and so large that I must nedys forgyff the myne evyll wyll."

And than sir Lameroke kneled adowne and unlaced fyrst his umbrere and than his owne, and than aythir kyssed othir with wepynge tearys. Than sir Lamerok led sir Bellyaunce to an abbey faste by, and there sir Lamerok wolde nat departe from sir Bellyaunce tylle he was hole. And than they were sworne togydyrs that none of hem sholde never fyght ayenste other.

So sir Lamerok departed and wente to the courte of Arthur. (450/25–451/28)

I have quoted this at length because it seems to me that it is precisely the ebb and flow of its overall movement that is crucial to its meaning. Sir Bellyaunce's revelation that he has killed his sons for Lamorak's sake comes out of the blue: we have never heard of it before and we shall never hear of it again. In a more realistic kind of narrative, we should expect either some preparation for such information, or some retrospective attempt to situate it in the narrative context; we should expect it, that is, to be woven into the broad band of experience that constitutes the field of the narrative action. In Malory's narrative, it is shorn of experiential context; it intrudes itself as an isolated and unexplained fact into a situation to which it stands in an utterly contradictory relation, as Lamorak's attempt to give up the fight once he has heard it indicates. Its function is merely to intensify to crisis point the distance already created by Lamorak's unintentional slaying of Sir Froll; Lamorak has killed the man he has just saved; Bellyaunce is trying to kill the man whose life he has saved by the sacrifice of his children; Lamorak is fighting the man who has saved his life.

Yet the ebb and flow of battle finally dissolves this distance in reconciliation. And significantly, it is not Lamorak's prayer for forgiveness, but the coming together in combat, that brings this about. It manifests itself in the apparently neutral impulses of the body: Bellyaunce's withdrawal to sit "a lytyll uppon an hylle," Lamorak's throwing his shield behind his back as he goes over to him.[5] Hatred is not intellectually argued away, it simply exhausts itself – an exhaustion expressed in the laconic exchange of Lamorak's enquiry "what chere" and Bellyaunce's "Well." Lamorak's refusal to press his advantage seems secondary to this physical relinquishing of hostility, merely finding a verbal expression for what has already been accomplished. Emotional distance is eradicated by the bodily engagement that expresses it. The scene ends with a concentrated series of images of wholeness: the knights kiss each other; Lamorak will "nat departe" from Sir Bellyaunce until he is made whole; they swear "togydyrs" that they will never fight against each other. An agonising sense of distance from self and other suddenly yields, for no rationally accountable reason, to an intense wholeness, of which the earlier encounter between Lamorak and Lancelot turns out to have been an adumbration.

It seems to me that the emotional counterpointing of distance and wholeness in this narrative sequence is the *only* meaning that it holds. It is in the "choreography" of the narrative, so to speak, its separations and its unions, whether of combat or of recognition, that its significance is expressed. The attempt to interpret it as if it were a novel – to try to guess at the past history of Lamorak's relation to Bellyaunce, or to criticize his conduct according to everyday ethical standards – produces only banality or nonsense. How would one begin to define a man's moral responsibilities to someone who has killed his sons for his sake? The romance narrative is deliberately emptied of realistic detail, its landscape almost featureless, its personages without name or history, as a sign that its interest is not in the intricate texture of cause and effect, the human responsibility for the development of events. Rather we are to read the action itself as a kind of balletic realization of important aspects of experience, which express themselves as mood or tone rather than as a rationally structured account of the world. The narrative, rather than its characters, embodies an urge towards integration which is fulfilled only unpredictably and briefly. The

5 For the importance of the body in Malory, see "Knightly Combat," 239–42 above.

emotional satisfaction of Lamorak's reconciliation with Bellyaunce inevitably gives way to distance: "So sir Lamerok departed and wente to the courte of Arthur" (451/28).

The themes of distance and wholeness are thus constantly played out in the routine activities of the knightly life: adventure, quest, combat. But they are equally evident in other areas covered by the narrative as well. They are, for example, intricately entwined in the opening account of Arthur's birth and the gradual acknowledgment of his identity as king of England. Distance lies at the very heart of Arthur's begetting: his mother Igrayne is distanced from her own action by the fact that she does not know that she is lying with King Uther and not with her husband the duke of Tintagel. As a result, Arthur too is distanced from himself and his destiny by ignorance of his true identity. And this identity is first revealed, not by any means that grounds itself in an intimate connection with the self – a birthmark, say, a family resemblance, or even an old nurse to testify to an early personal history – but by a means totally extraneous to the self, the sword that must be pulled from the stone.[6] The sense of distance between inner self and the identity which is destiny is expressed with dazzling clarity in the image of the sword fixed in the stone that identifies the one who is "rightwys kynge borne of all Englond" (12/36). Birth creates the self, but also delivers it to an alien destiny that enfolds it in its own mysterious imperatives.

So, when Arthur pulls the sword out of the stone, what he experiences is not so much the discovery of identity as the loss of identity. His foster-father Sir Ector and his foster-brother Sir Kay kneel to him, and he asks in dismay why his own father and brother should do so. "Nay, nay, my lord Arthur, it is not so," says Sir Ector, "I was never your fader nor of your blood" (14/36–7), and he reveals the history of his fostering. "Thenne Arthur made grete doole whan he understood that syre Ector was not his fadir" (15/1–2). The discovery of one father is the loss of another. The same combination of discovery of self and alienation from self reappears when the identification is repeated later on (just as identified knights become anonymous again, so Arthur's identity has to be established several times). Despite the fact that Merlin has announced his parentage and the manner of his conception to the kings who withstand his rule, Arthur himself seems to be sufficiently ignorant of his family relationships to form a brief sexual liaison with Queen Morgawse, who is his sister on his mother's side – an act which repeats the distancing from self created by his mother's ignorance at the time of his own begetting. When Merlin reveals to Arthur that Igrayne is his mother, he simultaneously reveals that Arthur has

6 See "'Taking the Adventure,'" 251–2, and n.18, above.

committed incest with his sister and "gotyn a childe that shall destroy you and all the knyghtes of youre realme" (44/18–19). The future acquires the inevitability of the past, distancing Arthur from a voluntary role in the creation of his own destiny. The full revelation of his birth leads to Arthur's reunion with his mother, which is the immediate consequence: "And therewith kyng Arthure toke his modir, quene Igrayne, in hys armys and kyssed her, and eythir wepte uppon other" (46/12–14). Arthur's identity is affirmed and integrated into the network of human relationships represented by kindred. But this experience of wholeness is counteracted by the sense of distance from self in the unwitting incest with his sister, resulting in the son who is to destroy him. Distanced from knowledge of itself and its true relations with the world, the self begets its own destruction, so that the discovery of identity is simultaneously the discovery of alienation.

There is a similar counterpointing of distance and wholeness in the early adventures of Tristram. He is born out of distance – that is, his mother's vain pursuit of his lost father – and his birth is his mother's death; he is born into loss. Wounded in his first battle with Marhalt, he is told he will never "be hole" unless he goes to Ireland (384/10–13), the country that is the source of the poison on the spear that wounded him. His quest for bodily wholeness thus, paradoxically, creates distance: exile from his native land, and distance from himself in the suppression of his identity that is necessary in the court of King Angwyssh, brother-in-law of Marhalt. His true identity is discovered when Angwyssh's queen notices the notch on his sword, and matches it to the sword fragment she had removed from her dead brother's skull. The reuniting of the sword fittingly reunites Tristram with his true identity, but at the same time it creates a dramatic severing of relations between Tristram and the Irish court – when a sword is made whole, one might say, it best severs. Tristram's farewell scene with Isode expresses the poignancy of this severance, and it does so largely because of the distance between words and feeling which is created by their dignified formality.

> "A, jantyll knyght!" seyde La Beale Isode, "full wo I am of thy departynge, for I saw never man that ever I ought so good wyll to," and therewithall she wepte hertyly.
>
> "Madam," seyde sir Trystramys, "ye shall undirstonde that my name ys sir Trystrames de Lyones, gotyn of a kynge and borne of a quene. And I promyse you faythfully, I shall be all the dayes of my lyff your knyght."
>
> "Gramercy," seyde La Beale Isode, "and I promyse you there agaynste I shall nat be maryed this seven yerys but by your assente, and whom that ye woll I shall be maryed to hym and he woll have me, if ye woll consente thereto."
>
> And than sir Trystrames gaff hir a rynge and she gaff hym another, and therewith he departed and com into the courte amonge all the barownes. (392/6–19)

We can feel a kind of betrothal being entered into in this exchange, but it is an essential part of its distanced quality that the intentions and feelings of each of the participants are implied rather than stated. Like Tristram and Isode themselves, we have to imagine the feelings that words carefully hold off from direct expression.

It is often suggested that Malory was not deeply interested in the love relationship between man and woman, and that his representations of it are lacking in passion and feeling. The reason for this belief – which I think mistaken – is in my view precisely that the sense of distance, here as in the accounts of knightly exploits, is his greatest source of emotional power. Love is most powerfully expressed in longing, in the severance that measures the strength of the desire for its elimination. So the most powerfully moving scene in the Tristram Book is not the drinking of the love potion and the first consummation of Tristram and Isode's love; it is a recognition scene which results not in joyful reunion but in bitter separation.[7] This is the scene that concludes Tristram's madness, which was originally caused by his belief that Isode had been unfaithful to him. Tristram's madness distances him doubly – from Isode, and from himself. Eventually, after he has, even in his madness, rescued one of King Mark's knights from a giant, he is brought to the court, where he is treated well despite being still unrecognized, until one day Isode and Brangwayne her woman go to look at this curiosity.

> So whan the quene loked uppon sir Trystramys she was nat remembird of hym, but ever she seyde unto dame Brangwayn,
>
> "Mesemys I shuld have sene thys man here before in many placis."
>
> But as sone as sir Trystramys sye her he knew her well inowe, and than he turned away hys vysage and wepte.
>
> Than the quene had allwayes a lytyll brachett that sir Trystramys gaff hir the first tyme that ever she cam into Cornwayle, and never wold that brachet departe frome her but yf sir Trystram were nyghe thereas was La Beall Isode. And thys brachet was firste sente frome the kynges doughter of Fraunce unto sir Trystrams for grete love.
>
> And anone thys lytyll brachet felte a savoure of sir Trystram. He lepte uppon hym and lycked his learys and hys earys, and than he whyned and quested, and she smelled at hys feete and at hys hondis and on all the partyes of hys body that she myght com to.

---

7 For a sensitive discussion of this scene in the context of medieval recognition scenes, see Piero Boitani's essay, "A Spark of Love: Medieval Recognitions," in his *The Tragic and the Sublime in Medieval Literature* (Cambridge, 1989), 115–41, 296–8.

> "A, my lady!" seyde dame Brangwayne, "Alas! I se hit ys myne owne lorde sir Trystramys."
>
> And thereuppon La Beall Isode felle downe in a sowne and so lay a grete whyle. And whan she myght speke she seyde,
>
> "A, my lorde, sir Trystram! Blyssed be God ye have youre lyff! And now I am sure ye shall be discoverde by this lityll brachet, for she woll never leve you. And also I am sure, as sone as my lorde kynge Marke do know you he woll banysh you oute of the contrey of Cornwayle, othir ellis he woll destroy you. And therefore, for Goddys sake, myne owne lorde, graunte kynge Marke hys wyll, and than draw you unto the courte off kynge Arthure, for there ar ye beloved. And ever whan I may I shall sende unto you, and whan ye lyste ye may com unto me, and at all tymys early and late I woll be at youre commaundement, to lyve as poore a lyff as ever ded quyene or lady."
>
> "A, madame!" seyde sir Trystramys, "go frome me, for much angur and daunger have I assayed for your love."
>
> Than the quene departed, but the brachet wolde nat frome hym, and therewithall cam kynge Marke, and the brachet sate uppon hym and bayed at them all. (501/20–502/24)

The ensuing recognition of Tristram by King Mark and his knights is a mere anti-climax. It is the mutual recognition of Tristram and Isode which is important. Yet the poignancy of this recognition is created precisely by distance – first, by the "displacement" of the identification from Isode to Brangwayne, and second, by the way that Isode's motions towards union are resisted: Tristram turns his head away and weeps, he bids Isode to go from him, and she wordlessly obeys. There is none of the intimacy of a lovers' quarrel; a cold formality which accepts distance as somehow inevitable creates a sense of bleak finality. Yet as the distance of their farewell in Ireland paradoxically testifies to the power of the emotions it is holding at bay, so here the wholeness of their love persists through the words and actions that contradict it, movingly embodied in the little brachet that would "never depart" from Isode except to go to Sir Tristram. The physical identification of Tristram by the little dog's whining and "questing," licking and smelling "all the partyes of hys body that she myght com to," is a displaced expression of the reunion that does not take place; it has nothing to do with sexual delight, it simply expresses identity as first and last a bodily truth, something that persists through spiritual or emotional change. And it is this *bodily* truth that holds Tristram and Isode together across the abyss of their separation; just as a note of distance so often sounds in the very heart of a scene of reunion and reconciliation, so in this moment of severance there is a stubborn survival of wholeness: "but the brachet wolde nat frome hym, and therewithall cam kynge Marke, and the brachet sate uppon hym and bayed at them all." Isode leaves, but the brachet is the part of her that stays and bays at them all.

Distance is likewise the source of emotional power in Malory's representation of the relationship between Lancelot and Guinevere. The most moving mutual expression of their love is their solemn leave-taking of each other as Mordred and Aggravain hammer at the queen's chamber door and they realize that "the day ys come that oure love muste departe" (1166/30). The "departure" is repeated after the destruction of the Round Table, when Guinevere declares her intention of entering the religious life, and Lancelot vows to do the same; it is intensified by Guinevere's refusal of Lancelot's request for a last kiss. Six years later, Lancelot is warned in a vision of Guinevere's approaching death, and he rides to the nunnery at Amesbury to find that she has died half an hour before, knowing of his imminent arrival, and yet constantly praying "I beseche Almyghty God that I may never have power to see syr Launcelot with my worldly eyen!" (1255/36–7). Her prayer appears to be the most absolute repudiation possible of her love for Lancelot, a fervent insistence on severance. And yet this very insistence is an oblique testimony to the undiminished power of her feelings: were she to set eyes on Lancelot again, it suggests, her long dedication to religion would crumble in an instant.[8] It is the need to hold Lancelot at a distance that expresses the power of her love.

Love and combat are thus linked by the themes of distance and wholeness. The importance of these themes in the conclusion to the whole work, the final fragmentation of the wholeness represented by the Round Table, is self-evident. Rather than turning to this part of Malory's work, therefore, I should like to devote my remaining time to the *Tale of the Sankgreal*. Despite the frequent critical assumption that the Grail Quest marks the introduction of a radical change in the nature of adventure and the knight's relation to it, if we examine the themes of distance and wholeness in the tale, we shall find that on the contrary it simply intensifies and deepens these themes by giving them a religious dimension.

This is apparent from the very beginning. The Tale opens with the assembly of the Round Table at Camelot for the feast of Pentecost, whence Lancelot is summoned away by a damsel who takes him to an abbey where he finds his two cousins, Bors and Lionel. The nuns then bring in Sir Galahad, who is named to us but not to Lancelot, and ask Lancelot to make him knight (853–4). This is the first meeting between father and son, but there is no recognition between them.

8 Cf. Larry D. Benson, *Malory's Morte Darthur* (Cambridge, MA, 1976), 242: "she still loves him, knows the power of her love, and therefore dares not look upon him."

Galahad was begotten when Lancelot lay with Elaine under the illusion that she was Guinevere – yet another procreative act in which one of the participants is "distanced" from his own action by ignorance of what he is doing. This meeting of father and son adumbrates wholeness, but maintains distance in the lack of mutual acknowledgment. It is also significant that it stands in oblique relation to the assembly of the Round Table at Camelot; "we wende to have founde you to-morne at Camelot," say Bors and Lionel to Lancelot (854/5–6), and Galahad himself is eventually to appear there too. The meeting of Lancelot and his kin, and Galahad in particular, is heavy with the suggestion of a central significance, yet it does not form part of the central narrative, which we take to be located with the main body of knights assembled at Camelot; it is marginalized, located away from the public centre of action, retaining its character as a separate incident that has yet to find its relation to the main narrative.

The return to Camelot strengthens the notes of wholeness sounded in this scene. King Arthur rejoices that Lancelot and his cousins have returned "hole and sounde" (855/34). The "felyship" of the Round Table is completed – made whole – by the arrival of Galahad to take the place miraculously marked out for him by the appearance of his name on the Siege Perilous, the last seat to remain empty. The preliminary inscription which proclaims the date when the seat is to be "fulfylled" is covered with a cloth of silk, which is later removed to reveal a new inscription with Galahad's name (855/14, 860/11). The act of uncovering emblematizes the removal of distance. Wholeness is also emblematized in the acquisition of a sword to fit Galahad's empty scabbard; it is, as Galahad explains, the sword of Balin, fixed in a stone by Merlin and left to float down the river to Camelot – an image of fixity within flux, of destiny borne on the waves of chance (856, 862–3). The river of the narrative thus links Balin with Galahad, bridging the distance between past and present. Galahad's words extend this process of "making whole" into the future, as he prophesies that it is he who will heal King Pelles of the wound given him by Balin, "the whych ys nat yett hole" (863/8).[9]

When the Grail finally appears, it attracts to itself these motions towards wholeness. It marks the consummation of the Round Table, its final meeting "holé togydirs" (864/7–12) – the phrase which is repeated no fewer than four times in the two sentences in which Arthur expresses his desire to see the Round Table joust one last time in celebration of its own completeness.[10] The

9 In contrast, anyone who tries to draw the sword and fails "shall resseyve a wounde by that swerde that he shall nat be longe hole afftir," as Lancelot explains (856/24–5).

10 See the fine discussion of this passage, and the similarly poignant celebration of wholeness in the Healing of Sir Urry, in Mark Lambert, *Malory: Style and Vision in Le Morte Darthur* (New Haven, CT, 1975), 64–5.

Grail satisfies the knights by giving them what food and drink they love best in the world; but it leaves them unsatisfied in that its covering of white samite still holds them at a distance.

> "Now," seyde sir Gawayne, "we have bene servyd thys day of what metys and drynkes we thought on. But one thyng begyled us, that we myght nat se the Holy Grayle: hit was so preciously coverde. Wherefore I woll make here a vow that to-morne, withoute longer abydynge, I shall laboure in the queste of the Sankgreall, and that I shall holde me oute a twelve-month and a day or more if nede be, and never shall I returne unto the courte agayne tylle I have sene hit more opynly than hit hath bene shewed here." (866/3–11)

This quest, that is, resembles other quests in expressing a desire to close the distance between self and adventure, to get closer to it in the simplest physical sense. This physical dimension is not discarded in the pursuit of spiritual advancement; it remains the vehicle through which spiritual advancement is expressed. The Grail Quest also resembles other quests in that this desire to close the distance between self and adventure immediately opens up a distance elsewhere, as Arthur's lamentation over this major "departure" makes clear.

> "Alas!" seyde kynge Arthure unto sir Gawayne, "ye have nygh slayne me for the avow that ye have made, for thorow you ye have berauffte me the fayryst and the trewyst of knyghthode that ever was sene togydir in ony realme of the worlde. For whan they departe frome hense I am sure they all shall never mete more togydir in thys worlde, for they shall dye many in the queste. And so hit forthynkith me nat a litill, for I have loved them as well as my lyff. Wherefore hit shall greve me ryght sore, the departicion of thys felyship, for I have had an olde custom to have hem in my felyship."
>
> And therewith the teerys felle in his yen, and than he seyde,
>
> "Sir Gawayne, Gawayne! Ye have sette me in grete sorow, for I have grete doute that my trew felyship shall never mete here more agayne." (866/19–867/8)

The word "depart" repeats itself with an increasing sense of foreboding throughout the rest of this section of the narrative, signalling the approach of a separation of more than routine importance.[11]

---

11 "And than they put on their helmys and departed and recommaunded them all hole unto the kynge and quene. And there was wepyng and grete sorow.

Than the quene departed into the chambir and holde hir there, that no man shold perceyve hir grete sorowys ...

Chastity assumes so much importance in the Grail Quest because it is an image of bodily wholeness. Galahad, his virginal intactness unbroken, is the embodiment of wholeness; he is the mender of swords and the healer of wounds. In contrast, the Grail Quest reveals Lancelot as fatally fragmented; unlike the author of the French *Queste*, Malory is not primarily concerned to stress the corruption of the sins of the flesh, but to show Lancelot, like Balin, confronted by an irreconcilable contradiction between two versions of his identity. This contradiction first comes to the fore in the aftermath of Lancelot's half-sleeping, half-waking vision of a sick knight being healed by the Grail – a vision of wholeness from which Lancelot is, significantly, distanced by his half-sleeping state. On waking, he hears a voice which orders him to leave, calling him "more harder than ys the stone, and more bitter than ys the woode, and more naked and barer than ys the lyeff of the fygge-tre" (895/25–7). Lamenting his loss of good fortune, Lancelot goes to a hermit and asks him to hear his confession. In Malory's source, the French *Queste del Saint Graal*, the hermit lectures Lancelot at length, humbling him by relating the parable of the talents to show him that the gifts God has so lavishly bestowed on him will be his condemnation unless he uses them in God's service.[12] Malory drastically shortens the hermit's speech to the point where the emphasis on Lancelot's knightly excellence overshadows the reference to his sinfulness.

> "Sir," seyde the ermyte, "ye ought to thanke God more than ony knyght lyvynge, for He hath caused you to have more worldly worship than ony knyght that ys now lyvynge. And for youre presumpcion to take uppon you in dedely synne for to be in Hys presence, where Hys fleyssh and Hys blood was, which caused you ye myght nat se hyt with youre worldely yen, for He woll nat appere where such synners bene but if hit be unto their grete hurte other unto their shame. And there is no knyght now lyvynge that ought to yelde God so grete thanke os ye, for He hath

---

Ryght so departed sir Launcelot and founde hys felyship that abode hys commyng, and than they toke their horsys and rode thorow the strete of Camelot. And there was wepyng of ryche and poore, and the kynge turned away and myght nat speke for wepyng.

So within a whyle they rode all togydirs tyll that they com to a cité, and a castell that hyght Vagon ...

And so on the morne they were all accorded that they sholde departe everych from othir. And on the morne they departed with wepyng chere, and than every knyght toke the way that hym lyked beste." (872/3–30)

12 See *La Queste del Saint Graal*, ed. Albert Pauphilet, Classiques Français du Moyen Âge (Paris, 1978), 63–71. For a translation, see *The Quest of the Holy Grail*, trans. P.M. Matarasso (Harmondsworth, 1969), 87–94.

yevyn you beauté, bownté, semelynes, and grete strengthe over all other knyghtes. And therefore ye ar the more beholdyn unto God than ony other man to love Hym and drede Hym, for youre strengthe and your manhode woll litill avayle you and God be agaynste you." (896/29–897/7)

Lancelot's sinfulness is not eliminated from the scene – the hermit's subsequent exposition of the meaning of the condemnatory voice makes it plain – but the greater simplicity of the conversation in Malory's version leaves this sinfulness in starker contrast to the emphasis on Lancelot's peerless nobility.[13] The impression is one of paradox rather than of humiliating qualification. There is a similar sense of paradox in another hermit's speech a bit later on: the hermit Nacien is explaining to Gawain that he will never succeed in the Grail Quest because he is "an untrew knyght and a grete murtherar" (948/19), and he goes on to draw a contrast with Sir Lancelot, which is Malory's own addition to the French source.

"For I dare sey, as synfull as ever sir Launcelot hath byn, sith that he wente into the queste of the Sankgreal he slew never man nother nought shall, tylle that he com to Camelot agayne; for he hath takyn upon hym to forsake synne. And ne were that he ys nat stable, but by hys thoughte he ys lyckly to turne agayne, he sholde be nexte to encheve hit sauff sir Galahad, hys sonne; but God knowith hys thought and hys unstableness. And yett shall he dye ryght an holy man, and no doute he hath no felow of none erthly synfull man lyvyng." (948/20–9)

Malory's paratactic style creates a sense of perpetual oscillation back and forth in this description of Sir Lancelot; the contradictions are not resolved into a

13 Cf. Larry Benson's comments on the changes Malory makes to his source, "considerably softening the effect of Lancelot's failure" (*Malory's Morte Darthur*, 218). Stephen C.B. Atkinson has discussed in detail Malory's "technique of heightening contrasts" in the portrayal of Lancelot in the Tale of the Sankgreal, but whereas he sees Malory's aim as "balance," I see it as a tragic contradiction ("Malory's Lancelot and the Quest of the Grail," in *Studies in Malory*, ed. James W. Spisak [Kalamazoo, MI, 1985], 129–52). Robert L. Kelly is nearer to my own view in concluding that "Malory leaves us with two Lancelots"; however he sees this as due to Malory's desire to preserve the "admirable Lancelot" for didactic purposes, and goes on to claim that this weakens the tragic implications of Malory's work by rupturing the link between character and action ("Wounds, Healing and Knighthood in Malory's Tale of Lancelot and Guenevere," in Spisak, *Studies in Malory*, 173–97, at 191–2). I cannot follow Kelly's logic here: in my view, it is precisely the irreparable split between essence and action in Malory's Lancelot that gives the narrative its tragic overtones, and in contrast, it is Tennyson's picture of Lancelot as corrupted by the insidious effects of adultery, which Kelly thinks to be truly tragic, that seems to me to merit the description of "didactic."

final synthesis, but are left confronting each other, the shifts between them becoming in themselves a sign of "unstableness."

Gawain's response to Nacien's revelation of his self is evasion: not staying to hear his counsel, he rides off after his fellow Sir Ector. In contrast, Lancelot's response is acceptance of the contradiction between his inner qualities and his relationship with Guinevere, an acceptance which realises itself in his confession. Distance and wholeness are complexly intertwined in this confession. The fragmentation of self and action is revealed, but also eliminated by being openly avowed; the self is recreated as a unity by the internal acceptance and external acknowledgment of its own contradictions. Lancelot's fragmentation is the "adventure" that he must "take" in the Grail Quest, just as the knight habitually "takes the adventure" in the sphere of physical combat. At the same time, Lancelot's confession creates another kind of distance, between himself and his love for Guinevere. But this repudiation of his past life nevertheless still keeps faith with its truest values; wholeness persists through the severance. In the French *Queste*, Lancelot bluntly avows "I have sinned unto death with my lady, she whom I have loved all my life, Queen Guinevere, the wife of King Arthur" – a confession whose explicit directness seems crudely to offer up Guinevere as a holocaust on the altar of Lancelot's new-found piety.[14] Malory's Lancelot keeps faith with his past self by the obliquity with which he expresses himself: "And than he tolde there the good man all hys lyff, and how he had loved a quene unmesurabely and oute of mesure longe" (897/15–16). The distant phrasing – "a quene" – leaves the feeling between Lancelot and Guinevere whole, intact, unviolated by direct revelation. It is in this delicate marginalization of Guinevere, as not to be degraded by his own acknowledgment of sinfulness, that we can feel the greater nobility of Malory's Lancelot over his French original.

Lancelot's fragmentation, then, is contrasted with Galahad's wholeness. And yet it is this very fragmentation that *results* in Galahad's wholeness. Lancelot is never more distanced from himself than in the begetting of Galahad – not only because this action represents the adultery that contaminates bodily wholeness, but also because he unknowingly belies himself by lying with Elaine in the belief that she is Guinevere. As the random separations of knightly adventure suddenly yield climactic moments of union, so Lancelot's distanced self paradoxically brings forth Galahad's perfect wholeness of being. The mysterious ties of blood assert a linkage between them which denies the divergence that

14 Ed. Pauphilet, 66: "Sire, fet Lancelot, il est einsi que je sui morz de pechié d'une moie dame que je ai amee toute ma vie, et ce est la reine Guenievre, la fame le roi Artus." The translation quoted in my text is Matarasso's, 89.

their different destinies in the Grail Quest create. So it is that the recognition of their blood relationship forms the climax of Lancelot's quest, bestowing the experience of wholeness that he is denied from the Grail itself. This substitution of Galahad for the Grail is foreshadowed at the very opening of the quest, when Galahad promises Guinevere that "he that ys my fadir shall be knowyn opynly and all betymys" (870/3–4). Coming as this does immediately after Gawain's vow to pursue the Grail in order to see it "more opynly" (866/9–10), these words make the open acknowledgment of Lancelot's relation to Galahad a parallel goal for the quest to achieve.

The mutual recognition of father and son eventually arrives after the month that Lancelot spends in the Grail ship with the dead body of Perceval's sister. In the French *Queste*, the boat has come to shore at a point where a forest runs down to the sea. Lancelot hears the noise of a knight riding through the trees; the knight rides up to the ship, boards it, is greeted by Lancelot, and the revelation of identity on both sides follows as a matter of course.[15] Malory makes a very small but very telling change to this simple narrative: he takes Lancelot *off the ship* before Galahad arrives. "And so on a nyght he wente to play hym by the watirs syde, for he was somwhat wery of the shippe" (1011/31–1012/1). He thus watches Galahad riding up to the ship from the sidelines, as it were; he is placed in a tangential relation to Galahad's goal. The direct trajectory of the French is deflected into obliquity.

> And than he lystened and herde an hors com and one rydyng uppon hym, and whan he cam nyghe hym semed a knyght, and so he late hym passe and wente thereas the ship was. And there he alyght and toke the sadyll and the brydill, and put the horse frome hym, and so wente into the shyppe. (1012/1–6)

The choreography of this scene is all-important, because it introduces the threat of distance. In the quest of the white hart, which I mentioned at the opening of this lecture, Pellinore refuses a damsel's request to turn aside from his quest to aid a wounded knight she holds in her arms; the result is that the knight dies and the lady kills herself from grief, so that when on his return to the court Pellinore rides past the spot again he finds two dead bodies, eaten by wild animals (114,118–19). Merlin then reveals that the lady was his own daughter (119). In adhering to the direct trajectory of his quest, Pellinore bypasses the fulfilment of a personal destiny; he misses an all-important moment of recognition, a wholeness that would counterbalance the lady's loss of her

15 Ed. Pauphilet, 250; trans. Matarasso, 257.

knight. In removing Lancelot from the Grail ship when Galahad arrives at it, I think Malory creates the momentary fear that something like this is about to happen again. Lancelot will remain a spectator on the sidelines; the two knights will simply miss each other. "And so he late hym passe ..." It seems that their different paths will never meet; the moment of confrontation and recognition will never come. But the fear is only momentary; distance is suddenly eradicated, obliquity effortlessly transforms itself into full engagement.

> And than sir Launcelot dressed hym unto the shippe and seyde, "Sir, ye be wellcom!"
>
> And he answerd, and salewed hym agayne and seyde, "Sir, what ys youre name? For much my herte gevith unto you."
>
> "Truly," seyde he, "my name ys sir Launcelot du Lake."
>
> "Sir," seyde he, "than be ye wellcom! For ye were the begynner of me in thys worlde."
>
> "A, sir, ar ye sir Galahad?"
>
> "Ye, forsothe."
>
> And so he kneled downe and askyd hym hys blyssynge. And aftir that toke of his helme and kyssed hym, and there was grete joy betwyxte them, for no tunge can telle what joy was betwyxte them. (1012/7–21)

The emotional power of this reunion comes from the way that it reverses the preceding pull towards distance with the sudden force of a recoil. With the same spontaneous yielding that makes the sword in the stone come with ease to the one who is destined to wield it, yet resist all efforts from those who are not, the distance created by anonymity, by the mysterious process of begetting, by disparity of spiritual state, by physical separation, suddenly and inexplicably gives way to the fulfilment of a personal destiny. Past and future meet and acknowledge the ties that hold them together; Lancelot's fragmented destiny is submerged in the wholeness of union with the son it has created.

II. The Distance of Narrative

In the first part of this essay I talked about distance as a narrative subject – that is, as an experience apprehended by the actors in the narrative and thus by its readers. But of course this sense of distance almost inevitably mediates itself through the mode of the narrative as much as through its content. Anonymity, for example, is not only a fact of knightly life, but a narratorial choice; whenever Malory writes "a knight," "a damsel," instead of writing "Lancelot" or "Pellinore's daughter," his narrative is creating or maintaining a distance between us and full knowledge of the world it reflects to us. And since the world of romance is so much a fictional artefact, something separate from any identifiable counterpart in reality, its mode becomes almost identical with its content; the laws of the romance world are the laws of its narrative. I want now to focus on distance as a principle of this narrative mode, although the distinction between mode and subject will often prove a rather artificial one.

The romance mode is characteristically episodic. Its different incidents are not linked together with the developmental logic of a plot; the story seems to be always "stopping and starting," reaching a halt on one line of action and starting again with another. This is a characteristic that can be manipulated so as to yield a sense of distance. The account of Arthur's incest with Morgawse, which I mentioned earlier, offers a good example. Arthur lies with Morgawse in ignorance that she is his sister; Merlin reveals to him the full meaning of his action. But the act is not immediately followed by the revelation of its meaning; a puzzlingly irrelevant episode intrudes between the two. First of all, Arthur has a dream that his land is inhabited by griffins and serpents, which he eventually slays. He gets up, still oppressed by his dream, and decides to go hunting to shake off this sense of oppression (41). We expect that somehow in the forest he will discover the truth of his relation with Morgawse – that what happens there will connect with the portentous event that still awaits his full recognition. What actually happens has nothing to do with the incest, and even little to do with Arthur. Arthur's horse drops dead from overexertion, and he is sitting by a spring waiting for a squire to bring him another, when an extraordinary beast, whose belly makes a noise like the barking of thirty pairs of hounds, comes to drink at the spring and then departs. Arthur marvels, but does not move; his non-involvement is underlined by the fact that he then falls asleep (42). A knight arrives, asks him if he has seen the strange beast, and as Arthur's squire arrives with a fresh horse for him, the knight seizes it and rides off, having violently rejected Arthur's offer to pursue the beast himself; it is a task, he says, reserved for himself and his near kindred (42–3). The knight departs, and immediately, as if somehow prompted by this episode, Merlin arrives, disguised as a fourteen-year-old child, and tells Arthur that he was begotten by King Uther on Igrayne. Arthur angrily refuses to believe him; Merlin leaves, and reappears as an eighty-year-old man who tells him that he has lain with his sister and begotten a child who will destroy him and all the knights of his realm (43–4).

The episode of the Questing Beast and the knight who pursues it (King Pellinore, as we, but not Arthur, are allowed to know) holds the two halves of the incest story apart, distancing the act itself from Merlin's revelation of its nature. Despite its apparent irrelevance to the incest story, it is a vital element in creating the sense of alienation from self that Merlin's revelation brings about.

Because what is striking about it is the way it displaces Arthur from a central role in the narrative; first reduced to a passive spectator of the marvellous beast, he is even further marginalized by Pellinore's seizure of his horse and refusal to allow him any part in the action. He is distanced from the adventure as the knights are distanced from the adventure of the white hart at his wedding feast, unable either to fathom its meaning or to involve himself in it through physical action. And it is this sense of being marginalized in relation to one's own story that carries through to colour Merlin's revelation of incest and final destruction with a strange sense of detachment from an inevitable destiny. Arthur's reaction concerns not the incest or the child he has begotten, but first of all Merlin himself ("What ar ye ... that telle me thys tydingis?": 44/20–21); Merlin's disguise emblematizes the way Arthur is placed at one remove from the truths of his own life. His next concern is with the nature of his future death ("I mervayle muche of thy wordis that I mon dye in batayle": 44/24–5). The revelatory moment is not a devastating Oedipal penetration to a central core of truth, but the detached contemplation of a self who remains strangely other. As a fourteen-year old-child, Merlin speaks for the past; as an eighty-year-old man, he speaks for the future. The instantaneous and enigmatic transformation from one to the other leaves the intervening period, which might create a meaningful transition from the past to the future, as an impenetrable blank.

The episodic quality of romance is one way in which a sense of distance can be created. Other types of narrative distancing were also part of Malory's inheritance from the romance genre. I want to illustrate one of them from the work of Chrétien de Troyes, to whose brilliant originality we owe the creation of so many of the familiar features of the romance world. At the opening of Chrétien's *Chevalier de la Charrete*, a strange knight challenges Arthur to send his queen, guarded by one of his knights, to a neighbouring wood. If the queen's escort can fend off the stranger's attack, he promises to release the Round Table knights he holds prisoner. Kay tricks Arthur into allowing him to be Guinevere's escort, and Gawain, who knows Kay is not equal to the task, persuades Arthur and the court that they should ride after them, to see what happens. It is in the next part of the narrative that we can feel distancing beginning to effect itself.

> And as they were thus approaching the forest, they saw come out of it Kay's horse, which they recognised, and they saw that both the reins of the bridle were broken. The horse had no rider, and the stirrup-leathers were stained with blood, and the saddle-bow was broken and damaged. There was no one who did not feel chagrin at this, and each one nudged the other. My lord Gawain was riding far ahead of the company, and it was not long before he saw a knight slowly making his way on a horse that was sore and tired, panting and covered with sweat. The knight first

> greeted my lord Gawain, and then Sir Gawain did the same to him. And the knight, who recognised my lord Gawain, stopped, and said: "Sir, do you not see how my horse is covered in sweat and of no more use? And I suppose that these two horses are yours; now I would beg you, on the understanding that I would reward you for the service and the favour, to give me either as a loan or a gift whichever you like." And he replied: "Choose whichever of the two you like." Then he, being in great need, did not pick out the better, the more handsome, or the larger, but mounted immediately on the one he found nearest to him and put him to the gallop. And the other [horse] which he had left behind fell dead, for he had worked him and ridden him so hard that day. The knight without delay went off through the forest in his armour, and my lord Gawain followed after him in hot pursuit, all the way down to the bottom of a hill. And when he had gone a long way, he found the horse he had given the knight lying dead, and he saw marks of the trampling of horses, and a lot of debris of shields and lances all around – it seemed to him that there had been a great combat between several knights, and he was very sorry and displeased not to have been there. He did not pause there, but went on at great speed until he saw the knight all alone on foot, fully armed, with his helmet laced on, his shield round his neck, and his sword girt round him – he had come up with a cart.[16]

By the end of this account, I think the reader has begun to feel that Gawain is not so much in pursuit of the queen as in pursuit of the story. It all seems to be happening somewhere else. All he encounters is what we might call the residue of narrative – the riderless horse, the trampled clearing, the broken shields and lances. And then there is the other knight, who seems to have entered the quest ahead of everybody else; despite the fact that the Arthurian court set out without delay in pursuit of the queen, and that Gawain rides at great speed, this knight has already been at it long and hard enough to have ridden one horse to death. This knight displaces Gawain from the narrative as Pellinore displaces Arthur in the Questing Beast episode; he takes Gawain's horse and rides ahead of him to become – presumably – part of the unseen narrative whose trail of wreckage Gawain finds himself following. The knight replaces Guinevere as the goal of Gawain's pursuit; coming up with him creates a temporary sense of achievement.

16 *Le chevalier de la charrete*, ed. Mario Roques, Classiques Français du Moyen Âge (Paris, 1968), 257–320. Translations are available in *Chretien de Troyes: Arthurian Romances*, trans. D.D.R. Owen (London, 1987), and *Chretien de Troyes: Arthurian Romances*, trans. William W. Kibler and Carleton W. Carroll (London, 1991); the translation in the text is my own.

Of course it could be said of this sequence that distance is a matter of its subject rather than its mode; it is not that the narrative is being pursued, it is that it is a narrative of pursuit. Narrative proximity to Gawain is what is important, not narrative distance from Guinevere and whatever it is that is going on in the wake of her abduction. But here again we are conscious of a narratorial choice conditioning our relation to the narrative – the choice that leads to the relation of Guinevere's abduction from this particular standpoint rather than from the point of view of the abducted queen herself, say, or even from the point of view of this mysterious knight. When the author of the prose *Lancelot* produced his version of this narrative sequence, he clearly found the distanced manner of the narration puzzling and unsatisfactory, for he turned it completely inside out, relating directly the events that Chrétien leaves us to guess at.[17] The narrative sticks with Kay and Guinevere as they leave the court; it relates their meeting with Meleagant, the arrival of "an armed knight" who is immediately named as Lancelot, Kay's unsuccessful combat with Meleagant, Lancelot's ensuing battle with Meleagant and his knights, and Gawain's encounter with Lancelot (who, as in Chrétien, recognizes Gawain, although Gawain does not recognize him). Then off the narrative goes with Lancelot in pursuit of Meleagant, relating the second great battle between them, in which Meleagant's men kill the horse Lancelot has taken from Gawain (thus accounting for Gawain's finding it dead), and finally Lancelot's encounter with the cart. The author obviously failed to see that the originality and interest of Chrétien's narrative lies precisely in the way that it deliberately stands off from direct relation of the very adventure that provides its motive force. The structure of the narrative is designed to make us feel a gradual displacement from what we apprehend as the centre of events. The entry of the unnamed knight increases this sense of displacement; what we had taken to be the only line of narrative turns out to be disconcertingly secondary. And his introduction also means that instead of following the quest with Gawain, a knight whose identity and whose relation to events are familiar to us, we find ourselves following the fortunes of a knight whose identity and involvement remain obscure; whatever our suspicions; he remains "the knight of the cart" until fully half the romance is over. His relation to the already enigmatic story is itself an enigma; the reader has no more sense of intimacy with the pursuer than with what is being pursued.

17 *Lancelot*, ed. Alexandre Micha, Textes Littéraires Français, 9 vols (Paris, 1978–83), 2:7–11 (XXXVI.13–23); trans. in *Lancelot-Grail. The Old French Arthurian Vulgate and Post-Vulgate in Translation*, ed. Norris J. Lacy, vol. 3 (New York, 1995), 5–6. Malory's version of the Knight of the Cart episode takes a different form – Meleagant simply kidnaps Guinevere while she is out riding, and Gawain is not involved (1121–3) – so that direct comparison cannot be made.

This brilliantly original sequence gives us the sense of encountering the residue of narrative, of coming in in the middle of a story that has been going on for some time, or indeed is virtually over. And in this respect it is akin to many of the favourite motifs of romance. There is, for example, the figure of the grieving girl who holds a dead knight in her arms, first encountered by Chrétien's Perceval the morning after his night at the Grail castle.[18] It is fitting that it is she who reveals to Perceval his unsuspected failure of the previous night in not questioning his host about the Grail procession as it passed before him, and likewise his sin in leaving his mother to die of grief at his departure; the dead knight she cradles in her arms confronts him with a narrative finality, the sense of encountering an unknown storial past frozen in its conclusion, mirroring his own confrontation with a retrospective and unalterable guilt which has no history to it, as it were, in terms of his own sense of his experience. The romance hero, one might say, is characteristically belated. He pursues events rather than driving them before him; he enters a narrative late in its development and never fully in possession of its beginnings and its meaning.

Malory's *Morte d'Arthur* is fully in line with the romance tradition initiated by Chrétien in these features and the narrative distancing they create. His landscape is littered with what I have called the residue of narrative – tombs, wounded knights, grieving women – bearing witness to a vanished story. The dead body of Perceval's sister adrift in the Grail ship (1011), Elaine of Ascolat floating in her barge down to Camelot (1095–6), the dead knight in a rich vessel found by Sir Tristram on "Humbir banke" (700/23), embody the residue of an antecedent narrative which is recorded on the letters they each carry in their hand. And as in Chrétien, so in Malory the knight often seems to be pursuing an infinitely receding narrative. Some pages of the Tristram Book will serve as a good example of both these things. Tristram comes upon nine knights engaged in battle with but a single opponent (560). He watches them fight for a while, and then, feeling sympathy with the solitary combatant, attempts to persuade his nine opponents to desist. They refuse to do so, and so Tristram himself enters the battle and puts them to flight. He returns to the knight he has rescued, and finds to his consternation that it is Sir Palomides, his enemy; he insists that Palomides should do battle with him, but is persuaded to delay the encounter until Palomides's wounds have healed (561–2). Tristram next asks why the nine knights had set upon Palomides. Palomides explains that he had come upon a lady weeping by the side of a dead knight, who had, she said, been

18 *Le Roman de Perceval*, ed. Keith Busby (Tübingen, 1993), 3422–611. For translations, see n. 16 above.

killed by Sir Brewnys Saunze Pité. Palomides had then undertaken to act as her protector until she had buried her husband, and as a result was attacked by Sir Brewnys and his men while riding past his castle (562). The narrative here pulls us steadily backward: drawn into an already ongoing sequence of events by his intervention on Sir Palomides's behalf, Tristram seeks for its source, which turns out to be Palomides's encounter with the residue of another narrative – the dead knight and the lady – into which Palomides likewise has let himself be drawn.

Tristram and Palomides next ride on together, and come upon a "fayre knyght" sleeping under a tree, fully armed, except that his helmet lies under his head (563/9). They awaken him roughly with the butt of Tristram's spear, and he responds by wordlessly mounting his horse and hurling both of them from their saddles with his spear, then riding off through the forest (563). Tristram resolves to ride in pursuit of him, and so takes leave of Palomides, admonishing him to appear at the appointed day for their battle. Riding in pursuit of the knight, Tristram finds yet another lady by the dead body of her husband, who has been slain by the stranger knight, because, the stranger says, he hates all those who belong to King Arthur's court (564). Continuing his pursuit, Tristram two days later comes upon Sir Gawain and Sir Bleoberys, both "sore wounded" (564/33). They confirm that they too are victims of the stranger knight, who may be known by the covered shield he bears (564–5). Tristram's next encounter is with Sir Kay and Sir Dinadan, who, on learning the object of his pursuit, inform him that they encountered the knight he is seeking in their lodging-place of the previous night, where he spoke ill of King Arthur and Queen Guinevere. Provoked by this slander, they had engaged him in battle that morning, but he had struck Kay from his horse and destroyed Dinadan's will to fight (565–6).

Tristram's pursuit of the stranger knight is thus a recuperation of other narratives; he tracks the marks of the stranger's passing without, apparently, gaining any ground on his receding goal. Like Chrétien's Gawain in pursuit of Guinevere, he finds a first-hand experience turning into a second-hand experience. His direct contact with the stranger in the initial joust is replaced by a mere recital of the stranger's jousts with others; the "real" story is always just out of his grasp. Yet he finally catches up with it just as it seems to have eluded him entirely. The pursuit seems to have petered out; Tristram finds a priory in a forest and stays there for six days, during which time he sends his squire Gouvernayle to fetch new armour (566). Eventually he sets out for his appointed battle with Sir Palomides, coping with a skirmish with Sir Sagramour and Sir Dodynas on the way (566–8). He arrives at the agreed rendezvous, which is itself the residue of a narrative, the marble tomb made by Merlin to commemorate the death of Launceor at the hands of Balin, and the subsequent suicide of Launceor's lady,

Columbe. Malory explicitly reminds us of this episode in the Tale of Balin, and likewise of Merlin's prophecy that this same spot will be the scene of a battle between "two the beste knyghtes that ever were in kynge Arthurs dayes, and two of the beste loveres" (568/19–20). Looking about him for Sir Palomides, Tristram sees a knight arrayed in white, carrying a covered shield, who greets him with the words "Ye be wellcom, sir knyght, and well and trewly have ye holdyn your promyse" – words which make it natural to assume that this is Sir Palomides (568/26–7). The battle duly commences and proves to be a mighty one – so mighty that doubts begin to creep in as to whether this is not a stronger knight than Palomides. Eventually, the blood-covered combatants pause to ask each other's names, and it is revealed that Tristram's opponent is not Sir Palomides but Sir Lancelot.

> "Fayre knyght, my name is sir Launcelot du Lake."
> "Alas!" seyde sir Trystram, "what have I done! For ye ar the man in the worlde that I love beste."
> "Now, fayre knyght," seyde sir Launcelot, "telle me your name."
> "Truly, sir, I hyght sir Trystram de Lyones."
> "A, Jesu!" seyde sir Launcelot, "what aventure is befall me!"
> And therwyth sir Launcelot kneled adowne and yeldid hym up his swerde. And therewithall sir Trystram kneled adowne and yeldid hym up his swerde, and so aythir gaff other the gre. And than they bothe forthwithall went to the stone and set hem downe uppon hit and toke of their helmys to keele them, and aythir kyste other an hondred tymes.
>
> (569/24–570/2)

The combat between Balin and the man he loves most, his brother Balan, repeats itself in the battle between Tristram and Lancelot. But here, instead of resulting in the tragic mutual slaying of brother by brother, the combat issues in joyful reconciliation, sealed by the ensuing installation of Sir Tristram as a knight of the Round Table (572). Once again the aimless wanderings of the narrative unpredictably arrive at a conclusion, a point of finality. And this conclusion resolves the identity of the stranger knight with the covered shield, who turns out to have been Sir Lancelot, attacking Round Table knights and speaking ill of Arthur and Guinevere in order to disguise his true identity (571). In the French prose *Tristan*, the stranger knight remains anonymous; Tristan loses track of him and he simply disappears from the narrative.[19] Vinaver supposes

19 See *Le Roman de Tristan en prose*, general ed. Philippe Ménard, vol. 3, ed. Gilles Roussineau (Geneva, 1991), 245–68 (sections 212–39).

that Malory was uneasy with this unresolved mystery, and therefore tidied up the loose end by identifying the stranger knight with Sir Lancelot. But in removing one enigma – the knight's identity – Malory creates another – the contradiction between Lancelot's actions and his true self, which Vinaver can only say he must have thought "the lesser evil."[20] It seems likely, on the contrary, that Malory positively wanted this deliberate alienation of actions from self, which leaves a note of distance counterpointing the scenes of joyous union that close the tale.[21] And the identification of Lancelot with the stranger knight also has another effect on the resolution – or non-resolution – of the narrative, which Vinaver does not notice. For if the combat with Lancelot unexpectedly provides a conclusion to Tristram's fruitless pursuit of the stranger knight by tracing the latter's exploits back to their source, it at the same time displaces the expected conclusion to the part of the narrative that concerns Sir Palomides. Lancelot's greeting to Tristram, with its reference to his keeping his promise, might lead us to believe that he was apprised of the arranged rendezvous between Tristram and Palomides, and that he has consciously taken Palomides's place, possibly at the latter's request. But this turns out not to be the case. Much later on we find Palomides explaining to Sir Dinadan that he could not keep his promise because he was held prisoner by a lord, and Dinadan in response tells him of the combat between Lancelot and Tristram, which is clearly all news to Palomides (595–6). It is only "by adventure," then, that Lancelot's combat with Tristram takes the place of the combat with Palomides, the part of the narrative that we thought had ended inconclusively is concluded, while the part that we thought was certain to reach its conclusion is left hanging in mid-air. Palomides, in fact, simply drops out of the narrative at this point, and re-enters it only much later and obliquely; characteristically, he has become anonymous again. We feel that we have lost contact with one line of the narrative – that it has wandered off beyond our reach.

The knight's encounters with the residue of narrative are one way of making us feel that the narrative we are reading is somehow distanced from the events that it wishes to embrace. The narrative tendency to divergence creates the same sense of distance; while we follow one line of the story, we are always conscious that we have lost sight of another, which may or may not re-emerge.

---

20 See Malory, *Works*, 1484.

21 Maureen Fries explains this enigma by suggesting that Lancelot is contaminated by the deceit that is endemic in Tristram's character and story ("Indiscreet Objects of Desire: Malory's 'Tristram' and the Necessity of Deceit," in *Studies in Malory*, ed. Spisak, 87–108, at 102–3). This censorious explanation seems to me to go against the grain of the admiration accorded to both Tristram and Lancelot throughout the Tristram Book.

The tripartite branching of the narrative in the early tales of Gawain, Torre, and Pellinore, and of Gawain, Ywain, and Marhalt, provides obvious examples of such narrative divergence; as the knights separate for their individual adventures they pull the narrative apart into different strands, leaving us always conscious of other stories going on elsewhere. The "interlacing" technique of Malory's French sources might be said to have the same effect, but its much more leisurely pace, and much greater immersion in the narrative details of the story that is before us at any one time, reduce our sense of urgency about catching up with lost lines of narrative. The incidents achieve a meaning in their own right, as coherent pieces of human action, whereas in Malory we are always left feeling that the secret explanation of the incident before us is perhaps to be found in some other area of the narrative. Larry Benson characterizes the difference between the two by calling Malory's technique "bracketing" rather than "interlacing."[22]

The opening of the *Book of Lancelot* illustrates this tendency for the narrative to split itself the moment it gets under way, leaving us uncertain as to which is its important line of development. Lancelot and his nephew Lionel ride out from the court, and take shelter from the noonday heat under an apple tree (253). Lancelot falls asleep; Lionel remains awake, and sees three knights fleeing with a single knight hotly pursuing them. The three are eventually overtaken, thrown from their horses and bound with their own bridles. Characteristically, Lionel watches this drama play itself out, and only when it is concluded does he mount his horse and challenge the knight himself – whereupon he too is overthrown, bound, led to the victor's castle, put in prison, and beaten with thorns on his naked flesh (254). Instead of returning to the sleeping Lancelot, the narrative now jumps to a different track altogether, relating Sir Ector de Marys's departure from the court in pursuit of Lancelot (254). We seem about to embark on another infinitely receding narrative, in which we get further and further away from the initial set of events. In fact the narrative does a sort of loop, bringing Sir Ector together with Sir Lionel, not Sir Lancelot. Ector finds a tree hung with the shields of Round Table knights, including Sir Lionel's; when he challenges the knight responsible, he too is overcome, taken captive, and put into the same prison as Sir Lionel (255–6). Their only hope is that Sir Lancelot will deliver them. The pursuer becomes a prisoner hoping to be found by the object of his pursuit. The narrative finally returns to the sleeping Sir Lancelot, who is found by Morgan le Fay and three other queens. They become instant rivals for his love; his sleep is prolonged by enchantment and he is transported to

22 *Malory's Morte Darthur*, 53–64.

a castle where he is to be held prisoner until he has chosen which of the queens he will honour with his love (256–7). The immediate concern of the narrative thus becomes Lancelot's escape from prison, which is effected through the help of a damsel who requires him to assist her father in a tournament as a reward (258–9). It is thus several pages of adventures later that Lancelot is finally free to "seke his brothir sir Lyonell that wente frome hym whan he slepte" (263/34–264/1). The aim of the narrative, that is, has become simply the restoration of its own *status quo ante*, the companionship of Sir Lancelot and Sir Lionel. In eliminating Sir Tarquin, the knight who holds Lionel and the rest prisoner, as he eventually does, Lancelot eliminates the cause of narrative divergence.

Yet the killing of Sir Tarquin and the freeing of his prisoners does not climax in the expected joyful reunion between Lancelot and his fellows; the restoration of the *status quo ante* is deferred. Instead, Lancelot rides off with the damsel who had initiated his encounter with Sir Tarquin in response to his request for some "adventures," and to whom he had in return promised that he would go to the aid of some distressed damsels (264, 268). So when Lionel and the rest come out of the prison, and are told by Sir Gaherys that they have been saved by Sir Lancelot, they vow that they will ride after Sir Lancelot to find him if they can (269). Once more the narrative turns round on itself: the pursuer becomes the pursued. No sooner has the knight reached the absent goal towards which his narrative tends, than he himself becomes the goal of an absent narrative of whose unseen pursuit we remain conscious as we follow his subsequent adventures.

The knight is characteristically thought of as the quester; it is surprising, then, to register how often he himself is the object of the quest. In the *Book of Tristram*, for example, King Arthur reproaches Lancelot for having caused Tristram's absence from the court by fighting him in a tournament; in response, Lancelot swears a formal oath on a book, with nine of his fellows, "never to reste one nyght where we reste another thys twelve-month, untyll that we fynde sir Trystram" (537/26–7). Their search is a true quest: they set forth "uppon theire queste togydirs" (538/2). After Lancelot and Tristram have fought their great battle and are riding back to Camelot, they meet Gawain and Gaherys, who have likewise sworn to King Arthur that they will not return to court without bringing Sir Tristram with them, and here too Lancelot refers to their search as a quest, telling them "Returne agayne ... for youre queste is done, for I have mette with sir Trystram. Lo, here is his owne person!" (570/8–10)

Like the knight, then, the narrative has no fixed goal; its motion can reverse itself as it loses contact with its original subject and strives to catch up with it again. Its only stable *point de repère*, like the knight's, is Camelot, where the divergent lines of narrative are reassembled in the knights' final relation of their different adventures. Away from the court, it is constantly running across other narratives, which deflect it from its course or draw it after them in pursuit. The knight's role as spectator is repeatedly used to make us conscious of the distance between these other narratives and the one on which we started out; time and again we find a knight gazing out of a window or across a plain, and becoming aware of a sequence of action already in motion in which he will become involved. One of the more dramatic examples occurs in the *Book of Lancelot*: Lancelot has taken lodging in the castle of Tintagell, and is already asleep in bed when he is woken by someone knocking at the gate in great haste.

> "Whan sir Launcelot herde this he arose up and loked oute at the wyndowe, and sygh by the moonelyght three knyghtes com rydyng aftir that one man, and all three laysshynge on hym at onys with swerdys; and that one knyght turned on hem knyghtly agayne and defended hym.
>
> "Truly," seyde sir Launcelot, "yondir one knyght shall I helpe, for hit were shame for me to se three knyghtes on one, and yf he be there slayne I am partener of his deth."
>
> (273/7–14)

Lancelot duly arms himself, lets himself down from his window by a sheet, and joins in the combat, rescuing the solitary knight, who turns out to be Sir Kay. Finally he knocks at the castle gate and is readmitted by his understandably startled host, who says "Sir ... I wente ye had bene in your bed." "So I was," says Sir Lancelot, "but I arose and lepe out at my wyndow for to helpe an olde felowe of myne" (274/18–20).

Apart from its rather comic conclusion, this is an utterly typical example of the knight as spectator, beholding an uncomprehended series of events in which he nevertheless engages himself, finding his position within them as they progress. The knight is not only characteristically a spectator; he is also very often an eavesdropper, another role that makes us conscious of encountering a narrative distanced from the one currently under attention. There is an early example in the conversation between two knights overheard by Pellinore. "What tydynges at Camelot?" asks one, and the other reports that Arthur has assembled there "the floure of chevalry," creating an invincible fellowship (118/11–16).

> "As for that," seyde the othir knyght, "I have brought a remedy with me that ys the grettist poysen that ever ye herde speke off. And to Camelot woll I with hit, for we have a frende ryght nyghe the kynge, well cheryshed, that shall poysen kynge Arthur." (118/19–23)

This plot to poison Arthur is never heard of again, and Pellinore does not even warn him of its existence on his immediately following return to Camelot. The overheard conversation functions, that is, simply as a window on to another narrative world, a momentary point of contact between two separated lines of action which merely emphasizes their general distance from each other.

The *Book of Tristram* has some interesting examples of eavesdropping which likewise create a sense of distance within narrative. Sitting by a fountain, King Mark eavesdrops on an unknown knight who is lamenting his love for Queen Morgawse, and who thus reveals himself to be Sir Lamorak (579). Again one feels one is coming upon another story, which remains in distant relation to the one in which one finds onself. A few pages later, another unidentified knight is overheard lamenting the pangs of love, first by King Mark, and then separately by Sir Dinadan; this time the lady in question is Isode, and the knight turns out to be Sir Palomides (591–2). But Palomides has only just separated from Mark and Dinadan, who have already discovered his identity from the servant of King Mark's whom he sends with a message to his mother (590). Palomides has only to ride off into the forest to become immediately anonymous again, to become merely "a man that made grete dole" (591/16). The anonymity suggests a fresh narrative start, despite the fact that the three participants in the eavesdropping scene are exactly the same ones who have figured in the immediately preceding action. The link between the two scenes is established by working backwards from the second one and not, as we might expect, forward from the first, across the barrier represented by Palomides's sudden recession into anonymity and the eavesdropping which suggests we are encountering a different story.

Even more important in creating a sense of distance within the narrative is the fact that so many of its important events happen "off-stage," so to speak. The most notorious example is the death of Sir Tristram. To the disappointment of many readers Malory concludes the *Book of Tristram* when he is no more than two-thirds of the way through his source, and so fails to relate the climactic death of Tristram and Isode. Only near the close of the whole work do we hear of Tristram's death, and then in a typically oblique manner. Urged by his kindred to take Queen Guinevere to Joyous Gard and there protect her from King Arthur's anger, as Tristram had kept Isode safe from King Mark in the same stronghold, Lancelot replies that this is not a good precedent,

> "for whan by meanys of tretyse sir Trystram brought agayne La Beall Isode unto kynge Marke from Joyous Garde, loke ye now what felle on the ende, how shamefully that false traytour kyng Marke slew hym as he sate harpynge afore hys lady, La Beall Isode. Wyth a grounden glayve he threste hym in behynde to the harte,

whych grevyth sore me," seyde sir Launcelot, "to speke of his dethe, for all the worlde may nat fynde such another knyght." (1173/13–20)

The relation of Tristram's death is thus distanced from the narrative to which it belongs, and it is also distanced in that we do not see it happen with our own eyes, but hear of it by a second-hand report which introduces it incidentally, not for its own sake. The death of Sir Lamorak is treated in much the same way in the *Book of Tristram* itself. Lamorak plays an important role in this Book: as Palomides is next in prominence after Sir Tristram, so Lamorak is next in importance after Sir Lancelot. His love for Queen Morgawse, and the consequent hatred of Morgawse's sons, Gawain, Gaherys, Mordred, and Aggravain, is a frequent focus of the narrative, and Morgawse's murder by her sons while she and Lamorak are in bed together is directly related. We should therefore expect Lamorak's death to be important enough to be recounted directly as well, but this is not the case. It is first referred to in a quite unsensational conversation about the relative strength of various knights. Sir Ector asks Palomides if he has ever been worsted by any knight other than Lancelot and Tristram. Yes, says Palomides, there was Sir Lamorak de Galys, who overthrew him and three other knights at a tournament, but was then treacherously slain by Gawain and his brothers as he rode away (687–8). Lamorak's brother Sir Perceval is present at this conversation, and swoons with grief on hearing this unexpected information of his brother's death. The obliquity with which it emerges adds to our feeling of distance; an important narrative event has simply taken place elsewhere, and enters the story we are hearing almost as an afterthought rather than as an important piece of news in its own right. References to Lamorak's death keep recurring in the subsequent narrative, like the ripples from a stone thrown into a pond reaching the shore one by one, and reminding us each time of our distance from the event itself (691, 698–9, 715–16, 809–10); we experience only its reverberations.

The narrative similarly distances itself from relating the death of Sir Lancelot directly. We are expecting it to come: Lancelot has fallen sick, is confessed, and given extreme unction. At night his fellows in the religious life go to their beds, and around midnight "the Bysshop that was hermyte" laughs aloud in his sleep. Woken by his fellows, he says he was never so merry in his life; he was dreaming that he saw Sir Lancelot being carried up by angels into heaven, a vision which Sir Bors rejects as "dretchyng of swevens" (1258/11). But when they go to Lancelot's room, they find him "starke dede; and he laye as he had smyled" (1258/16). The obliquity of narrative, its delicate removal to the next room, as it were, is here a means to emotional restraint; the counterpointing of the bishop's laughter, and the dead Lancelot's smile, with the grief that his death arouses, works in the same direction. Narrative distance also creates emotional restraint in the case of the deaths of Sir Lamorak and Sir Tristram. This emotional restraint is a pervasive feature of Malory's writing, as has often been recognized. His habitual use of the formal title *Sir* Lancelot, *Sir* Tristram, to which Mark Lambert has drawn attention, has a lot to do with it.[23] Its importance to the present discussion is the major contribution it makes to our sense of distance in the narrative. Emotional restraint is also the most notable quality of Malory's dialogue, which shows no gradations from formality to intimacy, not even when we hear private conversations between two lovers. All speech is conducted at the same level of formal dignity, even at its most passionate. The informal "thou" appears rarely, and mostly as an insult; to those they love, the knights habitually use the respectful "ye." Intimacy is achieved through the acceptance of distance. One other feature of Malory's style which is so pervasive as almost to escape notice, yet all-important in creating a sense of distance, is his use of the past tense.[24] We might think this almost inevitable in a prose narrative, but comparison with Malory's French sources, the texts that make up the so-called Vulgate cycle, and the prose romance of Tristan, shows that it is far from being the case. Alongside the preterite, the French prose narratives make a very free use of the historic present (as I have done myself in summarizing Malory); they also make frequent use of the perfect, which is of course in essence a present tense, although often translated by a preterite in English. Nor is this mixture of tenses alien to narrative writing in English; one has only to think of Chaucer or *Sir Gawain and the Green Knight* to see this. But Malory resolutely turned his back on it, adhering to the preterite with a relentless consistency throughout his work. His narrative never masquerades as a present event; it is always separated from us by a barrier of time that holds it at a distance.

I would like to illustrate this difference between Malory and his French sources with the final combat between Arthur and Sir Mordred, because it will also serve to round off my discussion by taking us back to distance and wholeness as narrative themes. In the French *Mort Artu*, the confrontation between Arthur and Mordred is provoked by Arthur's indignation when he sees Mordred kill Sagremor.

> "When the king sees this blow, he says very sorrowfully, "Ah, God, why do you allow me to be so greatly abased in worldly prowess? For the sake of this blow I vow to God that either Mordred or I must die here." He took a great and strong sword,

23 *Malory: Style and Vision*, 66–7.

24 Cf. P.J.C. Field's comment: "the simple past tense of the verbs puts the story firmly in a distant and unalterable past" (*Romance and Chronicle*, 146).

and spurs his horse forward as fast as he could, and Mordred, who knows well that the king is intent on nothing other than his death, did not avoid him, but turns the head of his horse to him, and the king, who comes at him with all his might, strikes him so hard that he bursts through the links of his mail coat and plunges the blade of his sword in his body; and the story says that after the sword was wrenched out, a ray of the sun passed through the wound so visibly that Girflet saw it, whence the local people said that this had been a sign of Our Lord's anger. When Mordred saw himself so wounded, he is convinced that he is wounded fatally; and he strikes King Arthur so hard on the helm that nothing prevents him from feeling the sword in his head, and he lost a piece of his skull. King Arthur was so dazed with this blow that he fell down from his horse to the earth, and so did Mordred; and they are both in such straits that neither of them has the power to get up, but the one lies by the other. So the father killed the son, and the son wounded the father fatally."[25]

The present tense is obviously used to give this combat drama and immediacy; it lends the account something of a "now read on" quality. The past tense in the final sentence sums it all up, closing it off as an incident. In contrast, when Malory recounts the same scene he uses the past tense throughout, giving it an air of finality from the beginning; it has the simplicity and inevitability of destiny.

Than the kynge gate his speare in bothe hys hondis, and ran towarde sir Mordred, cryyng and saying,

"Traytoure, now ys thy dethe-day com!"

And whan sir Mordred saw kynge Arthur he ran untyll hym with hys swerde drawyn in hys honde, and there kyng Arthur smote sir Mordred undir the shylde, with a foyne of hys speare, thorowoute the body more than a fadom. And whan sir Mordred felte that he had hys dethys wounde he threste hymselff with the myght that he had upp to the burre of kyng Arthurs speare, and ryght so he smote hys fadir, kynge Arthure, with hys swerde holdynge in both hys hondys, uppon the syde of the hede, that the swerde perced the helmet and the tay of the brayne. And therewith Mordred daysshed downe starke dede to the erthe. (1237/9–22)

Malory's unique version of this scene serves to intensify its function as a tragic climax of the themes of distance and wholeness. Instead of the French

25 *La Mort le Roi Artu*, ed. Jean Frappier, Textes Littéraires Français (Geneva, 1964), 244–5 (sections 190–1). For a translation, see *The Death of King Arthur*, trans. James Cable (Harmondsworth, 1971); the translation in the text is my own, and reproduces faithfully the shifts between past and present tenses in the original.

Mort's melodramatic detail about the wound in Mordred's body being large enough to let the sun be seen through it, Malory has Mordred struck by a spear, not a sword, and he then adds his own imaginative stroke: seeing that his wound is mortal, Mordred does not wrench himself free from the spear, but instead pushes himself forward along its full length so that he can get near enough to Arthur to strike a fatal blow. This grisly detail is, as I have observed elsewhere,[26] a grotesque parody of the chivalric ideal, the knightly willingness to "take the adventure," to accept destiny-in-chance with a stoic simplicity. Mordred "takes the adventure" of his death, but not in a spirit of self-abnegating resignation – rather, it is in order to have one last chance to destroy. And as his action travesties the chivalric acceptance of adventure, so it also travesties the closing of distance which characterizes the knight's relation to adventure. In the simplest physical sense, Mordred closes the gap between himself and Arthur, he eliminates distance, but the result is a final negation of wholeness. Father and son come face to face as in the meeting of Lancelot and Galahad, but the bonds of kindred are here brutally severed. The French text's rather ponderous signalling of the shocking fact that father has killed son, and son father, is reduced by Malory to the simple factuality of a single noun, which intrudes, with a sense of terrible travesty, at the very moment of destructive contact: "ryght so he smote his fadir, kynge Arthure, with hys swerde." The narrative embraces the fact of the father-son relationship with a restraint that has a far greater emotional effect than the hand-wringing of the French *Mort*.

Mordred dies here, before our eyes. But Arthur does not. As with so many of the important figures of the narrative, his end takes place off-stage. The barge with the black-hooded ladies comes and takes him away, as he says, "into the vale of Avylyon to hele me of my grevous wounde" – a departure with one last wistful hope of wholeness (1240/33–4). The narrative of his death eludes the narrator: "Thus of Arthur I fynde no more wrytten in bokis that bene auctorysed ... Now more of the deth of kynge Arthur coude I never fynde" (1242/3–4, 15–16). There is only the residue of a possible narrative, the tomb that mysteriously appears overnight with its inscription "HIC IACET ARTHURUS, REX QUONDAM REXQUE FUTURUS" (1242/29). The narrative proceeds through the separation of Lancelot and Guinevere, and their separate departures from life itself. Sir Ector's lament over Sir Lancelot mourns the flower of earthly knighthood as something irrecoverably past; an age has vanished. The narrative finally passes away from us completely, receding into the past where we have

26 " 'Taking the Adventure,' " 270 above.

always known it belongs. But it is only when it is thus finally distanced from us that it paradoxically achieves its own "wholeness," its completeness as a record of a wholeness that was once achieved, as Malory's final colophon makes clear:

> HERE IS THE ENDE OF THE HOOLE BOOK OF KYNG ARTHUR AND OF HIS NOBLE KNYGHTES OF THE ROUNDE TABLE, THAT WHAN THEY WERE HOLÉ TOGYDERS THERE WAS EVER AN HONDRED AND FORTY. AND HERE IS THE ENDE OF *The Deth of Arthur.* (1260/16–19)

Chapter Fifteen

Malory and the Grail Legend

The Grail first enters literature in the *Conte del Graal* of Chrétien de Troyes.[1] The title of this romance, which is given to it by Chrétien himself (line 66), seems to invest the Grail with a central importance. But when it makes its first appearance in the narrative, it is simply one of a number of striking features in the courtly procession that passes before the astonished Perceval as he sits at dinner talking to his host, the maimed Fisher King (lines 3190–253). First comes a boy holding a white lance, its point constantly dripping blood which falls on the boy's hand. Then there follow two other boys, holding candlesticks of gold, inlaid with black enamel-work. Behind them comes a girl, holding between her hands "un graal," made of gold and set with precious stones, which emits a light so brilliant that it eclipses the twenty candles in the two candlesticks. Then comes another girl, carrying a silver carving dish. One after another all these figures pass before Perceval and disappear into another room. With each course of dinner, the grail (and by implication the rest of the procession) passes by again.

To a modern reader, the most disconcerting feature of this narrative sequence is probably the use of the indefinite article: "*a* grail," not "*the* Grail." Not, that is, a unique object, designated by a proper name which labels it while leaving it uncategorized, enigmatic in nature. Instead, it is one of a class, even if it is a particularly splendid example of its kind. The definite article used in the title of the romance turns out not to indicate the grail's uniqueness, but simply to refer to the particular grail that figures in this story. "Graal" is a rather uncommon word in Old French, but it is attested, with the meaning "bowl" or "dish."[2]

1 *Le Roman de Perceval ou le conte du Graal*, ed. Keith Busby (Tübingen, 1993). Subsequent references to the line numbers of this edition are given in the text.

2 Tobler-Lommatzsch, s.v. *gräal*.

Helinand of Froidmont, a Cistercian monk writing in the late twelfth century, in the course of discussing the Grail legend defines a grail (Latin *gradalis, gradale*) as "a wide and slightly hollow dish," on which luxurious foods are served up to the wealthy.[3] Chrétien's Grail is thus not the chalice or goblet familiar from Pre-Raphaelite painting or Wagnerian opera; nor is there anything intrinsically "holy" about it. It is not carried by a priest or an acolyte, as would be proper for an object of a liturgical or religious nature, but by a girl. And however wonderful is the light that emanates from it, it is not as evidently puzzling as the bleeding lance which precedes it, and which seems to call even more urgently for some kind of explanation.

What gives the Grail its importance in Chrétien's romance is not its status as a sacral object, nor a previous history in Celtic myth or Christian legend, but Perceval's failure to ask about it. With the best of motives, he restrains his curiosity in obedience to the instructions of Gornemant, the "preudome sage" who had earlier impressed on him that he must not speak too much (lines 3244–7; cf. lines 1648–56). Next day, he awakes to find the castle deserted, and on riding away he meets a girl lamenting over the headless body of a knight, who questions him closely on the previous night's events. When he reveals that he had put no question to his host about the procession that had passed before him, she denounces him as "Perceval the wretch"; had he done so, she tells him, the Maimed King would at once have been cured. What is more, she continues, further ills will befall him and others as a result. And she blames his failure on his sin in leaving home and abandoning his mother, who has since died of grief (lines 3545–611). This denunciation is later repeated and extended by the Loathly Damsel who accuses Perceval in front of Arthur's court (lines

3 *Chronicon, PL* 212, col. 815: "Gradalis autem sive gradale Gallice dicitur scutella lata, et aliquantulum profunda; in qua pretiosae dapes cum suo jure divitibus solent apponi gradatim, unus morsellus post alium in diversis ordinibus; et dicitur vulgari nomine graalz, quia grata et acceptabilis est in ea comedenti: tum propter continens, quia forte argentea est, vel de alia pretiosa materia; tum propter contentum, id est ordinem multiplicem pretiosarum dapum" ("'Gradalis' or 'gradale' is in French the name of a wide and slightly hollowed dish, in which rich foods and their sauce are customarily carried to the wealthy in stages, one delicacy after another in different courses, and it is called 'grail' in the common tongue because it is pleasing ['grata'] and welcome to the one who eats from it, both because of the container, for it can be of silver, or some other precious substance, and also because of what is contained [in it], that is, the varied succession of rich foods"). One may suspect that Helinand's explanation of why a grail is so called is largely derived from a combination of close reading of Chrétien's *Perceval* and the employment of etymological ingenuity; but it is noteworthy that he does not take the word to be a proper name, even though the rest of his account shows that he is familiar with the legend that identifies the grail in the Perceval story with the vessel used to collect Christ's blood.

4610–83). The enigma of the Grail is thus a matter of narrative function, rather than of the properties of an object: the enigma lies in the contrast between the unambiguous boldness with which Perceval's guilt is asserted, and the difficulty of defining this guilt in terms of normal moral criteria. The most obvious reason for this difficulty is that the sequence of cause and effect which binds sin to disastrous consequence is obscure. Abandoning his mother may in itself be reprehensible, but it is difficult to see how this could have become the *cause* of his failure to ask the question, nor is it possible to understand how asking the question might have brought about the Maimed King's cure. In the second place, it seems unfair that Perceval should incur such blame when his fault is the result of trying his hardest to practise the rules of conduct that he has been taught.

The enigma of Perceval's guilt is never resolved. But a clue to understanding its significance within the narrative is supplied by Chrétien's own comment on Perceval's resolute silence: "I fear he may suffer for it, because I have heard it said that one can as easily be too silent on occasion as speak too much" (lines 3248–51). The question that Perceval is reproached for having failed to put is not "what is the grail?" but "who is served from the grail?" (lines 3244–5, 4660–1, 6379–80). This question is answered directly and without ceremony at a later point in the romance (lines 6417–31), when a hermit tells Perceval that the grail carries a single consecrated wafer, which for twelve years has been the sole sustenance of the Fisher King's father (who, like the hermit himself, is revealed to be Perceval's own uncle). It is thus not the answer to the question, but the *timing* of the question, that is the heart of the mystery. That is, the mystery that Perceval fails to penetrate is the mystery of courtly tact – the knowledge of when to speak and when to be silent. This is a knowledge that resides, not in rules that can be taught and learned, but in the instinctive responses of the courtly heart. The art of speaking and of being silent is one of the rituals and practices of court life that the Grail procession invests with mystique and wonder, a wonder heightened by the fact that Perceval has been brought up as a rustic in the woods, far away from civilized life. If the bleeding lance is a "marvel" (line 3202), so too is the lavish array of exotic fruits, wines, and spices served at dessert: "the young man marvelled greatly at all this, since he was unschooled in it" (line 3334–5). Courtly life becomes the object of awe and admiration as it is presented through the eyes of the untutored youth.

The consecrated wafer is the only feature in Chrétien's narrative that connects the Grail with religious ritual. Whether he intended to develop this aspect of the Grail must remain uncertain, since he left the *Conte del Graal* unfinished. But the various poets who wrote continuations of his romance seized on this detail and linked it with the enigmatic bleeding lance, in such a way as to create a religious pseudo-history for both objects.[4] The Grail, now first called "the holy grail" (112), is said to be the vessel in which the blood flowing from the crucified Christ was collected (160); the lance is identified as that with which Longinus pierced Christ's side (131–2). But at the same time the decor of the Grail procession remains courtly rather than religious: the Grail, and sometimes the lance too, is still carried by a girl (112, 180, 191), and it still forms part of the ritual of a courtly dinner, on one occasion serving up seven courses of food while magically circulating among the diners of its own accord (130). Meanwhile, the image of the bleeding lance, the agent of wounding which is itself wounded, is doubled in the appearance of a broken sword, which lies on the breast of a dead man whose bier is carried in the procession (112). Gawain twice tries to mend this broken sword and fails (113, 131); Perceval tries and succeeds (192).

The *Continuations* of the *Conte del Graal* thus adumbrate a religious history of the Grail, but fail to co-ordinate the bric-a-brac of proliferating imagery into a meaningful whole. It was Robert de Boron's *Estoire du Graal* which first shaped these scattered elements into a coherent narrative, by identifying the Grail as the vessel used by Christ and his disciples at the Last Supper, later passing into the hands of Joseph of Arimathea, who collected in it the blood from Christ's body as he prepared it for burial.[5] The *Estoire* goes on to relate how the Grail then became an object of veneration, the centre of a cult maintained by Joseph's descendants. It is this conception of the nature of the Grail and its history that reappears in the French prose *Queste del Saint Graal*, the immediate source of Malory's *Tale of the Sankgreal*.[6] Towards the end of this narrative, Galahad, Perceval, and Bors, along with nine other knights from other countries, see the Grail in the castle of Corbenic; it is again accompanied by the bleeding lance, which is now set upright in it. The Grail is then used as a Eucharistic vessel in the ceremony of the Mass; the celebrant (identified as Joseph, the son of Joseph of Arimathea) places in it a wafer, which is miraculously transformed into the figure of a child, and then becomes bread again. Joseph then vanishes, and out of the Grail comes a man who has (in Malory's words) "all

4 *The Continuations of the Old French Perceval of Chretien de Troyes*, ed. William Roach et al., 5 vols in 6 (Philadelphia, 1949–83); *Gerbert de Montreuil: La Continuation de Perceval*, ed. Mary Williams and Marguerite Oswald, 3 vols (Paris, 1922–75) The *Continuations* are also accessible in a translation-cum-summary appended to the translation of Chrétien's *Perceval* by Nigel Bryant (Cambridge, 1982). References in the text will be to the page-numbers of this translation.

5 Robert de Boron, *Le Roman de l'Estoire dou Graal*, ed. William A. Nitze (Paris, 1971).

6 *La Queste del Saint Graal*, ed. Albert Pauphilet (Paris, 1978); translated as *The Quest of the Holy Grail* by P.M. Matarasso (Harmondsworth, 1969).

the sygnes of the Passion of Jesu Cryste bledynge all opynly" (1030/4–5), who administers the Host to the knights. Finally, he identifies the Grail as "the holy dysshe wherein I ete the lambe on Estir Day" (1030/19–20) – that is, the vessel used in the Last Supper, when Christ identified the bread and wine he gave to his disciples as his own body and blood (Matt. 26:26–8; Mark 14:22–4; Luke 22:19–20). It is this occasion that is both commemorated and recreated in the Mass, when the consecration of bread and wine by the priest transforms them into the body and blood of Christ.

In both the French *Queste* and Malory, the Grail is thus a Eucharistic vessel.[7] The mystery that surrounds it is a religious mystery: it renders visible the transformation of bread and wine into body and blood, a transformation which is normally accessible to Christians only on the plane of belief. But why, one might ask, should such a penetration of the mystery of the Eucharist be the goal and climax of knightly endeavour? The conventional answer to this question is that the author of the French *Queste* was offering a challenge and a corrective to the secular ethos of chivalry that was celebrated in the verse and prose romances of his time. The knights in the *Queste* are frequently lectured by hermits on the distinction between the "earthly chivalry" ("chevalerie terriane") in which they have been engaged hitherto, and the "heavenly chivalry" ("chevalerie celestiel") which is demanded in the quest of the Grail. Critics of Malory have likewise seen his *Sankgreal* as the point at which the worldly values of the Round Table are judged by religious standards and found wanting; Lancelot's adultery is there revealed as the flaw which robs him of his pre-eminence, and which will lead eventually to the collapse of the whole Arthurian world in the *Morte*.[8]

Such interpretations of both the *Queste* and Malory are in the main following the lead of Albert Pauphilet, who in a widely influential book argued that the French *Queste* is deeply permeated by Cistercian spirituality; for Pauphilet, it represents a monastic attempt to appropriate the idiom of chivalric romance for religious ends.[9] The parallels with Cistercian writings and practice that Pauphilet claims are, however, weak and unconvincing, and there are other

7 W.E.M.C. Hamilton, "L'interprétation mystique de La Queste del Saint Graal," *Neophilologus* 27 (1942): 94–110; Jean Frappier, "Le Graal et la chevalerie," *Romania* 75: (1954), 165–210, at 166.

8 See, for example, Charles Moorman's analysis of the relation between Malory's *Sankgreal* and the French *Queste* in *Malory's Originality*, ed. R.M. Lumiansky (Baltimore, MD, 1964), 184–204.

9 *Études sur la Queste del Saint Graal* (Paris, 1921; repr. 1980), 53–84.

serious objections to this view of the *Queste*, the most powerful of which is that the early Cistercians, as Jean Frappier has observed, did not write romances;[10] the austerity of their order, which led even to the banishment of all church ornament, would hardly have tolerated engagement in so frivolous a pastime as the composition of vernacular fiction, even for religious ends. It is significant that Helinand of Froidmont mentions the Grail legend only to dismiss it as not worth wasting time on.[11] Emmanuèle Baumgartner has also stressed that the *Queste* was manifestly conceived and written in close relation to the prose *Lancelot*;[12] the first appearances of the Grail occur in the latter half of

10 "Le Graal et la chevalerie," 195. Frappier says of the author of the *Queste* "il ne saurait être question de voir en lui un moine de Cîteaux, ne fût-ce que pour cette raison péremptoire que les Cisterciens n'écrivaient pas des romans." This argument is reinforced and extended by Pauline Matarasso, *The Redemption of Chivalry: A Study of the Queste del Saint Graal* (Geneva, 1979), 225–8, but she still clings to a belief in the "Cistercian bias" (224) of the *Queste*, although the examples she cites are no more convincing than Pauphilet's (218–24); she tentatively concludes that the *Queste* may have been written by "a Cistercian seconded from his abbey to some lay or ecclesiastical dignitary" (241).

On the exclusion of profane literature (including classical Latin poetry) from Cistercian libraries, see Anne Bondéelle, "Trésor des moines. Les Chartreux, les Cisterciens et leurs livres," in *Histoire des bibliothèques françaises*, vol. 1, *Les bibliothèques médiévales du VIe siècle à 1530*, ed. André Vernet (Paris, 1988), 64–81; Birger Munk Olsen, "The Cistercians and Classical Culture," *Cahiers de l'institut du moyen-âge grec et latin* 47 (1984): 64–102; Christopher R. Cheney, "Les bibliothèques cisterciennes en Angleterre au XIIe siècle," in *Mélanges Saint Bernard: XXIVe Congrès de l'Association Bourguignonne des Sociétés Savantes, Dijon 1953* (Dijon, n.d.), 375–82. Cheney's view is endorsed by David N. Bell, *The Libraries of the Cistercians, Gilbertines and Premonstratensians*, Corpus of British Medieval Library Catalogues 3 (London, 1992), xxv (the vernacular romances listed under the abbey of Bordesley at Z.2 were a donation by Guy of Beauchamp, earl of Warwick, in 1306, and as Bell says, it is not known whether the abbey kept the books or sold them; in any case, they are highly untypical of Cistercian reading habits). The statutes of the Cistercian order forbade any abbot, monk, or novice to write books, except in the wholly unusual circumstance of their being given permission by the general chapter (David Knowles, *The Monastic Order in England*, 2nd ed. [Cambridge, 1963], 643–4). Around 1196 William of Newburgh, an Augustinian canon, was asked by Ernald, abbot of Rievaulx, to write a chronicle of English history, because Ernald did not wish the Rievaulx monks to be distracted from the monastic office by such work (*The History of William of Newburgh*, trans. Joseph Stevenson [London, 1856; repr. Felinfach, 1996], 397). Ailred of Rievaulx, who died thirty years earlier, represented a "contravention of both letter and spirit of the statute" (Knowles, *Monastic Order*, 644), but he was a notable exception.

11 Helinand complains that he cannot find a Latin version of the Grail legend, nor is it easy to find a complete version of the story in French. He prefers therefore to translate "more probable and useful" things ("verisimiliora et utiliora") into Latin (*PL* 212, col. 815).

12 *L'Arbre et le pain: Essai sur La Queste del Saint Graal* (Paris, 1981), 12, 21.

that work, as a kind of prelude to the *Queste*.[13] In only four of the forty-three manuscripts of the *Queste* does the work appear alone; usually it is either part of the whole Vulgate Cycle, or preceded by the end of the *Lancelot* or followed by the *Mort Artu*.[14] That is, the *Queste* is not conceived as a religious alternative to the secular prose romances, but as forming a continuum with them. Over fifty years ago, Jean Frappier presented a powerful case for reversing Pauphilet's view of the relation between chivalry and religion: that is, instead of representing an attempt to appropriate chivalry for religious ends, the Grail romances use religion as a means of exalting the dignity of the knightly class. They create a "messianic chivalry ... predestined, worthy of approaching, almost without intermediaries, the mysteries of the faith and of achieving knowledge of the divine."[15] The *Queste* in particular propagates, in Emmanuèle Baumgartner's words, "a class gospel" ("un évangile de classe," 146).

Against the background of this view of the Grail romances, it is worth re-posing the question: why should the mystery of the Eucharist be the goal and climax of knightly endeavour? The answer, I suggest, lies in the central elements of this religious mystery, the body and blood which are the concentrated symbols of Christ's redemptive suffering. For body and blood are also the central elements of the knightly experience: it is through hazarding his body in combat and shedding blood – both his own and his opponent's –that the knight realizes his worth and that of his fellows. Just as Christ's bodily suffering was, miraculously and mysteriously, the means through which redemption was accomplished on the spiritual plane, so the knight's bodily exploits are the vehicle through which his spiritual worth is realized. And blood is almost the only important bodily element in these exploits: the descriptions of knightly combat make no mention of muscles, nerves, sinews, sweat, pus, for example. The knightly body is represented in quasi-stylized form as a vessel containing blood, and in this it resembles the Grail itself.[16] What the knight sees in the Grail vision, therefore, is the apotheosis of his own existence.

---

13 *Lancelot*, ed. Alexandre Micha, 9 vols (Paris, 1978–83), 2:376–7 (LXVI.11–13); 4: 205–6 (LXXVIII.50), 270–1(LXXXI.11–12); 5: 255–6 (XCVIII.24–6), 267–71 (XCVIII.41–6); 6: 204–6 (CVI.43–5); trans. in *Lancelot-Grail. The Old French Arthurian Vulgate and Post-Vulgate in Translation*, ed. Norris J. Lacy, vol. 3 (New York, 1995), 100, 163–4, 179, 268–9, 271, 328–9.

14 Baumgartner, *L'Arbre et le pain*, 11–12.

15 Frappier, "Le Graal et la chevalerie," 170: "Ils parlent en effet d'une chevalerie messianique, enracinée dans les temps bibliques, présente à la Passion, prédestinée, digne d'approcher, presque sans médiation, des mystères de la foi et d'accéder à la connaissance du divin."

16 Charlotte C. Morse draws attention to the vessel-motif that links the Grail with the human body in *The Pattern of Judgment in the Queste and Cleanness* (Columbia, 1978); see especially 16.

The adventures of the Grail Quest thus follow, in intensified form, the pattern of the knightly adventure in general, which I have outlined on other occasions: they enact an elaborate interplay of distance and closeness, fragmentation and integration, separation and union.[17] Distanced from his world by his inability to understand the mysterious laws that govern it and produce its often bizarre events, the knight attempts to engage with it on the plane of physical action, using his body as the medium through which his destiny will be revealed. Coming together with his fellow knights, in extreme and violent form, in single combat, he ruptures the bodily integrity of his opponent and loses his own; but this rupture on the bodily plane often, paradoxically, leads to fellowship and union between the two combatants. The pursuit of an adventure is an attempt to close the gap between himself and the enigmatic challenges posed by the outside world, but it severs the knight from the fellows he leaves behind at court. At the close of the adventure, the movement is reversed and he is reintegrated into that fellowship.[18]

These patterns are repeated throughout the Arthurian narrative, but the Grail Quest sacralizes them by re-enacting them in a religious form. The French *Queste* is a symbolic narrative composed of a whole repertoire of images of wounding and healing, separation and union – images which reach a climactic expression in the final visions of the Grail, as we shall see. Malory's *Sankgreal* reproduces this symbolic narrative, but makes its patterns even clearer, not only by significant change at certain moments, but also by drastically reducing the religious interpretations of the narrative which in the *Queste* are regularly delivered by hermits and other religious. These religious commentaries not only blur the narrative line, they also tend to reduce its symbols to a set of cryptograms, whose imagistic power is discarded as they are decoded into moral instruction. In minimizing the role of these religious expositions, Malory makes the world of the *Sankgreal* consistent with that of the rest of his work: a world of pervasive enigma, in which explanation or understanding comes, if at all, fitfully and too late to have any bearing on action – a world in which the knight must engage in adventure without any clear notion of the consequences or character of his involvement. And here as elsewhere, adventure is heuristic: it reveals a knight's pre-existing worth rather than offering an opportunity to acquire it. Galahad's

17 See "Knightly Combat in Malory's *Morte d'Arthur*," "Taking the Adventure: Malory and the *Suite du Merlin*," and "The Narrative of Distance, The Distance of Narrative in Malory's *Morte d'Arthur*," 235–311 above.

18 The deeper resonances of the word "felyship" in Malory, as compared with the *Queste*'s "compaignie," are explored by Elizabeth Archibald, "Malory's Ideal of Fellowship," *Review of English Studies* n.s. 43 (1992): 311–28.

superiority is not a result of his trying harder, or of his resisting temptations more successfully; on the contrary, it is manifested in the fact that he is simply not tempted, as Perceval and Bors are.[19] His pre-eminence consists in his wholeness, which is his from the beginning, and which the events of the narrative are designed to express.

The symbolic patterns that I have attempted to describe are immediately visible in the opening sequence of the *Tale of the Sankgreal.* The fellowship of the Round Table, assembled for the feast of Pentecost, is made complete by the arrival of Galahad, who occupies the one empty seat, the Siege Perilous. His arrival is heralded by the miraculous appearance of gold letters on each seat bearing the name of the knight to whom it belongs; the Siege Perilous bears an inscription declaring that it will be "fulfylled" on this very day (855/14). The letters on the Siege Perilous are then covered with a silk cloth, which is removed on Galahad's arrival, revealing that the original inscription has been replaced by Galahad's name (860/8–11). The removal of the cloth represents the unveiling of a destiny, a moment of fulfilment, both for Galahad and the Round Table, which is imaged in the removal of this symbolic barrier. This moment of fulfilment is celebrated in the joust which is requested by King Arthur, so that he may see the Round Table "holé togydirs."

> "Now," seyde the kynge, "I am sure at this quest of the Sankegreall shall all ye of the Rownde Table departe, and nevyr shall I se you agayne holé togydirs, therefore ones shall I se you togydir in the medow, all holé togydirs! Therefore I woll se you all holé togydir in the medow of Camelot, to juste and to turney, that aftir youre dethe men may speke of hit that such good knyghtes were here, such a day, holé togydirs." (864/5–12)

The fourfold repetition of "holé togydir(s)" is Malory's own intensification of the single word "ensemble" in the *Queste* (13). But the sense of unity and completeness here is strengthened by the very thing that also undermines it – namely, Arthur's melancholy reference to the imminent departure of his knights on the quest of the Grail, and his conviction that they will never again be reassembled as a whole. The appearance of the Grail at the evening supper consecrates the completion of the Round Table, the eradication of its one remaining gap, but it also initiates the quest which will scatter the fellowship, and sever some of its members from it forever. And it introduces another barrier to be eradicated, a distance to be closed, in the form of the white samite covering that hides the

19 Cf. Matarasso, *The Redemption of Chivalry,* 85 n. 96.

Grail from view. Gawain is moved to initiate the quest because "we myght nat se the Holy Grayle: hit was so preciously coverde" (866/5–6). He proposes to pursue the Grail, not in order to take possession of it, but in order to see it "more opynly than hit hath bene shewed here" (866/10–11). The motive for the quest is the same impulse towards closeness that characterizes knightly engagement in adventure elsewhere. But this impulse towards closeness – again, as elsewhere – opens up a gap in another direction: Gawain's vow to undertake the quest provokes Arthur's bitter lament over "the departicion of thys felyship" (867/2–3); "For whan they departe frome hense I am sure they all shall never mete more togydir in thys worlde, for they shall dye many in the queste" (866/23–5). The dual meaning of "departe" in Middle English – "to leave" and "to separate" *(MED* la, 2a) – makes every departure in Malory's narrative a poignant image of severance, the loss of a fellowship temporarily achieved. But the departure on the Grail Quest is a "departicion" of a more final kind, precisely because it is a quest for a wholeness which is only to be realized beyond the confines of this world.

The veiling of the Grail is mirrored in the veiling of Galahad's identity. The *Sankgreal* opens with Lancelot being summoned away from the court to bestow the order of knighthood on the young Galahad, whom he does not know to be his son. When Galahad arrives at court, the revelation of his identity is adumbrated in the scene at the jousting where Guinevere asks him to remove his helmet, and surmises from his facial resemblance to Lancelot that they are father and son (864/34–865/3). But the final recognition of their relationship is deferred until later; until it takes place, there is another barrier towards whose removal the narrative aspires, another kind of wholeness which the quest can achieve.

The processes by which Galahad acquires his sword and his shield offer yet more images of wholeness and the loss of wholeness. The sword arrives at court before Galahad does: set in a stone which floats, miraculously, in the river, it bears an inscription proclaiming that it can be drawn out only by the knight for whom it is destined, who will be "the beste knyght of the worlde" (856/14–15). Declining to make the attempt, Sir Lancelot further reveals that "who that assayth to take hit and faylith of that swerde, he shall resseyve a wounde by that swerde that he shall nat be longe hole afftir" (856/23–5). This prediction is proved true on Gawain, who attempts to withdraw the sword, and is later severely wounded by Galahad with it (857/7–13; 982/5–10). Galahad, in contrast, withdraws the sword without difficulty and without suffering harm; his bodily invulnerability, that is, functions as the outward testimony of an inner perfection. Galahad then explains that the sword is the one with which Balin le Sauvage killed his brother Balan, "thorow a dolerous stroke that Balyn gaff unto kynge Pelles, the whych ys nat yett hole, nor naught shall be tyll that I hele hym"

(863/7–9). This explanation, which is Malory's own addition, makes the coming of Galahad into the completion of a history; the wound opened up by Balin is to be healed by Galahad. Himself the embodiment of a perfect wholeness, he is also the one who makes whole, and who brings the unfinished narrative to fulfilment.

The shield that Galahad later acquires likewise functions as a testimony to his wholeness. It too is destined for "the worthyest knyght of the worlde" (877/28–9), and is hedged about with a warning that "no man may bere hit aboute his necke but he be myscheved other dede within three dayes, other maymed for ever" (877/13–14). And again this prediction is fulfilled on another knight – in this case, King Bagdemagus, who takes the shield and is immediately wounded, near fatally, by a knight in white armour (878/2–16). The white knight then bids Bagdemagus's squire carry the shield to Galahad, who takes possession of it without further ado (878/17–879/10). His pre-eminence is demonstrated in his ability to remain invulnerable while bearing the shield, but this invulnerability is not a consequence of his superior strength or skill in combat; it is simply intrinsic to his being.

The events that follow also function as demonstrations of this quasi-magical wholeness. Bagdemagus's squire Melyas is knighted by Galahad, and asks if he may accompany him "tyll that som adventure departe us" (883/2–16). The severance of their temporary fellowship duly takes place a week later, when they come to a cross which (symbolically) "departed two wayes" (883/22), bearing a warning of the perils threatening the knight who takes either of them. Against Galahad's advice, Melyas insists on taking the left-hand path, the more arduous of the two. It leads him to a meadow in which stands a table set with food, and a chair with a golden crown on it. Melyas takes away the crown, and is then challenged by another knight who deals him an apparently fatal wound. Galahad arrives on the scene and engages with Melyas's assailant and a second knight, both of whom he overcomes. He then takes Melyas to an abbey so that he may be confessed; Melyas receives the Eucharist, and the tip of his opponent's spear is pulled from his body. He swoons, but does not die, and the monk who is tending to him declares that he can heal him within seven weeks (883–5).

The events in this short narrative sequence are shaped by a symbolic logic that works to contrast Melyas's vulnerability with Galahad's wholeness. The symbolic character of the narrative is made clear when a monk explains that Melyas's wound is due to his failure to make confession before being knighted (886/8–14). The left-hand path that he took signifies "the way of synnars and of myssebelevers" (886/15); the pride that led him to separate from Galahad, and the covetousness that led him to take the crown, are signified in the two knights against whom Galahad fought (886/20–30). The relation between narrative event and interpretation here, as elsewhere in the *Sankgreal*, is of a rather unusual kind. On the one hand, the interpretation is not far-reaching enough to convert the narrative into a full-blown allegory, such as Deguileville's *Pilgrimage of the Life of Man*: the two knights *signify* the two deadly sins which affect Melyas, but that is not to say that they *are* those sins. Yet at the same time the interpretation resists assimilation into a fully mimetic mode – that is, a mode in which ethical significance is intrinsic to the actions portrayed rather than symbolically expressed by them. Melyas's failure to be confessed may be deplorable, but it is not easy to see why it should be a cause of his being physically wounded. And if the left-hand path is in some literal sense "the way of synnars and of myssebelevers," why does Galahad urge Melyas to let him take it? Melyas does not become a sinner and a misbeliever by virtue of choosing a path that is intrinsically wicked; rather, this path becomes the way of sinners and misbelievers because the sinful Melyas chooses it. Again, if Melyas's covetousness in taking the crown is reprehensible, why does Galahad attack the knight who reproves Melyas for this action and tries to stop him? This narrative sequence is thus not designed to present a series of ethical choices which function as examples for everyday life; rather, like the final vision of the Grail, it manifests a spiritual reality on a physical plane, even though the relation between the spiritual and the physical remains inaccessible. So the lack of confession and the sin of pride manifest themselves in a physical separation from Galahad ("pryde ys hede of every synne: that caused thys knyght to departe frome sir Galahad" (886/22–4)) and a physical wound; confession, conversely, "makes whole" the spiritual wound and so initiates the process of physical healing.

The processes by which Galahad acquires first his sword and then his shield thus invest the knight's equipment with a special mystique. His arms are not merely the tools of his trade, but sacral objects which mark out his special destiny. The crown that Melyas takes seems, like the sword in the stone, to offer itself to all comers, but when he carries it off he finds that, like the sword, it chooses its owner, rather than the reverse. A king does not become king by seizing a crown; rather, the crown marks him out as the one who already is king. So it is with the knight: Galahad's arms are the symbols of a destinal election. This destinal role is reinforced by the account of the shield's history that the white knight gives Galahad: it goes back to the days of Joseph of Arimathaea, and was made for King Evelake to do battle against the Saracens. At the outset of the battle, it is covered with a cloth, which is removed at the most critical moment to reveal the figure of a crucified man. This image of suffering wins the battle, and also heals a man whose hand has been severed (880). Later, when Joseph of Arimathea is dying, he makes a cross on the shield with his own blood, and declares that no one will be able to own it with impunity but Galahad, the good knight, "laste of my lynage" (881/4–13). Again we have the unveiling of a destiny – a destiny expressed in an image of bodily suffering that conquers and heals. And this bodily suffering is elided with the knight's hazarding of himself in combat. Religious history thus finds its culmination in the knight; chivalry can trace its history back to the foot of the Cross.[20]

The dual role of blood, as symbol of both wounding and healing, is evident not only in the story of the shield but also elsewhere in the *Sankgreal*. The bleeding spear which accompanies the Grail, and which enigmatically unites the active and passive versions of wounding into a single image, is at the centre of this symbolic role. It is with the blood that drips from this spear that Galahad anoints the Maimed King and makes him "an hole man" (1031/8–15), after he and his companions have seen the man bearing the signs of Christ's Passion "bledynge all opynly" emerge from the Grail (1030/3–5). Bors's vision of the bird which dies giving blood for the life of its young is another image of the dual role of blood (956/6–13); so is the death of Perceval's sister, who consents to give a basinful of blood to heal a leper lady (1002–4). The simultaneity of wholeness and severance, bound together like substance and shadow, is expressed in the vocabulary Malory uses here: "Than asked she her Saveoure, and as sone as she had reseyved Hym the soule *departed* frome the body. So the same day was the lady *heled* whan she was anoynted with hir bloode" (1004/4–7; my italics).

Blood also creates a wholeness of another kind, as we are reminded when Galahad and Perceval find the tombs of the sixty maidens who have likewise died as a result of giving blood for the leper lady: the tombs bear their names "and of what bloode they were com off. And all were of kyngys bloode" (1005/16–17). Lineage and kin, the links created by blood, take on a special importance in the *Sankgreal*, working in both a horizontal and a vertical direction: blood relationship intensifies fellowship into a mystical bond; blood lineage is the carrier of destiny. Galahad is, as we have seen, the last of Joseph of Arimathaea's line; he is also the last knight of Solomon's kindred, as Perceval's sister reveals in her explanation of the three spindles on the ship (991/32, 994/13). The knightly stress on lineage unites with biblical genealogy to give a religious sanction to chivalry.[21] The quest for the Grail reveals kin relationships: Perceval finds an aunt and a sister, Lancelot a son.

20 Baumgartner, *L'Arbre et le pain*, 38.
21 As noted by Frappier, "Le Graal et la chevalerie," 173–4, 181–3.

Like blood, the body is an image of wholeness, expressed in the form of virginity. Galahad's perfection is manifested above all in the fact that he is "a clene virgyne above all knyghtes" (1025/12–13), and it is the magical power of his virginity that works to heal King Mordrains and restore his youth (1025/9–17). Similarly, the blood that Perceval's sister is required to give must come from "a maydyn, and a clene virgyne in wylle and in worke, and a kynges doughter" if it is to heal the leper lady (1002/20–2). It is because the intact, inviolate, virgin body is an image of spiritual wholeness that sexual temptations loom so large in the adventures of the Grail knights. Perceval is tempted by a lady who turns out to be a fiend in disguise; she plies him with food and drink, and then offers him her love. Perceval is ready to succumb, but he is saved by "adventure and grace."

> And than sir Percivale layde him downe by her naked. And by adventure and grace he saw hys swerde ly on the erthe naked, where in the pomell was a rede crosse and the sygne of the crucifixe therin, and bethought hym on hys knyghthode and hys promyse made unto the good man tofornehande, and than he made a sygne of the crosse in his forehed. And therewith the pavylon turned up-so-downe and than hit changed unto a smooke and a blak clowde. (918/28–919/1)

It is significant that Perceval is not saved by a moral struggle culminating in a deliberate choice, but rather by a semi-instinctive physical reaction prompted by chance – by adventure. The linking of "grace" with "adventure" fixes its meaning as "good fortune" (*MED* 3c) rather than "God's grace" *(MED* la); it is chance rather than God's will that is the operative force. Here, no less than in knightly combat, adventure works to reveal destiny. The symbolic nature of this scene is brilliantly conjured up by Malory's use of the word "naked," the adjective applied to both Perceval and his sword. The word "naked" makes the sword the image of the knight himself, again making his weapons the symbolic expression of his destined role. The "naked" sword is both vulnerable and dangerous – unprotected by its sheath, but at the same time ready to strike, to inflict a wound. So Perceval's naked body bespeaks vulnerability, the precarious fragility of his virginity, and yet it also bespeaks his openness to the power of "adventure" and "grace." It is his nakedness before the workings of chance that releases the power that saves him. Coming to his senses, Perceval punishes his unruly flesh by wounding himself in the thigh, so that "the blode sterte aboute hym" (919/15). The physical wound paradoxically heals his spiritual wound, the acknowledgment of guilt recreates wholeness on the spiritual plane.

Bors too is tempted by the offer of love from a lady who threatens to commit suicide, along with twelve of her gentlewomen, if he rejects her (965/4–34). The pressure is increased by the additional threat that rejection will also entail the death of his cousin Lancelot (963/36–964/1). Bors's response is to reflect "that levir he had they all had loste their soules than he hys soule" (966/4–5). The strange element of detachment in this reflection is also present in his assessment of the dilemma with which he is confronted – significantly, "at the departynge of ... two wayes" (960/22) – when he sees his brother Lionel, bound and bleeding, being led away on a horse by two knights on one hand, and on the other, a maiden about to be raped by a knight. Agonized, Bors decides to rescue the maiden, but he represents her plight not in terms of the physical or emotional trauma of rape, but in terms of the loss of virginity, whose very vulnerability gives it a quasi-magical status: "if I helpe nat the mayde she ys shamed, and shall lose hir virginité which she shall never gete agayne" (961/16–17). The claims of virginity here override the claims of blood; bodily wholeness entails separation, albeit accompanied by great emotional distress, from the bonds created by fellowship and kinship. The separateness which is the condition of this bodily wholeness is imaged both in Bors's prefatory dream of the two lily flowers which are "departed" by a good man (958/16–18), symbolizing the maiden and the would-be rapist (968/12–22), and in the issue of the final combat between the indignant Lionel and the reluctant Bors, when they are dramatically separated by a fiery cloud from heaven, and a voice commands Bors "go hens and beare felyship no lenger with thy brothir" (974/11–12). He is told to make his way to the sea, and join Perceval; the fellowship of the Grail, founded on bodily integrity, supersedes natural blood-ties.

The narrative imagery of wholeness and separation is woven into complicated and paradoxical patterns, as this sequence of adventures shows. Wholeness never brings unalloyed fulfilment; it always entails a corresponding separation, the rupture of another kind of unity, which imbues it with a sense of nostalgia or yearning. Malory inherits much of this complex narrative imagery from the *Queste,* although, as we have seen, he is also capable of extending and refining it. But his most imaginative development of the Grail narrative is in his conception of the role of Lancelot and his relation to Galahad. It is here that the *Sankgreal* achieves an emotional power which goes far beyond anything in the French source.

If Galahad embodies inner wholeness, Lancelot embodies an inner fragmentation. As Galahad's wholeness is expressed in his virginity, Lancelot's fragmentation resides in his relationship with Guinevere. The split at the centre of Lancelot's being can be seen in the comments made to Gawain by the hermit Nacien.

> "... as synfull as ever sir Launcelot hath byn, sith that he wente into the queste of the Sankgreal he slew never man nother nought shall, tylle that he com to Camelot

> agayne; for he hath takyn upon hym to forsake synne. And ne were that he ys nat stable, but by hys thoughte he ys lyckly to turne agayne, he sholde be nexte to encheve hit sauff sir Galahad, hys sonne; but God knowith hys thought and hys unstablenesse. And yett shall he dye ryght an holy man, and no doute he hath no felow of none erthly synfull man lyvyng." (948/20–9)

These words have no parallel in the French *Queste*, and they have often been attributed to Malory's partisan attachment to Lancelot, and consequent reluctance to admit that in the Grail Quest his hero becomes a failure. The function of Nacien's speech is not, however, to salvage Lancelot's reputation, but to show Lancelot as riven by a fundamental contradiction. The impression that Nacien's words give is not of qualification, of demotion to second best, but of paradox; what is taken away with one hand is immediately restored with the other, in a way that makes it impossible to arrive at a single unified view. The two occasions when Lancelot himself is lectured by a hermit show the same disorienting oscillation between praise and blame, producing the same sense of contradiction and paradox as fundamental to his being (896/29–897/7; 930/14–18).

Lancelot's inner fragmentation expresses itself in the events of the Grail Quest in terms of distance. Early in the quest, he has a vision of the Grail which appears before a sick knight and heals him; but throughout this vision he is "half wakyng and half slepynge" (894/9) and so is distanced from the wholeness it represents. Even in his final, most satisfying vision of the Grail, he has to watch from the chamber door, and when he tries to enter, invisible hands carry him outside and leave him in a trance before the door (1016/7–15). His distanced relation with his son Galahad is another sign of the lack of integration in his being. The distance is strikingly evident in the manner of Galahad's begetting: Lancelot is led by enchantment to believe that he is lying with Guinevere, when in fact it is Elaine to whom he is making love. Yet it is this action, which is at the furthest point of remove from his true self, that paradoxically produces the unflawed wholeness embodied in Galahad. Just as wholeness is never achieved without an accompanying severance, so fragmentation can miraculously issue in wholeness. Without Lancelot's adultery, Galahad's purity would not come into being.

If the Grail Quest lays bare the fragmented nature of Lancelot's being, it also allows him to achieve his own kind of wholeness. The first means to this end is confession: Lancelot cannot repair the fracture in his selfhood, but in openly acknowledging its existence, he eradicates the split between his outer reputation – his "worship," in Malory's words – and his inner being. The second way in which he achieves wholeness is in the mutual acknowledgment of his relationship with Galahad, which, significantly, is the prelude to his final vision of the

Grail. As Baumgartner has aptly observed with reference to the Grail narrative as a whole,[22] the quest for the Grail frequently turns into a quest for Galahad, who thus becomes a displaced figure of the Grail itself. So Lancelot's meeting with Galahad is a moving celebration of wholeness, symbolized in the mysterious ties of blood. Malory gives this scene an especial emotional power by altering the narrative of the *Queste* in one significant detail: in the *Queste,* Lancelot is alone on the ship which bears the dead body of Perceval's sister, and one night hears the arrival of a stranger knight who then identifies himself as Galahad. In Malory, Lancelot goes ashore, "for he was somwhat wery of the shippe" (1012/1); he then hears a knight going past him into the ship, whom he follows and accosts. Simple as this change of detail is, it nevertheless has a profound impact on the emotional charge of the ensuing recognition. For it introduces a distance, small but potentially decisive, between Lancelot and the recognition of his son. Removing Lancelot from the direct trajectory of Galahad's path creates the momentary possibility that the meeting may not be realized, that father and son will pass each other by, without ever acknowledging their relationship. The poignancy created by this sense of potential severance fills the recognition, when it is after all achieved, with a surge of emotional relief.

> And than he lystened and herde an hors com and one rydyng uppon hym, and whan he cam nyghe hym semed a knyght, and so he late hym passe and wente thereas the ship was. And there he alyght and toke the sadyll and the brydill, and put the horse frome hym, and so wente into the shyppe.
>
> And than sir Lancelot dressed hym unto the shippe and seyde,
>
> "Sir, ye be wellcom!"
>
> And he answerd, and salewed hym agayne and seyde,
>
> "Sir, what ys youre name? For much my herte gevith unto you."
>
> "Truly," seyde he, "my name ys sir Launcelot du Lake."
>
> "Sir," seyde he, "than be ye wellcom! For ye were the begynner of me in this worlde."
>
> "A, sir, ar ye sir Galahad?"
>
> "Ye, forsothe."
>
> And so he kneled downe and askyd hym hys blyssynge. And aftir that toke of his helme and kyssed hym, and there was grete joy betwyxte them, for no tunge can telle what joy was betwyxte them. And there every of them tolde othir the aventures that had befalle them syth that they departed frome the courte. (1012/1–23)

22 *L'Arbre et le pain,* 56.

The separate paths that their adventures have followed are united in their retelling and their convergence on this moment of union. Yet even here, distance is maintained in the formal mode of address – "sir Lancelot," "sir Galahad" – which reinforces the awareness of the preciousness and rarity of union.

The final reunion of Lancelot and Galahad is followed by their final separation: after they have spent half a year in adventures together, a knight armed in white bids Galahad leave the ship, and a heavenly voice tells them that they will not meet again before the Day of Judgment. Lancelot's response counterpoints the continuing bonds of blood with the finality of separation:

> "Now, my sonne, sir Galahad, sith we shall departe and nother of us se other more, I pray to that Hyghe Fadir, conserve me and you bothe." (1013/31–3)

The "departure" between father and son hangs over Lancelot's following vision of the Grail like a shadow, making the end of Lancelot's quest both severance and fulfilment.

The same is true of the original ending which Malory invents for the *Sankgreal* as a whole. After relating the death of Galahad, then of Perceval, the French *Queste* finally tells how Bors returned to King Arthur's court and related the adventures of the Grail, which were written down and kept in the library at Salisbury. Malory follows his source up to this point, but whereas the *Queste* ends with a reference to its own genesis in the fictive records at Salisbury, Malory introduces a completely original exchange between Bors and Lancelot. It is an exchange that emphasizes the permanent severance of Galahad and Perceval from the Round Table fellowship, sundered from it by death in a distant city, on the other side of the sea. But it is an exchange that also emphasizes wholeness, in the reassembling of the "hole courte" of Arthur at the conclusion of the Quest, in its reminiscence of the time that Lancelot and Galahad spent together, in its reminder of the ties of blood that link Galahad, Lancelot and Bors, and in Lancelot's final moving affirmation that he and Bors will never again "departe in sundir" so long as they live.

> And anone sir Bors seyde to sir Launcelot,
>
> "Sir Galahad, youre owne sonne, salewed you by me, and aftir you my lorde kynge Arthure and all the hole courte, and so ded sir Percivale. For I buryed them both myne owne hondis in the cité of Sarras. Also, sir Launcelot, sir Galahad prayde you to remembir of thys unsyker worlde, as ye behyght hym whan ye were togydirs more than halffe a yere."
>
> "Thys ys trew," seyde sir Launcelot, "now I truste to God hys prayer shall avayle me."

> Than sir Launcelot toke sir Bors in hys armys and seyde,
>
> "Cousyn, ye ar ryght wellcom to me! For all that ever I may do for you and for yours, ye shall fynde my poure body redy atte all tymes whyle the spyryte is in hit, and that I promyse you feythfully, and never to fayle. And wete ye well, gentyl cousyn sir Bors, ye and I shall never departe in sundir whylis oure lyvys may laste."
>
> "Sir," seyde he, "as ye woll, so woll I." (1036/23–1037/7)

Perfect wholeness, as represented by the full vision of the Grail granted to Galahad and his companions, is achieved only briefly, but fragmentary images of that wholeness are woven into the texture of knightly experience, sudden flowerings of fulfilment which bring renewed longing in their train.

The last two books of Malory's work trace the slow disintegration of the Round Table fellowship and the final loss of the wholeness which it had embodied. Yet just before he begins the final book, Malory introduces a powerful image of wholeness in "The Healing of Sir Urry," an episode which has no counterpart in the French source. It is an episode which, as Mark Lambert has noted, constitutes a kind of narrative pun on the word "hole":[23] the wounded knight Sir Urry seeks to be made whole by "the beste knyght of the worlde" (1146/12), the whole court attempts to heal him. The long roll-call of names emphasizes the wholeness of the Round Table fellowship, assembled one last time before the imminent end. Only Lancelot is absent, but he arrives just as all the other knights have tried and failed. Persuaded by Arthur to try in his turn, not out of presumption, but "for to beare us felyshyp, insomuche as ye be a felow of the Rounde Table" (1151/32–3), Lancelot prays to God to preserve his "symple worship and honesté" (1152/21–2), searches Sir Urry's wounds, and heals him. Lancelot's "worship" is proved on the body of Sir Urry, as the perfection of Galahad and Perceval is proved in acts of bodily healing. The healing of Sir Urry is a kind of secular counterpart to the final visions of the Grail in the *Sankgreal*, the first of which leads to the healing of the Maimed King, and the second of which leads to Galahad's absorption into the "feliship" of heaven (1034/14; 1035/1). But here too wholeness is counterpointed by separation, in the diverging responses to the healing of Sir Urry.

> Than kynge Arthur and all the kynges and knyghtes kneled downe and gave thankynges and lovynge unto God and unto Hys Blyssed Modir. And ever sir Launcelot wepte, as he had bene a chylde that had bene beatyn! (1152/33–6)

---

23 *Malory: Style and Vision in Le Morte Darthur* (New Haven, CT, 1975), 63.

The court rejoices; Lancelot weeps. This divergence at the very heart of the climactic moment of healing and fellowship expresses with delicate poignancy the precariousness and the preciousness of wholeness.

Malory, like the author of the *Queste*, sees the Grail narrative as the apotheosis of chivalric experience. But what for the French author is a story of chivalric success acquires in Malory a note of nostalgia and longing. In the French *Queste*, Galahad's role is to "put an end to" the adventures of Logres, as if they were an unpleasant interruption to normal life. In Malory, the ending of adventures brings sadness as well as a sense of fulfilment. The dominant mood of his work – particularly towards its end – is elegiac. If he celebrates the Arthurian world, he celebrates it as something lost forever, severed from the present by death and time. But the elegiac mood goes deeper still: it mediates a view of life as a constantly frustrated search for wholeness which is no sooner found than lost again. The *Sankgreal* situates the full realization of wholeness beyond earthly experience; its necessary condition is the severance from the world effected by death. So the "death and departynge" of King Arthur and his knights makes possible the completion of the "hoole book" that relates their adventures; earthly wholeness is realized only on the plane of narrative.

Bibliography

Primary Works

Alan of Lille. *De Planctu Naturae*. Edited by Nikolaus M. Häring, *Studi medievali*, 3rd ser. 19.2 (1978): 797–879.

– *Distinctiones dictionum theologicalium*. *PL* 210, cols 685–1012.

Andreas Capellanus. *On Love*, ed. P.G. Walsh. London, 1982.

Aquinas, Thomas. *Summa theologiae*. Blackfriars edition with English translation. 61 vols. London, 1964-80.

Aristoteles latinus, pars prior. Edited by Georges Lacombe. 2nd ed. Bruges, 1957.

Aristotle: *Ethica Nicomachea*. Edited by René Antoine Gauthier. *Aristoteles Latinus* XXVI.1–3. 5 vols. Leiden, 1972–5.

Augustine. *Confessionum Libri XIII*. Edited by L. Verheijen. Corpus Christianorum Series Latina 27. 2nd ed. Turnhout, 1981.

– *Saint Augustine. Confessions*. Translated by Henry Chadwick. Oxford, 1992.

– *De civitate dei*. Edited by B. Dombart and A. Kalb. 2 vols. Corpus Christianorum Series Latina 47–8. Turnhout, 1955.

Benoît de Sainte-Maure. *Le Roman de Troie*. Edited by Léopold Constans. Société des Anciens Textes Français. 6 vols. Paris, 1904–12.

Beowulf: *Klaeber's Beowulf*, 4th ed. Edited by R.D. Fulk, Robert E. Bjork, and John D. Niles. Toronto, 2008.

Beowulf. Edited and translated by Michael Swanton. Manchester, 1978.

Bernard: *Vita prima*, *PL* 185, cols 225–466.

Bernard: *St Bernard of Clairvaux. The Story of his Life as recorded in the Vita Prima Bernardi by certain of his contemporaries, William of St. Thierry, Arnold of Bonnevaux, Geoffrey and Philip of Clairvaux, and Odo of Deuil*. Translated by Geoffrey Webb and Adrian Walker. Westminster, MD, 1960.

Calcidius. *Timaeus*. Edited by J.H. Waszink. Plato Latinus, vol. 4. London, 1962.

Caxton, William. *The Recuyell of the Historyes of Troy*. Edited by H. Oskar Sommer. 2 vols. London, 1894.

– *The Book of the Ordre of Chyualry*. Edited by A.T.P. Byles. EETS o.s. 168. London, 1926.

Chaucer: *Troilus and Criseyde*. Edited by B.A. Windeatt. London, 1984.

Chrétien de Troyes. *Arthurian Romances: Chretien de Troyes*. Translated by D.D.R. Owen. London, 1987.

– *Le chevalier de la charrete*. Edited by Mario Roques. Paris, 1968.

– *Chretien de Troyes: Arthurian Romances*. Translated by William W. Kibler and Carleton W. Carroll. London, 1991.

– *Chrestien de Troyes. Yvain*. Edited by T.B.W. Reid. Manchester, 1942.

– *Le Roman de Perceval ou le conte du Graal*. Edited by Keith Busby. Tübingen, 1993.

– *Perceval: The Story of the Grail*. Translated by Nigel Bryant. Cambridge, 1982. [Includes selections from the *Continuations* of *Perceval.*]

Christine de Pisan, Jean Gerson, Jean de Montreuil, Gontier et Pierre Col. *Le débat sur Le Roman de la Rose*. Edited by Eric Hicks. Paris, 1977.

Cleanness: see *Pearl*.

The Continuations of the Old French Perceval of Chretien de Troyes. Edited by William Roach et al. 5 vols in 6. Philadelphia, 1949–83.

Dante Alighieri. *Convivio*. Edited by Cesare Vasoli and Domenico de Robertis. In *Dante Alighieri. Opere minore*. Vol. I, Part 2. Milan, 1988.

– *Dante: The Banquet*. Translated by Christopher Ryan. Saratoga, CA, 1989.

Dares: *Daretis Phrygii De Excidio Troiae Historia*. Edited by Ferdinand Meister. Leipzig, 1873.

Dymmok, Roger. *Liber Contra XII Errores et Hereses Lollardorum*. Edited by H.S. Cronin. London, n.d.

Fasciculi Zizaniorum. Edited by Walter Waddington Shirley. Rolls Series 5. London, 1858.

Gerbert de Montreuil: La Continuation de Perceval. Edited by Mary Williams and Marguerite Oswald. 3 vols. Paris, 1922–75.

Gower: *The English Works of John Gower*. Edited by G.C. Macaulay. 2 vols. EETS e.s. 81–2. London, 1900–1.

Grammatici Latini. Edited by H. Keil. 7 vols. Leipzig, 1857–80.

Guido delle Colonne, *Historia Destructionis Troiae*. Edited by Nathaniel E. Griffin. Cambridge, MA, 1936.

Helinand of Froidmont. *Chronicon*. *PL* 212, cols 771–1082.

Henryson: *The Poems of Robert Henryson*. Edited by Denton Fox. Oxford, 1981.

Historia Vitae et Regni Ricardi Secundi. Edited by George B. Stow. Philadelphia, 1977.

Hudson, Anne, ed. *Selections from English Wycliffite Writings*. Cambridge, 1978.

Ilias Latina. In *Poetae Latini Minores*, edited by Emil Baehrens. 5 vols. Leipzig, 1879–83. 3:3–59.

Isidore of Seville: *Isidori Hispalensis Etymologiarum sive Originum Libri XX*. Edited by W.M. Lindsay. 2 vols. Oxford, 1911.

Jerome. *Vita S. Pauli primi eremitae* [*Life of Paul of Thebes*]. *PL* 23, cols 17–28. Translated by Carolinne White, in *Early Christian Lives*. Harmondsworth, 1998.

John of Salisbury. *Policraticus*. Edited by C.J. Webb. 2 vols. Oxford, 1909.

Joseph of Exeter. *Frigii Daretis Yliados Libri Sex*. In *Joseph Iscanus Werke und Briefe*, edited by Ludwig Gompf. Leiden, 1970.

Julian of Norwich: *A Book of Showings to the Anchoress Julian of Norwich*. Edited by Edmund Colledge and James Walsh. 2 vols. Toronto, 1978.

Julian of Norwich: *The Writings of Julian of Norwich*. Edited by Nicholas Watson and Jacqueline Jenkins. University Park, PA, 2006.

King Horn: An Edition Based on Cambridge University Library MS Gg.4.27 (2). Edited by Rosamund Allen. New York, 1984.

Knighton's Chronicle 1337–1396. Edited and translated by G.H. Martin. Oxford, 1995.

Lancelot. Edited by Alexandre Micha. Textes Littéraires Français. 9 vols. Paris, 1978–83.

Lancelot-Grail: The Old French Arthurian Vulgate and Post-Vulgate in Translation. Edited by Norris J. Lacy. 5 vols. New York, 1993–6.

Langland, William. *The Vision of Piers Plowman: A Critical Edition of the B-Text*. Edited by A.V.C. Schmidt. 2nd edn, London, 1995.

– *William Langland. Piers Plowman: A Parallel-Text Edition of the A, B, C and Z Versions*. Edited by A.V.C. Schmidt. 2 vols. Vol. 1: London, 1995. Vol. 2: Kalamazoo, MI, 2008.

Livre de l'ordre de chevalerie. Edited by Vincenzo Minervini. Biblioteca di filologia romanza 21. Bari, 1972.

Lydgate, John. *Troy Book*. Edited by Henry Bergen. Parts 1–3, EETS e.s. 97, 103, 106. London, 1906–8. Reissued as 1 volume. Part 4, EETS e.s.126. London, 1935.

Malory, Sir Thomas. *The Morte Darthur: Parts Seven and Eight*. Edited by Derek S. Brewer. London, 1968.

Marie de France. *Lais*. Edited by A. Ewert. Oxford, 1944.

– *The Lais of Marie de France*, Translated by Glynn S. Burgess and Keith Busby. 2nd ed. London, 1999.

Matheolus: *Les Lamentations de Matheolus et le Livre de Leesce de Jehan le Fevre, de Ressons*. Edited by A.G. van Hamel. 2 vols. Bibliothèque des Hautes Études 95–6. Paris, 1893–1905.

Merlin: Roman en Prose du XIIIe Siècle, publié avec la mise en prose du Merlin de Robert de Boron d'après le manuscrit appartenant à M. Alfred H. Huth. Edited by Gaston Paris and Jacob Ulrich. Société des Anciens Textes Français. 2 vols. Paris, 1886.

Moore, Marianne. *Collected Poems*. London, 1951.

La Mort Le Roi Artu. Edited by Jean Frappier. Textes Littéraires Français. Geneva, 1964.

– *The Death of King Arthur*. Translated by James Cable. Harmondsworth, 1971.

Partenopeu de Blois. Edited by Joseph Gildea. 2 vols. Villanova, PA, 1967–8.
Pearl: Translated by Marie Borroff. *Pearl: A New Verse Translation*. New York, 1977.
Pearl: *The Poems of the Pearl Manuscript: Pearl, Cleanness, Patience, Sir Gawain and the Green Knight*. Edited by Malcolm Andrew and Ronald Waldron. 5th ed. Exeter, 2007.
Philippe de Mézières. *Letter to King Richard II*. Edited by G.W. Coopland. Liverpool, 1975.
Prudentius. Edited by H.J. Thomson, 2 vols. London, 1953–62.
La Queste del Saint Graal. Edited by Albert Pauphilet. Classiques Français du Moyen Âge. Paris, 1978.
– *The Quest of the Holy Grail*. Translated by P.M. Matarasso. Harmondsworth, 1969.
Recueil des croniques et anchiennes istories de la Grant Bretaigne, a present nomme Engleterre, par Jehan de Waurin, seigneur de Forestel ... 1399–1422. Edited by William Hardy. Rolls series 39, vol. 2. London, 1868.
Richard the Redeles. In *The Piers Plowman Tradition*, edited by Helen Barr, 99–133. London, 1993.
Robert de Boron. *Le Roman de L'Estoire dou Graal*. Edited by William A. Nitze. Paris, 1971.
Le Roman de Balain. Edited by M.D. Legge. Manchester, 1942.
Le Roman de la Rose. Edited by Felix Lecoy. Classiques Français du Moyen Âge, 3 vols. Paris, 1966–70.
Seneca. *Moral Essays*. Edited by J.W. Basore. 3 vols. Cambridge, MA, 1928–35. Reprinted 1958.
Silverstein, Theodore, ed. *Sir Gawain and the Green Knight*. Chicago, 1974.
Sir Orfeo. Edited by A.J. Bliss. Oxford, 1954.
Suite du Merlin. Edited by Gilles Roussineau. 2nd ed. 2 vols in one. Geneva, 2006.
Tristan: Le Roman de Tristan en prose. Edited by Renée L. Curtis. 3 vols. Cambridge, 1985. [Vol. 1: originally published in Munich, 1963. Vol. 2 originally published in Leiden, 1976.]
– *Le Roman de Tristan en prose*. General ed. Philippe Ménard. 9 vols. Geneva, 1987–97.
Troilus and Cressida. Edited by David M. Bevington. London, 1998.
Troilus and Cressida. Edited by Kenneth Palmer. London, 1982.
Les Troubadours. Edited and translated by René Lavaud and René Nelli. 2 vols. Paris, 1960–6.
The Vision of Edmund Leversedge. Edited by W.F. Nijenhuis. Nijmegen, 1991.
Walsingham: *The St Albans Chronicle. The Chronica maiora of Thomas Walsingham, I: 1376–1394*. Edited and translated by John Taylor, Wendy R. Childs, and Leslie Watkiss. Oxford, 2003.
William of Newburgh. *The History of William of Newburgh*. Translated by Joseph Stevenson. London, 1856. Reprinted Felinfach, 1996.
Ysengrimus: Text with Translation, Commentary, and Introduction. Edited and translated by Jill Mann. Leiden, 1987

Secondary Works

Adelman, Janet. "'This Is and Is Not Cressid': The Characterization of Cressida." In *The (M)other Tongue: Essays in Feminist Psychoanalytic Interpretation*, edited by Shirley Nelson Garner, Claire Kahane, and Madelon Sprengnether, 119–41. Ithaca, NY, 1985.

Aers, David. *Chaucer, Langland and the Creative Imagination*. London, 1980.

Alexander, Jonathan J.G. "Painting and Manuscript Illumination for Royal Patrons in the Later Middle Ages." In Scattergood and Sherborne, *English Court Culture*, 141–62.

– "The Portrait of Richard II in Westminster Abbey." In Gordon, Monnas, and Elam, *The Regal Image of Richard II*, 197–206.

Andrew, Malcolm. "Theories of Authorship." In Brewer and Gibson, *Companion to the Gawain-Poet*, 23–33.

Archibald, Elizabeth. "Malory's Ideal of Fellowship." *Review of English Studies* n.s. 43 (1992): 311–28.

Atkinson, Stephen C.B. "Malory's Lancelot and the Quest of the Grail." In Spisak, *Studies in Malory*, 129–52.

Auerbach, Erich. *Mimesis: The Representation of Reality in Western Literature*. Translated by Willard Trask. Princeton, NJ, 1953.

Barney, Stephen A. "Troilus Bound." *Speculum* 47 (1972): 445–58.

–, ed. *Chaucer's Troilus: Essays in Criticism*. London, 1980.

Barron, Caroline M. "Richard II and London." In *Richard II: The Art of Kingship*, edited by Anthony Goodman and James Gillespie, 129–54. Oxford, 1999.

– "Richard II: Image and Reality." In *Making and Meaning. The Wilton Diptych*, edited by Dillian Gordon, 13–19. London, 1993.

Bartlett, Robert. *Trial by Fire and Water: the Medieval Judicial Ordeal*. Oxford, 1986.

Bate, W. Jackson. *The Burden of the Past and the English Poet*. London, 1971.

Baumgartner, Emmanuèle. *L'Arbre et le pain: Essai sur La Queste del Saint Graal*. Paris, 1981.

Bayley, John. "Time and the Trojans." *Essays in Criticism* 25 (1975): 55–73.

– *Shakespeare and Tragedy*. London, 1981.

Beer, Gillian. *Arguing with the Past: Essays in Narrative from Woolf to Sidney*. London, 1989.

Beeston, John B. "How Much Was Known of the Breton Lai in Fourteenth-Century England?" In Benson, *The Learned and the Lewed*, 319–36.

Bell, David N. *The Libraries of the Cistercians, Gilbertines and Premonstratensians*. Corpus of British Medieval Library Catalogues 3. London, 1992.

Bennett, J.A.W. *Chaucer's Book of Fame: An Exposition of "The House of Fame."* Oxford, 1968.

Bennett, Michael J. *Community, Class and Careerism: Cheshire and Lancashire Society in the Age of Sir Gawain and the Green Knight*. Cambridge, 1983.

– "The Court of Richard II and the Promotion of Literature." In *Chaucer's England: Literature in Historical Context*, edited by Barbara Hanawalt, 3–20. Minneapolis, 1992.

– "Courtly Literature and Northwest England in the Later Middle Ages." In *Court and Poet. Selected Proceedings of the Third Congress of the International Courtly Literature Society (Liverpool 1980)*, edited by Glyn S. Burgess, 69–78. Liverpool, 1981.

– "'Good Lords' and King-Makers: The Stanleys of Lathom in English Politics, 1385–1485." *History Today* 31, no. 7 (July 1981): 12–17.

– "The Historical Background." In Brewer and Gibson, *Companion to the Gawain-Poet*, 71–90.

– "*Sir Gawain and the Green Knight* and the Literary Achievement of the North-West Midlands: The Historical Background." *Journal of Medieval History* 5 (1979): 63–88.

Benson, Larry D. *Art and Tradition in Sir Gawain and the Green Knight.* New Brunswick, NJ, 1965.

– *A Glossarial Concordance to the Riverside Chaucer.* New York and London, 1993.

–, ed. *The Learned and the Lewed: Studies in Chaucer and Medieval Literature.* Cambridge, MA, 1974.

– *Malory's Morte Darthur.* Cambridge, MA, 1976.

– "Sir Thomas Malory's *Le Morte Darthur.*" In *Critical Approaches to Six Major English Works*, edited by R. M. Lumiansky and Herschel Baker, 81–131. Philadelphia, PA, 1968.

Benson, Robert D.G. *Medieval Body Language: A Study of the Use of Gesture in Chaucer's Poetry.* Anglistica, 21. Copenhagen, 1980.

Binski, Paul. *Westminster Abbey and the Plantagenets. Kingship and the Representation of Power, 1200–1400.* New Haven, CT, 1995.

Blaess, Madeleine. "Predestination in Some Thirteenth-Century Prose Romances." *Currents of Thought in French Literature: Essays in Memory of G.T. Clapton*, 3–19. Oxford, 1965.

Blamires, Alcuin. *Chaucer, Ethics, and Gender.* Oxford, 2006.

– "The Wife of Bath and Lollardy." *Medium Ævum* 58 (1989): 224–42.

Bloom, Harold. *The Anxiety of Influence: A Theory of Poetry.* London, 1973.

Bloomfield, Morton W. "Distance and Predestination in *Troilus and Criseyde.*" *PMLA* 72 (1957): 14–26. Reprinted in Schoeck and Taylor, *Chaucer Criticism*, 2:196–210, and in Barney, *Chaucer's Troilus*, 75–90.

– "Episodic Motivation and Marvels in Epic and Romance." In Bloomfield, *Essays and Explorations: Studies in Ideas, Language and Literature*, 97–128. Cambridge, MA, 1970.

– "The Problem of the Hero in the Later Medieval Period." In *Concepts of the Hero in the Middle Ages and the Renaissance*, edited by Norman T. Burns and Christopher J. Reagan, 27–48. London, 1975.

Bogdanow, Fanni. *The Romance of the Grail.* New York, 1966.

Boitani, Piero. *Chaucer and the Imaginary World of Fame.* Cambridge, 1984.

– "Inferno XXXIII." In *Cambridge Readings in Dante's Comedy*, edited by Kenelm Foster and Patrick Boyde, 70–89. Cambridge, 1981.

– "Old Books Brought to Life in Dreams: the *Book of the Duchess*, the *House of Fame*, the *Parliament of Fowls*." In Boitani and Mann, *The Cambridge Companion to Chaucer*, 58–77.

– *The Tragic and the Sublime in Medieval Literature*. Cambridge, 1989.

Boitani, Piero and Jill Mann, eds. *The Cambridge Chaucer Companion*. Cambridge, 1986. Rev. ed., *The Cambridge Companion to Chaucer*. Cambridge, 2003.

Bondéelle, Anne. "Trésor des moines. Les Chartreux, les Cisterciens et leurs livres." In *Histoire des bibliothèques françaises*, vol. 1, *Les bibliothèques médiévales du VI*[e] *siècle à 1530*, edited by André Vernet, 64–81. Paris, 1988.

Borroff, Marie. "*Pearl*'s 'Maynful Mone': Crux, Simile, and Structure." In *Acts of Interpretation: The Text in its Contexts 700–1600. Essays on Medieval and Renaissance Literature in Honor of E. Talbot Donaldson*, edited by Mary J. Carruthers and Elizabeth D. Kirk, 159–72. Norman, OK, 1982.

Borthwick, Sister Mary Charlotte. "Antigone's Song as 'Mirour' in Chaucer's *Troilus and Criseyde*." *Modern Language Quarterly* 22 (1961): 227–35.

Bowers, John M. *The Politics of Pearl: Court Poetry in the Age of Richard II*. Cambridge, 2001.

– "Chaste Marriage: Fashion and Texts at the Court of Richard II." *Pacific Coast Philology* 30 (1995): 15–26.

Bradbrook, Muriel C. "What Shakespeare did to Chaucer's *Troilus and Criseyde*." In Bradbrook, *The Artist and Society in Shakespeare's England*, 133–43. Brighton, Sussex, 1982.

Bredero, Adriaan Hendrik. "Études sur la 'Vita prima' de Saint Bernard." *Analecta sacri ordinis cisterciensis* 17 (1961): 3–72.

Brewer, Derek S.. "Armour II: The Arming Topos as Literature." In Brewer and Gibson, *Companion to the Gawain-Poet*, 175–9.

– "The Present Study of Malory." *Forum for Modern Language Studies* 6 (1970): 83–97.

– "Some Metonymic Relationships in Chaucer's Poetry." *Poetica* 1 (1974): 1–20.

– *Tradition and Innovation in Chaucer*. London, 1982.

Brewer, Derek, and Jonathan Gibson, eds. *A Companion to the Gawain-Poet*. Cambridge, 1997.

Brewer, Elisabeth. *Sir Gawain and the Green Knight: Sources and Analogues*. Cambridge, 1992.

Brooke, George C. *English Coins from the Seventh Century to the Present Day*. 3rd edn. London, 1950.

Brooks, Douglas, and Alastair Fowler. "The Meaning of Chaucer's *Knight's Tale*." *Medium Ævum* 39 (1970): 123–46.

Brownlee, Kevin, and Walter Stephens. *Discourses of Authority in Medieval and Renaissance Literature*. Hanover, NH, 1989.

Burger, Glenn, and Steven F. Kruger, eds. *Queering the Middle Ages*. Minneapolis, MN, 2001.

Burgess, Glyn S., and Karen Pratt, eds. *The Arthur of the French: The Arthurian Legend in Medieval French and Occitan Literature*. Cardiff, 2006.

Burnley, J.D. *Chaucer's Language and the Philosophers' Tradition*. Cambridge, 1979.

Burrow, J.A. *Gestures and Looks in Medieval Narrative*. Cambridge, 2002.

– *A Reading of Sir Gawain and the Green Knight*. London, 1965.

– "Should We Leave Medieval Literature to the Medievalists?" *Essays in Criticism* 53 (2003): 278–83.

– "The Sinking Island and the Dying Author: R.W. Chambers Fifty Years On." *Essays in Criticism* 30 (1990): 1–23.

Bynum, Caroline Walker. *Jesus as Mother: Studies in the Spirituality of the High Middle Ages*. London, 1982.

Campbell, Marian. "'White Harts and Coronets': The Jewellery and Plate of Richard II," In Gordon, Monnas, and Elam, *The Regal Image of Richard II*, 95–114.

Cannon, Christopher. *The Grounds of English Literature*. Oxford, 2004.

Cannon, Christopher, and Maura Nolan, eds. *Medieval Latin and Middle English Literature: Essays in Honour of Jill Mann*. Cambridge, 2011.

Carlson, David. "English Poetry, July–October 1399, and Lancastrian Crime," *Studies in the Age of Chaucer* 29 (2007): 375–418.

Carruthers, Mary. "The Wife of Bath and the Painting of Lions." *PMLA* 94 (1979): 209–22.

Chambers, A.B. "Goodfriday, 1613. Riding Westward: The Poem and the Tradition." *ELH* 28 (1961): 31–53.

Cheney, Christopher R. "Les bibliothèques cisterciennes en Angleterre au XIIe siècle." In *Mélanges Saint Bernard: XXIVe Congrès de l'Association Bourguignonne des Sociétés Savantes, Dijon 1953*, 375–82. Dijon, n.d.

Chesterton, G.K. *Chaucer*. 1932. Reprinted London, 1962.

Chism, Christine, Theresa Coletti, Fiona Somerset, Sarah Stanbury, Anne Savage, and David Wallace. "Colloquium: *The Cambridge History of Medieval English Literature*." *Studies in the Age of Chaucer* 23 (2001): 473–519.

Cohen, Jeffrey Jerome, ed. *The Postcolonial Middle Ages*. New York, 2000.

Correale, Robert M., and Mary Hamel, eds. *Sources and Analogues of the Canterbury Tales*. 2 vols. Cambridge, 2002–5.

Corrie, Marilyn. "Self-determination in the Post-Vulgate *Suite du Merlin* and Malory's *Le Morte Darthur*." *Medium Ævum* 73 (2004): 273–89.

Courtenay, William J. "The King and the Leaden Coin: The Economic Background of 'Sine Qua Non' Causality." *Traditio* 28 (1972): 185–209.

Coward, Barry. *The Stanleys, Lords Stanley and Earls of Derby, 1385–1672*. Manchester, 1983.

Crane, Susan. *Gender and Romance in Chaucer's Canterbury Tales*. Princeton, NJ, 1994.
– *The Performance of Self. Ritual, Clothing, and Identity during the Hundred Years War.* Philadelphia, 2002.
Curry, Walter Clyde. "Destiny in *Troilus and Criseyde*." In *Chaucer and the Mediaeval Sciences*, 241–98. Rev. ed. New York, 1960. Reprinted in Schoeck and Taylor, *Chaucer Criticism*, 2:34–70.
Davies, R.R. "Richard II and the Principality of Chester 1397–9." In *The Reign of Richard II. Essays in Honour of May McKisack*, edited by F.R.H. Du Boulay and Caroline M. Barron, 256–79. London, 1971.
– "The Worshipful Way in Malory." In *Patterns of Love and Courtesy*, edited by John Lawlor, 157–77. London, 1966.
Delany, Sheila. *Chaucer's House of Fame: The Poetics of Skeptical Fideism*. Chicago, 1972.
Dinshaw, Carolyn. *Chaucer's Sexual Poetics*. Madison, WI, 1989.
– *Getting Medieval: Sexualities and Conventions, Pre- and Postmodern*. Durham, NC, 1999.
– "A Kiss Is Just a Kiss: Heterosexuality and its Consolations in *Sir Gawain and the Green Knight*." *Diacritics* 24 (1994): 205–26.
– "New Approaches to Chaucer." In Boitani and Mann, *The Cambridge Companion to Chaucer*, 270–89.
Dod, Bernard G. "Aristoteles latinus." In *The Cambridge History of Later Medieval Philosophy*, edited by Norman Kretzmann, Anthony Kenny, and Jan Pinborg, 45–79. Cambridge, 1982.
Donaldson, E. Talbot. "Criseide and her Narrator." In Donaldson, *Speaking of Chaucer*, 65–83. New York, 1970.
– "Designing a Camel; Or, Generalizing the Middle Ages." *Tennessee Studies in Literature* 22 (1977): 1–16.
– *The Swan at the Well: Shakespeare Reading Chaucer.* New Haven, CT, 1985.
Donoghue, Daniel, James Simpson, and Nicholas Watson, eds. *The Morton W. Bloomfield Lectures, 1989–2005*. Kalamazoo, MI, 2010.
Doyle, A.I. "The Manuscripts." In *Middle English Alliterative Poetry and its Literary Background*, edited by David A. Lawton, 88–100. Cambridge, 1982.
Dronke, Peter. "Chaucer and the Medieval Latin Poets: Part A." In *Writers and their Background: Geoffrey Chaucer*, edited by Derek Brewer, 154–72. London, 1974.
– *Fabula: Explorations in the Uses of Myth in Medieval Platonism*. Leiden, 1974.
Duggan, H.N. "Meter, Stanza, Vocabulary, Dialect." In Brewer and Gibson, *Companion to the Gawain-Poet*, 221–42.
Eagleton, Terry. *Shakespeare and Society.* London, 1970.
Eberle, Patricia. "The Politics of Courtly Style at the Court of Richard II." In *The Spirit of the Court. Selected Proceedings of the Fourth Congress of the International Courtly*

Literature Society (Toronto 1983), edited by Glyn S. Burgess and Robert A. Taylor, 168–78. Cambridge, 1985.

Edwards, A.S.G. "The Manuscript: British Library MS Cotton Nero A.x." In Brewer and Gibson, *Companion to the Gawain-Poet*, 197–219.

Elton, W.R. "Shakespeare's Ulysses and the Problem of Value." *Shakespeare Studies* 2 (1966): 95–111.

Field, P.J.C. *Romance and Chronicle*. London, 1971.

Fish, Stanley. *Is There a Text in This Class? The Authority of Interpretive Communities*. Cambridge, MA, 1980.

Fleming, John. "Chaucer's Clerk and John of Salisbury." *English Language Notes* 2 (1964): 5–6.

Fradenburg, Louise O. Aranye. *Sacrifice Your Love: Psychoanalysis, Historicism, Chaucer*. Minneapolis, MN, 2002.

Frappier, Jean. *Étude sur la Mort le Roi Artu*. Paris, 1936.

– "Le Graal et la chevalerie." *Romania* 75 (1954): 165–210.

Freccero, John. "Pilgrim in a Gyre." In Freccero, *Dante: The Poetics of Conversion*, 70–92. Cambridge, MA, 1986.

French, J. Milton. "A Defense of Troilus." *PMLA* 44 (1929): 1246–51.

Fries, Maureen. "Indiscreet Objects of Desire: Malory's 'Tristram' and the Necessity of Deceit." In Spisak, *Studies in Malory*, 87–108.

Gaylord, Alan T. "*Sentence* and *Solaas* in Fragment VII of the Canterbury Tales: Harry Bailly as Horseback Editor." *PMLA* 82 (1967): 226–35.

Gillespie, James L. "Richard II's Cheshire Archers." *Transactions of the Historic Society of Lancashire and Cheshire* 125 (1975): 1–39.

– "Richard II: King of Battles?" In *The Age of Richard II*, edited by James L. Gillespie, 139–64. Stroud, 1997.

Given-Wilson, Chris. *The Royal Household and the King's Affinity: Service, Politics and Finance in England 1360–1413*. New Haven, CT, 1986.

Gordon, Dillian, Lisa Monnas, and Caroline Elam, eds. *The Regal Image of Richard II and the Wilton Diptych*. London, 1997.

Gordon, Ida L. *The Double Sorrow of Troilus*. Oxford, 1970.

Grant, Edward. *Physical Science in the Middle Ages*. Cambridge, 1971.

Green, Richard Firth. *A Crisis of Truth: Literature and Law in Ricardian England*. Philadelphia, 1999.

– *Poets and Princepleasers. Literature and the English Court in the Late Middle Ages*. Toronto, 1980.

Green, Richard Hamilton "Gawain's Shield and the Quest for Perfection." *ELH* 29 (1962): 121–39. Reprinted in *Middle English Survey: Critical Essays*, edited by Edward Vasta. Notre Dame, 1965. 71–92.

Greenblatt, Stephen, gen. ed. *The Norton Anthology of English Literature*, 9th ed, vol.1. New York, 2012.

Greene, Gayle. "Shakespeare's Cressida: 'A kind of self.'" In *The Woman's Part: Feminist Criticism of Shakespeare*, edited by Carolyn Ruth Swift Lenz, Gayle Greene, and Carol Thomas Neely, 133–49. Urbana, IL, 1980.

Hamilton, Marie Padgett. "Echoes of Childermas in the Tale of the Prioress." In *Chaucer: Modern Essays in Criticism*, edited by Edward Wagenknecht, 88–97. New York, 1959.

Hamilton, W.E.M.C. "L'interprétation mystique de La Queste del Saint Graal." *Neophilologus* 27 (1942): 94–110.

Hammond, Eleanor Prescott. *Chaucer: A Bibliographical Manual*. New York, 1908.

Hanna, Ralph. "Defining Middle English Alliterative Poetry." In *The Endless Knot: Essays on Old and Middle English in Honor of Marie Borroff*, edited by M. Teresa Tavormina and R.F. Yeager, 43–64. Cambridge, 1995.

Hanning, Robert W. "From *Eva* to *Ave*: Chaucer's Insight into the Roles Women Play." *Signs* 2 (1977): 580–99.

– "Roasting a Friar, Mis-taking a Wife, and Other Acts of Textual Harassment in Chaucer's *Canterbury Tales*." *Studies in the Age of Chaucer* 7 (1985): 3–21.

Hansen, Elaine Tuttle. *Chaucer and the Fictions of Gender*. Berkeley, CA, 1992.

Harwood, B.J. "Language and the Real: Chaucer's Manciple," *Chaucer Review* 6 (1971–2): 268–79.

Hermann, John P. "Gesture and Seduction in *Troilus and Criseyde*." *Studies in the Age of Chaucer* 7 (1985): 107–35.

Hill, Thomas D. "Gawain's Jesting Lie: Towards an Interpretation of the Confessional Scene in *Gawain and the Green Knight*." *Studia Neophilologica* 52 (1980): 279–86.

Howard, Donald R. "Experience, Language and Consciousness: 'Troilus and Criseyde,' II, 596–931.' In *Medieval Literature and Folklore Studies: Essays in Honor of Francis Lee Utley*, edited by Jerome Mandel and Bruce A. Rosenburg, 173–92. New Brunswick, NJ, 1970. Reprinted in Barney, *Chaucer's Troilus*, 159–80.

Hulbert, James R. "A Hypothesis Concerning the Alliterative Revival." *Modern Philology* 28 (1931): 405–22.

Iser, Wolfgang. *The Act of Reading: A Theory of Aesthetic Response*. Baltimore, MD, 1978.

– *The Implied Reader: Patterns of Communication in Prose Fiction from Bunyan to Beckett*. Baltimore, MD, 1974.

Jacoff, Rachel. "The Hermeneutics of Hunger." In *Speaking Images: Essays in Honor of V.A. Kolve*, edited by Robert F. Yeager and Charlotte Morse, 95–110. Asheville, NC, 2001.

Jaeger, C. Stephen. "L'amour des rois: structure sociale d'une forme de sensibilité aristocratique." In Jaeger, *Scholars and Courtiers: Intellectuals and Society in the Medieval West*, VIII.547–71. Aldershot, Hants., 2002.

Jardine, Lisa. *Still Harping on Daughters: Women and Drama in the Age of Shakespeare*. Brighton, Sussex, 1983.

Jauss, Hans Robert. *Toward an Aesthetic of Reception*. Translated by Timothy Bahti. Brighton, Sussex, 1982.

Jefferson, Bernard L. *Chaucer and the Consolation of Philosophy of Boethius*. Princeton, NJ, 1917.

Jolivet, Jean. *Arts du langage et théologie chez Abélard*. Paris, 1969.

Justice, Steven. "Literary History." In *Chaucer: Contemporary Approaches*, edited by Susanna Fein and David Raybin, 199–214. University Park, PA, 2010.

– *Writing and Rebellion: England in 1381*. Berkeley, CA, 1994.

Kaye, Joel. *Economy and Nature in the Fourteenth Century*. Cambridge, 1998.

Keen, Maurice. "The Wilton Diptych: The Case for a Crusading Context." In Gordon, Monnas, and Elam, *The Regal Image of Richard II*, 189–96.

Keiser, Elizabeth. *Courtly Desire and Medieval Homophobia*. New Haven, CT, 1997.

Kelly, Robert L. "Malory's 'Tale of Balin' Reconsidered." *Speculum* 54 (1979): 85–99.

– "Wounds, Healing and Knighthood in Malory's Tale of Lancelot and Guenevere." In Spisak, *Studies in Malory*, 173–97.

Kermode, Frank. "'Opinion' in *Troilus and Cressida*." In *Teaching the Text*, edited by Susanne Kappeler and Norman Bryson, 164–79. London, 1983.

– "Opinion, Truth, and Value." *Essays in Criticism* 5 (1955): 181–7.

Kittredge, G.L. *Chaucer and His Poetry*. Cambridge, MA, 1915.

Kittredge, George Lyman. "Chaucer's Discussion of Marriage." *Modern Philology* 9 (1911–12): 435–67. Reprinted in *Chaucer: Modern Essays in Criticism*, edited by Edward Wagenknecht, 188–215. New York, 1959.

Knight, Rhonda. "All Dressed Up with Someplace To Go: Regional Identity in *Sir Gawain and the Green Knight*." *Studies in the Age of Chaucer* 25 (2003): 259–84.

Knight, Stephen. *The Structure of Sir Thomas Malory's Arthuriad*. Sydney, 1969.

– "Style and the Effects of Style in Malory's Arthuriad." *Parergon* 9 (Aug. 1974): 3–27.

Knowles, David. *The Monastic Order in England*. 2nd ed. Cambridge, 1963.

Kottler, Barnet, and Alan M. Markman, eds. *A Concordance to Five Middle English Poems*. Pittsburgh, 1966.

Kunz, George Frederick, and Charles Hugh Stevenson. *The Book of the Pearl*. London, 1908.

Lambert, Mark. *Malory: Style and Vision in Le Morte Darthur*. New Haven, CT, 1975.

– 'Telling the Story in *Troilus and Criseyde*.' In Boitani and Mann, *The Cambridge Companion to Chaucer*, 78–92.

Langholm, Odd. *Economics in the Medieval Schools*. New York, 1992.

– *Price and Value in the Aristotelian Tradition*. Bergen, 1979.

Levitan, Alan. "The Parody of Pentecost in Chaucer's *Summoner's Tale*." *University of Toronto Quarterly* 40 (1970–1): 236–46.

Lewis, C.S. *Studies in Medieval and Renaissance Literature*. Cambridge, 1966.

– *Studies in Words*. Cambridge, 1960.

Leyerle, John. "The Heart and the Chain." In Benson, *The Learned and the Lewed*, 113–45. Reprinted in Barney, *Chaucer's Troilus*, 181–209.

Long, A.A. *Problems in Stoicism*. London, 1971.

[Loomis], Laura A. Hibbard. "Malory's Book of Balin." In *Mediaeval Studies in Memory of Gertrude Schoepperle Loomis*, 175–95. Paris, 1927.

– "Chaucer and the Breton Lays of the Auchinleck Manuscript." *Studies in Philology* 38 (1941): 14–33.

Loomis, Roger Sherman, ed. *Arthurian Literature in the Middle Ages: A Collaborative History*. Oxford, 1959.

Lounsbury, Thomas R. *Studies in Chaucer*. 3 vols. London, 1892.

Lowes, John Livingston. "Chaucer's 'Etik.'" *Modern Language Notes* 25 (1910): 87–8.

– *Geoffrey Chaucer*. London, 1934.

Lumiansky, R.M. *Of Sondry Folk: The Dramatic Principle in the Canterbury Tales*. Austin, TX, 1955.

–, ed. *Malory's Originality: A Critical Study of Le Morte Darthur*. Baltimore, 1964.

Manly, John M. *Some New Light on Chaucer*. New York, 1926.

Mann, Jill. "Chaucer and Atheism." *Studies in the Age of Chaucer* 17 (1995): 5–19.

– *Chaucer and Medieval Estates Satire*. Cambridge, 1973.

– "Eating and Drinking in 'Piers Plowman.'" *Essays and Studies* 32 (1979): 26–43.

– *Feminizing Chaucer*. Cambridge, 2002.

– *From Aesop to Reynard: Beast Literature in Medieval Britain*. Oxford, 2009.

– *Geoffrey Chaucer*. Hemel Hempstead, 1991.

– "In Defence of Francesca: Human and Divine Love in Dante and Chaucer." *Strumenti critici* 131 (2013): 3–26

– "Langland and Allegory: The Morton W. Bloomfield Lectures on Medieval English Literature, II." Kalamazoo, MI, 1992. Reprinted in Donoghue, Simpson, and Watson, *The Morton W. Bloomfield Lectures*, 20–41.

– "The Nature of Need Revisited." *Yearbook of Langland Studies* 18 (2004): 3–29 .

– "The Planetary Gods in Chaucer and Henryson." In *Chaucer Traditions: Studies in Honour of Derek Brewer*, edited by Ruth Morse and Barry Windeatt, 91–106. Cambridge, 1990.

Martin, Priscilla. *Chaucer's Women: Nuns, Wives and Amazons*. Basingstoke, Hants, 1990.

Matarasso, Pauline. *The Redemption of Chivalry: A Study of the Queste del Saint Graal*. Geneva, 1979.

Mathew, Gervase. *The Court of Richard II*. London, 1968.

McIntosh, Angus. "A New Approach to Middle English Dialectology." *English Studies* 44 (1963): 1–11.

McIntosh, Angus, M.L. Samuels, and Michael Benskin, eds. *A Linguistic Atlas of Late Mediaeval English*. 4 vols. Aberdeen, 1986.

Meech, Sanford B. *Design in Chaucer's Troilus.* Syracuse, NY, 1959.

Micha, A. "L'épreuve de l'épée." *Romania* 70 (1948–9): 37–50.

Mieszkowski, Gretchen. "The Reputation of Criseyde 1155–1500." *Transactions of the Connecticut Academy of Arts and Sciences* 43 (1971): 71–153.

– "Revisiting Troilus's Faint." In *Men and Masculinities in Chaucer's Troilus and Criseyde*, edited by Tison Pugh and Marcia Smith Marzec, 43–57. Cambridge, 2008.

Miller, Jacqueline. *Poetic License: Authority and Authorship in Medieval and Renaissance Contexts.* New York, 1986.

– "The Writing on the Wall: Authority and Authorship in Chaucer's *House of Fame.*" *Chaucer Review* 17 (1982–3): 95–115.

Millett, Bella. "How Green is the Green Knight?" *Nottingham Medieval Studies* 38 (1994): 138–51.

Minnis, A.J., ed. *Chaucer's Boece and the Medieval Tradition of Boethius.* Cambridge, 1993.

Minnis, Alastair. *Medieval Theory of Authorship: Scholastic Literary Attitudes in the Later Middle Ages.* London, 1984.

Moorman, Charles. "'The Tale of the Sankgreall': Human Frailty." In Lumiansky, *Malory's Originality*, 184–204.

Morgan, Nigel. "The Signification of the Banner." In Gordon, Monnas, and Elam, *The Regal Image of Richard II*, 179–88.

Morse, Charlotte C. *The Pattern of Judgment in the Queste and Cleanness.* Columbia, 1978.

Munk Olsen, Birger. "The Cistercians and Classical Culture." *Cahiers de l'institut du moyen-âge grec et latin* 47 (1984): 64–102.

Muscatine, Charles. *Chaucer and the French Tradition.* Berkeley, CA, 1964.

Mustanoja, Tauno. *Middle English Syntax.* Part I. Helsinki, 1960.

Neilson, George. *Trial by Combat.* Glasgow, 1890.

Nelson, Cary. *The Incarnate Word: Literature as Visual Space.* Urbana, IL, 1973.

Nichols, Stephen G. "Writing the New Middle Ages." *PMLA* 120 (2005): 422–41.

Norris, Ralph. *Malory's Library.* Woodbridge, Suffolk, 2008.

North, J.D. *Chaucer's Universe.* Oxford, 1988.

Norton-Smith, John. *Geoffrey Chaucer.* London, 1974.

Nowottny, Winifred M.T. "'Opinion' and 'Value' in *Troilus and Cressida.*" *Essays in Criticism* 4 (1954): 282–96.

O'Connor, John J. "The Astronomical Dating of Chaucer's *Troilus.*" *Journal of English and Germanic Philology* 55 (1956): 556–62.

Osten, G. von der. "Job and Christ: The Development of a Devotional Image." *Journal of the Warburg and Courtauld Institutes* 16 (1953): 153–8.

Patch, Howard R. "Troilus on Determinism." *Speculum* 6 (1931): 225–43. Reprinted in Schoeck and Taylor, *Chaucer Criticism*, 2:71–85.

Patterson, Lee. *Acts of Recognition: Essays on Medieval Culture*. Notre Dame, IN, 2010.
– *Chaucer and the Subject of History*. Madison, WI, 1991.
– " 'For the Wyves love of Bathe': Feminine Rhetoric and Poetic Resolution in the *Roman de la Rose* and the *Canterbury Tales*." *Speculum* 58 (1983): 656–95.
– *Negotiating the Past: The Historical Understanding of Medieval Literature*. Madison, WI, 1987.
– *Temporal Circumstances: Form and History in the Canterbury Tales*. New York, 2006.
Pauphilet, Albert. *Études sur la Queste del Saint Graal*. Paris, 1921. Repr. 1980.
Payne, Robert O. *The Key of Remembrance: A Study of Chaucer's Poetics*. New Haven, CT, 1963.
Pearsall, Derek. "The Apotheosis of John Lydgate." *Journal of Medieval and Early Modern Studies* 25 (2005): 25–38.
– "Medieval Literature and History Enquiry." *Modern Language Review* 99.4 (2004): xxxi–xlii.
Pollock, Sir Frederick, and Frederic William Maitland. *The History of English Law Before the Time of Edward I*. 2nd ed. 2 vols. Cambridge, 1968.
Poulet, Georges. *The Metamorphoses of the Circle*. Translated by Carey Dawson and Elliott Coleman. Baltimore, MD, 1966.
Pratt, R.A. "Chaucer and the Hand that Fed Him." *Speculum* 41 (1966): 619–42.
Putter, Ad. *An Introduction to the Gawain-Poet*. London, 1996.
– *Sir Gawain and the Green Knight and French Arthurian Romance*. Oxford, 1995.
Putter, Ad, and Myra Stokes. "The *Linguistic Atlas* and the Dialect of the *Gawain* Poems." *Journal of English and Germanic Philology* 106 (2007): 468–91.
Rasmussen, Mark David. "Feminist Chaucer? Some Implications for Teaching." *Studies in Medieval and Renaissance Teaching* 5, no. 2 (1997): 77–85.
Raybin, David. "Critical Approaches." In *A Companion to Medieval English Literature and Culture, c.1350 –c.1500*, edited by Peter Brown, 9–24. Oxford, 2007.
Richards, I.A. *Speculative Instruments*. London, 1955.
Ricks, Christopher. *Keats and Embarrassment*. Oxford, 1974.
Ricoeur, Paul. *Freud and Philosophy: An Essay on Interpretation*. Translated by Denis Savage. New Haven, CT, 1970.
Riddy, Felicity. "Jewels." In Brewer and Gibson, *Companion to the Gawain-Poet*, 143–55.
Robertson, D.W. *A Preface to Chaucer*. Princeton, NJ, 1962.
Robinson, Ian. *Chaucer and the English Tradition*. Cambridge, 1972.
Rollins, Hyder E. "The Troilus–Cressida Story from Chaucer to Shakespeare." *PMLA* 32 (1917): 383–429.
Roover, Raymond de. *San Bernardino of Siena and Sant'Antonino of Florence: The Two Great Economic Thinkers of the Middle Ages*. Boston, MA, 1967.
Rossiter, A.P. *Angel with Horns and other Shakespeare Lectures*, edited by Graham Storey. London, 1961.

Rowe, Donald W. *O Love, O Charite! Contraries Harmonized in Chaucer's Troilus.* Carbondale, IL, 1976.

Saul, Nigel. *Richard II.* New Haven, CT, 1997.

Scala, Elizabeth. "Historicists and Their Discontents." *Texas Studies in Literature and Language* 44 (2002): 108–31.

Scattergood, V.J. "Literary Culture at the Court of Richard II." In Scattergood and Sherborne, *English Court Culture*, 29–43.

Scattergood, V.J., and J.W. Sherborne, eds. *English Court Culture in the Later Middle Ages.* London, 1983.

Schibanoff, Susan. "The New Reader and Female Textuality in Two Early Commentaries on Chaucer." *Studies in the Age of Chaucer* 10 (1988): 71–108.

Schoeck, Richard J., and Jerome Taylor, eds. *Chaucer Criticism.* 2 vols. Notre Dame, IN, 1961.

Scott, Kathleen L. *Later Gothic Manuscripts, 1390–1490.* 2 vols. London, 1996.

Severs, J. Burke. *The Literary Relationships of Chaucer's Clerke's Tale.* New Haven, CT, 1942.

Sherborne, J.W. "Aspects of English Court Culture in the Later Fourteenth Century." In Scattergood and Sherborne, *English Court Culture*, 1–27.

Shoaf, R.A. *The Poem as Green Girdle: Commercium in Sir Gawain and the Green Knight.* Gainesville, FL, 1984.

Simpson, James. *The Oxford English Literary History, Volume 2, 1350–1543: Reform and Cultural Revolution.* Oxford, 2002.

Smith, D. Vance. *Arts of Possession. The Middle English Household Imaginary.* Minneapolis, 2003.

Somerset, Fiona. *Clerical Discourse and Lay Audience in Late Medieval England.* Cambridge, 1998.

Spearing, A.C. *Criticism and Medieval Poetry.* 2nd ed. London, 1972.

– *The Gawain-Poet. A Critical Study.* Cambridge, 1970.

– *Medieval Dream-Poetry.* Cambridge, 1976.

– "Purity and Danger." In Spearing, *Readings in Medieval Poetry*, 173–94. Cambridge, 1987.

Spisak, James W., ed. *Studies in Malory.* Kalamazoo, MI, 1985.

Sponsler, Claire. "Narrating the Social Order: Medieval Clothing Laws." *Clio* 21, no. 3 (1992): 265–83.

Staley, Lynn. *Languages of Power in the Age of Richard II.* University Park, PA, 2005.

Stanesco, Michel. *Jeux d'errance du chevalier médiéval: Aspects ludiques de la fonction guerrière dans la littérature du moyen âge flamboyant.* Leiden, 1988.

Staniland, Kay. "Extravagance or Regal Necessity? The Clothing of Richard II." In Gordon, Monnas, and Elam, *The Regal Image of Richard II*, 85–93.

Stevens, John. *Medieval Romance.* London, 1973.

Stillwell, Gardiner. "Chaucer's 'Sad' Merchant." *Review of English Studies* 20 (1944): 1–18.

Stow, George B. "Richard II in Thomas Walsingham's Chronicles." *Speculum* 59 (1984): 68–102.

Strohm, Paul. *Hochon's Arrow: The Social Imagination of Fourteenth-Century Texts.* Princeton, NJ, 1992.

– *Social Chaucer*. Cambridge, MA, 1989.

– *Theory and the Pre-Modern Text*. Minneapolis, MN, 2000.

Szittya, Penn R. *The Antifraternal Tradition in Medieval Literature.* Princeton, NJ, 1986.

Tatlock, J.S.P. "The Siege of Troy in Elizabethan Literature: Especially in Shakespeare and Heywood." *PMLA* 30 (1915): 673–770.

Tatlock, John S.P., and Arthur G. Kennedy, eds. *A Concordance to the Complete Works of Geoffrey Chaucer*. Gloucester, MA, 1963.

Taylor, John. *English Historical Literature in the Fourteenth Century*. Oxford, 1987. Reprinted 2000.

Taylor, P.B. "Commerce and Comedy in *Sir Gawain*." *Philological Quarterly* 50 (1971): 1–15.

Thompson, Ann. *Shakespeare's Chaucer.* Liverpool, 1978.

Todorov, Tzvetan. *Mikhail Bakhtin: The Dialogical Principle*. Translated by Wlad Godzich. Manchester, 1984.

Tupper, Frederick. "The Quarrels of the Canterbury Pilgrims." *Journal of English and Germanic Philology* 14 (1915): 256–70.

Turville-Petre, Thorlac. "The *Pearl*-Poet in his 'Fayre Regioun.'" In *Essays on Ricardian Literature in Honour of J.A. Burrow*, edited by A.J. Minnis, Charlotte C. Morse, and Thorlac Turville-Petre, 276–94. Oxford, 1997.

Vale, Malcolm. *The Princely Court. Medieval Courts and Culture in North-West Europe 1270–1380.* Oxford, 2001.

Veblen, Thorstein. *Theory of the Leisure Class: An Economic Study in the Evolution of Institutions.* New York, 1899. Reprinted London, 1970.

Vinaver, Eugène. "La Genèse de la 'Suite du Merlin.'" In *Mélanges de philologie romane et de litterature médiévale offerts à Ernest Hoepffner*, 295–300. Paris, 1949.

– "King Arthur's Sword or the Making of a Medieval Romance." *Bulletin of the John Rylands Library* 40 (1957–8): 513–26.

– *The Rise of Romance.* Oxford, 1971.

Wallace, David, ed. *The Cambridge History of Medieval English Literature.* Cambridge, 1999.

Watson, Nicholas. "The *Gawain*-Poet as a Vernacular Theologian." In Brewer and Gibson, *Companion to the Gawain-Poet*, 293–313.

Weinstein, Donald, and Rudolph M. Bell. *Saints and Society. Christendom, 1000–1700.* Chicago, 1982.

Weiss, Judith. "Modern and Medieval Views on Swooning: the Literary and Medical Contexts of Fainting in Romance." In *Medieval Romance, Medieval Contexts*, edited by Rhiannon Purdie and Michael Cichon, 121–34. Cambridge, 2011.

– "The Wooing Woman in Anglo-Norman Romance." In *Romance in Medieval England*, edited by Maldwyn Mills, Jennifer Fellows, and Carol M. Meale, 149–61. Cambridge, 1991.

Weissman, Hope Phyllis. "Antifeminism and Chaucer's Characterization of Women." In *Geoffrey Chaucer: A Collection of Original Articles*, edited by George D. Economou, 93–110. New York, 1975.

Williams, Raymond. *Keywords: A Vocabulary of Culture and Society*. New York, 1976.

Wilson, Douglas B. "The Commerce of Desire: Freudian Narcissism in Chaucer's *Troilus and Criseyde* and Shakespeare's *Troilus and Cressida*." *English Language Notes* 21 (1983): 11–22.

Wilson, Edward. "*Sir Gawain and the Green Knight* and the Stanley family of Stanley, Storeton, and Hooton." *Review of English Studies* n.s. 30 (1979): 308–16.

Windeatt, Barry. "The Art of Swooning in Middle English." In *Medieval Latin and Middle English Literature: Essays in Honour of Jill Mann*, edited by Christopher Cannon and Maura Nolan, 211–30. Cambridge, 2011.

– "Gesture in Chaucer." *Medievalia et Humanistica* 9 (1979): 143–61.

Wood, Chauncey. *Chaucer and the Country of the Stars*. Princeton, NJ, 1970.

Woollcombe, W.W. *Essays on Chaucer*. London, 1896.

Wright, Thomas L. " 'The Tale of King Arthur': Beginnings and Foreshadowings." In Lumiansky, *Malory's Originality*, 9–66.

Yoder, R.A. " 'Sons and Daughters of the Game': An Essay on Shakespeare's 'Troilus and Cressida.' " *Shakespeare Survey* 25 (1972): 11–26.

Index

This index does not include editors or translators of medieval texts (unless their opinions are cited), or editors of modern essay collections, if the primary reference in the notes is to a contribution to the collection by another author.

www.ingramcontent.com/pod-product-compliance
Lightning Source LLC
LaVergne TN
LVHW090801070826
844660LV00022B/1053